Lecture Notes in Computer Science   11018

Commenced Publication in 1973
Founding and Former Series Editors:
Gerhard Goos, Juris Hartmanis, and Jan van Leeuwen

More information about this series at http://www.springer.com/series/7409

Patrice Bellot · Chiraz Trabelsi
Josiane Mothe · Fionn Murtagh
Jian Yun Nie · Laure Soulier
Eric SanJuan · Linda Cappellato
Nicola Ferro (Eds.)

Experimental IR Meets Multilinguality, Multimodality, and Interaction

9th International Conference
of the CLEF Association, CLEF 2018
Avignon, France, September 10–14, 2018
Proceedings

 Springer

Editors
Patrice Bellot (iD)
Aix-Marseille University
Marseille Cedex 20
France

Chiraz Trabelsi
Virtual University of Tunis
Tunis
Tunisia

Josiane Mothe (iD)
Systèmes d'informations, Big Data et Rec
Institut de Recherche en Informatique de
Toulouse Cedex 04
France

Fionn Murtagh (iD)
Department of Computer Science
University of Huddersfield
Huddersfield
UK

Jian Yun Nie
DIRO
Universite de Montreal
Montreal, QC
Canada

Laure Soulier (iD)
Pierre and Marie Curie University
Paris Cedex 05
France

Eric SanJuan
Université d'Avignon et des Pays de
Avignon
France

Linda Cappellato
Department of Information Engineering
University of Padua
Padua, Padova
Italy

Nicola Ferro (iD)
University of Padua
Padua
Italy

ISSN 0302-9743   ISSN 1611-3349   (electronic)
Lecture Notes in Computer Science
ISBN 978-3-319-98931-0   ISBN 978-3-319-98932-7   (eBook)
https://doi.org/10.1007/978-3-319-98932-7

Library of Congress Control Number: 2018950767

LNCS Sublibrary: SL3 – Information Systems and Applications, incl. Internet/Web, and HCI

This Springer imprint is published by the registered company Springer Nature Switzerland AG
The registered company address is: Gewerbestrasse 11, 6330 Cham, Switzerland

Preface

Since 2000, the Conference and Labs of the Evaluation Forum (CLEF) has played a leading role in stimulating research and innovation in the domain of multimodal and multilingual information access. Initially founded as the Cross-Language Evaluation Forum and running in conjunction with the European Conference on Digital Libraries (ECDL/TPDL), CLEF became a standalone event in 2010 combining a peer-reviewed conference with a multi-track evaluation forum. The combination of the scientific program and the track-based evaluations at the CLEF conference creates a unique platform to explore information access from different perspectives, in any modality and language.

The CLEF conference has a clear focus on experimental information retrieval (IR) as seen in evaluation forums (CLEF Labs, TREC, NTCIR, FIRE, MediaEval, RomIP, TAC, etc.) with special attention to the challenges of multimodality, multi-linguality, and interactive search ranging from unstructured, to semi-structured and structured data. CLEF invites submissions on significant new insights demonstrated by the use of innovative IR evaluation tasks or in the analysis of IR test collections and evaluation measures, as well as on concrete proposals to push the boundaries of the Cranfield/TREC/CLEF paradigm.

CLEF 2018[1] was jointly organized by Avignon, Marseille and Toulon Universities and was hosted by the University of Avignon, France, during September 10–14, 2018. The conference format consisted of keynotes, contributed papers, lab sessions, and poster sessions, including reports from other benchmarking initiatives from around the world.

The following scholars were invited to give a keynote talk at CLEF 2018: Gabriella Pasi (University of Milano-Bicocca, Italia), Nicholas Belkin (Rutgers University, NJ, USA), and Julio Gonzalo (UNED, Spain).

CLEF 2018 received a total of 39 submissions, of which a total of 13 papers (nine long, four short) were accepted. Each submission was reviewed by three Program Committee (PC) members, and the program chairs oversaw the reviewing and follow-up discussions. In all, 13 different countries are represented in the accepted papers. Many contributions this year tackle the medical e-Health and e-Health multimedia retrieval challenges in different ways: from medical image analysis to query suggestion. However, there are many other topics of research in the accepted papers such as document clustering, social biases in IR, social book search, personality profiling, to cite a few. As in previous editions since 2015, CLEF 2018 continued inviting CLEF lab organizers to nominate a "best of the labs" paper that was reviewed as a full paper submission to the CLEF 2018 conference according to the same review criteria and PC. Among the nine invited papers, six were accepted as long and three as short. Finally, eight posters were also accepted. Although they are not included in the LNCS

---

[1] http://clef2018.clef-initiative.eu/.

volume, posters give the opportunity to their authors to discuss their research during the conference and are accessible through the Web pages of the conference.

The conference integrated a series of workshops presenting the results of lab-based comparative evaluations. CLEF 2018 was the ninth year of the CLEF Conference and the 19th year of the CLEF initiative as a forum for IR Evaluation. The labs were selected in peer review based on their innovation potential and the quality of the resources created. The labs represented scientific challenges based on new data sets and real-world problems in multimodal and multilingual information access. These data sets provide unique opportunities for scientists to explore collections, to develop solutions for these problems, to receive feedback on the performance of their solutions, and to discuss the issues with peers at the workshops.

In addition to these workshops, the ten benchmarking labs reported results of their year-long activities in overview talks and lab sessions. Overview papers describing each of these labs are provided in this volume. The full details for each lab are contained in a separate publication, the *Working Notes*, which are available online[2].

The ten labs running as part of CLEF 2018 were as follows:

CENTRE@CLEF 2018 -CLEF/NTCIR/TREC Reproducibility[3] aims to run a joint CLEF/NTCIR/TREC task on challenging participants: (1) to reproduce the best results of the best/most interesting systems in previous editions of CLEF/NTCIR/TREC by using standard open source IR systems; (2) to contribute back to the community the additional components and resources developed to reproduce the results in order to improve existing open source systems.

CheckThat![4] aims to foster the development of technology capable of both spotting and verifying check-worthy claims in political debates in English and Arabic.

Dynamic Search for Complex Tasks[5]: The lab strives to answer one key question: How can we evaluate, and consequently build, dynamic search algorithms? The 2018 Lab focuses on the development of an evaluation framework, where participants submit "querying agents" that generate queries to be submitted to a static retrieval system. Effective "querying agents" can then simulate users toward developing dynamic search systems.

CLEFeHealth[6] provides scenarios that aim to ease patients, and nurses, understanding and accessing of e-Health information. The goals of the lab are to develop processing methods and resources in a multilingual setting to enrich difficult-to-understand e-Health texts, and provide valuable documentation. The tasks are: multilingual information extraction; technologically assisted reviews in empirical medicine; and patient-centered information retrieval.

ImageCLEF[7] organizes three main tasks and a pilot task: (1) a caption prediction task that aims at predicting the caption of a figure from the biomedical literature based

---

[2] http://ceur-ws.org/Vol-2125/.

[3] http://www.centre-eval.org/clef2018/.

[4] http://alt.qcri.org/clef2018-factcheck/.

[5] https://ekanou.github.io/dynamicsearch/.

[6] https://sites.google.com/view/clef-ehealth-2018/.

[7] http://www.imageclef.org/2018.

only on the figure image; (2) a tuberculosis task that aims at detecting the tuberculosis type, severity, and drug resistance from CT (computed tomography) volumes of the lung; (3) a lifelog task (videos, images, and other sources) about daily activities understanding and moment retrieval; and (4) a pilot task on visual question answering where systems are tasked with answering medical questions.

LifeCLEF[8] aims at boosting research on the identification of living organisms and on the production of biodiversity data in general. Through its biodiversity informatics-related challenges, LifeCLEF is intended to push the boundaries of the state of the art in several research directions at the frontier of multimedia information retrieval, machine learning, and knowledge engineering.

MC2[9] mainly focuses on developing processing methods and resources to mine the social media (SM) sphere surrounding cultural events such as festivals, music, books, movies, and museums. Following previous editions (CMC 2016 and MC2 2017), the 2018 edition focused on argumentative mining and multilingual cross SM search.

PAN[10] is a networking initiative for digital text forensics, where researchers and practitioners study technologies that analyze texts with regard to originality, authorship, and trustworthiness. PAN offered three tasks at CLEF 2018 with new evaluation resources consisting of large-scale corpora, performance measures, and Web services that allow for meaningful evaluations. The main goal is to provide for sustainable and reproducible evaluations, to get a clear view of the capabilities of state-of-the-art-algorithms. The tasks are: author identification; author profiling; and, author obfuscation.

Early Risk Prediction on the Internet (eRisk)[11] explores issues of evaluation methodology, effectiveness metrics, and other processes related to early risk detection. Early detection technologies can be employed in different areas, particularly those related to health and safety. For instance, early alerts could be sent when a predator starts interacting with a child for sexual purposes, or when a potential offender starts publishing antisocial threats on a blog, forum, or social network. Our main goal is to pioneer a new interdisciplinary research area that would be potentially applicable to a wide variety of situations and to many different personal profiles. eRisk 2018 had two campaign-style tasks: early detection of signs of depression and early detection of signs of anorexia.

Personalized Information Retrieval at CLEF (PIR-CLEF)[12] provides a framework for the evaluation of personalized information retrieval (PIR). Current approaches to the evaluation of PIR are user-centric, mostly based on user studies, i.e., they rely on experiments that involve real users in a supervised environment. PIR-CLEF aims to develop and demonstrate a methodology for the evaluation of personalized search that enables repeatable experiments. The main aim is to enable research groups working on PIR to both experiment with and provide feedback on the proposed PIR evaluation methodology.

---

[8] http://www.lifeclef.org/.
[9] https://mc2.talne.eu/.
[10] http://pan.webis.de/.
[11] http://early.irlab.org/.
[12] http://www.ir.disco.unimib.it/pir-clef2018/.

Avignon is famous for its medieval architecture and its international theater festival. The social program of CLEF 2018 set up a Science and Music Festival in medieval downtown at Theâtre des Halles[13] and surrounding gardens from Tuesday to Thursday. Music is a very popular hobby among members of the scientific community. Evenings were a mix of music and participatory science around PlantNet, OpenStreetMaps, and Wikipedia. Tuesday was especially devoted to welcoming students at CLEF. On Wednesday the focus was on IR scientific societies around the world mixing all CLEF languages in one evening. Finally, science outreach activities were carried out on Thursday; local musicians and students looking for a good time were invited to come and meet the participants of the CLEF conference.

The success of CLEF 2018 would not have been possible without the huge effort of several people and organizations, including the CLEF Association[14], the PC, the Lab Organizing Committee, the local organization committee in Avignon, the reviewers, and the many students and volunteers who contributed.

July 2018

Patrice Bellot
Chiraz Trabelsi
Josiane Mothe
Fionn Murtagh
Jian Yun Nie
Laure Soulier
Eric Sanjuan
Linda Cappellato
Nicola Ferro

---

[13] http://www.theatredeshalles.com/.
[14] http://www.clef-initiative.eu/association.

Organization

CLEF 2018, Conference and Labs of the Evaluation Forum – Experimental IR meets Multilinguality, Multimodality, and Interaction, was hosted by the University of Avignon and jointly co-organized by Avignon, Marseille and Toulon Universities, France.

General Chairs

Patrice Bellot	Aix-Marseille Université - CNRS LSIS, France
Chiraz Trabelsi	University of Tunis El Manar, Tunisia

Program Chairs

Josiane Mothe	SIG, IRIT, France
Fionn Murtagh	University of Huddersfield, UK

Lab Chairs

Jian Yun Nie	DIRO, Université de Montréal, Canada
Laure Soulier	LIP6, UPMC, France

Proceedings Chairs

Linda Cappellato	University of Padua, Italy
Nicola Ferro	University of Padua, Italy

Publicity Chair

Adrian Chifu	Aix-Marseille Université - CNRS LSIS, France

Science Outreach Program Chairs

Aurelia Barriere	UAPV, France
Mathieu FERYN	UAPV, France

Sponsoring Chair

Malek Hajjem	UAPV, France

Local Organization

Eric SanJuan (Chair)   LIA, UAPV, France
Tania Jimenez (Co-chair)   LIA, UAPV, France
Sebastien Fournier   Aix-Marseille Université - CNRS LIS, France
Hervé Glotin   Université de Toulon - CNRS LIS, France
Vincent Labatut   LIA, UAPV, France
Elisabeth Murisasco   Université de Toulon - CNRS LIS, France
Magalie Ochs   Aix-Marseille Université - CNRS LIS, France
Juan-Manuel   LIA, UAPV, France
   Torres-Moreno

Sponsors

Association francophone de Recherche d'Information et Applications

CLEF Steering Committee

Steering Committee Chair

Nicola Ferro   University of Padua, Italy

Deputy Steering Committee Chair for the Conference

Paolo Rosso   Universitat Politècnica de València, Spain

Deputy Steering Committee Chair for the Evaluation Labs

Martin Braschler   Zurich University of Applied Sciences, Switzerland

Members

Khalid Choukri	Evaluations and Language resources Distribution Agency (ELDA), France
Paul Clough	University of Sheffield, UK
Norbert Fuhr	University of Duisburg-Essen, Germany
Lorraine Goeuriot	Université Grenoble Alpes, France
Julio Gonzalo	National Distance Education University (UNED), Spain
Donna Harman	National Institute for Standards and Technology (NIST), USA
Djoerd Hiemstra	University of Twente, The Netherlands
Evangelos Kanoulas	University of Amsterdam, The Netherlands
Birger Larsen	University of Aalborg, Denmark
Séamus Lawless	Trinity College Dublin, Ireland
Mihai Lupu	Vienna University of Technology, Austria
Josiane Mothe	IRIT, Université de Toulouse, France
Henning Müller	University of Applied Sciences Western Switzerland (HES-SO), Switzerland
Maarten de Rijke	University of Amsterdam UvA, The Netherlands
Giuseppe Santucci	Sapienza University of Rome, Italy
Jacques Savoy	University of Neuchatel, Switzerland
Christa Womser-Hacker	University of Hildesheim, Germany

Past Members

Jaana Kekäläinen	University of Tampere, Finland
Carol Peters	ISTI, National Council of Research (CNR), Italy
	(Steering Committee Chair 2000–2009)
Emanuele Pianta	Centre for the Evaluation of Language
	and Communication Technologies (CELCT), Italy
Alan Smeaton	Dublin City University, Ireland

Contents

Short Papers

Best of CLEF 2017 Labs

CLEF 2018 Lab Overviews

Full Papers

Deep Multimodal Classification of Image Types in Biomedical Journal Figures

Vincent Andrearczyk[1]([✉]) and Henning Müller[1,2]

[1] University of Applied Sciences Western Switzerland (HES-SO), Sierre, Switzerland
`vincent.andrearczyk@hevs.ch`
[2] University of Geneva (UNIGE), Geneva, Switzerland

Abstract. This paper presents a robust method for the classification of medical image types in figures of the biomedical literature using the fusion of visual and textual information. A deep convolutional network is trained to discriminate among 31 image classes including compound figures, diagnostic image types and generic illustrations, while another shallow convolutional network is used for the analysis of the captions paired with the images. Various fusion methods are analyzed as well as data augmentation approaches. The proposed system is validated on the ImageCLEF 2013 and 2016 figure and subfigure classification tasks, largely improving the currently best performance from 83.5% to 93.7% accuracy and 88.4% to 89.0% respectively.

1 Introduction

The information contained in an image and the methods employed to extract it largely differ depending on its modality, making the latter a crucial aspect of medical image analysis and retrieval. An image type classification is, therefore, a useful preliminary filtering step prior to further analysis [2,16]. Besides this, the modality is a relevant information to be determined for medical image or document retrieval, allowing clinicians to filter their search by a particular modality, often specific to a pathology or organ of interest. Various modality classification tasks, among others, have been released through the ImageCLEF challenges [7,10]. We focus this work on the 2013 and 2016 ImageCLEF modality classification tasks, as they offer multimodal text and image data. The database is publicly available and the results are fully reproducible as a consequence. The database also originates from the PubMed Central database (it is a small subset of PubMed Central), allowing us to classify this large database for further processing and analysis. Much of the medical knowledge is stored in the medical literature, for example in the form of images and text, although the image type information is not available. Making this content accessible for research can help in many other tasks, such as retrieval or classification.

Multimodal analysis is commonly used to extract and fuse information from multiple modalities [11,24]. In this work, images and captions contain complementary information fused to boost the classification accuracy. Many methods

© Springer Nature Switzerland AG 2018
P. Bellot et al. (Eds.): CLEF 2018, LNCS 11018, pp. 3–14, 2018.
https://doi.org/10.1007/978-3-319-98932-7_1

have been used to extract high-level features from text and images independently and to fuse them. Convolutional Neural Networks (CNNs) have obtained state of the art performance in most computer vision [5,9] and biomedical image analysis [17] tasks. It is also well suited for text analysis [12]. This paper introduces several late fusion methods to combine powerful visual and textual CNNs.

2   Related Work

Multimodal textual and visual analysis has been widely studied for applications including annotation and captioning [11], image generation from text [24], text and image feature fusion for retrieval and classification [7]. A total of 51 runs from eight groups were presented in [7] for the ImageCLEF 2013 modality classification challenge. The best results (81.7% classification accuracy) were obtained by visual and textual fusion from the IBM Multimedia Analytics group [1] (see Table 1). A set of color and texture, local and global descriptors (including a color histogram, moments, wavelets, Local Binary Patterns (LPB) and Scale-Invariant Feature Transform (SIFT)) was extracted as visual descriptors and fused with multiple textual descriptors. The best results were obtained using a maximum late fusion with a classifier built on top of modality tailored keywords (with a hand-selected vocabulary that likely improved the performance) and a two-level Support Vector Machine (SVM) classification. The methods developed by other teams reported in [7] include various types of similar hand-crafted visual and textual descriptors combined by multiple fusion methods.

In [4], the authors build upon [1] to develop a more complex system. An ensemble of SVM models is trained on top of similar visual features, while the text is analyzed by scoring based on the detection of manually-selected patterns from the captions and from sentences in the body of the article. A weighted score average trained on a subset of the training data was used for fusing the visual and textual information. The best current system reached an accuracy of 83.5% on ImageCLEF 2013 modality classification.

Another set of hand-crafted visual and textual features are combined in [19]. The visual features include local and global texture and color features, while Bag-of-Words (BoW) features are used to analyze the captions. Multiple CNNs are combined in [23] by late fusion (average, maximum, majority and median), yet the resulting accuracy is lower than the shallow hand-crafted methods in [7]. More recently in [16,22], pre-trained deep visual CNNs are finetuned and their outputs are combined in an ensemble classifier with basic voting fusion methods. Besides this, deep pre-trained CNNs obtained better performance than shallower ones, motivating the use of very deep pre-trained networks even on these small datasets. A major drawback of combining multiple CNNs is the increase of computational complexity and redundancy of features to obtain only a limited accuracy improvement (less than 1% in [22]). A multimodal approach based on ensemble learning of various textual and visual features was proposed in [15], obtaining the state of the art results on the ImageCLEF 2016 subfigure modality classification task [8]. BoW textual features extracted from the article's text and captions are combined with visual features including hand-crafted shallow texture and color features, Bag-of-Visual-Words (BoVW) and deep features (ResNet152 [5]). The best results were obtained with an ensemble of SVMs trained on all the features (see Table 3).

3 Methods

3.1 ImageCLEF 2013 Modality Dataset

The goal of this task is to classify the images into medical modalities and other images types. Three main categories, namely compound figures, diagnostic images and generic illustrations are divided into 31 sub-categories [7,18]. The modality hierarchy and more details on the dataset can be found in [7]. A total of 2879 training and 2570 test images are provided. The classes are highly imbalanced, reflecting the distribution of the images in the data (PubMed Central[1]) containing a large proportion of compound figures.

3.2 ImageCLEF 2016 Modality Subfigures Dataset

The goal of this task is similar to the task in ImageCLEF 2013, although the images (subfigures) originate from a segmentation of larger compound figures. The modality hierarchy is the same as in 2013 without the compound figure category. The two main categories are diagnostic images and generic illustrations, further divided into 30 sub-categories [8]. A total of 6776 training and 4166 test images are provided. The captions are provided for the entire compound figures before segmentation and are therefore less specific than in the 2013 task. Although the classes are less imbalanced than ImageCLEF 2013 since the "compound figure" category is not present, the "GFIG" category (including statistical figures, graphs and charts) is strongly overrepresented with approximately 44% of the training samples while some classes contain less than 10 samples.

3.3 Overview of the Approach

An overview of the developed networks and fusion approaches is illustrated in Fig. 1. The components are described in more details in the following sections.

3.4 Visual Analysis

DenseNet [9] is a CNN having each layer connected to every other layer (within a dense block, see Fig. 1, right). The dense blocks are preceded by a 7×7 convolution layer and 3×3 max pooling. Each dense block is composed of densely connected 1×1 and 3×3 convolutions. The transitions between blocks contain a 1×1 convolution and 2×2 average pooling. All the convolutions are regularized with batch normalization and activated by a ReLU. The last dense block is globally down-sampled by a 7×7 average pooling and connected to a

---

[1] https://www.ncbi.nlm.nih.gov/pmc/.

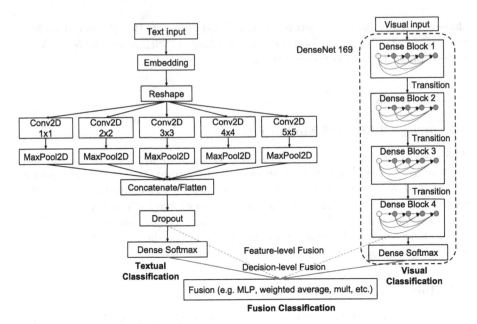

Fig. 1. Overview of the proposed deep learning visual and textual fusion method.

softmax activated dense layer with 30 or 31 neurons (number of classes). More details can be found in [9]. This architecture obtained excellent results on various image classification datasets while reducing the number of parameters and computation (floating point operations) as compared to other commonly used networks (e.g. AlexNet, VGG, GoogleNet and ResNet). On the proposed experiments, DenseNet169 obtained the best results as compared to DenseNet121 [9], ResNet50 and 152 [5], VGG19 [20], in line with recent computer vision and biomedical image analysis results. The training data are limited (2789 or 6776 images without data augmentation) and transfer learning is required to obtain a robust image classification. We use networks pre-trained on ImageNet and replace the last fully connected softmax activated dense layer by a layer of 31 or 30 neurons, equivalent to the number of classes in the ImageCLEF 2013 and 2016 datasets respectively.

To increase the visual training data, we explore two complementary data augmentation strategies. The first strategy uses extra training data from the other task, i.e. using ImageCLEF 2016 data for training ImageCLEF 2013 and vice versa. We also use images from the ImageCLEF 2016 compound figure detection task for training ImageCLEF 2013 as the compound class is not represented in the subfigure set. We ensure that no image is present twice in the training set or in both the training and test sets. The second data augmentation strategy consists of a set of random transformations applied to the training images including horizontal and vertical flips, width and height shift in the range of $[0, 0.1]$ of the total width and height respectively and a rotation in the range $[0°, 5°]$.

3.5   Text Analysis

We develop a CNN on top of word embeddings as inspired by [12], in which a CNN for sentence classification was developed. Our architecture is illustrated in Fig. 1 (left). The words are embedded into a low (300) dimensional space using fastText word embedding [3] pre-trained on Wikipedia data[2]. Similar results were obtained with a Global Vectors for word representation (GloVE) pre-trained on Wikipedia 2014 and Gigaword 5, while pre-training on biomedical text performed worse.

The maximum number of tokens was set to 20,000 and the maximum length of a caption was set to 200. The embedding layer is finetuned together with the network in order to adapt the embedding to this particular caption classification task and domain. We use convolution kernels ranging from 1×1 to 5×5 to perform a multi-scale analysis with scales that we deem relevant for the caption task. We confirmed experimentally that adding larger kernels does not improve the performance while significantly increasing the number of parameters. Recurrent Neural Networks (RNNs) may seem more intuitive than CNNs and better suited for natural language processing since local features captured by convolution filters are not as evident in text as they are in images. Captions, however, offer a relatively structured and controlled domain in which words are often organized in meaningful local features. CNNs are also better at detecting key phrases or combinations of words than RNNs, which is a useful asset for the evaluated task since the modality is often described by a single sentence or a group of words. The speed of convolution computations is an important aspect in the choice of the architecture. We also experimented with a 1D convolutional network, a Long Short-Term Memory (LSTM) network and a stacked LSTM network, resulting in a lower accuracy.

3.6   Decision-Level Fusion

The decision-level fusion combines the visual and textual predictions. We first train the visual and textual networks independently, then combine the class probabilities, i.e. outputs of the softmax layers. Simple fusions are used including (a) a weighted sum, (b) a maximum probability decision and (c) a product of probabilities (elementwise product of probability vectors). Equation 1 summarizes the class prediction of these three fusion methods.

$$
\begin{aligned}
c_{sum} &= amax(\alpha y_v + (1 - \alpha)y_t), \\
c_{max} &= amax(max(y_v, y_t)), \\
c_{prod} &= amax(y_v \circ y_t),
\end{aligned}
\tag{1}
$$

where c_{sum}, c_{max}, c_{prod} are the class predictions from (a), (b) and (c), y_v and y_t are the probability vectors of the visual and textual networks respectively. The weight $\alpha \in [0, 1]$ is used to balance the importance of the visual and textual parts

---

[2] https://dumps.wikimedia.org.

in (a). Another fusion method is to train a single layer Multi-Layer Perceptron (MLP) on top of the prediction layer. We freeze all previous layers to train only the last added layer. Using a two-layer MLP results in similar performance, yet increases the complexity. We do not use artificial data augmentation when training the MLP as the visual augmentation is learned when training DenseNet individually and then the network requires visual and textual pairs.

3.7   Feature-Level Fusion

The feature-level method fuses the outputs of intermediate layers from the visual and textual networks. We first train the two networks independently, then add one layer on top of the last layer before the softmax activated one and train similarly to the decision-level MLP. The networks' deep representations, inputs to the MLP, are richer and more complete than the decision-level ones ($\mathbb{R}^{2560}$ and $\mathbb{R}^{1664}$ for the textual and visual representations respectively, vs. $\mathbb{R}^N$, with $N = 31$, or $N = 30$ for the decision level).

4   Experimental Results

4.1   Network Setups

The networks are trained with an Adam [13] optimizer. The textual, visual and fusion MLP networks are trained for $N = 100$, $N = 25$ and $N = 50$ epochs respectively. The initial learning rate is set to 10^{-4} for finetuning the visual network and 10^{-3} for the textual network and MLP from scratch, average decays β_1 and β_2 are 0.9 and 0.999 respectively, the learning rate decay is $\frac{0.1}{N}$ and the batch size 32. Due to the high class imbalance in the training set, class weights are used during training for weighting the loss function as: $w_i = n_{max}/n_i$, where n_{max} and n_i are the number of training samples of the most represented class and of class i respectively. The most represented class is the one with most training samples, i.e. "compound figures" in ImageCLEF 2013 and "GFIG" in ImageCLEF 2016. For the visual network, class weights are not needed when artificial data augmentation is used.

4.2   Classification Results ImageCLEF 2013

The results are reported and compared with the best current systems in Table 1[3]. Best results of the 51 runs submitted by eight groups [7] are reported as well as the best results in the literature obtained after the challenge [4]. In [1,4], vocabularies and text patterns were manually selected, and in [4], the text in the body of the article was also used.

We do not use extra training data for the captions because in ImageCLEF 2016 the captions relate to the original compound figures from which the sub-figures are segmented. Consequently, the textual network is trained with only

---

[3] 34 images were removed from the 2013 dataset since the original challenge due to their presence in both training and test sets.

Table 1. Comparison of our methods with the best runs in ImageCLEF 2013.

Modality	Method	Accuracy
Textual	IBM_modality_run1 [1]	64.2%
	IBM textual [4]	69.6%
	textual CNN	**71.9%**
Visual	IBM_modality_run4 [1]	80.8%
	IBM visual [4]	82.2%
	DenseNet169 w/o data augm. w/o extra training	83.8%
	DenseNet169 w/ data augm. w/o extra training	84.5%
	DenseNet169 w/ data augm. w/ extra training	**86.8%**
Fusion	IBM_modality_run8 [1]	81.7%
	IBM fusion [4]	83.5%
	Weighted sum fusion w/ extra training	89.2%
	Maximum fusion w/ extra training	89.4%
	Product fusion w/ extra training	91.8%
	Decision-level MLP w/ extra training	86.0%
	Feature-level MLP w/ extra training	**93.7%**

ImageCLEF 2013 training data. For the same reason, the MLPs are also trained without extra training data in order to maintain pairs of visual and textual inputs. However, the visual network is first trained with artificial data augmentation and extra training data before being fused with the textual network.

The best fusion results are obtained with the feature-level MLP (93.7%). The previously best results (IBM [4]) on ImageCLEF 2013 were obtained without using extra data, yet our approach without extra data also outperforms them (91.9% vs. 83.5%, not reported in Table 1). The weighted loss described in Sect. 4.1 considerably improves the performance of our approach since the best performance obtained without weighted loss is 92.7% (not reported in the table) vs. 93.7% with. The confusion matrix of the best results (Feature-level MLP w/ extra training) is shown in Fig. 2.

The most relevant classes are the diagnostic images as they offer more potential in clinical applications such as retrieval. The confusion matrices for the three main categories (compound, diagnostic and generic illustrations) are illustrated in Fig. 3. It shows that our approach performs an excellent discrimination between diagnostic (e.g. MRI, CT, histopathology) and other images with lower relevance (e.g. compound figures, diagrams and maps), which was of critical importance for the development of the datasets in [6].

In order to evaluate the complementarity of the visual and textual information, we measured the overlap of correct classification. With the best MLP method previously described, the percentage of images correctly classified by both the visual and textual networks is 64.3%. 22.5% of the test set is correctly classified by the visual network but incorrectly classified by the textual

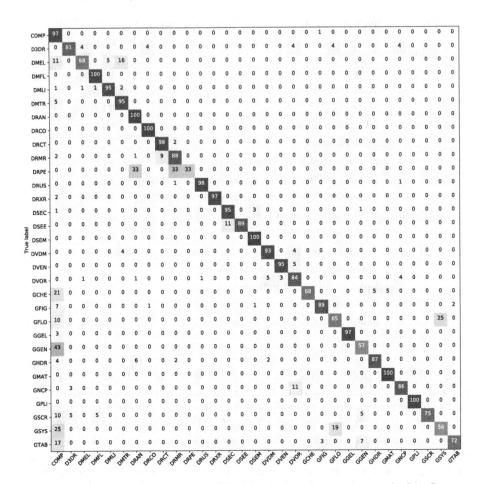

Fig. 2. Normalized confusion matrix (%) of the feature-level fusion method on Image-CLEF 2013. COMP stands for compound figures. Labels starting with D are diagnostic modalities, those with G are generic illustrations. The complete list of labels can be found in [7].

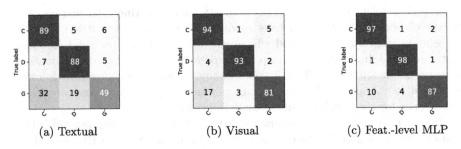

(a) Textual   (b) Visual   (c) Feat.-level MLP

Fig. 3. Normalized confusion matrices for the three main categories in ImageCLEF 2013: compound, diagnostic and generic illustrations.

one and, vice-versa, 7.6% is correctly classified using the caption but incorrectly classified using visual information. These results suggest, as confirmed by the fusion results in Table 1, that the visual and textual analyses offer some degree of complementarity to boost the final classification accuracy.

The accuracy obtained with multiple values of α in Eq. 1 is illustrated in Fig. 4. The best results with this weighted sum fusion are obtained with a contribution of the visual analysis slightly larger than the textual one ($\alpha = 0.51$), although a gradually reducing, yet neat, improvement from the single modality results is obtained with α values in the range $[0.51, 0.99]$.

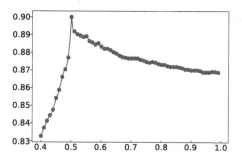

Fig. 4. Accuracy of the sum fusion method for various weights α on ImageCLEF 2013.

The networks are implemented in Keras with TensorFlow backend and written in Python. The computational training and test times are reported in Table 2 using a Titan Xp GPU.

Table 2. Computation time of the various networks on ImageCLEF 2013.

Method	Train time (nb. images)	Test time (nb. images)
Textual CNN	1,079 s (2789)	1.1 s (2570)
DenseNet169 w/o extra training	3,233 s (2789)	14.6 s (2570)
DenseNet169 w/ extra training	22,510 s (25880)	14.6 s (2570)
Feat.-level MLP w/ extra training	2,626 s (25880)	15.2 s (2570)

4.3 Classification Results ImageCLEF 2016

The results obtained on the ImageCLEF 2016 subfigure classification task are reported and compared with the best current systems in Table 3.

Our visual analysis based on DenseNet trained with class weights outperforms the complex ensemble classification of features in [15].

The textual analysis has less relevance in this challenge as the captions are only available for the compound figures from which multiple subfigures originate and not precisely for each subfigure, as such a separation is not done systematically. The textual analysis still brings complementary information to the

Table 3. Comparison of our methods with the best runs in ImageCLEF 2016.

Modality	Method	Accuracy
Textual	MLKD [21]	58.4%
	BCSG [15] w/ extra training	**72.2%**
	textual CNN	69.1%
	textual CNN w/ extra training	**72.2%**
Visual	IPL [21]	84.0%
	BCSG [15] w/ extra training	85.4%
	DenseNet169 w/o data augm. w/o extra training	86.2%
	DenseNet169 w/ data augm. w/o extra training	86.8%
	DenseNet169 w/ data augm. w/ extra training	**87.9%**
Fusion	BCSG [15] w/ extra training	88.4%
	weighted sum fusion w/ extra training	88.0%
	maximum fusion w/ extra training	87.8%
	product fusion w/ extra training	88.7%
	Decision-level MLP w/ extra training	88.5%
	Feature-level MLP w/ extra training	**89.0%**

visual analysis as shown by the fusion results. BCSG [15] makes use of the text and caption for the textual analysis. A class distribution of the test set is also learned based on the ImageCLEF 2015 dataset. We decided not to implement such approaches for a better generalization to unknown data without prior on the class distribution. Despite this simplified setup, our textual classifier is on a par with [15] (72.2%). Extra training data are also used in [15].

The best fusion method is again obtained with a feature-level MLP (89.0%). Slightly lower accuracy is obtained with the basic product fusion and decision-level MLP (88.7% and 88.5%).

5   Discussions and Future Work

As illustrated in the experiments, the proposed approach largely outperforms the state of the art [4] on the ImageCLEF 2013 dataset (93.7% vs. 83.5%). The results on ImageCLEF 2016 also outperform the best results [15] (89.0% vs. 88.4%). For this second experiment, our approach uses fewer data (only captions for the textual part) and no prior on the test data classes distribution. Besides this, our method jointly trains the visual and textural networks, whereas [15] requires learning an ensemble of hand-crafted and trainable features with multiple classifiers, which may limit its generalization and interpretability. The reported results demonstrated the major importance of the visual analysis in the developed method (86.8% and 87.5% accuracy), in line with the results and conclusions from the literature [1,4,7,14]. The visual data augmentation had an expected positive impact on the results with an increase of accuracy of 3% and 1.7%. The complementarity of textual and visual information was demonstrated by the series of experiments and analyses.

The proposed robust image modality classification enables to classify large datasets such as PubMed Central with over five million publicly available images and captions in 2017 and to use it as training or semi-supervised data for various medical image and text analysis tasks. In particular, it was used to develop the ImageCLEF 2018 caption prediction and concept detection challenges [6] by finding medical modality images (radiology, scanner etc.) to narrow the variability on these tasks.

In future work, we plan the use of attention mechanisms in the two modalities, which should greatly help the information extraction and classification.

Acknowledgments. The Titan Xp used for this research was donated by the NVIDIA Corporation.

References

1. Abedini, M., et al.: IBM research at ImageCLEF 2013 medical tasks. In: Proceedings of Workshop CLEF 2013 Working Notes, vol. 1179 (2013)
2. Bedrick, S., Radhouani, S., Kalpathy-Cramer, J.: Improving early precision in the ImageCLEF medical retrieval task. In: Müller, H., Clough, P., Deselaers, T., Caputo, B. (eds.) ImageCLEF. The Information Retrieval Series, vol. 32, pp. 397–413. Springer, Heidelberg (2010). https://doi.org/10.1007/978-3-642-15181-1_21
3. Bojanowski, P., Grave, E., Joulin, A., Mikolov, T.: Enriching word vectors with subword information (2017)
4. Codella, N., Connell, J., Pankanti, S., Merler, M., Smith, J.R.: Automated medical image modality recognition by fusion of visual and text information. In: Golland, P., Hata, N., Barillot, C., Hornegger, J., Howe, R. (eds.) MICCAI 2014. LNCS, vol. 8674, pp. 487–495. Springer, Cham (2014). https://doi.org/10.1007/978-3-319-10470-6_61
5. He, K., Zhang, X., Ren, S., Sun, J.: Deep residual learning for image recognition. In: Proceedings of the IEEE Conference on Computer Vision and Pattern Recognition, pp. 770–778 (2016)
6. García Seco de Herrera, A., Eickhoff, C., Andrearczyk, V., Müller, H.: Overview of the ImageCLEF 2018 caption prediction tasks. In: CLEF2018 Working Notes, CEUR Workshop Proceedings, CEUR-WS.org, 10–14 September 2018, Avignon, France (2018)
7. García Seco de Herrera, A., Kalpathy-Cramer, J., Demner Fushman, D., Antani, S., Müller, H.: Overview of the ImageCLEF 2013 medical tasks. In: Working Notes of CLEF 2013 (Cross Language Evaluation Forum), September 2013 (2013)
8. García Seco de Herrera, A., Schaer, R., Bromuri, S., Müller, H.: Overview of the ImageCLEF 2016 medical task. In: Working Notes of CLEF 2016 (Cross Language Evaluation Forum), September 2016 (2016)
9. Huang, G., Liu, Z., Weinberger, K.Q., van der Maaten, L.: Densely connected convolutional networks. In: Proceedings of the IEEE Conference on Computer Vision and Pattern Recognition (2017)

10. Kalpathy-Cramer, J., García Seco de Herrera, A., Demner-Fushman, D., Antani, S., Bedrick, S., Müller, H.: Evaluating performance of biomedical image retrieval systems: overview of the medical image retrieval task at ImageCLEF 2004–2014. Comput. Med. Imaging Graph. **39**, 55–61 (2015)
11. Karpathy, A., Fei-Fei, L.: Deep visual-semantic alignments for generating image descriptions. In: Proceedings of the IEEE Conference on Computer Vision and Pattern Recognition, pp. 3128–3137 (2015)
12. Kim, Y.: Convolutional neural networks for sentence classification. In: Proceedings of the Conference on Empirical Methods in Natural Language Processing (EMNLP), pp. 1746–1751 (2014)
13. Kingma, D., Ba, J.: Adam: a method for stochastic optimization. In: Proceedings of the 3rd International Conference on Learning Representations (ICLR) (2015)
14. Kitanovski, I., Dimitrovski, I., Loskovska, S.: FCSE at medical tasks of Image-CLEF 2013. In: Working Notes of CLEF 2013 (Cross Language Evaluation Forum), September 2013 (2013)
15. Koitka, S., Friedrich, C.M.: Traditional feature engineering and deep learning approaches at medical classification task of ImageCLEF 2016. In: CLEF2016 Working Notes, CEUR Workshop Proceedings, CEUR-WS.org, 5–8 September 2016, Évora, Portugal (2016)
16. Kumar, A., Kim, J., Lyndon, D., Fulham, M., Feng, D.: An ensemble of fine-tuned convolutional neural networks for medical image classification. IEEE J. Biomed. Health Inform. **21**(1), 31–40 (2017)
17. Litjens, G., et al.: A survey on deep learning in medical image analysis. Med. Image Anal. **42**, 60–88 (2017)
18. Müller, H., Kalpathy-Cramer, J., Demner-Fushman, D., Antani, S.: Creating a classification of image types in the medical literature for visual categorization. In: SPIE Medical Imaging (2012)
19. Pelka, O., Friedrich, C.: Modality prediction of biomedical literature images using multimodal feature representation. GMS Medical Informatics, Biometry and Epidemiology (MIBE) (2016)
20. Simonyan, K., Zisserman, A.: Very deep convolutional networks for large-scale image recognition. arXiv preprint arXiv:1409.1556 (2014)
21. Valavanis, L., Kalamboukis, T.: IPL at CLEF 2016 medical task. In: CLEF2016 Working Notes, CEUR Workshop Proceedings, CEUR-WS.org, 5–8 September 2016, Évora, Portugal (2016)
22. Yu, Y., Lin, H., Meng, J., Wei, X., Guo, H., Zhao, Z.: Deep transfer learning for modality classification of medical images. Information **8**(3), 91 (2017)
23. Yu, Y., et al.: Modality classification for medical images using multiple deep convolutional neural networks. J. Comput. Inf. Syst. **11**, 5403–5413 (2015)
24. Zhang, H., et al.: StackGAN: text to photo-realistic image synthesis with stacked generative adversarial networks. In: International Conference on Computer Vision (2017)

Multi-view Personality Profiling Based on Longitudinal Data

Kseniya Buraya[1]([✉]), Aleksandr Farseev[1,2], and Andrey Filchenkov[1]

[1] ITMO University, 49 Kronverksky Pr., St. Petersburg 197101, Russia
{ksburaya,afilchenkov}@corp.ifmo.ru
[2] SoMin Research, 221 Henderson Rd., Singapore 159557, Singapore
farseev@gmail.com

Abstract. Personality profiling is an essential application for the marketing, advertisement and sales industries. Indeed, the knowledge about one's personality may help in understanding the reasons behind one's behavior and his/her motivation in undertaking new life challenges. In this study, we take the first step towards solving the problem of automatic personality profiling. Specifically, we propose the idea of fusing multi-source multi-modal temporal data in our computational "PersonalL-STM" framework for automatic user personality inference. Experimental results show that incorporation of multi-source temporal data allows for more accurate personality profiling, as compared to non-temporal baselines and different data source combinations.

Keywords: User profiling · Social networks · Personality profiling

1 Introduction

User profiling plays an important role in various applications. One of the major components of user profiling is personality profiling, which is the identification of one's mental and emotional characteristics, such as personality type or mental status. These personal attributes allow for better understanding of the reasons behind one's behaviour [22], the selection of suitable individuals for particular tasks [27], and motivation of people in undertaking new life challenges.

There are several personality scales adopted by the research community. One of the most widely embraced typologies is called MBTI [18]. MBTI typology is designed to exhibit psychological preferences on how people perceive the world around them and distinguishes 16 personality types. It consists of four binary personality classes that form human personality type when being combined. Social scientists discovered that social media services exceedingly affect and reflect the way people communicate with the world and among themselves [11], which suggests that MBTI typology naturally fits social media research and can be used for assigning personality labels to user data when inferring users' behaviors and activities on social media.

© Springer Nature Switzerland AG 2018
P. Bellot et al. (Eds.): CLEF 2018, LNCS 11018, pp. 15–27, 2018.
https://doi.org/10.1007/978-3-319-98932-7_2

Several studies addressed the problem of personality profiling from social science perspective [22,24]. However, most of these works are descriptive in nature and based on manually collected data, which do not scale well to large-scale observations. At the same time, others [23,28] utilized the advantages of social network data for automatic personality profiling. However, most of these works are based on the data collected from a single data source (i.e. Twitter) or of a single data modality (i.e. text), which may lead to sub-optimal results in the real-world scenario. Indeed, taking into account that most of the social media users participate in more than one social network in their daily life [7], it is reasonable to utilize the data from multiple sources and modalities for automatic personality profiling. Another important aspect of social media data is its temporality, which is the tight dependence on user behavior on his/her temporal and spatial environment. For example, [2] found that one's relationship status (i.e. single/not single, which is closely related to one's personality) can be predicted from the history of users' check-ins. However, the temporal aspect of multi-source social media data was not yet comprehensively addressed in the literature [2]. Considering that user personality do not change a lot over time [18], it is essential to consider data temporality at the data modeling stage.

In this work, we focus on using multi-source multimodal temporal data for automatic personality profiling. We believe that the judicious fusion of multi-source heterogeneous temporal information sources would enrichment each other and facilitate more accurate detection of user personality traits, as compared to using single-source static data. We chose Twitter, Instagram, and Foursquare as the main data sources due to they are among the largest and diverse social media networks [4]. Specifically, we harvested Twitter as the textual data source; Instagram as the image data source; and Foursquare as the location data source.

Predicting user personality profiling from multi-source temporal data is a challenging problem due to the following issues:

- **Cross-Network User Account Disambiguation.** It is hard to align the accounts of the same user from different social media resources.
- **Incomplete Multi-Source Data Fusion.** Most social media users participate only in distinct sets of social media services (e.g. Twitter + Instagram or Foursquare + Twitter) and not always active in all of them. Both these factors introduce the problem of block-wise missing data, which is a significant challenge.
- **Incorporation of temporal data aspect.** Construction of multi-source learning models that take into account the temporal data dependencies is essential but was not well studied yet.

Inspired by the challenges above, in this study we seek to address the following research questions:

1. Is it possible to perform user personality profiling more accurately by learning from multiple incomplete data sources?
2. Is it possible to improve the performance of user personality profiling by leveraging on temporal aspect of data?
3. Which data sources contribute the most to user personality profiling?

To answer these research questions, we present our **idea of temporal learning from multiple social networks for automatic personality profiling**. Specifically, we utilize multi-modal longitudinal data from Twitter, Instagram, and Foursquare in our multi-source learning framework "PersonaLSTM". The framework simultaneously fuses multi-source multi-modal temporal data and performs personality predictions by following MBTI personality scale. The issue of block-vise incomplete data is solved by applying non-negative matrix factorization [13], while the data temporality is efficiently incorporated by using long-short-term memory neural networks [8]. The experimental results reveal the superiority of our proposed framework over non-temporal baselines and different data source combinations.

2   Problems with Current Approaches

It is worth mentioning that multiple research groups tackled the task of personality profiling from the Computational Social Science's point of view [1,9]. These works all observe that users' personality score is related to their behavior on social media platforms. Furthermore, Youyou et al. [30] mentioned that personality is a major driving force behind people's interactions, behavior, and emotions. Schwartz et al. [26] analyzed the Facebook messages of 75000 volunteers and demonstrated the correlations between words usage and personality traits. Unfortunately, these works are descriptive in nature and do not tackle the problem for automatic personality profiling.

Meanwhile, the problem of single-source personality profiling was addressed by several research groups. For example, Kosinski et al. [12] conducted an extensive correlation analysis over $180,000$ Facebook users by using different data representations, such as the size of individual social graph, the number of uploaded photos, and the number of attended events; and reported encouraging results on user extraversion prediction [12]. Later, Verhoeven et al. [28] revealed that such MBTI categories as "introversion—extraversion" and "thinking—feeling" can be successfully predicted from Twitter data, while the prediction of the other two categories is more challenging. Finally, Wei et al. [29] incorporated tweets, avatars, emoticons, and responsive patterns for predicting personality traits from Sina Weibo[1]. The aforementioned works made significant contributions to the field of automatic personality profiling. However, they are all limited due to the use of the single-source data, which is inadequate in the real-world scenario.

At the same time, several research works addressed the problem of user profiling from the multi-source learning perspective. One of the research groups [5] utilized multiple social networks for the task of user demographics profiling, while in [2] they demonstrated that the incorporation of multi-source data helps to increase the accuracy of relationship status prediction. Finally, Nie et al. [20] proposed an approach for seamless integration of information from multiple social networks for career path prediction. These works are related to our study regarding the incorporation of multi-source data for individual user profiling. However,

---

[1] http://weibo.com.

they do not incorporate the temporal aspect of multimedia data, which is one of the essential components of our study.

Finally, several works were dedicated to the usage of temporal data for user profiling. For example, Liu et al. [14] proposed a compositional recurrent neural network architecture to learn text representations at the character, word, and sentiment level for the task of personality trait inference. Another work [10] incorporated temporal aspect of the data for sentiment classification by using LSTMs. Finally, [25]) proposed "temporal continuity"-based version of nonnegative matrix factorization for emerging topic detection and reported its efficiency for Twitter stream analytics.

Even though the related works significantly contributed to user personality profiling, they did not address the problem of automatic personality profiling from multi-source temporal perspective. This work is the first attempt to fill this research gap.

3   Data Description

3.1   MBTI Scale

To obtain results on the type of personality, it is necessary to take the MBTI test, which consists of the answering a series of questions (from 72 to 222). The test is scored by evaluating each answer in terms of what it reveals about the taker. Each question is relevant to one of the MBTI category [15]: Extroversion/Introversion, Sensing/Intuition, Thinking/Feeling, Judging/Perceiving.

In this article, we name the MBTI category with the first letters of the two labels. It should be emphasized, that the labels for each category are not exactly inverse of each other. This is because the human can have in his/her character the part from both labels of MBTI category. The selected MBTI tests help to identify the predominant label for every MBTI category. Therefore we didn't choose any dominant label for each category.

3.2   Dataset Collection

The related works in the field of multi-source social media modeling proposed various approaches to solving the problem of cross-network user account disambiguation [4,6]. In this work, we adopt the so-called "cross-linking user account mapping" strategy, where Twitter is used as a "sink" that accumulates Instagram and Foursquare re-posts as well as Twitter tweets in one information channel. To obtain personality-related ground truth, we utilized Twitter search API[2] to perform a search for the results of trusted online MBTI tests, such as 16 Personalities[3], Jung Typology Test[4], and MBTI Online[5]. After collecting tweets

---

[2] http://dev.twitter.com/rest/public.

[3] http://16personalities.com.

[4] http://humanmetrics.com/.

[5] http://mbtionline.com.

with MBTI test results, we extracted MBTI ground truth labels from them. As a result, we obtained MBTI labels for 15,788 Twitter users. After collecting ground truth results and users' Twitter profiles, we downloaded all possible tweets, photos, and check-ins for each user (Table 1).

Table 1. Dataset statistics

	Twitter	Instagram	Foursquare
#users	15788	10254	3090
	tweets	**images**	**check-ins**
#posts	122,584,534	4,789,519	420,603

4 Data Representation

In this section, we overview the features that we extracted from our collected dataset.

Heuristically-Inferred and Lexicon Features. First, we counted the number of URLs, the number of hashtags and the number of user mentions. Second, we calculated the number slang words, the number of emotion words, the number of emoticons, and the average sentiment score. Third, we computed the linguistic style features, such as the number of repeated characters in words, number of misspellings, and number of unknown to spell checker words. Lastly, we utilized several crowd-sourced lexicons, which are associated with controversial subjects from the US press and healthiness categories. We also calculated the average level of user Twitter activity during eight daytime durations (3-h intervals) that could indirectly be related to users' activities. In total, we've extracted 53 heuristically-inferred and lexicon features.

Linguistic Features. We extracted LIWC features [21] that were found to be a powerful mechanism for personality, age, and gender prediction purposes [23]. For each user, we extracted 64 LIWC features.

LDA Features. For each user, we merged all his/her tweets into "documents" (one user - one document) and then projected these documents into a latent topic space by applying Latent Dirichlet Allocation (LDA). As a result, for each user, we extracted 50 LDA features[6].

Visual Features. We automatically mapped each Instagram photo to 1000 ImageNet [3] image concepts by using pre-trained GoogleNet model. We then summed up the predicted concept occurrence likelihoods for each user and divided the obtained vector to the total number of images posted by this user. In total, we extracted 1,000 image features for every user.

---

[6] We empirically set $\alpha = 0.5$, $\beta = 0.1$, $T = 50$ topics for 1,000 LDA iterations.

Location Features. We utilized 886 Foursquare venue categories to compute location features. For each user, we counted the total number of his/her Foursquare check-ins in venues of each venue category. Then, we divided the number of check-ins in each category by the total number of check-ins of the user.

5   Personality Profiling

This section presents our multi-view temporal data learning approach for the task of automatic personality profiling.

McCrae et al. [17] stated that personality traits in adulthood continuously evolve, but such changes are happening rare and over long periods of time. The above observation inspired us to incorporate temporal aspect in the form of not large time intervals. We thus divided user timelines into $k = 10$ time intervals of 142 days each, so that within **such summary interval user's personality is not expected to change significantly**. Such data division approach is expected to be helpful in identifying temporal user behavior patterns. According to [17] during all these time intervals user' personality will not significantly change, which means that we can use the same personality type for all time periods.

The original MBTI scheme assumes that each MBTI category represents distinct sides of a human character. For example, Mattare et al. [16] demonstrated that "sensing – intuition" category is related to human entrepreneur skills. In this work, we thus focus on the prediction of each MBTI category separately, so that they can later be aggregated into one of 16 MBTI personality types.

5.1   The PLSTM Framework

Long Short Term Memory neural networks (LSTMs) is a particular category of Recurrent Neural Networks (RNNs) that are capable of learning long-term temporal data dependencies. Such property fits well to our problem of temporal multi-source learning for personality profiling. The architecture of our PLSTM framework is illustrated on Figure ??. For the prediction of the full MBTI profile, four separate models will need to be trained for four MBTI categories, each of which consists of two labels. Each model predicts one final label for each MBTI category. For each model, the features extracted from the data that corresponds to the m time periods are used as inputs to the corresponding m LSTM layers. Each layer except the first one uses the learned information from the previous layers. In this way, the last layer represents the information for m periods of time. The output of the last layer is connected to the softmax layer, which consists of two neurons. Each neuron in the softmax layer corresponds to the probabilities of each label for a MBTI category. The final prediction is made by selecting the label with greater probability.

5.2   Missing Data Problem

As mentioned before, one of the major challenges in multi-source temporal data analysis is the modeling of block-wise missing data. Indeed, the number of users in our dataset who participate in all three social networks simultaneously is relatively small: 702 users. Moreover, the number of users who, at the same time, has performed activities in all $k = 10$ time periods is only 128, which is not sufficient for effective LSTM training. To tackle this problem, we utilize non-negative matrix factorization (NMF) [13] separately for the data from each period of time. For every time interval we try to recover the missing data modalities of those users who have contributed to at least one social network during that time interval. After applying NMF we obtained in total 5001 users with the automatically filled matrix of activities in all social networks and in all time periods (both with the real data and after filling missing data with NMF). For our final experiments, we selected only this group of users.

6   Evaluation

To answer our proposed research questions, we carried out two experiments. The first experiment aims to evaluate the importance of temporal data utilization; while the second one compares the results obtained by models trained on different data source combinations.

For evaluation, we divided the dataset into training, test and evaluation sets. First, we selected all users with the activities in any social network in all $k = 10$ time intervals. Second, we divided users into training (70%) evaluation (10%), and test (20%) sets, preserving the original distribution of data among MBTI types and the level of user activity in three social networks.

Although we perform binary classification on each label in each category, we cannot prioritize the label in each category since they are not exactly the inverse of each other. Because of this, we use "Macro-F1" metrics for evaluation in our experiments. This metrics represents the averaged "Recall", "Precision" and "F1" measures across two labels in each.

6.1   Model Training

In order to feed in the data into our LSTM neural network, for every user timeline in our dataset, we divided the data into $k = 10$ equal time periods of 142 days each. We then extracted the multi-source features for each time period as described in section above. We further defined a "window" as m consecutive time periods of user activity. We vary "window" size to find the best number of consecutive time periods for determining the dependencies between users' social activities and their personality and to test the sensitivity of time durations in inferring different personality concepts. We built an independent LSTM neural network for each of four personality categories. The trained LSTM models for all MBTI categories are then aggregated into the PersonalLSTM framework. It is noted, that the number of windows for train, test and validation sets for each *window* size is different. Let S be the number of windows for *window* os size m, then $S = k - m + 1$, where $k = 10$ is the total number of time periods in the dataset. From this formula, it follows, that the largest number of windows is for *window* size $m = 2$, while the smallest is for $m = 10$.

6.2   Baselines that Does Not Consider Temporal Aspect

We selected Gradient Boosting, Logistic Regression, and Naive Byes classifiers as our non-temporal baselines. These approaches achieved high performance when solving the problem of relationship status prediction [2] based on the early-fusion multisource data (when feature vectors from data modalities are combined into one feature vector). The task of relationship status profiling was reported to be semantically similar to user personality profiling [2], which implies that the above algorithms can be used as strong baselines for our task. The features for non-temporal baselines were computed as described in Section above and based on the whole history of user activities in our dataset. The key idea is to train the baseline models based on the whole period of data (from 1 January 2013 to 31 December 2016) and then compare them to our proposed temporal approach, which also utilizes the whole data, but divided the data into 10 periods of time.

6.3   Evaluation Against Non-temporal Baselines

First, we evaluated the performance of PersonaLSTM framework for different window sizes. We varied the window size m from 2 to 10 and trained LSTM network for each window size.

For each personality attribute the best performing window size is different. For example, the window size $m = 3$ (3 time periods of 142 days each, approximately 14 months) demonstrated the best performance for predicting MBTI category "extraversion – introversion". This category is related to the so-called "energy and motivation resources" for people of different types [18]. The small window size of the best-performing model could indicate that the "energy" acquisition resources do not depend on the temporal data aspect.

At the same time, the category "sensing – intuition" can be accurately predicted with the window size $m = 9$. We hypothesize that it is because the category depends on behavior patterns over long periods of time. The above observation is consistent with the description of "sensing – intuition" category in literature. Specifically, Mayers et al. [18] reported that "sensing" people pay attention to physical reality, while intuition people pay attention to impressions and the meaning of the information.

The best performing window size for the category "thinking – feeling" is $m = 7$ (approximately 2.7 years). Mayers et al. [18] mentioned that people of "feeling" type tend to be more aware of other humans' feelings and can "...relate more consistently well to people" [18]. At the same time, as noted in Nasca et al. [19], "thinking" people are considered to be less emotional. From the above definitions, it follows that the prediction results of "thinking – feeling" category can be explained by their dependence on users' reactions to surrounding life events.

Finally, for the category "judging – perception", the optimal window size is $m = 5$ (approximately 2 year interval). Based on Myers et al. [18] definition, "judging – perception" category separates judging people and perceiving individuals. At the same time, from Nasca et al. [19] it follows that people of "judging – perception" category "...do not show any particular relationship with communication apprehension" [19]. The above suggests that there are no strict communications patterns in social media data for predicting "judging – perception" category. At the same time, the results reveal that the temporal data helps to increase the quality of the predictions, which suggests that the temporal-enabled models can identify more complex behavior patterns that are not directly related to user conversations.

Based on the above results, we selected window sizes for temporal models that demonstrated the best results for each MBTI category and included them in the final configuration of PersonalLSTM framework. We then compared them with non-temporal baselines. The obtained results are presented in Table 2. From the Table, it can be seen that PersonalLSTM outperformed non-temporal baselines for "sensing – intuition" and "judging – perception" categories. At the same time, "introversion – extroversion" and "thinking – feeling" prediction performance is lower than those obtained by Gradient Boosting. Our obtained results are also consistent with Myers's definitions [18]. Precisely, "sensing – intuition" and "judging – perception" categories describe the "...reactions to different life changes" [18], which goes well with the temporality of social media data. At the same time, "introversion – extroversion" and "thinking – feeling" categories are more about life perception, which requires longer periods of data to be feed into personality profiling models. Based on the experimental outputs, we can **positively answer to our second research question**[7]. Specifically, we claim that it is possible to improve the performance of automatic personality profiling by leveraging on temporal data aspect for two MBTI categories: "sensing – intuition" and "judging – perception".

Table 2. Results obtained by non-temporal baselines and PLSTM framework. Evaluation metrics: macro F_1

	Gradient boosting	Logistic regression	Naive Bayes	LSTM
E/I	**0,715**	0,600	0,440	0,541
S/N	0,495	0,425	0,33	**0,724**
T/F	**0,670**	0,435	0,440	0,534
J/P	0,510	0,395	0,470	**0,750**

---

[7] Is it possible to improve the performance of user personality profiling by leveraging on temporal data aspect?

6.4   Evaluation Against Data Source Combinations

To understand the importance of different data sources for personality profiling as well as to answer our first and third research questions, in this section we compare the results obtained by PersonalLSTM trained based on different data source combinations.

The evaluation results are reported in Table 3. From the table, it can be seen that the incorporation of single data source always demonstrates lover prediction performance, as compared to multi-source utilization. Among the single data sources, the location data demonstrates the best performance for all categories except "sensing – intuition", which can be better predicted by leveraging textual data. These results are consistent with the definition of "sensing – intuition" type. Specifically, the category characterizes the way users receive new information from the outside world [18], which conforms well with the richness of the textual data modality.

Table 3. The results for combination of data of different modalities, the best window size is shown in brackets. Evaluation metrics: macro F_1.

	E/I	S/I	T/F	J/P
Text (T)	0,362 (2)	0,456 (8)	0,380 (6)	0,469 (9)
Media (M)	0,349 (2)	0,409 (5)	0,493 (9)	0,472 (7)
Location (L)	0,511 (4)	0,43 (4)	0,493 (9)	0,494 (5)
T, M	0,349 (3)	0,594 (3)	0,465 (9)	0,543 (2)
M, L	0,511 (4)	0,605 (5)	0,496 (4)	0,595 (3)
T, L	0,521 (5)	0,618 (3)	0,495 (3)	0,596 (7)
T, M, L	**0,541 (6)**	**0,724 (9)**	**0,534 (7)**	**0,750 (5)**

From the results of models that were trained on bi-source combinations, it can be seen that the best performance (ranging from 49.5% to 59.6%) for all MBTI categories was achieved by text and location combination. This is consistent with the results of models training on single modality data, where text and location were found to be the best among all single-source baselines. Thus, the results of experiments with a single source and bi-source data make it possible to **answer our third research question**[8] **that text and location modalities contribute the most to the task of automatic user personality profiling.**

Finally, it is noted that PersonalLSTM trained based on all three modalities, outperformed all other multi-source baselines, which **positively answers to our first**[9] **research question.** Specifically, we would like to highlight that **the**

---

[8] Which data sources contribute the most to user personality profiling?.

[9] Is it possible to perform user personality profiling more accurately by learning from multiple incomplete data sources?.

incorporation of multiple sources results from 28% boosting of personality profiling performance, as compared to single-source utilization. It is also worth mentioning that the best-performing window size varies from 5 to 9, which is the period from 1.5 years to 2.5 years. Such differences in the window size may be caused by differences in the essence of the each of the MBTI categories. Since each of MBTI categories characterizes the disjoint personality traits, the best time interval for determining each of MBTI category is also different.

6.5   Full MBTI Type Prediction

In this experiment, we aim to predicted the full MBTI type of users. First, we predicted each of the four MBTI categories separately and then combined the predicted categories into the full profile. The achieved results showed an accuracy of 20.3%. Even though these results are better than random prediction, their quality is insufficient for use in real-life settings. For real life applications, such as marketing and recommendations it is more reasonable to try to improve the quality of predictions of each MBTI category separately.

7   Conclusions and Future Work

In this work, we presented the first study of learning from multimodal temporal data of the task of automatic user personality profiling. Our proposed PersonalLSTM framework consists of multiple LSTM models trained based on temporal data from three social networks (Twitter, Instagram, Foursquare). The evaluation results demonstrate that for two MBTI categories the incorporation of temporal model increases the quality of automatic personality profiling, while the two MBTI categories can be better predicted by non-temporal models. At the same time, in all cases when the models are trained based on multiple data sources, the personality profiling performance is significantly better as compared to the single-source baselines. To facilitate further research, we released our multi-source multimodal temporal dataset for public use.

Our further research will include: (1) the extension of our current dataset; (2) the incorporation of new image features that will include visual sentiment estimations; (3) the incorporation of more detailed temporal data; and (4) the corresponding temporal regularization of PersonalLSTM framework.

References

1. Adali, S., Golbeck, J.: Predicting personality with social behavior. In: 2012 IEEE/ACM International Conference on Advances in Social Networks Analysis and Mining (ASONAM), pp. 302–309. IEEE (2012)
2. Buraya, K., Farseev, A., Filchenkov, A., Chua, T.S.: Towards user personality profiling from multiple social networks. In: Proceedings of the Thirty-First AAAI Conference on Artificial Intelligence (2017)

3. Deng, J., Dong, W., Socher, R., Li, L.J., Li, K., Fei-Fei, L.: Imagenet: a large-scale hierarchical image database. In: IEEE Conference on Computer Vision and Pattern Recognition, CVPR 2009, pp. 248–255. IEEE (2009)

4. Farseev, A., Akbari, M., Samborskii, I., Chua, T.S.: 360° user profiling: past, future, and applications. In: ACM SIGWEB Newsletter (Summer), vol. 4 (2016)

5. Farseev, A., Nie, L., Akbari, M., Chua, T.S.: Harvesting multiple sources for user profile learning: a big data study. In: Proceedings of the 5th ACM on International Conference on Multimedia Retrieval, pp. 235–242. ACM (2015)

6. Farseev, A., Samborskii, I., Chua, T.S.: bBridge: a big data platform for social multimedia analytics. In: Proceedings of the 2016 ACM on Multimedia Conference, pp. 759–761. ACM (2016)

7. Farseev, A., Samborskii, I., Filchenkov, A., Chua, T.S.: Cross-domain recommendation via clustering on multi-layer graphs. In: Proceedings of the 40th International ACM SIGIR Conference on Research and Development in Information Retrieval, pp. 195–204. ACM (2017)

8. Gers, F.A., Schraudolph, N.N., Schmidhuber, J.: Learning precise timing with LSTM recurrent networks. J. Mach. Learn. Res. 3(Aug), 115–143 (2002)

9. Golbeck, J., Robles, C., Turner, K.: Predicting personality with social media. In: CHI 2011 Extended Abstracts on Human Factors in Computing Systems, pp. 253–262. ACM (2011)

10. Huang, M., Cao, Y., Dong, C.: Modeling rich contexts for sentiment classification with LSTM. arXiv preprint arXiv:1605.01478 (2016)

11. Kaplan, A.M., Haenlein, M.: Users of the world, unite! the challenges and opportunities of social media. Bus. Horiz. 53(1), 59–68 (2010)

12. Kosinski, M., Stillwell, D., Graepel, T.: Private traits and attributes are predictable from digital records of human behavior. Proc. Natl. Acad. Sci. 110(15), 5802–5805 (2013)

13. Lee, D.D., Seung, H.S.: Learning the parts of objects by non-negative matrix factorization. Nature 401(6755), 788–791 (1999)

14. Liu, F., Perez, J., Nowson, S.: A language-independent and compositional model for personality trait recognition from short texts. arXiv preprint arXiv:1610.04345 (2016)

15. Martin, C.R.: Looking at Type: The Fundamentals. Center for Applications of Psychological Type, Gainesville (1997)

16. Mattare, M.: Revisiting understanding entrepreneurs using the Myers-Briggs type indicator®. J. Market. Dev. Competitiveness 9(2), 114 (2015)

17. McCrae, R.R., Costa, P.T.: Personality in Adulthood: A Five-Factor Theory Perspective. Guilford Press, New York (2003)

18. Myers, I.B., McCaulley, M.H., Most, R.: Manual, a Guide to the Development and Use of the Myers-Briggs Type Indicator. Consulting Psychologists Press, Mountain View (1985)

19. Nasca, D.: The impact of cognitive style on communication. NASSP Bull. 78(559), 99–107 (1994)

20. Nie, L., Zhang, L., Wang, M., Hong, R., Farseev, A., Chua, T.S.: Learning user attributes via mobile social multimedia analytics. ACM Trans. Intell. Syst. Technol. (TIST) 8(3), 36 (2017)

21. Pennebaker, J.W., Francis, M.E., Booth, R.J.: Linguistic Inquiry and Word Count: Liwc 2001. Lawrence Erlbaum Associates, Mahway (2001)

22. Pennebaker, J.W., Mehl, M.R., Niederhoffer, K.G.: Psychological aspects of natural language use: our words, our selves. Ann. Rev. Psychol. 54(1), 547–577 (2003)

23. Rangel, F., Rosso, P., Potthast, M., Stein, B., Daelemans, W.: Overview of the 3rd author profiling task at PAN 2015. In: CLEF. sn (2015)
24. Rushton, S., Morgan, J., Richard, M.: Teacher's Myers-Briggs personality profiles: identifying effective teacher personality traits. Teach. Teach. Educ. **23**(4), 432–441 (2007)
25. Saha, A., Sindhwani, V.: Learning evolving and emerging topics in social media: a dynamic NMF approach with temporal regularization. In: Proceedings of the Fifth ACM International Conference on Web Search and Data Mining, pp. 693–702. ACM (2012)
26. Schwartz, H.A., et al.: Personality, gender, and age in the language of social media: the open-vocabulary approach. PloS One **8**(9), e73791 (2013)
27. Song, X., Nie, L., Zhang, L., Akbari, M., Chua, T.S.: Multiple social network learning and its application in volunteerism tendency prediction. In: Proceedings of the 38th International ACM SIGIR Conference on Research and Development in Information Retrieval, pp. 213–222. ACM (2015)
28. Verhoeven, B., Daelemans, W., Plank, B.: Twisty: a multilingual Twitter stylometry corpus for gender and personality profiling. In: 10th International Conference on Language Resources and Evaluation (LREC 2016) (2016)
29. Wei, H., et al.: Beyond the words: predicting user personality from heterogeneous information. In: Proceedings of the Tenth ACM International Conference on Web Search and Data Mining, pp. 305–314. ACM (2017)
30. Youyou, W., Kosinski, M., Stillwell, D.: Computer-based personality judgments are more accurate than those made by humans. Proc. Natl. Acad. Sci. **112**(4), 1036–1040 (2015)

Using R Markdown for Replicable
Experiments in Evidence Based Medicine

Giorgio Maria Di Nunzio[1] and Federica Vezzani[2(✉)]

[1] Department of Information Engineering, University of Padua, Padova, Italy
giorgiomaria.dinunzio@unipd.it
[2] Department of Linguistic and Literary Studies, University of Padua, Padova, Italy
federica.vezzani@phd.unipd.it

Abstract. In this paper, we propose a methodology based on the R Markdown framework for replicating an experiment of query rewriting in the context of medical eHealth. We present a study on how to re-propose the same task of systematic medical reviews with the same conditions and methodologies to a larger group of participants. The task is the CLEF eHealth Task Technologically Assisted Reviews in Empirical Medicine which consists in finding all the most relevant medical documents, given an information need, with the least effort. We study how lay people, students of a master degree in languages in this case, can help the retrieval system in finding more relevant documents by means of a query rewriting approach.

1 Introduction

Systematic medical reviews are a method to collect the findings from multiple studies in a reliable way and are used to inform policy and practice [19]. During the 'screening' of documents, physicians look manually through collections of medical databases in order to identify most (if not all) the relevant documents pertaining the object of the search. In this context, Technology-Assisted Review (TAR) systems help the user to find as much relevant information as possible with reasonable effort [5]. The most successful TAR systems tackle the problem by training a classifier by means of a continuous active learning approach (each time a user reads a new document and judges it relevant or not, this information is immediately given as feedback to the system) [19,23]. There is also the problem related to how the user form the query in order to restrict the set of documents to be considered. The principal systems in current use are document databases supporting Boolean querying. Reviewers use such systems to incrementally build complex queries that may involve hundreds of terms, with the aim of including the great majority of relevant documents in the answer set. For example, in [14], the authors investigate a hybrid approach, where a Boolean search strategy is used to fetch an initial pool of candidate documents, and ranking is then applied to order the result set.

In this paper, we follow a similar approach to [14] and we present a methodology for replicating an experiment of query rewriting in the context of medical

© Springer Nature Switzerland AG 2018
P. Bellot et al. (Eds.): CLEF 2018, LNCS 11018, pp. 28–39, 2018.
https://doi.org/10.1007/978-3-319-98932-7_3

eHealth. In particular, the experiment consists in re-proposing a task previously performed by a team of researchers for the CLEF eHealth Task 2: "Technologically Assisted Reviews in Empirical Medicine" [7]. The task consists in retrieving all the relevant documents for medical specific domains as early as possible and with the least effort. The main goal of the experiment presented in this paper is to re-propose:

- the same task with
- the same conditions and
- the same methodologies
- to a larger group of participants.

In particular, we want to accomplish the goal of the 'Replication track' of this Task in order to disseminate solid and reproducible results, as also shown by [8].

1.1   Replicability Issues in IR Experiments

Replicable and reproducible methods are fundamental research tools because the lack of reproducibility in science causes significant issues for science itself. Research areas in Computer Science using linguistic resources in an extensive way have been addressed this problem in the last years. For example, the most important conferences in Information Retrieval (IR) support this kind of activities [9]: the open source information retrieval reproducibility challenge at SIGIR[1], the Reproducibility track at ECIR since 2016 [10], as well as some Labs at the Cross-Language Evaluation Forum (CLEF) that explicitly have a task on reproducibility, such as CLEF eHealth.[2] In 2018 the three major conferences in IR evaluation, TREC, CLEF and NTCIR made a joint effort to support replicable research through the CENTRE initiative.[3]

The Natural Language Processing (NLP) community has witnessed the same issue. In 2016, the "Workshop on Research Results Reproducibility and Resources Citation in Science and Technology of Language" at the Language Resources and Evaluation Conference (LREC) encouraged the discussion and the advancement on the reproducibility of research results and the citation of resources, and its impact on research integrity in the research area of language processing tools and resources [2]. In the very recent past, even the second edition of the 4REAL workshop at LREC 2018 aimed to contribute to the advancement of reproduction and replication of research results which are at the heart of the validation of scientific knowledge and scientific endeavor.

> "Everyone agrees that there's a problem: very often, results and conclusions in experimental science and some areas of engineering turn out to be unreliable or false. And everyone agrees that the solution is to put more effort into verifying such results and conclusions, by having other people re-do aspects of the research and analysis [17]".

---

[1] https://goo.gl/CePVzY.
[2] https://goo.gl/WgkqnZ.
[3] http://www.centre-eval.org.

Technical term: RADICULOPATHY				Traducente: RADICOLOPATIA			
Formal features				Caratteristiche formali			
Genre	Noun			Genere	s. f.		
Spelling	"th" pronounced as a voiceless dental non-sibilant fricative			Ortografia	niente da segnalare		
Tonic accent	/ radɪkjʊˈlɒpəθi/			Accento tonico	radicolopatia		
Derivation/Composition	Latin radicula + English -o- + -pathy First Known Use: 1942			Derivazione/Composizione	radicolopatia [comp. del lat. radicŭla (dim. di radix -icis xradìcex) e di -patia]		
Language Definition	Field	Register	Sources	Definizione in lingua	Dominio	Registro d'uso	Fonti
Dysfunction of one or more spinal nerve roots, characterized by pain and sensory and motor disturbances and often caused by compression	Pathology	Specialized	1	Qualsiasi alterazione a carico di una radice nervosa, determinata da cause varie: infiammatorie, compressive, tossiche, malformative, vascolari, ecc.	Patologia	Specializzato	1
/dysfunction/ /spinal nerve/ /root/ /body/ /living being/				/alterazione/ /radice/ /nervo/ /corpo/ /essere umano/			
Specialized contexts	Field	Register	Sources	Proposte di traduzione			
This is why neck problems that affect a cervical nerve root can cause pain and other symptoms through the arms and hands (radiculopathy), and low back problems that affect a lumbar nerve root can radiate through the leg and into the foot (radiculopathy, or sciatica), thus prompting leg pain and/or foot pain.	Pathology	Specialized	2	This is a semantically univocal term: the result is the perfect correspondence of units of sense. For this reason, the Italian translating candidate for "radiculopathy" is "radicolopatia".			
Risk factors for radiculopathy are activities that place an excessive or repetitive load on the spine.	Pathology	Specialized	3				
Ontological - encyclopedic illustrations	https://www.google.it/search?q=radiculopathy&rlz=1C1AVNE_enIT611IT611&source=lnms&tbm=isch&sa=X&ved=0ahUKEwiK-dKrw4nYAhVMCewKHUMZO0OQ_AUICigB&biw=1093&bih=470#imgrc=xQ8-SmJcQYTT8M:			Illustrazioni ontologiche - enciclopediche	https://neuroupdate.files.wordpress.com/2007/10/radicolopatia-s1.jpg		
Collocations - phraseology	RADICULOPATHY+VERB : R. occurs when [...], R. results when [...]			Collocazioni - fraseologia italiana	Soffrire di radicolopatia		
References				Riferimenti			
https://en.oxforddictionaries.com/definition/radiculopathy			1	https://www.treccani.it/vocabolario/radicolopatia/			1
https://www.spine-health.com/conditions/spine-anatomy/radiculopathy-radiculitis-and-radicular-pain			2	https://it.wikipedia.org/wiki/Radicolopatia			2
https://www.medicinenet.com/radiculopathy/article.htm			3				

Fig. 1. Multilingual terminological record: radiculopathy

The benefit of reproducibility is evident in cases where faithfully recreating the research conditions is impossible as the variables contributing to a particular instance of field observation are too hard to control in some cases [1]. Clearly, linguists cannot expect their colleagues to replicate data collection conditions, and doing so would not necessarily lead to replicated utterances, but reproducibility is a more realistic goal.

In this paper, in order to describe in detail the process of data preparation, we use the 'literate programming' approach proposed by Knuth [15]. Literate programming helps peers understand and replicate your results, find errors and suggest enhancements and, ultimately, produce better-quality programs.

We used the R Markdown framework[4] since it is considered one of the possible solutions to document the results of an experiment and, at the same time, reproduce each step of the experiment itself. Following the indications given by [11] and the suggestions discussed by [3], we developed the experimental framework in R and we share the source code on Github in order to allow other participants to reproduce and check our results.[5]

2 Linguistic Methodology for Query Rewriting

In this section, we outline the linguistic methodology that the participants of the experiment used to for rewrite the original query of the expert in order to capture different senses of the information need and retrieve more relevant documents. We proceeded by the reformulation of an initial query given by an expert by planning our working methodology on the analysis of some linguistic and terminological aspects functional to the process of query rewriting. This approach

---

[4] http://rmarkdown.rstudio.com.
[5] https://github.com/gmdn/CLEF2018.

has contributed to an effective and efficient reformulation for the retrieval of the most relevant documents for the research. The approach is divided into the following steps:

1. Identification of technical terms;
2. Manual extraction of technical terms;
3. Linguistic and semantic analysis;
4. Formulation of terminological records;
5. Query rewriting.

The basis of our methodology for query rewriting is a terminological and linguistic analysis of the initial query formulated by the expert. Given the short information need, we started with the identification of the technical terms, as all the terms that are strictly related to the conceptual and practical factors of a given discipline or activity [16]. Medical language has actually a specialised vocabulary composed of strictly specialised terms referring to this particular domain.

We then proceed with the manual extraction of such technical terms and started to conduct a linguistic and terminological analysis through the implementation of the core of our methodology for query rewriting, that is a new model of terminological record. Terminological records are commonly used in terminology and linguistics as a tool for the collection of terminological and linguistic data referring to a specific concept [12]. The term records proposed to the participants of the experiment is based on the model implemented in a linguistic resource aiming to provide a support eHealth tool for the study of the complexity of medical language from the semantic viewpoint: TriMED [24]. The new model of term record provide information both from a purely linguistic and from a translation point of view. TriMED is actually designed for technical-scientific translators who have the difficult task to decode and then transcode medical information from a source language into a target language. For this reason, the terminological record offers the same kind of information for the technical term and its equivalent in the target language. Figure 1 shows an example of a terminological record for the technical term *Radiculopathy* and its equivalent in Italian *Radicolopatia*.

Focusing on the linguistic aspects, these records provide a broad spectrum of information of the term analysed. We firstly decide to provide all the formal features related to the term that are necessary for its lexical framing:

- Genre;
- Spelling:
- Tonic accent;
- Derivation and composition.

In order to grasp the content of concepts, we provide the definition of the terms through the analysis of the meaning conventionally attributed to them by a community of people sharing the same knowledge and having a common goal. Definitions constitute a structured system of knowledge [18] in order to understand the meaning of a term. We extracted the definitions from reliable resources as Merriam-Webster Medical Dictionary[6] and MediLexicon[7] in particular for acronyms and abbreviations. Furthermore, we focus on the semantic viewpoint by providing the semic analysis of the term. Semic analysis is a methodology of study used in compositional semantics aiming to decompose the meaning of technical terms (that is the lexematic or morphological unit) into minimum unit of meaning that cannot be further segmented, known as semantic traits or semantic components. The union of multiple semantic traits makes up the meaning of a lexeme [21].

Moreover, participants were required to provide the context of use of the term. This is because, in a such specific domain, the context attributes the semantic value to the term. Participants considered phraseology (collocations in particular) in order to analyse the semantic behaviour of the terms related to their neighbours. Phrasemes are intended as the combinations whose overall meaning does not result from the sum of the meanings of the individual components [6]. Finally, terminological records offer ontological illustrations of the term and some references in order to track the retrieval of information.

With this kind of analysis participants were able to

1. create the basis of knowledge for the domain and the context of study;
2. propose the query variant through two different approaches.

The first variant of the query was a list of keywords that the participants obtained from the semic analysis of the technical terms contained in the initial query. The second variant is instead a human readable reformulation, therefore grammatically correct, and containing the fewest possible number of terms equal to the starting query. This reformulation is therefore made up of synonymic variants, acronyms, abbreviations or periphrases. Participants could exploit the information given by a document that could be relevant or not according to the initial query, the list of term frequencies, document frequency and the boolean query generated by PubMed.[8]

3   Experiments

The participants of this experiment were the students of the Master's Degree course in Modern Languages for International Communication and Cooperation of the University of Padua. The 90 students, all of them with different background, were divided into 30 groups of 3 people each. Each group has been entrusted with a specific information need for the medical field. The aim of the students was to reformulate the initial query by evaluating specific linguistic aspects in order to give two reformulations according to the above mentioned methodology. The result is a number of 60 reformulations, that is two variants of queries formulated by each group of students. Hereinafter an example of the two variants proposed by a group of students for a specific information need:

---

[6] https://www.merriam-webster.com/medical.

[7] http://www.medilexicon.com.

[8] https://www.ncbi.nlm.nih.gov/pubmed/.

- Initial query: *Physical examination for lumbar radiculopathy due to disc herniation in patients with low-back pain;*
- First variant: *Sensitivity, specificity, test, tests, diagnosis, examination, physical, straight leg raising, slump, radicular, radiculopathy, pain, inflammation, compression, compress, spinal nerve, spine, cervical, root, roots, sciatica, vertebrae, lumbago, LBP, lumbar, low, back, sacral, disc, discs, disk, disks, herniation, hernia, herniated, intervertebral;*
- Second variant: *Sensitivity and specificity of physical tests for the diagnosis of nerve irritation caused by damage to the discs between the vertebrae in patients presenting LBP (lumbago).*

At a later time, we asked to the students to reformulate an individual query different from the two variants previously proposed:

- Individual reformulation: *Patients with pain in the lower back need a check-up for the compression or inflammation of a spinal nerve caused by rupture of fibrocartilagenous material that surrounds the intervertebral disk.*

The first reformulation is therefore a list of keywords that tends to cover as much as possible the semantic sphere affected by the term analysed. The second human-readable reformulation is more focused on providing synonymic variants or acronyms in order to use the least possible number of terms of the initial query. Whereas, the individual reformulation does not follow a precise approach other than that of human interpretation resulting from the approximate study of the subject contained in the query. At the end of the experiment, 28 groups completed the task. We therefore received a total of 28 list of keywords, 28 human-readable reformulation and 66 individual reformulations.

3.1 Dataset and System Settings

The dataset provided by the TARs in Empirical Medicine Task at CLEF 2017 is based on 50 systematic reviews, or topics, conducted by Cochrane experts on Diagnostic Test Accuracy. The dataset consists of: a set of 50 topics (20 training and 30 test) and, for each topic, the set of PubMed Document Identifiers (PIDs) returned by running the query in Pubmed as well as the relevance judgments for both abstracts and documents [13].

The system that retrieves the documents that the user (the physician in our case) has to judge implements the AutoTAR Continuous Active Learning (CAL) method proposed by [4]. The system is based on a BM25 weighting scheme [22] which is updated whenever the system identifies a document for assessment and the relevance judgment (provided with the CLEF dataset) is used as a feedback [20]. The system has only two parameters that can be set to adjust the amount of documents that a physician is willing to review: the *percentage p* of documents over the number of documents retrieved by the original boolean query, the *threshold t* of the number of documents to read. The parameter p is used to find the initial estimates of the probabilities of each term in the ranking phase while t sets the maximum number of documents that a physician is willing to read before the final round of classification.

In our experiments, we used only the relevance judgments of the abstracts and we did not use any training topic to optimize the system. We used the source code provided by [20] for the Continuous Active Learning method [5] to simulate the interaction with a physician who gives a relevance feedback for each abstract retrieved. Following the indications given by the authors, we vary the parameter p from 10% to 50% and set t equal to 500 and 1000, respectively. For each combination of values of p and t, 10 in total, we produce three types of runs: a run named 'expert' with the query variants produced by the two experts in linguistics, a run named 'group' with the query variants created by each group of students, a run named 'individual' with the variants written by each student of each group.

4   Results

For the evaluation of our experiments, we used the official scripts provided by the organizers of the CLEF eHEalth task.[9] This repository also contains the official results of all the participants to the task, we use these results as a baseline for our analyses. We present the results of the experiments in three parts: a comparison with the official runs of the CLEF 2017 task, an analysis among the top performing runs, a brief failure analysis.

Comparison with CLEF 2017 Runs. In Fig. 2a, we show a comparison between the performances of the runs with threshold $t = 500$ and $t = 1000$ and those of the official runs of CLEF 2017. On the abscissa we have the number of documents shown (the documents that are actually shown to the physician for relevance judgment), on the ordinate the average recall over the 30 topics. The grey points represent the performance of the CLEF 2017 runs, and the dotted grey line the Pareto frontier[10] of the best runs. The coloured lines represent the performance of the three types of runs (expert, group, individual). Each line connects five points relative to the five values of p (from $p = 10$ to $p = 50$). All our runs dominate the Pareto frontier across all the range of documents shown. In particular, the best runs with threshold $t = 500$ achieve the same recall of the best CLEF run with the same recall using around 20,000 documents less (40,000 vs 60,000), while the best runs with $t = 1000$ achieve almost the same perfect recall of the CLEF run (0.993 vs 0.998) using 25,000 documents less (63,000 vs 88,000).

Comparison Across Runs. In Fig. 2b, we show a close-up of Fig. 2a for the six runs. By increasing p the average recall increases consistently, especially from $p = 10\%$ to $p = 20\%$ and from $p = 20\%$ to $p = 30\%$. When $p = 50\%$

---

[9] https://github.com/leifos/tar.
[10] https://en.wikipedia.org/wiki/Pareto_efficiency.

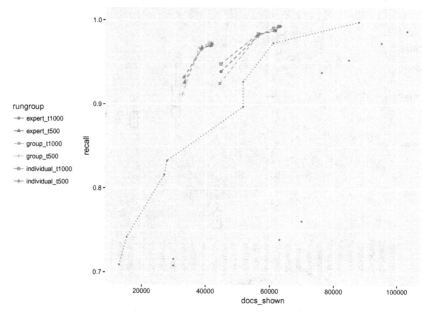

(a) Grey dots are the official CLEF 2017 runs

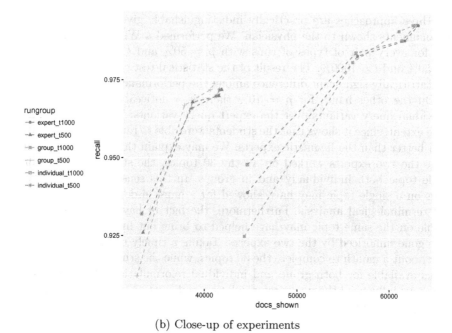

(b) Close-up of experiments

Fig. 2. Average recall at total number of documents shown.

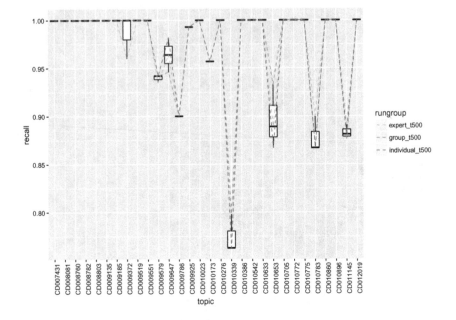

Fig. 3. Recall per topic for runs with $t = 500$ and $p = 50$.

the three approaches are practically indistinguishable given the same number of documents shown to the physician. We performed a Wilcoxon paired signed test for every pair of types of runs with $p = 50\%$ and $t = 500\%$, as well as $p = 50\%$ and $t = 1000\%$. The result of the statistical test confirms that there is no statistically significant difference among the performances of the runs.

On the other hand, for $p = 10\%$ there is a noticeable advantage of the individual query variants over the expert query variants. This is surprising to some extent, since it shows that the students were able to rewrite the information need better than the linguistic experts. We may explain this behaviour because while the two experts worked on all the 30 topics, the students worked on a single topic both individually and in groups. In this sense, the possibility to focus on a single topic may have allowed for a more in-depth domain research and terminological analysis. Furthermore, the fact of having worked in three people on the same topic may have helped to bring out linguistic aspects that have gone unnoticed by the two experts. Taking a timely estimate, the experts took about a month to complete the 30 topics, while the students had about two weeks available for both group and individual reformulation. All these factors may have influenced the query reformulation and consequently the effectiveness of the performance.

Low Recall Topics. We perform a failure analysis on those topics for which the system did not achieve a recall of 100%. Since for $t = 1000$ we obtain an almost perfect recall and there are no noticeable differences among the three types of runs, we decided to investigate the runs with threshold $t = 500$ and $p = 50\%$ since they achieve a good balance between recall, close to 0.95, and number of documents shown, around 40,000. In Fig. 3, the box-plot summarizes the values of recall of the three runs for each topic, while the coloured lines highlight the (possible) differences among the three types of runs. There are only 10 topics that do not achieve a perfect recall. Among these topics, we focus topic CD010653 since it is the one with the largest difference in performance among the runs. From a linguistic point of view it is interesting to note the differences between the expert keywords reformulation and the individual variant: on one hand, the first reformulation uses a lexical morphological approach; more variants (inflected forms) of the same term are proposed such as *diagnosis, diagnostic* or *schneider, schneiderian, and non-schneiderian*. The individual variant 2, on the other hand, aims at covering the involved semantic sphere: the participant uses terms such as *psychopathology, pathognomonic, specificity, ICD and meta analysis* that are not present in other reformulations. The reformulation approach adopted, the morphological or the semantic one, may therefore have influenced the results of the performance, but we shall analyze in more detail this particular emerging feature in future works.

5   Conclusions

In this paper, we presented a methodology for replicating an experiment of query rewriting in the context of medical eHealth. Following the approach by [14], we devised an active learning strategy that combines the information need and the boolean query of the physician with a ranked list of documents organized by the search engine in a continuous active learning framework which involved non-experts of the field of medicine.

The experiment consisted in re-proposing a task previously performed by a team of researchers for the CLEF eHealth Task 2: "Technologically Assisted Reviews in Empirical Medicine". Our working methodology was based on the analysis of linguistic and terminological aspects functional for the query rewriting in order to produce two variants of the same information need. The participants of this experiment were the students of the Master's Degree course in Modern Languages for International Communication and Cooperation of the University of Padua. They were required to rewrite the initial information need retrieve all the relevant documents for medical specific domains through the reformulation of an initial query given by an expert.

Experimental results showed that our approach allowed the TAR system to achieve a perfect recall on almost all the topics of the task with few significantly less documents compared to other CLEF participants of the same task. In terms of costs, the experts took about a month to complete the 30 topics, which means one day of work per topic, while the students had about two weeks available for both group and individual reformulation.

References

1. Berez-Kroeker, A.L., et al.: Reproducible research in linguistics: a position statement on data citation and attribution in our field. Linguistics **561**(1), 1–18 (2017)
2. Branco, A., Cohen, K.B., Vossen, P., Ide, N., Calzolari, N.: Replicability and reproducibility of research results for human language technology: introducing an LRE special section. Lang. Resour. Eval. **51**(1), 1–5 (2017)
3. Cohen, K.B., Xia, J., Roeder, C., Hunter, L.: Reproducibility in natural language processing: a case study of two R libraries for mining PubMed/MEDLINE. In: LREC 4REAL Workshop: Workshop on Research Results Reproducibility and Resources Citation in Science and Technology of Language, pp. 6–12. European Language Resources Association (ELRA) (2016)
4. Cormack, G.V., Grossman, M.R.: Scalability of continuous active learning for reliable high-recall text classification. In: Proceedings of the 25th ACM International on Conference on Information and Knowledge Management, CIKM 2016, pp. 1039–1048. ACM, New York (2016)
5. Cormack, G.V., Grossman, M.R.: Technology-assisted review in empirical medicine: waterloo participation in CLEF ehealth 2017. In: Working Notes of CLEF 2017 - Conference and Labs of the Evaluation Forum, Dublin, Ireland, 11–14 September 2017 (2017)
6. Cowie, A.P.: Phraseology: Theory, Analysis, and Applications. Oxford Studies in Lexicography and Lexicology. OUP Oxford, Oxford (1998)
7. Di Nunzio, G.M., Beghini, F., Vezzani, F., Henrot, G.: An interactive two-dimensional approach to query aspects rewriting in systematic reviews. IMS unipd at CLEF ehealth task 2. In: Working Notes of CLEF 2017 - Conference and Labs of the Evaluation Forum, Dublin, Ireland, 11–14 September 2017 (2017)
8. Di Nunzio, G.M., Beghini, F., Vezzani, F., Henrot, G.: A reproducible approach with R markdown to automatic classification of medical certificates in French. In: Proceedings of the Fourth Italian Conference on Computational Linguistics (CLiC-it 2017), Rome, Italy, 11–13 December 2017 (2017)
9. Ferro, N.: Reproducibility challenges in information retrieval evaluation. J. Data Inf. Qual. **8**(2), 8:1–8:4 (2017)
10. Ferro, N., et al. (eds.): Advances in Information Retrieval. LNCS, vol. 9626. Springer, Cham (2016). https://doi.org/10.1007/978-3-319-30671-1
11. Gandrud, C.: Reproducible Research with R and R Studio, 2nd edn. Chapman and Hall/CRC, Boca Raton (2015)
12. Gouadec, D.: Terminologie: constitution des données. AFNOR gestion. AFNOR (1990)
13. Kanoulas, E., Li, D., Azzopardi, L., Spijker, R. (eds.) CLEF 2017 technologically assisted reviews in empirical medicine overview. In: Working Notes of CLEF 2017 - Conference and Labs of the Evaluation Forum, Dublin, Ireland, 11–14 September 2017, CEUR Workshop Proceedings. CEUR-WS.org (2017)
14. Karimi, S., Pohl, S., Scholer, F., Cavedon, L., Zobel, J.: Boolean versus ranked querying for biomedical systematic reviews. BMC Med. Inform. Decis. Mak. **10**, 58–58 (2010)
15. Knuth, D.E.: Literate programming. Comput. J. **27**(2), 97–111 (1984)
16. L'Homme, M.-C.: Sur la notion de "terme". Meta **50**(4), 1112–1132 (2005)

17. Liberman, M.: Validation of results in linguistic science and technology: terminology, problems, and solutions. In: Branco, A., Calzolari, N., Choukri, K. (eds.) Proceedings of the Eleventh International Conference on Language Resources and Evaluation (LREC 2018), Paris, France, May 2018. European Language Resources Association (ELRA) (2018)
18. Martín, A.S., L'Homme, M.-C.: Definition patterns for predicative terms in specialized lexical resources. In: Proceedings of the Ninth International Conference on Language Resources and Evaluation, LREC 2014, Reykjavik, Iceland, 26–31 May 2014, pp. 3748–3755 (2014)
19. Miwa, M., Thomas, J., O'Mara-Eves, A., Ananiadou, S.: Reducing systematic review workload through certainty-based screening. J. Biomed. Inform. **51**, 242–253 (2014)
20. Di Nunzio, G.M.: A study of an automatic stopping strategy for technologically assisted medical reviews. In: Pasi, G., Piwowarski, B., Azzopardi, L., Hanbury, A. (eds.) ECIR 2018. LNCS, vol. 10772, pp. 672–677. Springer, Cham (2018). https://doi.org/10.1007/978-3-319-76941-7_61
21. Rastier, F.: Sémantique interprétative. Formes sémiotiques. Presses universitaires de France, Paris (1987)
22. Robertson, S.E., Walker, S., Jones, S., Hancock-Beaulieu, M., Gatford, M.: Okapi at TREC-3. In: Proceedings of the Third Text REtrieval Conference, TREC 1994, Gaithersburg, Maryland, USA, 2–4 November 1994, pp. 109–126 (1994)
23. Singh, G., Thomas, J., Shawe-Taylor, J.: Improving active learning in systematic reviews. CoRR, abs/1801.09496 (2018)
24. Vezzani, F., Di Nunzio, G.M., Henrot, G.: Trimed: a multilingual terminological database. In: Proceedings of the Eleventh International Conference on Language Resources and Evaluation, LREC 2018, Miyazaky, Japan, 7–12 May 2018 (2018, in press)

Rethinking the Evaluation Methodology of Authorship Verification Methods

Oren Halvani$^{(\boxtimes)}$ and Lukas Graner

Fraunhofer Institute for Secure Information Technology,
Rheinstraße 75, 64295 Darmstadt, Germany
oren.halvani@sit.fraunhofer.de

Abstract. Authorship verification (AV) concerns itself with the task to judge, if two or more documents have been written by the same person. Even though an increase of research activities in the last years can be observed, it can also be clearly seen that AV suffers of well-defined evaluation standards. Based on a comprehensive literature review of more than 50 research works including conference papers, journals, bachelor's/master's theses and doctoral dissertations, we could not identify consistent evaluation procedures that adequately reflect the reliability of AV methods. To counteract this, we propose an alternative evaluation methodology based on the construction of reliable corpora in combination with a more suitable performance measure. In an experimental setup our approach reveals the weakness of a number of existing and successful AV methods, in particular, when it comes to accept as many documents of the true author, while at the same time reject as many documents of other authors, as possible.

Keywords: Authorship verification · Evaluation · Cohen's Kappa

1 Introduction

Authorship verification (AV) is a subdiscipline of authorship analysis, a branch of digital text forensics. The goal of AV is to determine if a set of documents $\{\mathcal{D}_{\mathcal{U}}\} \cup \mathbb{D}_{\mathcal{A}}$ stem from the **same** author. Here, $\mathcal{D}_{\mathcal{U}}$ denotes an **unknown** document and $\mathbb{D}_{\mathcal{A}} = \{\mathcal{D}_1, \mathcal{D}_2, \ldots\}$ a set of reference documents of the **known** author $\mathcal{A}$ such that the question we wish to answer is, if either $\mathcal{U} = \mathcal{A}$ or $\mathcal{U} \neq \mathcal{A}$ holds. AV has numerous application possibilities across many domains. In the social media domain, for example, AV can serve as a helpful supplement for the identification of **compromised accounts** [1] or **fake news detection** [25]. In information retrieval (IR), AV can be used as an extension to **enhance IR systems** [26], which allows to aggregate retrieved documents by their underlying writing style. In the IT security domain, AV can be used for **continuous authentication** [4] or the investigation of **malicious e-mails** [13].

From a machine learning point of view, AV belongs to the family of **one class classification** (OCC) problems. Existing research works in the field of AV that

P. Bellot et al. (Eds.): CLEF 2018, LNCS 11018, pp. 40–51, 2018.
https://doi.org/10.1007/978-3-319-98932-7_4

support this statement are for instance [14, 15, 18, 19, 23, 30]. However, in order to perform a reasonable evaluation, it is clear that both must be present the **target** class $\mathcal{A}$ holding sample documents of the known author and the **outlier** class $\neg\mathcal{A}$, which comprises documents not authored by $\mathcal{A}$. Based on these, an OCC system has to consider the following four possible outcomes: hit, false alarm, miss, and correct rejection which, in context of AV, have the following meaning: **Hits** refer to the true positives (**TP**), which are cases where we correctly predict $\mathcal{A}$. **False alarms** denote the false negatives (**FN**) that are cases, in which we predict $\neg\mathcal{A}$, whereas $\mathcal{A}$ is correct. On the other hand, **misses** describe the false positives (**FP**) that are cases, where we falsely predict $\mathcal{A}$, while $\neg\mathcal{A}$ is indeed correct. Finally, **correct rejections** represent the true negatives (**TN**) that are cases, where we correctly predict $\neg\mathcal{A}$. Given these outcomes, a variety of measures can be defined in order to determine the performance of AV methods.

In contrast to related fields such as authorship attribution or author profiling, AV is a young and underresearched field. Therefore, it is not surprising that up to the present date no standardized performance measure exists, accepted by the majority of the research community. This fact can be observed through the inspection of existing research works in AV, where a variety of measures have been proposed and used so far including Accuracy, F_1, AUC, c@1, AUC $\cdot$ c@1, Equal Error Rate, False Acceptance/Rejection Rate, Precision/Recall-curves and others. However, the evaluation of corpora (as used in the past) based on these measures not adequately reflects the reliability of AV methods. Under the term "**reliable AV methods**", we understand such methods that **accept** as many documents of the true author as possible, while simultaneously **reject** as many documents of other authors as possible.

The purpose of this paper is to rethink previous evaluation methodologies and to propose an alternative strategy that fits more realistic AV cases which occur, for example, in digital text forensics. The remainder of the paper is structured as follows. In Sect. 2 we describe how AV methods have been evaluated in the past and, in particular, which performance measures were involved. Based on these, we highlight in Sect. 3 a number of observed problems and propose in Sect. 4 our evaluation strategy, which involves the construction of suitable corpora for the task, together with a performance measure that better reflects the reliability of AV methods. In Sect. 5 we present our experimental setup and the observations we made regarding two self-compiled AV corpora. Finally, we draw our conclusions in Sect. 6 and provide ideas for future work.

2   Related Work

In contrast to authorship attribution, there is a lack of well-defined evaluation standards in AV, in particular the way how test corpora are constructed and the choice of suitable performance measures. In the following, we review previous evaluation methodologies that will be subsequently analyzed in Sect. 3.

2.1   The PAN Competitions

In the PAN competitions of 2013–2015 [16,28,29] the organizers put a lot of effort on increasing the number of research activities in the field of AV. Among others, the organizers compiled several corpora for a number of languages that follow a uniform format. A PAN corpus consists of n **problems**, where each one has the form of $(\mathcal{D}_\mathcal{U}, \mathbb{D}_\mathcal{A}, \alpha)$. Here, $\alpha \in \{Y, N\}$ denotes the ground truth for the problem, while the labels Y and N represent a **true** and **false** authorship, respectively. Each corpus was constructed in such a way that the underlying problems were evenly distributed (**balanced**) regarding their Y/N labels.

   In the first PAN competition on the AV task [16], the organizers used two performance measures to evaluate 18 AV methods, submitted by the competitors. The first was a variant of F_1, a common measure for binary classification tasks in IR, which in its original form ignores the true negatives TN. However, in order to take TN into account, the organizers redefined **precision** (P) and **recall** (R) as follows: P = (Number of correct answers)/(Total number of answers) and R = $(1/n)$(Number of correct answers). Afterwards, they combined both measures via $F_1 = 2PR/(P + R)$ into the variant, which we denote by $F_{1\,(\text{Pan})}$. During our literature review, we observed that besides the PAN 2013 competition, a number of other works [2,22,30] also made use of F_1. However, it remains unclear whether the original or the modified version regarding P and R were chosen by the researchers. The second measure was the **AUC**, a scalar obtained from the area under the ROC curve. The latter represents a graph, where the x-axis denotes the false positive rate ($\mathbf{FPR} = \frac{\text{FP}}{\text{FP} + \text{TN}}$) and the y-axis the true positive rate ($\mathbf{TPR} = \frac{\text{TP}}{\text{TP+FN}}$). The resulting AUC is a value ranging from zero to one (the best possible value) which represents the probability that a randomly selected Y-problem is ranked higher than a randomly selected N-problem. Beyond the PAN competitions, AUC was used in a number of other works in the field of AV, for instance, by Stamatatos and Potha [23,24].

   In the second and third PAN competitions [28,29] the organizers again used AUC but, in addition, introduced a new performance measure named **c@1** which is defined as $(1/n)(n_c + (1/n)(n_u \cdot n_c))$. Here, n_c denotes the number of correct answers and n_u the number of **unanswered** problems. The intention behind this measure was to give the participants the option to leave some problems unanswered in case of uncertainty by providing a U-label. c@1 obeys the following properties: It rewards AV methods that maintain the same number of correct answers and decrease the number of wrong answers by leaving some problems unanswered [29]. If, on the other hand, all problems are left unanswered, then c@1 will be zero. During our literature review we observed that in some AV works [6,17] evaluation results were based solely on c@1.

2.2   Other Evaluation Methodologies

In 2004, Koppel and Schler [18] introduced the well-known meta learning AV approach **Unmasking**, where its success was repeatedly confirmed in a number of other AV research works (e. g., [21,25,30]). In order to evaluate their method,

Koppel and Schler used **Accuracy** $= (TP + TN)/(TP + TN + FP + FN)$, which measures the proportion of correct Y- and N-answers, against all existing problems in a corpus. Probably due to its easy comprehensibility, the measure has been used in a number of AV works (for example [3,15]). However, Accuracy suffers from a number of drawbacks, making it an unsuitable choice, not only when evaluating an AV method in isolation, but also when comparing several AV methods to each other. In the next section we will explore this in more detail.

3   Analysis of Previous Evaluation Methodologies

In the following, we highlight a number of problems we observed in previous evaluation methodologies regarding different performance measures.

3.1   Accuracy, $F_{1\,(Pan)}$ and c@1

Even though Accuracy is a compact and simple measure, it also suffers from a number of problems. One obvious drawback is that it is not suitable for corpora with an unequal distribution of Y and N problems. Koppel and Schler [18], for example, compiled such an imbalanced corpus, where as a data basis they used a collection of twenty-one 19th century English books covering a variety of genres, which were written by 10 different authors. Each book was chunked into sections of nearly equal length (≈ 58 sections per book), where each chunk comprised at least 500 words. Based on these chunks, the imbalanced corpus resulted in 209 AV problems (20 Y- and 189 N-cases). Even though, their AV approach clearly performs very well (95.7% in terms of Accuracy, based on $n = 209$, $TP = 19$, $TN = 181$) its potential is not reflected by this measure. To explain this, we consider the following simple example: Imagine we are given a corpus with 10 Y- and 990 N-problems as well as an AV method that predicts nothing but N. Then, we trivially can achieve a nearly perfect result, since $TP = 0$, $TN = 990$, $FP = 0$ and $FN = 10$ leads to $\frac{990}{1000} = 99\%$ Accuracy. In other words, the overrepresented class N benefits from this measure.

The modified F_1 measure $F_{1\,(Pan)}$, which has been used in the first PAN AV competition in 2013 [16] also suffers from this problem, as it equals the Accuracy in a specific situation. Let n_a = "number of answers", $n_c = TP + TN$ = "number of correct answers" and $n = TP + TN + FP + FN$ = "total number of problems". When an AV method predicts for each problem an answer (Y or N) then $n_a = n$ holds such that:

$$F_{1\,(Pan)} = \frac{2PR}{P+R} = \frac{2 \cdot \frac{n_c}{n} \cdot \frac{n_c}{n}}{\frac{n_c}{n} + \frac{n_c}{n}} = \frac{n_c}{n} = \frac{TP + TN}{TP + TN + FP + FN} = Accuracy$$

In addition to $F_{1\,(Pan)}$, c@1 is also affected by the same problem, when an AV method provides solely Y- or N-answers for all verification problems in a corpus, since $n_u = 0$ leads to $(1/n)(n_c + (1/n)(0 \cdot n_c)) = n_c/n = Accuracy$. Based on this, all three measures suffer from the same problem and are, therefore, not suitable for imbalanced AV corpora. Leaving problems unanswered is generally a bad advice, since it leads to an unexpected evaluation behavior regarding any performance measure that relies on the four possible outcomes.

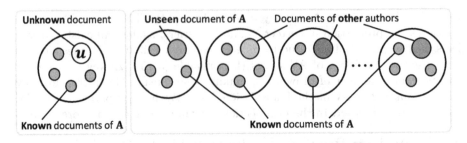

Fig. 1. Left: A common evaluation strategy as used in the previous PAN competitions [16,28,29]. **Right:** Our proposed approach.

3.2   AUC

The AUC, which has been used widely in the field of AV (alone or in combination with c@1), is a robust performance measure that can also handle imbalanced corpora. Under lab conditions, AUC is quite effective to measure how well a model behaves across all possible thresholds and, by this, helps to compare several AV methods against each other. However, in real-world forensic scenarios we cannot rely on an AV method that has been optimized against an threshold-independent performance measure. Instead, we wish to have a system that is bounded to a **fixed threshold** and based on it, to make a reasonable, reliable and reproducible Y/N-decision regarding the authorship. To take fixed thresholds into account, the organizers of the PAN competitions of 2014 and 2015 [28,29] introduced the product of AUC and c@1 as an alternative measure. However, AUC · c@1 does not solve the aforementioned dilemma, since c@1 is not suitable for imbalanced corpora.

4   Proposed Evaluation Strategy

In the following, we introduce our evaluation methodology that represents an enhanced version of the AV task, as has been considered in previous research works and AV competitions. For this, we no longer consider to verify a single verification problem $\rho = (\mathcal{D}_{\mathcal{U}}, \mathbb{D}_{\mathcal{A}}, \alpha)$ regarding a known author $\mathcal{A}$. Instead, we construct m verification problems $\rho_1 = (\mathcal{D}_{\mathcal{U}_1}, \mathbb{D}_{\mathcal{A}}, \mathbf{Y}), \rho_2 = (\mathcal{D}_{\mathcal{U}_2}, \mathbb{D}_{\mathcal{A}}, \mathbf{N}), \ldots, \rho_m = (\mathcal{D}_{\mathcal{U}_m}, \mathbb{D}_{\mathcal{A}}, \mathbf{N})$ for each $\mathcal{A}$, where only one ρ_i contains an unseen document of $\mathcal{A}$, while the remaining problems contain unknown documents from other $m - 1$ (disjoint) authors. Our intention is to make the AV task more realistic such that the goal is not only to **recognize** the true authorship for ρ_i, but also to **reject** the false authorship for all other constructed problems, given the same reference texts $\mathbb{D}_{\mathcal{A}}$ of the true author $\mathcal{A}$. Figure 1 illustrates the idea.

4.1   Corpus Construction

As a prerequisite, a set of document collections $\mathbb{D}_{\mathbb{A}} = \{\mathbb{D}_{\mathcal{A}_1}, \mathbb{D}_{\mathcal{A}_2}, \ldots, \mathbb{D}_{\mathcal{A}_\ell}\}$ belonging to set of ℓ authors $\mathbb{A} = \{\mathcal{A}_1, \mathcal{A}_2, \ldots, \mathcal{A}_\ell\}$ is required, where each

$\mathbb{D}_{\mathcal{A}}$ has the form of $\{\mathcal{D}_1, \mathcal{D}_2, \ldots\}$. Given a predefined percentage value, we split $\mathbb{D}_{\mathbb{A}}$ into two subsets $\mathbb{D}_{\text{train}}$ and $\mathbb{D}_{\text{test}}$. Next, we construct a training corpus $\mathcal{C}_{\text{train}}$ from $\mathbb{D}_{\text{train}}$ and a test corpus $\mathcal{C}_{\text{test}}$ from $\mathbb{D}_{\text{test}}$, in the following manner.

Training Corpus: To construct $\mathcal{C}_{\text{train}}$ the following steps are performed. First, we define a set $\mathbb{D}_\dagger = \{\mathcal{D}^\dagger_{\mathcal{A}_1}, \mathcal{D}^\dagger_{\mathcal{A}_2}, \ldots, \mathcal{D}^\dagger_{\mathcal{A}_\ell}\}$, where each $\mathcal{D}^\dagger_{\mathcal{A}}$ denotes the longest document that has been taken out from $\mathbb{D}_{\mathcal{A}}$. Next, we generate for each $\mathbb{D}_{\mathcal{A}} \in \mathbb{D}_{\text{train}}$ a Y-problem of the form $(\mathcal{D}_{\mathcal{U}} = \mathcal{D}^\dagger_{\mathcal{A}}, \mathbb{D}_{\mathcal{A}} \setminus \{\mathcal{D}^\dagger_{\mathcal{A}}\}, \text{Y})$ and a N-problem of the form $(\mathcal{D}_{\mathcal{U}} = \mathcal{D}^\dagger_{\mathcal{A}'}, \mathbb{D}_{\mathcal{A}} \setminus \{\mathcal{D}^\dagger_{\mathcal{A}}\}, \text{N})$. The latter is constructed for a randomly chosen Author $\mathcal{A}' \neq \mathcal{A}$. Note that in our scheme it cannot happen that the same author $\mathcal{A}'$ is used twice. In total, $\mathcal{C}_{\text{train}}$ results in a **balanced** corpus comprising 2ℓ problems. The reason we choose $\mathcal{C}_{\text{train}}$ to be balanced is because we wanted to keep the original training procedure of the involved AV methods consistent.

Test Corpus: Based on $\mathbb{D}_{\text{test}}$, the compilation of $\mathcal{C}_{\text{test}}$ is performed in a similar way to $\mathcal{C}_{\text{train}}$. While the construction of Y-problems is identical to $\mathcal{C}_{\text{train}}$, the generation of N-problems is slightly different. Instead of only one, we generate $\ell - 1$ N-problems for each author in the corpus. More precisely, for each $\mathbb{D}_{\mathcal{A}} \in \mathbb{D}_{\text{train}}$ we construct $\ell - 1$ N-problem of the form $(\mathcal{D}_{\mathcal{U}} = \mathcal{D}^\dagger_{\mathcal{A}'}, \mathbb{D}_{\mathcal{A}} \setminus \{\mathcal{D}^\dagger_{\mathcal{A}}\}, \text{N})$ not for all a **single** author $\mathcal{A}' \neq \mathcal{A}$ but for **all** authors other than $\mathcal{A}$. In total, $\mathcal{C}_{\text{test}}$ results in an **imbalanced** corpus of $n = \ell^2$ problems (ℓ Y- and $\ell^2 - \ell$ N-problems).

4.2   Proposed Performance Measure

In order to reflect the reliability of AV methods regarding the mentioned imbalanced corpora, we suggest to use Cohen's Kappa (κ), a well-established statistic that measures the inter-rater reliability (sometimes called inter-observer agreement). According to our literature review, this is the first time κ is used to evaluate AV methods. Note that in the context of AV, there are no "raters" but instead a ground truth and the corresponding predictions. Based on the four possible outcomes regarding the predicted authorship, κ is calculated as:

$$n = \text{TP} + \text{FN} + \text{FP} + \text{TN}$$
$$p_0 = n^{-1}(\text{TP}+\text{TN})$$
$$p_c = n^{-2}\left((\text{TP}+\text{FN})(\text{TP}+\text{FP}) + (\text{FP}+\text{TN})(\text{FN}+\text{TN})\right)$$
$$\kappa = \frac{p_0 - p_c}{1 - p_c}.$$

Here, p_0 refers to the observed level of **agreement** ($p_0 = \text{Accuracy}$), while p_c denotes the **expected agreement**. When in comes to interpret κ, it turns out to be not entirely trivial. The easy cases occur for $\kappa = 0$ (agreement equivalent to **chance**), $\kappa = 1$ (**perfect** agreement) or the rare case $\kappa < 0$ (agreement behaves **inverse**). On the other hand, the difficult part occurs when κ takes values between 0 and 1. Here, there is no absolute standard, since κ is scaled by the proportion of each class (Y/N). However, in the next section we provide a better picture regarding this, where we focus on imbalanced corpora.

5   Experimental Evaluation

In the following, we describe our experimental setup, where we first present our two compiled corpora for the AV task. Next, we mention the reimplemented AV methods that were trained and evaluated regarding these corpora. Finally, we present the results and summarize our observations.

5.1   Corpora

In contrast to other research disciplines, only few corpora for AV have been made publicly available. To our best knowledge, the most well-known AV corpora are those used in the previous PAN competitions [16, 28, 29] that have also been used in other research works. Unfortunately, the PAN corpora are not suitable for the proposed evaluation strategy, as no author meta-information is provided, needed to construct the overrepresented outlier class $\neg\mathcal{A}$. Therefore, we decided to compile our own AV corpora, which we make available[1] for other researchers in this field. Note that both corpora are **compatible** regarding the existing PAN corpora, where the only **difference** is the additional author meta-information.

The Enron AV Corpus: As a first corpus, we compiled $\mathcal{C}_{\mathrm{Enron}}$, a derivate of the *Enron Email Dataset*[2], which has been used across different research domains. $\mathcal{C}_{\mathrm{Enron}}$ comprises emails of 80 authors, where for each author $\mathcal{A}$ there are 2–4 texts. Most of the texts were aggregated from several mails of $\mathcal{A}$, in order to have a sufficient length that captures $\mathcal{A}$'s writing style. The length of each text ranges from 2,200–5,000 characters. All texts in $\mathcal{C}_{\mathrm{Enron}}$ were preprocessed by hand, which resulted in an overall processing time of more than 30 h. First, we performed de-duplication, normalization of utf-8 symbols and removed URLs, e-mail headers and other metadata. Next, we removed greetings/closing formulas, signatures, (telephone) numbers, various repetitions, named entities (names of people, companies, locations, etc.) as well as quotes. As a last preprocessing step, we substituted multiple successive blanks, newlines and tabs with a single blank. Afterwards, we applied our proposed corpus construction procedure, which resulted in a balanced training corpus of 48 problems and an imbalanced test corpus of 3,136 problems (56 Y- and 3,080 N-problems).

The C50 AV Corpus: As a second corpus, we compiled $\mathcal{C}_{\mathrm{c50}}$, a derivate of the *Reuters_50_50* (c50) dataset, which is a subset of the *Reuters Corpus Volume 1 (RCV1)* [20]. The c50 dataset has been used in many authorship attribution studies and comprises a **training** and a **test** corpus. In each corpus there are 50 authors, where for each one there are 50 documents. All texts in c50 are manually categorized newswire stories that cover **corporate** and **industrial** related topics. To construct $\mathcal{C}_{\mathrm{c50}}$, we used the **test** corpus within c50 and picked out

---

[1] Available under: http://bit.ly/CLEF_2018.
[2] Available under: https://www.cs.cmu.edu/~enron.

for each author the top 5 documents in terms of length. Similar to C_{Enron}, here we also applied a number of preprocessing steps including deletion of citations, telephone/fax numbers as well as substitution of multiple blanks. The final corpora resulted in a balanced training corpus of 30 problems and an imbalanced test corpus of 1,225 problems (35 Y- and 1,190 N-problems).

5.2   Authorship Verification Methods

In order to perform a reasonable evaluation, we decided to use eight existing AV methods. Four of these (OCCAV [8], MOCC [9], COAV [10] and AVeer [11]) were developed by us, while the other four[3] methods (GLAD [12], CNG [14], Stat14 [23], and GI [27]) were reimplementations of AV approaches that have shown their potentials in existing papers and previous AV competitions. Each AV method was trained regarding its (hyper-)parameters on the training corpora of C_{Enron} and C_{c50}, according to the procedure described in the respective literature.

5.3   Evaluation Results

After finishing the training of all involved AV methods, we applied them together with their corresponding models on both evaluation corpora C_{Enron} and C_{c50}. The results are given in Table 1. Note that none of the involved AV methods left problems unanswered such that $c@1 = F_1 =$ Accuracy holds. Therefore, we list only the results for $c@1$. As can be seen from Table 1, a number of observations can be inferred. First, it is remarkable that none of the involved AV methods was able to significantly maximize TP and TN and at the same time minimize FP and FN, which results in low κ values. However, we can still see differences regarding κ among the methods for each corpus. Even tough these differences are primarily caused by the internal (decision) threshold of the methods, both COAV and GI seem to yield the best compromise between the four outcomes. In order to gain a better picture of how κ behaves on imbalanced corpora, we varied the TPR and FPR from 0 to 1 with a step size of 0.02 and map the κ-values to corresponding colors. As can be seen from the left plot in Fig. 2 the FPR clearly dominates the resulting κ, where higher values can only be approached in a very narrow corridor. For comparison, we also performed the same procedure for Accuracy (right plot in Fig. 2), where it can be seen easily how misleading this performance measure behaves on imbalanced corpora.

6   Conclusion and Future Work

We have highlighted a number of problems and drawbacks regarding previous evaluation procedures in AV, including the way how corpora were constructed and which performance measures have been used. Based on these, we proposed

---

[3] In fact, we reimplemented two additional AV approaches [2,4], but due to reproduction problems we had to discard them.

Table 1. Evaluation results regarding $\mathcal{C}_{Enron}$ and $\mathcal{C}_{c50}$ in terms of κ, AUC·c@1, AUC, c@1 and the four possible outcomes. Entries are sorted by κ in descending order.

	Method	Outcome				Performance measure			
		TP	FN	FP	TN	κ	AUC·c@1	AUC	c@1
$\mathcal{C}_{Enron}$	COAV	40	16	165	2,915	0.286	0.857	0.909	0.942
	GI	49	7	865	2,215	0.106	0.652	0.896	0.722
	OCCAV	45	11	656	2,424	0.089	0.688	0.874	0.787
	MOCC	37	19	593	2,487	0.078	0.669	0.832	0.805
	AVeer	45	11	946	2,134	0.054	0.606	0.873	0.695
	Stat14	42	14	944	2,136	0.048	0.577	0.831	0.695
	CNG	47	9	1,169	1,911	0.041	0.500	0.800	0.624
	GLAD	52	4	1,447	1,633	0.034	0.421	0.784	0.537
$\mathcal{C}_{c50}$	COAV	27	8	181	1,009	0.182	0.744	0.880	0.846
	OCCAV	24	11	171	1,019	0.168	0.693	0.814	0.851
	GI	28	7	283	907	0.164	0.683	0.886	0.763
	AVeer	22	13	169	1,021	0.154	0.681	0.800	0.851
	MOCC	18	17	143	1,047	0.143	0.621	0.715	0.869
	Stat14	29	6	308	882	0.110	0.633	0.851	0.744
	GLAD	34	1	593	597	0.051	0.417	0.809	0.515
	CNG	25	10	456	734	0.046	0.463	0.747	0.620

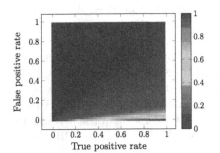 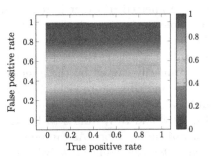

Fig. 2. Behavior of κ (**left**) and Accuracy (**right**) for imbalanced corpora with a size of $n = 2,500$ problems comprising 50 Y- and 2,450 N-problems. (Color figure online)

an alternative evaluation methodology that better reflects the reliability of AV methods. In an experimental setup, we revealed how challenging the AV task is in realistic scenarios, where as many text samples of the true author as possible must be accepted, while simultaneously as many documents of other authors as possible must be rejected. Such cases occur often in digital text forensics and require a more reliable form of evaluation regarding the involved AV method(s), which according to the reviewed literature was rarely investigated in previous research works. To achieve this, we suggested to use Cohen's Kappa κ which in fact is more suitable for imbalanced AV corpora, in contrast to other performance measures. In comparison to these measures, obtaining high κ-values is in fact much more difficult and strengthens the idea to rethink the way how AV methods should be evaluated. One idea for future work is to experiment with other measures, build on top of Cohen's Kappa as for instance the little known "area under the κ-curve". Another idea for future work is to investigate the question, if using imbalanced corpora together with κ during training yields better results, in contrast to the original training procedures of AV methods.

Acknowledgments. This work was supported by the German Federal Ministry of Education and Research (BMBF) under the project "DORIAN" (Scrutinise and thwart disinformation). We would like to thank our mock reviewer Christian Winter for his valuable comments that helped to improve the quality of this paper.

References

1. Barbon Jr., S., Igawa, R.A., Bogaz Zarpelão, B.: Authorship verification applied to detection of compromised accounts on online social networks. Multimed. Tools Appl. **76**(3), 3213–3233 (2017)
2. Boukhaled, M.A., Ganascia, J.-G.: Probabilistic anomaly detection method for authorship verification. In: Besacier, L., Dediu, A.-H., Martín-Vide, C. (eds.) SLSP 2014. LNCS (LNAI), vol. 8791, pp. 211–219. Springer, Cham (2014). https://doi.org/10.1007/978-3-319-11397-5_16
3. Brennan, M.R., Greenstadt, R.: Practical attacks against authorship recognition techniques. In: Haigh, K.Z., Rychtyckyj, N. (eds.) IAAI. AAAI (2009)
4. Brocardo, M.L., Traore, I., Woungang, I.: Toward a framework for continuous authentication using stylometry. In: 2014 IEEE 28th International Conference on Advanced Information Networking and Applications, pp. 106–115, May 2014
5. Cappellato, L., Ferro, N., Jones, G.J.F., San Juan, E. (eds.): Working Notes for CLEF 2015 Conference, Toulouse, France, 8–11 September 2015, CEUR Workshop Proceedings, vol. 1391. CEUR-WS.org (2015)
6. Castro Castro, D., Adame Arcia, Y., Pelaez Brioso, M., Muñoz Guillena, R.: Authorship verification, average similarity analysis. In: Proceedings of the International Conference Recent Advances in Natural Language Processing, pp. 84–90. INCOMA Ltd., Shoumen (2015)
7. Forner, P., Navigli, R., Tufis, D., Ferro, N. (eds.): Working Notes for CLEF 2013 Conference, Valencia, Spain, 23–26 September 2013, CEUR Workshop Proceedings, vol. 1179. CEUR-WS.org (2014)
8. Halvani, O., Graner, L., Vogel, I.: Authorship verification in the absence of explicit features and thresholds. In: Pasi, G., Piwowarski, B., Azzopardi, L., Hanbury, A. (eds.) ECIR 2018. LNCS, vol. 10772, pp. 454–465. Springer, Cham (2018). https://doi.org/10.1007/978-3-319-76941-7_34
9. Halvani, O., Steinebach, M.: An efficient intrinsic authorship verification scheme based on ensemble learning. In: Ninth International Conference on Availability. Reliability and Security, ARES 2014, Fribourg, Switzerland, 8–12 September 2014, pp. 571–578. IEEE Computer Society, Washington, DC (2014)
10. Halvani, O., Winter, C., Graner, L.: On the usefulness of compression models for authorship verification. In: Proceedings of the 12th International Conference

on Availability, Reliability and Security, ARES 2017, pp. 54:1–54:10. ACM, New York (2017)

11. Halvani, O., Winter, C., Pflug, A.: Authorship verification for different languages, genres and topics. Digit. Investig. 16(S), S33–S43 (2016)

12. Hürlimann, M., Weck, B., von den Berg, E., Šuster, S., Nissim, M.: GLAD: groningen lightweight authorship detection. In: Cappellato et al. [5]

13. Iqbal, F., Khan, L.A., Fung, B.C.M., Debbabi, M.: e-Mail authorship verification for forensic investigation. In: Proceedings of the 2010 ACM Symposium on Applied Computing, SAC 2010, pp. 1591–1598. ACM, New York (2010)

14. Jankowska, M., Milios, E.E., Keselj, V.: Author verification using common n-gram profiles of text documents. In: Hajic, J., Tsujii, J. (eds.) 25th International Conference on Computational Linguistics, Proceedings of the Conference: Technical Papers, COLING 2014, Dublin, Ireland, 23–29 August 2014, pp. 387–397. ACL (2014)

15. Noecker Jr., J., Ryan, M.: Distractorless authorship verification. In: Calzolari, N., et al. (eds.) Proceedings of the Eight International Conference on Language Resources and Evaluation (LREC 2012). European Language Resources Association (ELRA), Istanbul, May 2012

16. Juola, P., Stamatatos, E.: Overview of the author identification task at PAN 2013. In: Forner et al. [7]

17. Kocher, M., Savoy, J.: A simple and efficient algorithm for authorship verification. J. Assoc. Inf. Sci. Technol. 68(1), 259–269 (2017)

18. Koppel, M., Schler, J.: Authorship verification as a one-class classification problem. In: Brodley, C.E. (ed.) Machine Learning, Proceedings of the Twenty-First International Conference (ICML 2004), ACM International Conference Proceeding Series, Banff, Alberta, Canada, 4–8 July 2004, vol. 69. ACM (2004)

19. Koppel, M., Schler, J., Bonchek-Dokow, E.: Measuring differentiability: unmasking pseudonymous authors. J. Mach. Learn. Res. 8, 1261–1276 (2007)

20. Lewis, D.D., Yang, Y., Rose, T.G., Li, F.: RCV1: a new benchmark collection for text categorization research. J. Mach. Learn. Res. 5, 361–397 (2004)

21. Meister, J.C. (ed.): Evaluating Unmasking for Cross-Genre Authorship Verification. Hamburg, Germany (2012)

22. Petmanson, T.: Authorship verification of opinion pieces in Estonian. Eesti Rakenduslingvistika Uhingu Aastaraamat 10, 259–267 (2014)

23. Potha, N., Stamatatos, E.: A profile-based method for authorship verification. In: Likas, A., Blekas, K., Kalles, D. (eds.) SETN 2014. LNCS (LNAI), vol. 8445, pp. 313–326. Springer, Cham (2014). https://doi.org/10.1007/978-3-319-07064-3_25

24. Potha, N., Stamatatos, E.: An improved *impostors* method for authorship verification. In: Jones, G.J.F., et al. (eds.) CLEF 2017. LNCS, vol. 10456, pp. 138–144. Springer, Cham (2017). https://doi.org/10.1007/978-3-319-65813-1_14

25. Potthast, M., Kiesel, J., Reinartz, K., Bevendorff, J., Stein, B.: A stylometric inquiry into hyperpartisan and fake news. ArXiv e-prints, February 2017

26. Rexha, A., Kröll, M., Ziak, H., Kern, R.: Extending scientific literature search by including the author's writing style. In: Mayr, P., Frommholz, I., Cabanac, G. (eds.) Proceedings of the Fifth Workshop on Bibliometric-enhanced Information Retrieval (BIR) Co-located with the 39th European Conference on Information Retrieval (ECIR 2017), Aberdeen, UK, 9th April 2017. CEUR Workshop Proceedings, vol. 1823, pp. 93–100. CEUR-WS.org (2017)

27. Seidman, S.: Authorship verification using the impostors method notebook for PAN at CLEF 2013. In: Forner et al. [7]

28. Stamatatos, E., et al.: Overview of the author identification task at PAN 2015. In: Cappellato et al. [5]
29. Stamatatos, E., et al.: Overview of the author identification task at PAN 2014. In: Cappellato, L., Ferro, N., Halvey, M., Kraaij, W. (eds.) Working Notes for CLEF 2014 Conference, Sheffield, UK, 15–18 September 2014. CEUR Workshop Proceedings, vol. 1180, pp. 877–897. CEUR-WS.org (2014)
30. Stein, B., Lipka, N., zu Eissen, S.M.: Meta analysis within authorship verification. In: 19th International Workshop on Database and Expert Systems Applications (DEXA 2008), Turin, Italy, 1–5 September 2008, pp. 34–39. IEEE Computer Society (2008)

Learning-to-Rank and Relevance Feedback for Literature Appraisal in Empirical Medicine

Athanasios Lagopoulos$^{(\boxtimes)}$ ⑩, Antonios Anagnostou⑩, Adamantios Minas⑩,
and Grigorios Tsoumakas⑩

Aristotle University of Thessaloniki, 54124 Thessaloniki, Greece
{lathanag,anagnoad,adamantcm,greg}@csd.auth.gr

Abstract. The constantly expanding medical libraries contain immense amounts of information, including evidence from healthcare research. Gathering and interpreting this evidence can be both challenging and time-consuming for researchers conducting systematic reviews. Technologically assisted review (TAR) aims to assist this process by finding as much relevant information as possible with the least effort. Toward this, we present an incremental learning method that ranks documents, previously retrieved, by automating the process of title and abstract screening. Our approach combines a learning-to-rank model trained across multiple reviews with a model focused on the given review, incrementally trained based on relevance feedback. The classifiers use as features several similarity metrics between the documents and the research topic, such as Levenshtein distance, cosine similarity and BM25, and vectors derived from word embedding methods such as Word2Vec and Doc2Vec. We test our approach using the dataset provided by the Task II of CLEF eHealth 2017 and we empirically compare it with other approaches participated in the task.

Keywords: Learning to rank · Relevance feedback
Technology-assisted reviews · Empirical Medicine

1 Introduction

Evidence-Based Medicine (EBM) is an approach to medical practice that makes thorough and explicit use of the current best evidence in making decisions about the care and treatment of patients. Clinicians practice EBM by integrating their expertise with the best available external clinical evidence from systematic reviews [25]. A systematic review attempts to collect all empirical evidence that fits pre-specified eligibility criteria in order to answer a specific research question by minimizing the bias and thus providing more reliable findings [9]. The creation of a systematic review usually includes the following three stages [13]:

P. Bellot et al. (Eds.): CLEF 2018, LNCS 11018, pp. 52–63, 2018.
https://doi.org/10.1007/978-3-319-98932-7_5

Listing 1.1. Part of a boolean query constructed by Cochrane experts. Retrieved from Task II of CLEF eHealth 2017 (Topic ID: CD007394).

```
exp Ovarian Neoplasms/
Fallopian Tube Neoplasms/
((ovar* or fallopian tube*) adj5 (cancer* or tumor*
or tumour* or adenocarcinoma* or carcino* or
cystadenocarcinoma* or choriocarcinoma* or malignan*
or neoplas* or metasta* or mass or masses)).tw,ot.
```

1. **Document retrieval:** Information specialists build a Boolean query and submit it to a medical database, which returns a set of possibly relevant studies. Boolean queries typically have very complicated syntax and consist of multiple lines. An example of such a query can be found for reference in Listing 1.1.
2. **Title and abstract screening:** Domain experts go through the title and abstract of the set of documents retrieved by the previous stage, perform a first level of screening and remove irrelevant studies.
3. **Document screening:** Experts go through the full text of each document that passes the screening of the previous stage to decide whether it will be included in their systematic review.

Considering the rapid pace with which medical databases are expanding and the amount of information they contain, collecting and interpreting evidence into reviews requires time, skills and resources making it very challenging for health care providers and researchers. Organizations such as Cochrane[1], the Centre for Reviews and Dissemination[2] and the Joanna Briggs Institute[3] respond to this challenge by producing high-quality systematic reviews in health care. However, the specificity of boolean searches is usually low, hence the reviewers often need to look manually through thousands of articles, in tight timescales, in order to identify only the relevant ones [17]. Therefore, identifying *all* relevant studies and minimizing the bias in the selection are still very complex tasks [3,20].

This paper presents an approach for assisting experts in the second stage of creating systematic reviews, by ranking the set of documents retrieved by a Boolean query search. Our approach is based on text mining techniques and combines an inter-review learning-to-rank method with an intra-review incremental training method. Both similarity measures and vectors extracted by word embedding methods are used as features to the classifiers. We test our approach using the dataset provided by Task II [13] of the CLEF eHealth 2017 lab [7] and compare it with other approaches submitted to the task. Finally, we evaluate the performance of the different features extracted. A preliminary version of this work [2] was presented at the CLEF eHealth 2017 lab.

---

[1] http://www.cochrane.org/.
[2] https://www.york.ac.uk/crd/.
[3] http://joannabriggs.org/.

The rest of the paper is organized as follows: After providing related work in Sect. 2, we introduce our approach in ranking documents retrieved by a boolean query in Sect. 3. In Sect. 4, we describe our empirical study by presenting the data and the evaluation process we followed for our classification methods, while final conclusions and future work are outlined in Sect. 5.

2   Related Work

Several approaches have been proposed in the past to automate the different processes of creating a systematic review. Most of them are particularly focused on reducing the burden of screening for reviewers. These approaches are based on text mining [11,20,31] along with active learning [8,30] or learning-to-rank [22]. Furthermore, different systems and platforms have been developed. Abstrackr [23] and Rayyan [21] use a semi-automatic active learning way to perform citation screening, while Cochrane Crowd[4] is an online collaborative platform that categorizes health care evidence.

The recently organized task on Technologically Assisted Reviews in Empirical Medicine [13] of CLEF eHealth 2017 [7], with a focus on Diagnostic Test Accuracy (DTA), aimed to bring together academic, commercial, and government researchers that conduct experiments and share results on automatic methods to retrieve relevant studies. Specifically, a set of research topics were provided to the participants. The topics were constructed by Cochrane experts and each topic contained the title of a systematic review and the corresponding boolean query. The set of documents returned from the query were also provided. The participants were asked to rank the documents so as: (i) to produce an efficient ordering of the documents such that all of the relevant abstracts are retrieved as early as possible, and (ii) to identify a subset of documents which contains all or as many of the relevant abstracts for the least effort (i.e. total number of abstracts to be assessed). Fourteen teams participated in the task and presented their work. Several teams developed Learning-to-Rank approaches [4,10,26], while others adopted active learning techniques [6,32]. Two teams worked with neural networks and deep learning [16,27]. Furthermore, participants represented the textual data in a variety of ways, including topic models [12,29], TF-IDF [1] and n-grams [19].

3   Our Approach

Our approach comprises two consecutive supervised learning models. The first model is a learning-to-rank binary classifier that considers a topic-document pair as input and whether the document is relevant to the systematic review or not as output (Fig. 1). This inter-review model is used at the first stage of our approach in order to obtain an initial ranking of all documents returned by the Boolean query of an unseen test topic. The second model is a standard

---

[4] http://crowd.cochrane.org/.

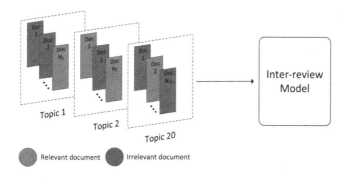

Fig. 1. Training of the inter-review model.

binary classifier that considers a document of the given test topic as input and whether this document is relevant to the test topic as output. This intra-review model is incrementally trained based on relevance feedback that it requests after returning one or more documents to the user. The first version of this model is trained based on feedback obtained from the top k ranked documents by the inter-review model (Fig. 2). The re-ranking of subsequent documents is from then on based solely on the intra-review model (Fig. 3).

3.1   Inter-review Model

The inter-review model is a learning-to-rank model that ranks the set of documents according to their relevance and importance to the topic. Each topic-document pair is represented by a multi-dimensional feature vector, and each dimension of the vector is a feature indicating how relevant or important the document is with respect to the topic [22]. In total, 31 features were extracted. Most of the features (1–26) are simple similarity features and they are computed by considering the similarity of different fields of the document (title, abstract), with different fields of the topic (title, boolean query), using a variety of similarity measures, such as the number of common terms between the topic and the

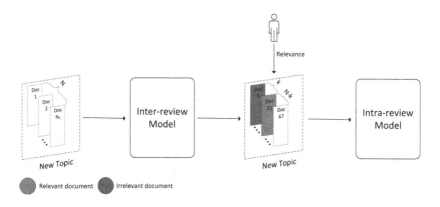

Fig. 2. Ranking with the inter-review model. Initial training of the intra-review model.

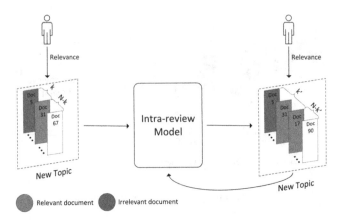

Fig. 3. Continuous re-ranking of subsequent documents and incremental re-training of the intra-review model.

document parts, Levenshtein distance, cosine similarity and BM25 [28]. The text in these cases is represented either as simple word tokens or as TF-IDF vectors. The remaining 5 features (27–31) are also similarity measures between the topic and the document but the text representations are word embeddings extracted from methods such as Word2Vec [18] and Doc2Vec [15].

Table 1 presents the features which we employed in our model. Two of these features depend only on the topic, denoted with T in the *Category* column of Table 1, as opposed to the rest of the features that are dependent on both the topic and the document, denoted with $T - D$. Details about the features are listed below.

1. We consider two fields of a document d: the title and the abstract. The column *Document field* indicates which field is used by the feature.
2. We consider two fields of a topic: the title t, consisting of tokens t_i, and the Medical Subject Headings (MeSH) m extracted from the boolean query.
3. $|C|$ is the total number of documents in the document collection. $|d|$ denotes the length, the number of tokens d_j, of a document d considering a specific field. Document frequency $df(t_i)$ is the number of documents containing t_i.
4. The number of occurrences of title tokens or MeSH of the topic in a document d is denoted as $c(t, d)$ and $c(m, d)$, respectively.
5. In features 1–20 a simple string tokenization of the text is considered.
6. The $levenshtein(x, y)$ stands for the Levenshtein distance string metric. The v value is user defined.
7. The BM25 score is computed as in [24].
8. The vocabulary and inverse-term frequency (idf) of tf-idf is fitted on the topic's title.
9. In feature 25–26, we follow a standard Latent Semantic Analysis (LSA). A Singular Value Decomposition (SVD) is performed upon the tf-idf, which is fitted on the documents' title and abstract. The cosine similarity is estimated from the reduced vectors of the two fields.

10. In feature 27–28, the vector of each field is the averaging vector of the word vectors produced by a Word2Vec model.
11. In feature 29–30, the Word Mover's Distance (WMD) of the word vectors is computed as in [14].
12. In feature 31, the vector of each field is produced by a Doc2Vec model [15].

Table 1. Set of features employed by the inter-review model.

ID	Description	Category	Topic field	Document field
1	$\sum_{t_i \in t \cap d} c(t_i, d)$	$T - D$	Title	Title
2	$\sum_{t_i \in t \cap d} \log(c(t_i, d))$	$T - D$	Title	Title
3	$\sum_{t_i \in t \cap d} c(t_i, d)$	$T - D$	Title	Abstract
4	$\sum_{t_i \in t \cap d} \log(c(t_i, d))$	$T - D$	Title	Abstract
5	$\sum_{m_i \in t \cap d} c(m_i, d)$	$T - D$	Query	Title
6	$\sum_{m_i \in t} \sum_{d_j \in d} levenshtein(m_i, d_j)$	$T - D$	Query	Title
7	$\sum_{m_i \in t} \sum_{d_j \in d} levenshtein(m_i, d_j)$ if $levenshtein(m_i, d_j) < k$	$T - D$	Query	Title
8	$\sum_{m_i \in t \cap d} \log(c(m_i, d))$	$T - D$	Query	Title
9	$\sum_{m_i \in t \cap d} c(m_i, d)$	$T - D$	Query	Abstract
10	$\sum_{m_i \in t \cap d} \log(c(m_i, d))$	$T - D$	Query	Abstract
11	$\sum_{m_i \in t} \log(\frac{|C|}{df(t_i)})$	T	Title	-
12	$\sum_{m_i \in t} \log(\log(\frac{|C|}{df(t_i)}))$	T	Title	-
13	BM25	$T - D$	Title	Title
14	BM25	$T - D$	Title	Abstract
15	BM25	$T - D$	Query	Title
16	BM25	$T - D$	Query	Abstract
17	log(BM25)	$T - D$	Title	Title
18	log(BM25)	$T - D$	Title	Abstract
29	log(BM25)	$T - D$	Query	Title
20	log(BM25)	$T - D$	Query	Abstract
21	cos(tf-idf)	$T - D$	Title	Title
22	cos(tf-idf)	$T - D$	Title	Abstract
23	cos(tf-idf)	$T - D$	Query	Title
24	cos(tf-idf)	$T - D$	Query	Abstract
25	cos(SVD(tf-idf))	$T - D$	Title	Title
26	cos(SVD(tf-idf))	$T - D$	Title	Abstract
27	cos(Word2Vec)	$T - D$	Title	Title
28	cos(Word2Vec)	$T - D$	Title	Abstract
29	WMD(Word2Vec)	$T - D$	Title	Title
30	WMD(Word2Vec)	$T - D$	Title	Abstract
31	cos(Doc2Vec)	$T - D$	Title	Abstract

3.2   Intra-review Model

The intra-review model is a standard binary model which classifies a document as relevant or not to a certain topic. Initially, the intra-review model is trained based on the top k documents as ranked by the inter-review model. It then iteratively re-ranks the rest of the documents, expanding the training set of the intra-review model with the top-ranked document, until the whole list has been added to the training set or a certain threshold is reached. The expansion of the training set can be configured with user-defined steps. After the initial training with k documents, an initial expansion step is defined ($step_{init}$) until a certain threshold (t_{step}) is reached. Then, the step is increased to a secondary step ($step_{secondary}$). The secondary step is used until the final threshold (t_{final}). This iterative feedback and re-ranking mechanism is described in detail in Algorithm 1. The use of different steps and thresholds reduces the cost of feedback and the time needed to produce predictions since the classifier is considered sufficiently trained when a certain amount of documents is used in the training set. For this classifier, a standard *tf-idf* vectorization was used, enhanced with English stop word removal.

4   Empirical Study

This section initially describes the data we used for our empirical study and gives details about the implementation and the technologies underneath our approach. It then presents the evaluation process we followed for our models and, finally, it discusses the evaluation results and compares them with the results presented in Task II of CLEF eHealth 2017 lab.

4.1   Data and Preprocessing

We experimented with the development set distributed by the Task II of CLEF eHealth 2017 lab. In total, the set contains 50 topics, 20 topics in the training set and 30 topics in the test set. However, 8 topics were later marked as unreliable from the organizers, reducing the number of total topics to 42. Each topic contains an ID, a systematic review title, a boolean query in Ovid MEDLINE format and set of MEDLINE document's PIDs returned from the boolean query. The title and the boolean query are constructed by Cochrane experts. Each MEDLINE document contains the title, the abstract text and the MeSH headings. Along with the topics, the corresponding relevance sheet were also provided, denoting the positive or negative relevance of a document to a topic as derived from an abstract-level screening. The percentage of relevant documents at abstract level for the 42 topics is 4.07%. The full dataset is publicly available at the official GitHub repository of the task[5].

In order to use the rich information available in the boolean query field of the topics and be able to construct the features described in Table 1 we used Polyglot[6], a JavaScript tool that can parse and produce a full syntactical tree of

---

[5] https://github.com/CLEF-TAR/tar.
[6] https://github.com/CREBP/sra-polyglot.

Algorithm 1. Iterative relevance feedback algorithm of the intra-review model

---

    Input   : The ranked documents R, of length n, as produced by the inter-review model, initial training step k, initial local training step $step_{init}$, secondary local training step $step_{secondary}$, step change threshold t_{step}, final threshold t_{final} (optional)

    Output: Final ranking of documents R - $finalRanking$

1   $finalRanking \leftarrow ()$;   `// empty list`

2   **for** $i = 1$ **to** k **do**

3     $finalRanking_i \leftarrow R_i$

4   $k' \leftarrow k$;

5   **while** *not* $finalRanking$ *contains both* **relevant** *and* **irrelevant** *documents* **do**

6     $k' \leftarrow k' + 1$;

7     $finalRanking_{k'} = R_{k'}$;

8   **while** *not* $length(finalRanking) == n$ **OR** $length(finalRanking) == t_{final}$ **do**

9     $train(finalRanking)$;   `// Train a local classifier by asking for` `abstract or document relevance for these documents`

10    $localRanking = rerank(R - finalRanking)$; `// Rerank the rest of the` `initial list` R `from the predictions of the local classifier`

11   **if** $length(finalRanking) < t_{step}$ **then**

12      $step = step_{init}$;

13   **else**

14      $step = step_{secondary}$;

15   **for** $i = k'$ **to** $k' + step$ **do**

16      $finalRanking_i \leftarrow localRanking_{i-k'}$;

17 **return** $finalRanking$;

Ovid MEDLINE boolean queries. In particular, we extracted those MeSH that *should* characterize the retrieved documents, avoiding the ones that are negated in the query syntax.

4.2 Evaluation Process and Results

We split our evaluation process into two stages. The first stage is focused solely on the evaluation of the inter-review model and how different sets of features affect its performance. In the second stage we try to utilize the parameters of the intra-review model to make better use of the output, the initial ranking, of the inter-review model.

For all our experiments, we employ the XGBoost algorithm [5] to learn the inter-review model and linear support vector machines (SVMs), from the scikit-learn library[7], to learn the intra-review models. We use the default parameter settings for the XGBoost classifier and we set the C parameter of linear SVM to 0.1. Furthermore, for feature 7 we set v to 5 and for features 25–26 we set

---

[7] http://scikit-learn.org/.

the number of output dimensions of SVD to 200. The Word2Vec model used for features 27–30 was obtained from the BioASQ challenge[8]. This model has been trained on 10,876,004 English abstracts of biomedical articles from PubMed resulting in 1,701,632 distinct word vectors. The Doc2Vec model used in feature 31 is trained with all the documents associated with a topic retrieved from PubMed Central (PMC). Finally, we use all 42 topics for our evaluation and we perform cross validation using the Leave-One-(Topic)-Out method. Evaluation measures are computed using the script provided by the task[9] based on relevant judgment at the abstract level.

The first stage of our evaluation process focuses on the inter-review model. We first evaluate the features used in this model by performing an Anova F-test between each feature and the class. Table 2 shows the top-10 features along with their scores. We notice that all the features in which tf-idf is computed (21–26) are included in the top-10 with the ones using SVD to be the highest-ranked, which highlights the importance of semantic analysis. The list is completed with two Word2Vec features (27, 30) and two features that depend only on the topic (11–12). These features are related to the frequency of terms t_i in the title of the topic and are most probably regulating the importance of other features based on t_i, such as features 1–4.

To evaluate our model we perform three experiments using different sets of features. The first experiment makes use of features 1–24 which are standard LtR features. Our submission in Task II of CLEF eHealth 2017 lab also included the same features [2]. The second experiment consists of the full list of features 1–31 which includes advanced text representations derived from word embedding methods. The final experiment uses the top-10 features determined by the Anova F-test. Table 3 shows the Average Precision (AP), the normalized cumulative gain (NCG) at 10% and 20% and the minimum number of documents returned to retrieve all relevant documents (Last Relative - LR) of the three models described above. We first notice that using the full list of features achieves better scores than using just the top-10 features or the simple LtR features, beating our previous approach. Besides the increase in average precision, we also see an increase of NCG@10 and NCG@20 which indicates that more relevant documents appear first when using the additional features. This also hints at the need of a highly complex model that can overcome the high bias due to our very unbalanced dataset. Furthermore, the fact that the model using just the top-10 features achieves better results than the model using the simple LtR features highlights the strong influence of these specific features.

In the second stage of our evaluation process we explore the parameter space of the intra-review model as described in Sect. 3.2. Table 4 presents the final results of our approach using different parameter sets. The inter-review model using the full list of features is employed. We notice that integrating the intra-review model greatly increases the scores in all four metrics compared with the sole use of the inter-review model. The intra-review model not only ranks

---

[8] http://bioasq.org/.
[9] https://github.com/CLEF-TAR/tar.

Table 2. The scores of the top-10 features as measured by the F-test in ANOVA.

Rank	Feature ID	F-score	Rank	Feature ID	F-score
1	25	7013.55	6	12	2682.01
2	26	6363.41	7	11	2613.24
3	21	5252.00	8	30	1541.90
4	22	3289.95	9	24	501.01
5	27	2700.76	10	23	373.70

Table 3. Results concerning the inter-review model using different sets of features.

Features	AP	NCG@10	NCG@20	LR
Simple LtR (1–24)	0.171	0.363	0.594	4085.643
Full list (1–31)	0.187	0.382	0.613	3776.262
Top-10	0.177	0.372	0.601	3993.167

the relevant documents higher, as indicated by the NCG@ metrics, but also decreases, almost in half, the total number of documents returned to retrieve all relevant documents (LR metric).

Table 4. Results of our approach using different parameters of the intra-review model.

Run	k	$step_{init}$	t_{step}	$step_{sec}$	t_{final}	AP	NCG@10	NCG@20	LR
1	5	1	200	100	2000	0.309	0.533	0.819	2109.83
2	10	1	200	100	2000	0.309	0.536	0.820	2106.43
3	15	1	200	100	2000	0.304	0.533	0.820	2109.95
4	10	1	300	100	2000	0.310	0.534	0.824	2104.97
5	10	1	500	100	2000	0.311	0.538	0.822	2108.93

5   Conclusion and Future Work

We introduced a classification approach for automatic title and abstract screening for systematic reviews. Our approach constructs a global inter-review classification model based on LtR features of the topics and documents, produces an initial ranking for the test documents and then a second model iteratively asks for feedback and re-ranks them based on the acquired relevance feedback.

In the future, we plan to work more on the tuning and extraction of better features for the inter-review model and produce a better representation for the intra-review model using word embedding methods. Moreover, it would be worthy to experiment with other classification approaches as well, such as convolutional and recurrent neural networks.

References

1. Alharbi, A., Stevenson, M.: Ranking abstracts to identify relevant evidence for systematic reviews: the university of Sheffield's approach to CLEF eHealth 2017 task 2: working notes for CLEF 2017. In: CEUR Workshop Proceedings, vol. 1866 (2017)
2. Anagnostou, A., Lagopoulos, A., Tsoumakas, G., Vlahavas, I.: Combining inter-review learning-to-rank and intra-review incremental training for title and abstract screening in systematic reviews. In: CEUR Workshop Proceedings, vol. 1866 (2017)
3. Bastian, H., Glasziou, P., Chalmers, I.: Seventy-five trials and eleven systematic reviews a day: how will we ever keep up? PLoS Med. **7**(9), e1000326 (2010). https://doi.org/10.1371/journal.pmed.1000326
4. Chen, J., et al.: ECNU at 2017 eHealth task 2: technologically assisted reviews in empirical medicine. In: CEUR Workshop Proceedings, vol. 1866 (2017)
5. Chen, T., Guestrin, C.: XGBoost: reliable large-scale tree boosting system. arXiv, pp. 1–6 (2016). https://doi.org/10.1145/2939672.2939785
6. Cormack, G.V., Grossman, M.R.: Technology-assisted review in empirical medicine: waterloo participation in CLEF eHealth 2017. In: CEUR Workshop Proceedings, vol. 1866 (2017)
7. Goeuriot, L., et al.: CLEF 2017 eHealth evaluation lab overview. In: Jones, G.J.F., et al. (eds.) CLEF 2017. LNCS, vol. 10456, pp. 291–303. Springer, Cham (2017). https://doi.org/10.1007/978-3-319-65813-1_26
8. Hashimoto, K., Kontonatsios, G., Miwa, M., Ananiadou, S.: Topic detection using paragraph vectors to support active learning in systematic reviews. J. Biomed. Inform. **62**, 59–65 (2016). https://doi.org/10.1016/j.jbi.2016.06.001
9. Higgins, J.P., Green, S.: Cochrane Handbook for Systematic Reviews of Interventions. Wiley, Hoboken (2011). www.handbook.cochrane.org
10. Hollmann, N., Eickhoff, C.: Ranking and feedback-based stopping for recall-centric document retrieval. In: CEUR Workshop Proceedings, vol. 1866 (2017)
11. Howard, B.E., et al.: SWIFT-review: a text-mining workbench for systematic review. Syst. Rev. **5**(1), 87 (2016). https://doi.org/10.1186/s13643-016-0263-z
12. Kalphov, V., Georgiadis, G., Azzopardi, L.: SiS at CLEF 2017 eHealth TAR task. In: CEUR Workshop Proceedings, vol. 1866 (2017)
13. Kanoulas, E., Li, D., Azzopardi, L., Spijker, R.: CLEF 2017 technologically assisted reviews in empirical medicine overview. In: CEUR Workshop Proceedings, vol. 1866 (2017)
14. Kusner, M.J., Sun, Y., Kolkin, N.I., Weinberger, K.Q.: From word embeddings to document distances. In: Proceedings of the 32nd International Conference on Machine Learning, vol. 37, pp. 957–966 (2015)
15. Le, Q., Mikolov, T.: Distributed representations of sentences and documents. In: International Conference on Machine Learning, ICML 2014, vol. 32, pp. 1188–1196 (2014). https://doi.org/10.1145/2740908.2742760
16. Lee, G.E.: A study of convolutional neural networks for clinical document classification in systematic reviews: sysreview at CLEF eHealth 2017. In: CEUR Workshop Proceedings, vol. 1866 (2017)
17. Lefebvre, C., Manheimer, E., Glanville, J.: Searching for studies. In: Cochrane Handbook for Systematic Reviews of Interventions. Cochrane Book Series, pp. 95–150 (2008). https://doi.org/10.1002/9780470712184.ch6
18. Mikolov, T., Corrado, G., Chen, K., Dean, J.: Efficient estimation of word representations in vector space. In: Proceedings of the International Conference on

Learning Representations (ICLR 2013), pp. 1–12 (2013). https://doi.org/10.1162/153244303322533223

19. Norman, C., Leeflang, M., Névéol, A.: LIMSI@CLEF eHealth 2017 task 2: logistic regression for automatic article ranking. In: CEUR Workshop Proceedings, vol. 1866 (2017)

20. O'Mara-Eves, A., Thomas, J., McNaught, J., Miwa, M., Ananiadou, S.: Using text mining for study identification in systematic reviews: a systematic review of current approaches. Syst. Rev. **4**(1), 1–22 (2015). https://doi.org/10.1186/2046-4053-4-5

21. Ouzzani, M., Hammady, H., Fedorowicz, Z., Elmagarmid, A.: Rayyan-a web and mobile app for systematic reviews. Syst. Rev. **5**(1), 210 (2016). https://doi.org/10.1186/s13643-016-0384-4

22. Qin, T., Liu, T.Y., Xu, J., Li, H.: LETOR: a benchmark collection for research on learning to rank for information retrieval. Inf. Retr. **13**(4), 346–374 (2010). https://doi.org/10.1007/s10791-009-9123-y

23. Rathbone, J., Hoffmann, T., Glasziou, P.: Faster title and abstract screening? Evaluating Abstrackr, a semi-automated online screening program for systematic reviewers. Syst. Rev. **4**(1), 80 (2015). https://doi.org/10.1186/s13643-015-0067-6

24. Robertson, S.: The probabilistic relevance framework: BM25 and beyond. Found. Trends® Inf. Retr. **3**(4), 333–389 (2010). https://doi.org/10.1561/1500000019

25. Sackett, D.L.: Evidence-based medicine. Semin. Perinatol. **21**(1), 3–5 (1997). https://doi.org/10.1016/S0146-0005(97)80013-4

26. Scells, H., Zuccon, G., Deacon, A., Koopman, B.: QUT ielab at CLEF eHealth 2017 technology assisted reviews track: initial experiments with learning to rank. In: CEUR Workshop Proceedings, vol. 1866 (2017)

27. Singh, G., Marshall, I., Thomas, J., Wallace, B.: Identifying diagnostic test accuracy publications using a deep model. In: CEUR Workshop Proceedings, vol. 1866 (2017)

28. Sparck Jones, K., Sparck Jones, K., Walker, S., Walker, S., Robertson, S.E., Robertson, S.E.: A probabilistic model of information retrieval: development and comparative experiments part 2. Inf. Process. Manage. **36**, 809–840 (2000). https://doi.org/10.1016/S0306-4573(00)00016-9

29. Van Altena, A.J., Olabarriaga, S.D.: Predicting publication inclusion for diagnostic accuracy test reviews using random forests and topic modelling. In: CEUR Workshop Proceedings, vol. 1866 (2017)

30. Wallace, B.C., Small, K., Brodley, C.E., Trikalinos, T.A.: Active learning for biomedical citation screening. In: Proceedings of the 16th ACM SIGKDD International Conference on Knowledge Discovery and Data Mining, KDD 2010, p. 173 (2010). https://doi.org/10.1145/1835804.1835829

31. Wallace, B.C., Trikalinos, T.A., Lau, J., Brodley, C.E., Schmid, C.H.: Semi-automated screening of biomedical citations for systematic reviews. BMC Bioinform. **11**(1), 55 (2010). https://doi.org/10.1186/1471-2105-11-55

32. Yu, Z., Menzies, T.: Data balancing for technologically assisted reviews: undersampling or reweighting. In: CEUR Workshop Proceedings, vol. 1866 (2017)

Combining Tags and Reviews to Improve Social Book Search Performance

Messaoud Chaa[1,2(✉)], Omar Nouali[1], and Patrice Bellot[3]

[1] Centre de Recherche sur l'Information Scientifique et Technique, Alger, Algeria
{mchaa,onouali}@cerist.dz
[2] Université de Bejaia, 06000 Bejaia, Algeria
[3] Aix-Marseille Université, CNRS, LSIS UMR 7296, 13397 Marseille, France
patrice.bellot@lsis.org

Abstract. The emergence of Web 2.0 and social networks have provided important amounts of information that led researchers from different fields to exploit it. Social information retrieval is one of the areas that aim to use this social information to improve the information retrieval performance. This information can be textual, like tags or reviews, or non textual like ratings, number of likes, number of shares, etc. In this paper, we focus on the integration of social textual information in the research model. As it seems logical that integrating tags in the retrieval model should not be in the same way taken to integrate reviews, we will analyze the different influences of using tags and reviews on both the settings of retrieval parameters and the retrieval effectiveness. After several experiments, on the CLEF social book search collection, we concluded that combining the results obtained from two separate indexes and two models with specific parameters for tags and reviews gives good results compared to when using a single index and a single model.

Keywords: Social information retrieval · Social book search
Document length normalization · User-generated content
Tag Based Model · Review Based Model

1 Introduction

The rise of social media has changed the role of users in the Web. From simple users who just consume information to users that can produce it. Many kinds of social information are generated like tags, reviews, rating, users' relation or users' interests. This social information has been exploited in several application domains such as marketing [11], commerce [20], etc. The field of information retrieval is no exception to this. A few years ago, a new area of research namely social information retrieval (SIR) emerged and gained popularity. The objective of SIR systems is to identify and integrate that social information (tags, reviews, ratings...) in a search process in order to improve the IR performance [3,17].

© Springer Nature Switzerland AG 2018
P. Bellot et al. (Eds.): CLEF 2018, LNCS 11018, pp. 64–75, 2018.
https://doi.org/10.1007/978-3-319-98932-7_6

On the other hand, social digital libraries such as LibraryThing[1] and Goodreads[2] are social cataloging websites for books that enable users to store and share book catalogues. Users can rate, review, tag, and discuss their books. They can also create groups with other members, create discussions, and ask for book recommendations. While suggestions and recommendations can be sent to users in response to their request. This generates a large volume of data for books and represent a great challenge for information retrieval tasks in general and book search in particular. In order to exploit this wealth of information, the CLEF track social book search (SBS) has come to use the social information to search and develop techniques to support users in book search tasks.

2 Social Book Search

Social book search (SBS)[3] was a CLEF lab (2011–2016) that particularly investigated book search in social media. It was interested in the use of user-generated content from social media to support users of LibraryThing forum in finding documents (books)[4] that interest them and that are relevant to their request [13,14]. The organizers of INEX SBS have used Amazon[5] and Librarything (LT) to provide a document collection which consists of 2.8 million books. This collection contains both textual and non-textual social information about books. Textual social information consists of users' reviews and tags that are respectively extracted from Amazon and LT. As to non-textual information like rating, number of time a book is catalogued, etc., they are extracted from LT whereas ratings, number of reviews, of total votes and helpful votes are extracted from Amazon. In order to evaluate systems in SBS, a set of topics with relevance assessments are provided. These topics are based on discussion threads from LT forums, where users express their needs and ask suggestions and recommendations about books to other forum users. These topics contain many fields: group, title, narrative and examples (see Fig. 1). The group field designates the discussion group in which a user posts their thread, the title is the short representation of the topic which often contains a brief summary about the user's need. Narrative is a long representation of the topic in which the user utilizes natural language to explain their needs in details. As to the field examples, it consists of some similar books add by some LT users in order to indicate the kind of books they want.

3 Related Works

Since its first edition in 2011, participants of SBS have proposed approaches and submitted their results (runs) to get them evaluated. The majority of these

---

[1] www.librarything.com.
[2] www.goodreads.com.
[3] www.social-book-search.humanities.uva.nl.
[4] We use the terms "document" and "book" interchangeably in this paper.
[5] www.amazon.com.

```
<topic id="41306"> <request>Spanish Civil War : For Whom The Bell Tolls :: French
Revolution: ?? I don't think there's a right answer, I'm just looking for suggestions for
a good fictional book set during the French Revolution. (My interest was piqued after
reading the Jim Shepard short story "Sans Farine" in The Best American Short Stories
2007.) <request>
<group>Book talk</group>
<title>Fill in this historical fiction analogy</title>
<examples>
<example>
<booktitle>For Whom the Bell Tolls</booktitle>
<author>Ernest Hemingway</author>
<workid>10084</workid>
</example>
<example>
<booktitle>The Best American Short Stories 2007</booktitle>
<author>Stephen King</author>
<workid>3539369</workid>
</example>
</examples>
```

Fig. 1. XML file representing an example topic in social book search.

approaches use textual information (tags and reviews) to estimate the initial score of books then non-textual information like (rating, popularity, number of tags, number of reviews, profile of user, etc.) is used to re-rank the initial ranking and improve the initial text-based search results.

The authors in [2] used the language modeling with Jelinek-Mercer (JM) smoothing to build the initial content based results. They also experimented different re-ranking approaches using different information sources, such as user ratings, tags, authorship, and Amazon's similar products. The results show that the re-ranking approaches are often successful.

In [7,22], the probability of the query content produced by the language model is used to rank the documents based on textual information. Ratings, number of reviews, popularity and high frequent books are then used to re-rank the initial ranking. Finally, random forest was used to learn the different combinations of scores and the results are better than the initial ranking.

In [8] the BM25F model was used to optimize the weight of the four book fields (title, summary, tags, reviews). Popularity, reputation, ratings and similarity between users were used to improve the results however, their integration did not give any improvement. [10] employ the textual model BM25 and enhance it by using social signals such as rating. Finally, they applied a random forest learning to improve the results by including non-textual modalities like price and number of pages according to the user's preferences. This approach improves the results and shows good performances.

The authors in [1] used two textual retrieval model Divergence from randomness model (DFR) and Sequential Dependence Model (SDM) before combining the results with the ratings of books. The best results were obtained when using

DFR model with textual information only. In [4,5], the authors use only tags as textual information about books. They investigate the representation of the query by transforming the long verbose queries to a reduced queries before applying the BM15 retrieval model. The result of this approach shows also good performance despite not using Amazon reviews at all.

To sum up, the majority of these works used textual information as a baseline before using non-textual information for reranking. As for indexing, they used users' tags and reviews together to represent books. However, some of them [2,8, 12,14] studied the influence of using tags only, reviews only or tags with reviews as books representation on the retrieval performance. To our knowledge, there is no study that has adapted a specific model for each document representation. Hence, when combining tags and reviews, the authors in [2,8,12,14] used the same retrieval model to compute scores and rank documents for each query.

In this paper, we use both textual and non textual information of books as used in the studies mentioned above. However, instead of using one index for all textual fields and one function to compute scores of documents, we build a separate index for each field. We build two models, Tag Based Model (TBM) and Review Based Model (RBM) which respectively use the index of tags and the index of reviews. Then, we analyse the different influences of using tags and reviews on the settings of retrieval parameters as well as on the retrieval effectiveness. Then, we combine the results of the two models to form the textual score. Finally, we combine textual and non textual score to form the final result.

4   Experimental Setup

In our experiments we have used the collection provided by the organizers of SBS. For documents, we have considered two kinds of representations: LT users' tags and Amazon users' reviews. Table 1 summarizes the statistics of the collection. The numbers of tokens and single terms are calculated after stopword removal and Porter stemming. Table 1 shows that the number of books that have been tagged is greater than the number of books that have been reviewed however, the number of tokens (all occurrences) in reviews are greater than those of tags. This because, for reviews the users use natural language to give their opinions and speak freely about books. However for tags the users assign a few keywords or terms to describe books.

Table 1. Statistics on tags and reviews of SBS collection

Number of books	2,781,400
Number of books that have been reviewed at least once	1,915,336
Number of books that have been tagged at least once	2,306,368
Number of tokens in reviews	1,161,240,462
Number of single terms in reviews	1,135,910
Number of tokens in tags	246,552,598
Number of single terms in tags	194,487

As to queries, we have used all the six-year topics (1646 topics) provided by SBS from 2011 to 2016. Because each query is composed of title and narrative, we have considered two types of queries: short and long queries. The short query is constructed from the title of the topic while the long query is the narrative and title + narrative.

The prime target of our study is to investigate the impact of using the different query representations as well as the two representations of documents on the retrieval performance. To achieve this, we built three indexes, the first contains tags assigned by users to books in LT, the second contains reviews extracted from Amazon while the last one merges tags and reviews in the same index. The Terrier IR platform [16] was used to index the collection by applying basic stopword filtering and Porter stemming algorithm. The BM25 model [18] was used for querying. Using the BM25 model, the relevance score of a book d for query Q is given by:

$$S(d,Q) = \sum_{t \in Q} \frac{(k_1 + 1)tf_{td}}{tf_{td} + k_1(1 - b + b.\frac{|D|}{avgdl})}.idf(t).\frac{(k_3 + 1)tf_{tq}}{k_3 + tf_{tq}} \tag{1}$$

Where tf_{td} and tf_{tq} are respectively the frequency of term t in document d and in query Q. The three free parameters of the function are: k_1 and k_3 that respectively controls term frequency scaling of the document and the query, the parameter b controls the document length normalization. $idf(t)$ is the inverse document frequency of term t, given as follow:

$$idf(t) = log\frac{|D| - df(t) + 0.5}{df(t) + 0.5} \tag{2}$$

Where $df(t)$ is the number of documents where the term t appears, and $|D|$ is the number of documents in the collection.

4.1   Length Normalization vs Document and Query Representation

Document length normalization is a technique that attempts to adjust the term frequency or the relevance score in order to normalize the effect of document length on the document ranking. Several works [6,9,15] show that this technique has an important impact on the performance of the model.

In order to determine the sensitivity of the model performance as to the length normalization, using the different cases of document representations as well as query representations, we have set the BM25 standard parameters for $k1$ and $k3$ ($k1 = 2$, $k3 = 1000$) and varied the length normalization parameter b from 0 to 0.75 (in steps of 0.05) then we evaluated the results in terms of NDCG@10 on both indexes (tags and reviews). The results obtained for all queries together are shown in Fig. 2.

From Fig. 2, we can see that in TBM, the performance of the model is very sensitive to the normalization of the length of the document. NDCG@10 drops from 0.1415 (b = 0) to 0.0375 (b = 0.75) in the case of title (short queries). It increases from 0.0368 (b = 0) to 0.0961 (b = 0.05) then drops to 0.0321 (b = 0.75)

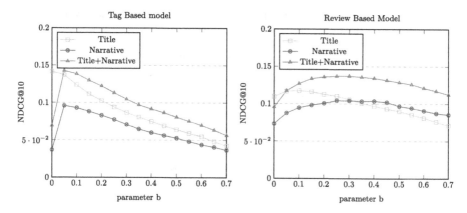

Fig. 2. Sensitivity of ndcg@10 for length normalization for Tag Based Model and Review Based Model.

when using narrative (long queries). The same sensitivity of the model was shown When combining title and narrative to represent the query, NDCG@10 increases from 0.0695 (b = 0) to 0.1429 (b = 0.1) and then drops to 0.0490 (b = 0.75).

In the case of RBM, the model performance is not very sensitive to the normalization of the document length compared to TBM. The values of NDCG@10 are very close so there is no big difference between them especially when varying b from 0 to 0.35. NDCG@10 is 0.1096 (b = 0) and 0.1003 (b = 0.35) in the case of short queries. The same measure increases from 0.0731 (b = 0) to 0.1042 (b = 0.25) and then decreases to 0.0803 (b = 0.75) in the case of long queries. In the same way, the NDCG@10 increases from 0.0957 (b = 0) to 0.1370 (b = 0.25) and then decreases to 0.1062 (b = 0.75) when combining title and narrative.

The same figure clearly shows that in short queries the best performance is obtained when b is very small, b = 0 for the tags (no length normalization is required) and b = 0.1 for reviews. However, when using long queries we find that the best performance is obtained when b = 0.1 for tags and b = 0.25 for reviews (length normalization is required). We can conclude that the setting parameters of the model are not the same in the TBM model or in the RBM model. Each of them has its specific parameters.

Because these evaluations are obtained for all queries together and to make our results more meaningful, we have decided to learn the parameter b by selecting the set of topics of each year as the testing set and the remaining sets of topics (of other years) as the training set. The evaluation in term of NDCG@10 of the results, for Single index($b = 0.3$), TBM model ($b = 0.05$) and RBM Model($b = 0.25$), obtained after training and testing is shown in Table 2.

As shown in Table 2, TBM gave the best results, compared to RBM and Single index, except for 2011 when RBM gave the best results. By the way, we were surprised that, in most cases, using tags only (TBM) or reviews only (RBM) to index documents gave better results compared to when using tags and reviews together. The only exceptional case was in 2011 where single index (NDCG = 0.2810) was better than TBM (NDCG = 0.2459).

Table 2. Results in term of NDCG@10 of the three index, using Title + Narrative as a representation of the topic; best results are shown in bold.

Year	Single index	TBM	RBM
2011	0.2810	0.2459	**0.3007**
2012	0.1387	**0.2012**	0.1479
2013	0.1143	**0.1193**	0.1191
2014	0.1169	**0.1291**	0.1175
2015	0.0682	**0.1222**	0.0794
2016	0.0803	**0.0951**	0.0906
All	0.1307	**0.1429**	0.1370

4.2 Query Expansion Using Example Books

In addition to title and narrative, the topics of SBS contain an example field which includes a list of books that the user has mentioned in their topic to show the kind of books he/she requests. In our approach, we consider this list of books as relevant books; therefore we use the query expansion technique to extract the highly relevant terms of these books and expand the original query. The Rocchio function [19] used to expand the query is as follows:

$$\vec{Q}_{new} = \vec{Q}_{T+N} + \frac{\beta}{|EXP|} \sum_{d \in EXP} \vec{d} \qquad (3)$$

Where $\vec{Q}_{new}$ is the expansion query, $\vec{Q}_{T+N}$ is the original query represented by Title + Narrative. $\vec{d}$ denotes the weighted term vector of the example book d using the default term weighting model Bo1 (Bose-Einstein 1). EXP is the set of example books and $/EXP/$ is the number of example books mentioned in the topic. The function was used with their default parameter settings $\beta = 0.4$, and the number of terms selected from each example book was set to 10.

Table 3 shows the results after the query expansion for the Single index, TBM model as well as for the RBM model. The same table shows that the query expansion technique has improved the results for the three indexes. We also notice that TBM gave the best results for all cases except for 2011 when RBM gave the best NDCG@10 (0.3418) and for 2013 when Single index has an NDCG@10 = 0.1496.

4.3 Combining the Scores of the Two Models

Once the parameters of TBM and RBM are optimized, a combination of the two scores obtained is necessary to obtain the final textual score of each book with respect to the query. The linear combination function is as follows:

$$S(d,Q) = \alpha.S_{TBM}(d,Q) + (1-\alpha).S_{RBM}(d,Q) \qquad (4)$$

Table 3. NDCG@10 results obtained after applying a query expansion technique.

Year	Single index		TBM		RBM	
	Before expansion	After expansion	Before expansion	After expansion	Before expansion	After expansion
2011	0.281	0.3310	0.2459	0.2725	0.3007	**0.3418**
2012	0.1387	0.1667	0.2012	**0.2341**	0.1479	0.1754
2013	0.1143	**0.1496**	0.1193	0.1452	0.1191	0.1478
2014	0.1169	0.1436	0.1291	**0.1525**	0.1175	0.1423
2015	0.0682	0.0887	0.1222	**0.1409**	0.0794	0.0907
2016	0.0803	0.1088	0.0951	**0.1367**	0.0906	0.1205
All	0.1307	0.1619	0.1429	**0.1686**	0.1370	0.1639

Where $S(d, Q)$ is the final score of document d with respect to query Q. $S_{TBM}(d, Q)$ and $S_{RBM}(d, Q)$ are the scores of document d with respect to query Q respectively obtained from TBM and RBM models. The query Q is represented by Title + Narrative and expanded using similar books as explained in the previous section. α [0 1] is a free parameter that controls the weight of the two models. This parameter was tuned using six-fold cross-validation in the same way it was performed to tuned the parameter b as indicated in Sect. 4.1. Thus, a single set of topics of one year is used for testing the model and the remaining five-year topics are used as a training set. After the process is repeated six times (once for each year), the results have been summed up in Table 4. This table shows the results in term of NDCG@10 obtained from the combination and compares them to the results obtained from the previous experiments. The best results of the combination are obtained when $\alpha \in$ is set to 0.4.

Table 4. NDCG@10 obtained by the combination after tuning the parameter α using six-fold cross-validation compared to a single index, RBM model and TBM Model. Asterisks indicate statistically significant differences compared with single index (Student's t-test, P < 0.05)

Year	Single index	TBM	RBM	Combination
2011	0.3310	0.2725	0.3418	**0.3595**
2012	0.1667	0.2341	0.1754	**0.2425***
2013	0.1496	0.1452	0.1478	**0.1888***
2014	0.1436	0.1525	0.1423	**0.1886***
2015	0.0887	0.1409	0.0907	**0.1526***
2016	0.1088	0.1367	0.1205	**0.1793***
All	0.1619	0.1686	0.1639	**0.2091***

From the results, we note that for all years the combination of the two scores gave good results, compared to the results of each index. For all queries, the NDCG@10 increased from 0.1619 (single model), 0.1686 (TBM model) and 0.1639 (RBM model) to 0.2091 when combining the two scores so there is an improvement of 29.15%, 24.02% and 27.54% compared to the three models. This results shows that the technique of using two separate indexes and combining the results is an effective technique to get best results.

4.4   Non Textual Information to Re-rank Documents

The non textual information of documents in social media like number of likes, number of rating, number of times the document was catalogued or rated represents an important information and can be used to re-rank the documents to improve the results. Several Re-ranking approaches were proposed by [22] at INEX2014 and [2] in 2012, which proved to be effective. In this paper we combine the textual score obtained above with the number of times the book was rated to re-rank the documents. The combination of scores is calculated by the flowing function:

$$S(d, Q) = \lambda . S_{Textual}(d, Q) + (1 - \lambda) . S_{Non-textual}(d) \tag{5}$$

where $S(d, Q)$ is the final score of document d with respect to query Q. $S_{Textual}(d, Q)$ is the textual score of document d obtained by combining the scores of TBM and RBM as explained in the previous section. λ [0 1] is a free parameter that controls the weight of the two scores. $S_{Non-textual}(d)$ is the normalized non-textual score of document d calculated as follow:

$$S_{Non-textual} = \frac{Nb\_rated - Min\_nb\_rated}{Max\_nb\_rated - Min\_nb\_rated} \tag{6}$$

Where nb_rated is the number of times the document is rated, Min_nb_rated and Max_nb_rated is the minimum and the maximum of the number of times that all books of the collection have. Table 5 shows the results obtained when using the non-textual information for re-ranking. The best results obtained when $\lambda \in$ was set to 0.9. From this Table we show that when using the Non-Textual information to re-rank documents gave good results of all years of topics, except in 2011 when the NDCG@10 (0.3595) obtained by using the textual information only is better than the NDCG@10 (0.3551) after re-ranking the documents.

Finally, we compare the performance of our best results, obtained by our approach, to the best official and non official runs. The official runs are those that have been submitted by participants to SBS during the six last years. The non official runs are the results obtained recently in the works of [21,23]. Table 6 represents the comparative results. The results show that the NDCG@10 value of our approach is better than the best official runs of the four years (2011, 2012, 2013 and 2014) but lower than the best runs of the two years (2015 and 2016). This table shows also that our approach gave good results in the three first years compared to the non official runs.

Table 5. NDCG@10 obtained by the combination of Textual and Non-textual scores

	Textual score only	Textual and non-textual scores
2011	**0.3595**	0.3551
2012	0.2425	**0.2469**
2013	0.1888	**0.1907**
2014	0.1886	**0.1943**
2015	0.1526	**0.1585**
2016	0.1793	**0.1935**
All	0.2091	**0.2133**

Table 6. Comparison between the results of our approach and the best runs submitted to the different years of SBS; best results are shown in bold.

	Our approach	Best non official runs	Best official runs
2011	**0.3551**	0.3423	0.3101
2012	**0.2469**	0.2325	0.1456
2013	**0.1907**	0.1856	0.1361
2014	0.1943	**0.1960**	0.1420
2015	0.1585	**0.2040**	0.1870
2016	0.1935	**0.2157**	**0.2157**

5   Analysis

From the results, we have noticed that TBM model requires a smaller value of b for optimal performance whether for short or long queries compared to RBM model. This led us to ask the following question:

Why document length normalization is required when using reviews as a document representation and not required when using tags as document representation?

As an answer to the question, this may be due to the fact that the users' reviews are a natural language text in which users can repeat freely the same term many times in the same review. Hence, the frequency value of any given term present in the query will be increased thereby increasing the relevance scores of long documents that contain long reviews. That is why document length normalization is required to penalize very long documents. Contrary to the reviews, the users' tags are keywords that users assign them to documents and the same user can not assign the same term many times to the same document. Hence, for long documents when the frequency value of any query term is great this means that this document was tagged by several users using the same term then it is relevant to the topic and it is unreasonable to penalize them. Therefore, the document length normalization is not required for tag representation.

6   Conclusion

In this paper, we have studied the exploitation of user tags and reviews in social book search. Three indexes have been created, the first for tags, the second for reviews and the third that merges the two. After several experimentations, we concluded that the Tag Based Model does not require a document length normalization especially for short queries. The best results of this model were obtained when b has very low values, This may be due to the fact that the number of tags assigned to books by users cannot be regarded as a length of text documents. However, the Review Based Model requires the document length normalization, this may be because the user reviews are long and be seen as a classical textual document. We have noticed that using two indexes for tags and reviews separately and combining the results of the models gives good and better results compared to when using a single index and a single model. We have also demonstrated that the proposed combination has given satisfactory results, especially when using non-textual information to re-rank documents, and outperforms the best runs submitted to SBS in the four first years.

References

1. Benkoussas, C., Hamdan, H., Albitar, S., Ollagnier, A., Bellot, P.: Collaborative filtering for book recommandation. In: CLEF (Working Notes), pp. 501–507 (2014)
2. Bogers, T., Larsen, B.: RSLIS at INEX 2012: social book search track. In: INEX, vol. 12, pp. 97–108 (2012)
3. Bouadjenek, M.R., Hacid, H., Bouzeghoub, M.: Social networks and information retrieval, how are they converging? A survey, a taxonomy and an analysis of social information retrieval approaches and platforms. Inf. Syst. **56**, 1–18 (2016)
4. Chaa, M., Nouali, O., Bellot, P.: Verbose query reduction by learning to rank for social book search track. In: CLEF (Working Notes), pp. 1072–1078 (2016)
5. Chaa, M., Nouali, O., Bellot, P.: New technique to deal with verbose queries in social book search. In: Proceedings of the International Conference on Web Intelligence, pp. 799–806. ACM (2017)
6. Cummins, R., O'Riordan, C.: The effect of query length on normalisation in information retrieval. In: Coyle, L., Freyne, J. (eds.) AICS 2009. LNCS (LNAI), vol. 6206, pp. 26–32. Springer, Heidelberg (2010). https://doi.org/10.1007/978-3-642-17080-5_5
7. Feng, S.H., et al.: USTB at social book search 2016 suggestion task: active books set and re-ranking. In: CLEF (Working Notes), pp. 1089–1096 (2016)
8. Hafsi, M., Géry, M., Beigbeder, M.: LaHC at INEX 2014: social book search track. In: Working Notes for CLEF 2014 Conference (2014)
9. He, B., Ounis, I.: Term frequency normalisation tuning for BM25 and DFR models. In: Losada, D.E., Fernández-Luna, J.M. (eds.) ECIR 2005. LNCS, vol. 3408, pp. 200–214. Springer, Heidelberg (2005). https://doi.org/10.1007/978-3-540-31865-1_15
10. Imhof, M., Badache, I., Boughanem, M.: Multimodal social book search. In: 6th Conference on Multilingual and Multimodal Information Access Evaluation (CLEF 2015), p. 1 (2015)

11. Kim, A.J., Ko, E.: Do social media marketing activities enhance customer equity? An empirical study of luxury fashion brand. J. Bus. Res. **65**(10), 1480–1486 (2012)
12. Koolen, M.: "User reviews in the search index? That'll never work!". In: de Rijke, M., et al. (eds.) ECIR 2014. LNCS, vol. 8416, pp. 323–334. Springer, Cham (2014). https://doi.org/10.1007/978-3-319-06028-6_27
13. Koolen, M., et al.: Overview of the CLEF 2015 social book search lab. In: Mothe, J., et al. (eds.) CLEF 2015. LNCS, vol. 9283, pp. 545–564. Springer, Cham (2015). https://doi.org/10.1007/978-3-319-24027-5_51
14. Koolen, M., Kamps, J., Kazai, G.: Social book search: comparing topical relevance judgements and book suggestions for evaluation. In: Proceedings of the 21st ACM International Conference on Information and Knowledge Management, pp. 185–194. ACM (2012)
15. Lv, Y., Zhai, C.: Lower-bounding term frequency normalization. In: Proceedings of the 20th ACM International Conference on Information and Knowledge Management, pp. 7–16. ACM (2011)
16. Ounis, I., Amati, G., Plachouras, V., He, B., Macdonald, C., Lioma, C.: Terrier: a high performance and scalable information retrieval platform. In: Proceedings of the OSIR Workshop, pp. 18–25 (2006)
17. Park, D.H., Liu, M., Zhai, C., Wang, H.: Leveraging user reviews to improve accuracy for mobile app retrieval. In: Proceedings of the 38th International ACM SIGIR Conference on Research and Development in Information Retrieval, pp. 533–542. ACM (2015)
18. Robertson, S.E., Walker, S., Beaulieu, M.: Experimentation as a way of life: Okapi at TREC. Inf. Process. Manag. **36**(1), 95–108 (2000)
19. Rocchio, J.J.: Relevance feedback in information retrieval. The Smart retrieval system-experiments in automatic document processing (1971)
20. Swamynathan, G., Wilson, C., Boe, B., Almeroth, K., Zhao, B.Y.: Do social networks improve e-commerce? A study on social marketplaces. In: Proceedings of the First Workshop on Online Social Networks, pp. 1–6. ACM (2008)
21. Yin, X.C., et al.: ISART: a generic framework for searching books with social information. PLoS One **11**(2), e0148479 (2016)
22. Zhang, B.W., et al.: USTB at INEX2014: social book search track. In: CLEF (Working Notes), pp. 536–542 (2014)
23. Zhang, B.W., Yin, X.C., Zhou, F., Jin, J.L.: Building your own reading list anytime via embedding relevance, quality, timeliness and diversity. In: Proceedings of the 40th International ACM SIGIR Conference on Research and Development in Information Retrieval, pp. 1109–1112. ACM (2017)

Fast and Simple Deterministic Seeding of KMeans for Text Document Clustering

Ehsan Sherkat[1(✉)], Julien Velcin[2], and Evangelos E. Milios[1]

[1] Dalhousie University, Halifax, Canada
ehsansherkat@dal.ca, eem@cs.dal.ca
[2] University Lyon 2, Lyon, France
julien.velcin@univ-lyon2.fr

Abstract. KMeans is one of the most popular document clustering algorithms. It is usually initialized by random seeds that can drastically impact the final algorithm performance. There exists many random or order-sensitive methods that try to properly initialize KMeans but their problem is that their result is non-deterministic and unrepeatable. Thus KMeans needs to be initialized several times to get a better result, which is a time-consuming operation. In this paper, we introduce a novel deterministic seeding method for KMeans that is specifically designed for text document clustering. Due to its simplicity, it is fast and can be scaled to large datasets. Experimental results on several real-world datasets demonstrate that the proposed method has overall better performance compared to several deterministic, random, or order-sensitive methods in terms of clustering quality and runtime.

Keywords: Document clustering · Text · KMeans initialization
Deterministic

1 Introduction

The objective of KMeans is to assign similar data points to the same cluster while they are dissimilar to other clusters. The gradient descent method is usually used for optimizing the objective function and due to the non-convex nature of KMeans, the initial seeds play an important role in the quality of the clustering. There are several research works that try to provide good seeds for the KMeans. These methods can be divided into two major categories of non-deterministic and deterministic methods [12].

The non-deterministic methods are random or order-sensitive in nature. KMeans++ is a well known seeding method that incrementally selects initial seeds one at a time [3]. In each step, a data point is selected with a probability proportional to the minimum distance to the previously selected seeds. Because the first seed in KMeans++ is determined randomly and next seeds are selected based on a probabilistic method, the initial seeds are not repeatable. The KMC2 method improves the KMeans++ sampling step by Markov chain Monte Carlo

© Springer Nature Switzerland AG 2018
P. Bellot et al. (Eds.): CLEF 2018, LNCS 11018, pp. 76–88, 2018.
https://doi.org/10.1007/978-3-319-98932-7_7

based approximation [4]. Similarly to KMeans++, KMC2 starts with a uniformly random seed then the next seeds are selected by Markov chains of size m. The key factor for speeding up the KMC2 is that for each seed selection, it does not need to fully pass through all the data points and it only needs to compute the distance between m data points and previously selected seeds. The m is a fixed value, independent of the number of data points.

While there are many non-deterministic seeding methods, there exist few deterministic ones. The deterministic approaches need to be run only once and it makes them more practical for larger datasets. The comparison between different deterministic methods is presented by [11]. The KKZ method is one of the first deterministic seeding methods for KMeans [17]. It first sorts the data points by their vector's norm and the one with the highest value is selected as the first seed. The next seeds will be selected from data points that have the largest distance to the closest previously selected seeds. The most important drawback of this method is that it is sensitive to outliers. To avoid selecting an outlier as the initial seed, the ROBIN approach [16] uses local outlier factor (LOF) method [9]. This method first starts with a reference point r that usually is the origin of data points. Then it sorts the data points in decreasing order of their minimum distances from r. It then traverses the sorted list and selects the first non-outlier node, based on its LOF value. For the next steps, it sorts the data points in decreasing order by their minimum distance to the previous seeds and, again, the first non-outlier node is the next seed. The LOF method is not applicable to high dimensional and sparse datasets, which is an important issue in textual document collections [2].

The PCA-part and VAR-part are two popular deterministic hierarchical initialization methods for KMeans [21]. They start with all data points as a single cluster and then divide the data point into two halves based on Principle Component Analysis (PCA) [1]. This process continues and at each step, the half with largest average distance to its centroid is divided into two parts until the required number of seeds is reached. The result of the previous steps is an approximate clustering of data points; the centroid of the clusters are used for initializing KMeans.

There are some applications that require determinism. Interactive document clustering is a task that involves a human domain expert in the clustering procedure [7]. First, the clustering algorithm provides the user with initial clustering results, then the user provides feedback to reflect her idea of a meaningful clustering. If the initial result is non-deterministic, the user may get confused by the inconsistent clustering result. It is possible to store the initial data points to make the result of a non-deterministic method repeatable, but it may lead to a bad quality solution unless one initializes the clustering algorithm several times and then consider the one which has optimized the objective function the most, which is a very time-consuming process. In a medical domain, such as cancer subtype prediction, it is essential to have deterministic clusters for making a consistent decision and for being able to compare the clustering results with other clustering algorithms [20]. There is a particular treatment plan for each

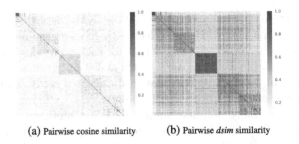

(a) Pairwise cosine similarity   (b) Pairwise *dsim* similarity

Fig. 1. The comparative result of pairwise cosine and *dsim* similarity of Newsgroup5 dataset. The darker color indicates the higher similarity between two documents. The documents are sorted by their class labels and five clusters are clearly detectable in both heatmaps. (Color figure online)

cancer subtype and in case that a subtype is clustered differently with different seeds it may impact the patients treatment procedure.

In this paper, we introduce a simple deterministic seeding method for KMeans algorithm, called DSKM (Deterministic Seeding KMeans), with the target of text document clustering. The proposed method is not only deterministic and reproducible but also improves the overall clustering results. The proposed method tries to find initial seeds that are as diverse as possible which consequently lead to a better clustering result. The KMeans need to be initialized by DSKM only once and this makes it fast and can be applied on large datasets. The code to the paper is publicly available[1].

2   Proposed Method

The key idea of the proposed method is to select k data points that are far from each other and, at the same time, have a high L_1 norm. These data points are used to initialize the KMeans algorithm. Steps of the proposed method are described in the following.

Step 1. First the document vectors are created based on terms of document collection after removing numbers, punctuations and stop-words. The document-term matrix produced as a result of this step is the input of the Algorithm 1. Let D be the set of documents and d a document in D. The TF-IDF weight of term w in document d is defined as Eq. 1, which has smoothed variant of the IDF.

$$TF\_IDF(w, d, D) = f(w, d) \times log \frac{|D| + 1}{|x \in D : w \in x| + 1} + 1. \tag{1}$$

where $f(w, d)$ is the frequency of term w in document d. Each document vector is then normalized by the L_2 norm. The high dimension of vectors may impact the results of the clustering algorithm. To reduce the dimension, we use a

---

[1] https://github.com/ehsansherkat/DSKM.

Algorithm 1. Deterministic seeding KMeans (DSKM)

---

input : k: Number of clusters, Data$^{|D| \times |W|}$: document-term matrix   // Step1
output: S:$\{s_1, s_2, ..., s_k\}$ = Set of seed documents index

1 **Function** $T(s_i)$:   // Threshold function
2 $\quad$ **return** $\frac{1}{|D|} \sum_{j=1}^{|D|} dsim(d_j, s_i)$;
3 **end**

4 $C^{|D| \times |D|} \leftarrow$ pairwise-similarity(Data, 'cosine');
5 A:$\{a_1, a_2, ..., a_{|D|}\} \leftarrow$ sort(Data, 'L_1 norm');
6 $s_0 \leftarrow C[a_1]$ $\quad$ // Set starting point. C[i] is row vector. Step2;
7 $S \leftarrow \{\}$

8 **for** $i \leftarrow 1$ **to** $|D|$ **do**   // Step 3
9 $\quad$ **if** $dsim(C[s_0], C[a_i]) < T(s_0)$ **then**
10 $\quad\quad$ $S \leftarrow a_i$;
11 $\quad\quad$ **break**;
12 $\quad$ **end**
13 **end**
14 **while** $|S| < k$ **do**   // Step 4
15 $\quad$ found $\leftarrow$ False;
16 $\quad$ **for** $i \leftarrow 1$ **to** $|D|$ **do**
17 $\quad\quad$ **if** $dsim(C[s_j], C[a_i]) < T(s_j), \forall s_j \in S, a_i \notin S$ **then**
18 $\quad\quad\quad$ $S \leftarrow a_i$;
19 $\quad\quad\quad$ found $\leftarrow$ True;
20 $\quad\quad\quad$ **break**;
21 $\quad\quad$ **end**
22 $\quad$ **end**
23 $\quad$ **if** $found == False$ **then**
24 $\quad\quad$ $S \leftarrow argmin(\sum_{j=1}^{|S|} dsim(a_i, s_j)), \forall a_i \in A, a_i \notin S$
25 $\quad$ **end**
26 **end**
27 **return** S

---

simple but effective approach for pruning: the terms with a lower *mean-TF-IDF score* than the average mean-TF-IDF of all terms. For each term, the *mean-TF-IDF score* is calculated based on Eq. 2.

$$mean\_TF\_IDF(w, D) = \frac{1}{|D|} \times \sum_{d \in D} TF\_IDF(w, d, D). \tag{2}$$

Step 2. The rows of the document-term matrix are sorted by L_1 norm in a way that the first row of the matrix is the document with the highest L_1 norm. Documents with a higher L_1 norm have more impact on grouping similar documents because of having more key-terms. Therefore, we select the document with the highest L_1 norm as the starting data point (s_0). This procedure will generally not select an outlier document as a seed document.

Step 3. In the third step, we find a data point that is far from the starting data point and consider it as the first seed. Let $C^{|D| \times |D|}$ be the pairwise cosine similarity matrix between each pair of documents. Let c_{d_i} be the i-th row of C. c_{d_i} corresponds to the vector of similarities of document d_i with every other document. It has been shown that the cosine similarity is a better metric than the Euclidean distance for comparing textual documents [6]. We define the double similarity (*dsim*) between the document d_i to document d_j as Eq. 3.

$$dsim(d_i, d_j) = \frac{c_{d_i} \cdot c_{d_j}}{\|c_{d_i}\|_2 \|c_{d_j}\|_2}. \tag{3}$$

The insight for using *dsim* is that not only two documents, but also their similar documents, should be far from each other. Using *dsim* can help to achieve this goal. The comparison between heatmaps of pairwise cosine and *dsim* similarity of Newsgroup5 dataset is depicted in Fig. 1. The darker colors in the *dsim* heatmap indicates that two documents may have considerable number of common similar documents. It means that two documents may be more similar to each other if we compare their similar documents with each other than directly comparing them.

Let A be the list of document indexes sorted in decreasing order by their L_1 norm. The goal of the third step is finding the first document which has *dsim* similarity less than a specific threshold from the starting point (s_0) by traversing from the first of list A (Lines 8–13 Algorithm 1). Let S be the set of seed documents and $s_i \in S$ be the document index of seed i. The similarity threshold (Lines 1–3 Algorithm 1) is calculated based on Eq. 4.

$$T(s_i) = \frac{1}{|D|} \sum_{j=1}^{|D|} dsim(d_j, S_i). \tag{4}$$

$T(s_0)$ is the threshold for finding the first seed based on the starting data point s_0. We do not consider the starting data point as the first seed but we will give the chance for it to be selected in the next steps. Using Eq. 4 as the threshold prevents to select documents that are at the very end of list A which have low L_1 norm and less impact on grouping similar documents. After having found the first document s_1 that passes the threshold, we stop considering other documents and we add it to the seed document set S. Now, the seed documents set has the size of 1.

Step 4. We find $k - 1$ seed documents in this step. Starting from the beginning of set $A - S$ and find the first document which is far from every seed in set S based on the threshold defined by Eq. 4. We iterate this step until k seeds are determined (Lines 16–22 Algorithm 1). If there is no document far from all the seeds in S, the following objective function is considered, with the goal of finding the document, which has the lowest cumulative *dsim* to every other seed document (Lines 23–25 Algorithm 1).

$$argmin(\sum_{j=1}^{|S|} dsim(d_i, s_j)), \quad 1 \leq i \leq |D|, \quad d_i \notin S. \tag{5}$$

This step ensures that the proposed method can always find k seed documents in every document collection.

After finding the initial seeds, we can directly initialize the KMeans algorithm. Based on our experiments, we can achieve a higher quality of result if for each seed document we find a few similar documents based on cosine similarity and then consider their centroid as the final seed. In our experiments, we extended each seed document with first 15 most similar documents to it by calculating the cosine similarity.

Complexity Analysis: Let $|D| = n$ be the number of documents and m the number of unique terms after applying Eq. 2 filter. The time complexity of sorting document-term-matrix and calculating the cosine similarity matrix is $O(n \log n)$ and $O(n^2 m/2)$ while the time complexity of finding seed documents based on $dsim$ is $O(n^2 k)$. Calculating the cosine similarity matrix is the most time-consuming step of the proposed method but it could easily be processed in parallel. In reality, the size of m will be less than a few thousand even for large textual datasets after selecting important terms, which makes the proposed approach practically feasible.

3 Experiments

In this section, first we introduce the baseline methods including state-of-the-art deterministic and non-deterministic initialization algorithms. The datasets' description and the evaluation metrics are in Sect. 3.2. Finally, the extensive experimental results is reported in Sect. 3.3.

Table 1. Description of datasets. The Eq. 2 is used for feature selection for the first 7 datasets and for the rest only stop-words and words with frequency less than 20 are removed.

#	Dataset	#Samples	#Dim.	#Classes	#	Dataset	#samples	#Dim.	#classes
1	Newsgroup5	400	1450	5	8	BBCsport	737	969	5
2	Yahoo6	600	2206	6	9	BBC	2225	3121	5
3	R8	7674	1997	8	10	Wikilow	4986	15441	10
4	Newsgroup20	18846	11556	20	11	WikiHigh	5738	17311	6
5	WebKB	4199	1578	4	12	Guardian	6520	10801	6
6	NewsSeparate	381	380	13	13	Irishtimes	3246	4823	7
7	SMS	5549	858	2					

3.1 Baseline Methods

We compared three random or order-sensitive seeding methods, Points, KMeans++, and KMC2 with the proposed method. In the Points method, uniformly k randomly selected data points are considered as the initial seeds for the KMeans algorithm. The KMeans++ is one of the most widely used seeding methods which has been demonstrated to achieve better performance result than the Points method [3]. KMeans++ starts with a random seed, then it tries to find the next one as far as possible from the first seed based on a probability sampling method called D^2-sampling. In this sampling method, data points that have higher distance to the previously selected seeds will more likely be selected as the next seed. This process continues until k initial seeds are detected. The KMC2 method is speeding up the KMeans++ algorithm by Markov chain Monte Carlo sampling based approximation [4]. It has been reported that the KMC2 has a better quality of results and computational cost than the KMeans++ algorithm. In our experiments, we used the assumption-free version of KMC2 with m equals to 200.

Two widely used deterministic seeding methods of PCA-part and VAR-part are compared with the proposed method. The PCA-part method hierarchically divides the data points into two halves based on PCA. First, it starts with calculating the centroid of all data points as a single cluster, and the principal eigenvector of the cluster covariance matrix. Second, it passes an hyperplane orthogonal to the principal eigenvector of the cluster which passes from the cluster centroid to create two sub-clusters. The sum distance of each data points in each sub-cluster to its centroid is calculated and the sub-cluster with a higher value is divided in the next step. Finally, this procedure is continued until k clusters are obtained. The VAR-part (variance partitioning) is an approximation to the PCA-part method [21]. In VAR-part the covariance matrix of the cluster is assumed to be diagonal. In each partitioning stage, the hyperplane is diagonal to the dimension with the largest variance. Based on our experiments, using the Euclidean distance leads to similar initialized seeds compared to cosine distance for VAR-par and PCA-part in all datasets; therefore we used the Euclidean distance for both methods.

In our experiments, we used the Spherical version of the KMeans algorithm. In Spherical KMeans the feature vectors is projected to the unit sphere equipped with the cosine similarity which performs better than Euclidean distance for text document clustering [14]. We compared the Spherical KMeans with different seeding methods with Fuzzy CMeans and Von Mises-Fisher Mixture methods. In the Fuzzy CMeans algorithm the data points can belong to more than one cluster with different membership values rather than distinct membership to only one cluster [8]. In our experiments, we used cosine similarity for the distance measure of the Fuzzy CMeans. The Von Mises-Fisher Mixture methods is a mixture model for clustering data distributed on the unit hypersphere based on Von Mises-Fisher distribution [5].

Table 2. Comparing precision of seeds. The average (±std) over 50 runs is reported for the Points, KMeans++, and KMC2 methods.

Dataset	DSKM	Points	KMeans++	KMC2
Newsgroup5	**0.800**	0.684 ± 0.145	0.636 ± 0.182	0.692 ± 0.134
Yahoo6	**1.000**	0.700 ± 0.115	0.613 ± 0.131	0.677 ± 0.070
R8	**0.750**	0.393 ± 0.120	0.495 ± 0.135	0.443 ± 0.137
Newsgroup20	**0.700**	0.634 ± 0.064	0.617 ± 0.072	0.638 ± 0.060
WebKB	**1.000**	0.660 ± 0.179	0.610 ± 0.151	0.655 ± 0.165
NewsSeparate	**0.846**	0.582 ± 0.084	0.563 ± 0.089	0.614 ± 0.103
SMS	**1.000**	0.620 ± 0.214	0.630 ± 0.219	0.610 ± 0.207
BBCsport	**0.800**	0.660 ± 0.140	0.576 ± 0.148	0.656 ± 0.133
BBC	**0.800**	0.668 ± 0.153	0.580 ± 0.146	0.688 ± 0.145
Wikilow	**0.800**	0.646 ± 0.090	0.556 ± 0.098	0.676 ± 0.111
WikiHigh	**0.833**	0.653 ± 0.152	0.627 ± 0.131	0.687 ± 0.123
Guardian	**1.000**	0.643 ± 0.105	0.577 ± 0.138	0.667 ± 0.120
Irishtimes	**0.857**	0.611 ± 0.114	0.509 ± 0.149	0.643 ± 0.112

3.2 Datasets and Evaluation Metrics

Datasets. The description of datasets is provided in Table 1. We obtained dataset Newsgroup5 by selecting 5 categories of the Newsgroup20[2] dataset each containing 80 randomly chosen documents. The Newsgroups20 dataset consists of nearly 20,000 messages of Internet news articles with 20 categories. The Yahoo6 is a sub-collection of questions and answers extracted from the Yahoo! Answers website [13]. We used 6 sub-categories with 100 randomly selected question and answer pairs. R8 is a subset of *Reuters-21578* dataset containing 8 categories and can be downloaded from Ana Cachopo's homepage[3]. The WebKB dataset consists of 4199 faculty, student, project, and course websites collected from the four universities on January 1997[4]. The NewsSeparate dataset is a subset of RSS news feeds from BBC, CNN, Reuters and Associated Press manually categorized into 13 categories [19]. The SMS dataset is a set of labeled SMS messages for spam research[5].

Datasets number 8 to 13 are taken from [15] and can be downloaded from their web-page[6]. The BBCsport, BBC, Irishtimes, and Guardian are news articles and WikiHigh and Wikilow are a subset of a Wikipedia dump from January 2014.

---

[2] http://qwone.com/~jason/20Newsgroups/.
[3] http://ana.cachopo.org.
[4] https://www.cs.cmu.edu/afs/cs/project/theo-20/www/data/.
[5] http://www.dt.fee.unicamp.br/~tiago/smsspamcollection/.
[6] http://mlg.ucd.ie/howmanytopics/index.html.

Table 3. Comparing clustering accuracy. For the deterministic approaches the McNemar's test is used. The P-value less than 0.05 indicates that the clustering algorithm does not have the same error rate as DSKM approach. The average over 50 runs with standard deviation is reported for the random or order-sensitive methods in which the m shows the minimum and the M shows the maximum of 50 runs.

Dataset	KMeans (DSKM)	KMeans (PCA-part)	KMeans (VAR-part)	KMeans (Points)	KMeans (KMeans++)	KMeans (KMC2)	Fuzzy CMeans (Points)	Von Mises Fisher Mixture
Newsgroup5	**0.850**	0.740 $p<0.05$	0.525 $p<0.05$	0.687 ± 0.082 m:0.522 M:0.91	0.696 ± 0.095 m:0.555 M:0.922	0.706 ± 0.080 m:0.542 M:0.912	0.719 ± 0.056 m:0.505 M:0.785	0.666 ± 0.073 m:0.497 M:0.820
Yahoo6	**0.850**	0.827 $p>0.05$	0.803 $p<0.05$	0.756 ± 0.079 m:0.553 M:0.847	0.740 ± 0.072 m:0.577 M:0.850	0.746 ± 0.070 m:0.620 M:0.843	0.798 ± 0.062 m:0.633 M:0.830	0.645 ± 0.052 m:0.457 M:0.757
R8	**0.688**	0.411 $p<0.05$	0.537 $p<0.05$	0.468 ± 0.060 m:0.332 M:0.605	0.476 ± 0.052 m:0.381 M:0.585	0.474 ± 0.064 m:0.361 M:0.612	0.457 ± 0.045 m:0.368 M:0.539	0.431 ± 0.054 m:0.271 M:0.513
Newsgroup20	0.485	**0.517** $p<0.05$	0.386 $p<0.05$	0.478 ± 0.037 m:0.399 M:0.565	0.496 ± 0.041 m:0.378 M:0.605	0.484 ± 0.039 m:0.410 M:0.595	0.119 ± 0.003 m:0.114 M:0.126	0.343 ± 0.024 m:0.303 M:0.407
WebKB	0.65	0.609 $p<0.05$	0.529 $p<0.05$	0.609 ± 0.029 m:0.521 M:0.669	0.604 ± 0.033 m:0.539 M:0.661	0.605 ± 0.039 m:0.529 M:0.692	0.603 ± 0.041 m:0.514 M:0.660	-
NewsSeparate	**0.861**	0.711 $p<0.05$	0.766 $p<0.05$	0.727 ± 0.072 m:0.562 M:0.89	0.713 ± 0.059 m:0.583 M:0.861	0.748 ± 0.066 m:0.622 M:0.864	0.747 ± 0.048 m:0.627 M:0.874	0.679 ± 0.066 m:0.507 M:0.824
SMS	0.597	0.904 $p<0.05$	**0.907** $p<0.05$	0.675 ± 0.142 m:0.502 M:0.907	0.646 ± 0.139 m:0.502 M:0.907	0.667 ± 0.143 m:0.505 M:0.907	0.797 ± 0.037 m:0.721 M:0.839	-
BBCsport	0.856	0.670 $p<0.05$	**0.951** $p<0.05$	0.783 ± 0.115 m:0.521 M:0.961	0.789 ± 0.117 m:0.620 M:0.958	0.800 ± 0.124 m:0.514 M:0.958	0.869 ± 0.123 m:0.626 M:0.955	0.803 ± 0.122 m:0.528 M:0.955
BBC	0.956	**0.958** $p>0.05$	0.953 $p>0.05$	0.870 ± 0.116 m:0.654 M:0.962	0.817 ± 0.133 m:0.493 M:0.965	0.833 ± 0.142 m:0.443 M:0.965	0.948 ± 0.035 m:0.704 M:0.953	0.809 ± 0.108 m:0.539 M:0.953
Wikilow	0.763	**0.969** $p<0.05$	0.834 $p<0.05$	0.803 ± 0.101 m:0.466 M:0.968	0.771 ± 0.096 m:0.581 M:0.964	0.793 ± 0.097 m:0.477 M:0.967	0.843 ± 0.075 m:0.702 M:0.964	0.751 ± 0.067 m:0.590 M:0.870
WikiHigh	0.715	**0.861** $p<0.05$	0.658 $p<0.05$	0.774 ± 0.087 m: 0.544 M:0.88	0.774 ± 0.087 m:0.487 M:0.890	0.785 ± 0.069 m:0.655 M:0.874	0.851 ± 0.026 m:0.712 M:0.867	0.629 ± 0.062 m:0.496 M:0.730
Guardian	**0.951**	0.951 $p>0.05$	0.950 $p>0.05$	0.834 ± 0.104 m: 0.583 M:0.954	0.832 ± 0.108 m:0.574 M:0.955	0.837 ± 0.121 m:0.554 M:0.954	0.945 ± 0.013 m:0.856 M:0.947	0.851 ± 0.097 m:0.661 M:0.945
Irishtimes	**0.871**	0.772 $p<0.05$	0.626 $p<0.05$	0.695 ± 0.083 m: 0.518 M:0.871	0.671 ± 0.085 m:0.505 M:0.837	0.678 ± 0.084 m:0.498 M:0.827	0.784 ± 0.074 m:0.625 M:0.877	0.704 ± 0.059 m:0.574 M:0.837

Evaluation Metrics. The clustering quality is measured by two widely used document clustering evaluation metrics of Normalized Mutual Information (NMI) and Accuracy (Acc) [10]. These metrics generate values between 0 and 1 in which values closer to 1 shows better performance. To match the predicted labels with actual labels for calculating the accuracy, we used the Hungarian method [18].

We compare the precision of initial seeds of methods defined by Eq. 6. The true label of each initial seed is used to find the diversity of seed labels. The method with more diverse (their true labels be different) initial seeds is better because it is able to introduce a better representative seed for each cluster. The comparative result of seed precision of evaluation methods is given in Table 2. The PCA-part and VAR-part produce initial centroids instead of initial seeds so it is not possible to evaluate their seed precision.

$$SeedPrecision = \frac{\#diverse\ labels}{k}. \tag{6}$$

The NMI score of the proposed method compared to other methods is summarized in Table 4. The DSKM outperforms in most of the datasets. The same trend of performance similar to the accuracy score can be observed for NMI score as well. KMC2 has slightly better NMI score compared to KMeans++ and Points.

Table 4. Comparing clustering NMI score. The average 50 runs with standard deviation is reported forthe random or order-sensitive approaches in which the m shows the minimum and the M shows the maximum of 50 runs.

Dataset	KMeans (DSKM)	KMeans (PCA-part)	KMeans (VAR-part)	KMeans (Points)	KMeans (KMeans++)	KMeans (KMC2)	Fuzzy CMeans (Points)	Von Mises Fisher Mixture
Newsgroup5	**0.781**	0.742	0.513	0.663 ± 0.075 m:0.437 M:0.829	0.667 ± 0.074 m:0.511 M:0.821	0.665 ± 0.066 m:0.550 M:0.815	0.663 ± 0.032 m:0.537 M:0.706	0.622 ± 0.069 m:0.442 M:0.777
Yahoo6	**0.704**	0.684	0.645	0.631 ± 0.043 m:0.492 M:0.700	0.621 ± 0.044 m:0.538 M:0.693	0.629 ± 0.041 m:0.532 M:0.694	0.664 ± 0.028 m:0.585 M:0.678	0.538 ± 0.03 m:0.449 M:0.615
R8	**0.575**	0.534	0.509	0.515 ± 0.032 m:0.420 M:0.567	0.520 ± 0.027 m:0.460 M:0.580	0.527 ± 0.029 m:0.453 M:0.600	0.480 ± 0.032 m:0.425 M:0.548	0.397 ± 0.057 m:0.260 M:0.495
Newsgroup20	**0.539**	0.533	0.467	0.498 ± 0.023 m:0.453 M:0.554	0.509 ± 0.028 m:0.439 M:0.578	0.501 ± 0.024 m:0.456 M:0.567	0.234 ± 0.002 m:0.232 M:0.239	0.412 ± 0.018 m:0.365 M:0.45
WebKB	**0.388**	0.320	0.353	0.362 ± 0.017 m:0.324 M:0.396	0.362 ± 0.017 m:0.316 M:0.395	0.363 ± 0.016 m:0.322 M:0.394	0.349 ± 0.023 m:0.307 M:0.377	-
NewsSeparate	**0.872**	0.809	0.829	0.819 ± 0.035 m:0.729 M:0.899	0.813 ± 0.033 m:0.742 M:0.882	0.833 ± 0.031 m:0.777 M:0.893	0.826 ± 0.022 m:0.767 M:0.894	0.77 ± 0.036 m:0.679 M:0.868
SMS	0.123	0.409	**0.414**	0.120 ± 0.128 m:0.000 M:0.414	0.135 ± 0.115 m:0.002 M:0.413	0.140 ± 0.115 m:0.000 M:0.414	0.267 ± 0.043 m:0.165 M:0.317	-
BBCsport	0.761	0.716	**0.858**	0.742 ± 0.077 m:0.583 M:0.881	0.742 ± 0.079 m:0.578 M:0.876	0.752 ± 0.089 m:0.570 M:0.876	0.816 ± 0.066 m:0.692 M:0.869	0.743 ± 0.091 m:0.461 M:0.876
BBC	0.865	**0.871**	0.857	0.806 ± 0.072 m:0.663 M:0.880	0.772 ± 0.091 m:0.536 M:0.891	0.774 ± 0.090 m:0.557 M:0.889	0.851 ± 0.020 m:0.708 M:0.856	0.718 ± 0.086 m:0.494 M:0.859
Wikilow	0.867	**0.934**	0.897	0.862 ± 0.040 m:0.730 M:0.933	0.853 ± 0.037 m:0.781 M:0.930	0.862 ± 0.039 m:0.740 M:0.931	0.879 ± 0.027 m:0.825 M:0.927	0.774 ± 0.031 m:0.713 M:0.832
WikiHigh	0.723	**0.740**	0.642	0.707 ± 0.047 m:0.580 M:0.761	0.702 ± 0.043 m:0.548 M:0.764	0.704 ± 0.037 m:0.633 M:0.759	0.721 ± 0.016 m:0.620 M:0.727	0.552 ± 0.041 m:0.479 M:0.667
Guardian	**0.862**	0.862	0.861	0.805 ± 0.054 m:0.627 M:0.870	0.803 ± 0.056 m:0.647 M:0.872	0.807 ± 0.062 m:0.644 M:0.871	0.852 ± 0.015 m:0.748 M:0.856	0.786 ± 0.055 m:0.639 M:0.848
Irishtimes	**0.783**	0.720	0.642	0.681 ± 0.049 m:0.575 M:0.759	0.672 ± 0.055 m:0.564 M:0.761	0.680 ± 0.052 m:0.573 M:0.761	0.741 ± 0.032 m:0.666 M:0.780	0.672 ± 0.036 m:0.595 M:0.740

3.3   Experimental Results

The accuracy result of the DSKM in comparison to other methods is summarized in Table 3. For random or order-sensitive methods, we report the average over 50 runs with its standard deviation, the minimum, and the maximum result. In order to have a fair comparison, we only initialize KMeans once for the non-deterministic methods. For the PCA-part and VAR-part methods, the McNemar's test is applied to determine whether their clustering result has the same error rate as DSKM. The Hungarian algorithm is used to map the cluster labels to actual labels. The deterministic approaches are superior in accuracy score compared to the average score of random or order-insensitive methods. Better performance result for deterministic methods on non-textual and Synthetic datasets has been reported by [12]. A possible reason is that the deterministic methods are running once and the seeding step can be viewed as an approximate clustering of data points. The DSKM method has similar or even better accuracy compared to the maximum accuracy score of the random or order-sensitive methods on Yahoo6, R8, WebKB, NewSeparate, BBC, Guardian, and Irishtimes. The SMS dataset is an unbalanced dataset and DSKM does not perform well on it although it was able to find 100% diverse initial seeds (Table 2). PCA-part, and VAR-part performed well on the SMS dataset which demonstrates their effectiveness for unbalanced datasets. Fuzzy CMeans has the best average and Von Mises Fisher Mixture the lowest accuracy score on most of the datasets

Table 5. Running time (seconds) of seeding methods. A random single run of KMeans++ and KMC2 is reported. Datasets are sorted by the sample size.

Dataset	DSKM	PCA-part	VAR-part	KMeans++	KMC2
NewsSeparate	0.03	0.74	0.03	0.02	**0.01**
Newsgroup5	**0.03**	5.27	**0.03**	0.05	**0.03**
Yahoo6	0.02	10.08	0.04	**0.01**	0.02
BBCsport	0.06	4.79	0.03	**0.01**	**0.01**
BBC	0.38	94.93	0.39	0.08	**0.07**
Irishtimes	0.99	410.3	1.25	0.22	**0.14**
WebKB	0.72	-	-	0.11	**0.06**
Wikilow	7.02	6849.23	5.62	1.45	**0.70**
SMS	0.77	7.92	0.11	**0.02**	0.03
WikiHigh	8.75	8725.6	5.59	1.21	**0.71**
Guardian	6.02	3681.96	3.88	0.82	**0.44**
R8	3.22	172.67	0.90	**0.25**	0.47
Newsgroup20	55.96	19712.72	39.56	8.28	**6.28**

among random or order-sensitive methods. On the Newsgroup20 dataset, Fuzzy CMeans does not perform well, which indicates that this method has difficulty on large datasets with a high number of clusters. The Points, KMeans++, and KMC2 have similar average accuracy results on most datasets. This shows that KMeans++ and KMC2 are performing better for very large datasets which is a case for Newsgroup20 and R8 datasets.

We compared the running time of the seeding methods in Table 5. Although the PCA-part has better performance result than the VAR-part, its running time makes it not practical for large datasets. The DSKM method has acceptable running time even for large datasets. The KMC2 is the fastest seeding algorithm compared to the others and based on its accuracy and NMI performance, it is the best random or order-sensitive method. Due to the random nature of the KMeans++ and KMC2, the Kmeans is initialized several times by them and the clustering which optimizes the KMeans objective function is selected. The impact of the number of initializations on the accuracy performance of the KMeans++ and KMC2 for NewsSeparate is depicted in Fig. 2. In order to have stable results, we reported the average of 50 runs for KMC2 and KMeans++. As the number of initialization increases, the accuracy of the KMC2 and KMeans++ increases and converges to a stable value. On the other hand, the running time increases as the number of initializations is increased. This indicates that the DSKM method could be even faster than the random or order-sensitive methods in practice because it does not need to run several times.

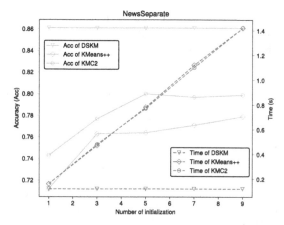

Fig. 2. The impact of number of initialization on the Accuracy performance and running time. Each initialization of the KMeans++ and KMC2 is the result of average 50 runs.

4 Conclusion

In this paper, we propose a new deterministic seeding algorithm for the KMeans algorithm called DSKM. The key idea of the DSKM is that the initial seeds should be as far as possible from each other. Two data points that not only themselves but their similar documents are less similar to each other are good candidates and that is why we defined the *dsim* similarity. For finding seeds we start from documents with higher L_1 norm. Experimental results on several real world textual datasets shows that DSKM outperforms the other deterministic, random or order-sensitive methods in terms of clustering accuracy and NMI score. The proposed methods have an acceptable running time even for large datasets.

References

1. Abdi, H., Williams, L.J.: Principal component analysis. Wiley Interdiscip. Rev.: Comput. Stat. **2**(4), 433–459 (2010)
2. Aggarwal, C.C., Yu, P.S.: Outlier detection for high dimensional data. In: Proceedings of the 2001 ACM SIGMOD International Conference on Management of Data, SIGMOD 2001, pp. 37–46. ACM, New York (2001)
3. Arthur, D., Vassilvitskii, S.: K-means++: the advantages of careful seeding. In: Proceedings of the Eighteenth Annual ACM-SIAM Symposium on Discrete Algorithms, SODA 2007, pp. 1027–1035. Society for Industrial and Applied Mathematics, Philadelphia (2007)
4. Bachem, O., Lucic, M., Hassani, H., Krause, A.: Fast and provably good seedings for k-means. In: Lee, D.D., Sugiyama, M., Luxburg, U.V., Guyon, I., Garnett, R. (eds.) Advances in Neural Information Processing Systems 29, pp. 55–63. Curran Associates, Inc. (2016)

5. Banerjee, A., Dhillon, I.S., Ghosh, J., Sra, S.: Clustering on the unit hypersphere using von mises-fisher distributions. J. Mach. Learn. Res. **6**, 1345–1382 (2005)
6. Basu, S., Davidson, I., Wagstaff, K.: Constrained Clustering: Advances in Algorithms, Theory, and Applications, 1st edn. Chapman & Hall/CRC, Boca Raton (2008)
7. Bekkerman, R., Raghavan, H., Allan, J., Eguchi, K.: Interactive clustering of text collections according to a user-specified criterion. In: Proceedings of the 20th International Joint Conference on Artifical Intelligence, IJCAI 2007, pp. 684–689. Morgan Kaufmann Publishers Inc., San Francisco (2007)
8. Bezdek, J.C.: A convergence theorem for the fuzzy ISODATA clustering algorithms. IEEE Trans. Pattern Anal. Mach. Intell. **2**(1), 1–8 (1980)
9. Breunig, M.M., Kriegel, H.P., Ng, R.T., Sander, J.: LOF: identifying density-based local outliers. In: Proceedings of the 2000 ACM SIGMOD International Conference on Management of Data, SIGMOD 2000, pp. 93–104. ACM, New York (2000)
10. Cai, D., He, X., Han, J.: Document clustering using locality preserving indexing. IEEE Trans. Knowl. Data Eng. **17**(12), 1624–1637 (2005)
11. Celebi, M.E., Kingravi, H.A.: Linear, deterministic, and order-invariant initialization methods for the k-means clustering algorithm. In: Celebi, M.E. (ed.) Partitional Clustering Algorithms, pp. 79–98. Springer, Cham (2015). https://doi.org/10.1007/978-3-319-09259-1_3
12. Celebi, M.E., Kingravi, H.A., Vela, P.A.: A comparative study of efficient initialization methods for the k-means clustering algorithm. Expert Syst. Appl. **40**(1), 200–210 (2013)
13. Chang, M., Ratinov, L., Roth, D., Srikumar, V.: Importance of semantic representation: dataless classification. In: AAAI, July 2008
14. Dhillon, I.S., Modha, D.S.: Concept decompositions for large sparse text data using clustering. Mach. Learn. **42**(1–2), 143–175 (2001)
15. Greene, D., O'Callaghan, D., Cunningham, P.: How many topics? stability analysis for topic models. In: Calders, T., Esposito, F., Hüllermeier, E., Meo, R. (eds.) ECML PKDD 2014 Part I. LNCS (LNAI), vol. 8724, pp. 498–513. Springer, Heidelberg (2014). https://doi.org/10.1007/978-3-662-44848-9_32
16. Hasan, M.A., Chaoji, V., Salem, S., Zaki, M.J.: Robust partitional clustering by outlier and density insensitive seeding. Pattern Recogn. Lett. **30**(11), 994–1002 (2009)
17. Katsavounidis, I., Kuo, C.C.J., Zhang, Z.: A new initialization technique for generalized Lloyd iteration. IEEE Sig. Process. Lett. **1**(10), 144–146 (1994)
18. Kuhn, H.W.: The Hungarian method for the assignment problem. Nav. Res. Logist. Q. **2**(1–2), 83–97 (1955)
19. Martins, R.M., Coimbra, D.B., Minghim, R., Telea, A.: Visual analysis of dimensionality reduction quality for parameterized projections. Comput. Graph. **41**, 26–42 (2014)
20. Nidheesh, N., Nazeer, K.A., Ameer, P.: An enhanced deterministic k-means clustering algorithm for cancer subtype prediction from gene expression data. Comput. Biol. Med. **91**, 213–221 (2017)
21. Su, T., Dy, J.G.: In search of deterministic methods for initializing k-means and Gaussian mixture clustering. Intell. Data Anal. **11**(4), 319–338 (2007)

Medical Image Classification with Weighted Latent Semantic Tensors and Deep Convolutional Neural Networks

Spyridon Stathopoulos[(✉)] and Theodore Kalamboukis

Information Processing Laboratory, Department of Informatics,
Athens University of Economics and Business, 76 Patission Str, 10434 Athens, Greece
{spstathop,tzk}@aueb.gr
http://ipl.cs.aueb.gr/index_eng.html

Abstract. This paper proposes a novel approach for identifying the modality of medical images combining Latent Semantic Analysis (LSA) with Convolutional Neural Networks (CNN). In particular, we aim in investigating the potential of Neural Networks when images are represented by compact descriptors. To this end, an optimized latent semantic space is constructed that captures the affinity of images to each modality using a pre-trained network. The images are represented by a Weighted Latent Semantic Tensor in a lower space and they are used to train a deep CNN that makes the final classification. The evaluation of the proposed algorithm was based on the datasets from the ImageCLEF Medical Subfigure classification contest. Experimental results demonstrate the effectiveness and the efficiency of our framework in terms of classification accuracy, achieving comparable results to current state-of-the-art approaches on the aforementioned datasets.

Keywords: Latent Semantic Analysis · Latent Semantic Tensors
Deep learning · Convolutional Neural Networks · Image classification
Modality classification

1 Introduction

Images from many diagnostic modalities, such as Radiology, visible light photography, Microscopy etc., are actively used to support clinical decisions, medical research and education. Identifying these modalities is an important part of medical retrieval allowing to filter only a subset from a diverse collection and thus, aiding the retrieval process. Traditionally, the modality of medical images is extracted from the surrounding text or their caption although it is quite common that the text does not describe the image-modality. This has motivated researchers to develop methods for modality identification from the image itself using various supervised machine learning techniques [1,2]. Many of those solutions are based on extracting and combining several compact descriptors for

© Springer Nature Switzerland AG 2018
P. Bellot et al. (Eds.): CLEF 2018, LNCS 11018, pp. 89–100, 2018.
https://doi.org/10.1007/978-3-319-98932-7_8

training a classifier. Therefore, their performance is limited by the quality and the representation capabilities of these descriptors.

More recently, deep neural networks and specifically deep CNNs [3] have exhibited quite promising results in the field of computer vision and image classification. CNNs are able to learn features through the training process, thus, eliminating the need for designing specialized hand-crafted descriptors.

In this work, we investigate the potentials of using compact descriptors with CNNs. We argue that several hand-crafted features, when extracted locally, can capture important information from an image and can be used for constructing higher level descriptors. We therefore, propose the use of Weighted Latent Semantic Tensors (WLST) for training a CNN aimed to predicting the modality of biomedical images.

With the use of a pre-trained residual network, a probability is assigned to each image-modality. Based on these probabilities, a weighted LSA kernel is calculated and is used to project each image into a localized semantic tensor of lower size. Finally a second CNN classifier is trained from those latent tensors that makes the final decision. Our experimental results show that the proposed Weighted Latent Semantic Tensor (WLST) representation of images improves classification accuracy with comparable results to the current state-of-the-art methods.

The rest of this paper is organized as follows. Section 2 presents a brief overview of similar approaches in the literature and relevant work applied in the medical domain. Section 3 describes the details of our proposed WLST method. In Sects. 4 and 5 our evaluation framework is discussed with experimental results and finally concluding remarks are summarized in Sect. 6.

2   Related Work

In this section we focus on research related to the modality identification of medical images. In particular we review on approaches that achieve state-of-the-art results on the same datasets, as those used in the ImageCLEF contest, that enables us to draw more clear conclusions on the progress achieved so far in terms of classification accuracy. The results from these approaches are presented in Sect. 5.

Various feature engineering methods have been used successfully, with the most prominent ones being the Compact Composite Descriptors (CCD) [4]. These descriptors, combined with classifiers, such as Support Vector Machines (SVM), have been used over the years with promising results [1,2]. Another approach to image representation, inspired from text retrieval, is based on the construction of visual vocabularies [5]. Two are the main representatives of this approach: the Bag-of-Visual-Words (BoVW) model based on local descriptors such as the Scale Invariant Feature Transform (SIFT) [6] and the Bag-of-Colors (BoC) model for certain color descriptors [7]. In [8], a BoC representation was successfully combined with the BoVW-SIFT model in a late fusion manner. A generalized version of BOC that incorporates spatial information was proposed in

[9]. In this work images are split into quadrants of homogeneous colors. Similarly spatial information is introduced in the BoVW model constructing a pyramid histogram of visual words after the partitioning the images into 1×1, 2×2 and 4×4 regions of equal size.

With the recent breakthroughs of deep learning in computer vision and image classification, several models using deep CNNs have been proposed for classifying biomedical images. CNNs are used in two ways: (i) as an image feature-vector extractor to be used for training multi-class SVMs and (ii) as a classifier generating softmax probabilities. The posterior probabilities from the ensemble of SVMs and softmax classifiers are used to determine the final class of the images. Wang et al. [10] explores several approaches for the task of modality classification on the dataset of ImageCLEF 2016. Three pre-trained deep CNNs, namely VGG-16, VGG-19 [11] and ResNet-50 [12] were used to extract features from images. Those features together with 10 more compact visual descriptors were jointly used to train a stacked SVM classifier. Similarly, Koitka et al. [13] apply an ensemble of classifiers by combining an SVM classifier based on 11 traditional visual descriptors and the pre-trained deep CNN ResNet-152 with transfer learning. Moreover in [14], they perform data analysis to improve the image pre-processing prior to training. The adjusted re-sizing and pre-processing method combined with an ensemble of five fine-tuned deep CNNs show a significant performance increase.

In the work of Yu et al. [15], an architecture with three different types of deep CNNs was proposed. Two pre-trained CNNs, VGGNet-16 and ResNet-50 were combined with a third one composed of 6 weighted layers, trained exclusively on the ImageCLEF dataset. A similar approach is followed in [16], where two CNNs based on the AlexNet [17] and GoogLeNet [18] architectures are used to compose an ensemble of classifiers. A Synergic Deep Learning (SDL) approach is proposed by Zhang et al. [19], composed of a data pair input layer connected with a dual deep convolutional network. A synergic signal system is used to verify whether the input pair belongs to the same category and provides corrective feedback of the synergic error.

Most of the proposed methods so far either used only raw image pixels as input to CNNs or compact descriptors through ensemble methods by training a separate classifier. However, by extracting these descriptors locally, a feature map can be created and used as input to a CNN instead of raw pixel values. In this work, we explore this approach in combination with LSA to extract a Weighted Latent Semantic Tensor (WLST). These enhanced feature tensors are used as input in a CNN classifier. The following sections provide a detailed description of the proposed algorithm.

3 Proposed Algorithm

The method proposed in this work, exploits low-level image information captured by a pre-trained CNN in order to boost higher level latent semantic features. This is accomplished in two steps. In the first step, a localized LSA is applied on the instances of each modality and a pre-trained CNN is used to built a weighted latent semantic kernel that projects the data into a lower dimensionality space. At the second step, the latent semantic features are used to train a second CNN that makes the final prediction. In the next sections we give a detailed description of the proposed method, which in brief is described in the following steps:

Training Phase

1. Transfer learning with Pre-trained CNNs.
2. Localized feature extraction and image representation.
3. Per-modality Latent semantic analysis.
4. WLST calculation and feature projection.
5. WLST CNN training.

Testing Phase

1. Pre-trained CNN prediction.
2. WLST calculation and feature projection.
3. WLST CNN prediction.

3.1 Transfer Learning with Pre-trained CNNs

As it is known, CNNs achieve high performance but require a large number of examples for their training. The main approaches to overcome this issue are data augmentation and transfer learning. The former involves enhancing the training set by creating artificial images from the original ones. This is usually accomplished by randomly translating and rotating images from the train set. Transfer learning on the other hand, is the process of using a CNN pre-trained on a large dataset, like ImageNet [20]. The feature maps of the last convolution layer are vectorized and fed into Fully-Connected (FC) layers followed by a soft-max logistic regression layer with a number of neurons equal to the number of classes. The last FC layer is replaced to contain $|\mathcal{T}|$ neurons where $\mathcal{T}$ is the number of categories in the new dataset and the network is re-trained keeping the weights of the convolution layers fixed. In our experiments, we explore two approaches for connecting the last convolution layer and the final FC layer. The first approach adds a FC layer with 256 neurons and the ReLU activation function. In the second approach we replace the FC layer with a Global Average Pooling (GAP) layer. In [21], GAP is proposed to replace the fully connected layers and the idea is to generate a feature map for each category of the classification task in the last convolutional layer. Instead of adding fully connected layers on top of the feature maps, the average of each feature map is taken, and the resulting vector is fed directly into the soft-max layer.

In this work, ResNet-50 [12], a deep residual network with a depth of 50 weighted layers is used to appropriately calculate weights of a latent semantic feature matrix as described in the following sections. This extremely deep CNN is pre-trained on the ImageNet dataset with 1, 000 classes, on which it obtained state-of-the-art results.

3.2   Localized Feature Extraction

As mentioned in Sect. 2, visual features are extracted locally. Each image is first re-scaled to 256 × 256 pixels, and then is divided into 16 × 16 disjoint square blocks of equal size. From each block, a feature vector of size f is extracted. These localized compact descriptors are used in the next step to calculate a per-modality Latent Semantic Analysis. Placing these feature vectors into a 16 × 16 grid, each image is represented by a 3D feature-tensor of size $16 \times 16 \times f$. Those feature tensors are used in the sequel to train a deep CNN.

Although a large number of visual descriptors, with various characteristics and capabilities are proposed in the literature, here, we will present results only from the top performing ones. Those descriptors were:

1. Color Layout (CL) represents effectively the spatial distribution of the dominant colors on a grid imposed on an image (vector size = 120 features).
2. Color and Edge Directivity Descriptor (CEDD) [4], a compact low-level visual feature that combines color and edge information (vector size = 144 features).
3. Fuzzy Color and Texture Histogram (FCTH) [4], a feature that combines, in one histogram, color and texture information (vector size = 192 features).
4. QBoC histogram [9], using a quad-tree decomposition of the image. The features were extracted using a learned palette of 128 RGB colors.

3.3   Per-modality Latent Semantic Analysis

To follow the details of the proposed algorithm we give here a description of our problem in mathematical notation.

Let $\mathcal{Y}$ be a set of predefined categories and $\mathcal{T} = \{(x_i, y) : x_i \in R^n, y \in \mathcal{Y}\}$ a training set. Let $\mathcal{T}_i \subset \mathcal{T}$, be the subset of the training data that contains all the images within a category $y_i \in \mathcal{Y}$. This subset is considered as the semantic group of the category y_i and it is represented by a matrix $X_i = [x_1, ..., x_{ni}]$ where ni is the size of the subset $\mathcal{T}_i$. In our case each image belongs to a unique category and therefore we have a multi-class classification problem. For a given test-image, J, we aim to assign a category (label), y, such that

$$y = argmax \ p(y_i|J)$$

As we previously mention, each image is represented by a 3D tensor $(nb \times nb \times f)$. Unfolding this tensor in the 3rd dimension we get a square matrix $nb^2 \times f$. To capture the latent relations among the features within a semantic group and reduce the computational cost, we apply dimensionality reduction by employing LSA. LSA is applied locally by performing a separate Singular Value Decomposition (SVD) on the matrices defined by each semantic group. Following the same strategy as in [22], we solve the partial (rank-k) eigenvalue problem for the matrix $X_i \cdot X_i^T$: $[U_i, L_i] = eigs(X_i \cdot X_i^T, k)$ were $eigs$ is the eigenvalue decomposition function and k defines the rank-k approximation. The function returns the eigenvectors (U_i) corresponding to the k-largest eigenvalues (L_i) of the matrix $X_i X_i^T$. Preliminary experiments with 5-fold cross-validation revealed that a value of $k = 64$ results in an efficient semantic space.

3.4 Weighted Latent Semantic Tensors

Each image plays a different role to the final feature space and it is expected that relevant images to a topic will contribute more to the semantic space of this topic than non relevant ones. Thus, we classify each image, x, using the pre-trained CNN, discussed in Sect. 3.1, and allocate weights $(p = [p_1, p_2, ..., p_{|T|}])$ to classes defined by the probabilities $p_i = p(y_i|x)$ derived from the classifier. A weighted latent space is defined by:

$$U_x = \sum_{i=1}^{|T|} U_i \cdot p_i \tag{1}$$

which is used to project the localized vectors of each block of the image x. To reduce the noise from classes with low probability, we keep only the t-largest probabilities in Eq. 1. Details on determining the value of t are given in Sect. 5.

The reduced feature vectors are placed into an $nb \times nb$ grid. Thus each image is now represented by a Weighted Latent Semantic Tensor (WLST) T of size $16 \times 16 \times k$.

3.5 WLST CNN Training

The Weighted Latent Semantic Tensors (WLST) representing the dataset's images are used to train a second CNN classifier. This CNN has a similar architecture with [15, 23] (see image 1). The first two convolutional layers contain 128 kernels of size 3×3, and the second two have 256 kernels of size 3×3. The second and fourth convolutional layers are interleaved with max pooling layers of dimension 2×2 with a dropout of 0.25 neurons. The architecture of our CNN is presented in Fig. 1 and the pseudocode of the testing phase is listed in Algorithm 1.

Algorithm 1. WLST CNN Classification algorithm

---

  for $J \in$ TestSet **do**
     $[p]$=ResNet50.predict(J);
     $U_J = \sum_{i=1}^{|T|} U_i \cdot p_i$
     blocks=split(J, nb, nb);
     for $J_k \in$ blocks **do**
       $[f_k]$=extractFeatures(J_k);
       $\tilde{J}_k = U_J^T f_k$
       $[m, n] = blockPosition(\tilde{J}_k)$;
       $T_J(m, n) = \tilde{J}_k$;
     end for
     y=CNN2.predict(T_J);
  end for

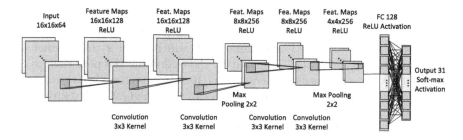

Fig. 1. CNN Architecture with WLST input for ImageCLEF 2013

4   Benchmark Datasets

The presented algorithms were evaluated on the classification problem with the data sets of ImageCLEF contest of the years 2013 and 2016. Detailed descriptions of the data sets can be found on the contest website[1] and their corresponding overview papers [1,2]. The ImageCLEF collections contain a wide range of heterogeneous images (such as MR, x-rays or even tables) from single to multi-pane images from different categories (compound), originating from various medical acquisition methods and articles. Accessing or classifying a sub-image of a multi-pane one makes the retrieval and classification a hard to solve problem. In the 2013 dataset, 2,957 training and 2,582 test images were provided with a class hierarchy of 31 categories. In the 2016 contest, the dataset contained 6,776 images in the train set and 4,166 in the test set.

However, both sets, train and test are quite unbalanced with one very large category (GFIG, 2,085) and some other categories that contain just a few instances (GPLI, 2) or (DSEE, 3). Thus for the 2016 data we present results from two different sets of experiments: one with the original data of the competition and another with the training set enriched with the images of the train and test sets of the 2013 contest (2016 enriched). Moreover, for compatibility with the performance measures used in the contest and most state-of-the-art results presented in Table 2 we adopted the accuracy measure, defined by the proportion of correct predictions in the test set.

5   Evaluation Results

To evaluate the performance of our proposed framework we first conducted experiments using compact descriptors with deep CNNs. To this end, we used the architecture depicted in Fig. 1 adapted for using the locally extracted CCDs as input. Several descriptors and their combinations were used which have shown a comparable performance with raw pixels. Due to space limitations we do not present those results here.

---

[1] http://www.imageclef.org/.

The second set of experiments aims at determining the performance of applying transfer learning with residual neural networks (ResNet) and our proposed method of WLSA learning. The parameter, t, which denotes the number of terms in calculating Eq. 1 was estimated by the evaluating the performance of the ResNet-50. Considering as a success for the ResNet classifier when the correct prediction is included in the t predicted classes with the highest probabilities, we observed that more than 98% of the correct assignments lie in the top 6 returned classes (Fig. 2a). In addition, by calculating the performance of the WLST for different values of t (Fig. 2b), we see that the best performance is achieved for the value $t = 6$.

To further increase the training set, a data augmentation technique was applied. This is accomplished by randomly shifting original images horizontally and vertically by 10% of the total width and height respectively. Results in Table 1 show a significant performance gain with WLST and compact descriptors over transfer learning and raw pixels as input. By *CNN-FC* we refer to runs using the architecture with Fully Connected neurons as the last hidden layer and *CNN-GAP* refers to runs using Global Average Pooling. Our method achieves the best performance to date as shown in Table 2 which summarizes the results of all the existing, to our knowledge, solutions on the ImageCLEF 2016 dataset.

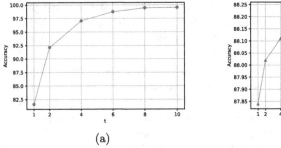
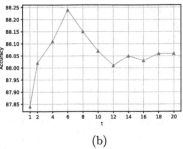

(a)   (b)

Fig. 2. (a) Estimated accuracy of the ResNet-50 considering as a success of the classifier when the correct prediction is included in the t predicted classes with highest probabilities. (b) Accuracy of WLST (second CNN) as a function of t using the descriptors CEDD, FCTH, CL and QBOC with the ImageCLEF-13 dataset.

Although the accuracy captures the overall performance for all modalities, it is also interesting to examine the classification performance per modality. Figure 3 depicts the confusion matrix for our best run, WLST (CEDD, FCTH, CL, QBOC) & data augmentation. As we observe from this matrix, there are some evident misclassifications. Most false positives were observed in the category GFIG. This is mainly due to the large variety of images in this category, including charts and diagrams bearing similarities with other modalities like Electrocardiography (DSEC) and System overviews (GSYS). Other evident misclassifcations are between related modalities like Electron microscopy (DMEL),

Table 1. Classification accuracy of localized compact descriptors and CNN

Algorithm	CLEF2013		CLEF2016		CLEF2016 enriched	
	CNN-FC	CNN-GAP	CNN-FC	CNN-GAP	CNN-FC	CNN-GAP
ResNet-50	81.33	82.03	85.21	85.31	86.08	85.09
ResNet-50 & data aug.	81.60	82.61	85.24	85.26	86.10	85.67
WLST (raw pixels)	83.66	85.17	86.92	87.06	87.28	87.25
WLST (CEDD, FCTH, CL, QBOC)	**87.49**	**87.57**	**87.47**	**87.69**	**87.97**	**88.00**
WLST (raw pixels) & data aug.	85.34	85.63	87.11	87.21	87.59	87.47
WLST (CEDD, FCTH, CL, QBOC) & data aug.	**88.23**	**88.30**	**88.43**	**88.31**	**88.45**	**88.50**

Table 2. Classification accuracy of the best-performing solutions on the Image-CLEF2016 dataset

Method	Accuracy
Koitka et al. [14] (Inception-V4, image pre-processing)	88.48
Yu et al. [15] ensemble of CNNs	87.37
Zang et al. [19] (SDL model)	86.58
Wang et al. [10] (10 handcrafted & CNN features with stacked SVMs)	85.62
Koitka et al. [13] (ResNet-152)	85.38
Valavanis et al. [9] (QBoC+PHOW)	85.19
Koitka et al. [13] (11 handcrafted features)	84.46
Valavanis et al. [24]	84.01
Kumar et al. [16] (ensemble of CNNs)	82.48

Fluorescence microscopy (DMFL), Light microscopy (DMLI) and Transmission microscopy (DMTR), all belonging to the same parent class of Microscopy.

Finally, to compare the scalability and computational complexity of the proposed method, we examine the execution time for training and evaluation presented in Table 3. Experiments were carried out on a system with I5 Processor 3.6 GHz, 16 GB RAM and a NVIDIA GTX 750-TI GPU. It should be noted however that the execution times for our WLSTs method were obtained without programming optimization and fully use of the GPU card thus they can be further improved. The reported times refer to the CNN-GAP architectures. The fully connected architectures were slightly slower due to the increased number of weights.

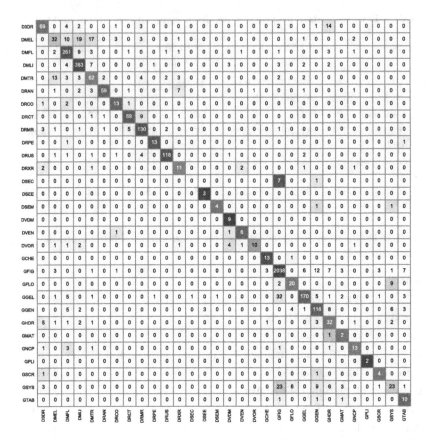

Fig. 3. Confusion matrix for the classification of ImageCLEF 2016 enriched with WLST (CEDD, FCTH, CL, QBOC) & data augmentation

Table 3. Execution times for training and evaluating images of the ImageCLEF 2016 dataset

Method	Training time	Evaluation time
ResNet 50	4.8 h	18 ms/image
CEDD & CNN	14.66 min	765 μs/image
FCTH & CNN	14.65 min	641 μs/image
CL & CNN	14.66 min	441 μs/image
QBOC & CNN	17.33 min	895 μs/image
CEDD + FCTH & CNN	17.33 min	855 μs/image
CEDD + FCTH + CL & CNN	18.66 min	867 μs/image
CEDD + FCTH + CL + QBOC & CNN	29.95 min	5 ms/image
WLSTs (raw pixels)	1.36 h	0.72 s/image
WLSTs (CEDD + FCTH + CL + QBOC)	2.10 h	0.85 s/image

6   Conclusions

In this work, a novel approach to modality classification of medical images was presented. We have investigated the potentials of Local LSA to capture important information for each class and construct local semantic spaces that improve the discrimination between modalities. With the help of a pre-trained CNN, a Weighted LSA Kernel is computed optimized for each image, capturing the semantic affinity with the most relevant classes. Results in Table 1 indicate that the proposed approach has improved performance compared to the state-of-the-art methods considering that most of them have either altered or enhanced in some way the original dataset through image pre-processing or external sources.

The results are very promising although only a pure visual approach is applied ignoring any textual information in the captions that usually accompany these images. Further research directions include the investigation of approaches for efficient utilization of textual information to supplement the classification procedure. Furthermore, due to the tendency of deep CNNs architectures to overfit on small datasets, further exploration with data augmentation techniques could improve the overall performance.

References

1. García Seco de Herrera, A., Kalpathy-Cramer, J., Demner-Fushman, D., Antani, S.K., Müller, H.: Overview of the ImageCLEF 2013 medical tasks. In: Working Notes for CLEF 2013 Conference (2013)
2. García Seco de Herrera, A., Schaer, R., Bromuri, S., Müller, H.: Overview of the ImageCLEF 2016 medical task. In: Working Notes of CLEF 2016 Conference, pp. 219–232 (2016)
3. Schmidhuber, J.: Deep learning in neural networks: an overview. CoRR abs/1404.7828 (2014)
4. Chatzichristofis, S.A., Boutalis, Y.S.: Compact Composite Descriptors for Content Based Image Retrieval: Basics, Concepts, Tools. VDM Verlag Dr. Müller, Saarbrücken (2011)
5. Li, F., Perona, P.: A Bayesian hierarchical model for learning natural scene categories. In: 2005 IEEE Computer Society Conference on Computer Vision and Pattern Recognition (CVPR 2005), 20–26 June 2005, San Diego, CA, USA, pp. 524–531 (2005). https://doi.org/10.1109/CVPR.2005.16
6. Lowe, D.G.: Object recognition from local scale-invariant features. In: ICCV, pp. 1150–1157 (1999). https://doi.org/10.1109/ICCV.1999.790410
7. Wengert, C., Douze, M., Jégou, H.: Bag-of-colors for improved image search. In: MM 2011 - 19th ACM International Conference on Multimedia, Scottsdale, United States, pp. 1437–1440. ACM, November 2011
8. García Seco de Herrera, A., Markonis, D., Müller, H.: Bag–of–colors for biomedical document image classification. In: Greenspan, H., Müller, H., Syeda-Mahmood, T. (eds.) MCBR-CDS 2012. LNCS, vol. 7723, pp. 110–121. Springer, Heidelberg (2013). https://doi.org/10.1007/978-3-642-36678-9_11
9. Valavanis, L., Stathopoulos, S., Kalamboukis, T.: Fusion of bag-of-words models for image classification in the medical domain. In: Jose, J.M., et al. (eds.) ECIR 2017. LNCS, vol. 10193, pp. 134–145. Springer, Cham (2017). https://doi.org/10.1007/978-3-319-56608-5_11

10. Wang, H., Zhang, J., Xia, Y.: Jointly using deep model learned features and traditional visual features in a stacked SVM for medical subfigure classification. In: Sun, Y., Lu, H., Zhang, L., Yang, J., Huang, H. (eds.) IScIDE 2017. LNCS, vol. 10559, pp. 191–199. Springer, Cham (2017). https://doi.org/10.1007/978-3-319-67777-4_17

11. Simonyan, K., Zisserman, A.: Very deep convolutional networks for large-scale image recognition. CoRR abs/1409.1556 (2014)

12. He, K., Zhang, X., Ren, S., Sun, J.: Deep residual learning for image recognition. In: 2016 IEEE Conference on Computer Vision and Pattern Recognition, CVPR 2016, Las Vegas, NV, USA, 27–30 June 2016, pp. 770–778 (2016). https://doi.org/10.1109/CVPR.2016.90

13. Koitka, S., Friedrich, C.M.: Traditional feature engineering and deep learning approaches at medical classification task of imageCLEF 2016. In: Working Notes of CLEF 2016 - Conference and Labs of the Evaluation forum, Évora, Portugal, 5–8 September, 2016, pp. 304–317 (2016)

14. Koitka, S., Friedrich, C.M.: Optimized convolutional neural network ensembles for medical subfigure classification. In: Jones, G.J.F., et al. (eds.) CLEF 2017. LNCS, vol. 10456, pp. 57–68. Springer, Cham (2017). https://doi.org/10.1007/978-3-319-65813-1_5

15. Yu, Y., Lin, H., Meng, J., Wei, X., Guo, H., Zhao, Z.: Deep transfer learning for modality classification of medical images. Information 8(3), 91 (2017). https://doi.org/10.3390/info8030091

16. Kumar, A., Kim, J., Lyndon, D., Fulham, M., Feng, D.: An ensemble of fine-tuned convolutional neural networks for medical image classification. IEEE J. Biomed. Health Inform. 21(1), 31–40 (2017). https://doi.org/10.1109/JBHI.2016.2635663

17. Krizhevsky, A., Sutskever, I., Hinton, G.E.: ImageNet classification with deep convolutional neural networks. In: Proceedings of the 25th International Conference on Neural Information Processing Systems, NIPS 2012, vol. 1, pp. 1097–1105. Curran Associates Inc., New York (2012)

18. Szegedy, C., et al.: Going deeper with convolutions. CoRR abs/1409.4842 (2014)

19. Zhang, J., Xia, Y., Wu, Q., Xie, Y.: Classification of medical images and illustrations in the biomedical literature using synergic deep learning. CoRR abs/1706.09092 (2017)

20. Russakovsky, O., et al.: Imagenet large scale visual recognition challenge. Int. J. Comput. Vis. 115(3), 211–252 (2015). https://doi.org/10.1007/s11263-015-0816-y

21. Lin, M., Chen, Q., Yan, S.: Network in network. CoRR abs/1312.4400 (2013)

22. Stathopoulos, S., Kalamboukis, T.: Applying latent semantic analysis to large-scale medical image databases. Comp. Med. Imaging Graph. 39, 27–34 (2015)

23. Yu, Y., Lin, H., Meng, J., Wei, X., Zhao, Z.: Assembling deep neural networks for medical compound figure detection. Information 8(2), 48 (2017). https://doi.org/10.3390/info8020048

24. Valavanis, L., Stathopoulos, S., Kalamboukis, T.: IPL at CLEF 2016 medical task. In: Working Notes of CLEF 2016 - Conference and Labs of the Evaluation forum, Évora, Portugal, 5–8 September, 2016, pp. 413–420 (2016)

Effects of Language and Terminology of Query Suggestions on the Precision of Health Searches

Carla Teixeira Lopes[✉] and Cristina Ribeiro

DEI, Faculdade de Engenharia, Universidade do Porto and INESC TEC,
Rua Dr. Roberto Frias, s/n, 4200-465 Porto, Portugal
{ctl,mcr}@fe.up.pt

Abstract. Health information is highly sought on the Web by users that naturally have different levels of expertise in the topics they search for. Assisting users with query formulation is important when users are searching for topics about which they have little knowledge or familiarity. To assist users with health query formulation, we developed a query suggestion system that provides alternative queries combining Portuguese and English language with lay and medico-scientific terminology. Here, we analyze how this system affects the precision of search sessions. Results show that a system providing these suggestions tends to perform better than a system without them. On specific groups of users, clicking on suggestions has positive effects on precision while using them as sources of new terms has the opposite effect. This suggests that a personalized suggestion system might have a good impact on precision.

Keywords: Query suggestion · Health · Language · Terminology
English proficiency · Health literacy · Topic familiarity

1 Introduction

Health information is an online popular pursuit being sought by 80% of U.S. Internet users [2]. In this type of searches, users frequently have difficulties finding the correct terms to include in their queries [7,21], lacking the knowledge of the proper medical terms [19,22] or misspelling them [6,13]. For these reasons, support in query formulation may contribute to an improved retrieval experience.

Previous findings [8,9] led us to develop a system that, based on an initial user query, suggests 4 different queries combining two languages (English and Portuguese) and two bodies of terminology (lay and medico-scientific). To the best of our knowledge, no previous works have explored cross-language query suggestions in the health domain.

The usage given to the suggestions provided by this system was studied before [10] as well as their effect on the medical accuracy of the knowledge acquired during the search session, considering different user characteristics [18].

© Springer Nature Switzerland AG 2018
P. Bellot et al. (Eds.): CLEF 2018, LNCS 11018, pp. 101–111, 2018.
https://doi.org/10.1007/978-3-319-98932-7_9

In this work we assess the impact of presenting and using these suggestions on the precision of the search session. As search assistance should be personalized to achieve its maximal outcome [4], we have considered users' English proficiency, health literacy and topic familiarity in this analysis.

2   Related Work

Query formulation is one of the most important aspects of information seeking. Query suggestion provides alternative ways to help users formulate queries and explore less familiar topics [5]. This technique is particularly important in topics about which users have little knowledge or familiarity. In these situations, users lack of vocabulary and knowledge may hinder query formulation.

In the health domain, the terminology gap between medical experts and lay people often causes additional difficulties in searches conducted by consumers [23]. To mitigate some of these difficulties, different query modification approaches have been proposed. Most of the approaches use specialized vocabularies from the Unified Medical Language System (UMLS). This is the case of the assistant proposed by Zeng et al. [21] that compute the semantic distance between the query and suggested terms using co-occurrences in medical literature and log data as well as UMLS semantic relations. iMed [11] and MedSearch [12] are two health search engines that suggest related medical phrases to help the user refine the query. In these systems, the phrases are extracted and ranked based on MeSH (Medical Subject Headings), the collection of crawled webpages, and the query. Similarly to our two-terminology query suggestion system, Zarro and Lin [20] also use MeSH along with social tagging to provide users with medico-scientific and lay terms.

All these works assess their systems through user studies, although focusing on different issues. In three of them [11,12,21], users were randomized into 2 groups, one receiving suggestions and the other not receiving them. In the study conducted by Zarro and Lin [20], 10 subjects were lay and the other 10 were expert. All subjects used the same system. The evaluation that is most resembled with a precision assessment is conducted by Luo et al. [12]. Authors combine relevance and diversity in a metric they call usefulness and each document is either useful or not. This metric is then used to compute the NDCG metric. Zeng et al. [21] assess the rates of successful queries, i.e., queries with at least one relevant result among the top 10. In the assessment of iMed [11], a search session is considered successful if the user can list one of the correct diseases associated with the medical case's situation. Note that this evaluation does not consider the relevance of each document. Zarro and Lin [20] focused on the differences between lay and expert subjects. Zarro and Lin [20] found that both user groups preferred MeSH terms because their quality was considered superior to the quality of social tags. All the assistance approaches described here were considered successful.

Regarding multilingual query suggestion, Gao et al. [3] proposed a system providing suggestions in a language different from the original query's language.

After using query logs to translate queries, authors used word translation relations and word co-occurrence statistics to estimate the cross-lingual query similarity. They used French-English and Chinese-English tasks for the evaluation and found that these suggestions, when used in combination with pseudo-relevance feedback, improved the effectiveness of cross-language information retrieval.

Since 2014, the Conference and Labs of the Evaluation Forum (CLEF) eHealth lab began to propose a multilingual information user-centred health retrieval task, incorporating queries in several languages in its dataset. The low number of teams proposing multilingual approaches makes us conclude that this type of approaches could be more explored.

3 Suggestion Tool

We developed a search suggestion system that, given a health query, suggests queries in two languages, Portuguese (PT) and English (EN), using medico-scientific (MS) and lay terminology.

In Fig. 1, we present the architecture of the suggestion tool, which will be briefly described in the following paragraphs. More details on the suggestion system can be found in a previous publication [18].

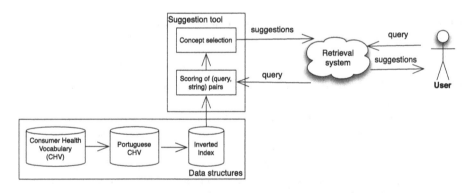

Fig. 1. Architecture of the suggestion tool [18].

Our system uses the Consumer Health Vocabulary (CHV) [14], a vocabulary that connects informal expressions about health to technical terms used by health care professionals. Each expression is associated with an Unified Medical Language System (UMLS) concept which, in turn, may be associated with several expressions or strings. Each string is associated with a CHV and an UMLS preferred names. Given that queries will probably be formulated in Portuguese, we use a Portuguese translation of the CHV.

After stemming the terms included in the CHV, we created an inverted index in which we associate each term with an inverse string frequency (isf_t) and a postings list, i.e., a list of the strings in which the stemmed term appears. The inverse string frequency is computed as $isf_t = log(N/sf_t)$, where sf_t is the number of strings in which the term appears and N is the total number of strings.

As the probability of finding multiple occurrences of the same term in a string is very small, we decided to ignore the term frequency in each string ($tf_{t,s}$). Each (query, string) pair is assigned the following $score(q, s) = \sum_{t \in (q \cap s)} isf_t$. Because the length of strings and queries has a very small variance, we decided to not normalize the above formula.

To limit the number of suggestions, for each query, we only select the string with the maximum score. For this string, we identify the associated concept and return its CHV and UMLS preferred names in English and Portuguese. This results in a maximum of 4 suggestions for each query. As an example, a set of suggestions could be: "colectomia", "remoção do cólon", "colectomy" and "colon removal".

Our retrieval system used the Bing Search API to obtain web results for users' queries. To increase the usability of the interface with regard to learning, we decided to keep the interfaces very simple and similar to those used in the most popular search engines. All the suggestions are presented in a single line.

4   Experiment

We conducted a user study with 40 participants (24 female; 16 male), with a mean age of 23.48 years (standard deviation = 7.66). English proficiency was evaluated using an instrument developed by the European Council that grades English proficiency in the Common European Framework of Reference for Languages, a widely accepted European standard for this purpose. To evaluate the users' health literacy, we have used the Medical Term Recognition Test, a brief and self-administered instrument proposed by Rawson et al. [15]. Users' familiarity with each topic was self-assessed on a five-level scale. The sample of users is heterogeneous in these characteristics.

Each user was assigned a set of 8 tasks, half of them conducted in a system presenting the suggestions (SYS+) and the other half on a system without suggestions (SYS). Each task was associated with a simulated work task situation [1]. Situations were rotated and counter-balanced across subjects and systems. Before the user study, to define these situations, we asked 20 persons with no medical expertise from 30 to 68 years old and a wide range of education levels (from high school to PhD) to state the health topic for which they had most recently searched on the Web. From these, we randomly selected 8 and created a scenario for each. Note that these persons were not participants of the study. The information situations were described to the users in Portuguese.

In each task the user had to formulate 3 queries in a language of their choice and assess the relevance of the top 10 results for each query, considering his own context in a 3-value scale. In the first query, users formulated the query without help from the system. Users had no restrictions in query formulation, being able to use their preferred language and terminology. Based on the initial query, the system presents suggestions that can, or not, be used for the formulation of the second query. The same happens when the user is moving from the second to the third iteration. The set of 3 iterations constituted a search session. After the third iteration, they were asked to evaluate the feeling of success with the iterations in a 5-level scale. More details on the user study can be found in a previous publication [18].

Our experiment was motivated by the following research questions: (1) Does a system that includes this suggestion tool lead to a higher precision? (2) How does clicking on a suggestion and using suggestions as sources of terms affect precision? (3) Does this effect differ with the language and terminology of the suggestions? (4) Does this effect differ with the English proficiency, health literacy and topic familiarity of the user?

5   Data Analysis

To evaluate the impact of suggestions provided by this system, we considered that users might use them as suggestions, clicking or not on them, or as a source of terms they can use in later queries. Considering this last scenario, we computed the proportion of suggestion's terms that were used in the subsequent query (termsUsed) and the proportion of the suggestion's terms that were used in the following query and were not used in the previous query (newTermsUsed). The former is useful to assess the quality of suggestions' terms and the latter is also useful to assess the utility of the suggestions for the users. Let Q_{it} be the set of unique stemmed terms belonging to the query of the iteration it and S_{it} the set of unique stemmed terms belonging to the suggestion presented in the iteration it, these proportions are computed as follows: $termsUsed_{it} = \frac{|Q_{it} \cap S_{it}|}{|S_{it}|}$ and $newTermsUsed_{it} = \frac{|(Q_{it} \cap S_{it}) \setminus Q_{it-1}|}{|S_{it}|}$. With these proportions, we were able to analyze three scenarios of suggestions' use as source of terms: using or not using suggestions' terms (Terms?), using or not using all the terms of a suggestion (All terms?), using or not using suggestions' terms that were not used in the previous query (NewTerms?). Note that users may use all the terms from a suggestion without clicking it, or they can change the order of the terms or even mix them with other terms.

We used Graded Average Precision (GAP), a measure proposed by Robertson et al. [16], based on a probabilistic model that generalizes average precision to the case of multi-graded relevance in which the user has a binary view of relevance even when using a non-binary scale of relevance. Based on the results presented by GAP's proponents, we used an equally balanced g_1 and g_2, i.e., $g_1 = g_2 = 0.5$, meaning that the levels 1 and 2 of our relevance scale have the same probability of being the grade from which the user starts considering the documents relevant.

The analysis was done comparing iterations where suggestions were used with iterations where suggestions were not used. We compared GAP means between groups of iterations (with and without the use of suggestions) using the Student's t-test. When the assumption of homogeneity of variances was not verified, we applied the Welch t-test. To compare groups of users, we applied the one-way ANOVA and the Tukey's test to locate the differences. Reporting our results, we use a * to mark significant results at $\alpha = 0.05$ and a ** to mark significant results at $\alpha = 0.01$.

6   Results

We found that the first iteration has a higher mean GAP than the second iteration (Tukey's adj. p = 0.009**) and the third iteration (Tukey's adj. p = 3.3e−06**). Differences may be explained by users' criteria in judging relevance. We found that documents with reoccurring contents, because they are no longer useful, are assigned lower relevance scores. Given these differences, we decided to base our analysis on the variation of GAP between iterations. For each iteration we have therefore computed a $\Delta GAP_{it} = GAP_{it} - GAP_{it-1}$. We found no significant differences between ΔGAP_2 and ΔGAP_3.

In SYS+, GAP tends to decrease less (Δ GAP mean of −0.031) than in SYS (Δ GAP mean of −0.033). In all the four use scenarios (Terms?, All terms?, NewTerms? and Click?), we did not find significant differences between using or not using suggestions. After this general analysis, we repeated it by suggestion's language and terminology. Almost all the comparisons were non-significant. The only exceptions occur when new terms from Portuguese (t(147.5) = 2.4, p = 0.01**) or lay (t(139.5) = 2.78, p = 0.003**) suggestions are used, situations in which the impact of suggestions on precision is negative.

6.1   Analysis by English Proficiency

We compared the mean Δ GAP in the four use scenarios, in each group of English proficiency (Table 1). With respect to Portuguese suggestions, although we haven't found significant differences, the general tendency is to have higher precision when users do not use the suggestions. In terms of English suggestions, we found an opposite effect when a suggestion is clicked or when all the terms of a suggestion are used. Yet, this tendency is only significant when *proficient* users click on English suggestions. Proficient users tend to benefit when they use new terms from an English suggestion and, surprisingly, the same happens with *basic* proficiency users when they use terms from English suggestions.

6.2   Analysis by Health Literacy

Comparing the precision of lay and medico-scientific queries by level of health literacy, we found few significant differences. As can be seen in Table 2, two of the three exceptions occur when *marginal* (t(89.9) = 2.3, p = 0.01*) and *functional* (t(33.7) = 2.0, p = 0.03*) health literate users employ terms from lay suggestions they have not used before. These suggestions have a negative impact on the precision of the search sessions of these users. The use of lay suggestions tends to be beneficial to precision when *low* health literate users use all the suggestion's

Table 1. Δ GAP means by language. Boldface represents the maximum in each group and scenario. Square brackets are used there are significant differences between scenarios. EP stands for English proficiency.

	Terms? [w/o — w/]	All terms? [w/o — w/]	NewTerms? [w/o — w/]	Click? [w/o — w/]
Portuguese				
Basic EP	**−0.05 — −0.03**	**−0.04 — −0.05**	**−0.04 — −0.08**	**−0.04 — −0.05**
Independent EP	**−0.01 — −0.04**	**−0.02 — −0.06**	**−0.02 — −0.06**	−0.02 — −0.02
Proficient EP	**−0.03 — −0.08**	**−0.04 — −0.05**	**−0.03 — −0.10**	−0.04 — −0.04
English				
Basic EP	**−0.04 — −0.03**	**−0.04 — −0.03**	**−0.04 — −0.06**	**−0.04 — −0.03**
Independent EP	**−0.02 — −0.05**	**−0.02 — −0.01**	**−0.02 — −0.08**	−0.02 — −0.01
Proficient EP	**−0.04 — −0.05**	**−0.05 — 0.01**	**−0.04 — −0.02**	[−0.05 — **0.03**]*

terms and when these users and the *marginal* health literate users click in the suggestions.

In medico-scientific suggestions, the use of all the suggestion' terms tends to be favorable to precision in all levels of health literacy. Moreover, the use of new terms from suggestions and suggestions' clicks are beneficial to precision in the *low* and *functional* health literacy groups. Of these, the only significant difference occurs when *low* literate users click medico-scientific suggestions (t(35.4) = −1.9, p = 0.03*), showing the positive impact of this type of suggestions.

6.3   Analysis by Topic Familiarity

Considering topic familiarity, whose results are also in Table 2, we found that *familiar* users (TF2) have significantly higher precision in iterations in which they do not use new terms from lay (t(72.9) = 2.2, p = 0.01*) or medico-scientific suggestions (t(76.4) = 2.0, p = 0.02*). We also found that *extremely familiar* users tend to have higher precision with medico-scientific suggestions or when they click or use all the terms from lay suggestions. *Non-familiar* users also seem to benefit from clicks in both lay and medico-scientific suggestions.

Comparing the mean Δ GAP of the several topic familiarity levels in each scenario and type of terminology, we found that, when using new terms from medico-scientific suggestions, *non-familiar* users have a significantly higher precision than *familiar* users (Tukey's adjusted p = 0.01*). This is simultaneously due to the increase in precision in *non-familiar* users and the significant decrease found in the *familiar* users, when using these suggestions.

7   Discussion

On Table 3 we summarize the significant findings previously reported, only found when users use new terms from suggestions or when they click on them.

Answering the first research question, the system with suggestions (SYS+) tended to demonstrate better performance in terms of precision. The positive

Table 2. ΔGAP means by terminology. Boldface represents the maximum in each group and scenario. Square brackets are used there are significant differences between scenarios. HL stands for Health Literacy.

	Terms? [w/o — w/]	All terms? [w/o — w/]	NewTerms? [w/o — w/]	Click? [w/o — w/]
Lay				
Low HL	**−0.04** — −0.06	−0.05 — **−0.03**	**−0.04** — −0.07	−0.05 — **0.00**
Marginal HL	**−0.02** — −0.04	**−0.02** — −0.04	[−0.02 — −0.08]**	−0.03 — **−0.01**
Functional HL	**−0.04** — −0.10	**−0.05** — 0.10	[−0.05 — −0.11]**	**−0.05** — −0.09
Not familiar	**0.01** — −0.03	**0.00** — −0.03	**0.00** — −0.06	0.00 — **0.02**
Familiar	**−0.04** — −0.06	**−0.04** — −0.05	[−0.03 — −0.11]*	**−0.04** — −0.04
Extremely familiar	−0.04 — −0.05	−0.05 — **−0.04**	**−0.04** — −0.06	−0.05 — **−0.01**
MS				
Low HL	**−0.04** — −0.04	−0.04 — **−0.05**	**−0.04** — −0.04	[−0.05 — **0.01**]*
Marginal HL	**−0.02** — −0.03	−0.03 — −0.03	**−0.02** — −0.06	**−0.03** — −0.04
Functional HL	**−0.04** — −0.08	−0.06 — **−0.03**	−0.05 — −0.05	−0.05 — **−0.04**
Not familiar	**0.00** — −0.01	0.00 — **0.02**	0.00 — **0.01**	0.00 — **0.03**
Familiar	**−0.04** — −0.06	**−0.04** — −0.06	[−0.03 — −0.10]*	**−0.04** — −0.06
Extremely familiar	−0.05 — **−0.04**	−0.05 — **−0.04**	**−0.05** — −0.04	−0.05 — **−0.04**

effects of the suggestion system has also been previously shown in the medical accuracy of the knowledge obtained in the session [18].

Pertaining the second research question, we found no significant differences between using or not using the overall set of suggestions, either as a whole or as a source of terms. Answering the third research question, negative effects of language and terminology are found when users use new terms from Portuguese and lay suggestions. No other significant effect was found.

Moving on to the fourth research question, as seen in Table 3, the effect differs in the two use scenarios, clicking on suggestions has positive effects on precision and using new terms from them has negative effects. English suggestions are advantageous to *proficient* users when they click on them. The use of lay and medico-scientific suggestions has also a good effect on precision. Surprisingly, lay suggestions increase precision not only in *non-familiar* users but also in the *extremely familiar* group.

The precision increase found when *low* health literate users click on medico-scientific suggestions is consistent with what has been found in a previous study, that is, "less subject expertise seems to lead to more lenient and relatively higher relevance ratings" [17]. This means that these users may be assessing documents regarding their relation with the topic instead of their utility to themselves. Findings in *non-familiar* users could be explained the same way but, since we have found in a previous study [18] that medico-scientific suggestions increase their answers' correct contents and tends to decrease their incorrect contents, we have reasons to believe this is not the case. Moreover, this agrees with what we found in a previous study [9] where we concluded that health literacy is more important to comprehend medico-scientific documents than topic familiarity.

Table 3. Summary of the significant findings. ↑ denotes increases and ↓ decreases in each outcome.

	NewTerms?	Click?
General		
English		Proficient EP (↑)
Portuguese	General (↓)	
Lay	General (↓)	
	Marginal HL (↓)	Non-familiar (↑)
	Functional HL (↓)	Extremely familiar (↑)
	Familiar (↓)	
Medico-scientific	Familiar (↓)	Low HL (↑)
		Non-familiar (↑)
		Extremely familiar (↑)

With the use of new terms from suggestions, precision decreases with the use of Portuguese and lay suggestions. The same happens with lay suggestions in higher levels of health literacy and with both lay and medico-scientific suggestions in users familiar with the topic.

We have also compared the performance of different groups of users in each use scenario for each type of suggestion. In these comparisons, we found that users *familiar* with the topic have lower precision than *non-familiar* users when new terms from medico-scientific suggestions are used. This may be explained by the benefits that *non-familiar* users seem to obtain from medico-scientific suggestions in every scenario.

8   Conclusion

We describe a query suggestion system for the health domain and study its impact on the precision of the search session considering several user characteristics. This analysis takes into account the utility of the suggestions as new whole queries and as sources of terms.

We found that a system with these suggestions is beneficial for the precision of the search session. In a previous work we have reached a similar conclusion regarding medical accuracy [18]. The best precision effects of the suggestion tool are achieved when users use it strictly as a suggestion tool, that is, when they click in suggestions.

Previously, we found that English suggestions are preferred to the Portuguese by the general user, both in terms of clicks and as source of new terms [10]. We have also found that clicking English suggestions is beneficial for the medical accuracy of the knowledge acquired during the search session. In this work, we have shown that the benefit of whole English suggestions is not restricted to medical accuracy but also applies to precision if the user is proficient in this language. The benefits of these suggestions allied with users preference for them show the potential of English suggestions for users with other native languages in the health domain. This corroborates the finding of a previous study [8] that suggest that non-English–speaking users having at least elementary English proficiency can benefit from a system that suggests English alternatives for their queries.

In terms of terminology, medico-scientific suggestions are preferred to lay ones by the general user, in clicks and as source of terms, a preference that increases with health literacy [10].

In terms of medical accuracy, both terminologies are favourable to the general user. In the present work we found that both terminologies are advantageous to specific groups of users but not to the general user. This suggests that personalizing the suggestion system might have good effects on precision.

As future work, we would like to explore the effects of this suggestion system on motivational relevance.

Acknowledgments. This work was supported by Project "NORTE-01-0145-FEDER-000016" (NanoSTIMA), financed by the North Portugal Regional Operational Programme (NORTE 2020), under the PORTUGAL 2020 Partnership Agreement, and through the European Regional Development Fund (ERDF).

References

1. Borlund, P.: The IIR evaluation model: a framework for evaluation of interactive information retrieval systems. Inf. Res. **8**(3) (2003). http://informationr.net/ir/8-3/paper152.html
2. Fox, S.: Health topics. Technical report, Pew Internet & American Life Project, Washington, DC (2011)
3. Gao, W., Niu, C., Nie, J.Y., Zhou, M., Wong, K.F., Hon, H.W.: Exploiting query logs for cross-lingual query suggestions. ACM Trans. Inf. Syst. **28**(2), 1–33 (2010). https://doi.org/10.1145/1740592.1740594
4. Jansen, B.J., McNeese, M.D.: Evaluating the effectiveness of and patterns of interactions with automated searching assistance. J. Am. Soc. Inf. Sci. **56**(14), 1480–1503 (2005). https://doi.org/10.1002/asi.20242
5. Kelly, D., Gyllstrom, K., Bailey, E.W.: A comparison of query and term suggestion features for interactive searching. In: Proceedings of the 32nd International ACM SIGIR Conference on Research and Development in Information Retrieval, SIGIR 2009, pp. 371–378. ACM, New York (2009). https://doi.org/10.1145/1571941.1572006
6. Kogan, S., Zeng, Q., Ash, N., Greenes, R.A.: Problems and challenges in patient information retrieval: a descriptive study. In: Proceedings AMIA Symposium, pp. 329–333 (2001). http://www.ncbi.nlm.nih.gov/pmc/articles/PMC2243602/
7. Kriewel, S., Fuhr, N.: Evaluation of an adaptive search suggestion system. In: Gurrin, C., et al. (eds.) ECIR 2010. LNCS, vol. 5993, pp. 544–555. Springer, Heidelberg (2010). https://doi.org/10.1007/978-3-642-12275-0_47
8. Lopes, C.T., Ribeiro, C.: Measuring the value of health query translation: an analysis by user language proficiency. J. Am. Soc. Inf. Sci. Technol. **64**(5), 951–963 (2013). https://doi.org/10.1002/asi.22812

9. Lopes, C.T., Ribeiro, C.: Effects of terminology on health queries: an analysis by user's health literacy and topic familiarity, vol. 39, chap. 10, pp. 145–184. Emerald Group Publishing Limited (2015). https://doi.org/10.1108/S0065-283020150000039013

10. Lopes, C.T., Ribeiro, C.: Effects of language and terminology on the usage of health query suggestions. In: Fuhr, N., et al. (eds.) CLEF 2016. LNCS, vol. 9822, pp. 83–95. Springer, Cham (2016). https://doi.org/10.1007/978-3-319-44564-9_7

11. Luo, G., Tang, C.: On iterative intelligent medical search. In: Proceedings of the 31st Annual International ACM SIGIR Conference on Research and Development in Information Retrieval, SIGIR 2008, pp. 3–10. ACM, New York (2008). https://doi.org/10.1145/1390334.1390338

12. Luo, G., Tang, C., Yang, H., Wei, X.: MedSearch: a specialized search engine for medical information retrieval. In: Proceeding of the 17th ACM Conference on Information and Knowledge Mining, CIKM 2008, pp. 143–152. ACM, New York (2008). https://doi.org/10.1145/1458082.1458104

13. McCray, A.T., Tse, T.: Understanding search failures in consumer health information systems. In: AMIA Annual Symposium Proceedings, pp. 430–434 (2003). http://www.ncbi.nlm.nih.gov/pmc/articles/PMC1479930/

14. NLM: 2012AA consumer health vocabulary source information (2012). http://www.nlm.nih.gov/research/umls/sourcereleasedocs/current/CHV/index.html

15. Rawson, K.A., et al.: The METER: a brief, self-administered measure of health literacy. J. Gen. Intern. Med. **25**(1), 67–71 (2010). https://doi.org/10.1007/s11606-009-1158-7

16. Robertson, S.E., Kanoulas, E., Yilmaz, E.: Extending average precision to graded relevance judgments. In: Proceeding of the 33rd International ACM SIGIR Conference on Research and Development in Information Retrieval, SIGIR 2010, pp. 603–610. ACM, New York, July 2010. https://doi.org/10.1145/1835449.1835550

17. Saracevic, T.: Relevance: a review of the literature and a framework for thinking on the notion in information science. Part III: behavior and effects of relevance. J. Am. Soc. Inf. Sci. Technol. **58**(13), 2126–2144 (2007)

18. Lopes, C.T., Paiva, D., Ribeiro, C.: Effects of language and terminology of query suggestions on medical accuracy considering different user characteristics. J. Assoc. Inf. Sci. Technol. **68**(9), 2063–2075 (2017). https://doi.org/10.1002/asi.23874

19. Toms, E.G., Latter, C.: How consumers search for health information. Health Inform. J. **13**(3), 223–235 (2007). https://doi.org/10.1177/1460458207079901

20. Zarro, M., Lin, X.: Using social tags and controlled vocabularies as filters for searching and browsing: a health science experiment. In: Fifth Workshop on Human-Computer Interaction and Information Retrieval, October 2011

21. Zeng, Q.T., Crowell, J., Plovnick, R.M., Kim, E., Ngo, L., Dibble, E.: Assisting consumer health information retrieval with query recommendations. J. Am. Med. Inform. Assoc. (JAMIA) **13**(1), 80–90 (2006). https://doi.org/10.1197/jamia.m1820

22. Zhang, Y.: Contextualizing consumer health information searching: an analysis of questions in a social Q&A community. In: Proceedings of the 1st ACM International Health Informatics Symposium, pp. 210–219 (2010)

23. Zielstorff, R.: Controlled vocabularies for consumer health. J. Biomed. Inform. **36**(4–5), 326–333 (2003). https://doi.org/10.1016/j.jbi.2003.09.015

Short Papers

Automatic Query Selection for Acquisition and Discovery of Food-Drug Interactions

Georgeta Bordea[1]([✉]), Frantz Thiessard[1,2], Thierry Hamon[3,4], and Fleur Mougin[1]

[1] University of Bordeaux, Inserm, Bordeaux Population Health Research Center, team ERIAS, UMR 1219, 33000 Bordeaux, France
{georgeta.bordea,frantz.thiessard,fleur.mougin}@u-bordeaux.fr
[2] CHU de Bordeaux, Pole de sante publique, 33000 Bordeaux, France
[3] LIMSI, CNRS, Université Paris-Saclay, Orsay, France
hamon@limsi.fr
[4] Université Paris 13, Villetaneuse, France

Abstract. Food-drug interactions can profoundly impact desired and adverse effects of drugs, with unexpected and often harmful consequences on the health and well-being of patients. A growing body of scientific publications report clinically relevant food-drug interactions, but conventional search strategies based on handcrafted queries and indexing terms suffer from low recall. In this paper, we introduce a novel task called food-drug interaction discovery that aims to automatically identify scientific publications that describe food-drug interactions from a database of biomedical literature. We make use of an expert curated corpus of food-drug interactions to analyse different methods for query selection and we propose a high-recall approach based on feature selection.

Keywords: Query selection · Corpus construction · Feature selection
Food-drug interactions

1 Introduction

With the rising popularity of neural networks and word embeddings [12,13] for various information extraction tasks, there is an increased need to collect large domain-specific corpora. This is especially true for specialised domains such as the biomedical [5,8] or the legal domain [9] where many concepts are poorly represented in general purpose corpora derived from the web. In this paper, we address the problem of automatically constructing a relevant corpus of scientific articles that describe Food-Drug Interactions (FDIs). Food-drug interactions are generally related to the absorption of a drug into the body with respect to mealtimes and are systematically analysed as part of clinical trials required prior to drug marketing. But certain foods contain chemical substances and compounds that are susceptible of dramatically increasing or reducing the effect of

© Springer Nature Switzerland AG 2018
P. Bellot et al. (Eds.): CLEF 2018, LNCS 11018, pp. 115–120, 2018.
https://doi.org/10.1007/978-3-319-98932-7_10

a drug, with unexpected results including treatment failure, toxicity and higher risk of side-effects. For example, grapefruit contains bioactive furocoumarins and flavonoids that activate or deactivate many drugs in ways that can be life-threatening [3]. While drug-drug interactions can be investigated systematically, there is a much larger number of possible FDIs. Therefore, these interactions are generally discovered and reported after a drug is administered on a wide scale during post-marketing surveillance. Currently, information about FDIs is available to medical practitioners from online databases and compendia such as the Stockley's Drug Interactions [2], but these resources have to be regularly updated to keep up with a growing body of evidence from biomedical articles.

The extraction of drug-drug interactions from scientific articles has received a considerable amount of interest in the context of a SemEval shared task [15], but similar progress is currently hindered by a lack of resources for FDIs. Although a first corpus of MEDLINE abstracts about FDIs was recently made available [6], this corpus called POMELO covers a limited number of FDIs. The authors rely on PubMed to retrieve all the articles indexed with the *Food-Drug Interactions* term from the MeSH thesaurus[1]. While the number of articles annotated with *Drug Interactions* is abundant, there is a much smaller number of documents indexed with *Food-Drug Interactions*. A bibliographic analysis of the references cited in the Stockley's Drug Interactions in relation to foods shows that only 11% of these articles are indexed with *Food-Drug Interactions*, although almost 70% of the articles are available in PubMed. The POMELO corpus has a more narrow focus on articles related to adverse effects, therefore it covers only 3% of the references provided in the Stockley compendium. Although biomedical articles are thoroughly annotated using a well-known vocabulary, constructing a high-coverage corpus of FDIs using MeSH terms and PubMed is not trivial.

In this paper, the problem of food-drug interaction discovery from biomedical literature is limited to the task of interaction candidates search, that is the task of finding documents that describe FDIs from a large bibliographic database. We make use of a large corpus of relevant publications to investigate indexing terms used to annotate articles about FDIs and we propose an automated method for query selection that increases recall.

2   Related Work

Using hand-crafted queries based on MeSH terms is a popular technique for retrieving documents related to adverse drug effects [4], but there is a much smaller number of documents available for specific types of adverse effects such as FDIs and herb-drug interactions. The problem of building queries for finding documents related to drug interactions has been recently tackled for herb-drug interactions [10]. This work addresses a less challenging usage scenario where users have in mind a pair of herbs and drugs and are interested in finding evidences of interaction. Queries are manually constructed by a domain expert using MeSH synonyms for herbs and drugs together with the following MeSH qualifiers:

---

[1] https://www.nlm.nih.gov/mesh/.

adverse effects, *pharmacokinetics*, and *chemistry*. Two additional heuristics rank higher retrieved articles that are annotated with the MeSH terms *Drug Interactions* and *Plant Extracts/pharmacology*. Another limitation of this work is the size of the evaluation dataset that is based on a single review paper [7] that provides about 100 references. In contrast, we propose an automated approach for query selection and we make use of a considerably larger dataset of relevant publications for training and evaluation. The food-drug interaction discovery task proposed here is similar in setting with the subtask on prior art candidates search from the intellectual property domain [14]. In the CLEF-IP datasets, topics are constructed using a patent application and the task is to identify previously published patents that potentially invalidate this application. Keyphrase extraction approaches were successfully applied to generate queries from patent applications [11,16]. The input is much larger for our task, that is a corpus of scientific articles that describe FDIs manually annotated with indexing terms from the MeSH thesaurus. A main difference between our work and the CLEF-IP task is that we mainly focus on evaluating different methods for query selection by relying on the PubMed search engine. This makes our task more similar to the term extraction task [1], as we aim to identify relevant terms for a broad domain rather than for a specific document, as done in keyphrase extraction.

3   Proposed Query Selection Approaches

Given a test collection C of size n where each document c_i is associated with a vector of indexing terms v_i of a variable size from a set V of size n defined as follows:

$$v_i = \{t_1, \ldots, t_k\}$$

where t_j is a term from a controlled vocabulary that describes the contents of document c_i, and k is the number of indexing terms used to annotate the document. We assume that a subset D of size m of relevant documents known to report FDIs is also given, where $m < n$. The subset of indexing vectors associated with relevant documents is the set V' of size m and each relevant document d_i is annotated with a vector v' of indexing terms. We also assume there is a fixed retrieving function S, where $S(q, d)$ gives the score for document d with respect to query q.

We define query selection as the problem of finding a query scoring function R, that gives the score $R(D, q)$ for query q with respect to the collection of relevant documents D. A desired query scoring function would rank higher the queries that perform best when selecting relevant documents. In our experiments we consider as candidate queries single terms but more complex queries that combine multiple index terms can also be envisaged. We consider two types of scoring functions, first based on simple frequency counts of indexing terms and a second type of scoring functions inspired by existing approaches for feature selection used in supervised classification. The most basic query scoring function is frequency, denoted as the count $c(V', q)$ of query q with respect to the set V' of indexing vectors associated with relevant documents. The TF-IDF scoring function $tfidf(V', V, q)$ of query q with respect to the set of indexing vectors associated with relevant documents V' discriminated against the full set of indexing terms V is defined as:

$$tfidf(V', V, q) = c(V', q)/ln(c(V, q))$$

For the second category of scoring functions, we consider a binary classifier that distinguishes between relevant documents D and an equal number m of randomly selected documents from the test collection C. Assuming that the size of the test collection is much larger than the number of documents known to be relevant, there is a high probability that randomly selected documents are irrelevant. The features considered for classification are all the indexing terms that are used to annotate a predefined minimum number of documents. The first scoring function is the information gain defined as follows:

$$InfoGain(Class, t) = H(Class) - H(Class|t)$$

where the entropy H of a class with two possible values (i.e., relevant *pos* and irrelevant *neg*) is defined based on their probability p as:

$$H(Class) = -p(pos) * log(p(pos)) - p(neg) * log(p(neg))$$

The gain ratio is further defined as the information gain divided by the entropy of the term t:

$$GainR(Class, t) = InfoGain(Class, t)/H(t)$$

Finally, we also consider the Pearson's correlation as a query scoring function for the same binary classifier.

4   Experimental Settings and Results

The corpus used in our experiments is constructed by collecting references provided in the Stockley compendium in relation to food. We manually identify references from pages listed in the index under individual foodstuffs and *Foods*, for a total of 912 references and 460 references, respectively. Using the title and the year of each reference, we retrieve 802 unique PubMed identifiers. Additionally, we consider an update of the POMELO corpus by retrieving PubMed documents with the same query that was used to gather the original corpus. The updated POMELO corpus contains 846 articles, including 207 articles that were published since the corpus was originally collected. All together, the corpus contains 1610 relevant documents and we also collect an equal number of randomly selected documents for a total of 3220 documents. We retrieve MeSH terms assigned to each article and we use for classification all the terms that are mentioned in at least 10 documents for a total of 623 terms. An SVM classifier achieves an F-score of 96% on this dataset using 10-fold cross-validation.

The classical measures of precision, recall and F-score are adapted for our task to reflect our interest in discovering unseen documents. We use our high-performance classifier to predict the relevance of retrieved documents instead of computing precision based on the documents known to be relevant alone. The high precision achieved by the classifier allows to compute a reliable estimate of precision avoiding the need for manual annotation. Recall is calculated for a limited number of retrieved documents as some of the MeSH indexing terms such as *Humans* and *Animals* are broad enough to be used for annotating most of the documents in the test collection. Table 1 gives an overview of the results obtained by each scoring function discussed in the previous section. Performance is computed for the top 20 ranked queries for each method. All the methods score high the *Food-Drug interactions* term but we remove this term from the results because it was used to construct the FDIs corpus. Overall, the best performance is obtained by the Gain ratio scoring function. Selected queries using this approach include: *Biological Availability*, *Drug Interactions*, and *Intestinal Absorption*. Gain ratio outperforms other approaches because it penalizes high frequency terms that are too broad such as *Adult*, *Aged*, and *Female*.

Table 1. Scoring functions evaluated for the top 20 MeSH terms using predicted precision at top 100, recall at top 16k and the combined predicted F-score

Scoring function	Predicted P@100	Recall @16k	Predicted F-score
Frequency	0.2020	0.0032	0.0584
TF-IDF	0.2590	0.0084	0.0784
Information gain	0.2755	0.0084	0.0812
Gain ratio	**0.3755**	**0.0557**	**0.0970**
Correlation	0.2590	0.0081	0.0770

5   Conclusions

In this paper, we made use of a large dataset of articles that describe food-drug interactions annotated with indexing terms to investigate an approach for query selection that allows us to discover other food-drug interactions. We proposed an automatic evaluation of retrieved results using a high-performance classifier and we showed that feature selection approaches outperform frequency-based approaches for this task, with an approach based on gain ratio achieving the best results in terms of predicted F-score. In this work, we focus on queries constructed using a single indexing term, therefore a first improvement would be to investigate more complex queries that combine multiple terms. Another improvement would be to compare our results with keyphrase extraction approaches and to generate queries using background knowledge about drugs and foods. The MeSH hierarchy could also be used to distinguish indexing terms related to foods and drugs.

Acknowledgements. This work was supported by the MIAM project and Agence Nationale de la Recherche through the grant ANR-16-CE23-0012 France.

References

1. Aubin, S., Hamon, T.: Improving term extraction with terminological resources. In: Salakoski, T., Ginter, F., Pyysalo, S., Pahikkala, T. (eds.) FinTAL 2006. LNCS (LNAI), vol. 4139, pp. 380–387. Springer, Heidelberg (2006). https://doi.org/10.1007/11816508_39

2. Baxter, K., Preston, C.: Stockley's Drug Interactions, vol. 495. Pharmaceutical Press, London (2010)

3. Dahan, A., Altman, H.: Food-drug interaction: grapefruit juice augments drug bioavailability—mechanism, extent and relevance. Eur. J. Clin. Nutr. **58**(1), 1 (2004)

4. Gurulingappa, H., Rajput, A.M., Roberts, A., Fluck, J., Hofmann-Apitius, M., Toldo, L.: Development of a benchmark corpus to support the automatic extraction of drug-related adverse effects from medical case reports. J. Biomed. Inform. **45**(5), 885–892 (2012)

5. Habibi, M., Weber, L., Neves, M., Wiegandt, D.L., Leser, U.: Deep learning with word embeddings improves biomedical named entity recognition. Bioinformatics **33**(14), i37–i48 (2017)

6. Hamon, T., Tabanou, V., Mougin, F., Grabar, N., Thiessard, F.: POMELO: medline corpus with manually annotated food-drug interactions. In: Recent Advances in Natural Language Processing (RANLP), pp. 73–80 (2017)

7. Izzo, A.A., Ernst, E.: Interactions between herbal medicines and prescribed drugs. Drugs **69**(13), 1777–1798 (2009)

8. Jiang, Z., Li, L., Huang, D., Jin, L.: Training word embeddings for deep learning in biomedical text mining tasks. In: International Conference on Bioinformatics and Biomedicine (BIBM), pp. 625–628. IEEE (2015)

9. Landthaler, J., Waltl, B., Holl, P., Matthes, F.: Extending full text search for legal document collections using word embeddings. In: JURIX, pp. 73–82 (2016)

10. Lin, K., Friedman, C., Finkelstein, J.: An automated system for retrieving herb-drug interaction related articles from medline. AMIA Summits Transl. Sci. Proc. **2016**, 140 (2016)

11. Lopez, P., Romary, L.: Experiments with citation mining and key-term extraction for prior art search. In: CLEF 2010-Conference on Multilingual and Multimodal Information Access Evaluation (2010)

12. Mikolov, T., Chen, K., Corrado, G., Dean, J.: Efficient estimation of word representations in vector space. arXiv preprint arXiv:1301.3781 (2013)

13. Pennington, J., Socher, R., Manning, C.: GloVe: global vectors for word representation. In: Proceedings of the 2014 Conference on Empirical Methods in Natural Language Processing (EMNLP), pp. 1532–1543 (2014)

14. Piroi, F., Lupu, M., Hanbury, A., Zenz, V.: CLEF-IP 2011: retrieval in the intellectual property domain. In: CLEF (notebook papers/labs/workshop) (2011)

15. Segura-Bedmar, I., Martínez, P., Zazo, M.H.: SemEval-2013 task 9: extraction of drug-drug interactions from biomedical texts (ddiextraction 2013). In: Second Joint Conference on Lexical and Computational Semantics (*SEM), Volume 2: Proceedings of the Seventh International Workshop on Semantic Evaluation (SemEval 2013), vol. 2, pp. 341–350 (2013)

16. Verma, M., Varma, V.: Exploring keyphrase extraction and IPC classification vectors for prior art search. In: CLEF (Notebook Papers/Labs/Workshop) (2011)

Addressing Social Bias in Information Retrieval

Jahna Otterbacher[1,2]([✉]) [iD]

[1] Open University of Cyprus, Nicosia, Cyprus
`jahna.otterbacher@ouc.ac.cy`
[2] Research Centre on Interactive Media Smart Systems and Emerging Technologies,
Nicosia, Cyprus

Abstract. Journalists and researchers alike have claimed that IR systems are socially biased, returning results to users that perpetuate gender and racial stereotypes. In this position paper, I argue that IR researchers and in particular, evaluation communities such as CLEF, can and should address such concerns. Using as a guide the *Principles for Algorithmic Transparency and Accountability* recently put forward by the Association for Computing Machinery, I provide examples of techniques for examining social biases in IR systems and in particular, search engines.

Keywords: Social biases · Ranking algorithms · Crowdsourcing

1 Introduction

The social impact of algorithmic systems – including information retrieval (IR) systems – is being discussed extensively in the media. Eye-catching titles often convey sweeping claims such as "AI learns to be sexist and racist[1]" or "Biased algorithms are everywhere, and no one seems to care[2]." IR systems – particularly search engines – are often the target of more specific accusations of *social bias*, for instance: "Google has a striking history of bias against black girls[3]" or "Google's algorithm shows prestigious job ads to men, but not to women[4]."

At the same time, there is growing recognition from the scientific community that algorithms – especially those that are opaque to the user – can and do bring about negative consequences, some of which are systematic. Several communities have started initiatives to promote the alignment of algorithmic systems with

Partially supported by the European Union's Horizon 2020 Research and Innovation Programme under grant agreement No. 739578.

[1] http://www.newsweek.com/2017/12/22/ai-learns-sexist-racist-742767.html.
[2] https://www.technologyreview.com/s/608248/biased-algorithms-are-everywhere-and-no-one-seems-to-care/.
[3] http://time.com/5209144/google-search-engine-algorithm-bias-racism/.
[4] https://www.independent.co.uk/life-style/gadgets-and-tech/news/googles-algorithm-shows-prestigious-job-ads-to-men-but-not-to-women-10372166.html.

P. Bellot et al. (Eds.): CLEF 2018, LNCS 11018, pp. 121–127, 2018.
https://doi.org/10.1007/978-3-319-98932-7_11

human values. For example, in April 2016, the IEEE launched its Global Initiative on Ethics of Autonomous and Intelligent Systems, to demonstrate that taking into consideration the human and ethical aspects of design can have a positive impact on innovation[5]. The deliverables of the initiative include a collaboratively produced document, *Ethically Aligned Design*, which summarizes input from hundreds of stakeholders, as well as a set of standards projects (e.g., IEEE P7003 Standard for Algorithmic Bias Considerations working group[6]).

Another recent development is the Association for Computing Machinery's *Statement on Algorithmic Transparency and Accountability*, which has been approved by both the ACM U.S. Public Policy Council and the Europe Policy Committee[7]. The statement notes that many algorithmic processes are opaque and that the reasons for this may vary. For instance, it is more often than not difficult to interpret results from models induced by new machine learning techniques such as deep learning (i.e., there are significant technical challenges for transparency). In addition to this, there are social and economic challenges for achieving algorithmic transparency, such as the need for developers/owners of such processes to protect trade secrets, or even the privacy concerns of users.

The ACM Statement puts forward a set of seven principles, which can be used by system developers and owners for promoting algorithmic transparency and accountability. The principles include Data Provenance (i.e., scrutinizing the processes by which training data is generated) and Validation and Testing (i.e., routine assessments as to whether an algorithm's outputs result in discriminatory harm, and making the assessment results public). Inspired by the principles, as well as a recent presentation by Margaret Mitchell[8], Fig. 1 presents three known sources of human biases (data, development process, user behaviors) in a typical pipeline involving an algorithmic system and a human end-user, as well as possible opportunities to promote transparency (i.e., "interventions").

I shall return to these principles, and how they might be applied in the context of IR system development and evaluation. Next, I provide a working definition for the term *social bias* and briefly summarize some recent work that has revealed social biases in IR systems and in particular, *image search engines*.

1.1   Social Biases in Search Engines

While it has long been accepted that information systems bring a slant in their presentation of information to users, there is a need to determine if and when a system is *biased* and when intervention is necessary. Writing long before the age of Big Data, Friedman and Nissenbaum [2] outlined two conditions under which a system could be considered biased: (1) its results are slanted in unfair

---

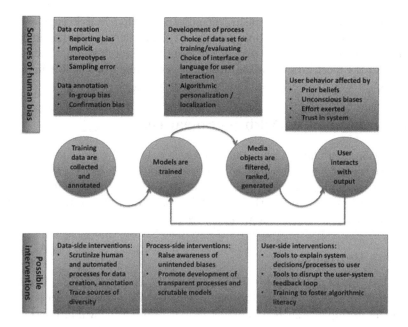

Fig. 1. Sources of human bias in algorithmic systems and interventions.

discrimination against particular persons or groups, and (2) the observed discrimination is systematic within the system. Indeed, over the past years, many researchers have found that search engines, through the result sets they present to users, tend to reinforce a view of the social world that aligns with the status quo.

For instance, a study by Kay, Matuszek and Munson [3] found that Google image search results present a gendered view of the professions, amplifying existing stereotypes. For queries related to professions (e.g., doctor vs. nurse, engineer vs. teacher), they showed that the engine systematically returned more/fewer images of stereotype congruent/incongruent individuals, as compared to U.S. labor statistics. This work also demonstrated the power of search on users' perceptions; when participants were shown gender-biased search results and were asked to estimate the corresponding labor statistic, this skewed their estimates of the distribution of women/men in a particular profession.

My colleagues and I [6] considered the gendering of image search results, although in the context of the Microsoft Bing search engine, to which we submitted queries involving character traits (e.g., intelligent person vs. emotional person). Grounding our study in social psychology theory surrounding person perception, we found that Bing more often associated images of women with warm traits (e.g., kind, emotional) whereas images of men were typically featured in results sets on searches for agentic traits (e.g., assertive, intelligent). In addition, we found a backlash effect, in term of the nature of the images retrieved, which penalized stereotype-incongruent individuals (i.e., agentic women).

Research over the past years has demonstrated that search engine results can and do shape the public's opinion (e.g., [1]). Furthermore, it has long been known that users place great trust in the results of search engines, and rarely look beyond the most highly-ranked results [8]. For these reasons, it is important to promote greater transparency in search algorithms.

2 Interventions to Address Social Bias

In this section, I briefly present some approaches that my colleagues and I have used in our recent work, in order to explore various sources of social biases in search engines. Guided by Fig. 1, I consider Data Provenance, Validation and Testing procedures as well as the role of the user's own biases in perpetuating social stereotypes in image search engine results.

2.1 Data Provenance

The fifth principle in the ACM Statement is that of *Data Provenance*. Researchers are called to scrutinize the means by which training data sets are built. As an example of such "data-side interventions," as shown in Fig. 1, I have conducted a series of studies, to better understand the extent to which social stereotypes are conveyed in crowdsourced descriptions of people-related media. In [4], I analyzed the "Small ESP Game Dataset"[9], consisting of images collected from the Web, and labeled through the well-known ESP game [9], which asks players to describe images in their own words. The analysis revealed systematic gender-based differences in the way that people-images were described by ESP players. Specifically, images of women were labeled more frequently with subjective adjectives, as compared to images of men. Furthermore, images depicting women received more labels related to appearance, in contrast to images of men, which more often had labels related to the person's occupation.

While the above study showed evidence that crowdsourced image annotations can perpetuate gender stereotypes (i.e., that women should be attractive and men career-oriented), it did not examine how worker demographics are correlated to the process, nor could it control the parameters of the labeling task or the nature of the content of the images. Therefore, in [5], I conducted a controlled experiment with workers at Amazon Mechanical Turk, who were located in the U.S. and who identified as being Caucasian, native English speakers. In a between-subjects study, I asked workers to label images of professionals depicted in similar scenarios. However, the gender and race of the depicted person were manipulated. Among other findings, there was evidence of systematic differences in the language used to describe black versus white professionals, a phenomenon known as *linguistic bias*. Interestingly, the biases were more pronounced in the image descriptions produced by men workers, as compared to women workers, demonstrating that, depending on the nature of the task and the intended use of the resulting data, the use of anonymous crowdworkers can be problematic.

---

[9] http://www.cs.cmu.edu/~biglou/resources.

2.2   Validation and Testing

The seventh principle in the ACM Statement describes the need to "routinely perform tests to assess and determine whether the model generates discriminatory harm." In the context of our study of the Bing search engine and the perpetuation of gender stereotypes based on character traits [6], we developed a process for post-processing the first 1.000 images retrieved for a given query. More specifically, we used machine vision to process the images retrieved, in order to determine the gender distribution of the depicted individuals in the results set. This allowed us to study how a wide range of character traits are gendered by Bing, which would not be possible if we relied on manual analysis of the images. In addition, we were able to compare the gendering of traits across search markets, comparing four large anglophone markets (U.K., U.S., India and South Africa). It must be noted that our testing procedure for Bing's output relied on another algorithm for processing the images. Therefore, we first tested the performance of the procedure, comparing its accuracy on inferring the gender(s) of the depicted person(s) against that of human analysts.

2.3   The Role of the User

The ACM Statement's first principle is *Awareness* – that all stakeholders, from system designers and engineers, to the end users, should be aware of possible biases of the system as well as their potential harms. To this end, in [7], my colleagues and I explored users' awareness of gender bias in image search results sets. We hypothesized that users who are more sexist, would be less likely to indicate that a heavily gender-imbalanced set of images is "subjective" as compared to less sexist users. We again conducted an experiment with crowdworkers, this time at the Crowdflower platform. Without priming workers on the topic of our experiment, we first showed them a set of images, which we knew to be either heavily gender-skewed toward depicting men or women, or gender balanced. We then asked them to describe to us what they saw, and specifically, what keywords best describe the set of images. Next, we informed them that the images were in fact retrieved from a search engine using the given query, asking them to assess the objectivity/subjectivity of results set as a 7-point item. Finally, the workers were asked to take a standardized psychological test to assess their level of sexism. The correlation between sexism and the evaluation of gender bias in the image set results was as expected. However, an interesting finding was that more/less sexist users described the images in a very similar manner, suggesting few differences in how the images were perceived. The study demonstrates how studying users' prejudices and beliefs can help us better understand how they engage with and evaluate search technologies.

3 Conclusion

I have argued in favor of IR researchers and the evaluation community more broadly, addressing the issue of social biases in information retrieval systems. To this end, I have presented examples from my recent work, which considers the perpetuation of social stereotypes in three areas (i.e., potential sources of biases in the system development pipeline): training data sets, search result sets, and users' own biases.

More concretely, the CLEF community could consider the introduction of new tracks or labs to tackle social bias in IR. One could envision data-focused tasks, such as the development of metrics to audit search benchmark data and even techniques to prevent bias in evaluation corpora. Similarly, in the spirit of the ACM Statement's seventh principle, the community might discuss what a standardized "routine assessment" of algorithmic output in various IR tasks should look like. In conclusion, while many may argue that the issue of social biases is beyond the scope of an IR researcher or developer's work, given the recent attention to the social and ethical dimensions of algorithmic and intelligent systems, I hope that this paper will stimulate fruitful discussion amongst those who aim to effectively evaluate IR system performance in a holistic manner.

References

1. Epstein, R., Robertson, R.E.: The search engine manipulation effect (SEME) and its possible impact on the outcomes of elections. Proc. Nat. Acad. Sci. **112**(33), E4512–E4521 (2015). https://doi.org/10.1073/pnas.1419828112. http://www.pnas.org/content/112/33/E4512
2. Friedman, B., Nissenbaum, H.: Bias in computer systems. ACM Trans. Inf. Syst. (TOIS) **14**(3), 330–347 (1996)
3. Kay, M., Matuszek, C., Munson, S.A.: Unequal representation and gender stereotypes in image search results for occupations. In: Proceedings of the 33rd Annual ACM Conference on Human Factors in Computing Systems, pp. 3819–3828. ACM (2015)
4. Otterbacher, J.: Crowdsourcing stereotypes: linguistic bias in metadata generated via gwap. In: Proceedings of the 33rd Annual ACM Conference on Human Factors in Computing Systems, CHI 2015, pp. 1955–1964. ACM, New York (2015). https://doi.org/10.1145/2702123.2702151
5. Otterbacher, J.: Social cues, social biases: stereotypes in annotations on people images. In: Proceedings of the Sixth AAAI Conference on Human Computation and Crowdsourcing (HCOMP-2018). AAAI Press, Palo Alto (2018)
6. Otterbacher, J., Bates, J., Clough, P.: Competent men and warm women: gender stereotypes and backlash in image search results. In: Proceedings of the 2017 CHI Conference on Human Factors in Computing Systems, CHI 2017, pp. 6620–6631. ACM, New York (2017). https://doi.org/10.1145/3025453.3025727
7. Otterbacher, J., Checco, A., Demartini, G., Clough, P.: Investigating user perception of gender bias in image search: the role of sexism. In: Proceedings of the 41st International ACM SIGIR Conference on Research and Development in Information Retrieval (SIGIR-2018). ACM Press, New York (2018)

8. Pan, B., Hembrooke, H., Joachims, T., Lorigo, L., Gay, G., Granka, L.: In google we trust: users decisions on rank, position, and relevance. J. Comput. Med. Commun. **12**(3), 801–823 (2007). https://doi.org/10.1111/j.1083-6101.2007.00351.x
9. Von Ahn, L., Dabbish, L.: Labeling images with a computer game. In: Proceedings of the SIGCHI Conference on Human Factors in Computing Systems, pp. 319–326. ACM (2004)

Analyzing and Visualizing Translation Patterns of Wikidata Properties

John Samuel[(✉)]

CPE Lyon, Université de Lyon, Villeurbanne Cedex, France
john.samuel@cpe.fr

Abstract. From multi-domain multilingual Wikipedia websites to a single-domain multilingual Wikidata site, online collaboration has taken a major stride. However, achieving a multilingual experience is a rather challenging task for a highly evolving site like Wikidata built with the collaboration of contributors from around the world. It is important to let the contributors analyse and discover how properties are translated and also detect potential problems. This article focuses on developing a tool for understanding and visualizing the translation patterns of Wikidata.

Keywords: Online collaboration · Multilingualism
Ontology development · Wikidata

1   Introduction

Wikidata [11] is a multilingual, linked, open and structured knowledge base started by the Wikimedia Foundation in 2012. Since then, it has seen a tremendous growth and is widely used and studied by a number of researchers focusing on many aspects including collaboration and multilingual features [4,5,7,10] of the project. Unlike its sister project, Wikipedia that has a dedicated sub-domain[1] for every supported language (currently around 300 languages), Wikidata is a single domain website[2] with the capability to let users change the language settings. Such a change enables different users to view the same URL in different languages. That means a user can share these URLs to any other user of a different language and she can see the details in her own native language. For e.g., https://www.wikidata.org/wiki/Q9143 refers to the entity 'programming language' (en) or 'langage de programmation' (fr).

One interesting aspect is the way Wikidata identifies the items. It uses Q-numbers[3] for entities called items and P-numbers[4] to describe the properties.

---

[1] e.g., https://[en,fr,ml].wikipedia.org.
[2] https://www.wikidata.org.
[3] e.g., https://www.wikidata.org/wiki/Q9143.
[4] https://www.wikidata.org/wiki/Property:P279.

© Springer Nature Switzerland AG 2018
P. Bellot et al. (Eds.): CLEF 2018, LNCS 11018, pp. 128–134, 2018.
https://doi.org/10.1007/978-3-319-98932-7_12

A first-time user looking at an entity URL cannot say what it's about unlike a Wikipedia URL (See footnote 4) or even a DBpedia URL[5], another structured knowledge store.

Labels form a crucial part of Wikidata [10]. They are short texts to identify a given Wikidata entity in a given language. Additionally, every item two other attributes: description and alias. Both of these are human-understandable texts available in different Wikidata-supported languages to specify a long description and any additional labels respectively.

Wikidata is a collaborative [5,7] website, i.e., contributors can create, update or delete new items on the site. However, creation (and deletion) of Wikidata properties is a very long process. Wikidata, with its goal to represent data belonging to multiple domains uses both discussion and subsequent voting for the property creation/deletion. Properties form the key part of Wikidata since they are used to describe the various entities. Take for example, P856, one of the highly used properties is used to specify the official website of an entity. Its English label is 'official website'. But given the collaborative nature, labels, descriptions and aliases can be changed by any contributor. Hence any changes must be properly monitored to detect any possible vandalism since it may affect the semantics of thousands (or even millions) of Wikidata entries.

Secondly, it is also important to analyze and visualize the way by which properties are translated. As discussed in [7,8], though Wikidata provides a number of templates for multilingual discussion, properties are translated in other languages after their creation. Therefore, the role played by bilingual or even multilingual speakers in Wikidata cannot be undermined. Therefore, it is important to visualize the property translation process at a much more granular level not only to detect possible vandalism but also to get useful insights into the translation process.

Instead of doing one-time cumulative analysis of all the properties based on a data dump on a given period, it is important that the contributors can see, analyse and validate the results as well as suggest useful insights at a more granular level. With these goals, the web application WDProp[6][8] is built providing Wikidata users and contributors information concerning the properties, though primarily focusing on their multilingual translation. In this article, we will focus on how WDProp is further extended to obtain the details of property translation process.

Section 2 will briefly describe WDProp, its various objectives and its current capabilities. The implementation of the visualization process along with the results are described in Sect. 3. Section 4 presents various related works in multilingual collaborative ontology development and the role of visualization towards this goal. Section 5 briefly describes the future course of actions and concludes the article.

---

[5] e.g., http://dbpedia.org/ontology/ProgrammingLanguage.
[6] https://tools.wmflabs.org/wdprop/.

2   WDProp

WDProp[7][8] is an online application developed with the goal of understanding and improving multilingual and collaborative ontology development on Wikidata. Based on the translation status in different languages, properties can be separated into two categories: translated and untranslated properties. For example, statistics showing already translated properties[8] and languages with no translated properties[9] are shown in Fig. 1. The key advantage of this tool is the ability to navigate the properties in different ways including based on the (missing) translation status, property datatypes, curated property classes, curated WikiProjects etc. Every link is bookmarkable and gives statistics on the fly.

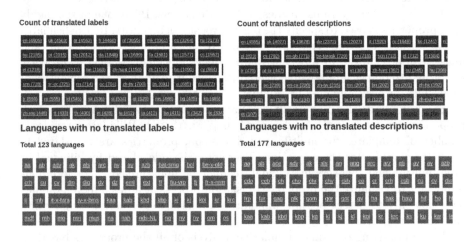

Fig. 1. Statistics on WDProp with clickable and bookmarkable links

WDProp also lets the users to search properties by their labels, compare translation statistics among different languages, view already translated labels, descriptions, aliases and the different property discussion templates.

3   Implementation

In addition to showing translation statistics for every property, WDProp is further extended to show the translation pattern. To implement this feature, it goes through the edit history of a given property. Any edit on Wikidata results in a message is prepended with a phrase given in Table 1. There are also other

---

[7] https://doi.org/10.5281/zenodo.1174371.

[8] https://tools.wmflabs.org/wdprop/translated.html.

[9] https://tools.wmflabs.org/wdprop/untranslated.html.

phrases like 'wbeditentity-create', 'wbsetaliases-add-remove', 'wbsetlabeldescrip-tionaliases' to detect when a property is created, an alias is added or removed or when all the three attributes are set in a single edit. The presence of these patterns are checked to understand the objective of each edit.

Table 1. Edit message for changes related to labels, descriptions and aliases of Wikidata properties

Attribute	Add	Update	Remove
Label	wbsetlabel-add	wbsetlabel-set	wbsetlabel-remove
Description	wbsetdescription-add	wbsetdescription-set	wbsetdescription-remove
Alias	wbsetaliases-add	wbsetaliases-add-remove	wbsetaliases-remove

We color code the actions and also show the associated time when a given action is made and use the colors blue to show addition, light blue to show any update and the color red to show removal. For each action, we also show the Wikidata language codes (e.g., en for English, fr for French etc.)

Development: WDProp is developed using web technologies like HTML, Javascript and CSS. This has an additional advantage that developers can download, setup and use it on their personal desktop or even integrate it with their internal servers. It makes use of Wikidata SPARQL endpoint[10] to obtain the data on the fly.

Results: Figure 2 shows the results of the translation path of property P856[11]) in chronological order, with four columns: time, label, description and alias. Some more translation paths[12] are given in the Fig. 3. Contributors can also look at the colors light blue and red to detect any possible problems and if needed, go to Wikidata site to revert them. Some interesting questions can be: is English always the first language used for translation?, is it common to see multiple label or description changes in a given language? Which language immediately follows French? etc.

Limitations: Our approach has certain limits. If multiple changes are made in one single edit by bots, it is currently not possible to detect them. It may require additional information like the actual content changes. For properties that have a long edit history, the SPARQL query may timeout, thereby showing no results.

---

[10] https://query.wikidata.org/.
[11] https://tools.wmflabs.org/wdprop/path.html?property=P856.
[12] https://tools.wmflabs.org/wdprop/path.html?property=P4290.

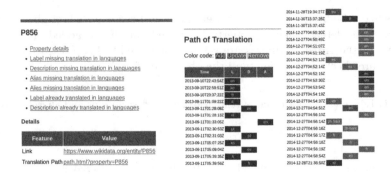

Fig. 2. Details of property P856, especially the translation path. Note the red color boxes. Some of these changes were later reverted. (Color figure online)

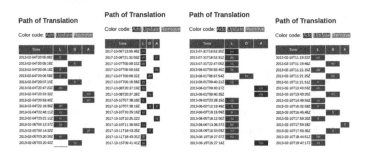

Fig. 3. Translation path of P18, P4290, P735, P106 (Color figure online)

4   Related Works

There is a growing interest in building collaborative approaches for knowledge management. Wikipedia, OntoWiki [2], Wikidata [11] are some major examples. All of these follow Wiki-style editing, i.e., users can create, edit, correct, delete, discuss or revert changes to articles. A number of research works are now available especially for Wikipedia that can visualize the above actions. Visualization of deletion discussions is considered by Notabilia [9]. [1,3] focuses on analyzing how information flows across different language editions.

Even though Wikidata is a recent entry in this picture, the above questions still remain important. There are several research works that has focused on its multilingual [4,10] and collaborative aspects [5]. Recent work on property label stability[13][10] shows the growing importance on the need of maintaining the stability in property labels and detect any undesired changes.

The goal of WDProp is to take these research works into consideration and provide on-the-fly statistics to Wikidata users and contributors so that they can

---

[13] https://thomas.pellissier-tanon.fr/wikidata/labels-timeline.html?entity=P279& lang=en.

find by themselves any linguistic influence [3, 6] patterns, possible vandalism or any new insight in a transparent, reproducible and shareable manner.

5   Conclusion

Labels and descriptions of Wikidata properties are very important since they form a major role in describing numerous items. In this article, we looked at obtaining the translation path of every property and visualizing them with the online application called WDProp. Visualizing the translation process helps not only in detecting any possible vandalism but also in understanding how more tools and alert systems can be made for bilingual or multilingual speakers. By basing on web technologies and SPARQL endpoint, this work may be extended to other private or independent multilingual Wikibase instances. Our future course of actions include optimizing the performance of results especially for highly used properties with a long edit history.

References

1. Borra, E., et al.: A platform for visually exploring the development of Wikipedia articles. In: Proceedings of the Ninth International Conference on Web and Social Media, ICWSM 2015, University of Oxford, Oxford, UK, 26–29 May 2015, pp. 711–712. AAAI Press (2015). http://www.aaai.org/ocs/index.php/ICWSM/ICWSM15/paper/view/10565
2. Frischmuth, P., Martin, M., Tramp, S., Riechert, T., Auer, S.: Ontowiki - an authoring, publication and visualization interface for the data web. Semant. Web **6**(3), 215–240 (2015). https://doi.org/10.3233/SW-140145
3. Gottschalk, S., Demidova, E.: MultiWiki: interlingual text passage alignment in Wikipedia. TWEB **11**(1), 6:1–6:30 (2017). https://doi.org/10.1145/3004296
4. Kaffee, L., Piscopo, A., Vougiouklis, P., Simperl, E., Carr, L., Pintscher, L.: A glimpse into babel: an analysis of multilinguality in Wikidata. In: Proceedings of the 13th International Symposium on Open Collaboration, OpenSym 2017, Galway, Ireland, 23–25 August 2017, pp. 14:1–14:5. ACM (2017). https://doi.org/10.1145/3125433.3125465
5. Müller-Birn, C., Karran, B., Lehmann, J., Luczak-Rösch, M.: Peer-production system or collaborative ontology engineering effort: what is Wikidata? In: Proceedings of the 11th International Symposium on Open Collaboration, San Francisco, CA, USA, 19–21 August 2015, pp. 20:1–20:10. ACM (2015). https://doi.org/10.1145/2788993.2789836
6. Samoilenko, A., Karimi, F., Kunegis, J., Edler, D., Strohmaier, M.: Linguistic influence patterns within the global network of Wikipedia language editions. In: Proceedings of the ACM Web Science Conference, WebSci 2015, Oxford, United Kingdom, 28 June–1 July 2015, pp. 54:1–54:2. ACM (2015). https://doi.org/10.1145/2786451.2786497
7. Samuel, J.: Collaborative approach to developing a multilingual ontology: a case study of Wikidata. In: Garoufallou, E., Virkus, S., Siatri, R., Koutsomiha, D. (eds.) MTSR 2017. CCIS, vol. 755, pp. 167–172. Springer, Cham (2017). https://doi.org/10.1007/978-3-319-70863-8_16

8. Samuel, J.: Towards understanding and improving multilingual collaborative ontology development in Wikidata. In: Wikidata Workshop 2018 (2018). http://wikiworkshop.org/2018/papers/wikiworkshop2018_paper_12.pdf
9. Stefaner, M., Taraborelli, D., Ciampaglia, G.L.: Notabilia-visualizing deletion discussions on Wikipedia (2011). http://well-formed-data.net/archives/570/notabilia-visualizing-deletion-discussions-on-wikipedia
10. Tanon, T.P., Kaffee, L.: Property label stability in Wikidata: evolution and convergence of schemas in collaborative knowledge bases. In: Companion of the the Web Conference 2018 on the Web Conference 2018, WWW 2018, Lyon, France, 23–27 April 2018, pp. 1801–1803. ACM (2018). https://doi.org/10.1145/3184558.3191643
11. Vrandecic, D., Krötzsch, M.: Wikidata: a free collaborative knowledgebase. Commun. ACM **57**(10), 78–85 (2014). https://doi.org/10.1145/2629489

Character N-Grams for Detecting Deceptive Controversial Opinions

Javier Sánchez-Junquera[1]([✉]), Luis Villaseñor-Pineda[1,3],
Manuel Montes-y-Gómez[1], and Paolo Rosso[2]

[1] Laboratorio de Tecnologías del Lenguaje, Instituto Nacional de Astrofísica,
Óptica y Electrónica, San Andres Cholula, Mexico
jjsjunquera@gmail.com, {villasen,mmontesg}@inaoep.mx
[2] PRHLT Research Center, Universitat Politècnica de València, Valencia, Spain
prosso@dsic.upv.es
[3] Centre de Recherche en Linguistique Française GRAMMATICA (EA 4521),
Université d'Artois, Arras, France

Abstract. Controversial topics are present in the everyday life, and opinions about them can be either truthful or deceptive. Deceptive opinions are emitted to mislead other people in order to gain some advantage. In the most of the cases humans cannot detect whether the opinion is deceptive or truthful, however, computational approaches have been used successfully for this purpose. In this work, we evaluate a representation based on character n-grams features for detecting deceptive opinions. We consider opinions on the following: abortion, death penalty and personal feelings about the best friend; three domains studied in the state of the art. We found character n-grams effective for detecting deception in these controversial domains, even more than using psycholinguistic features. Our results indicate that this representation is able to capture relevant information about style and content useful for this task. This fact allows us to conclude that the proposed one is a competitive text representation with a good trade-off between simplicity and performance.

Keywords: Deception detection · Controversial opinions
char n-gram

1 Introduction

An opinion is a belief that a person has formed about a topic or issue. It may be about, ideas, laws or experiences, and can be stated with informative purpose or commenting one's own belief about a controversial issue (e.g., politics, health, education, sex, etc.). People need to be provided with significant opinions on current important issues, to form a personal judgment that can impact their future decisions. In order to gain some advantage, there are dishonest opinions whose aim is to mislead thousands of people. Despite the importance of detecting deceptive opinions, psychologists and computational works have proven that it is a very difficult task even for human judges.

© Springer Nature Switzerland AG 2018
P. Bellot et al. (Eds.): CLEF 2018, LNCS 11018, pp. 135–140, 2018.
https://doi.org/10.1007/978-3-319-98932-7_13

Controversial topics are intensively debated in digital media, with opinions expressed in a variety of online forums, newspaper articles, blogs and comments by readers. Even if humans could detect deception effectively, it is inconceivable to manually ensure the authenticity of such opinions.

In previous works, some computational findings are in contrast to psycholinguistic studies of deception. For instance, in [8] the authors observed a lack of negative emotion terms in online hotel reviews, while authors of [2,11] associated negative emotions (e.g. guilt and fear) with interpersonal deception. Thus, cues of deception not only depend on the domain, but also depend on the emotions that a deceiver has about deceiving and its consequences.

Domains of very different nature are, for example, opinion spam and controversial opinions. On hotel reviews, deceivers probably do not have a real opinion about the hotel, so they would be far from having an internal struggle derived from their deception. On the other hand, for a person with an opinion formed about death penalty, to lie about their real point of view is to be against their beliefs, ideals, ethics or religion. In the first case the arguments would be more concrete than in the second, in which the opinion is more philosophical. We presume it is more difficult to detect deception in controversial opinions, [7,8].

Several works have evaluated different text representations for detecting deception in controversial opinions. In [7], some datasets were collected with opinions on abortion, death penalty and personal feelings about the best friend. Using words as features the authors showed that truthful and lying texts are separable. On the same datasets, other approaches have been used with more complex representations such as a combination of words with deep syntactic patterns [4] and with features obtained through Latent Dirichlet Allocation (LDA)[6], both combinations showed good results. Although embeddings are effective in semantically characterizing texts, they do not facilitate the explanation of results, and consequently they have not been popular in this task.

Recently, some character n-grams approaches have been tested for detecting opinion spam. For example, [1,3,5] achieved a very good performance using character n-grams as text representation. Despite several works have employed complex features for the same task in controversial opinions, character n-grams, which are extremely simple features, have not been evaluated in such domains. For these reasons, in this paper we are motivated to evaluate how good character n-grams are in controversial opinions while considering the good precedent performance in opinion spam detection and the great difference between opinion spam and controversial opinions. Our purpose is to observe the suitability of character n-gram features for deception detection in domains very different from opinion spam, rather than to overcome all the baselines in controversial opinions.

2   Text Representation

Character n-grams are sequences of n characters present in the text, which are able to capture lexical and stylistic information. In this work, we evaluate different values for n and ten categories of n-grams with the purpose of finding the most effective ones. These categories are related to three linguistic aspects: morpho-syntax, thematic content and style [10], as illustrated below:

- PREFIX: The first n characters of a word: "is killing".
- SUFFIX: The last n characters of a word: "is killing".
- SPACE_PREFIX: The first $n-1$ characters of a word, beginning with a space : "is killing".
- SPACE_SUFFIX: The last $n-1$ characters of a word ending with a space: "is killing".
- WHOLE_WORD: A whole word with n characters: "not moral".
- MID_WORD: n consecutive characters of a word, without the first and the last: "killing".
- MULTI_WORD: Include a space in the middle of the n-gram: "this person".
- BEG_PUNCT: A character n-gram where the first character is a punctuation: "essay. it would".
- MID_PUNCT: A character n-gram containing a punctuation mark: "essay. it".
- END_PUNCT: A character n-gram where only the last character is a punctuation: "essay.".

3 Experiments

3.1 Datasets Description

For both Abortion and Death Penalty domains, opiners were asked to express both the true opinion and the opposite on the topic, imaging that they were taking part in a debate. In the Best Friend domain, opiners were asked to write about their best friend and describe the detailed reasons for their friendship. Subsequently, they were asked to think about a person they could not tolerate, and describe her/him as if s/he were their best friend [9]. Table 1 shows the statistics of the three used datasets.

Table 1. Statistics for the datasets. Each domain has the information related to the deceptive (D) and truthful (T) classes: number of instances, the instances' vocabulary size, as well as the instances' length in characters and words.

	Instance		Length(ch)		Vocabulary		Length	
Domain	T	D	T	D	T	D	T	D
Abortion	100	100	499	359	64	50	101	73
Best friend	100	100	337	266	51	40	72	57
Death penalty	100	100	463	395	60	54	93	78

3.2 Experimental Setup

Preprocessing: We maintain all the characters present in the texts (e.g., punctuation marks, numbers, delimiters, etc.). The only normalization process was to convert all words to lowercase letter.

Feature Extraction and Selection: We considered char n-grams with n from 3 to 7, and discarded all features with a corpus frequency less than 3.

Classification: We used the Naïve Bayes (NB) and Support Vector Machine (SVM)[1] algorithms with a binary[2] weighting scheme.

Evaluation: We applied a 10-fold cross-validation procedure and used the accuracy as evaluation measure.

---

[1] SVM from *sklearn* with linear kernel, and default parameters.

[2] *tf* and *tf-idf* weighting also were used, but with binary weighting the classifiers achieve better results.

3.3 Results

This section presents the results achieved with character n-grams. We considered n-grams from 3 to 7, but character 5-grams showed slightly better performance taking into account the three datasets. Therefore, the following analyses were carried out with character 5-grams.

Table 2 shows the results obtained with character 5-grams, as well as the results from main related works. Interestingly, this simple representation is able to capture relevant information for detecting deception in controversial opinions. The results achieved with these simple sequences of characters are better than those obtained with a more complex, linguistically-motivated, representation using LIWC [9], which may be due to the fact that character n-grams combine information about style and content more specific to the domain at hand. However, approaches using *deep syntax* and LDA topics better discriminate between deceptive and truthful classes.

Table 2. Comparison of our results with other works on the same corpora. The classifier used by each author is given in the same cell as the accuracy.

Work	Abortion		Best friend		Death penalty	
words [7]	70%	NB	77%	SVM	67.4%	NB
LIWC [9]	73.03%	SVM	75.98%	SVM	60.36%	SVM
Deep syntax + words [4]	77%	SVM	85%	SVM	71%	SVM
LDA+words[6]	87.5%	SVN	87%	SVN	80%	SVN
character 5-grams	74%	NB	80.15%	SVM	63.95%	SVM

Qualitative Analysis. One single character n-gram can capture different things, for example, the 5-gram *count* can represent a prefix in *count*ry and a suffix in ac*count*. With the purpose of analyzing if char n-grams lose information for this phenomena, we divided them into the ten categories described in Sect. 2. Table 3 shows the three categories with the best results in at least one domain. In Abortion all the categories are almost equally important, while in Best Friend and Death Penalty the content and the way in which punctuation marks are used are the most important respectively.

Table 3. Accuracy with each category of character 5-grams using Naïve Bayes. Boldface indicates the highest value for each column.

Type of character 5-gram	Abortion	Best friend	Death Penalty
SPACE_SUFFIX	60%	**79%**	53%
BEG_PUNCT	60%	67%	**62%**
MULTI_WORD	66%	**79%**	60%
character 5-gram	**74%**	**79%**	54%

Table 4. Top 10 highest relevant features in the deceptive class. Each character 5-gram is highlighted in yellow and inserted in a context of each dataset.

<table>
<tr><td colspan="3" align="center">(a) Relevant words</td><td colspan="3" align="center">(b) Relevant character 5-grams</td></tr>
<tr><th>Abortion</th><th>Best Friend</th><th>Death Penalty</th><th>Abortion</th><th>Best Friend</th><th>Death Penalty</th></tr>
<tr><td>god</td><td>does</td><td>having</td><td>is murder</td><td>this person</td><td>convicted of</td></tr>
<tr><td>killing</td><td>this</td><td>him</td><td>is murder</td><td>would never</td><td>killing another</td></tr>
<tr><td>babies</td><td>person</td><td>man</td><td>deserves a</td><td>this person</td><td>man</td></tr>
<tr><td>murder</td><td>his</td><td>practice</td><td>is morally</td><td>this individual</td><td>having</td></tr>
<tr><td>necessary</td><td>guy</td><td>rid</td><td>is killing</td><td>this person</td><td>having</td></tr>
<tr><td>chance</td><td>nice</td><td>lesson</td><td>babies</td><td>he is</td><td>no matter</td></tr>
<tr><td>morally</td><td>how</td><td>around</td><td>killing</td><td>he does</td><td>easy. it would</td></tr>
<tr><td>evil</td><td>never</td><td>they</td><td>way of</td><td>this guy</td><td>no matter</td></tr>
<tr><td>mistake</td><td>trustworthy</td><td>chance</td><td>babies to be</td><td>is a great</td><td>matter what</td></tr>
<tr><td>innocent</td><td>wonderful</td><td>her</td><td>not moral</td><td>of his</td><td>need to</td></tr>
</table>

Another qualitative analysis was carried out to find the most relevant features. This was done evaluating the *mutual information* between features and classes (i.e. deceptive, truthful). Table 4 shows the 10 most representative words and character 5-grams used by deceivers in each topic. We observe that two differences among these representations arise from this table: (i) while one word could be taken as one feature in the word representation, many features are derived from the same word in character 5-grams, which is better for dealing with misspellings; (ii) the same character 5-gram can come from two different but related words, making it possible for two words that are semantically related to be reduced to a single feature, such is the case of *moral* in a*moral* and *morally*.

From the 5-grams given in Table 4b, and their respective contexts, we can draw the following conclusions: (i) deceivers tend to associate abortion with *murder* or *killing*, (ii) tend to distance themselves from their "best friend" (*this person/guy/individual*), and (iii) affirm their fake beliefs denying the importance of other factors. Additionally, we also noticed that in the Best Friend domain, deceivers tend to use expressions with *he is/does*, while non-deceivers use plural first person pronouns to talk about activities they do together; in truthful opinions is more common expressions that emphasize that what they say is what they really believe (e.g. *I believe that abortion is...; My honest opinion about...*); finally, non-deceivers tend to offer more detailed opinions.

4   Conclusions and Future Work

In this paper we addressed the problem of deceptive detection in controversial opinions using character n-grams as features. These features have not been studied in controversial opinions, although their simplicity and good results in opinion spam detection. Our experiments reported encouraging accuracies, between 63.95% and 80.15%, which suggest that character n-grams are effective for detecting deception in controversial domains, even better than using more complex representations based on linguistic features from LIWC. Character n-grams were able to capture shallow stylistic and thematic patterns not only useful for the classification, but also for helping humans to analyze deceptive behaviors. According to their simplicity and performance, character n-grams are almost as satisfactory as more sophisticated representations. However, it seems that within our best results reported with character n-grams in these controversial domains, deep syntax and topic modeling must be considered in order to achieve high levels of accuracy.

In the future, we plan to analyze the relevant features obtained in all the domains and use them in cross-domain scenarios.

Acknowledgments. We would like to thank CONACyT for partially supporting this work under grants 613411, CB-2015-01-257383, and FC-2016/2410. The work of the last author was partially funded by the Spanish MINECO under the research project SomEMBED (TIN2015-71147-C2-1-P).

References

1. Aritsugi, M., et al.: Combining word and character n-grams for detecting deceptive opinions, vol. 1, pp. 828–833. IEEE (2017)
2. Buller, D.B., Burgoon, J.K.: Interpersonal deception theory. Commun. Theory **6**(3), 203–242 (1996)
3. Cagnina, L.C., Rosso, P.: Detecting deceptive opinions: intra and cross-domain classification using an efficient representation. Int. J. Uncertainty Fuzziness Knowl. Based Syst. **25**(Suppl. 2), 151–174 (2017)
4. Feng, S., Banerjee, R., Choi, Y.: Syntactic stylometry for deception detection, pp. 171–175. Association for Computational Linguistics (2012)
5. Fusilier, D.H., Montes-y-Gómez, M., Rosso, P., Cabrera, R.G.: Detection of opinion spam with character n-grams. In: Gelbukh, A. (ed.) CICLing 2015. LNCS, vol. 9042, pp. 285–294. Springer, Cham (2015). https://doi.org/10.1007/978-3-319-18117-2_21
6. Hernández-Castañeda, Á., Calvo, H., Gelbukh, A., Flores, J.J.G.: Cross-domain deception detection using support vector networks. Soft Comput. **21**(3), 1–11 (2016)
7. Mihalcea, R., Strapparava, C.: The lie detector: explorations in the automatic recognition of deceptive language. In: Proceedings of the ACL-IJCNLP 2009 Conference Short Papers, pp. 309–312. Association for Computational Linguistics (2009)
8. Ott, M., Choi, Y., Cardie, C., Hancock, J.T.: Finding deceptive opinion spam by any stretch of the imagination. In: Proceedings of the 49th Annual Meeting of the Association for Computational Linguistics: Human Language Technologies-Volume 1, pp. 309–319. Association for Computational Linguistics (2011)
9. Pérez-Rosas, V., Mihalcea, R.: Cross-cultural deception detection. In: Proceedings of the 52nd Annual Meeting of the Association for Computational Linguistics (Volume 2: Short Papers), vol. 2, pp. 440–445 (2014)
10. Sapkota, U., Solorio, T., Montes-y-Gómez, M., Bethard, S.: Not all character n-grams are created equal: a study in authorship attribution. In: Proceedings of the 2015 Conference of the North American Chapter of the Association for Computational Linguistics: Human Language Technologies, pp. 93–102 (2015)
11. Vrij, A.: Detecting Lies and Deceit: Pitfalls and Opportunities. Wiley, Hoboken (2008)

Best of CLEF 2017 Labs

Simply the Best: Minimalist System Trumps Complex Models in Author Profiling

Angelo Basile[1,3], Gareth Dwyer[3], Maria Medvedeva[3], Josine Rawee[2,3], Hessel Haagsma[3], and Malvina Nissim[3]✉

[1] Faculty of ICT, University of Malta, Msida, Malta
angelo.basile.17@um.edu.mt
[2] Center for Mind/Brain Sciences, University of Trento, Rovereto, Italy
josinenelleke.rawee@studenti.unitn.it
[3] Center for Language and Cognition,
University of Groningen, Groningen, The Netherlands
garethdwyer@gmail.com, {m.medvedeva,hessel.haagsma,m.nissim}@rug.nl

Abstract. A simple linear SVM with word and character n-gram features and minimal parameter tuning can identify the gender and the language variety (for English, Spanish, Arabic and Portuguese) of Twitter users with very high accuracy. All our attempts at improving performance by including more data, smarter features, and employing more complex architectures plainly fail. In addition, we experiment with joint and multitask modelling, but find that they are clearly outperformed by single task models. Eventually, our simplest model was submitted to the PAN 2017 shared task on author profiling, obtaining an average accuracy of 0.86 on the test set, with performance on sub-tasks ranging from 0.68 to 0.98. These were the best results achieved at the competition overall. To allow lay people to easily use and see the value of machine learning for author profiling, we also built a web application on top our models.

Keywords: Author profiling · Linear models · Gender prediction
Language variety identification · Multitask learning

1 Introduction and Background

Profiling authors, that is, inferring personal characteristics from text, can reveal many things, such as their age, gender, personality traits, and/or location, even though writers might not consciously choose to put indicators of those characteristics in the text. The uses for this are obvious, for cases like targeted advertising and security, but it is also interesting from a linguistic standpoint. With the rise of social media, more and more people acquire some kind of on-line presence or persona, mostly made up of images and text. This means that these people can be considered authors, and thus that we can profile them as such.

© Springer Nature Switzerland AG 2018
P. Bellot et al. (Eds.): CLEF 2018, LNCS 11018, pp. 143–156, 2018.
https://doi.org/10.1007/978-3-319-98932-7_14

In this contribution we explore two specific author traits, namely gender and native language variety of Twitter users, across four languages. In addition to experimenting with a variety of features and algorithms for developing systems geared to optimal performance, we specifically investigate the benefits of modelling these two different axes *separately* or *jointly*.

Previous work has shown that the very same features could be reliable clues for classification. Indeed, for both profiling authors on Twitter as well as for discriminating between similar languages, word and character n-grams have proved to be the strongest predictors of gender as well as language varieties. For language variety discrimination, the systems that performed best at the Discriminating between Similar Languages (DSL) shared task in 2016 (on test set B, i.e. social media) used word/character n-grams, independently of the algorithm [12]. The crucial contribution of these features was also observed by [3,17], who participated in the 2017 DSL shared task with the two best performing systems. For author profiling, it has been shown that tf-idf weighted n-gram features, both in terms of characters and words, are very successful in capturing especially gender distinctions [25].

If different aspects, such as language variety and gender of a Twitter user, might be captured by the same features, can both tasks be modelled with the same approach? Also, if these are distinct but somewhat similar aspects, to what extent is it beneficial to model them together? We investigate such questions by building models that address the tasks separately but rely on the same set of features, and also explore the feasibility of modelling both tasks at the same time.

We built two simple SVM models based on n-gram features, using identical settings for both gender and language variety prediction (Sect. 3). Over such settings, we experimented with a variety of enhancements to our models which however turned out to be detrimental to performance. These include manipulating the data itself (adding more, and changing preprocessing) and using a large variety of features (Sect. 4.1), as well as changing strategies in modelling the problem. Specifically, we used different algorithms and paradigms, and tried to learn the two tasks jointly via Multitask Learning (Sect. 4.2).

We observe that simple models outperform complex models under all settings, confirming the predictive power of word and character n-grams for author profiling. The best model described in this paper (Sect. 3) was submitted as an official participation to the PAN 2017 shared task on author profiling (22 participants), and achieved best results overall. The system is also made available to the general public via a simple web interface.

2   Data

We use data from the 2017 shared task on author profiling [24], organised within the PAN framework [21]. Data is provided in four languages: English, Spanish,

Arabic, and Portuguese, for a total of 11400 sets of tweets, each set representing a single author.[1]

Gender is provided as a binary label (male/female), whereas language variety differs per language, from 2 varieties for Portuguese (Brazil and Portugal) to 7 varieties for Spanish (Argentina, Chile, Colombia, Mexico, Peru, Spain, Venezuela). For each variety in each language the dataset consists of 1,000 authors, with 100 tweets each. This means that there is more data overall for the languages with the most varieties. Of these 1,000 authors per variety, 500 are male and 500 are female. The test set of each *gender × variety* subset contains 200 authors and the training set 300.

In order to better understand the data and gain some insights that could help the feature engineering process, we used two visualisations, one for each task. For the variety label we trained a decision tree classifier using word unigrams for English. Although the performance is poor (accuracy score of 0.63) it allowed us to see which feature values where the most distinctive (i.e. the first splits of the decision tree). We find that the most important indicators of language variety are simply geographical names: "NZ","Dublin", "Australia", etc.

For gender, we used the Scattertext tool [9] to compare the most frequent words used by males and females in the English dataset. This revealed several interesting things about the gendered use of language. The words used often by males and very seldom by females are sport-related, and include words such as "league", and "chelsea". Conversely, tokens used frequently by females and infrequently by males include several emojis, e.g. "😫", "😊", as well as words like "kitten", "mom", "sister" and "chocolate". This kind of stereotypical usage was also observed by [26].

We also found distinctive words include both time-specific ones, like "gilmore" and "imacelebrityau", and general words from everyday life, which are less likely to be subject to time-specific trends, like "player", and "chocolate". Although time-specific words are highly useful as features within this experimental setup, where training and evaluation data are from the same time periods, the usage of such features might hamper the predictive capability on unseen future data.

3   Basic Models

Previous work suggests that character and word n-grams as features of an SVM system are excellent at capturing both gender and language variety [12,24]. Using the scikit-learn LinearSVM implementation [20], we built a simple SVM system that uses character 3- to 5-grams and word 1- to 2-grams. We employ tf-idf weighting with sublinear term frequency scaling, where instead of the standard term frequency we use: $1 + \log(tf)$.

To optimise parameters, we ran an extensive grid search over both tasks and all languages on a 64-core machine with 1 TB RAM (see Table 1 for the

---

[1] This is the training set released at PAN 2017. An additional test set was available for testing models during the campaign, but not anymore at the time of writing.

list of values over which the grid search was performed). The full search took about a day to complete. In particular, using min_df = 2 (i.e. excluding all terms that are used by only one author) seems to have a strong positive effect and greatly reduces the feature size as there are many words that appear only once. Having different optimal parameters for different languages provided only a slight performance boost for each language. We decided that this increase was too small to be significant, so we used the same parameter values for all languages and both tasks. Similarly, after experimenting with different tokenisation techniques for the different languages, we decided to use the default scikit-learn tokeniser for all languages as average results did not improve. Table 2 shows the results of this base system. All reported results are on the PAN 2017 training data using five-fold cross-validation, unless otherwise specified.

Table 1. The list of parameter values included in the grid search. The optimal values that we use then in our system are in **bold**.

Name	Values	Description
lowercase	**True**, False	Lowercase all words
max_df	1, **100**, None	Exclude terms appearing in more than $n\%$ documents
min_df	1, **2**, 3	Exclude terms appearing in fewer than n documents
use_idf	**True**, False	Use Inverse Document Frequency weighting
sublinear_tf	**True**, False	Replace term frequency (tf) with $1 + log(tf)$
C	0.1, 0.5, **1**, 1.5, 5	Penalty parameter for the SVM

Table 2. Accuracy of the base system using 5-fold cross-validation on the PAN 2017 training set. "Joint": single models predict gender and language variety, and the joint accuracy is inferred afterwards for global evaluation. "Merged": one models predicts the merged labels directly.

Language	Gender	Variety	Joint	Merged
Arabic	0.800	0.831	0.683	0.630
English	0.823	0.898	0.742	0.645
Spanish	0.832	0.962	0.803	0.686
Portuguese	0.845	0.981	0.828	0.792

Aside from evaluating the performance of the classifier on the two separate tasks, we also evaluated its global performance over the correct prediction of both labels at the same time. For example, for a female American user, predicting female British would lead to a correct gender prediction, a wrong prediction for variety, and therefore also a wrong prediction of the profile as a whole. Results for this joint evaluation are shown in Table 2, under the "Joint" column.

With an eye to the performance on the whole profile, we also trained our system to predict both language variety and the gender of each user simultaneously, instead of predicting each task separately, by simply merging the two labels. As expected, since the task is harder, the performance goes down when compared to a model trained independently on each task. In other words: the derived joint prediction is better than the joint prediction learnt directly from the merged labels (see Table 2).

4 Variations

4.1 Data and Features

As potential improvements over the base models, we experimented with more training data, and by including more features.

Adding Previous PAN Data. We extended the training dataset by adding data and gender labels from the PAN 16 Author Profiling shared task [25], based on the expectation that having a larger amount of training data might yield better performance. To confirm this, we attempted to train on English data from PAN 17 and predict gender labels for the English data from PAN 16, as well as vice versa. Training on the PAN 16 data resulted in an accuracy score of 0.754 for the PAN 17 task, and training on PAN 17 gave an accuracy score of 0.700 for PAN 16, both scores significantly lower than cross-validated results.

One possible explanation for this is that our unigram model captures aspects that are tied specifically to the PAN 17 dataset, because it contains topics that may not be present in datasets that were collected in a different time period. This is in line with previous findings, as [16] show that simple author profiling models tend to generalise poorly to datasets from different genres or time periods.

Using the Twitter 14k Dataset. We attempted to classify the English tweets by Gender using only the data collected by [1]. This dataset consists of aggregated word counts by gender for about 14,000 Twitter users and 9 million Tweets. We used this data to calculate whether each word in our dataset was a 'male' word (used more by males), or a 'female' word, and classified users as male or female based on a majority count of the words they used. Using this method we achieved 0.712 accuracy for the English gender data, showing that this simple method can provide a reasonable baseline to the gender task.

PoS Tags. We added PS-tags to the English tweets using the $spaCy^2$ tagger, and experimented with a model that included both regular unigrams and part-of-speech information. The results of both models are shown in Table 3. Compared

---

[2] https://spacy.io/.

to the model using only unigrams performance dropped slightly for gender and a bit more for variety. It is not clear whether the missed increase in performance is due to the fact that the PoS tagger does not perform well on Twitter data (the PoS tagger is not Twitter specific) or to the fact that our classifier does not perform well with PoS tags.

Table 3. Accuracy scores on gender and variety classification of only an only unigram model with and without part-of-speech tags on the PAN 17 English training data using 5-fold cross-validation

	Gender	Variety
Unigrams	0.826	0.895
Unigrams + Part-of-Speech	0.818	0.853

Emojis (😃😁😆😄😁😆😊😈😉 😊)

In April 2015, SwiftKey did an extensive report[3] on emoji use by country. They discovered that emoji use varies across languages and across language varieties. For example, they found that Australians use double the average amount of alcohol-themed emoji and use more junk food and holiday emoji than anywhere else in the world.

We tried to leverage these findings but the results were disappointing. We used a list of emojis[4] as a vocabulary for the td/idf vectorizer. Encouraged by the data in the SwiftKey report, we tried first to use emojis as the only vocabulary for predicting gender. The results on the Spanish training set using 5-fold cross validation are surprisingly high (0.67 accuracy) and clearly higher than a random baseline, but fall clearly short of the score of the simple unigram model (0.79 accuracy). Adding emojis as extra features to the unigram model did not yield any improvement.

Excluding Specific Word Patterns. We looked at accuracy scores for the English gender and variety data more closely. We tried different representations of the tweet texts, to see what kind of words were most predictive of variety and gender. Specifically, we look at using only words that start with an uppercase letter, only words that start with a lowercase letter, only Twitter handles (words that start with an "@") and all the text excluding the handles. Results are presented in Table 4.

It is interesting that the accuracies are so high although we are using only a basic unigram model, without looking at the character n-grams that we include in our final model. Representing each text only by the Twitter handles used in

---

[3] https://blog.swiftkey.com/americans-love-skulls-brazilians-love-cats-swiftkey-emoji-meanings-report/.

[4] http://www.unicode.org/emoji/charts/full-emoji-list.html.

that text results in 0.77 accuracy for variety, probably because users tend to interact with other users who are in the same geographic area. However, excluding handles from the texts barely decreases performance for the variety task, showing that while the handles can be discriminative, they are not necessary for this task. It is also interesting to note that for this dataset, looking only at words beginning with an uppercase character results in nearly the same score for the gender task as we get when using all of the available text, while using only lowercase words decreases performance. The opposite is true for the variety task, where using lowercase-only words results in as good performance as using all the text, but using only uppercase words decreases accuracy by over 10%.

Table 4. Accuracy scores on gender and variety prediction using 5-fold cross-validation with the base system on the English training data, with and without the exclusion of specific groups of words.

	Gender	Variety
All text	0.816	0.876
Handles only	0.661	0.769
Exclude handles	0.814	0.869
Uppercase only	0.802	0.767
Lowercase only	0.776	0.877

Place Names and Twitter Handles. We tried enriching the data to improve the unigram model. For each of the language varieties, we obtained 100 geographical location names, representing the cities with the most inhabitants. When this location was mentioned in the tweet, the language variety the location was part of was added to the tweet.

We attempted to use Twitter handles in a similar manner. The 100 most-followed Twitter users per language variety were found and the language variety was added to the text when one of its popular Twitter users was mentioned.

Unfortunately, these methods did not improve our model's performance. We suspect that the information is already captured by the word n-grams, so encoding this information explicitly does not improve performance.

GronUP Combinations. We have tried the partial setup of last year's winning system, GronUP [5], with the distinction that we had to classify language variety instead of age groups. We have excluded the features that are language-dependent (i.e. PoS-tagging and misspelling/typos), and experimented with various feature combinations of the rest while keeping word and character n-grams the same. We achieved average accuracy scores ranging from 0.810 to 0.830, which is clearly lower than our simple final model, which achieved an average accuracy score of 0.872 using 5 fold cross validation of the training data.

4.2 Different Approaches

As an alternative to adding data and features, we tried to improve the performance of our base system employing different algorithms and modelling strategies.

FastText. We experimented with Facebook's FastText system, which is an out-of-the-box supervised learning classifier [8]. We used only the data for the English gender task, trying both tweet-level and author-level classification. We pre-processed all text with the NLTK Tweet Tokenizer and used the classification-example script provided with the FastText code base.

Training on 3,000 authors and testing on 600 authors gave an accuracy score of 0.64, compared to average English gender performance of SVM of 0.823. Changing the FastText parameters such as number of epochs, word n-grams, and learning rate showed no improvement. We achieved an accuracy of 0.79 when we attempted to classify on a per-tweet basis (300,000 tweets for training and 85,071 for test), but this is an easier task as some authors are split over the training and test sets. There are various ways to summarise per-tweet predictions into author-predictions, but we did not experiment further as the SVM system clearly worked better for the amount of data we have.

Multi-task Learning. Multi-task learning (MTL, [6]) has proven successful in a variety of NLP tasks [4,7,10,15], including author profiling [2]. Usually, one main task is learned while one or more auxiliary tasks are learned at the same time in order to provide some additional signal, and reduce overfitting.

We used MTL to investigate whether learning the two tasks at the same time would be beneficial. Practically, we used the *DyNet* framework [19] to build a neural network that learns both tasks simultaneously, defining gender as the main task, and language variety as the auxiliary task. The reason for this choice is the observation that, while language variety is predicted by the SVM with high accuracy, performance on gender is lower, suggesting that it could benefit from an additional signal.

We compute two different losses, one per task, and back-propagate their sum to train the model. Our network structure consists of an embedding layer, two Bi-LSTM layers, and two multi-layer perceptrons on top, one for each task. The hidden layers are shared. We trained the network for 20 iterations, using a constant learning rate. For these experiments, the only pre-processing that we applied consisted of lower-casing all the words.

The final accuracy of the MTL model is 48.3%, thus below the baseline. Due to resource constraints, we did not perform proper tuning of the hyper-parameters of the network, which can be a reason for the low performance. For the moment, to better understand and contextualise these results, we trained the same network two more times, one per task, thus treating them separately again, and using a single loss. The rationale behind this is to verify whether it is the architecture itself that is not learning the two problems well, or whether the poor performance derives mainly by treating them jointly.

Accuracy is 70.2% for the language variety model, and 51.4% for the gender model. The models are slightly better than chance at predicting gender, while for variety there seems to be some signal that could potentially be amplified with more training data and/or hyper-parameter tuning. With the current settings, results are still far below what we achieved with our n-gram based SVM. As such, it is likely that the low MTL performance is due to the chosen network architecture, and not necessarily due to the joint learning of the two tasks.

5   The System in Practice

5.1   Participation in the PAN 2017 Shared Task

N-GrAM (New Groningen Author-profiling Model), our best system as described in Sect. 3, was submitted as official participant to the PAN 2017 evaluation campaign on author profiling. Overall, N-GrAM came first in the shared task, with a score of 0.8253 for gender 0.9184 for variety, a joint score of 0.8361 and an average score of 0.8599 (final rankings were taken from this average score) on the official PAN 2017 test set [24]. For the global scores, all languages are combined.

Table 5. Results (accuracy) on the test set for variety, gender and their joint prediction.

Task	System	Arabic	English	Portuguese	Spanish	Average	+ 2nd
Gender	N-GrAM	**0.8006**	**0.8233**	**0.8450**	**0.8321**	**0.8253**	0.0029
	LDR	0.7044	0.7220	0.7863	0.7171	0.7325	
Variety	N-GrAM	**0.8313**	0.8988	0.9813	0.9621	0.9184	0.0013
	LDR	0.8250	**0.8996**	**0.9875**	**0.9625**	**0.9187**	
Joint	N-GrAM	**0.6831**	**0.7429**	**0.8288**	**0.8036**	**0.7646**	0.0101
	LDR	0.5888	0.6357	0.7763	0.6943	0.6738	

We present finer-grained scores showing the breakdown per language in Table 5. We compare our gender and variety accuracies against the LDR-baseline [23], a low dimensional representation especially tailored to language variety identification, provided by the organisers. The final column, + 2nd shows the difference between N-GrAM and the score achieved by the second-highest ranked system (excluding the baseline).

Results are broken down per language, and are summarised as both *joint* and *average* scores. The joint score is the percentage of texts for which both gender and variety were predicted correctly at the same time, while still running single models. The average is calculated as the mean over all languages.

N-GrAM ranked first in all cases except for the language variety task. In this case, the baseline was the top-ranked system, and ours was second by a minimal margin. Our system significantly out-performed the baseline on the joint evaluation, as the baseline scored significantly lower for the gender task than for the variety task. These scores are highly similar to the scores on the cross-validated training set that were described in Table 2.

N-GrAM Compared to Other Systems. Although we have tried a large amount of different approaches to the task, everything boiled down to a simple Linear SVM system with n-gram features and slightly adapted tf-idf parameters.

When looking at the other participating systems at the PAN 2017 shared task, it appears we were not alone [24]. Out of the top-ranked seven teams (including us), six used Logistic Regression [14,22] or SVMs [11,13,27] and only one used Neural Attention Networks [18]. Interestingly, the latter system performed much better than any other system when predicting Portuguese gender, but was beaten by linear classifiers in other subtasks.

Although many participants have experimented with various preprocessing methods and normalisation, such as removing Twitter handles, URLs and lower-casing, as well as tried to take advantage of emojis, the majority of the systems have also used n-grams as the main set of features and the difference in scores often came down to small alternation within n-gram length.

5.2   Online System Demonstration

We worked with a group of software engineers to make author profiling and author identification more accessible, even outside an academic context. Under our direction, these engineers built a web application through which anyone can easily submit text and see instant author profiling results, with no need for any technical or academic experience.

The web application encompasses author attribution as well as author profiling. The author profiling follows the PAN 2016 settings [25], attempting to predict gender and age instead of gender and variety. Nonetheless, the model used for gender identification is built on N-GrAM.

Users of the web application do not require any software except a standard web browser. On visiting the page, they see a brief description of what author profiling is. After navigating to the author profiling page, they can choose to paste text into a box, upload a plain text file, or load an example. After submitting text through any of the three options, they see some visualisations which depict the predicted gender and age of the text's author. The submission screen of the web application can be seen in Fig. 1 and the full application can be used online.[5]

We believe that taking research such as ours, which is all-too-often presented only in academic papers and code repositories, and making it available to and accessible by members of the public who are not necessarily academics or programmers, is highly important. Not only does it help solve a disconnect between active areas of research and the public perception of research, but it furthermore

---

[5] https://aabeta.herokuapp.com.

Profiling

The Author Profiling System will, given a text, try to predict its author's age and gender.

Profiling text

Place here the text of which the author is unknown. The text can either be pasted directly, or one file can be uploaded.

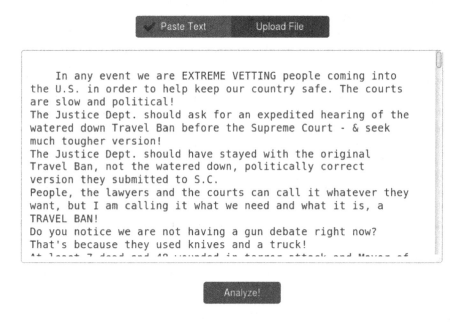

Fig. 1. Example page from the author analysis web application.

moves towards a goal of ensuring that a gap does not develop between those who understand and can use machine learning and those who cannot. This is part of a larger conversation which is well summarised in a feature released by Microsoft, titled *Democratizing AI.*[6]

---

[6] https://news.microsoft.com/features/democratizing-ai/.

6   Conclusion

For the author profiling task at hand, a seemingly simple system using word and character n-grams and an SVM classifier proves very hard to beat. Indeed, our simple system, N-GrAM, turned out to be the best-performing out of the 22 systems submitted in the PAN 2017 shared task. Using additional training data, 'smart' features, and hand-crafted resources hurt rather than helped performance. A possible lesson to take from this would be that manually crafting features serves only to hinder a machine learning algorithm's ability to find patterns in a dataset, and perhaps it is better to focus one's efforts on parameter optimisation instead of feature engineering.

Our preliminary experiments, including a setting that has proved beneficial for a variety of language processing tasks, namely multitask learning, do not however show the superiority of neural models compared to the SVM that one might have expected. Nevertheless, we believe that this is too strong a conclusion to draw from this limited study, since several factors specific to this setting need to be taken into account. We expect that while an SVM is the best choice for the given amount of training data, with more training data, and proper parameter optimisation, a neural network-based approach might achieve better results.

Regarding the frustrating lack of benefit from more advanced features than n-grams, a possible explanation comes from a closer inspection of the data. Both the decision tree model and the Scattertext visualisation give us an insight in the most discriminating features in the dataset. In the case of language variety, we see that place names can be informative features, and could therefore be used as a proxy for geographical location, which in turn serves as a proxy for language variety. Adding place names explicitly to our model did not yield performance improvements, which we take to indicate that this information is already captured by n-gram features.

In the case of gender, many useful features are ones that are highly specific to the Twitter platform (*#iconnecthearts*), time (*cruz*), and topics (*pbsnewshour*) in this dataset, which have been shown not to carry over well to other datasets [16], but provide high accuracy in this case. Conversely, features designed to capture gender in a more general sense do not yield any benefit over the more specific features, although they would likely be useful for a robust, cross-dataset system and should definitely be further investigated.

Acknowledgements. We are grateful to the organisers of PAN 2017 for making the data available. We also would like to thank Barbara Plank for her advice on the MTL architecture and the anonymous reviewers for providing valuable insights.

References

1. Bamman, D., Eisenstein, J., Schnoebelen, T.: Gender identity and lexical variation in social media. J. Socioling. **18**(2), 135–160 (2014)
2. Benton, A., Mitchell, M., Hovy, D.: Multitask learning for mental health conditions with limited social media data. In: Proceedings of the 15th Conference of the European Chapter of the Association for Computational Linguistics: Volume 1, Long Papers, vol. 1, pp. 152–162 (2017)
3. Bestgen, Y.: Improving the character NGRAM model for the DSL task with BM25 weighting and less frequently used feature sets. In: Proceedings of the VarDial Workshop (2017)
4. Bordes, A., Glorot, X., Weston, J., Bengio, Y.: Joint learning of words and meaning representations for open-text semantic parsing. In: AISTATS, vol. 351, pp. 423–424 (2012)
5. Busger op Vollenbroek, M., et al.: GronUP: Groningen user profiling. In: Working Notes of CLEF, CEUR Workshop Proceedings, pp. 846–857. CEUR-WS.org (2016)
6. Caruana, R.: Multitask learning. Mach. Learn. **28**, 41–75 (1997)
7. Collobert, R., Weston, J., Bottou, L., Karlen, M., Kavukcuoglu, K., Kuksa, P.: Natural language processing (almost) from scratch. J. Mach. Learn. Res. **12**(Aug), 2493–2537 (2011)
8. Joulin, A., Grave, E., Bojanowski, P., Mikolov, T.: Bag of tricks for efficient text classification. arXiv preprint arXiv:1607.01759 (2016)
9. Kessler, J.S.: Scattertext: a browser-based tool for visualizing how corpora differ. In: Proceedings of the 54th Annual Meeting of the Association for Computational Linguistics (ACL): System Demonstrations. Association for Computational Linguistics, Vancouver (2017)
10. Liu, X., Gao, J., He, X., Deng, L., Duh, K., Wang, Y.Y.: Representation learning using multi-task deep neural networks for semantic classification and information retrieval. In: Proceedings of NAACL (2015)
11. López-Monroy, A.P., Montes-y Gómez, M., Escalante, H.J., Villaseñor-Pineda, L., Solorio, T.: Social-media users can be profiled by their similarity with other users. In: Working Notes of CLEF, CEUR Workshop Proceedings. CEUR-WS.org (2017)
12. Malmasi, S., Zampieri, M., Ljubešić, N., Nakov, P., Ali, A., Tiedemann, J.: Discriminating between similar languages and Arabic dialect identification: a report on the third DSL shared task. In: Proceedings of the Third Workshop on NLP for Similar Languages, Varieties and Dialects (VarDial3), pp. 1–14. The COLING 2016 Organizing Committee, Osaka, December 2016
13. Markov, I., Gómez-Adorno, H., Sidorov, G.: Language-and subtask-dependent feature selection and classifier parameter tuning for author profiling. In: Working Notes of CLEF, CEUR Workshop Proceedings. CEUR-WS.org (2017)
14. Martinc, M., Škrjanec, I., Zupan, K., Pollak, S.: Pan 2017: author profiling - gender and language variety prediction. In: Working Notes of CLEF, CEUR Workshop Proceedings. CEUR-WS.org (2017)
15. Martínez Alonso, H., Plank, B.: When is multitask learning effective? Semantic sequence prediction under varying data conditions. In: Proceedings of the 15th Conference of the European Chapter of the Association for Computational Linguistics: Volume 1, Long Papers, pp. 44–53. Association for Computational Linguistics, Valencia, April 2017. http://www.aclweb.org/anthology/E17-1005

16. Medvedeva, M., Haagsma, H., Nissim, M.: An analysis of cross-genre and in-genre performance for author profiling in social media. In: Jones, G.J.F., et al. (eds.) CLEF 2017. LNCS, vol. 10456, pp. 211–223. Springer, Cham (2017). https://doi.org/10.1007/978-3-319-65813-1_21

17. Medvedeva, M., Kroon, M., Plank, B.: When sparse traditional models outperform dense neural networks: the curious case of discriminating between similar languages. In: Proceedings of the Fourth Workshop on NLP for Similar Languages, Varieties and Dialects, pp. 156–163. Association for Computational Linguistics (2017)

18. Miura, Y., Taniguchi, T., Taniguchi, M., Ohkuma, T.: Author profiling with word+character neural attention network. In: Working Notes of CLEF, CEUR Workshop Proceedings. CEUR-WS.org (2017)

19. Neubig, G., et al.: DyNet: the dynamic neural network toolkit. arXiv preprint arXiv:1701.03980 (2017)

20. Pedregosa, F., et al.: Scikit-learn: machine learning in Python. J. Mach. Learn. Res. **12**, 2825–2830 (2011)

21. Potthast, M., Rangel, F., Tschuggnall, M., Stamatatos, E., Rosso, P., Stein, B.: Overview of PAN 2017. In: Jones, G.J.H., et al. (eds.) CLEF 2017. LNCS, vol. 10456, pp. 275–290. Springer, Cham (2017). https://doi.org/10.1007/978-3-319-65813-1_25

22. Poulston, A., Waseem, Z., Stevenson, M.: Using TF-IDF n-gram and word embedding cluster ensembles for author profiling. In: Working Notes of CLEF, CEUR Workshop Proceedings. CEUR-WS.org (2017)

23. Rangel, F., Franco-Salvador, M., Rosso, P.: A low dimensionality representation for language variety identification. arXiv preprint arXiv:1705.10754 (2017)

24. Rangel, F., Rosso, P., Potthast, M., Stein, B.: Overview of the 5th author profiling task at PAN 2017: gender and language variety identification in Twitter. In: Cappellato, L., Ferro, N., Goeuriot, L., Mandl, T. (eds.) Working Notes Papers of the CLEF 2017 Evaluation Labs, CEUR Workshop Proceedings. CLEF and CEUR-WS.org (2017)

25. Rangel, F., Rosso, P., Verhoeven, B., Potthast, W.D.M., Stein, B.: Overview of the 4th author profiling task at PAN 2016: cross-genre evaluations. In: Working Notes of CLEF, pp. 750–784 (2016)

26. Schwartz, H.A., et al.: Personality, gender, and age in the language of social media: the open-vocabulary approach. PLoS one **8**(9), e73791 (2013)

27. Tellez, E.S., Miranda-Jiménez, S., Graff, M., Moctezuma, D.: Gender and language variety identification with MicroTC. In: Working Notes of CLEF, CEUR Workshop Proceedings. CEUR-WS.org (2017)

Textured Graph-Based Model of the Lungs: Application on Tuberculosis Type Classification and Multi-drug Resistance Detection

Yashin Dicente Cid[1,2(✉)], Kayhan Batmanghelich[3], and Henning Müller[1,2]

[1] University of Applied Sciences Western Switzerland (HES-SO), Sierre, Switzerland
yashin.dicente@hevs.ch
[2] University of Geneva, Geneva, Switzerland
[3] University of Pittsburgh, Pittsburgh, USA

Abstract. Tuberculosis (TB) remains a leading cause of death worldwide. Two main challenges when assessing computed tomography scans of TB patients are detecting multi-drug resistance and differentiating TB types. In this article we model the lungs as a graph entity where nodes represent anatomical lung regions and edges encode interactions between them. This graph is able to characterize the texture distribution along the lungs, making it suitable for describing patients with different TB types. In 2017, the ImageCLEF benchmark proposed a task based on computed tomography volumes of patients with TB. This task was divided into two subtasks: multi-drug resistance prediction, and TB type classification. The participation in this task showed the strength of our model, leading to best results in the competition for multi-drug resistance detection (AUC = 0.5825) and good results in the TB type classification (Cohen's Kappa coefficient = 0.1623).

Keywords: Lung graph model · 3D texture analysis · Tuberculosis

1 Introduction

Tuberculosis (TB) is an infectious disease that remains a persistent threat and a leading cause of death worldwide. An important task is to detect when the TB organisms become resistant to standard drugs. The multi-drug resistant (MDR) form of the disease is a difficult and expensive form to recover from. The gold-standard methods for MDR detection are expensive and may take up to several months [1]. Therefore, there is a need for quick and cheap methods of MDR detection. The identification of TB types (TBT) is another important task, as different types of TB may require different treatments. Several visual patterns can be seen in a Computed Tomography (CT) volume of a patient with TB in the lungs, some of them characteristic of a specific TB type. However, the final classification of the disease requires additional analyses, besides the

© Springer Nature Switzerland AG 2018
P. Bellot et al. (Eds.): CLEF 2018, LNCS 11018, pp. 157–168, 2018.
https://doi.org/10.1007/978-3-319-98932-7_15

CT images [2]. An automatic image analysis system that can identify holistic patterns of lungs with TB, not evident through simple visual assessment of CT images, can be very useful for radiologists.

Graph modeling is a complete framework that was previously proposed for brain connectivity analysis but has rarely been applied to other organs [3]. Graph methods divide the brain into fixed anatomical regions and compare neural activations between regions [4]. In [5], we presented a basic graph model of the lungs capable of differentiating between pulmonary hypertension and pulmonary embolism. Both diseases present similar visual defects in lung CT scans. However, they differ in their distribution throughout the lung. The graph was based on dividing the lung into several regions and using these regions as nodes of a graph. The regions were described using Hounsfield Unit (HU) distributions, extracted from Dual Energy CT (DECT) scans. Preliminary results showed that a single CT did not contain enough information about the HU distribution to differentiate between the diseases and a more advanced description of the regions was needed.

In this article, we present a more complex version of the graph model to characterize the lungs. The new model describes each region of the lung using state-of-the-art 3D texture descriptors. Our hypothesis is that a holistic analysis of the relations between regional texture features is able to encode subtle differences between patients with separate TB types and to assist in an early detection of drug resistance patients. We tested our texture-based graph model of the lungs in the ImageCLEF 2017 TB challenge, where it was compared against 8 other methods, obtaining the best results in the MDR detection task. The following section contains a brief overview of the subtasks and dataset of the ImageCLEF 2017 TB task. More detailed information on the task can be found in the overview article [6]. Section 3 explains the process of building the texture graph model of the lungs and all the variations tested for this task in detail. The results obtained by this approach in the task are shown in Sect. 4. Finally, Sect. 5 concludes with lessons learned working on the data with our approach.

2   ImageCLEF Challenge

The ImageCLEF (Image retrieval and image analysis evaluation campaign of the Cross-Language Evaluation Forum, CLEF) has organized challenges on image classification and retrieval since 2003 [7]. Since 2004, medical image retrieval and analysis tasks have been organized [8,9]. The ImageCLEF 2017 [10] challenge included a task based on CT volumes of patients with TB, the ImageCLEF 2017 TB task [6]. In this task, a dataset of lung CT scans was provided and two subtasks were proposed. For both subtasks volumetric chest CT images with different voxel sizes and automatic segmentations of the lungs were provided.

MDR Detection Task: This subtask was a 2-class problem that consisted on detecting MDR based on a series of CT images. The dataset was composed of 444 CT volumes, divided into training and test sets as shown in Table 1. By

Table 1. Number of CT images for the MDR detection and TBT classification tasks.

MDR dataset				TBT dataset		
Patient set	Train	Test		Patient set / TBT	Train	Test
DS	134	101		Infiltrative	140	80
MDR	96	113		Focal	120	70
Total patients	230	214		Tuberculoma	100	60
				Miliary	80	50
				Fibro–cavernous	60	40
				Total patients	500	300

visual inspection, the CT volumes of this task did not present any relevant visual difference that distinguished MDR from drug-sensitive (DS) patients.

TBT Classification Task: The TBT subtask was a classification problem with five classes, corresponding to five TB types: Infiltrative, focal, tuberculoma, miliary, and fibro-cavernous. The patterns present in the several TBT patients were already quite discriminative, *e.g.* the patients with fibro-cavernous TB presented distinctive caverns in their CT image (see Fig. 1). The dataset for this subtask consisted of 800 CT volumes. The detailed number of patients for each class is shown in Table 1.

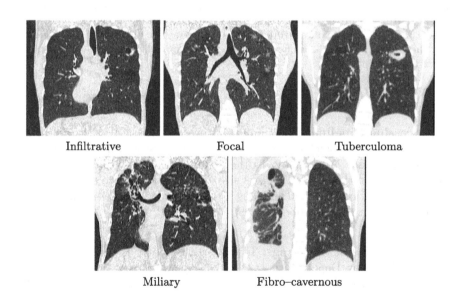

Infiltrative   Focal   Tuberculoma

Miliary   Fibro–cavernous

Fig. 1. Examples of the five tuberculosis types in the TBT subtask. The CT slices are shown using a HU window with center at -500 HU and width of 1400 HU

3   Texture-based Graph Model of the Lungs

We propose a general pipeline (see Fig. 2) to automatically obtain a texture-based graph model of the lungs that is composed of four steps: (1) automatic segmentation of the lung fields; (2) division of the lung mask into regions; (3) extraction of local biomedical texture features in each region; and (4) construction of the lung graph encoding the comparison between the regional features. Following this general pipeline, several graph models were investigated in this work and tested on the ImageCLEF 2017 TB task. The models obtained were produced varying the texture descriptors used in each lung region, the number of connections used to build the graph (edges), and the type of comparison between the regional features (weights).

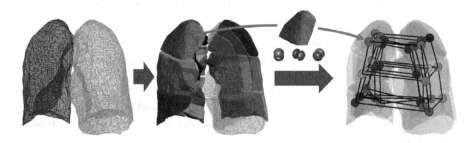

Fig. 2. Construction pipeline of a texture-based graph model of the lungs: First, the lungs are automatically segmented. Then, they are divided using a geometric atlas with 36 regions. From each region, texture features are extracted. Finally, the graph is built using the regions in the atlas as nodes. The edges contain the similarities between the 3D texture descriptors.

Preprocessing Pipeline: The graphs built were based on 3D texture features that require having isometric voxels. Therefore, we first resampled the CT volumes and the masks. After analyzing the multiple resolutions and the inter-slice distances found in the dataset, a voxel size of 1 mm was used to capture a maximum of information. We used the lung masks provided by the organizers, that were obtained with the method described in [11].

Geometric Atlas of the Lungs: In this article we use as a lung division the atlas introduced by Depeursinge *et al.* [12]. This atlas contains 36 geometric regions produced by intersecting four axis segmentations: coronal (right/left), sagital (anterior/posterior), vertical (apical/central/basal), and axial (peripheral/middle/central). These regions are based on the 3D model of the lung presented by Zrimec *et al.* [13]. Each region of the atlas is referred to as r. Figures 2, 3, and 4 contain a 3D visualization of this atlas.

3.1 3D Texture Features

Two state-of-the-art 3D texture feature types were selected to describe the texture in each atlas region r. The first method is a histogram of gradients based on the Fourier transform HOG (FHOG) introduced in [14]. We used 28 3D directions for the histogram obtaining a 28-dimensional feature vector per image voxel v ($\mathbf{f}_H(v) \in \mathbb{R}^{28}$). The second descriptor is the locally-oriented 3D Riesz-wavelet transform introduced by Dicente *et al.* in [15]. The parameters used in this work correspond to the ones obtaining the best classification results of synthetic 3D textures in the above mentioned article. These are: 3rd-order Riesz transform, 4 scales and 1st-order alignment. This configuration provides 40-dimensional feature vectors for each image voxel. The feature vector for a single voxel was then defined as the weighted sum of the absolute Riesz response along the 4 scales, obtaining a 10-dimensional feature vector ($\mathbf{f}_\mathcal{R}(v) \in \mathbb{R}^{10}$). Finally, the average (μ) and standard deviation (σ) of these descriptors were extracted from each region r, hence obtaining four region descriptors (see Eq. 1).

$$
\begin{aligned}
\boldsymbol{\mu}_H(r) &= \mu_{v \in r}(\mathbf{f}_H(v)) & \boldsymbol{\mu}_\mathcal{R}(r) &= \mu_{v \in r}(\mathbf{f}_\mathcal{R}(v)) \\
\boldsymbol{\sigma}_H(r) &= \sigma_{v \in r}(\mathbf{f}_H(v)) & \boldsymbol{\sigma}_\mathcal{R}(r) &= \sigma_{v \in r}(\mathbf{f}_\mathcal{R}(v))
\end{aligned}
\tag{1}
$$

3.2 Graph Model of the Lungs

A graph is a structure that contains a set of nodes $\mathcal{N}$ and a set of relations between the nodes, called set of edges $\mathcal{E}$. In particular, edge-weighted graphs are graphs in which a value is assigned to each edge, *i.e.*, there is a function $w : \mathcal{E} \to \mathbb{R}$. From now on, the graphs in this work are considered to be edge-weighted graphs with no self-loops.

Given a division of the lungs with n regions $\{r_1, \ldots, r_n\}$, we define a *graph model of the lungs* $\mathcal{G} = (\mathcal{N}, \mathcal{E})$ as a set of n nodes $\mathcal{N} = \{N_1, \ldots, N_n\}$ connected by a set of m edges $\mathcal{E}$. $E_{i,j}$ is defined as the edge connecting nodes N_i and N_j with associated weight $w_{i,j}$. The weights are functions of the texture features extracted in the lung regions. Using the 36-region atlas as a lung division, the graphs were finite with 36 nodes, *i.e.*, $\mathcal{N} = \{N_1, \ldots, N_{36}\}$. Figure 3 contains a 3D visualization of the graph elements using this atlas.

Using a fixed number of nodes and the same connections for all patients allow us to compare the patient graphs by comparing their adjacency matrices. Given a graph $\mathcal{G} = (\mathcal{N}, \mathcal{E})$ with 36 nodes, its adjacency matrix $\mathcal{A}$ is defined as the 36×36 square matrix with elements $a_{i,j} = w_{i,j}$ if $E_{i,j}$ exists, and $a_{i,j} = 0$ otherwise. Since no self-loops are allowed, $a_{i,i} = 0 \ \forall i \in \{1, \ldots, 36\}$. These matrices can be characterized by the ordered list of their elements in a vector form. Then, the comparison of graphs of different patients can be reduced to a vector comparison, where standard machine learning techniques can be directly applied. For a patient p with graph $\mathcal{G}_p$ and adjacency matrix $\mathcal{A}_p$, we define the *patient descriptor* $\boldsymbol{w}_p$ as the ordered list of weights $w_{i,j}$, using the order induced by the vectorization of the matrix $\mathcal{A}_p$.

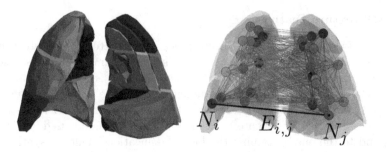

Fig. 3. Prototype visualization of the graph elements defined in Sect. 3.2. Left: 3D visualization of the geometric atlas used where six regions are not visible to show the atlas interior divisions. Right: Complete graph built from the geometric atlas. N_i and N_j are the nodes corresponding to regions r_i and r_j, respectively. $E_{i,j}$ is the edge connecting the nodes N_i and N_j. All the other edges are shown in light gray.

3.3 Graph Architectures

Using the geometric atlas with 36 regions as a base, several undirected weighted graphs were defined varying the number of edges and their weights. The number of edges varied according to the connections considered between the nodes. The different configurations of node connections correspond to different pruning levels of the complete graph with 36 nodes and we refer to them as *graph architectures*. Three graph architectures were designed (shown in Fig. 4), each one with a different adjacency matrix $\mathcal{A}$. Figure 5 shows the matrix $\mathcal{A}$ for each graph architecture using the same local features. The difference between them is the number of elements $a_{i,j} \in \mathcal{A}$ informed.

- *Graph_Complete:* This is the complete 36-node graph. For every pair of nodes N_i and N_j with $i \neq j$ an undirected edge $E_{i,j}$ exists. The total number of edges in this case is 630 ($\frac{36 \cdot 35}{2}$).
- *Graph_66:* Based on the region adjacency defined by the geometric atlas, there is an edge $E_{i,j}$ between nodes N_i and N_j if regions r_i and r_j are neighbors in the atlas, *i.e.*, if the regions are 3D adjacent. This graph contains in total 66 edges.
- *Graph_84:* This graph architecture has the same 66 edges as Graph_66. In addition, it includes 18 edges connecting each pair of nodes representing symmetric regions in the atlas with respect to the left-right division of the lungs.

3.4 Graph-Based Patient Descriptors

The weight $w_{i,j}$ of an edge $E_{i,j}$ was defined using four different measures between the features of the corresponding nodes N_i and N_j. Considering $\mathbf{f}_i$ and $\mathbf{f}_j$ the feature vectors of regions r_i and r_j respectively, the measures used are:

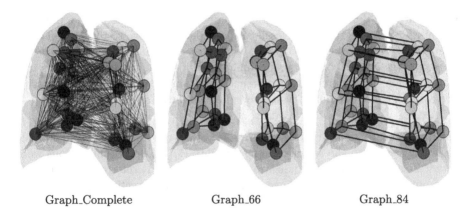

Graph_Complete   Graph_66   Graph_84

Fig. 4. 3D visualization of the three graph architectures (or pruning levels) designed.

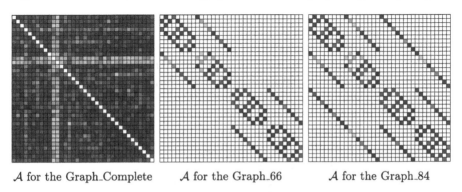

$\mathcal{A}$ for the Graph_Complete $\mathcal{A}$ for the Graph_66 $\mathcal{A}$ for the Graph_84

Fig. 5. Example of adjacency matrices for the three graph architectures shown in Fig. 4. The matrices were created using the same features in each atlas region. Hence, the elements present in the three matrices contain the same values. The adjacency matrices differ in the non informed elements (blanks).

- *Correlation distance (corr):* $w_{i,j} = 1 - corr(\mathbf{f}_i, \mathbf{f}_j)$.
- *Cosine similarity (cos):* $w_{i,j} = 1 - cos(\mathbf{f}_i, \mathbf{f}_j)$.
- *Euclidean distance (euc):* $w_{i,j} = \|\mathbf{f}_i - \mathbf{f}_j\|_2$.
- *Norm of the sum (sumNorm):* $w_{i,j} = \|\mathbf{f}_i + \mathbf{f}_j\|_2$.

The feature vector $\boldsymbol{w}_p$ of a patient p is defined as the ordered list of weights $w_{i,j}$ (see Sect. 3.2). The adjacency matrices $\mathcal{A}_p$ are symmetric, and only half of the elements are needed to characterize them. Depending on the graph used, this feature vector is 630-, 66-, or 84-dimensional.

3.5   Graph-Based Patient Descriptor Fusion and Classification

Given a graph model of the lungs, a patient descriptor vector $\boldsymbol{w}_p$ was obtained. In particular, for each of the regional texture descriptors extracted ($\boldsymbol{\mu}_H$, $\boldsymbol{\mu}_\mathcal{R}$,

σ_H, and $\sigma_{\mathcal{R}}$), a different graph model was obtained, thus generating a different patient descriptor w_p. For the classification experiments, we tested several combinations of these patient descriptors. Therefore, we defined the *derived patient descriptor vector* $\hat{w}_p$, containing a combination of these patient descriptors w_p. In this section, the different steps designed to obtain the derived patient descriptor vectors $\hat{w}_p$ are explained. Moreover, the classification setup is detailed.

Patient Descriptor Normalization: The patient descriptors w_p were normalized with respect to the set of training patients P_{trn}. Two normalizations were tested: Z-score and box normalization between 0 and 1, referred to as *Gauss-Norm* and *[0,1]* respectively. Since each component of a vector w_p corresponds to the weight of a different edge in the graph, the normalizations were performed over all the vector components together to preserve the relations induced by the graph structure. $\bar{w}_p$ denotes the normalized patient descriptor of a patient p.

Patient Descriptor Concatenation: Fixing a graph structure (Graph_Complete, Graph_66, or Graph_84) and a measure between the regional features (*corr*, *cos*, *euc*, or *sumNorm*) (see Sects. 3.3 and 3.4), four normalized patient descriptor vectors $\bar{w}_p$ were obtained. These are: $\bar{w}_{\mu_H}$, $\bar{w}_{\sigma_H}$, $\bar{w}_{\mu_{\mathcal{R}}}$, and $\bar{w}_{\sigma_{\mathcal{R}}}$. Five concatenations of these descriptors were tested in our experiments in order to better describe each patient:

- Mean and std of FHOG: $\hat{w} = (\bar{w}_{\mu_H} || \bar{w}_{\sigma_H})$.
- Mean and std of 3DARiesz: $\hat{w} = (\bar{w}_{\mu_{\mathcal{R}}} || \bar{w}_{\sigma_{\mathcal{R}}})$.
- Mean of FHOG and 3DARiesz: $\hat{w} = (\bar{w}_{\mu_H} || \bar{w}_{\mu_{\mathcal{R}}})$.
- Std of FHOG and 3DARiesz: $\hat{w} = (\bar{w}_{\sigma_H} || \bar{w}_{\sigma_{\mathcal{R}}})$.
- Mean and std of FHOG and 3DARiesz: $\hat{w} = (\bar{w}_{\mu_H} || \bar{w}_{\sigma_H} || \bar{w}_{\mu_{\mathcal{R}}} || \bar{w}_{\sigma_{\mathcal{R}}})$.

Feature Space Reduction: The dimension of the feature space was much larger than the number of patients in some of the experiments, *e.g.* when using the Graph_Complete architecture or the feature concatenations. To avoid the known problems of overfitting, two feature space reduction techniques were tested, both applied in the training phase. The first one selected the dimensions that best correlated with the training labels. The second one only kept those dimensions with a standard deviation higher than the mean standard deviation of all dimensions. Both techniques reduced the size of the feature space by two approximately and are referred as to *mostCorr* and *mostStd*, respectively.

Classification: Multi-class SVM classifiers with RBF kernel were used in both subtasks, particularly, 2-class SVMs for the MDR task and 5-class SVMs for the TBT task. Grid search over the RBF parameters (cost C and gamma γ) was applied. Since the data were normalized, both C and γ varied in $\{2^{-10}, 2^{-9}, \ldots, 2^{10}\}$. The best C and γ combination for a run was set as the one with highest cross-validation (CV) accuracy (10-fold) in the training set of each subtask.

4   Experiments

The ImageCLEF 2017 TB task was divided into two phases. In the first phase, the organizers released for each subtask a set of patient CT volumes as training set with their lung masks and ground truth labels. In the second phase, the test set with the corresponding lung segmentations were provided. However, the test labels were never released. The evaluation of the methods was performed by the organizers of the task based on the predicted labels submitted by the participants. In this section we detail the tested and submitted runs. Moreover the results of other participants provided by the organizers of the task are detailed.

4.1   Tested Runs

Considering all the different configurations explained in Sect. 3, 648 runs were obtained per subtask. Table 2 summarizes all possible options for each configuration step using the same codename as in the result tables.

Table 2. Possible configurations for each step. With these variations there were 648 combinations: 3 graph architectures × 4 edge weights × 3 texture features × 3 feature measures × 2 feature normalizations × 3 feature reductions.

Graph model property	Options
Graph architecture	Graph_Complete, Graph_66, Graph_84
Edge weight	corr, cos, euc, sumNorm
Texture feature	FHOG, 3DARiesz, FHOG and 3DARiesz
Feature measure	mean, std, mean and std
Feature normalization	[0,1], GaussNorm
Feature reduction	none, mostCorr, mostStd

4.2   Submitted Runs

A total of ten runs could be submitted in the ImageCLEF 2017 TB task, considering the submitted runs of both subtasks. Therefore, five runs were submitted for each subtask. For both subtasks, we first selected the five runs with best scores considering only the CV accuracy on the training set (Acc_{trn}). Tables 3 and 4 show the identifier and run setup of the five selected runs with top Acc_{trn} for each subtask, respectively. Then, subgroups of these five runs were combined using late fusion to obtain new run files. Four new run files were obtained per subtask, identified by the suffixes *TopBest2*, *TopBest3*, *TopBest4*, and *TopBest5*. The late fusion was computed using the probabilities that the SVM classifier returned and the mean probability of belonging to each class. Finally, we submitted three original runs with the best scores and two fused runs per subtask.

The following tables show the results obtained by the submitted runs on the training set (Acc_{trn}) and the final performance in the competition (Acc_{tst}).

Table 3. Runs for the MDR subtask with the best scores based on the CV accuracy in the training set.

Run Id.	Graph	Texture features	F. measure	E. weight	F. norm.	F. reduct.	Acc_{trn}
MDR_Top1	Graph_84	FHOG and 3DARiesz	mean and std	corr	GaussNorm	mostCorr	0.6900
MDR_Top2	Graph_66	FHOG and 3DARiesz	std	cos	[0,1]	mostCorr	0.6856
MDR_Top3	Graph_84	FHOG	mean	corr	[0,1]	none	0.6812
MDR_Top4	Graph_66	FHOG and 3DARiesz	mean and std	corr	[0, 1]	mostCorr	0.6725
MDR_Top5	Graph_66	FHOG	mean	corr	GaussNorm	mostCorr	0.6725

Table 4. Runs for the TBT subtask with the best scores based on the CV accuracy in the training set.

Run Id.	Graph	Texture features	F. measure	E. weight	F. norm.	F. reduct.	Acc_{trn}
TBT_Top1	Graph_66	FHOG and 3DARiesz	mean and std	sumNorm	GaussNorm	None	0.5276
TBT_Top2	Graph_84	FHOG and 3DARiesz	mean and std	sumNorm	GaussNorm	None	0.5174
TBT_Top3	Graph_66	FHOG and 3DARiesz	mean and std	sumNorm	[0, 1]	None	0.5112
TBT_Top4	Graph_66	FHOG and 3DARiesz	mean and std	sumNorm	GaussNorm	mostCorr	0.5112
TBT_Top5	Graph_84	FHOG and 3DARiesz	mean and std	sumNorm	[0, 1]	None	0.5092

The final ranking was based on the AUC for the MDR subtask and on the unweighted Cohen's Kappa coefficient (Kappa) for the TBT task. Table 5 shows the results for the MDR subtask provided by the task organizers. The run identifiers *MDR_TopBest3* and *MDR_TopBest5* were obtained by late fusion of the 3 and 5 best runs respectively. The results for the TBT task are shown in Table 6. Again, the run identifiers *TBT_TopBest3* and *TBT_TopBest5* correspond to the late fusion of the 3 and 5 best runs respectively.

Table 5. Results of the MDR detection task. We participated as the MedGIFT group.

Group name	Run Id.	AUC	Acc_{tst}	Acc_{trn}	#Rank
MedGIFT	MDR_Top1	0.5825	0.5164	0.6900	1
MedGIFT	MDR_TopBest3	0.5727	0.4648	–	2
MedGIFT	MDR_TopBest5	0.5624	0.4836	–	3
SGEast	MDR_LSTM_6_probs	0.5620	0.5493	–	4
SGEast	MDR_resnet_full	0.5591	0.5493	–	5
MedGIFT	MDR_Top2	0.5337	0.4883	0.6856	10
MedGIFT	MDR_Top3	0.5112	0.4413	0.6725	17

5   Discussion and Conclusions

This article presents a novel graph-based framework to model the lung fields based on regional 3D texture features. The parts of this framework can be

Table 6. Results of the TBT classification task. We participated as the MedGIFT group.

Group name	Run Id.	Kappa	Acc_{tst}	Acc_{trn}	#Rank
SGEast	TBT_resnet_full	0.2438	0.4033	–	1
SGEast	TBT_LSTM_17_wcrop	0.2374	0.3900	–	2
MEDGIFT UPB	TBT_T_GNet	0.2329	0.3867	–	3
SGEast	TBT_LSTM_13_wcrop	0.2291	0.3833	–	4
Image processing	TBT-testSet-label-Apr26-XGao-1	0.2187	0.4067	–	5
MedGIFT	TBT_Top1	0.1623	0.3600	0.5276	10
MedGIFT	TBT_TopBest3	0.1548	0.3500	–	12
MedGIFT	TBT_TopBest5	0.1410	0.3367	–	15
MedGIFT	TBT_Top4	0.1352	0.3300	0.5112	16
MedGIFT	TBT_Top2	0.1235	0.3200	0.5174	17

adapted to describe multiple diseases affecting the lung parenchyma. In particular, more than 600 configurations were tested to describe patients with TB. The participation in the ImageCLEF 2017 TB task provides an objective comparison between methods, since the ground truth for the test set was never released. The global description of the lungs provided by the graph model allowed the detection of MDR patients better than any other approach submitted in this challenge. Moreover, it also showed to be useful in the distinction of the different TB types. According to the results in the ImageCLEF 2017 TB task, the new representation of the lungs as a graph entity showed to be promising, reaching better results than for example deep learning approaches. Our method was robust enough to provide a better characterization of the several classes in both subtasks only with the available number of patients in the task. If added to the clinical workflow, physicians can benefit of a new way of visualizing and interpreting the lung parenchyma, in a systematic and schematic fashion.

For the MDR subtask, the graph model participated with five runs and obtained the 1st, 2nd and 3rd place in the challenge. The results obtained by the participants confirmed the difficulty of this subtask. Independently of the technique applied, all runs remained close to the performance of a random classifier, meaning that there is likely a high potential for improvements.

On the other hand, the results support the suitability of the imaging techniques for the TBT task. Five runs were also submitted to the TBT subtask but the best rank obtained by the texture-based graph model was 10. For this particular task, deep learning methods worked better than other approaches, obtaining the 6 best results. The results underline the difficulty of both tasks and the suitability of the graph model for describing TB patients. However, the strong differences in the accuracies obtained for the training and test sets (see Tables 5 and 6) suggest some overfitting in the training phase. The graph model describes each patient with a single vector in a relativity large feature space. Therefore, more training data may be needed to build a stable model of each class.

Acknowledgements. This work was partly supported by the Swiss National Science Foundation in the project PH4D (320030-146804).

References

1. Bento, J., Silva, A.S., Rodrigues, F., Duarte, R.: Diagnostic tools in tuberculosis. Acta Med. Port. **24**(1), 145–154 (2011)
2. Jeong, Y.J., Lee, K.S.: Pulmonary tuberculosis: up-to-date imaging and management. Am. J. Roentgenol. **191**(3), 834–844 (2008)
3. Richiardi, J., Achard, S., Bunke, H., Van De Ville, D.: Machine learning with brain graphs: predictive modeling approaches for functional imaging in systems neuroscience. IEEE Sig. Process. Mag. **30**(3), 58–70 (2013)
4. Richiardi, J., Eryilmaz, H., Schwartz, S., Vuilleumier, P., Van De Ville, D.: Decoding brain states from fMRI connectivity graphs. NeuroImage **56**(2), 616–626 (2011)
5. Dicente Cid, Y., et al.: A lung graph-model for pulmonary hypertension and pulmonary embolism detection on DECT images. In: Müller, H., et al. (eds.) MCV/BAMBI -2016. LNCS, vol. 10081, pp. 58–68. Springer, Cham (2017). https://doi.org/10.1007/978-3-319-61188-4_6
6. Dicente Cid, Y., Kalinovsky, A., Liauchuk, V., Kovalev, V., Müller, H.: Overview of ImageCLEFtuberculosis 2017 - predicting tuberculosis type and drug resistances. In: CLEF 2017 Labs Working Notes, CEUR Workshop Proceedings, Dublin, Ireland. CEUR-WS.org, 11–14 September 2017. http://ceur-ws.org
7. Müller, H., Clough, P., Deselaers, T., Caputo, B. (eds.): ImageCLEF - Experimental Evaluation in Visual Information Retrieval. The Springer International Series On Information Retrieval, vol. 32. Springer, Heidelberg (2010). https://doi.org/10.1007/978-3-642-15181-1
8. Kalpathy-Cramer, J., de Herrera, A.G.S., Demner-Fushman, D., Antani, S., Bedrick, S., Müller, H.: Evaluating performance of biomedical image retrieval systems: Overview of the medical image retrieval task at ImageCLEF 2004–2014. Comput. Med. Imaging Graph. **39**, 55–61 (2015)
9. Villegas, M., et al.: General overview of ImageCLEF at the CLEF 2015 labs. In: Mothe, J., et al. (eds.) CLEF 2015. LNCS, vol. 9283, pp. 444–461. Springer, Cham (2015)
10. Ionescu, B., et al.: Overview of ImageCLEF 2017: information extraction from images. In: Jones, G.J.F., et al. (eds.) CLEF 2017. LNCS, vol. 10456, pp. 315–337. Springer, Cham (2017)
11. Dicente Cid, Y., Jimenez-del-Toro, O., Depeursinge, A., Müller, H.: Efficient and fully automatic segmentation of the lungs in CT volumes. In: Goksel, O., Jimenez-del-Toro, O., Foncubierta-Rodriguez, A., Müller, H. (eds.) Proceedings of the VISCERAL Challenge at ISBI, CEUR Workshop Proceedings, vol. 1390, pp. 31–35, April 2015
12. Depeursinge, A., Zrimec, T., Busayarat, S., Müller, H.: 3D lung image retrieval using localized features. In: Medical Imaging 2011: Computer-Aided Diagnosis, vol. 7963, p. 79632E. SPIE (2011)
13. Zrimec, T., Busayarat, S., Wilson, P.: A 3D model of the human lung. In: Barillot, C., Haynor, D.R., Hellier, P. (eds.) MICCAI 2004. LNCS, vol. 3217, pp. 1074–1075. Springer, Heidelberg (2004)
14. Liu, K., et al.: Rotation-invariant hog descriptors using fourier analysis in polar and spherical coordinates. Int. J. Comput. Vis. **106**(3), 342–364 (2014)
15. Dicente Cid, Y., Müller, H., Platon, A., Poletti, P.A., Depeursinge, A.: 3-D solid texture classification using locally-oriented wavelet transforms. IEEE Trans. Image Process. **26**(4), 1899–1910 (2017)

Plant Classification Based on Gated Recurrent Unit

Sue Han Lee[1]([✉]), Yang Loong Chang[1], Chee Seng Chan[1], Joly Alexis[2],
Pierre Bonnet[3] [iD], and Herve Goeau[3]

[1] Center of Image and Signal Processing,
Faculty of Computer Science and Information Technology, University of Malaya,
Kuala Lumpur, Malaysia
{leesuehan,yangloong}@siswa.um.edu.my, cs.chan@um.edu.my
[2] INRIA, Montpellier, France
alexis.joly@inria.fr
[3] CIRAD-Amap, Montpellier, France
pierre.bonnet@cirad.fr, herve.goeau@inria.fr

Abstract. Classification of plants based on a multi-organ approach is
very challenging due to the variability in shape and appearance in plant
organs. Despite promising solutions built using convolutional neural network (CNN) for plant classification, the existing approaches do not consider the correspondence between different views captured of a plant. In
fact, botanists usually observe and study simultaneously a plant from
different vintage points, as a whole and also analyse different organs in
order to disambiguate species. Driven by this insight, we introduce a new
framework for plant structural learning using the recurrent neural network (RNN) approach. This novel approach supports classification based
on a varying number of plant views composed of one or more organs of
a plant, by optimizing the dependencies between them. We also present
the qualitative results of our proposed models by visualizing the learned
attention maps. To our knowledge, this is the first study to venture into
such dependencies modeling and interpret the respective neural net for
plant classification. Finally, we show that our proposed method outperforms the conventional CNN approach on the PlantClef2015 benchmark.
The source code and models are available at https://github.com/cs-
chan/Deep-Plant.

Keywords: Plant classification · Deep learning
Recurrent neural network

1 Introduction

Plants are the backbone of all life on earth providing us with food and oxygen. A
good understanding of plants is essential to help in identifying new or rare plant

© Springer Nature Switzerland AG 2018
P. Bellot et al. (Eds.): CLEF 2018, LNCS 11018, pp. 169–180, 2018.
https://doi.org/10.1007/978-3-319-98932-7_16

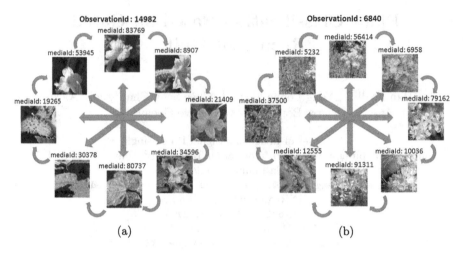

Fig. 1. (a) and (b) Represent examples of plant images taken from the plants tagged with ObservationID 14982 and 6840 respectively in PlantClef2015 dataset [15]. Different plant views captured of a plant exhibit correlated characteristic in their organ structures. Best viewed in color.

species in order to improve the drug industry, balance the ecosystem as well as the agricultural productivity and sustainability. Ever since LifeCLEF, one of the foremost visual image retrieval campaigns hosted a plant identification challenge, researchers have started to focus on automatic analysis of multiple images exploiting different views of a plant capturing one or more organs. From year 2014, it has provided up to seven different plant views which are entire plant, branches, flower, leaf, leaf scan, fruit, and stem. Indeed, [14] has shown that combining different types of views in a query can increase the species identification rate. Previously, researchers [14,20] consider that different images are independent from each other. A straightforward fusion scheme such as the mean of the categorical distributions predicted for each image is generally employed to combine the information contained in each image. However, in reality, different views are far from being independent because they correspond to multiple views of the same individual specimen. For example, as shown in Fig. 1, different plant views (or organs) captured of a plant exhibit correlated or overlapping characteristics in their organ structures, nonetheless these traits are distinctive between different plants. This information inevitably can be seen as one of the important cue to help differentiate species. Majority studies have used CNN to classify plant images [18,21]. This approach however was designed to capture similar region-wise patterns within an image, thus disregarding the correlation between different plant views of a plant. In this work, we propose a new framework based on RNN [12] to model the dependencies between different plant views where the probability of a view is conditioned by the other views. Specifically, it takes in a varying number of plant view images composed of one or more organs, and optimizes the dependencies between them for species classification. Additionally, we introduce a Coarse-to-Fined Attention (*CFA*) module where it can locate the local regions that are highly voted by the RNN method in each plant view. Our contributions are summarized as follows:

1. We propose a RNN based approach to model different plant views capturing one or more organs of plant for species classification.
2. We introduce *CFA* module that provides a better visual understanding on the local features emphasized by the RNN method in plant views dependencies modeling.
3. Our proposed model achieves a better performance compared to the conventional CNN approach on PlantClef2015 benchmark.

2 Related Works

Plant Identification. Over the past few years, researchers have worked on recognizing plant species using solely a single plant organ. A majority of the studies have utilized leaves to identify species. Leaf characters such as shape, texture, and venation are the most generally used features to distinguish leaves of different species [18]. To fit better with a real scenario where people generally try to identify a plant by observing several plant organs or a similar organ from different viewpoints, researchers in computer vision have focused on designing an automated plant classification system to identify multi-organ plant images. Earliest attempts [11,27,33] in general, adopt organ-specific features for discrimination. Specifically, they first group the images of plants into their respective organ categories. Then, based on each organ category, organ-specific features are extracted using feature engineering approaches. Ever since, DL has been proved extremely high recognition capabilities in dealing with very large datasets, [10] proposed using an end-to-end CNN to replace those hand-crafted feature extractors. They introduced organ-specific CNN models where each model is trained on dedicated plant organs. There are also researchers [6,24] focused on using CNN to learn generic features of plants, irrespective of their organ information. Lately, [21] showed that using the HGO-CNN which incorporates both the organ-specific and generic features could provide the best result in the LifeClef2015 challenge. Despite promising results obtained using CNN based approach, the representation learned focuses only on the information contained in each image, but fails to capture the high-level semantics corresponding to the interaction between different plant views (organs). Henceforth, this work moves beyond existing practice, venturing into a new alternative to solve this problem.

RNN Based Classification. The RNN has always been used to process sequential data such as language translation [17,30] and action recognition [22,29]. Lately, CNN and RNN have been employed to combine information, integrating the domain of computer vision and natural language processing [9,28,31,32,34]. Despite using RNN to model complex structures of video or language, a few publications have showed the capability of RNN in processing variable length of fixed-sized data in a sequential manner though data originally is not in a form of sequences. For example, it has been actively explored in segmentation [23,25], scene labeling [4,26], object recognition [2,3] as well as image generation [13]. In such case, RNN is used to model the dependencies between pixels or regions within an image. In our work, we formulate RNN to the contrary, to learn the structure of an object based on its different views which do not have a form of sequences. We introduce a probabilistic model to process different plant views captured of a plant where each state variable is conditioned upon all other states, and not only its previous ones.

3   Approach

Notations. We denote the plant view images as $I_t \in \{I_1, I_2, \cdots, I_T\}$ where $t = 1, \cdots, T$ are the states corresponding to the indices of plant view images of the same plant. Each I_t is associated with a species annotation (I_t, r_t) where r_t is a one hot vector with only the species label set as positive. For each plant view image, we extract its convolutional features from a CNN model, $\delta_t \in \{\delta_1, \delta_2, \cdots, \delta_T\}$, $\delta_t \in \mathbb{R}^{H \times W \times C}$ where H, W and C are the height, width and number of channels of feature maps.

Architecture. It is known that human brain processes information iteratively, where it keeps the current state in an internal memory and uses it to infer future observation, capturing the potential relationships between them [8]. Driven by this insight, we build a new plant classification framework upon the RNN based approach, which can hold and relate different structural information of a plant. Moreover, it is versatile to an arbitrary number of plant images. In this work, the Gated Recurrent Unit (GRU) [7], one of the gating mechanism in RNNs, is adopted for a more light-weight and simple network structure. The activation h_t is a linear interpolation between the previous activation h_{t-1} and the current candidate activation $\tilde{h}_t$: $h_t = (1 - z_t)h_{t-1} + z_t\tilde{h}_t$ where z_t is the update gate that decides how much of the previous state should be kept around. The z_t is computed as $z_t = \sigma(W_{z1}x_t + W_{z2}h_{t-1})$. The candidate activation $\tilde{h}_t$ which is processed with a hyperbolic tangent is formulated as follows: $\tilde{h}_t = \tanh(W_{h1}x_t + W_{h2}(v_t \odot h_{t-1}))$ where v_t is the reset gate that determines to which extent the new input should be combined with the previous state and $\odot$ is an element-wise multiplication operator. The v_t is formulated as follows: $v_t = \sigma(W_{v1}x_t + W_{v2}h_{t-1})$. The activations of both gates are element-wise logistic sigmoid functions σ. It maps v_t and z_t in between 0 to 1. All the W matrices are trained parameters. The network is fed by the current input vector x_t, while all the W matrices are trained parameters.

Attention (attn). The attention module is used to reduce the dimensionality of convolutional features in order to ease the computational burden of a network [5]. The attention map λ_t controls the contribution of convolutional features at the t-th state. Larger value in λ_t indicates higher importance. The term ϵ_t

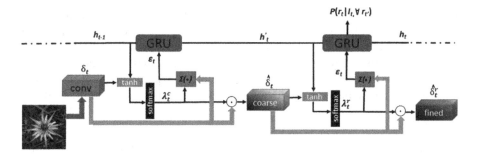

Fig. 2. The proposed Coarse-to-Fined Attention module. Best viewed in color.

introduced as the weighted average of convolutional features that is dependent on the previous activation $\mathbf{h_{t-1}}$ and convolutional features δ_t. The attention function $g : \delta_t, \mathbf{h_{t-1}} \rightarrow \epsilon_t$ is defined as follows:

$$\zeta_t = \{\tanh(\delta_t \mathbf{W}_\delta + \mathbf{h_{t-1}} \mathbf{W_h})\} \mathbf{W_a} \tag{1}$$

$$\lambda_t = softmax(\zeta_t) \tag{2}$$

$$\epsilon_t = \sum_{i,j} \lambda_{t,ij} \delta_{t,ij} \tag{3}$$

where the embedding matrices $\mathbf{W}_\delta \in \mathbb{R}^{C \times C}$, $\mathbf{W_h} \in \mathbb{R}^{E \times C}$, $\mathbf{W_a} \in \mathbb{R}^{p \times 1}$, E is the dimensionality of GRU cell, $p = H \times W$ and $\delta_{t,ij}$ denotes convolutional feature at location $(i, j) \in p$.

Coarse-to-Fined Attention (*CFA*). Using the aforementioned attention mechanism (Eqs. 1–3), the GRU decodes species prediction based on global image features attained from a CNN. The attention mechanism trained by such global image features might not be able to infer the discriminative local features of plant structures. To gain a better visual understanding on which part of a plant view image is mostly emphasized by the RNN based approach, a better localization of the attention map is inevitably necessary. To this end, we refine the attention map acquired in each state t by proposing *CFA* module as shown in Fig. 2. Basically, the convolutional feature δ_t is first processed to obtain a coarse attention map λ_t^c. The λ_t^c is then element-wise multiplied with the δ_t to produced a masked convolutional feature $\hat{\delta}_t$ which is to be fed to the following GRU. The attention mechanism at the later stage is therefore trained to look for pertinent features from this refined image feature $\hat{\delta}_t$ and identify the best local features. With the use of the refined attention map produced as λ_t^r, we can eventually locate these local features in each plant view.

Training. Contrary to modeling video or language data where variable number of inputs are conditioned upon their previous states $P(r_t | \mathbf{I_t}, r_1, \cdots, r_{t-1})$, in our case, it is logical to condition the inputs upon all other states information for the plant structural modeling, $P(r_t|\mathbf{I_t}, \{r_d\}_{d \neq t})$. The reason is that, states in our context are analogous to the collections of different plant views captured from a similar plant, so the relationships between these states are interrelated. Henceforth, to tackle this challenge, we design in such a way that it would be able to iteratively classify images of a plant while conjointly operate on all of its related instances. In particular, we build a bidirectional states modeling mechanism where the forward neuron activations $\overrightarrow{\mathbf{h}}$ models $P_{fw} = P(r_t|\mathbf{I_t}, r_1, \cdots, r_{t-1})$ and the backward neuron activations $\overleftarrow{\mathbf{h}}$ models $P_{bw} = P(r_t|\mathbf{I_t}, r_{t+1}, \cdots, r_T)$. Then, we put in correspondence between both neurons for every state and train them upon the respective species classes. In this manner, each state t can be considered as condition upon the collections of the related plant images from states $1, \cdots, t-1, t+1, \cdots, T$. In order to correlate between both states, the output activations of the forward and backward GRU are cascaded as follows: $\mathbf{h_t} = [\overrightarrow{\mathbf{h}}_t, \overleftarrow{\mathbf{h}}_t]$. Then, we multiply $\mathbf{h_t}$ with a class embedding matrix, $\mathbf{W_{em}}$, which is $\mathbf{s}(\mathbf{I_t}) = \mathbf{W_{em}}\mathbf{h_t}$ before normalizing it with a softmax function: $P(r_t|\mathbf{I_t}, \{r_d\}_{d \neq t}) = \frac{e^{s_r(\mathbf{I_t})}}{\sum_{m=1}^{M} e^{s_m(\mathbf{I_t})}}$ where M and r stand for the total number of classes and the target class respectively. We perform the softmax operation for every state t preceding the computation of the overall cross entropy function: $L_{psn} = \frac{1}{T} \sum_{t=1}^{T} L_t$, where $L_t = -logP(r_t|\mathbf{I_t}, \{r_d\}_{d \neq t})$.

4   Datasets and Evaluation Metrics

Dataset. The PlantClef2015 dataset [15] was used. It has 1000 plant species classes. Training and testing data comprise 91759 and 21446 images respectively. Each image is associated with a single organ type (branch, entire, flower, fruit, leaf, stem or leaf scan).

Evaluation Metrics. We employ the *observation* and *image-centered* scores [15] to evaluate the model's performance. The purpose of the observation score is to evaluate the ability of a model to predict the correct species labels for all the users. To this end, the observation score is the mean of the average classification rate per user as defined: $S_{obs} = \frac{1}{U} \sum_{u=1}^{U} \frac{1}{P_u} \sum_{p=1}^{P_u} S_{u,p}$ where U represents the number of users, P_u is the number of individual plants observed by the u-th user, and $S_{u,p}$ is the score between 0 and 1 as the inverse of the rank of the correct species (for the p-th plant observed by the u-th user). Each query observation is composed of multiple images. To compute $S_{u,p}$, we adopt the Borda count (BD) to combine the scores of multiple images: $BD = \frac{1}{n} \sum_{k=1}^{n} score_k$ where n is the total number of images per query observation and $score$ is the softmax output score, which describes the ranking of the species.

Next, the image-centered score evaluates the ability of a system to provide the correct species labels based on a single plant observation. It calculates the average classification rate for each individual plant defined as: $S_{img} = \frac{1}{U} \sum_{u=1}^{U} \frac{1}{P_u} \sum_{p=1}^{P_u} \frac{1}{N_{u,p}} \sum_{n=1}^{N_{u,p}} S_{u,p,n}$ where U and P_u are explained earlier in the text, $N_{u,p}$ is the number of pictures taken from the p-th plant observed

Table 1. Performance comparison between the E-CNN [20] and the GRU architecture.

Method	Acc	S_{img}	S_{obs}
E-CNN [19, 20]	0.635	0.710	**0.737**
GRU ($conv7$) + $attn$	0.669	0.709	0.718
GRU ($conv5\_3$) + CFA	0.662	0.711	0.723
GRU ($conv5\_3$) + $attn$	**0.686**	**0.718**	0.726

by the u-th user and $S_{u,p,n}$ is the score between 0 and 1 equal to the inverse of the rank of the correct species (for the n-th picture taken from the p-th plant observed by the u-th user). We compute the rank of the correct species based on its softmax scores. Besides S_{obs} and S_{img}, we also compute the top-1 classification result to infer the robustness of the system: $Acc = T_r/T_s$ where T_r is the number of true species prediction and T_s represents total number of testing data.

5 Experiments

We firstly group the training and testing images into their respective observation ID. Note that, each observation ID consists of T number of plant images captured from a p-th plant observed by a u-th user. By doing so, we have 27907 and 13887 observation IDs for training and testing respectively. Next, we apply the multi-scale image generation process proposed in [19] on these images. For each plant image, we extract its image representation using the enhanced HGO-CNN (E-CNN) [19,20]. We train the architecture based on random sequence, disregarding the order of the plant images fed into the network. This is driven by our understanding that botanists usually observe and study a plant from different vintage points simultaneously, as a whole and also analyse different organs, and this is done without specific order. We test the performance of GRU architecture using different levels of image abstraction representation. We use $conv5\_3$ and $conv7$ features extracted from the last convolutional layer of generic and species layer of E-CNN [20] respectively. The GRU architecture is trained using the Tensorflow library [1]. We use the ADAM optimizer [16] with the parameters $\alpha = 1e-08$, $\beta1 = 0.9$ and $\beta2 = 0.999$. We applied L_2 weight decay with penalty multiplier set to 1×10^{-4}, and dropout ratio set to 0.5, respectively. We set the learning rate to 1×10^{-3}, and, reduce it to 1×10^{-4} when the training performance stops improving. Mini-batch size is set to 15.

5.1 Performance Evaluation

In Table 1, we compare the performance of the GRU architecture with the E-CNN baseline [19,20]. It can be seen that using the GRU with $conv5\_3$ input layer, achieved the highest top-1 accuracy of 0.686, outperforms the previous

Table 2. Comparison of top-1 classification accuracy for different categories of observation ID. Note that, Category A = a single image per observation ID; Category B = number of images ≥ 2 per observation ID

Category	A	B
Total number of training images for each category	11690	80069
Total number of testing images for each category	9905	11541
E-CNN [19, 20]	**0.634**	0.637
GRU ($conv5\_3$) + $attn$	0.607	**0.754**

Table 3. Classification performance comparison of each content based on S_{img}.

Method	Branch	Entire	Flower	Fruit	Leaf	LeafScan	Stem
E-CNN [19, 20]	0.564	0.573	0.801	0.657	0.666	0.759	0.384
GRU ($conv5\_3$) + $attn$	**0.650**	**0.643**	**0.823**	**0.709**	**0.729**	**0.790**	**0.546**
Gain (%)	+15.2	+12.2	+2.7	+7.9	+9.5	+4.1	+42.2

E-CNN [19, 20]. However, we found that its S_{img} and S_{obs} do not seem to have much improvement. We then explore the cause and observe that most of the misclassifications occur when there is only one testing image per observation ID. Table 2 shows that there is a total of 9905 testing images that fall in category A, which is nearly 47% of the testing set. The GRU performs noticeably better in category B than A (top-1 accuracy of 0.754 compared to 0.607), while E-CNN [19,20] performs almost equally in all cases for category A and B (top-1 accuracy of 0.634 and 0.637). This can be deduced from the characteristic of both E-CNN and GRU based models used in this context. To recognize a plant image, the E-CNN based model is trained to find similar patterns on all different subfields of an image, while the GRU based model is trained to look for higher level features, modeling the dependencies between a series of images. Next, we noticed that the number of training samples in category A is significantly less than category B. Such imbalanced training set might be another factor that affects the performance of the GRU in predicting species for category A. Based on these findings, we therefore deduce that the poor performance of the GRU based model is most likely due to the inadequate samples of plants given one observation ID. Besides, we found that using GRU + CFA module, the S_{img} and S_{obs} are 0.711 and 0.723 respectively, which are comparable to the $attn$ module but the top-1 accuracy on the other hand is only 0.662. This is probably due to the absence of global information when the network is explicitly forced to focus on local regions of plant structures. Moreover, using the GRU with the $conv5\_3$ as the input layer is proven to be better compared to the $conv7$. We attribute this performance difference to $conv5\_3$ features being more generic compared to $conv7$, as we note that there is a transition from generic to class specific features within the CNNs. Hence, the generic features are more versatile when

Table 4. Percentage of testing images that fall under category A for each organ category (%)

Branch	Entire	Flower	Fruit	Leaf	LeafScan	Stem
56.49	68.17	64.81	50.98	33.59	64.23	25.77

re-purposed for a new task. Additionally, training the GRU with generic features does not make any explicit use of the organ tags, which inevitably reduces the complexity in model training.

5.2 Detailed Scores for Each Plant Organ

In this section, we analyse the classification performance for each of the organ based on the image-centered score, S_{img}. We observe that the GRU model essentially improved the recognition performance of each organ, especially the 'stem' organ. As shown in Table 3, the improvement gained is 42.2% which is considerably significant compared to other organs. This is due to the fact that the stem organ has the least number of images in category A compared to other organs. That is the majority of stem images co-exists with other plant images in one observation ID. For this reason, we can see that although the stem organ is considered as the least informative one compared to other organs, using the RNN method, we can successfully boost its classification performance. Besides, note that, although improvement gained for the 'flower' is not as high as the 'stem' organ, its performance is the highest for the overall plant views. This shows that flower is the most effective organ to identify plant species (Table 4).

5.3 Qualitative Analysis

Contrary to CNN, RNN learns the high-level structural features of a plant by modeling the dependencies between different plant views. Besides quantitative analysis, we go deeper into exploring, analyzing and understanding the learned features by using both, the *attn* and the *CFA* modules. Figure 3 shows the visualisation results of the GRU(*conv5_3*) + *attn* and the GRU(*conv5_3*) + *CFA*. It is noticed that, using the *attn* module, the highly activated regions mostly fall on the holistic plant structures. Hence, we deduce that the GRU(*conv5_3*) + *attn* is able to locate the pertinent foreground regions that are analogous to the plant structures. On the other hand, using the *CFA* module to recurrently refine the attention regions can precisely locate the discriminative local regions of plant structures, which are voted the most by the RNN method. Based on the visualisation results in Fig. 3, we can notice that the refined features are focused on the boundary of the flower's petals as well as the center of the compound leaflets, radiating from the tip of the petiole. This shows that the *CFA* can provide more localized attention that emphasizes the most distinctive local regions rather than the holistic plant structures. These insights therefore provide us with a better visual understanding from the global to the local perspective of image representation learned through the RNN in modeling plant views correlation.

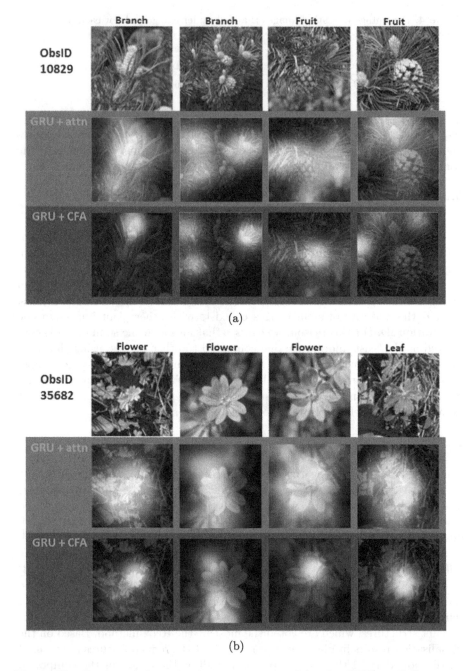

Fig. 3. Visualisation of the activation maps generated by the GRU(*conv5_3*) + *attn* and GRU(*conv5_3*) + *CFA* for plant samples tagged with observation ID (a)10829 and (b) 35682 in PlantCLef 2015 dataset. It can be seen that the CFA module can refine the attention regions to locate the most distinctive local regions rather than the holistic plant structures. Best viewed in color.

6 Conclusion

We presented a novel plant classification framework based on RNN approach where it supports classification based on a varying number of plant views composed of one or more organs of a plant, by optimizing the dependencies between them. Experiments on the PlantClef 2015 benchmark showed that modeling the higher level features of plant views interaction can essentially improve the classification performance, especially for the less distinctive 'stem' organ. Furthermore, with the help of the proposed *CFA* module, we can achieve better insights of the discriminative subparts of the plant structures which are voted the most by the RNN approach for species classification.

References

1. Abadi, M., et al.: Tensorflow: a system for large-scale machine learning. In: OSDI, vol. 16, pp. 265–283 (2016)
2. Ba, J., Mnih, V., Kavukcuoglu, K.: Multiple object recognition with visual attention. arXiv preprint arXiv:1412.7755 (2014)
3. Bell, S., Lawrence Zitnick, C., Bala, K., Girshick, R.: Inside-outside net: detecting objects in context with skip pooling and recurrent neural networks. In: CVPR, pp. 2874–2883 (2016)
4. Byeon, W., Breuel, T.M., Raue, F., Liwicki, M.: Scene labeling with LSTM recurrent neural networks. In: CVPR, pp. 3547–3555 (2015)
5. Cho, K., Courville, A., Bengio, Y.: Describing multimedia content using attention-based encoder-decoder networks. IEEE Trans. Multimed. **17**(11), 1875–1886 (2015)
6. Choi, S.: Plant identification with deep convolutional neural network: SNUMedinfo at lifeCLEF plant identification task 2015. In: CLEF (Working Notes) (2015)
7. Chung, J., Gulcehre, C., Cho, K., Bengio, Y.: Empirical evaluation of gated recurrent neural networks on sequence modeling. arXiv preprint arXiv:1412.3555 (2014)
8. Clark, A.: Whatever next? Predictive brains, situated agents, and the future of cognitive science. Behav. Brain Sci. **36**(3), 181–204 (2013)
9. Fu, K., Jin, J., Cui, R., Sha, F., Zhang, C.: Aligning where to see and what to tell: image captioning with region-based attention and scene-specific contexts. IEEE Trans. Pattern Anal. Mach. Intell. **39**(12), 2321–2334 (2017)
10. Ge, Z., McCool, C., Sanderson, C., Corke, P.: Content specific feature learning for fine-grained plant classification. In: CLEF (Working Notes) (2015)
11. Goëau, H., et al.: Plantnet participation at lifeCLEF2014 plant identification task. In: CLEF2014 Working Notes, Working Notes for CLEF 2014 Conference, Sheffield, UK, 15–18 September 2014, pp. 724–737. CEUR-WS (2014)
12. Graves, A., Mohamed, A.R., Hinton, G.: Speech recognition with deep recurrent neural networks. In: 2013 IEEE International Conference on Acoustics, Speech and Signal Processing (ICASSP), pp. 6645–6649 (2013)
13. Gregor, K., Danihelka, I., Graves, A., Rezende, D.J., Wierstra, D.: Draw: a recurrent neural network for image generation. arXiv preprint arXiv:1502.04623 (2015)
14. Joly, A., et al.: Interactive plant identification based on social image data. Ecol. Inf. **23**, 22–34 (2014)
15. Joly, A., et al.: LifeCLEF 2016: multimedia life species identification challenges. In: Fuhr, N., et al. (eds.) CLEF 2016. LNCS, vol. 9822, pp. 286–310. Springer, Cham (2016). https://doi.org/10.1007/978-3-319-44564-9_26

16. Kingma, D.P., Ba, J.: Adam: a method for stochastic optimization. arXiv preprint arXiv:1412.6980 (2014)
17. Kumar, A., et al.: Ask me anything: dynamic memory networks for natural language processing. In: ICML, pp. 1378–1387 (2016)
18. Lee, S.H., Chan, C.S., Mayo, S.J., Remagnino, P.: How deep learning extracts and learns leaf features for plant classification. Pattern Recogn. **71**, 1–13 (2017)
19. Lee, S.H., Chan, C.S., Remagnino, P.: Multi-organ plant classification based on convolutional and recurrent neural networks. IEEE Trans. Image Process. **27**(9), 4287–4301 (2018)
20. Lee, S.H., Chang, Y.L., Chan, C.S.: LifeCLEF 2017 plant identification challenge: classifying plants using generic-organ correlation features. In: Working Notes of CLEF 2017 (2017)
21. Lee, S.H., Chang, Y.L., Chan, C.S., Remagnino, P.: HGO-CNN: hybrid generic-organ convolutional neural network for multi-organ plant classification. In: ICIP, pp. 4462–4466 (2017)
22. Ng, J.Y.H., Hausknecht, M., Vijayanarasimhan, S., Vinyals, O., Monga, R., Toderici, G.: Beyond short snippets: deep networks for video classification. In: CVPR, pp. 4694–4702 (2015)
23. Ren, M., Zemel, R.S.: End-to-end instance segmentation with recurrent attention. arXiv preprint arXiv:1605.09410 (2017)
24. Reyes, A.K., Caicedo, J.C., Camargo, J.E.: Fine-tuning deep convolutional networks for plant recognition. In: CLEF (Working Notes) (2015)
25. Romera-Paredes, B., Torr, P.H.S.: Recurrent instance segmentation. In: Leibe, B., Matas, J., Sebe, N., Welling, M. (eds.) ECCV 2016. LNCS, vol. 9910, pp. 312–329. Springer, Cham (2016). https://doi.org/10.1007/978-3-319-46466-4_19
26. Shuai, B., Zuo, Z., Wang, B., Wang, G.: Dag-recurrent neural networks for scene labeling. In: CVPR, pp. 3620–3629 (2016)
27. Szűcs, G., Papp, D., Lovas, D.: Viewpoints combined classification, method in image-based plant identification task. In: CLEF (Working Notes), vol. 1180, pp. 763–770 (2014)
28. Vinyals, O., Toshev, A., Bengio, S., Erhan, D.: Show and tell: lessons learned from the 2015 MSCOCO image captioning challenge. IEEE Trans. Pattern Anal. Mach. Intell. **39**(4), 652–663 (2017)
29. Wu, Z., Jiang, Y.G., Wang, X., Ye, H., Xue, X.: Multi-stream multi-class fusion of deep networks for video classification. In: Proceedings of the 2016 ACM on Multimedia Conference, pp. 791–800 (2016)
30. Xiong, C., Merity, S., Socher, R.: Dynamic memory networks for visual and textual question answering. In: ICML, pp. 2397–2406 (2016)
31. Xu, H., Saenko, K.: Ask, attend and answer: exploring question-guided spatial attention for visual question answering. In: Leibe, B., Matas, J., Sebe, N., Welling, M. (eds.) ECCV 2016. LNCS, vol. 9911, pp. 451–466. Springer, Cham (2016). https://doi.org/10.1007/978-3-319-46478-7_28
32. Yang, Z., He, X., Gao, J., Deng, L., Smola, A.: Stacked attention networks for image question answering. In: CVPR, pp. 21–29 (2016)
33. Yanikoglu, B., Tolga, Y., Tirkaz, C., FuenCaglartes, E.: Sabanci-Okan system at lifeCLEF 2014 plant identification competition. In: CLEF (Working Notes) (2014)
34. Yu, H., Wang, J., Huang, Z., Yang, Y., Xu, W.: Video paragraph captioning using hierarchical recurrent neural networks. In: CVPR, pp. 4584–4593 (2016)

Microblog Contextualization: Advantages and Limitations of a Multi-sentence Compression Approach

Elvys Linhares Pontes[1,2,3]([✉]), Stéphane Huet[1],
and Juan-Manuel Torres-Moreno[1,2,3]

[1] LIA, Université d'Avignon et des Pays de Vaucluse, 84000 Avignon, France
elvys.linhares-pontes@alumni.univ-avignon.fr
[2] Polytechnique Montréal, Montréal, QC, Canada
[3] Université du Québec à Montréal, Montréal, QC, Canada

Abstract. The content analysis task of the MC2 CLEF 2017 lab aims to generate small summaries in four languages to contextualize microblogs. This paper analyzes the challenges of this task and also details the advantages and limitations of our approach using a cross-lingual compressive text summarization. We split this task in several subtasks in order to discuss their setup. In addition, we suggest an evaluation protocol to reduce the bias of the current metrics toward the approaches by extraction.

Keywords: Microblog contextualization
Multi-sentence compression · Word embedding · Wikipedia

1 Introduction

The MC2 CLEF 2017 [3] lab analyzed the context and the social impact of microblogs. This lab was composed of three main tasks: (1) Content Analysis, (2) Microblog Search, and (3) Time Line Illustration. The Content Analysis task involved itself several items: classification, filtering, language recognition, localization, entity extraction, linking open data, and summarization of Wikipedia pages and microblogs. Specifically, the summarization item, on which we focus here, aims to generate a textual summary using Wikipedia pages to contextualize a microblog in four languages (English, French, Portuguese, and Spanish).

This paper aims to present the complexity and challenges of the MC2 task to contextualize microblogs in four languages. We also carry out an analysis of our last year's participation (named CLCTS) [5] that proposed a cross-language compressive text summarization method to extract information from several language versions of Wikipedia in order to enhance informativeness. Our approach analyzes this task in several subtasks, each being prone to errors; this requires to measure how each subtask acts on the quality of summaries. Therefore, we propose an evaluation protocol to evaluate this task in two ways: end-to-end and by subtask.

© Springer Nature Switzerland AG 2018
P. Bellot et al. (Eds.): CLEF 2018, LNCS 11018, pp. 181–190, 2018.
https://doi.org/10.1007/978-3-319-98932-7_17

This paper is organized as follows. Section 2 briefly describes a baseline approach and an overview of the CLCTS architecture to tackle the MC2 task. Next, in Sects. 3 and 4, we analyze the challenges of this task, the advantages and limitations of our approach. Then, we propose a protocol to evaluate this task in several ways in Sect. 5. Finally, we compare our approach with other state-of-the-art methods and we make final conclusions in Sects. 6 and 7, respectively.

2   System Architecture

A simple baseline for the MC2 task aims to retrieve information about a festival in a microblog from the Wikipedia databases in four languages (English, French, Portuguese, and Spanish). Then, this system selects the most relevant sentences that describe a festival to generate a short summary of 120 words independently for each language version. However, this approach does not cross-check the facts between languages and an extractive summarization may contain several irrelevant words that reduce the informativeness of summaries.

In order to improve the informativeness, we jointly take into account several language versions of Wikipedia and the sentences are compressed in order to retain only the relevant information. However, this analysis increases the complexity of the MC2 task. Considering these problems, we divided this task into subtasks. In this regard, we present their challenges, advantages, and limitations.

We first divided our system into two main parts. The first one (see Fig. 1, left side) aims to retrieve the Wikipedia pages that best describe the festival mentioned in a microblog (Sect. 3). Then, we scored these Wikipedia pages according to their relevance with respect to a microblog.

The second part of our system (see Fig. 1, right side) analyzes the best scored pages, then it extracts the relevant information from this subset in order to generate a short text summary. Our approach creates clusters of similar sentences, then we use a Cross-Language Compressive Text Summarization (CLCTS) system (Sect. 4) to compress the clusters and then generate summaries in four languages describing a festival.

3   Wikipedia Document Retrieval

The set of CLEF microblogs is composed of tweets in several languages related to festivals around the world. Wikipedia provides a description of a given festival in several languages (e.g. the Avignon Festival has a dedicated page in 17 languages). We independently analyze four language versions of Wikipedia (en, es, fr, and pt) for each microblog, by repeating the whole process first to retrieve the best Wikipedia pages and then to summarize the pages for the four versions of Wikipedia.

The following subsections describe the procedure to analyze and to retrieve the Wikipedia pages which are the most related to a festival in a microblog.

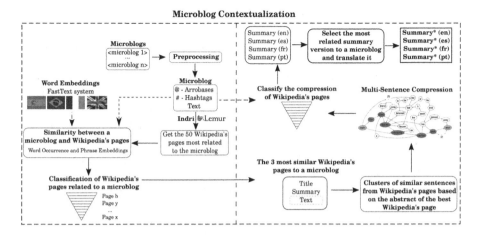

Fig. 1. Our system architecture to contextualize the microblogs.

3.1 Wikipedia Page Retrieval

The first challenge of the MC2 task is to retrieve the Wikipedia pages that best describe a festival in a microblog. A microblog is written in a specific language and contains usernames, hashtags, text, and punctuation marks. Based on this microblog, a system has to identify the most relevant Wikipedia pages in four languages with respect to a festival.

We assume that hashtags and usernames represent the keywords of a tweet, and they are independent of the language. In other words, the festival name, its geographic localization, or a show name normally have the same name in different languages (e.g. "Festival d'Avignon" in French and "Avignon Festival" in English share the same keywords). We remove all punctuation marks. From hashtags, usernames, and the plain text (i.e. the tweet without hashtags, usernames, and punctuation), we create Indri queries to retrieve 50 Wikipedia documents per each microblog[4]. These Indri queries have hashtags, usernames, and the word "festival" as keywords.

The procedure described above is simple but has several limitations. Some language versions of the Wikipedia database have very little information or no page at all about a festival. In this case, the Indri system may retrieve pages about other festivals (e.g. "Avignon Festival" is not available in Portuguese). Besides, some of these festivals have names that vary according to the language and our system does not translate these names to retrieve these pages in other languages. Another characteristic that we do not take into account is the date of a microblog. Normally, people write their microblogs during festivals, therefore timestamp could have helped us to identify the correct festival.

---

[4] https://www.lemurproject.org/indri.php.

3.2   Selection of Wikipedia Pages

The Wikipedia pages retrieved by the Indri system may contain several subjects. Indri returns these pages sorted by relevance, where the first page is the most relevant, the second is less relevant and so on. However, the quality of these results depends on the Indri query and the amount of information available about a festival. Some microblogs only contain limited information about a festival, e.g. the location of a festival or the name of a show. In this case, a system has to identify the correct festival among several with similar characteristics, presentations in common, or in the same location.

To confirm the relevance of the Wikipedia pages retrieved by Indri, we select the pages most related to a microblog. Normally, the title of a Wikipedia document has few words and contains the core information, while the summary of the document, which is usually made of the first paragraphs of the article before the start of the first section, is larger and provide additional information[5]. Therefore, we consider Eq. (4) to compute the relevance score of the Wikipedia document D with respect to the microblog T.

$$\text{score}_{title} = \alpha_1 \times \text{sim}(ht, title) + \alpha_2 \times \text{sim}(un, title) + \alpha_3 \times \text{sim}(nw, title) \quad (1)$$

$$\text{score}_{sum} = \beta_1 \times \text{sim}(ht, sum) + \beta_2 \times \text{sim}(un, sum) + \beta_3 \times \text{sim}(nw, sum) \quad (2)$$

$$\text{sim}(x, y) = \gamma_1 \times \text{cosine}(x, y) + \gamma_2 \times \text{occur}(x, y) \quad (3)$$

$$\text{score}_{doc} = \text{score}_{title} + \text{score}_{summary} \quad (4)$$

where ht are the hashtags of the tweet T, un the usernames of T, nw the normal words of T, and sum the summary of D. $\text{occur}(x, y)$ represents the number of occurrences of x in y, while $\text{cosine}(x, y)$ is the cosine similarity between x and y using Continuous Space Vectors[6] [2].

We empirically set up the parameters as follows: $\alpha_1 = \alpha_2 = 0.1, \alpha_3 = 0.01, \beta_1 = \beta_2 = 0.05, \beta_3 = 0.005, \gamma_1 = 1$ and $\gamma_2 = 0.5$. These coefficients give more weights to hashtags than usernames and the tweet text, and compensate the shorter length of the titles of Wikipedia articles with respect to their summary. These pages may contain several subjects and we only want to keep the pages that describe the festival of the microblog. Therefore, we finally keep in each language the three Wikipedia documents with the highest scores to be analyzed by the Text Compression (TC) system.

Our system prioritizes the information in hashtags and arrobases; however, a microblog has few information about a festival and, sometimes, this information is too general or too specific to easily identify a festival. Another problem is that the Wikipedia dataset has several kinds of pages, e.g. lists of festivals based on

---

[5] We did not consider the whole text of Wikipedia pages because it is sometimes huge and we preferred to rely on the work of the contributors to build the summary of the article.

[6] We used the pre-trained word embeddings (en, es, fr, and pt) of FastText system [2] that is available in https://github.com/facebookresearch/fastText/blob/master/pretrained-vectors.md.

a show, cities, or types of festival. These pages contain irrelevant information about a particular festival and may reduce the informativeness of summaries.

4   Text Summarization

One of the biggest challenges of the Microblog Contextualization task is to summarize all the information available in a correct and informative summary about a festival. As we described before, the retrieved pages may contain wrong information because they may be in different languages and describe various festivals.

While famous festivals have several Wikipedia pages that describe in detail all previous editions, less prominent ones have only one page or no article at all in Wikipedia. For this reason, we use the best scored page as the reference for the contextualization of microblogs. This analysis helps to have access to the correct subject and avoid using information about other subjects. The abstract provided at the start of the Wikipedia pages is assumed to be good enough to be coherent and to provide a basic explanation about a festival. However, relying only on this part of the article may lead to miss relevant information about the festival that could be obtained from other sections or even other pages. For this reason, we preferred to use the summary of the top article as a basic abstract and to improve its quality with relevant information using Multi-Sentences Compression (MSC) (i.e. generate sentences that are shorter and more informative than the original sentences of the summary). Then, we translate the best summaries for the languages that have poor summaries.

In the case some Wikipedia pages do not have an abstract, the whole text is analyzed. Nevertheless, this text may have additional information that is not relevant to contextualize a festival in only 120 words. Therefore, our approach strongly depends on the best scored page abstract to generate a correct summary.

4.1   Clustering

Clustering enables the identification of subjects and relevant information inside a document. These clusters are composed of similar sentences. The objective of this process is to divide a document in topics where each cluster describes a specific topic.

As we consider the sentences of the summary of the best scored page as key sentences, we create clusters made of sentences from the three first retrieved pages, and similar to each key sentence. Two sentences are considered as similar if the cosine similarity between them is bigger than a threshold[7].

It can happen that some festivals have only a single relevant Wikipedia page. The cosine similarity normally helps in selecting only pertinent sentences; however, particularly in this case, sentences which are similar to key sentences may deal with different subjects and may still be included in clusters with irrelevant information.

---

[7] We empirically set up a threshold of 0.4 to consider two sentences as similar.

4.2   Multi-sentence Compression

The problematics of text summarization is to produce summaries that are both grammatical and informative while meeting length restrictions, 120 words in the task considered here. Since most of sentences in Wikipedia are long, we attempt to compress them to preserve only the relevant information. We use a MSC method to generate a shorter and hopefully more informative compression for each cluster. Our MSC method adopts the approach proposed by Linhares Pontes et al. [6,8] to model a document D as a Word Graph (WG), where vertices represent words and arcs represent the cohesion of the words. The weights of the arcs represent the level of cohesion between the words of two vertices based on the frequency and the position of these words in the sentences (Eq. 5).

$$w(e_{i,j}) = \frac{\text{cohesion}(e_{i,j})}{freq(i) \times freq(j)}, \tag{5}$$

$$\text{cohesion}(e_{i,j}) = \frac{freq(i) + freq(j)}{\sum_{f \in D} dist(f,i,j)^{-1}}, \tag{6}$$

$$dist(f,i,j) = \begin{cases} pos(f,i) - pos(f,j), & \text{if } pos(f,i) < pos(f,j) \\ 0, & \text{otherwise} \end{cases} \tag{7}$$

This approach relies on the analysis of keywords, in order to ensure to keep the core information of the cluster, and the 3-grams of the document, in order to preserve the grammaticality. Since each cluster to compress is composed of similar sentences, we consider that there is only one topic; the Latent Dirichlet Allocation (LDA) method is used to identify the keywords of this topic [1].

From the weights of 2-grams (Eq. 5), the relevance of a 3-gram is based on the relevance of the two 2-grams, as described in Eq. 8:

$$3\text{-gram}(i,j,k) = \frac{qt_3(i,j,k)}{\max_{a,b,c \in WG} qt_3(a,b,c)} \times \frac{w(e_{i,j}) + w(e_{j,k})}{2}, \tag{8}$$

In order to generate a better compression, the objective function expressed in Eq. 9 is minimized in order to improve the informativeness and the grammaticality.

$$\text{Minimize} \left(\alpha \sum_{(i,j) \in A} b_{i,j} \cdot x_{i,j} - \beta \sum_{k \in K} c_k \cdot w_k - \gamma \sum_{t \in T} d_k \cdot z_t \right) \tag{9}$$

where x_{ij} indicates the existence of the arc (i,j) in the solution, $w(i,j)$ is the cohesion of the words i and j (Eq. 5), z_t indicates the existence of the 3-gram t in the solution, d_t is the relevance of the 3-gram t (Eq. 8), c_k indicates the existence of a word with label (keyword) k and β is the geometric average of the arc weights in the graph (more details in [6,8]). Finally, the 50 best solutions are computed according to the objective (9) and we select the sentence with the lowest final score (Eq. 10) as the best compression.

$$score_{norm}(f) = \frac{e^{score_{opt}(f)}}{||f||}, \tag{10}$$

where $score_{opt}(f)$ is the value of the path to generate the compression f from Eq. 9. Like Linhares Pontes et al. [8], we set up the parameters to $\alpha = 1.0$, $\beta = 0.9$ and $\gamma = 0.1$.

Our approach assumes that clusters are composed of only correct sentences (subject + verb + object) to generate correct compressions. Another limitation is the similarity of sentences in a cluster. A cluster has to describe a single topic; otherwise, the MSC will merge information of several subjects and generate a compression with wrong information.

4.3   Summary Generation

The last step of summarization is the generation of summaries. While original sentences are likely to be more grammatically correct than compressions, the compressed sentences are by definition shorter and have in principle more relevant information. Therefore, we prefer to add a compression in the summary if this compression is considered more relevant than the original sentences.

We generate summaries by concatenating the most similar compression to a microblog without redundant sentences. The relevance of sentences/compressions is calculated based on the average TF-IDF. We add a sentence/compression to the summary only if the cosine similarity between this compression and the sentences already added in the summary is lower that a threshold of 0.4.

Let us note that our approach does not check the time of facts and consequently, it may generate summaries that do not preserve the sequence of facts.

4.4   Best Summary

The best possible scenario is the generation of a summary for each language version of Wikipedia. However, some language versions do not have a page or have a small text describing a specific festival. Therefore, we analyzed four summaries (one for each language version) for each microblog and we only retain the summary which contains the best description. We consider a summary as relevant if it is similar to the microblog. As the translation process generates some errors, we translate a language version summary only if the quality of the best summary is much better than other versions[8]. Therefore, we used the Yandex library[9] to translate the kept summary into other languages (en, es, fr, and pt).

---

[8] We translate a summary into a target language only if the summary in the target language has a similarity score (cosine similarity between the summary and the microblog) lower by 0.2 than the similarity score between the best summary and the microblog.

[9] https://tech.yandex.com/translate/.

The pipeline made of the summarization and translation processes is prone to errors, which reduces the quality of summaries. However, we have to use information from other language versions of Wikipedia when the available information about a festival in a language is poor or does not exist.

5   Evaluation Protocol

The MC2 task contains several subtasks and the automatic evaluation of this task as an end-to-end problem generates incomplete results. In our opinion, the best way to evaluate this task is to split it in two subtasks (Wikipedia page retrieval and Text Summarization (TS)). In this case, we can estimate the impact of each subtask in the contextualization.

Our proposition for the evaluation protocol is composed of three steps: Wikipedia pages retrieval, TS and microblog contextualization (Fig. 2). For the Wikipedia pages retrieval subtask, systems have to determine which Wikipedia pages describe a festival in a microblog. The TS subtask consists in generating a summary of a festival based on one or several Wikipedia pages. Finally, the microblog contextualization task is composed of both subtasks.

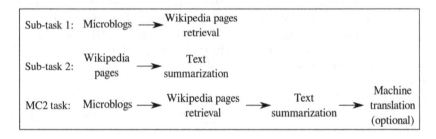

Fig. 2. Proposition of an evaluation protocol for MC2 task composed of two subtasks.

The Wikipedia pages retrieval subtask can be evaluated with a list of the Wikipedia pages related to a microblog. We can evaluate the performance of a system if it retrieves the correct Wikipedia pages for each microblog. The TS subtask and microblog contextualization task can be analyzed in several ways: automatic, semi-automatic and manual evaluations. Automatic (FRESA [9]) and semi-automatic (ROUGE [4]) evaluation systems analyze the overlap of n-grams between reference summaries and candidate summaries (or original text) to determine the quality of candidate summaries. However, compression and translation methods change the structure of sentences by generating paraphrases and new n-grams that may not exist in reference summaries (or source document), thereby reducing ROUGE (or FRESA) scores. In this case, a manual evaluation is required to evaluate the quality of these summaries.

6   Related Work and Propositions

Several studies have analyzed Text Summarization (TS) and Cross-Language Text Summarization (CLTS) [7,10,11]. TS aims to create a short, accurate, and fluid summary of a longer text document; CLTS also generates a summary but the language of the summary is different from the language of the source documents. As we described before, some language versions of Wikipedia have a limited content so the CLTS can produce more correct and informative summaries.

Wan [10] considered the information in the source and in the target language to estimate the relevance of sentences for cross-lingual summarization. He proposed a graph-based summarization method (CoRank) that considers a sentence as relevant if this sentence in both languages is heavily linked with other sentences in each language separately (source-source and target-target language similarities) and between languages (source-target language similarity). Zhang *et al.* [11] analyzed Predicate-Argument Structures (PAS) to obtain an abstractive English-to-Chinese CLTS. They split parallel sentences at the level of bilingual concepts and facts and use the CoRank method to fuse these structures and to generate cross-lingual summaries considering their saliency and their translation quality. Linhares Pontes *et al.* have published a recent work about cross-language text summarization of multiple texts written about the same topic [7]. Their method analyzes the information in both languages (source and target languages) to extract as much information as possible about documents. In addition, they use SC and MSC to compress and improve the informativeness of sentences and, consequently, the quality of the summary.

The methods described above need a group of documents that describe a same subject to generate a correct summary; however, the MC2 task does not necessarily provide correct documents about a festival and the use of these methods can generate bad summaries. A possible solution is to ensure the quality of the source documents about a same subject and to adapt these methods to analyze Wikipedia pages.

7   Conclusion

The Microblog Contextualization task is composed of several challenges that can modify the quality of results. Depending on the microblog, this task may require the generation of multi-lingual and cross-lingual summaries. We proposed a solution for each subtask in order to generate more informative summaries; however, this task involves several subtasks and the performance of our system depends on all these subtasks. This pipeline of subtasks complicates the identification of errors and the performance analysis of our approach. Another major problem is the lack of a training corpus to test and to adapt our system for this task.

We hope the organizers will make available a complete training/test dataset with all information about the main task and its subtasks in the next edition of Microblog Contextualization task. Our system is modular and can contextualize microblogs with several approaches. For example, we can remove the MSC and/or the automatic translation methods in our approach. With this dataset, we could evaluate and improve our system.

Acknowledgement. This work was partially financed by the European Project CHISTERA-AMIS ANR-15-CHR2-0001.

References

1. Blei, D.M., Ng, A.Y., Jordan, M.I.: Latent Dirichlet allocation. J. Mach. Learn. Res. **3**, 993–1022 (2003). http://dl.acm.org/citation.cfm?id=944919.944937
2. Bojanowski, P., Grave, E., Joulin, A., Mikolov, T.: Enriching word vectors with subword information. arXiv preprint arXiv:1607.04606 (2016)
3. Ermakova, L., Goeuriot, L., Mothe, J., Mulhem, P., Nie, J.-Y., SanJuan, E.: CLEF 2017 microblog cultural contextualization lab overview. In: Jones, G.J.F., et al. (eds.) CLEF 2017. LNCS, vol. 10456, pp. 304–314. Springer, Cham (2017). https://doi.org/10.1007/978-3-319-65813-1_27
4. Lin, C.Y.: ROUGE: a package for automatic evaluation of summaries. In: Workshop Text Summarization Branches Out (ACL), pp. 74–81 (2004)
5. Linhares Pontes, E., Huet, S., Torres-Moreno, J.M., Linhares, A.C.: Microblog contextualization using continuous space vectors: multi-sentence compression of cultural documents. In: Working Notes of the CLEF Lab on Microblog Cultural Contextualization, vol. 1866. CEUR-WS.org (2017)
6. Linhares Pontes, E., Huet, S., da Silva, T.G., Linhares, A.C., Torres-Moreno, J.M.: Multi-sentence compression with word vertex-labeled graphs and integer linear programming. In: Workshop on Graph-Based Methods for Natural Language Processing, TextGraphs-12. Association for Computational Linguistics (2018)
7. Linhares Pontes, E., Huet, S., Torres-Moreno, J.-M., Linhares, A.C.: Cross-language text summarization using sentence and multi-sentence compression. In: Silberztein, M., Atigui, F., Kornyshova, E., Métais, E., Meziane, F. (eds.) NLDB 2018. LNCS, vol. 10859, pp. 467–479. Springer, Cham (2018). https://doi.org/10.1007/978-3-319-91947-8_48
8. Linhares Pontes, E., da Silva, T.G., Linhares, A.C., Torres-Moreno, J.M., Huet, S.: Métodos de otimização combinatória aplicados ao problema de compressão multi-frases. In: Anais do XLVIII Simpósio Brasileiro de Pesquisa Operacional (SBPO), pp. 2278–2289 (2016)
9. Torres-Moreno, J.M.: Automatic Text Summarization. Wiley, Hoboken (2014)
10. Wan, X.: Using bilingual information for cross-language document summarization. In: ACL, pp. 1546–1555 (2011)
11. Zhang, J., Zhou, Y., Zong, C.: Abstractive cross-language summarization via translation model enhanced predicate argument structure fusing. IEEE/ACM Trans. Audio Speech Lang. Process. **24**(10), 1842–1853 (2016)

Early Detection of Depression Based on Linguistic Metadata Augmented Classifiers Revisited

Best of the eRisk Lab Submission

Marcel Trotzek[1](✉) (iD), Sven Koitka[1,2,3](✉) (iD),
and Christoph M. Friedrich[1,4](✉) (iD)

[1] Department of Computer Science,
University of Applied Sciences and Arts Dortmund (FHDO),
Emil-Figge-Str. 42, 44227 Dortmund, Germany
mtrotzek@stud.fh-dortmund.de,
{sven.koitka,christoph.friedrich}@fh-dortmund.de
[2] Department of Computer Science, TU Dortmund University, Dortmund, Germany
[3] Department of Diagnostic and Interventional Radiology and Neuroradiology,
University Hospital Essen, Essen, Germany
[4] Institute for Medical Informatics, Biometry and Epidemiology (IMIBE),
University Hospital Essen, Essen, Germany

Abstract. Early detection of depression based on written texts has become an important research area due to the rise of social media platforms and because many affected individuals are still not treated. During the eRisk task for early detection of depression at CLEF 2017, FHDO Biomedical Computer Science Group (BCSG) submitted results based on five text classification models. This paper builds upon this work to examine the task and especially the $ERDE_o$ metric in further detail and to analyze how an additional type of metadata features can help in this task. Finally, different prediction thresholds and ensembles of the developed models are utilized to investigate the possible improvements, and a newly proposed alternative early detection metric is evaluated.

Keywords: Depression · Early detection · Linguistic metadata
Neural networks

1 Introduction

World Health Organization (WHO) ranks depression as the largest contributor to global disability with more than 300 million people affected worldwide [28]. WHO also estimates that 788,000 people have died by suicide in 2015, to which depression is a large contributor. As depression occurs in any group and is not limited to specific life situations, it is often described to be accompanied by paradoxes caused by the contrast between an affected individual's self-image and the actual facts [4]. Although the prevalence and severity of depression are

© Springer Nature Switzerland AG 2018
P. Bellot et al. (Eds.): CLEF 2018, LNCS 11018, pp. 191–202, 2018.
https://doi.org/10.1007/978-3-319-98932-7_18

well-known, it was estimated in 2007 that only half of the individuals suffering from any mental disorder in Europe are treated [2].

From another perspective, studies have shown that people with stigmatized illnesses are more likely to use the internet to obtain information [5], connect with other affected individuals, share experiences, and help each other [10]. In combination with the growth of social media platforms, this emphasizes how important it is to find ways to assist individuals that are at risk of or already suffering from depression based on texts written on such platforms. Results could not only be used for direct intervention by trained counselors but, for example, also serve as an important additional resource for professional therapists.

The eRisk pilot task for early detection of depression at CLEF 2017 [16] was therefore created to foster research in this area and evaluate first models with an emphasis on early depression classification based on as few writings as possible. This paper extends the research done by this team during the eRisk task, which was focussed on the concept of combining user-level linguistic metadata with different text classification methods. After examining some related work in the area of text-based mental health classification in Sect. 2, Sect. 3 gives new insights into the dataset and the $ERDE_o$ metric for early detection systems, which was first used for eRisk. Section 4 examines a new type of linguistic metadata features, namely emotion and sentiment information, and its viability for this specific dataset. Finally, Sect. 5 contains additional results obtained from the models used during the task and also shows the evaluation of an alternative early detection metric.

2   Related Work

Detecting mental health status based on language use dates back to speech studies [6,27] that found an elevated use of first person singular pronouns in the spoken words of depression patients. Similar research based on written texts [20] reported, for example, a more frequent use of the word "I" in particular and more negative emotion words. A recent study [1] also found more absolutist words (like "absolutely", "completely", "every", or "nothing") in English forum posts related to depression, anxiety, and suicidal ideation than in posts from completely unrelated areas as well as in posts concerning asthma, diabetes, or cancer.

The knowledge that mental state has various effects on a person's language has driven the development of language analysis tools like Linguistic Inquiry and Word Count (LIWC) [23], which allows researchers to calculate a total of 93 lexicon-based features for any given text. Similar to the eRisk task at CLEF, social media texts have already been used in a shared task concerning the detection of depression and post-traumatic stress disorder (PTSD) [7]. Apart from shared tasks, several different approaches have been used to detect depression on platforms like Facebook, Twitter, and reddit [11].

3   Dataset and Task

The eRisk 2017 dataset contains chronological text sequences written by 486 training users (83 depressed users, 295,023 documents total) and 401 test users

(52 depressed users, 236,371 documents total) on the social platform reddit.com. Depressed users were selected based on the fact that they mentioned an explicit diagnosis in one of their messages and not further validated. Users for the control group were selected randomly from users that had posted recently when the dataset was collected. Each document is represented by a *title* and *text* field, of which one may be empty depending on the message type, and a timestamp of when the message was posted. Since reddit provides all timestamps in UTC, there is no way to know the actual timezone of the user, which would most likely lead to misleading results when comparing timestamps between users. To simulate the early detection aspect, chunks of 10% of each user's messages were provided on a weekly basis. Participants had to decide whether their models were confident enough to predict a user or whether they wanted to wait for more messages in the following week. Any submitted prediction was final.

Because of the way control group users were selected, their distribution over time does not match the distribution of the depressed users. As soon as the latest messages of each user are available in the final week, the latest timestamp at which a user has posted contains a powerful hidden feature that could potentially be exploited at this point: Using the time of the latest post per user in seconds since epoch as only input for a logistic regression classifier results in an F_1 score of 0.78 for the test data, which is far better than any actual submission to the task. Figure 1 shows boxplots of this feature (converted to days since epoch) and illustrates how easily the classes can be separated for both the training and test data. The maximum value of 16,638.6 corresponds to 2015-07-23 when the dataset was collected. As the results show, no team has actually exploited this fact for the models that submitted predictions only in the final week. To prevent such an exploit in future tasks, the control and target groups should either be collected with a similar distribution over time or the timestamp feature should be completely removed or limited to a less precise format for future tasks.

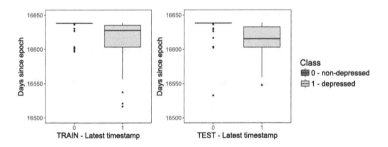

Fig. 1. Boxplot of the latest time a user has written a post in days since epoch with two decimal places. Lower outliers have been omitted to enhance visibility.

Submissions to the eRisk task were evaluated based on the standard F_1 score and based on the Early Risk Detection Error (ERDE), which was defined by the organizers of this task [15, pp. 7–8]. Mainly, this score includes a punishment for late predictions of true positives based on the number of documents seen before the prediction. The cost for true positives is defined as $lc_o(k) \cdot c_{tp}$. For the eRisk task, c_{tp} was set to $c_{tp} = c_{fn} = 1$, making a late prediction equal to no prediction at all [16, p. 5], while $lc_o(k)$ defines after how many messages k the cost grows and is given by [15, p. 8]:

$$lc_o(k) = 1 - \frac{1}{1 + e^{k-o}}, \tag{1}$$

with the free parameter o controlling the center of this sigmoid function. Figure 2 displays the cost function $lc_o(k)$ of $ERDE_5$ and $ERDE_{50}$, which were used for the task. Because this leads to a true positive cost that grows rapidly to the same value used for false negatives and the cost is based on the absolute number of documents, $ERDE_o$ cost has some issues in the context of shared tasks. Since the eRisk task required participants to read whole chunks of between 1 and 200 documents per user each week, it was impossible to predict several depressed users correctly: $ERDE_5$ could only result in a cost close to 1 for users with more than around 10 messages per week (100 messages total) and the same applies to $ERDE_{50}$ and users with more than around 55 messages per week (550 messages total). Since the test data of eRisk 2017 only contains 18 depressed users with less than 10 documents per week, the remaining 34 depressed users had nearly no effect on $ERDE_5$ at all. In fact, the best possible $ERDE_5$ score would have been 10.60%, while predicting only these 18 users as positive leads to a value of 10.61%. $ERDE_o$ is therefore hard to interpret and would actually require an equal amount of available messages per user to be viable in such a chunk-based shared task.

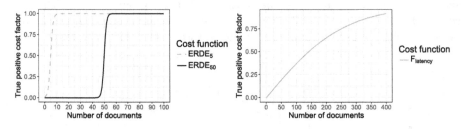

Fig. 2. Plot of the true positive cost functions used for $ERDE_5$ and $ERDE_{50}$ (left) as well as for $F_{latency}$ with $p = 0.0078$ (right).

Based on similar findings, an alternative score for early detection systems, namely $F_{latency}$, was recently proposed by another participating team of eRisk 2017 [21]. This metric incorporates the standard F_1 measure and uses a cost factor based on the latency of the classification, which is defined as the median number of messages read before predicting a depressed user. Based on this, they define their cost function $P_{latency}$ and the corresponding score $F_{latency}$ as [21, p. 497]:

$$P_{latency}(u, sys) = -1 + \frac{2}{1 + e^{-p \cdot (time(u,sys)-1)}} \tag{2}$$

$$F_{latency}(U, sys) = F_1(U, sys) \cdot \left(1 - \operatorname*{median}_{u \in U \wedge ref(u)=+} P_{latency}(u, sys)\right), \quad (3)$$

with $time(u, sys)$ denoting the number of documents seen for user u by system sys, the free parameter p to modify how the cost grows, the standard F_1 score $F_1(U, sys)$ calculated over all users in the dataset U, and $ref(u) = +$ referring to a user with a positive (depressed) label. In addition to the true positive cost function of $ERDE_o$, Fig. 2 also displays a plot of the cost function used for $F_{latency}$: It shows $P_{latency}$ with $p = 0.0078$ as proposed in the paper, which results in a cost of 0.5 for the median number of posts per user (142 for eRisk 2017). This results in a less rapid growth of the cost function, fewer parameters as there are no fixed cost values to define, and already incorporates F_1, which makes this score more meaningful alone. To compare the scores and provide further baseline results for $F_{latency}$, Sect. 5 also includes evaluations of this score for all models utilized by BCSG. Still, the cost is based on the absolute number of read documents, which leads to the same problem as discussed above for chunk-based shared task scenarios. A modified version of $ERDE_o$ based on the fraction of documents instead of the absolute number was thus proposed and evaluated in another paper by BCSG [25].

4   Linguistic Metadata

Using linguistic metadata features on user basis as an additional input to all classification models was one of the main concepts behind this team's participation in the eRisk 2017 task. The detailed description of these features is beyond the scope of this follow-up paper that will only focus on examining possible additional metadata features. Details about the features used during the task can be found in the corresponding working notes paper [24].

In particular, this follow-up work examines metadata features based on the emotions, opinions, and sentiments contained in a user's writings. This is based on the assumption that writings containing indications of depression might contain more negative emotions and an overall rather negative sentiment than writings of the control group. Since sentiment analysis in particular is a very broad and active research area [19], a variety of methods could be used to extract a sentiment feature from the reddit messages. This work is focussed on using lexica to calculate the sentiment and emotional content based on the words used in a message.

Several lexica specific to the task of sentiment or emotion detection have been collected by various researchers. The ones selected for this task are the NRC Emotion Lexicon [18], the Opinion Lexicon[1], the VADER Sentiment Lexicon [13], and SentiWordNet [3]. The NRC Emotion Lexicon contains 14,182 words that are assigned to one or more of the categories "positive", "negative", "anger", "anticipation", "disgust", "fear", "joy", "sadness", "surprise", and "trust". The

---

[1] https://www.cs.uic.edu/~liub/FBS/sentiment-analysis.html#lexicon, accessed on 2018-04-12.

respective features for each document are calculated by counting the words of each category and dividing these counts by the total number of lexicon words present in the document. The Opinion Lexicon consists of a list of 2,006 positive and a list of 4,783 negative words that can be used to similarly calculate two features. In contrast, the VADER Sentiment Lexicon contains 7,517 terms (including emoticons) with their average sentiment score based on ten human annotators on a scale between -4 (extremely negative) to 4 (extremely positive). A single VADER feature is therefore calculated as the mean sentiment score of a document's words that occur in the lexicon.

While the first three lexica directly consist of word lists with either an associated score or a categorization, SentiWordNet is based on the sets of synonyms (synsets) assigned to any word by WordNet [17] and contains a positivity, negativity, and objectivity score for each synset. Calculating the score for a message therefore requires to first obtain the fitting synset for each word based on the part of speech (POS) it represents in its sentence. POS tagging and the lookups of WordNet and SentiWordNet are all done based on the Python NLTK framework[2] for this work. The final SentiWordNet score of a message $SWN(d)$ is calculated as:

$$SWN(d) = \frac{1}{n_w} \cdot \sum_{w \in d} SWN_{pos}\left(w, POS_w\right) - SWN_{neg}\left(w, POS_w\right), \quad (4)$$

with n_w denoting the number of words in message d, the part of speech represented by a word POS_w, the positivity score of a word $SWN_{pos}(w, POS_w)$, and the negativity score of a word $SWN_{neg}(w, POS_w)$. Words that do not exist in WordNet are removed from the document before the calculation.

Similar to the other metadata features, the sentiment and emotion features described above are averaged over all documents of a user to obtain a user-level metadata vector. Figure 3 shows boxplots of all features extracted from the NRC Emotion Lexicon and also includes an additional feature based on the number of lexicon words present in the documents. Contrary to the original assumption, all kinds of emotions, as well as positive and negative words, tend to occur more often in documents of depressed users in this dataset. In general, the most indicative feature based on these boxplots seems to be the number of lexicon words present in a document.

Figure 4 displays a correlation matrix of all described sentiment and emotion features and also includes the class label information (0 for non-depressed and 1 for depressed). While the correlations among these features show how negative emotions indeed lead to lower VADER and SentiWordNet score and vice versa, all features have a slight positive correlation with the class label. The amount of positive and negative opinion words based on the Opinion Lexicon is also strongly correlated, showing that users with more positive words also use more negative words. This matches the insights given by the above boxplots and shows that all kinds of lexicon words occur more often in the depressed class and that the calculated sentiment scores based on VADER and SentiWordNet have no

---

[2] https://www.nltk.org/, accessed on 2018-04-12.

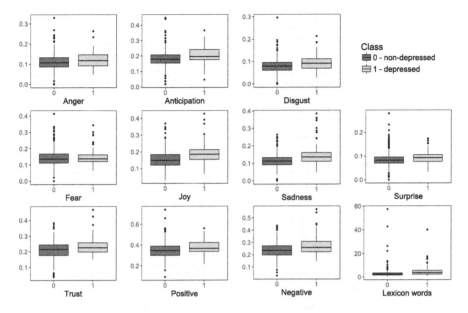

Fig. 3. Boxplot of the user-level emotion features based on the NRC Emotion Lexicon.

interesting correlation at all. As this indicates, experiments have shown that these features are not viable to enhance the previous models for early detection of depression based on the eRisk 2017 dataset.

The limited meaning of these features is likely due to the character of this specific dataset. While it could be speculated that depressed individuals indeed use more emotions of any kind in online discussions, the messages of the control group differ too drastically to make any general assumptions based on these observations. Since the control group has been selected randomly and therefore contains messages from all kinds of subreddits, the overall text quality and writing style cannot be compared to the target group. Another dataset used for the detection of anxiety on reddit [22] was explicitly collected in a way to obtain similar writings in both the control and target group. By only selecting messages from specific subreddits, the researchers considered their observation that "anxiety-related posts are overwhelmingly from a first-person point-of-view" [22, p. 59]. As the eRisk control group also contains many writings that only contain news headlines, a single short sentence, or even a single word, comparing them to messages of individuals who discuss their personal problems is often difficult. Based on these findings, choosing the control group users more selectively could be an interesting plan for future eRisk tasks, although this could potentially also lead to an unwanted bias that does not resemble real-world data on a social platform.

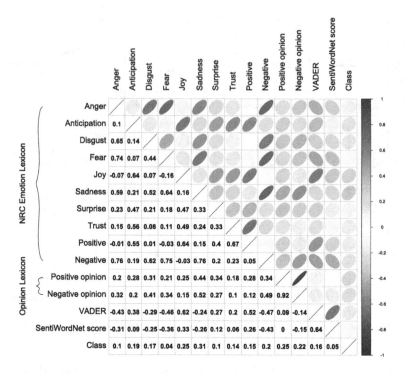

Fig. 4. Correlation matrix of user-based emotion and sentiment features including the class information (non-depressed/depressed).

5   Additional Results

The participation of this team in the eRisk 2017 task was based on five text classification models. The first four of these models (denoted as BCSGA/B/C/D) were used to predict a probability for the test users each week, while the final model (denoted as BCSGE) was only utilized in the final week to examine the effects of a late prediction model on all scores. Using these models, BCSG obtained the best results according to $ERDE_5$ and F_1 score and the second-best result according to $ERDE_{50}$ during the task. The first seven rows of Table 1 display the best results achieved within the scope of the pilot task and also contains the $F_{latency}$ scores of this team's models. A detailed description of the models is beyond the scope of this paper but can be found in the corresponding working notes paper [24]. In short, BCSG's models were created as follows:

BCSGA. The best F_1 score was obtained using this ensemble of four logistic regression classifiers based on three bags of words with different term weightings and n-grams and the user-based metadata features described in Sect. 4. The bags of words were calculated by first concatenating all available documents of a user.

BCSGB. Another logistic regression ensemble obtained the best $ERDE_5$ score: The two classifiers used in this case were again based on the user metadata and on a concatenation of document embeddings from two self-trained Paragraph Vector [14] models. The document classification was done by first calculating the average of all document embeddings for a user.

BCSGC. This model as well as the following two were based on a Recurrent Neural Network (RNN) [9] with a Long Short-Term Memory (LSTM) [12] layer to process a sequence of documents. In this case, the network input was created by first calculating a bag of words for each document separately and reducing them to 100 dimensions by using Latent Semantic Analysis (LSA) [8]. For all three neural network models the user metadata features were added as an additional input and merged with the LSTM output vector.

BCSGD. The second LSTM model was setup similar to BCSGC but used the document embeddings obtained from the Paragraph Vector models of BCSGB as input.

BCSGE. As already described, this final model was only used to submit any predictions in the final week of the task and was therefore not focussed on early detection. It was generally identical to BCSGD but used two new Paragraph Vector models with twice as many dimensions, an additional fully connected layer, weight decay and learning rate decay.

Table 1. Results on the eRisk 2017 test dataset during the task and based on later modifications of the same models. Rows with gray background contain the best results published by other teams and p denotes the prediction threshold for depressed predictions.

Model	$ERDE_5$	$ERDE_{50}$	F_1	$F_{latency}$
UNSLA [16]	13.66	9.68	0.59	-
UArizonaB [16]	13.07	11.63	0.30	-
BCSGA ($p > 0.5$) [16]	12.82	9.69	**0.64**	0.42
BCSGB [16]	12.70	10.39	0.55	0.34
BCSGC [16]	13.24	10.56	0.56	0.38
BCSGD [16]	13.04	10.53	0.57	0.37
BCSGE [16]	14.16	12.42	0.60	0.21
UNSL TVT-NB [26]	13.13	8.17	0.54	-
UNSL TVT-RF [26]	12.30	8.95	0.56	-
UArizona SVM [21]	13.10	9.70	0.51	0.39
BCSGA ($p > 0.4$)	13.17	8.47	0.62	**0.48**
BCSGA no meta ($p > 0.3$)	14.42	8.33	0.49	0.44
BCSGA no meta ($p > 0.5$)	13.09	9.76	0.63	0.39
Meta only ($p > 0.5$)	13.56	9.20	0.51	0.39
Meta only ($p > 0.7$)	12.73	9.92	0.60	0.38
ABCD ensemble ($p > 0.3$)	13.49	8.33	0.51	0.43
ABCD ensemble ($p > 0.4$)	12.69	9.44	0.59	0.39
ABCD ensemble ($p > 0.6$)	**12.24**	10.27	0.52	0.32
ABC ensemble ($p > 0.3$)	14.20	**8.11**	0.47	0.42
ACD ensemble ($p > 0.3$)	13.03	8.19	0.55	0.46

The second group of results in Table 1 shows two results that have been achieved by another team shortly after the ground truth had been released and the best baseline result for $F_{latency}$ published in the corresponding paper. All following results are based on the exact probabilities obtained from BCSG's models used during eRisk 2017. They illustrate the effect of modified prediction thresholds, possible results when evaluating BCSGA without metadata, and results obtained from the metadata features alone. Finally, some ensembles of three or four of these models are evaluated.

The results show, for example, that BCSGA would have obtained a drastically better $ERDE_{50}$ score if the prediction threshold had been set to 0.4 instead of 0.5 without seriously harming other scores and that discarding the metadata for this model could have resulted in an even better $ERDE_{50}$ but a much worse F_1 score in exchange. The evaluated ensembles unfortunately lead to slightly worse F_1 scores but result in the best overall $ERDE_o$ scores. In terms of $F_{latency}$, several models achieve a better score than the published baseline.

6 Conclusions

This paper has provided new insights into the dataset and evaluation metric used for the eRisk pilot task at CLEF 2017 that can serve as a basis for discussions about future workshops. The detailed analysis of the $ERDE_o$ score (and $ERDE_5$ in particular) has shown that it might not represent an interpretable result in a chunk-based shared task. An examination of lexicon-based sentiment and emotion features as additional linguistic metadata has shown that these features are unfortunately not helpful for depression detection using this specific dataset. A possible explanation for this fact has been found in the different text quality and style between the depressed users and the control group. The further evaluations of new combinations and prediction thresholds for the same models utilized during the task have provided new insights into the effect of the metadata features and varying thresholds.

Future work in this area and within the eRisk workshop in particular, should focus on the discussion of a modified evaluation metric. In addition, it could be interesting to provide a dataset with a control group that more closely resembles the depressed group regarding writing style and text quality. This could enable (and maybe even force) systems to find smaller differences in language use instead of separating users based on the pure text quality. Overall, the eRisk workshop has fostered research in this challenging and important area and has shown that there is a lot of room for future improvements.

Acknowledgment. The work of Sven Koitka was partially funded by a PhD grant from University of Applied Sciences and Arts Dortmund, Germany.

References

1. Al-Mosaiwi, M., Johnstone, T.: In an absolute state: elevated use of absolutist words is a marker specific to anxiety, depression, and suicidal ideation. Clin. Psychol. Sci. (2018, prepublished). https://doi.org/10.1177/2167702617747074
2. Alonso, J., et al.: Population level of unmet need for mental healthcare in Europe. Br. J. Psychiatr. **190**(4), 299–306 (2007)
3. Baccianella, S., Esuli, A., Sebastiani, F.: SentiWordNet 3.0: an enhanced lexical resource for sentiment analysis and opinion mining. In: Proceedings of the 7th International Conference on Language Resources and Evaluation (LREC 2010), Valletta, Malta, vol. 10 (2010)
4. Beck, A.T., Alford, B.A.: Depression: Causes and Treatment, 2nd edn. University of Pennsylvania Press, Philadelphia (2009)
5. Berger, M., Wagner, T.H., Baker, L.C.: Internet use and stigmatized illness. Soc. Sci. Med. **61**(8), 1821–1827 (2005)
6. Bucci, W., Freedman, N.: The language of depression. Bull. Menninger Clin. **45**(4), 334–358 (1981)
7. Coppersmith, G., Dredze, M., Harman, C., Hollingshead, K., Mitchell, M.: CLPsych 2015 shared task: depression and PTSD on Twitter. In: Proceedings of the 2nd Workshop on Computational Linguistics and Clinical Psychology: From Linguistic Signal to Clinical Reality (CLPsych 2015), Denver, Colorado, USA, pp. 31–39 (2015)
8. Deerwester, S., Dumais, S.T., Furnas, G.W., Landauer, T.K., Harshman, R.: Indexing by latent semantic analysis. J. Am. Soc. Inf. Sci. **41**(6), 391–407 (1990)
9. Goodfellow, I., Bengio, Y., Courville, A.: Deep Learning. MIT Press, Cambridge (2016)
10. Gowen, K., Deschaine, M., Gruttadara, D., Markey, D.: Young adults with mental health conditions and social networking websites: seeking tools to build community. Psychiatr. Rehabil. J. **35**(3), 245–250 (2012)
11. Guntuku, S.C., Yaden, D.B., Kern, M.L., Ungar, L.H., Eichstaedt, J.C.: Detecting depression and mental illness on social media: an integrative review. Curr. Opin. Behav. Sci. **18**, 43–49 (2017)
12. Hochreiter, S., Schmidhuber, J.: Long short-term memory. Neural Comput. **9**(8), 1735–1780 (1997)
13. Hutto, C.J., Gilbert, E.E.: VADER: a parsimonious rule-based model for sentiment analysis of social media text. In: Proceedings of the 8th International AAAI Conference on Weblogs and Social Media (ICWSM 2014), Ann Arbor, Michigan, USA, pp. 216–225 (2014)
14. Le, Q.V., Mikolov, T.: Distributed representations of sentences and documents. In: Proceedings of the 31st International Conference on Machine Learning (ICML 2014), Beijing, China, vol. 14, pp. 1188–1196 (2014)
15. Losada, D.E., Crestani, F.: A test collection for research on depression and language use. In: Experimental IR Meets Multilinguality, Multimodality, and Interaction: 7th International Conference of the CLEF Association, CLEF 2016, Évora, Portugal, pp. 28–39 (2016)
16. Losada, D.E., Crestani, F., Parapar, J.: eRISK 2017: CLEF lab on early risk prediction on the internet: experimental foundations. In: Proceedings Conference and Labs of the Evaluation Forum CLEF 2017, Dublin, Ireland (2017)
17. Miller, G.A.: WordNet: a lexical database for English. Commun. ACM **38**(11), 39–41 (1995)

18. Mohammad, S.M., Turney, P.D.: Crowdsourcing a word-emotion association lexicon. Comput. Intell. **29**(3), 436–465 (2013)
19. Pang, B., Lee, L.: Opinion mining and sentiment analysis. Found. Trends Inf. Retr. **2**(1–2), 1–135 (2008)
20. Rude, S., Gortner, E.-M., Pennebaker, J.: Language use of depressed and depression-vulnerable college students. Cogn. Emot. **18**(8), 1121–1133 (2004)
21. Sadeque, F., Xu, D., Bethard, S.: Measuring the latency of depression detection in social media. In: Proceedings of the 11th ACM International Conference on Web Search and Data Mining (WSDM 2018), Los Angeles, California, USA, pp. 495–503 (2018)
22. Shen, J.H., Rudzicz, F.: Detecting anxiety through reddit. In: Proceedings of the Fourth Workshop on Computational Linguistics and Clinical Psychology. From Linguistic Signal to Clinical Reality (CLPsych 2017), Vancouver, Canada, pp. 58–65 (2017)
23. Tausczik, Y.R., Pennebaker, J.W.: The psychological meaning of words: LIWC and computerized text analysis methods. J. Lang. Soc. Psychol. **29**(1), 24–54 (2010)
24. Trotzek, M., Koitka, S., Friedrich, C.M.: Linguistic metadata augmented classifiers at the CLEF 2017 task for early detection of depression. In: Working Notes Conference and Labs of the Evaluation Forum CLEF 2017, Dublin, Ireland (2017). http://ceur-ws.org/Vol-1866/paper_54.pdf. Accessed 29 Mar 2018
25. Trotzek, M., Koitka, S., Friedrich, C.M.: Utilizing neural networks and linguistic metadata for early detection of depression indications in text sequences. arXiv preprint arXiv:1804.07000 [cs.CL] (2018)
26. Villegas, M.P., Funez, D.G., Ucelay, M.J.G., Cagnina, L.C., Errecalde, M.L.: LIDIC - UNSL's participation at eRisk 2017: pilot task on early detection of depression. In: Working Notes Conference and Labs of the Evaluation Forum CLEF 2017, Dublin, Ireland (2017). http://ceur-ws.org/Vol-1866/paper_107.pdf. Accessed 29 Mar 2018
27. Weintraub, W.: Verbal Behavior: Adaptation and Psychopathology. Springer, New York (1981)
28. World Health Organization: Depression and Other Common Mental Disorders: Global Health Estimates (2017)

Deep Learning for ICD Coding: Looking for Medical Concepts in Clinical Documents in English and in French

Zulfat Miftahutdinov[1,2] and Elena Tutubalina[1,2(✉)]

[1] Kazan (Volga Region) Federal University, Kazan, Russia
zulfatmi@gmail.com, ElVTutubalina@kpfu.ru
[2] Neuromation OU, 10111 Tallinn, Estonia

Abstract. Medical Concept Coding (MCD) is a crucial task in biomedical information extraction. Recent advances in neural network modeling have demonstrated its usefulness in the task of natural language processing. Modern framework of sequence-to-sequence learning that was initially used for recurrent neural networks has been shown to provide powerful solution to tasks such as Named Entity Recognition or Medical Concept Coding. We have addressed the identification of clinical concepts within the International Classification of Diseases version 10 (ICD-10) in two benchmark data sets of death certificates provided for the task 1 in the CLEF eHealth shared task 2017. A proposed architecture combines ideas from recurrent neural networks and traditional text retrieval term weighting schemes. We found that our models reach accuracy of 75% and 86% as evaluated by the F-measure on the CépiDc corpus of French texts and on the CDC corpus of English texts, respectfully. The proposed models can be employed for coding electronic medical records with ICD codes including diagnosis and procedure codes.

Keywords: ICD coding · ICD codes · Medical concept coding
Medical record coding · Computer assisted coding
Recurrent neural network · Encoder-decoder model · Deep learning
Machine learning · Death certificates · CépiDc corpus · CDC corpus
Healthcare · CLEF eHealth

1 Introduction

Medical concept coding is an important task of biomedical information extraction (IE), which is also a central concern of the text mining research community in recent years. The goal of IE is to automatically detect a textual mention of a named entity in free-form texts and map the entity mention to a unique concept in an existing ontology after solving the homonymy problem [1]. There are several widely used ontologies of medical concepts such as the Unified Medical Language System (UMLS), SNOMED CT, and International Classification of Diseases (ICD, ICD-10).

© Springer Nature Switzerland AG 2018
P. Bellot et al. (Eds.): CLEF 2018, LNCS 11018, pp. 203–215, 2018.
https://doi.org/10.1007/978-3-319-98932-7_19

The problem of homonymy, i.e., of disambiguation of unrelated word meanings, is one of the well-known challenges in natural language processing (NLP), which could be found in each and every NLP sub-fields and related areas like information retrieval. The drug discovery application sub-field is no exception in that regard, but it also has its own unique features. Namely, it is typical for the field that semantic unit here is an entity consisting typically of two and more words or abbreviations. Thus, one needs to disambiguate the meaning of an entity rather than a single word. For example, "headache" could mean migraine, or dizziness, or a few additional discrepant medical terms. This task in the field is called medical concept mapping, and disambiguation is one of its main features.

In this paper, we focus on the problem of ICD-10 coding, the aim is to assign codes from the International Classification of Diseases to fragments of texts. Computer-assisted coding (CAC) can help reduce the coding burden. CAC systems are already in use in many healthcare facilities as a helpful tool for increasing medical coder productivity [2]. Thus, progress in automated methods for ICD coding is expected to directly impact real-world operations.

The problem of accurate identification of ICD codes based on verbal description of medical conditions naturally lends itself to using NLP approaches for the task at hand. Since manual coding is time-consuming and error-prone, automatic coding has been studied for many years. Two basic methods of identifying ICD codes are dictionary matching and pattern matching [3]. Recent advances in neural networks have deeply reshaped NLP research because of their capability to learn representations from data without feature engineering in an end-to-end manner. Recent studies treat the medical concept coding task as a supervised sequence labeling problem. For instance, Miftahutdinov and Tutubalina [4] proposed an encoder-decoder model based on bidirectional recurrent neural networks (RNNs) to translate a sequence of words into a sequence of medical codes; experiments were carried out on the English corpus of death certificates. Karimi et al. [5] leveraged a simple convolutional neural network with a fully-connected layer to assign a label (a diagnosis code) for entries in a dataset of radiology reports written in English. Duarte et al. [6] applied a deep neural network that processes the texts of clinical reports from the Portuguese Ministry of Health. These works demonstrate the first attempts to use deep learning methods for ICD coding.

This work is a significantly extended version of the previously reported study [4]; here, we extended experiments to employ novel RNN architectures. In addition to Long Short-Term Memory (LSTM), we utilize Gated Recurrent Units (GRU) used for sequence learning. We explore the impact of different word embeddings and the length of output sequences of ICD codes. We conduct extensive experiments on the French and English datasets from the CLEF eHealth shared task 2017 and demonstrate the efficiency of our approach.

2   Related Work

Different approaches have been developed for medical concept coding task, mainly falling into two categories: (i) knowledge-based methods [7–11]; and (ii) machine learning approaches [12–14].

The *ShARe/CLEF eHealth 2013* lab addressed the problem of identification and normalization of disorders from clinical reports in Task 1 [15]. Leaman et al. introduced a DNorm system for assigning disease mentions from PubMed abstracts [16]. The *CLEF Health 2016 and 2017* labs addressed the problem of mapping death certificates to ICD codes. Death certificates are standardized documents filled by physicians to report the death of a patient [17]. For the CLEF eHealth 2016 lab, five teams participated in the shared task 2 about the ICD-10 coding of death certificates in French [18]. Most submitted methods utilized dictionary-based semantic similarity and, to some extent, string matching. Mulligen et al. [9] obtained the best results in task 2 by combining a Solr tagger with ICD-10 terminologies. The terminologies were derived from the task training set and a manually curated ICD-10 dictionary. They achieved an F-measure of 84.8%. Zweigenbaum and Lavergne [19] utilized a hybrid method combining pre-processing steps (stop word removal, diacritic removal, correction of some spelling errors), simple dictionary projection, and mono-label supervised classification. They used Linear SVM trained on the full training corpus and the 2012 dictionary provided for CLEF participants. This hybrid method obtained an F-measure of 85.86%. The participants of the CLEF eHealth 2016 task 2 did not use word embeddings or deep neural networks.

The CLEF eHealth 2017 ICD-10 coding task provided datasets which consisted of death certificates in French and English [17]. Nine teams participated in the shared task 1. Cabot et al. [20] applied a combination of a dictionary-based approach and fuzzy match algorithms. Their system obtained an F-measures of 76.36% on French records and 80.38% on English records. Zweigenbaum and Lavergne extended their hybrid method [19] to multi-label classification. They obtained F-measures of 82.5% and 84.7% on French and English texts, respectively. Miftakhutdinov and Tutubalina [4] obtained the best results in the CLEF eHealth 2017 task 1, training an LSTM-based encoder-decoder architecture. As input, the network uses the certificates' text lines containing terms that could be directly linked to a single ICD-10 code or several codes. As output, the network predicts a sequence of codes. The model obtained an F-measure of 85% on English texts. In this paper, we extend experiments with neural networks on a corpus of French certificates.

Although deep neural network models and word embedding techniques are widely used in most natural language processing task, so far they have found limited use for the medical domain texts. Nevertheless, first studies towards using neural networks for medical concept coding could be noticed [4–6,21,22]. For instance, Karimi et al. [5] leveraged a simple convolutional neural network and fully-connected layer to assign a single label (an ICD code) on a dataset of radiology reports. Duarte et al. [6] applied bidirectional GRU-based neural networks for the assignment of ICD-10 codes to the death certificates, together with the associated autopsy reports and clinical bulletins, from the Portuguese Ministry of Health. We note that those works did not discuss experimental comparison of their methods for one-label and multi-label classification of clinical texts.

2.1   Materials and Methods

In this section, we discuss challenges in the task, our datasets, and proposed approaches. There are several challenges to concept coding as well as entity and word disambiguation:

- **Textual variations**. Clinical records have multiple mention forms, including lexical, morphological, and syntactic variations, synonyms (hypertension vs. high blood pressure disorder), abbreviations (attention deficit hyperactivity disorder vs. ADDH vs. ADHD), alternate spellings or grammatical errors (diarrheas vs. diarrhoea).
- **Multiple overlapping entities**. Boundaries of different entities in the text could be not well defined. For example, the sentence "metastatic adencarcinoma of lung to brain"is associated with two concepts:"Malignant neoplasm of unspecified part of bronchus or lung" (C349) and "Secondary malignant neoplasm of brain and cerebral meninges" (C793).
- **Ambiguity**. A single mention, like aspiration, can match multiple UMLS entries, e.g. Endotracheal aspiration, Pulmonary aspiration, Aspiration Pneumonia, Aspiration precautions. We note that a great number of ambiguous words in the biomedical domain are actually abbreviations [23].

The combination of these challenges makes concept coding especially challenging with simple string matching algorithms and dictionary-based approaches.

2.2   Corpora

We briefly describe two real-world datasets used in our study. **The CépiDc corpus** and **the CDC corpus** consist of free-form text death certificates in French and English, respectively. These corpora were provided for the task of ICD10 coding in CLEF eHealth 2017 (Task 1).

The CépiDc corpus was provided by the French institute for health and medical research (INSERM). It consists of free text death certificates collected from physicians and hospitals in France over the period of 2006–2014. The corpus consists of 65,844, 27,850, and 31,690 raw texts for training, developing and testing, respectively. The full set includes 131,426 codes (2,527 unique codes). Statistics of the corpus are presented in Table 1. We note that the CépiDc corpus contains 6 times more certificates than the CDC corpus. We utilize the 'raw' version of the CépiDc corpus for further experiments.

The CDC corpus was provided by the American Center for Disease Control (CDC). The corpus consists of free text death certificates collected electronically in the United States during the year 2015. The corpus consists of 13,330 and 14,833 raw texts for training and testing, respectively. Additionally, the CDC test set includes the "external" test set which is limited to textual fragments with ICD codes linked with a particular type of deaths, called"external causes" or violent deaths. The full set includes 18,928 codes (900 unique codes), while the "external" set includes only 126 codes (28 unique codes). Statistics of the corpus are presented in Table 2. Examples of raw texts from death certificates with medical concepts and ICD codes are presented in Table 3.

Table 1. Statistics of the CépiDc corpus from [24].

	Train	Development	Test
Certificates	65,844	27,850	31,690
Year	2006–2012	2013	2014
Lines	195,204	80,899	91,962
Tokens	1,176,994	496,649	599,127
Total ICD codes	266,808	110,869	131,426
Unique ICD codes	3,233	2,363	2,527
Unique unseen ICD codes	-	224	266

Table 2. Statistics of the CDC American death certificates corpus from [24].

	Train	Test
Certificates	13,330	6,665
Year	2015	2015
Lines	32,714	14,834
Tokens	90,442	42,819
Total ICD codes	39,334	18,928
Unique ICD codes	1,256	900
Unique unseen ICD codes	-	157

3   Our Approach

The basic idea of our approach is to map the input sequence to a fixed-sized vector, more precisely, some semantic representation of this input, and then unroll this representation in the target sequence using a neural network model. This intuition is formally captured in an encoder-decoder architecture. The output sequence is not a tagging sequence with one-to-one matching like in Part-of-Speech tagging task. It is the sequence of medical concepts corresponding to input sequence semantics. In fact, this architecture is aimed to solve multi-label classification problem, since output sequence could be interpreted as a set of labels for a sample input sequence.

3.1   Recurrent Neural Networks

RNNs are naturally used for sequence learning, where both input and output are word and label sequences, respectively. RNN has recurrent hidden states, which aim to simulate memory, i.e., the activation of a hidden state at every time step depends on the previous hidden state [25]. The recurrent unit computes a weighted sum of the input signal. There is the difficulty of training RNNs to capture long-term dependencies due to the effect of vanishing gradients [26], so

Table 3. Examples of raw texts from death certificates with medical concepts and ICD codes.

#	Sample	Medical Concept Code
1	CKD STAGE III, CHF, SEVERE OSTEOPOROSIS	
		Chronic kidney disease, stage 3 N183
		Congestive ventricular heart failure I500
		Osteoporosis M819
2	CAD / s/p CABG / Volume overload	
		Acute coronary artery disease I251
		Fluid overload E877
3	F.T.T.	
		Failure to thrive syndrome R628
4	Neutropenic fever, pneumonia	
		Chronic Neutropenia D70
		Fever R509
		Pneumonia J189

the most widely used modifications of a RNN unit are the Long Short-Term Memory (LSTM) [27] and the Gated Recurrent Unit (GRU) [28].

An important modification of the basic RNN architecture is bidirectional RNNs, where the past and the future context is available in every time step [29]. Bidirectional LSTMs, developed by Graves and Schmidhuber [30,31], contain two chains of LSTM cells flowing in both forward and backward direction, and the final representation is either a linear combination or simply concatenation of their states.

3.2   Encoder-Decoder Model

As shown in Fig. 1, the model consists of two components based on RNNs: an encoder and a decoder. The encoder processes the input sequence, while the decoder generates the output sequence.

We adopted the architecture as described in [4,28]. The input layer of our model is vector representations of individual words. Word embedding models represent each word using a single real-valued vector. Such representation groups together words that are semantically and syntactically similar [32].

In order to incorporate prior knowledge, we additionally concatenated cosine similarity vector to the encoded state using on tf-idf representation. CLEF participants were provided with a manually created dictionary. The tf-idf score of a word, as defined by Salton and Buckley [33], is a reasonable measure of word importance. This score privileges the words that not only mention frequently in a given document, but also appear rarely in other documents of a corpus.

Cosine similarity vector was calculated as follows. First, for each ICD-10 code present in the dictionary, we construct a document by simply concatenating diagnosis texts belonging to that code. For the resulting document set, the

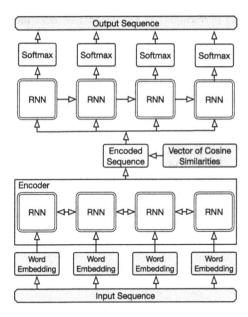

Fig. 1. An illustration of the encoder-decoder architecture.

tf-idf transformation was computed; thus, every ICD-10 code was provided with a vector representation. For a given input sequence, the tf-idf vector representation was calculated. Using the vector representation of the input sequence and each ICD-10 code, the vector of cosine similarities was constructed such as follows: the i-th position of vector is the cosine distance between input sequence representation and i-th ICD code representation. We have made the implementation of our model available at the github repository[1]. We consider pairs (diagnosis text, ICD1) from the dictionary for our system since most entries in the dictionary are associated with these codes.

Neural networks require word representations as inputs. We investigate the use of several different pre-trained word embeddings. We utilize word embeddings named *HealthVec*: publicly available 200-dimensional embeddings that were trained on 2,607,505 unlabeled user comments from health information websites using the Continuous Bag-of-Words model in [34]. We adopt 300-dimensional embeddings trained on the French version of Wikipedia using fasttext [35]. We also experiment with another published 200-dimensional embeddings named *PubMedVec*, which were trained on biomedical literature indexed in PubMed [36].

4 Experiments

In this section, we discuss the performance of neural networks.

---

[1] https://github.com/dartrevan/clef_2017.

Table 4. ICD-10 coding performance of the encoder-decoder model on the CDC test set of English texts (left) and the CépiDc test set of French texts (right).

	P	R	F
Encoder-decoder LSTM	.907	**.817**	**.860**
Official results from [24]			
KFU-run1 (ours)	.893	.811	.850
TUC-MI-run1	**.940**	.725	.819
SIBM-run1	.839	.783	.810
WBI-run1	.616	.606	.611
LIRMM-run1	.691	.514	.589
Average score	.670	.582	.622
Median score	.646	.606	.611
Non-off. from [24]			
LIMSI-run2	.899	.801	.847

	P	R	F
Encoder-decoder LSTM	.848	.673	.750
Official results from [24]			
SIBM-run1	.857	.689	.764
LITL-run2	.666	.414	.510
LIRMM-run1	.541	.480	.509
LIRMM-run2	.540	.480	.508
Average score	.475	.358	.406
Median score	.541	.414	.508
Non-off. from [24]			
LIMSI-run2	.872	**.784**	**.825**
TUC-MI-run1	**.883**	.539	.669

4.1 Settings

To find optimal neural network configuration and word embeddings, the 5-fold cross-validation procedure was applied to the training CDC set. We compared architectures with different numbers of neurons in hidden layers of the encoder and the decoder. The best cross-validation F-score was obtained for the architecture with 600 neurons in the hidden layer of the encoder and 1000 neurons in the hidden layer of the decoder. We tested bidirectional LSTM as decoder but did not achieve an improvement over the left-to-right LSTM. Additionally, we utilized the encoder with attention mechanism but did not achieve an improvement on the validation set. We also established that 10 were enough for stable performance on the validation sets. In contrast with our previous model [4], we set the decoder to predict ICD codes from the training set, not all codes from the dictionary. We adopted the train and validation sets of the CépiDc corpus for training.

We have implemented networks with the Keras library [37]. LSTM is trained on top of the embedding layer. We used the 600-dimensional hidden layer for the encoder RNN chain. Finally, the last hidden state of LSTM chain output concatenated with cosine similarities vector was fed into a decoding LSTM layer with 1000-dimensional hidden layer and softmax activation. In order to prevent neural networks from overfitting, we used dropout of 0.5 [38]. We used categorical cross entropy as the objective function and the Adam optimizer [39] with the batch size of 20.

4.2 Results

Our neural models were evaluated on texts in English using evaluation metrics of task 1 such as precision (P), recall (R) and balanced F-measure (F).

Table 4 presents results of the LSTM-based encoder-decoder model trained with PubMedVec and several official results of participants' methods (TUC-

Table 5. Performance of the encoder-decoder model on the CDC test sets.

Networks' settings			= 1 code			≥2 codes			Full set		
encoder	decoder	emb	P	R	F	P	R	F	P	R	F
biLSTM	LSTM	random, 100 d.	.935	.899	.916	**.837**	.605	.702	.908	.813	.858
biLSTM	LSTM	random, 200 d.	.934	.900	.917	**.837**	.603	.701	.903	.816	.857
biLSTM	LSTM	random, 300 d.	.932	.899	.915	.827	.606	.699	.904	.814	.857
biLSTM	LSTM	HealthVec	.932	.899	.915	.813	.601	.691	.902	.814	.856
biLSTM	LSTM	PubMedVec	**.937**	**.904**	**.920**	.803	.623	.702	**.907**	.817	.860
biGRU	LSTM	PubMedVec	.931	.901	.916	.829	**.631**	**.717**	.904	**.823**	**.861**
biGRU	GRU	PubMedVec	.927	.896	.912	.800	.627	.703	.892	.819	.854

Table 6. Performance of the encoder-decoder model on the CépiDc full sets.

Networks' settings				= 1 code			≥2 codes			Full set		
encoder	decoder	emb	sim.	P	R	F	P	R	F	P	R	F
biLSTM	LSTM	random, 100 d.	no	.868	.721	.787	.799	.340	.477	.832	.658	.735
biLSTM	LSTM	HealthVec	no	.874	.725	.793	.799	.340	.477	.836	.660	.737
biLSTM	LSTM	PubMedVec	no	.876	.728	.795	.806	.350	.488	.838	.669	.744
biLSTM	LSTM	PubMedVec	yes	.877	.728	.796	.815	.350	.490	.847	.673	.750
biLSTM	LSTM	French Wiki	no	**.879**	**.730**	**.798**	.815	**.355**	**.495**	.845	**.677**	**.752**
biLSTM	LSTM	French Wiki	yes	.874	.723	.792	**.821**	.350	.491	.848	.673	.750

MI, SIBM, LIMSI teams, etc.) which did not resort to RNNs [19,20,24]. On the CDC test set, LSTM-based encoder-decoder model obtained F-measure of 86.0% with significant improvement as compared to other methods. The neural network obtained comparable results with the LIMSI team that combined SVM with the dictionary for multi-label classification and submitted unofficial runs due to conflict of interest. On the CépiDc test set, our neural network obtained F-measure of 75.2% (without additional knowledge) and 75.0% (with similarity vector) which is comparable results with SIBM team (F-measure of 76.4%).

The experiments with neural networks are presented in Tables 5 and 6. Each dataset was divided into two parts: the one part contains records with only one corresponding label, so we may consider this task to be single-label classification; the other part contains records with two or more corresponding labels which makes it multi-label classification task. The full dataset is also considered as multi-labeled.

Table 5 presents results for the English dataset. The best achieved F-measure on single-label classification task is 92% for biLSTM with PubMedVec. For two multi-label classification tasks (on the second part of the dataset and on the full dataset) the best model was biGRU with PubMedVec achieving 72% and 86% of F-measure, respectively. The second result is the best among all the participants of this challenge. Interestingly the best precision on the experiment with second class only is achieved by systems using random vectors. Overall the quality of underlying vectors has limited influence on system performance.

Table 6 presents results for the French dataset. These results are comparable with approaches presented by challenge participants, but our solution does not use large vocabulary as additional input. The lowered system performance in comparison with English dataset could be explained by two main reasons: (I) the large number of Out-of-Vocabulary (OOV) words (app. 64% words of the vocabulary) for French language which were not associated with embeddings, (II) we did not perform language-dependent pre-processing steps including diacritic removal and correction of some spelling errors (as in the LIMSI's system), and (III) unlike the CDC dataset, the CépiDc train and test sets have records from different years, so the results could be influenced by changes in ICD-10 itself. Interestingly, the vectors for the English language actually improve system's performance, which can be explained by the significant percentage of French loan words in English language and consequently vocabulary sharing between these two datasets.

5   Conclusion

In this paper, we introduce a neural network architecture with a specific application to medical concept coding, i.e. linking the free-form language of clinical records to particular entries in the International Classification of Diseases. We find that by combining the encoder-decoder framework with cosine similarity metrics and a traditional tf-idf weighting scheme, we achieve the state-of-the-art results on the CDC corpus of English texts. Although we focus on ICD-10 coding of death certificates, our model is extensible without any task-specific manual feature engineering effort to other multi-label document tagging tasks, including prediction of diagnoses and procedures.

We foresee three directions for future work. First, we plan to carry out experiments on other datasets for medical code prediction including both MIMIC-II and MIMIC-III datasets. Second, we believe attention should be given to infrequent codes since ICD-10-CM has more than 70,000 codes. From the system perspective, future research might focus on embedding code descriptions and ICD hierarchy to a latent space. If we can better incorporate prior knowledge about codes, we may be able to infer rare medical events. From the medical side, future work might focus on applying our automatic coding model to find misclassification in clinical records coded manually. The third promising direction for research is to investigate multilingual models on datasets provided by CLEF eHealth 2017 and 2018 challenges.

Acknowledgements. This work was supported by the Russian Science Foundation grant no. 18-11-00284. The authors are grateful to Prof. Alexander Tropsha and Valentin Malykh for useful discussions about this study.

References

1. Pradhan, S., Elhadad, N., Chapman, W.W., Manandhar, S., Savova, G.: SemEval-2014 task 7: analysis of clinical text. In: SemEval@ COLING, pp. 54–62 (2014)
2. Dougherty, M., Seabold, S., White, S.E.: Study reveals hard facts on CAC. J. AHIMA **84**(7), 54–56 (2013)
3. Stanfill, M.H., Williams, M., Fenton, S.H., Jenders, R.A., Hersh, W.R.: A systematic literature review of automated clinical coding and classification systems. J. Am. Med. Inform. Assoc. **17**(6), 646–651 (2010)
4. Miftahutdinov, Z., Tutubalina, E.: KFU at CLEF ehealth 2017 task 1: ICD-10 coding of English death certificates with recurrent neural networks. In: CEUR Workshop Proceedings, vol. 1866 (2017)
5. Karimi, S., Dai, X., Hassanzadeh, H., Nguyen, A.: Automatic diagnosis coding of radiology reports: a comparison of deep learning and conventional classification methods. In: BioNLP 2017, pp. 328–332 (2017)
6. Duarte, F., Martins, B., Pinto, C.S., Silva, M.J.: Deep neural models for ICD-10 coding of death certificates and autopsy reports in free-text. J. Biomed. Inform. **80**, 64–77 (2018)
7. Zhang, Y., et al.: Uth_CCB: a report for SemEval 2014-task 7 analysis of clinical text. In: SemEval 2014, p. 802 (2014)
8. Ghiasvand, O., Kate, R.J.: UWM: disorder mention extraction from clinical text using CRFS and normalization using learned edit distance patterns. In: SemEval@ COLING, pp. 828–832 (2014)
9. Van Mulligen, E., Afzal, Z., Akhondi, S.A., Vo, D., Kors, J.A.: Erasmus MC at CLEF eHealth 2016: concept recognition and coding in French texts. In: CLEF (2016)
10. Cabot, C., Soualmia, L.F., Dahamna, B., Darmoni, S.J.: SIBM at CLEF eHealth evaluation lab 2016: extracting concepts in French medical yexts with ECMT and CIMIND. In: CLEF (2016)
11. Mottin, L., Gobeill, J., Mottaz, A., Pasche, E., Gaudinat, A., Ruch, P.: BiTeM at CLEF eHealth evaluation lab 2016 task 2: multilingual information extraction. In: CEUR Workshop Proceedings, vol. 1609, pp. 94–102 (2016)
12. Dermouche, M., Looten, V., Flicoteaux, R., Chevret, S., Velcin, J., Taright, N.: ECSTRA-INSERM@ CLEF eHealth2016-task 2: ICD10 code extraction from death certificates. In: CLEF (2016)
13. Zweigenbaum, P., Lavergne, T.: LIMSI ICD10 coding experiments on CépiDC death certificate statements. In: CLEF (2016)
14. Leaman, R., Khare, R., Lu, Z.: NCBI at 2013 shARe/CLEF ehealth shared task: disorder normalization in clinical notes with DNorm. Radiology **42**(21.1), 1–941 (2011)
15. Suominen, H., et al.: Overview of the ShARe/CLEF eHealth evaluation lab 2013. In: Forner, P., Müller, H., Paredes, R., Rosso, P., Stein, B. (eds.) CLEF 2013. LNCS, vol. 8138, pp. 212–231. Springer, Heidelberg (2013). https://doi.org/10.1007/978-3-642-40802-1_24
16. Leaman, R., Islamaj Doğan, R., Lu, Z.: DNorm: disease name normalization with pairwise learning to rank. Bioinformatics **29**(22), 2909–2917 (2013)
17. Névéol, A., et al.: CLEF ehealth 2017 multilingual information extraction task overview: ICD10 coding of death certificates in English and French. In: CLEF 2017 Evaluation Labs and Workshop: Online Working Notes, CEUR-WS (2017)

18. Névéol, A., et al.: Clinical information extraction at the CLEF eHealth evaluation lab 2016. In: Proceedings of CLEF 2016 Evaluation Labs and Workshop: Online Working Notes, CEUR-WS, September 2016 (2016)
19. Zweigenbaum, P., Lavergne, T.: Hybrid methods for ICD-10 coding of death certificates. In: EMNLP 2016, p. 96 (2016)
20. Cabot, C., Soualmia, L.F., Darmoni, S.J.: SIBM at CLEF ehealth evaluation lab 2017: multilingual information extraction with CIM-IND. In: CLEF (2017)
21. Tutubalina, E., Miftahutdinov, Z., Nikolenko, S., Malykh, V.: Medical concept normalization in social media posts with recurrent neural networks. J. Biomed. Inform. **84**, 93–102 (2018)
22. Rios, A., Kavuluru, R.: EMR coding with semi-parametric multi-head matching networks. In: Proceedings of the 2018 Conference of the North American Chapter of the Association for Computational Linguistics: Human Language Technologies, Volume 1 (Long Papers), vol. 1, pp. 2081–2091 (2018)
23. Schuemie, M.J., Kors, J.A., Mons, B.: Word sense disambiguation in the biomedical domain: an overview. J. Comput. Biol. **12**(5), 554–565 (2005)
24. Névéol, A., et al.: CLEF eHealth 2017 Multilingual information extraction task overview: ICD10 coding of death certificates in English and French. In: Working Notes of Conference and Labs of the Evaluation (CLEF) Forum, CEUR Workshop Proceedings (2017)
25. Elman, J.L.: Finding structure in time. Cogn. Sci. **14**(2), 179–211 (1990)
26. Bengio, Y., Simard, P., Frasconi, P.: Learning long-term dependencies with gradient descent is difficult. IEEE Trans. Neural Netw. **5**(2), 157–166 (1994)
27. Greff, K., Srivastava, R.K., Koutník, J., Steunebrink, B.R., Schmidhuber, J.: LSTM: a search space odyssey. IEEE Trans. Neural Netw. Learn. Syst. **28**(10), 2222–2232 (2016)
28. Cho, K., et al.: Learning phrase representations using RNN encoder-decoder for statistical machine translation. arXiv preprint arXiv:1406.1078 (2014)
29. Schuster, M., Paliwal, K.K.: Bidirectional recurrent neural networks. IEEE Trans. Sig. Proc. **45**(11), 2673–2681 (1997)
30. Graves, A., Fernández, S., Schmidhuber, J.: Bidirectional LSTM networks for improved phoneme classification and recognition. In: Duch, W., Kacprzyk, J., Oja, E., Zadrożny, S. (eds.) ICANN 2005. LNCS, vol. 3697, pp. 799–804. Springer, Heidelberg (2005). https://doi.org/10.1007/11550907_126
31. Graves, A., Schmidhuber, J.: Framewise phoneme classification with bidirectional LSTM networks. In: Proceedings of IEEE International Joint Conference on Neural Networks, IJCNN 2005, vol. 4, pp. 2047–2052. IEEE (2005)
32. Mikolov, T., Sutskever, I., Chen, K., Corrado, G.S., Dean, J.: Distributed representations of words and phrases and their compositionality. In: Advances in Neural Information Processing Systems, pp. 3111–3119 (2013)
33. Salton, G., Buckley, C.: Term-weighting approaches in automatic text retrieval. Inf. Proc. Manag. **24**(5), 513–523 (1988)
34. Miftahutdinov, Z., Tutubalina, E., Tropsha, A.: Identifying disease-related expressions in reviews using conditional random fields. In: Proceedings of International Conference on Computational Linguistics and Intellectual Technologies Dialog, vol. 1, pp. 155–167 (2017)
35. Bojanowski, P., Grave, E., Joulin, A., Mikolov, T.: Enriching word vectors with subword information. Trans. Assoc. Comput. Linguist. **5**, 135–146 (2017)
36. Moen, S., Ananiadou, T.S.S.: Distributional semantics resources for biomedical text processing (2013)

37. Chollet, F., et al.: Keras (2015). https://github.com/fchollet/keras
38. Srivastava, N., Hinton, G.E., Krizhevsky, A., Sutskever, I., Salakhutdinov, R.:
    Dropout: a simple way to prevent neural networks from overfitting. J. Mach. Learn.
    Res. **15**(1), 1929–1958 (2014)
39. Kinga, D., Adam, J.B.: A method for stochastic optimization. In: International
    Conference on Learning Representations (ICLR) (2015)

Hierarchical Clustering Analysis: The Best-Performing Approach at PAN 2017 Author Clustering Task

Helena Gómez-Adorno[1,2](✉), Carolina Martín-del-Campo-Rodríguez[2],
Grigori Sidorov[2], Yuridiana Alemán[3], Darnes Vilariño[3], and David Pinto[3]

[1] Engeneering Institute (II), Universidad Nacional Autónoma de México (UNAM),
Mexico City, Mexico
hgomeza@iingen.unam.mx

[2] Instituto Politécnico Nacional (IPN), Center for Computing Research (CIC),
Mexico City, Mexico
cm.del.cr@gmail.com, sidorov@cic.ipn.mx

[3] Faculty of Computer Science (FCC),
Benemérita Universidad Autónoma de Puebla (BUAP), Puebla, Mexico
yuridiana.aleman@gmail.com, dvilarinoayala@gmail.com, dpinto@cs.buap.mx

Abstract. The author clustering problem consists in grouping documents written by the same author so that each group corresponds to a different author. We described our approach to the author clustering task at PAN 2017, which resulted in the best-performing system at the aforementioned task. Our method performs a hierarchical clustering analysis using document features such as typed and untyped character n-grams, word n-grams, and stylometric features. We experimented with two feature representation methods, log-entropy model, and TF-IDF, while tuning minimum frequency threshold values to reduce the feature dimensionality. We identified the optimal number of different clusters (authors) dynamically for each collection using the Caliński Harabasz score. The implementation of our system is available open source (https://github.com/helenpy/clusterPAN2017).

Keywords: Author clustering · Hierarchical clustering
Authorship-link ranking

1 Introduction

Authorship Attribution consists in identifying the author of a given document in a collection. There are several subtasks within the Authorship Attribution field such as author verification [18], author clustering [15], and plagiarism detection [16]. This paper focuses on the author clustering task, which is defined as follows: given a document collection, the task is to group documents written by the same author so that each group corresponds to a different author. Applications of this problem include automatic text processing in repositories (Web), retrieval of documents written by the same author, among others.

© Springer Nature Switzerland AG 2018
P. Bellot et al. (Eds.): CLEF 2018, LNCS 11018, pp. 216–223, 2018.
https://doi.org/10.1007/978-3-319-98932-7_20

The author clustering evaluation campaign was introduced in PAN 2016 [15], including the authorship-link ranking subtask. PAN[1] is a CLEF Lab on uncovering plagiarism, authorship, and social software misuse. Our approach outperforms the best-performing systems of PAN 2017 author clustering task [5,19].

The evaluation corpus at PAN 2017 contains documents in three languages (English, Dutch, and Greek) and two genres (newspaper articles and reviews). Two application scenarios are analyzed in this paper:

Complete Author Clustering: We approach the first scenario using a hierarchical clustering technique with different linkage strategies. As document features, we extract word and character n-grams, and stylometric features. We evaluate the contribution of the document features individually and in combination. We perform a detailed analysis to identify the number k of different authors (clusters) in a collection, then we assign each document to exactly one of the k clusters.

Authorship-Link Ranking: In this scenario, we explore the collection of documents as a retrieval task. We aim to establish authorship links between documents and provide a list of document pairs ranked by a confidence score. For this, we calculate the pairwise similarity between each pair of documents in every problem using the cosine similarity metric.

The research questions addressed in this paper are the following:

- How can we find the optimal number of clusters for each clustering problem?
- Is it possible to find an optimal feature representation scheme for every clustering problem?
- Which distance measure is better for document clustering problems?

2 Related Work

A wide range of approaches have been proposed to tackle the author clustering task. The PAN evaluation campaign, has been organized annually since 2013 to promote studies on several authorship identification-related tasks. For this paper, the best approaches of the last two editions of the author clustering task at PAN will be discussed.

Bagnall [2], achieved the best results in the author clustering task at PAN 2016. He used a multi-headed recurrent neural network to train a character n-gram model with a softmax output for each text in all problems. Later, he applied a method to turn multiple softmax outputs into clustering decisions. The goal of the training phase was to optimize the F-Bcubed score. Kocher's system [6] was ranked second. The author proposed an unsupervised approach using simple features and a distance measure called SPATIUM-L1. The features extracted when computing the distance between a pair of documents corresponded to the

---

[1] https://pan.webis.de/.

top m most frequent terms in the first document of the pair, hence the distance being asymmetric $\Delta_{A,B} \neq \Delta_{B,A}$.

In the 2017 edition of the author clustering evaluation campaign our methodology obtained the first place [5]. The second place was obtained by García-Mondeja et al. [4], they used β-compact graph-based clustering. The documents belong to the same group as long as the similarity between them exceeds the threshold β and it is the maximum similarity with respect to other documents. The authors evaluated different linguistic features and similarity measures presented in previous works on authorship analysis task.

3   Methodology

3.1   Feature Representation

Previous work on authorship attribution found that character n-grams are highly effective features, regardless of the language the texts are written in [11,13]. We examined the following document features: typed character n-grams ($n = 3$ and $n = 4$), untyped character n-grams (with n ranging between 2 and 8), and word n-grams (with n varying from 1 to 5). Typed character n-grams are character n-grams classified into ten categories based on affixes, words, and punctuation, which were introduced by Sapkota et al. [17].

We also examined the following language independent stylometric features:

- Punctuation: the count of occurrences of punctuation marks (colon, semicolon, comma, period, question mark, exclamation mark).
- Upper case: the number of words whose first letter is capital.
- Digits: number of digits in the document.
- Words number: number of words in the document.
- Length text: number of characters in the text.
- Length of words: average length of words, average number of words per sentence, average length of word per sentence.
- Ratio per word: ratio of words in the document to the dictionary of words of the document with frequency 1, 4 and 6.

The performance of each of the feature sets was evaluated separately and in different combinations. The N most frequent terms in the vocabulary of each problem were selected based on a grid search and optimized based on the F-Bcubed score on the entire training set. We evaluated the N terms from 1 to 60,000 with a step of 50.

Finally, we examined two feature representations based on a global weighting scheme: log-entropy and TF-IDF.

TF-IDF: Is the product of the frequency of the term and the inverse document frequency. It is a numerical statistic that aims to reflect how important a word is for a document in a collection or corpus. To calculate TF-IDF the following equation is used:

$$tf\text{-}idf_{t,d} = tf_{t,d} \times idf_t \qquad (1)$$

where $tf_{t,d}$ is the number of occurrences of the term t in the document d.

Log-Entropy: Global weighting functions measure the importance of a term across the entire collection of documents. Previous research on document similarity judgments [8,12] has shown that entropy-based global weighting is generally better than the TF-IDF model. The log-entropy (le) weight is calculated with the following equation (Eq. 2):

$$le_{ij} = e_i \times \log(tf_{ij} + 1) \tag{2}$$

$$e_i = 1 + \sum_j \frac{p_{ij} \times \log p_{ij}}{\log n} \quad where \quad p_{ij} = \frac{tf_{ij}}{gf_i} \tag{3}$$

where n is the number of documents, tf_{ij} is the frequency of the term i in document j, and gf_i is the frequency of term i in the whole collection. A term that appears once in every document will have a weight of zero. A term that appears once in one document will have a weight of one. Any other combination of frequencies will assign a given term a weight between zero and one.

3.2   Complete Author Clustering

For the complete author clustering, we apply a Hierarchical Cluster Analysis (HCA) using an agglomerative [7] (bottom-up) approach. In this approach, each text starts in its own cluster and in each iteration we merge pairs of clusters using a linkage strategy.

We evaluate the following linkage algorithms:

Single: combines two clusters that contain the closest pair of elements not yet belonging to the same cluster.

Complete: combines two clusters that contain the closest pair of elements among those elements that are farthest away from each other (one in each cluster).

Average: combines two clusters that contain the minimum average distance between all elements in the two considered clusters.

Ward: combines two clusters that minimize the total within-cluster variance.

We use the Caliński Harabasz score [3] to evaluate the clustering model, where a higher Caliński-Harabasz score relates to a model with better defined clusters. In order to determine the number of clusters in each problem we perform the clustering process using a range of k values (with k varying from 1 to the number of samples in each problem) and choose the value of k with the highest Caliński Harabasz score. For k clusters, the Caliński Harabasz score is given as the ratio of the between-clusters dispersion mean and the within-cluster dispersion. This score is higher when clusters are dense and well separated, which means that different authors are probably well grouped in separate clusters.

3.3   Authorship-Link Ranking

In order to establish the authorship links, we simply calculate the pairwise similarity between each pair of documents in each problem using the cosine similarity metric. The vector space model is built in the same manner as the complete author clustering subtask, i.e., the same features and the same weighting schemes.

4 Experimental Results

4.1 Evaluation Measures

Two measures were used to estimate the performance of the submitted systems to the PAN@CLEF 2017 campaign. The F-Bcubed [2] score [1] was used to evaluate the clustering output. This measure corresponds to the harmonic mean between the Bcubed precision and recall. On one hand, the Bcubed precision (P-Bcubed) represents the ratio of documents written by the same author in the same cluster. On the other, the Bcubed recall (R-Bcubed) represents the ratio of documents written by an author that appear in its cluster. The Mean Average Precision (MAP) [9] is used to evaluate the authorship-link ranking. The MAP measures the average area under the precision-recall curve for a set of problems.

4.2 Corpus

The training corpus of PAN author clustering corpus contains 60 problems divided by genre (articles and reviews) and language (Dutch, English or Greek). There are 10 problems for each genre/language pair, with approximately 20 documents each. In the training corpus, most of the clustering problems include 10 documents, whereas in the testing set the number of document in each problem is 20. In both corpora the average of authors is 6. A detailed description of the training and testing corpus can be found in [19].

4.3 Official Results at PAN 2017

For our first submission, we used the k-means algorithm with TF-IDF weighting scheme and the Silhouette Coefficient for choosing the number of clusters. In the final submission, we used a hierarchical clustering with log-entropy weighting scheme and the Caliński Harabasz score for choosing the number of clusters.

Table 1 presents the results of our first submission obtained on the PAN author clustering 2017 test dataset evaluated on the TIRA platform [14]. In this submission, we came across a problem with our authorship-link ranking module due to which the MAP evaluation measure is not available.

We found that when selecting the most frequent 20,000 features we achieved the highest F-Bcubed score on the entire training set. Hence, for the final submission we fixed this threshold for all the languages but selected the features separately for each problem. Table 2 presents the results of our final submission obtained on the PAN author clustering 2017 test dataset. Our final system increased the performance of our early bird submission by 2.5% in terms of the

---

[2] https://github.com/hhromic/python-bcubed

Table 1. Early bird submission results in the author clustering subtask.

Language	F-Bcubed	R-Bcubed	P-Bcubed
English	0.5868	0.6858	0.5914
Greek	0.5372	0.6306	0.5461
Dutch	0.5372	0.6306	0.5461
Average	0.5483	0.6630	0.5479

mean F-Bcubed score. We also observed a similar improvement on the training set, where the final configuration of the system achieved 3% more than our baseline system in terms of the mean F-Bcubed score. Our system was ranked first in both subtasks, author clustering (evaluated with the mean F-Bcubed score) and authorship-link ranking (evaluated with the MAP score).

Table 2. Results on the author clustering 2017 test dataset.

Language	F-Bcubed	R-Bcubed	P-Bcubed	MAP
English	0.5913	0.6175	0.6483	0.5211
Greek	0.5517	0.5743	0.6222	0.4220
Dutch	0,5765	0.7204	0.5508	0.4224
Average	0.5733	0.6379	0.6069	0.4554

5   Conclusions

We presented our approach to the author clustering task in the context of PAN 2017 evaluation lab, where it showed the best results of ten participating teams. We carried out experiments using different features: typed and untyped character n-grams, word n-grams, and stylometric features. Our best approach configuration implemented log-entropy weighting scheme on the combination of the 20,000 most frequent features with hierarchical clustering using an average linkage strategy. We optimized the number of clusters in each problem using the Caliński Harabasz score.

Our main contributions are: (1) the use of the Caliński Harabasz score for optimizing the number of clusters (k) for each problem instead of the commonly used silhouette score, (2) the implementation of the log-entropy weighting scheme, which provided a better weighting strategy for document clustering, and (3) the use of the cosine distance, which is better suited for document vectors than the Euclidean distance.

In future research, we plan to adapt the feature set for each language (subcorpus), as described in [10], in order to improve system performance for each of the languages individually.

Acknowledgments. This work was partially supported by the Mexican Government (CONACYT projects 240844 and 002225 SNI, COFAA-IPN, SIP-IPN).

References

1. Amigó, E., Gonzalo, J., Artiles, J., Verdejo, F.: A comparison of extrinsic clustering evaluation metrics based on formal constraints. Inf. Retr. **12**(4), 461–486 (2009)
2. Bagnall, D.: Authorship clustering using multi-headed recurrent neural networks—notebook for PAN at CLEF 2016. In: Balog, K., Cappellato, L., Ferro, N., Macdonald, C. (eds.) CLEF 2016 Evaluation Labs and Workshop - Working Notes Papers, Évora, Portugal, 5–8 September 2016
3. Caliński, T., Harabasz, J.: A dendrite method for cluster analysis. Commun. Stat. **3**(1), 1–27 (1974)
4. García-Mondeja, Y., Castro-Castro, D., Lavielle-Castro, V., Muñoz, R.: Discovering author groups using a β-compact graph-based clustering. In: CLEF (Working Notes), CEUR Workshop Proceedings, vol. 1866. CEUR-WS.org (2017)
5. Gómez-Adorno, H., Aleman, Y., Vilariño, D., Sanchez-Perez, M.A., Pinto, D., Sidorov, G.: Author clustering using hierarchical clustering analysis. In: CLEF 2017 Working Notes. CEUR Workshop Proceedings (2017)
6. Kocher, M.: UniNE at CLEF 2016: author clustering—notebook for PAN at CLEF 2016. In: Balog, K., Cappellato, L., Ferro, N., Macdonald, C. (eds.) CLEF 2016 Evaluation Labs and Workshop - Working Notes Papers, Évora, Portugal, 5–8 September 2016
7. Layton, R., Watters, P., Dazeley, R.: Automated unsupervised authorship analysis using evidence accumulation clustering. Nat. Lang. Eng. **19**, 95–101 (2013)
8. Lee, M.D., Navarro, D.J., Nikkerud, H.: An empirical evaluation of models of text document similarity. In: Proceedings of the Cognitive Science Society, vol. 27 (2005)
9. Manning, C.D., Raghavan, P., Schütze, H., et al.: Introduction to Information Retrieval, vol. 1. Cambridge University Press, Cambridge (2008)
10. Markov, I., Gómez-Adorno, H., Sidorov, G.: Language- and subtask-independent feature selection and classifier parameter tuning for author profiling. In: Cappellato, L., Ferro, N., Goeuriot, L., Mandl, T. (eds.) Working Notes Papers of the CLEF 2017 Evaluation Labs, CEUR Workshop Proceedings. CLEF and CEUR-WS.org (2017)
11. Markov, I., Stamatatos, E., Sidorov, G.: Improving cross-topic authorship attribution: the role of pre-processing. In: Proceedings of the 18th International Conference on Computational Linguistics and Intelligent Text Processing, CICLing 2017. Springer, Heidelberg (2017)
12. Pincombe, B.: Comparison of human and latent semantic analysis (LSA) judgements of pairwise document similarities for a news corpus. Technical report, Defense Science and Technology Organization Salisbury (Australia) Info Science Lab (2004)
13. Posadas-Durán, J., Gómez-Adorno, H., Sidorov, G., Batyrshin, I., Pinto, D., Chanona-Hernández, L.: Application of the distributed document representation in the authorship attribution task for small corpora. Soft. Comput. **21**, 627–639 (2016)
14. Potthast, M., Gollub, T., Rangel, F., Rosso, P., Stamatatos, E., Stein, B.: Improving the reproducibility of PAN's shared tasks: plagiarism detection, author identification, and author profiling. In: Information Access Evaluation meets Multilinguality, Multimodality, and Visualization. 5th International Conference of the CLEF Initiative. CLEF 2014, pp. 268–299 (2014)

15. Rosso, P., Rangel, F., Potthast, M., Stamatatos, E., Tschuggnall, M., Stein, B.: Overview of PAN'16—new challenges for authorship analysis: cross-genre profiling, clustering, diarization, and obfuscation. In: Fuhr, N., et al. (eds.) Experimental IR Meets Multilinguality, Multimodality, and Interaction, 7th International Conference of the CLEF Initiative (CLEF 2016), Heidelberg (2016)
16. Sanchez-Perez, M.A., Gelbukh, A., Sidorov, G.: Adaptive algorithm for plagiarism detection: the best-performing approach at PAN 2014 text alignment competition. In: Mothe, J., et al. (eds.) CLEF 2015. LNCS, vol. 9283, pp. 402–413. Springer, Cham (2015). https://doi.org/10.1007/978-3-319-24027-5_42
17. Sapkota, U., Bethard, S., Montes-y-Gómez, M., Solorio, T.: Not all character n-grams are created equal: a study in authorship attribution. In: Proceedings of the 2015 Annual Conference of the North American Chapter of the ACL: Human Language Technologies. NAACL-HLT 2015, pp. 93–102. Association for Computational Linguistics (2015)
18. Stamatatos, E., et al.: Overview of the author identification task at PAN 2015. In: Cappellato, L., Ferro, N., Jones, G., San Juan, E. (eds.) CLEF 2015 Evaluation Labs and Workshop - Working Notes Papers (2015)
19. Tschuggnall, M., et al.: Overview of the author identification task at PAN 2017: style breach detection and author clustering. In: Cappellato, L., Ferro, N., Goeuriot, L., Mandl, T. (eds.) Working Notes Papers of the CLEF 2017 Evaluation Labs, CEUR Workshop Proceedings (2017)

Attention-Based Medical Caption Generation with Image Modality Classification and Clinical Concept Mapping

Sadid A. Hasan[1(✉)], Yuan Ling[1], Joey Liu[1], Rithesh Sreenivasan[2],
Shreya Anand[2], Tilak Raj Arora[2], Vivek Datla[1], Kathy Lee[1], Ashequl Qadir[1],
Christine Swisher[3], and Oladimeji Farri[1]

[1] Artificial Intelligence Lab, Philips Research North America, Cambridge, MA, USA
{sadid.hasan,yuan.ling,joey.liu,vivek.datla,kathy.lee_1,ashequl.qadir,
dimeji.farri}@philips.com
[2] Philips Innovation Campus, Bengaluru, India
{rithesh.sreenivasan,shreya.anand,tilak.arora}@philips.com
[3] Human Longevity, Inc., San Diego, CA, USA
christinelswisher@gmail.com

Abstract. This paper proposes an attention-based deep learning framework for caption generation from medical images. We also propose to utilize the same framework for clinical concept prediction to improve caption generation by formulating the task as a case of sequence-to-sequence learning. The predicted concept IDs are then mapped to corresponding terms in a clinical ontology to generate an image caption. We also investigate if learning to classify images based on the modality e.g. CT scan, MRI etc. can aid in generating precise captions.

Keywords: Caption prediction · Concept detection · Attention

1 Introduction

Automatically describing the content of an image is a key challenge in artificial intelligence at the intersection of computer vision and natural language processing. This could especially be beneficial to clinicians for useful insights and reduction of the significant burden on the overall workflow in patient care. The recent advances in deep neural networks have been shown to work well for large scale image analysis tasks [2,4]. Hence, we use an encoder-decoder based deep neural network architecture [4] to address the task of medical image caption generation, where the encoder uses a deep CNN [2] to encode a raw medical image to a feature representation, which is in turn decoded using an attention-based RNN to generate the most relevant caption for the given image. We also utilize the

---

C. Swisher—The author was affiliated with Philips Research at the time of this work.

P. Bellot et al. (Eds.): CLEF 2018, LNCS 11018, pp. 224–230, 2018.
https://doi.org/10.1007/978-3-319-98932-7_21

same framework for clinical concept prediction to improve caption generation. Additionally, we investigate if learning to classify image modalities can aid in generating precise captions by efficiently capturing the specific characteristics of an image modality. Our experiments are conducted on an open access biomedical image corpus. The results show the effectiveness of our approach.

2   Approach

We use an encoder-decoder-based framework that uses a CNN-based architecture to extract the image feature representation and a RNN-based architecture with an attention-based mechanism to translate the image feature representation to relevant captions [4] (Fig. 1).

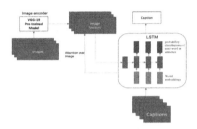

Fig. 1. The overall framework for medical image caption generation.

2.1   Image Encoder

We encode image features in two ways. First, we use the VGGnet-19 [2] deep CNN model (Fig. 1) pre-trained on the ImageNet dataset [3] with fine tuning on the open access PubMed Central biomedical image corpus to extract the image feature representation from a lower convolution layer. Second, we modify the VGG-19 network architecture by including an additional softmax layer at the end for classifying medical images into N imaging modality classes including CT, MR, Ultrasound, X-ray, Pathology, Endoscopy etc. (Fig. 2). The results of imaging modality classes are combined with other image features (directly learned using the pre-trained VGG-19 model from the medical images) into an image vector representation.

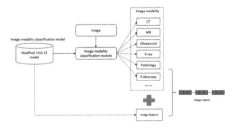

Fig. 2. Image vector representation with image modality classification.

2.2   LSTM-Based Decoder

The decoder uses a long short-term memory (LSTM) network with a soft attention mechanism [4] that generates a caption by predicting one word at every time step based on a context vector (which represents the important parts of the image to focus on), the previous hidden state, and the previously generated words. In particular, during training of the caption generation module, the image features are given as input to the first LSTM cell along with the first caption word, and the sequence of words are similarly passed along to the subsequent LSTM cells. Image weights are shared across all LSTM steps during the decoding stage to learn the association between image features and caption words. We use an attention mechanism over the image features in the decoder such that the caption words can learn the inherent alignments for important image regions without explicitly relying on segmentation information. Ultimately, the series of LSTM cells learns the probabilities of the next word given an input word and a medical image. The resulting model is able to generate a caption given a medical image.

2.3   Concept Mapping

To generate clinically relevant text, the training data should contain relevant clinical concepts embedded as part of captions. Because, biomedical images generally indicate certain anatomies, findings, diagnoses, location descriptors etc., which are usually available as clinical terms in a comprehensive ontology. Hence, it could be interesting to see if clinical concepts can be identified from the captions using a clinical NLP engine [5,7] to prepare a dataset of biomedical images and their corresponding clinical concepts per image. Such a dataset can be utilized to formulate a clinical concept prediction task from images. We cast this task as a sequence-to-sequence learning problem. The predicted clinical concept IDs are later replaced by all possible terms from a clinical ontology such as UMLS metathesaurus to generate a caption of an image (Fig. 3).

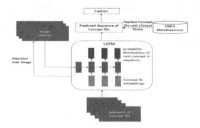

Fig. 3. Biomedical image caption generation with clinical concept mapping.

3   Experimental Setup

3.1   Corpus

We use the 2017 ImageCLEF caption prediction and concept detection task datasets [1] for our experiments. For the caption prediction task, the training data contained 164,614 biomedical images along with their captions extracted from PubMed Central. Furthermore, 10K images with captions were provided as the validation set while 10 K additional images were provided as the test set. The same collection was used for the concept detection task, except a set of clinical concepts is associated with each biomedical image instead of the caption.

3.2   Training

We use a one-hot vector approach to represent the words or clinical concept IDs in all models. Each LSTM in the decoder is built with 1024 hidden units. Our models are trained with stochastic gradient descent (SGD) using Adam as the adaptive learning rate algorithm and dropout as the regularization mechanism. The update direction of the SGD algorithm is computed using a mini batch size of 32 image-caption pairs. We use TensorFlow and a publicly available repository of encoder-decoder templates[1] for our experiments. Our models are trained with two NVIDIA Tesla M40 GPUs for approximately one month.

3.3   Models for Comparison

For comparison and analysis, we propose four models for biomedical image caption generation as follows: **Model1:** The entire training and validation sets are used to train this model without considering any semantic pre-processing of the captions, **Model2:** This model considers semantic pre-processing of captions using MetaMap [5] and the UMLS metathesaurus [6], initially trained on the modified VGG19 model with a randomly selected subset of 20K ImageCLEF training images to automatically generate image features and classify the imaging modality, and then finally trained with a random subset of 24K training images and 2K validation images to minimize time and computational complexity, **Model3:** This model is similar to Model1 with automatic generation of UMLS CUIs using the training dataset for the concept detection task, and then replacing the CUIs (generated for the test set) with the longest relevant clinical terms from the UMLS metathesaurus as the caption, and **Model4:** This model is similar to Model3 except we replace the CUIs with all relevant clinical terms (including synonyms) from the UMLS metathesaurus to generate a possible caption.

For the concept detection task, we prepared three models as follows: **Concept-Model1:** In this model, we consider the task as a sequence-to-sequence generation problem similar to caption generation, where the CUIs associated with an image are simply treated as a sequence of concepts, **Concept-Model2:** This model is created by simply transforming the generated captions

---

[1] https://github.com/yunjey/show-attend-and-tell.

(for the test set) from Model1 of the caption prediction task by replacing clinical terms with the best possible CUIs from the UMLS metathesaurus, and **Concept-Model3:** This model is created by simply transforming the generated captions (for the test set) from Model2 of the caption prediction task by replacing clinical terms with the best possible CUIs from the UMLS metathesaurus.

3.4 Evaluation and Analysis

The evaluation for the caption prediction task is conducted using BLEU whereas F1 score is used to evaluate the concept detection task. Tables 1 and 2 show the evaluation results.

Table 1. Evaluation of caption prediction models

Caption generation models	Mean BLEU score
Model1	0.2638
Model2	0.1107
Model3	0.1801
Model4	**0.3211**

Table 2. Evaluation of concept detection models

Concept prediction models	Mean F1 score
Concept-Model1	**0.1208**
Concept-Model2	0.0234
Concept-Model3	0.0215

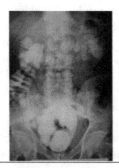

Ground Truth:	Pouchogram of the patient with entero-pouch fistula.
Model1	barium enema showing a distended rectum .
Model2	x ray showed radiolucent area
Model3	loops large intestine colon gastrointestinal tract small intestine
Model4	intestinum intestine colons colonic tenue intestinal large small colon intestines tract loops gastrointestinal bowel structure nos

Fig. 4. Example outputs of caption prediction from different models.

For the caption prediction task (Table 1), Model4 and Model1 achieved high scores denoting the effectiveness of our approach. Overall, our system was ranked first in the caption prediction task in ImageCLEF 2017 [1,8]. Model4 is better as it includes all possible terms from the ontologies in the generated caption but trades-off the coherence of the caption. Hence, this approach increases the BLEU scores, which essentially computes exact word overlaps between the generated and the ground truth captions. Model2 likely suffered from the limited training data whereas Model3 has a lower score as it accepts only the longest possible clinical term as a replacement for a CUI in the caption. As evident from the example in Fig. 4, Model4 generates the longest caption while compromising with the coherence aspect; however, we find its effectiveness in improving the BLEU scores justifying our hypothesis that concept mapping can indeed increase the coverage of words in a caption to improve its potential overlap with the ground truth caption. Model2 is the only successful model to predict that Pouchogram is a type of X-ray test, showing the usefulness of image modality classification in generating a precise caption. However, Model2 states *a radiolucent area*, while the large intestine shown is radio-opaque. For Model1 we see that *barium enema* is a likely differential diagnosis. For the concept detection task (Table 2), Concept-Model1 performed reasonably well, but shows that there is still room for improvement. We may consider treating the task as a multi-label classification problem to achieve possible improvements. Concept-Model2 and Concept-Model3 were limited due to the 2-step translation of clinical terms to CUIs from the generated captions of the other task, which potentially indicates propagation of errors in learning the captions to the downstream task.

4 Conclusion

We presented an attention-based deep learning framework for caption generation from medical images. We also proposed to utilize the same framework for clinical concept prediction to improve caption generation. Our experiments conducted on an open access PubMed Central biomedical image corpus demonstrated that generating medical image captions by first predicting clinical concept IDs and then mapping them to all possible clinical terms in the ontology helps to improve the overall coverage of words in predicted captions compared to ground truth captions. Our experiments also revealed the usefulness of image modality classification in generating precise captions. In the future, we would extend this work by leveraging advanced deep learning algorithms and larger datasets.

References

1. Eickhoff, C., et al.: Overview of imageCLEFcaption 2017 - image caption prediction and concept detection for biomedical images. In: CLEF Labs Working Notes (2017)
2. Simonyan, K., Zisserman, A.: Very deep convolutional networks for large-scale image recognition (2014). arXiv:1409.1556

3. Krizhevsky, A., et al.: ImageNet classification with deep convolutional neural networks. In: NIPS, pp. 1106–1114 (2012)
4. Xu, K., et al.: Show, attend and tell: neural image caption generation with visual attention. In: ICML (2015)
5. Aronson, A.R.: Effective mapping of biomedical text to the UMLS metathesaurus: the MetaMap program. In: AMIA (2001)
6. Bodenreider, O.: The unified medical language system (UMLS): integrating biomedical terminology. Nucleic Acids Res. 32(Suppl. 1), D267–D270 (2004)
7. Datla, V., et al.: Automated clinical diagnosis: the role of content in various sections of a clinical document. In: IEEE BIBM-BHI, pp. 1004–1011 (2017)
8. Hasan, S.A., et al.: PRNA at imageCLEF 2017 caption prediction and concept detection tasks. In: Working Notes of CLEF (2017)

A Compound Model for Consumer Health Search

Hua Yang[1,2](✉) and Teresa Gonçalves[1](✉)

[1] Computer Science Department, University of Évora, Évora, Portugal
tcg@uevora.pt
[2] ZhongYuan University of Technology, Zhengzhou, China
huayangchn@gmail.com

Abstract. General search engines are still far from being effective in addressing complex consumer health queries. The language gap between the consumers and the medical resources can confuse non-expert consumers, and may cause problems like the growing concerns about common symptoms. Current methods in addressing this issue are primarily based on modern information retrieval approaches and query expansion is one of the primes. In this paper, an investigation on merging new schemes into state of the art techniques is made and a new compound system based on query expansion approach is presented. This system takes into account the characteristics of medical language and combines Natural Language Processing techniques with traditional query expansion to overcome the query expansion approach shortcomings of not paying enough attention to the specialty of the medical language. The system is evaluated on the CLEF 2017 eHealth IR challenge data and its effectiveness is demonstrated.

Keywords: Health information search · Consumer health
Query expansion · UMLS · Word vectors

1 Introduction

It is a common activity for consumers to use the World Wide Web as a source for health information and general search engines are popularly used for it. A report from 2013 [2] shows that 73% of US people use Internet, and 71% of them use Internet to search health information. However, general search engines are still far from being effective in addressing complex consumer health queries [9,10]. Related research work has shown that the language gap between the consumers and the complex medical resources confuses a non-expert consumer [3].

To solve the language gap problem, different ideas and corresponding methods have been proposed. Current consumer health search systems are designed primarily by employing state-of-the-art information retrieval techniques and partially take into account the characteristics of medical language. These systems make use of domain specific thesauri and show some effectiveness in search performance. Query expansion technique uses an existing medical thesaurus to find

© Springer Nature Switzerland AG 2018
P. Bellot et al. (Eds.): CLEF 2018, LNCS 11018, pp. 231–236, 2018.
https://doi.org/10.1007/978-3-319-98932-7_22

query term synonyms and expand the query with them. A participate team explored an unique expansion approach based on mined results from Google. The results obtained the highest effectiveness among the submissions for CLEF 2015 eHealth IR task [7]. Lopes *et al.* [4] state they implemented several query expansion strategies using various term resources and various techniques to select the terms to expand the original query. Locally trained word vectors models using medical corpora have been researched and employed in the area of consumer health search. The words that share common contexts in one corpus are located in close proximity in a vector space [5]. oh *et al.* [6] constructed a word vector model from medical Wikipedia with word2vec tools aiming to use the model to properly understand the information need of a query. Budaher *et al.* [1] researched the effectiveness of word embeddings for query expansion in the health domain.

Based on previous work [10], this paper integrates several Natural Language Processing techniques into more traditional ones. The remaining of this paper is organized as follows: Sect. 2 presents the proposed approach and the applied methods; Sect. 3 describes the designed experiments and presents the evaluation results; finally Sect. 4 concludes the paper.

2   Methods

Considering the speciality of the medical language and the gap between the consumer and the medical language resources, in this work the proposal was to integrate various Natural Language Processing techniques into traditional query expansion. The methods presented were mainly based on the following two assumptions: (1) the query terms do not contribute equally to a query when searching relevant documents; (2) the phrases are more effective than single, separate terms when finding relevant documents.

Based on the above ideas, a compound system which merges new schemes into the state-of-the-art information retrieval techniques was proposed. Figure 1 illustrates the complete framework used. First the original query was pre-processed; next, the query expansion was done applying specific query expansion methods to the pre-processed query. For the query expansion phase, three different approaches were tested using: a medical concept model, a trained word vectors model and the classic pseudo relevance feedback method. The expanded query was then presented to the retrieval platform that, in turn, using a weighting model returns a ranked list of documents. The rest of this section introduces the system modules in detail.

Medical Concepts Model. First the medical concepts presented in a query were identified; next different processing were taken on phrase or term medical concepts; then query expansion was performed using UMLS; finally the new terms were added building the new expanded query.

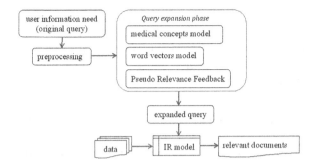

Fig. 1. System framework for improved query expansion

Apache cTAKES [1] is an existing Natural Language Processing tool and was used to identify the medical concepts presented in a query. Query terms not identified by cTAKES or identified as belonging to the types of *Procedure* or *Finding* were discarded. Besides, as noted above in assumption two, a phrase concept and a term concept contribute differently, so a further classification in one of these two types of concepts was done. An undemanding phrase was introduced and denoted as **loose phrase**. In a loose phrase, a maximum number of words between two terms was allowed. Based on that, an identified phrase concept was reconstructed into a loose phrase allowing a maximum number of words within. Then, this reconstructed loose phrase was added to the query. Further on, a phrase concept was assumed to definitely contribute to the query and it was processed as a must check item during the retrieval process. As noted in assumption one, for a term identified as a concept, its contribution was deemed to be higher and an extra weight was assigned to that term. Then, the term concept with an extra weight was then added to the original query. The third way to identify medical concepts was to use UMLS to find synonyms and related words for an identified phrase or term concept. Still based on the above assumptions, the expanded synonyms words were treated differently: synonyms expanded from a phrase concept, would have a higher extra weight than the synonyms expanded from a term concept.

Word Vectors Model. According to assumption two, the most related terms in a query will more likely reflect the user's need compared to other terms. In this work a pre-trained word vectors model was to find the most related terms inside a query.

Word2vec tools were adopted to train the word vector model [5]. As training data, a snapshot (dated on 16th Feb, 2017) of the PMC Open Access Subset[2] was done. The CBOW architecture was used and the dimension of the word vector was set to 200. A file containing $25,140,380$ vectors (number of distinct

---

[1]   http://ctakes.apache.org/index.html.

[2]   https://www.ncbi.nlm.nih.gov/pmc/tools/openftlist/.

terms) with size 200 was obtained. The two most related terms in a query were to be found using the trained model. Using the same method described in Sect. 2, the two most similar terms were reconstructed into a loose phrase. The loose phrase was then added to the original query. In the same way, this new phrase was regarded as a must check item during the retrieval process.

Pseudo Relevance Feedback. Pseudo relevance feedback for automatic expansion during retrieval process was also tested. The number of words to expand a query was set to 10 and the number of top-ranked documents from which those words are extracted was set to 3 in the retrieval system.

3   Experiments and Results

Dataset. This system was evaluated in the CLEF 2017 eHealth IR challenge. There is a total of 300 queries, that were generated by mining posts published in public health web forums. These are considered to be real health information needs expressed by the general public. Those public posts were extracted from the AskDocs section of Reddit[3]. The task uses the ClueWeb12-B13 dataset[4], which was created to support research on information retrieval and related technologies. ClueWeb12-B13 dataset contains more than 52 million web pages and a higher-fidelity representation of a common Internet crawl [8].

Experiments. Terrier[5] platform version 4.17 was chosen as IR model of the system. The Okapi BM25 weighting model was used with all the parameters set to default values. All queries were pre-processed by lower-casing characters, removing stop words and applying stemming with the Porter Stemmer. The default stop words list available in the IR platform was used. Five experiments, using the data from CLEF 2017 eHealth IR task, were conducted. Experiment 1, 2 and 3 are based on the Medical Concepts Model: 1 and 2 are based on different techniques discussed in Sect. 2 and experiment 3 uses combined schemes of experiment 1 and 2. Experiment 4 is based on the Word Vectors Model (see Sect. 2) and experiment 5 is a combination of experiment 3 and 4.

Results. To assess the topic relevance, two measures are used. P@10 is computed using the binary relevance assessment; NDCG@10 is computed using the graded relevance assessments. The formulation of understandability assessment is based on the Rank Biased Precision (RBP). Its variants uRBP and uRBPgr are taken as the understandability biased evaluation measures. uRBP uses binary understandability assessments while uRBPgr uses graded understandability assessments [7,11].

---

[3]   https://www.reddit.com/r/AskDocs/.

[4]   https://www.lemurproject.org/clueweb12.php/.

[5]   http://terrier.org/.

Table 1 presents the topical relevance assessments for the experiments over CLEF 2017 eHealth IR task dataset. Experiment 1, 2 and 3 based on medical concept model achieved better results than experiments using word vectors model (experiment 4 and 5). The best result was achieved by experiment 3. Also, using UMLS expansion obtained higher score than phrase search (comparing experiment 2 to experiment 1). Singly using word vectors model (experiment 4) led to low result scores and combining word vectors model with medical concept model (experiment 5) led to an increase as expected. Table 2 presents the understandability assessment results using understandability measures uRBP and uRBPg. The best understandability scores were obtained with experiment 3. Comparing experiment 2 to experiment 1, one can state that using UMLS expansion techniques achieves lower understandability scores than using phrase search[6].

Table 1. Results measured with p@10 and ndcg@10.

Nr.	Methods	p@10	ndcg@10
1	Medical concept model (phrase search, term weighting)	0.1411	0.1045
2	Medical concept model (UMLS, term weighting)	0.1422	0.1038
3	Combination of experiments 1 and 2	0.1504	0.1108
4	Word vectors model	0.0996	0.0756
5	Combination of experiments 3 and 4	0.1159	0.0886

Table 2. Results measured with understandability assessments.

Nr.	Methods	uRBP	uRBPgr
1	Medical concept model (phrase search, term weighting)	0.0123	0.0083
2	Medical concept model (UMLS, term weighting)	0.0077	0.0060
3	Combination of experiment 1 and 2	0.0126	0.0095

---

[6] Since understandability assessments are calculated based on topical relevance, experiments 1, 2 and 3 with high topical relevance scores were selectively evaluated in understandability assessment.

4 Conclusion

In this paper, an approach to integrate Natural Language Processing methods into query expansion was introduced. Five experiments were performed and the results were assessed using both topical relevance and understandability assessments with the standard CLEF 2017 eHealth IR task Qrel files. From the results, one can conclude that merging Natural Language Processing methods with state-of-the-art query expansion techniques is a feasible and effective way in consumer health search.

Acknowledgement. This work was supported by EACEA under the Erasmus Mundus Action 2, Strand 1 project LEADER - Links in Europe and Asia for engineering, eDucation, Enterprise and Research exchanges.

References

1. Budaher, J., Almasri, M., Goeuriot, L.: Comparison of several word embedding sources for medical information retrieval. In: CLEF (Working Notes), pp. 43–46 (2016)
2. Fox, S., Duggan, M.: Health online 2013. In: Health 2013, pp. 1–55 (2013)
3. Hollada, J.L., et al.: Readability assessment of patient-centered outcomes research institute public abstracts in relation to accessibility. Epidemiology **28**(4), e37–e38 (2017)
4. Lopes, C.T., Ribeiro, C.: Effects of language and terminology on the usage of health query suggestions. In: Fuhr, N., et al. (eds.) CLEF 2016. LNCS, vol. 9822, pp. 83–95. Springer, Cham (2016). https://doi.org/10.1007/978-3-319-44564-9_7
5. Mikolov, T., et al.: Effcient estimation of word representations in vector space. In: arXiv preprint arXiv:1301.3781 (2013)
6. Oh, H.S., Jung, Y.: KISTI at CLEF eHealth 2016 task 3: ranking medical documents using word vectors. In: CLEF (Working Notes), pp. 103–108 (2016)
7. Palotti, J.R., et al.: CLEF eHealth evaluation lab 2015, task 2: retrieving information about medical symptoms. In: CLEF (Working Notes) (2015)
8. Palotti, J., et al.: CLEF 2017 task overview: the IR task at the ehealth evaluation lab. In: Working Notes of Conference and Labs of the Evaluation (CLEF) Forum, CEUR Workshop Proceedings (2017)
9. Sinha, M., Mannarswamy, S., Roy, S.: CHIS@ FIRE: overview of the shared task on consumer health information search. In: FIRE (Working Notes), pp. 193–196 (2016)
10. Yang, H., Goncalves, T.: Promoting understandability in consumer health information search. In: Jose, J.M., et al. (eds.) ECIR 2017. LNCS, vol. 10193, pp. 727–734. Springer, Cham (2017). https://doi.org/10.1007/978-3-319-56608-5_72
11. Zuccon, G.: Understandability biased evaluation for information retrieval. In: Ferro, N., et al. (eds.) ECIR 2016. LNCS, vol. 9626, pp. 280–292. Springer, Cham (2016). https://doi.org/10.1007/978-3-319-30671-1_21

CLEF 2018 Lab Overviews

Overview of CENTRE@CLEF 2018: A First Tale in the Systematic Reproducibility Realm

Nicola Ferro[1], Maria Maistro[1(✉)], Tetsuya Sakai[2], and Ian Soboroff[3]

[1] Department of Information Engineering, University of Padua, Padua, Italy
{ferro,maistro}@dei.unipd.it
[2] Waseda University, Tokyo, Japan
tetsuyasakai@acm.org
[3] National Institute of Standards and Technology (NIST), Gaithersburg, USA
ian.soboroff@nist.gov

Abstract. Reproducibility has become increasingly important for many research areas, among those IR is not an exception and has started to be concerned with reproducibility and its impact on research results. This paper describes our first attempt to propose a lab on reproducibility named CENTRE and held during CLEF 2018. The aim of CENTRE is to run a reproducibility challenge across all the major IR evaluation campaigns and to provide the IR community with a venue where previous research results can be explored and discussed. This paper reports the participant results and preliminary considerations on the first edition of CENTRE@CLEF 2018, as well as some suggestions for future editions.

1 Introduction

Reproducibility is becoming a primary concern in many areas of science [14] as well as in computer science, as also witnessed by the recent ACM policy on result and artefact review and badging[1]. *Information Retrieval (IR)* is especially interested in reproducibility [10,11,28] since it is a discipline strongly rooted in experimentation where experimental evaluation represents a main driver of advancement and innovation.

Even if reproducibility has become part of the review forms at major conferences like SIGIR, this is more a qualitative assessment performed by a reviewer on the basis of what can be understood from a paper rather than an actual "proof" of the reproducibility of the experiments reported in the paper. Since 2015, the ECIR conference started a new track focused on reproducibility of previously published results. This conference track led to a stable enough flow of 3–4 reproducibility papers accepted each year but, unfortunately, this valuable effort did not produce a systematic approach to reproducibility: submitting authors adopted different notions of reproducibility, they adopted very diverse

---

[1] https://www.acm.org/publications/policies/artifact-review-badging.

© Springer Nature Switzerland AG 2018
P. Bellot et al. (Eds.): CLEF 2018, LNCS 11018, pp. 239–246, 2018.
https://doi.org/10.1007/978-3-319-98932-7_23

experimental protocols, they investigated the most disparate topics, resulting in a very fragmented picture of what was reproduced and what not, and the outcomes of these reproducibility papers are spread over a series of potentially disappearing repositories and Web sites.

Moreover, if we consider open source IR systems, they are typically used as:

- starting point by new-comers in the field, which take them almost off-the-shelf using default configuration to begin experience with IR and/or specific search tasks;
- base system on top of which to add a new component/technique you are interested to develop, keeping all the rest in the default configuration;
- baseline for comparison, again using default configuration.

Nevertheless, it has been repeatedly shown that best TREC systems still outperform off-the-shelf open source systems [2–4,20,21]. This is due to many different factors, among which lack of tuning on a specific collection when using default configuration, but it is also caused by the lack of the specific and advanced components and resources adopted by the best systems. It has been also shown that additivity is an issue, since adding a component on top of a weak or strong base does not produce the same level of gain [4,20]. This poses a serious challenge when off-the-shelf open source systems are used as stepping stone to test a new component on top of them, because the gain might appear bigger starting from a weak baseline. Overall, the above considerations stress the need and urgency for a systematic approach to reproducibility in IR.

Therefore, the goal of CENTRE@CLEF 2018[2] is to run a joint task across CLEF/NTCIR/TREC on challenging participants:

- to reproduce best results of best/most interesting systems in previous editions of CLEF/NTCIR/TREC by using standard open source IR systems;
- to contribute back to the community the additional components and resources developed to reproduce the results in order to improve existing open source systems.

The paper is organized as follows: Sect. 2 introduces the setup of the lab; Sect. 3 discusses the participation and the experimental outcomes; and, Sect. 4 draws some conclusions and outlooks possible future works.

2   Evaluation Lab Setup

2.1   Tasks

The CENTRE@CLEF 2018 lab offered two pilot tasks:

- *Task 1 - Replicability:* the task focused on the replicability of selected methods on the same experimental collections;

---

[2] http://www.centre-eval.org/clef2018/.

- *Task 2 - Reproducibility:* the task focused on the reproducibility of selected methods on the different experimental collections.

where we adopted the ACM Artifact Review and Badging definition of replicability and reproducibility:

- *Replicability (different team, same experimental setup):* the measurement can be obtained with stated precision by a different team using the same measurement procedure, the same measuring system, under the same operating conditions, in the same or a different location on multiple trials. For computational experiments, this means that an independent group can obtain the same result using the author's own artifacts.
  In CENTRE@CLEF 2018 this meant to use the same collections, topics and ground-truth on which the methods and solutions have been developed and evaluated.
- *Reproducibility (different team, different experimental setup):* The measurement can be obtained with stated precision by a different team, a different measuring system, in a different location on multiple trials. For computational experiments, this means that an independent group can obtain the same result using artifacts which they develop completely independently.
  In CENTRE@CLEF 2018 this meant to use a different experimental collection, but in the same domain, from those used to originally develop and evaluate a solution.

2.2   Replicability and Reproducibility Targets

Below we list the runs selected as targets of replicability and reproducibility among which the participants can choose. For each run, it is specified the collection for replicability and the collections for reproducibility; for more information, the list also provides references to the papers describing those runs as well as the overviews describing the overall task and collections.

Since these runs were not originally thought for being used as targets of a replicability/reproducibility exercise, we contacted the authors of the papers to inform them and ask their consent to use the runs.

- **Run:** AUTOEN [16]
  - **Task type:** CLEF Ad Hoc Multilingual Task
  - **Replicability:** Multi-8 Two Years On with topics of CLEF 2005 [9]
  - **Reproducibility:** Multi-8 with topics of CLEF 2003 [5,25]
- **Run:** AH-TEL-BILI-X2EN-CLEF2008.TWENTE.FCW [24]
  - **Task type:** CLEF Ad Hoc, Bilingual Task
  - **Replicability:** TEL English (BL) with topics of CLEF 2008 [1]
  - **Reproducibility:** TEL French (BNF) and TEL German (ONB) with topics of CLEF 2008 [1]
    TEL English (BL), TEL French (BNF) and TEL German (ONB) with topics of CLEF 2009 [13]
- **Run:** AH-TEL-BILI-X2DE-CLEF2008.KARLSRUHE.AIFB_ONB_EN [26]

- **Task type:** CLEF Ad Hoc, Bilingual Task
- **Replicability:** TEL German (ONB) with topics of CLEF 2008 [1]
- **Reproducibility:** TEL English (BL) and TEL French (BNF) with topics of CLEF 2008 [1]
  TEL English (BL), TEL French (BNF) and TEL German (ONB) with topics of CLEF 2009 [13]
- **Run:** UDInfolabWEB2 [27]
  - **Task type:** TREC Ad Hoc Web Task
  - **Replicability:** ClueWeb12 Category A with topics of TREC 2013 [7]
  - **Reproducibility:** ClueWeb09 Category A and B with topics of TREC 2012 [6]
    ClueWeb12 Category B with topics of TREC 2013 [7]
    ClueWeb12 Category A and B with topics of TREC 2014 [8]
- **Run:** uogTrDwl [23]
  - **Task type:** TREC Ad Hoc Web Task
  - **Replicability:** ClueWeb12 Category A with topics of TREC 2014 [8]
  - **Reproducibility:** ClueWeb09 Category A and B with topics of TREC 2012 [6]
    ClueWeb12 Category A and B with topics of TREC 2013 [7]
    ClueWeb12 Category B with topics of TREC 2014 [8]
- **Run:** RMIT-E-NU-Own-1 and RMIT-E-NU-Own-3 [15]
  - **Task type:** NTCIR Ad Hoc Web Task
  - **Replicability:** ClueWeb12 Category B with topics of NTCIR-13 [22]
  - **Reproducibility:** ClueWeb12 Category A with topics of NTCIR-13 [22]

2.3   Evaluation Measures

The quality of the replicability runs has been evaluated from two points of view:

- *Effectiveness:* how close are the performance scores of the replicated systems to those of the original ones. This is measured using the *Root Mean Square Error (RMSE)* [19] between the new and original *Average Precision (AP)* scores:

$$\text{RMSE} = \sqrt{\frac{1}{m} \sum_{i=1}^{m} \left(AP_{orig,i} - AP_{replica,i} \right)^2} \tag{1}$$

where m is the total number of topics, $AP_{orig,i}$ is the AP score of the original target run on topic t_i and $AP_{replica,i}$ is the AP score of the replicated run on topic t_i.
- *Ranked result lists:* since different result lists may produce the same effectiveness score, we also measure how close are the ranked results list of the replicated systems to those of the original ones. This is measured using Kendall's τ correlation coefficient [18] among the list of retrieved documents for each

topic, averaged across all the topics. The Kendall's τ correlation coefficient on a single topic is given by:

$$\tau_i(orig, replica) = \frac{P - Q}{\sqrt{(P + Q + T)(P + Q + U)}}$$

$$\bar{\tau}_i(orig, replica) = \frac{1}{m} \sum_{i=1}^{m} \tau_i(orig, replica)$$

(2)

where m is the total number of topics, P is the total number of concordant pairs (document pairs that are ranked in the same order in both vectors) Q the total number of discordant pairs (document pairs that are ranked in opposite order in the two vectors), T and U are the number of ties, respectively, in the first and in the second ranking.

Since for the reproducibility runs we do not have an already existing run to compare against, we planned to compare the reproduced run score with respect to a *baseline run* to see whether the improvement over the baseline is comparable between the original and the new dataset. However, we did not receive any reproducibility runs so we cannot put in practice this part of the evaluation task.

3   Participation and Outcomes

17 groups registered for participating in CENTRE@CLEF2018 but, unfortunately, only one group succeeded in submitting one replicability run.

Technical University of Wien (TUW) [17] replicated the run by Cimiano and Sorg, i.e. `AH-TEL-BILI-X2DE-CLEF2008.KARLSRUHE.AIFB_ONB_EN`, the code they used to replicate the run is available online[3].

The paper by Cimiano and Sorg [26] uses *Cross-Lingual Explicit Semantic Analysis (CL-ESA)* to leverage Wikipedia articles to deal with multiple languages in a uniform way.

TUW encountered the following issues in replicating the original run:

- the Wikipedia underlying database dump of 2008 was no longer available and they have to resort to the static HTML dump of Wikipedia in the same period;
- the above issue caused a processing of Wikipedia articles sensibly different from the original one in [26] and had to rely on several heuristics to cope with HTML;
- they fixed an issue in the *Inverse Document Frequency (IDF)* computation, which might result in negative values according to the equation provided by [26];
- they had to deal with redirect pages in the static HTML dump of Wikipedia in order to find links across wiki pages in multiple languages;

---

[3] https://bitbucket.org/centre_eval/c2018_dataintelligence/src/master/.

– they had to find an alternative interpretation language identification heuristics.

All these issues prevented TUW from successfully replicating the original run. Indeed the *Mean Average Precision (MAP)* of the run by Cimiano and Sorg was 0.0667 while the MAP of the run by TUW is 0.0030. This is further stressed by the RMSE, computed according to Eq. (1), which is 0.1132 and the average Kendall's τ correlation among the ranked lists of retrieved documents, computed according to Eq. (2), which is $-5.69 \cdot 10^{-04}$.

4   Conclusions and Future Work

This paper reports the results on the first edition of CENTRE@CLEF2018. A total of 17 participants enrolled in the lab, however just one group managed to submit a run. As reported in the results section, the group encountered many substantial issues which prevented them to actually replicate the targeted run, as described in more detail in their paper [17].

These results support anecdotal evidence in the field about how difficult it is to actually replicate (and even more reproduce) research results, even in a field with such a long experimental tradition as IR is. However, the lack of participation is a signal that the community is somehow overlooking this important issue. As it also emerged from a recent survey within the SIGIR community [12], while there is a very positive attitude towards reproducibility and it is considered very important from a scientific point of view, there are many obstacles to it such as the effort required to put it into practice, the lack of rewards for achieving it, the possible barriers for new and inexperienced groups, and, last but not least, the (somehow optimistic) researcher's perception that their own research is already reproducible.

For the next edition of the lab we are planning to propose some changes in the lab organization to increase the interest and participation of the research community. First, we will target for newer and more popular systems to be reproduced, moreover we will consider other tasks than the AdHoc, as for example the medical or other popular domains.

References

1. Agirre, E., Di Nunzio, G.M., Ferro, N., Mandl, T., Peters, C.: CLEF 2008: ad hoc track overview. In: Peters, C., et al. (eds.) CLEF 2008. LNCS, vol. 5706, pp. 15–37. Springer, Heidelberg (2009). https://doi.org/10.1007/978-3-642-04447-2_2
2. Arguello, J., Crane, M., Diaz, F., Lin, J., Trotman, A.: Report on the SIGIR 2015 workshop on reproducibility, inexplicability, and generalizability of results (RIGOR). SIGIR Forum 49(2), 107–116 (2015)
3. Armstrong, T.G., Moffat, A., Webber, W., Zobel, J.: Has adhoc retrieval improved since 1994? In: Allan, J., Aslam, J.A., Sanderson, M., Zhai, C., Zobel, J. (eds.) Proceedings of the 32nd Annual International ACM SIGIR Conference on Research and Development in Information Retrieval (SIGIR 2009), pp. 692–693. ACM Press, New York (2009)

4. Armstrong, T.G., Moffat, A., Webber, W., Zobel, J.: Improvements that don't add up: ad-hoc retrieval results since 1998. In: Cheung, D.W.L., Song, I.Y., Chu, W.W., Hu, X., Lin, J.J. (eds.) Proceedings of the 18th International Conference on Information and Knowledge Management (CIKM 2009), pp. 601–610. ACM Press, New York (2009)

5. Braschler, M.: CLEF 2003 – overview of results. In: Peters, C., Gonzalo, J., Braschler, M., Kluck, M. (eds.) CLEF 2003. LNCS, vol. 3237, pp. 44–63. Springer, Heidelberg (2004). https://doi.org/10.1007/978-3-540-30222-3_5

6. Clarke, C.L.A., Craswell, N., Voorhees, E.M.: Overview of the TREC 2012 web track. In: Voorhees, E.M., Buckland, L.P. (eds.) Proceedings of the Twenty-First Text REtrieval Conference (TREC 2012), pp. 1–8. National Institute of Standards and Technology (NIST), Special Publication 500–298, Washington (2013)

7. Collins-Thompson, K., Diaz, F., Clarke, C.L.A., Voorhees, E.M.: TREC 2013 web track overview. In: Voorhees, E.M. (ed.) Proceedings of the Twenty-Second Text REtrieval Conference (TREC 2013). National Institute of Standards and Technology (NIST), Special Publication 500–302, Washington (2014)

8. Collins-Thompson, K., Macdonald, C., Bennett, P.N., Voorhees, E.M.: TREC 2014 web track overview. In: Voorhees, E.M., Ellis, A. (eds.) Proceedings of the Twenty-Third Text REtrieval Conference (TREC 2014). National Institute of Standards and Technology (NIST), Special Publication 500–308, Washington (2015)

9. Di Nunzio, G.M., Ferro, N., Jones, G.J.F., Peters, C.: CLEF 2005: ad hoc track overview. In: Peters, C., et al. (eds.) CLEF 2005. LNCS, vol. 4022, pp. 11–36. Springer, Heidelberg (2006). https://doi.org/10.1007/11878773_2

10. Ferro, N.: Reproducibility challenges in information retrieval evaluation. ACM J. Data Inf. Qual. (JDIQ) **8**(2), 8:1–8:4 (2017)

11. Ferro, N., Fuhr, N., Järvelin, K., Kando, N., Lippold, M., Zobel, J.: Increasing reproducibility in IR: findings from the Dagstuhl seminar on "reproducibility of data-oriented experiments in e-science". SIGIR Forum **50**(1), 68–82 (2016)

12. Ferro, N., Kelly, D.: SIGIR initiative to implement ACM artifact review and badging. SIGIR Forum **52**(1) (2018)

13. Ferro, N., Peters, C.: CLEF 2009 ad hoc track overview: TEL and Persian tasks. In: Peters, C., et al. (eds.) CLEF 2009. LNCS, vol. 6241, pp. 13–35. Springer, Heidelberg (2010). https://doi.org/10.1007/978-3-642-15754-7_2

14. Freire, J., Fuhr, N., Rauber, A. (eds.): Report from Dagstuhl seminar 16041: reproducibility of data-oriented experiments in e-science. Dagstuhl Reports, vol. 6, no 1. Schloss Dagstuhl-Leibniz-Zentrum für Informatik, Germany (2016)

15. Gallagher, L., Mackenzie, J., Benham, R., Chen, R.C., Scholer, F., Culpepper, J.S.: RMIT at the NTCIR-13 we want web task. In: Kando, N., Fujita, S., Kato, M.P., Manabe, T. (eds.) Proceedings of the 13th NTCIR Conference on Evaluation of Information Access Technologies, pp. 402–406. National Institute of Informatics, Tokyo (2017)

16. Guyot, J., Radhouani, S., Falquet, G.: Ontology-based multilingual information retrieval. In: Peters, C., Quochi, V., Ferro, N. (eds.) CLEF 2005 Working Notes. CEUR Workshop Proceedings. CEUR-WS.org (2005). http://ceur-ws.org/Vol-1171/. ISSN 1613–0073

17. Jungwirth, M., Hanbury, A.: Replicating an experiment in cross-lingual information retrieval with explicit semantic analysis. In: Cappellato, L., Ferro, N., Nie, J.Y., Soulier, L. (eds.) CLEF 2018 Working Notes. CEUR Workshop Proceedings. CEUR-WS.org (2018). ISSN 1613–0073

18. Kendall, M.G.: Rank Correlation Methods. Griffin, Oxford (1948)

19. Kenney, J.F., Keeping, E.S.: Mathematics of Statistics - Part One, 3rd edn. D. Van Nostrand Company, Princeton (1954)
20. Kharazmi, S., Scholer, F., Vallet, D., Sanderson, M.: Examining additivity and weak baselines. ACM Trans. Inf. Syst. (TOIS) **34**(4), 23:1–23:18 (2016)
21. Lin, J., et al.: Toward reproducible baselines: the open-source IR reproducibility challenge. In: Ferro, N., et al. (eds.) ECIR 2016. LNCS, vol. 9626, pp. 408–420. Springer, Cham (2016). https://doi.org/10.1007/978-3-319-30671-1_30
22. Luo, C., Sakai, T., Liu, Y., Dou, Z., Xiong, C., Xu, J.: Overview of the NTCIR-13 we want web task. In: Kando, N., Fujita, S., Kato, M.P., Manabe, T. (eds.) Proceedings of the 13th NTCIR Conference on Evaluation of Information Access Technologies, pp. 394–401. National Institute of Informatics, Tokyo (2017)
23. McCreadie, R., et al.: University of Glasgow at TREC 2014: experiments with terrier in contextual suggestion, temporal summarisation and web tracks. In: Voorhees, E.M., Ellis, A. (eds.) Proceedings of the Twenty-Third Text REtrieval Conference (TREC 2014). National Institute of Standards and Technology (NIST), Special Publication 500–308, Washington (2015)
24. Nguyen, D., Overwijk, A., Hauff, C., Trieschnigg, D.R.B., Hiemstra, D., de Jong, F.: WikiTranslate: query translation for cross-lingual information retrieval using only Wikipedia. In: Peters, C., et al. (eds.) CLEF 2008. LNCS, vol. 5706, pp. 58–65. Springer, Heidelberg (2009). https://doi.org/10.1007/978-3-642-04447-2_6
25. Savoy, J.: Report on CLEF-2003 multilingual tracks. In: Peters, C., Gonzalo, J., Braschler, M., Kluck, M. (eds.) CLEF 2003. LNCS, vol. 3237, pp. 64–73. Springer, Heidelberg (2004). https://doi.org/10.1007/978-3-540-30222-3_6
26. Sorg, P., Cimiano, P.: Cross-lingual information retrieval with explicit semantic analysis. In: Borri, F., Nardi, A., Peters, C., Ferro, N. (eds.) CLEF 2008 Working Notes. CEUR Workshop Proceedings. CEUR-WS.org (2008). http://ceur-ws.org/Vol-1174/. ISSN 1613–0073
27. Yang, P., Fang, H.: Evaluating the effectiveness of axiomatic approaches in web track. In: Voorhees, E.M. (ed.) Proceedings of the Twenty-Second Text REtrieval Conference (TREC 2013). National Institute of Standards and Technology (NIST), Special Publication 500–302, Washington (2014)
28. Zobel, J., Webber, W., Sanderson, M., Moffat, A.: Principles for robust evaluation infrastructure. In: Agosti, M., Ferro, N., Thanos, C. (eds.) Proceedings of the Workshop on Data infrastructurEs for Supporting Information Retrieval Evaluation (DESIRE 2011), pp. 3–6. ACM Press, New York (2011)

Overview of LifeCLEF 2018: A Large-Scale Evaluation of Species Identification and Recommendation Algorithms in the Era of AI

Alexis Joly[1]([⊠]), Hervé Goëau[2], Christophe Botella[1,3], Hervé Glotin[4],
Pierre Bonnet[2], Willem-Pier Vellinga[5], Robert Planqué[5], and Henning Müller[6]

[1] Inria, LIRMM, Montpellier, France
alexis.joly@inria.fr
[2] CIRAD, UMR AMAP, Montpellier, France
[3] INRA, UMR AMAP, Montpellier, France
[4] AMU, Univ. Toulon, CNRS, ENSAM, LSIS UMR 7296, IUF,
Marseille, France
[5] Xeno-canto foundation, Amsterdam, The Netherlands
[6] HES-SO, Sierre, Switzerland

Abstract. Building accurate knowledge of the identity, the geographic distribution and the evolution of living species is essential for a sustainable development of humanity, as well as for biodiversity conservation. Unfortunately, such basic information is often only partially available for professional stakeholders, teachers, scientists and citizens, and often incomplete for ecosystems that possess the highest diversity. In this context, an ultimate ambition is to set up innovative information systems relying on the automated identification and understanding of living organisms as a means to engage massive crowds of observers and boost the production of biodiversity and agro-biodiversity data. The Life-CLEF 2018 initiative proposes three data-oriented challenges related to this vision, in the continuity of the previous editions, but with several consistent novelties intended to push the boundaries of the state-of-the-art in several research directions. This paper describes the methodology of the conducted evaluations as well as the synthesis of the main results and lessons learned.

1 LifeCLEF Lab Overview

Identifying organisms is a key for accessing information related to the uses and ecology of species. This is an essential step in recording any specimen on earth to be used in ecological studies. Unfortunately, this is difficult to achieve due to the level of expertise necessary to correctly record and identify living organisms (for instance flowering plants are one of the most difficult groups to identify with an estimated number of 400,000 species). This *taxonomic gap* has been recognized since the Rio Conference of 1992, as one of the major obstacles to the global

© Springer Nature Switzerland AG 2018
P. Bellot et al. (Eds.): CLEF 2018, LNCS 11018, pp. 247–266, 2018.
https://doi.org/10.1007/978-3-319-98932-7_24

implementation of the Convention on Biological Diversity. Among the diversity of methods used for species identification, Gaston and O'Neill [10] discussed in 2004 the potential of automated approaches typically based on machine learning and multimedia data analysis methods. They suggested that, if the scientific community is able to (i) overcome the production of large training datasets, (ii) more precisely identify and evaluate the error rates, (iii) scale up automated approaches, and (iv) detect novel species, it will then be possible to initiate the development of a generic automated species identification system that could open up vistas of new opportunities for theoretical and applied work in biological and related fields.

Since the question raised in Gaston and O'Neill [10], *automated species identification: why not?*, a lot of work was done on the topic (*e.g.* [7,23,30,45–47]) and it is still attracting much research today, in particular using deep learning techniques. In parallel to the emergence of automated identification tools, large social networks dedicated to the production, sharing and identification of multimedia biodiversity records have increased in recent years. Some of the most active ones like eBird[1] [43], iNaturalist[2], iSpot [39], Xeno-Canto[3] or Tela Botanica[4] (respectively initiated in the US for the two first ones and in Europe for the three last ones), federate tens of thousands of active members, producing hundreds of thousands of observations each year. Noticeably, the Pl@ntNet initiative was the first one attempting to combine the force of social networks with that of automated identification tools [23] through the release of a mobile application and collaborative validation tools. As a proof of their increasing reliability, most of these networks have started to contribute to global initiatives on biodiversity, such as the Global Biodiversity Information Facility (GBIF[5]) which is the largest and most recognized one. Nevertheless, this explicitly shared and validated data is only the tip of the iceberg. The real potential lies in the automatic analysis of the millions of raw observations collected every year through a growing number of devices but for which there is no human validation at all. However, this is still a challenging task: state-of-the-art multimedia analysis and machine learning techniques are actually still far from reaching the requirements of an accurate biodiversity monitoring system working. In particular, we need to progress on the number of species recognized by these systems. Indeed, the total number of living species on earth is estimated to be around 10K for birds, 30K for fishes, more than 400K for flowering plants (cf. State of the World's Plants 2017[6]) and more than 1.2M for invertebrates [2]. To bridge this gap, it is required to boost research on large-scale datasets and real-world scenarios.

---

[1] http://ebird.org/content/ebird/.

[2] http://www.inaturalist.org/.

[3] http://www.xeno-canto.org/.

[4] http://www.tela-botanica.org/.

[5] http://www.gbif.org/.

[6] https://stateoftheworldsplants.com/.

To evaluate the performance of automated identification technologies in a sustainable, repeatable and scalable way, the LifeCLEF[7] research platform was created in 2014 as a continuation of the plant identification task [24] that was run within the ImageCLEF lab[8] the three years before [13–15,33]. LifeCLEF enlarged the evaluated challenge by considering birds and marine animals in addition to plants, and audio and video content in addition to images. In this way, it aims at pushing the boundaries of the state-of-the-art in several research directions at the frontier of information retrieval, machine learning and knowledge engineering including (i) large scale classification, (ii) scene understanding, (iii) weakly-supervised and open-set classification, (iv) transfer learning and fine-grained classification and (v), humanly-assisted or crowdsourcing-based classification. As described in more detail in the following sections, each task is based on big and real-world data and the measured challenges are defined in collaboration with biologists and environmental stakeholders so as to reflect realistic usage scenarios. The main novelties of the 2018 edition of LifeCLEF compared to the previous years are the following:

1. **Expert vs. Machines plant identification challenge:** As the image-based identification of plants has improved considerably in the last few years (in particular through the PlantCLEF challenge), the next big question is how far such automated systems are from the human expertise. To answer this question, following the study of [4], we launched a new challenge, ExpertLifeCLEF, which involved 9 of the best expert botanists of the French flora who accepted to compete with AI algorithms.

2. **Location-based species recommendation challenge:** Automatically predicting the list of species that are the most likely to be observed at a given location is useful for many scenarios in biodiversity informatics. To boost the research on this topic, we also launched a new challenge called GeoLifeCLEF.

Besides these two main novelties, we decided to continue running the BirdCLEF challenge without major changes over the 2017 edition. The previous results actually showed that there was still a large margin of progress in terms of performance, in particular on the *soundscapes* data (long audio recordings). More generally, it is important to remind that an evaluation campaign such as LifeCLEF has to encourage long-term research efforts so as to (i) encourage non-incremental contributions, (ii) measure consistent performance gaps, and (iii), enable the emergence of a strong community.

Overall, 57 research groups from 22 countries registered to at least one of the three challenges of the lab. 12 of them finally crossed the finish line by participating in the collaborative evaluation and by writing technical reports describing in details their evaluated system. In the following sections, we provide a synthesis of the methodology and main results of each of the three challenges of LifeCLEF2018. More details can be found in the overview reports of each challenge and the individual reports of the participants (references provided below).

---

[7] http://www.lifeclef.org.
[8] http://www.imageclef.org/.

2   Task1: ExpertLifeCLEF

Automated identification of plants has improved considerably in the last few years. In the scope of LifeCLEF 2017 in particular, we measured impressive identification performance achieved thanks to recent convolutional neural network models. This raised the question of how far automated systems are from the human expertise and of whether there is a upper bound that can not be exceeded. A picture actually contains only a partial information about the observed plant and it is often not sufficient to determine the right species with certainty. For instance, a decisive organ such as the flower or the fruit, might not be visible at the time a plant was observed. Some of the discriminant patterns might be very hard or unlikely to be observed in a picture such as the presence of pills or latex, or the morphology of the root. As a consequence, even the best experts can be confused and/or disagree between each other when attempting to identify a plant from a set of pictures. Similar challenges arise for most living organisms including fishes, birds, insects, etc. Quantifying this intrinsic data uncertainty and comparing it to the performance of the best automated systems is of high interest for both computer scientists and expert naturalists.

2.1   Dataset and Evaluation Protocol

Test Set: to conduct a valuable experts vs. machines experiment, image-based identifications from the best of the best experts in the plant domain in France were collected according to the following procedure. 125 plants were photographed between May and June 2017, in a botanical garden called the *Parc floral de Paris* and in a natural area located in the north of Montpellier city (southern part of France, close to the Mediterranean sea). The photos were produced with two best-selling smartphones by a botanist and an amateur under his supervision. The species were selected by several criteria including (i) their membership to a difficult plant group (*i.e.* a group known as being the source of many confusions), (ii) the availability of well developed specimens with visible organs on the spot and (iii), the diversity of the selected set of species in terms of taxonomy and morphology. About fifteen pictures of each specimen were acquired to cover all the informative parts of the plant. However, only 1 to 5 pictures were randomly selected for all specimen to intentionally hide a part of the information and increase the difficulty of the identification. In the end, the set contains 75 plants illustrated by a total of 216 images and is related to 33 families and 58 genera. The species labels were cross-validated by other experts in order to have a near-perfect gold standard. Finally, the set was mixed into a larger one containing about 2000 observations (and about 7000 associated images) coming from the data flow of the mobile application Pl@ntNet[9,10]. The added observations are necessarily related to species belonging to the list of the 10,000 species of the training set and are mainly wild plant species coming from

---

[9] https://itunes.apple.com/fr/app/plantnet/id600547573?mt=8.
[10] https://play.google.com/store/apps/details?id=org.plantnet.

the Western European flora and the North American flora but also plant species used all around the world as cultivated or ornamental plants including some endangered species.

Training Set(s): As training data, all the datasets of the previous PlantCLEF challenges were made available to the participants. It can be divided into 3 subsets: first a **"Trusted"** training set contains 256,287 pictures related to the 10,000 most populated species in the online collaborative Encyclopedia Of Life (EoL) after a curation pipeline made by the organizers of the PlantCLEF 2017 task (taxonomic alignment, duplicates removal, herbaria sheets removal, no plant pictures removal). A second *Noisy* training set is an extension of the *Trusted* training set adding about 900,000 images collected through the Bing image search engine during Autumn 2016 (and to a lesser extent with the Google image search engine). Lastly, a *PlantCLEFPrevious* training set is the concatenation of images collected through the Pl@ntNet project and shared during the challenges PlantCLEF 2011 to 2017, related to more than 100,000 images and 1100 species. In the end, the whole training set contains more than 1.2 million pictures and has the specificity to be strongly unbalanced with for instance a minimum of 4 pictures for the *Plectranthus sanguineus* species while the a maximum is 1732 pictures for *Fagus grandifolia*.

Task and Evaluation: the goal of the task was to return the most likely species list by decreasing probability for each observation of the test set, and the main evaluation metric was the top-1 accuracy.

2.2   Participants and Results

28 research groups registered for the LifeCLEF plant challenge 2018 and downloaded the dataset. Only 4 research groups succeeded in submitting *runs*, i.e., files containing the predictions of the system(s) they ran. Details of the methods and systems used in the runs are synthesized in the overview working notes paper of the task [12] and further developed in the individual working notes of the participants (CMP [42], MfN [29], Sabanci [1] and TUC MI [21]. We report in Fig. 1 the performance achieved by the 19 collected runs and the 9 participating human experts, while Fig. 2 reports the results on the whole test dataset.

The main outcomes we derived from the results of the evaluation are the following ones:

A Difficult Task, Even for Experts: as a first noticeable outcome, none of the botanist correctly identified all observations. The top-1 accuracy of the experts is in the range 0.613–0.96. with a median value of 0.8. This illustrates the difficulty of the task, especially when reminding that the experts were authorized to use any external resource to complete the task, Flora books in particular. It shows that a large part of the observations in the test set do not contain enough

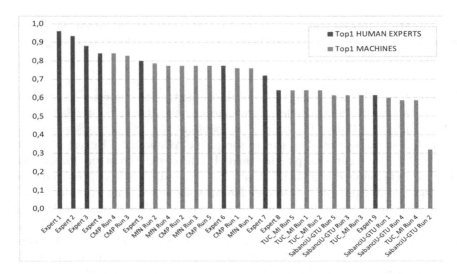

Fig. 1. ExpertLifeCLEF 2018 results: identification performance achieved by the evaluated systems and the participating human experts

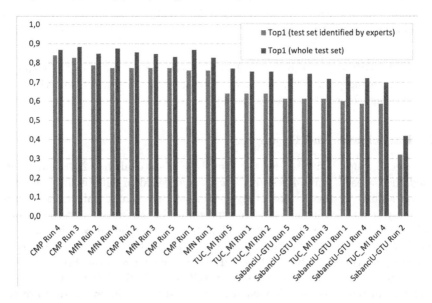

Fig. 2. Identification performance achieved by machines: top-1 accuracy on the whole test dataset and on the subpart also identified by the human experts.

information to be identified with confidence when using classical identification keys. Only the four experts with an exceptional field expertise were able to correctly identify more than 80% of the observations.

Deep Learning Algorithms were Defeated by the Best Experts: but the margin of progression is becoming tighter and tighter. The top-1 accuracy of the evaluated systems is in the range 0.32–0.84 with a median value of 0.64. This is globally lower than the experts but it is noticeable that the best systems were able to perform better than 5 of the highly skilled participating experts.

We give hereafter more details of the 2 systems that performed the best.

CMP System [42]: used an ensemble of a dozen Convolutional Neural Networks (CNNs) based on 2 state-of-the-art architectures (Inception-ResNet-v2 and Inception-v4). The CNNs were initialized with weights pre-trained on ImageNet, then fine-tuned with different hyper-parameters and with the use of data augmentation (random horizontal flip, color distortions and random crops for some models). Each single test image is also augmented with 14 transformations (central/corner crops, horizontal flips, none) to combine and improve the predictions. Still at test time, the predictions are computed using the *Exponential Moving Average* feature of TensorFlow, *i.e.* by averaging the predictions of the set of models trained during the last iterations of the training phase (with an exponential decay). This popular procedure is inspired from Polyak averaging method [36] and is known to sometimes produce significantly better results than using the last trained model solely. As a last step in their system, assuming that there is a strong unbalanced distribution of the classes between the test and the training sets, the outputs of the CNNs are adjusted according to an estimation of the class prior probabilities in the test set based on an Expectation Maximization algorithm. The best score of 88.4% top-1 accuracy during the challenge was obtained by this team with the largest ensemble (CMP Run 3). With half less combined models, the CMP Run 4 reached a close top-1 accuracy and even obtained a slightly better accuracy on the smaller test subset identified by human experts. It can be explained by the strategy during the training of using the trusted and noisy sets: a comparison between CMP Run 1 and 4 clearly illustrates that refining further a model with only the trusted training set after learning it on the whole noisy training set is not relevant. CMP Run 3 which combines all the models seems to have its performances degraded by the inclusion of the models refined on the trusted training set when we compare it with CMP Run 4 on the test subset identified by human experts.

MfN System [29]: followed quite similar approaches used last year during the PlantCLEF2017 challenge [27]. This participant used an ensemble of fine-tuned CNNs pretrained on ImageNet, based on 4 architectures (GoogLeNet, ResNet-152, ResNeXT, DualPathNet92), each trained with bagging techniques. Data augmentation was used systematically for each training, in particular random cropping, horizontal flipping, variations of saturation, lightness and rotation. For the three last transformations, the intensity of the transformation is correlated to the diminution of the learning rate during training to let the CNNs see patches progressively closer to the original image at the end of the training. Test images followed similar transformations for combining and boosting the accuracy of the predictions. MfN Run 1 used basically the best and winning approach during PlantCLEF2017 by averaging the prediction of 11 models based on 3 architectures (GoogLeNet, ResNet-152, ResNeXT). However, surprisingly, the runs MfN Run 2 and 3, which are based on only one architecture (respectively ResNet152 and DualPathNet92), performed both better than the Run 1 combining several architectures and models. The combination of all the approaches in MfN Run 4 seems even to be penalized by the winning approach during PlantCLEF2017.

3 Task2: BirdCLEF

The general public as well as professionals like park rangers, ecological consultants and of course ornithologists are potential users of an automated bird song identifying system. A typical professional use would be in the context of wider initiatives related to ecological surveillance or biodiversity conservation. Using audio records rather than bird pictures is justified [6,7,45,46] since birds are in fact not that easy to photograph and calls and songs have proven to be easier to collect and have been found to be species specific.

The 2018 edition of the task shares similar objectives and scenarios with the previous edition: (i) the identification of a particular bird species from a recording of one of its sounds, and (ii) the recognition of all species vocalising in so-called *soundscapes* that can contain up to several tens of birds vocalising. The first scenario is aimed at developing new automatic and interactive identification tools, to help users and experts to assess species and populations from field recordings obtained with directional microphones. The soundscapes, on the other side, correspond to a much more passive monitoring scenario in which any multi-directional audio recording device could be used without or with very light user's involvement. These (possibly crowdsourced) passive acoustic monitoring scenarios could scale the amount of annotated acoustic biodiversity records by several orders of magnitude.

3.1 Data and Tasks Description

SubTask1: Monospecies (Monophone) Recordings: The dataset was the same as the one used for BirdCLEF 2017 [17], mostly based on the contributions of the Xeno-Canto network. The training dataset contains 36,496 recordings covering 1500 species of south America (more precisely species observed in Brazil, Colombia, Venezuela, Guyana, Suriname, French Guiana, Bolivia, Ecuador and Peru) and it is the largest bioacoustic dataset in the literature to our knowledge. It has a massive class imbalance with a minimum of four recordings for *Laniocera rufescens* and a maximum of 160 recordings for *Henicorhina leucophrys*. Recordings are associated to various metadata such as the type of sound (call, song, alarm, flight, etc.), the date, the location, textual comments of the authors, multilingual common names and collaborative quality ratings. The test set for the monophone sub-task contains 12,347 recordings of the same type (mono-phone recordings). More details about that data can be found in the overview working note of BirdCLEF 2017 [17].

The goal of the task is to identify the species of the most audible bird (*i.e.* the one that was intended to be recorded) in each of the provided test recordings. Therefore, the evaluated systems have to return a ranked list of possible species for each of the 12,347 test recordings. The used evaluation metric is the Mean Reciprocal Rank (MRR), a statistic measure for evaluating any process that produces a list of possible responses to a sample of queries ordered by probability of correctness. The reciprocal rank of a query response is the multiplicative inverse of the rank of the first correct answer. The MRR is the average of the reciprocal ranks for the whole test set:

$$MRR = \frac{1}{|Q|} \sum_{i=1}^{Q} \frac{1}{rank_i}$$

where $|Q|$ is the total number of query occurrences in the test set.

SubTask2: Soundscape Recordings: As the soundscapes appeared to be very challenging during the 2015 and 2016 (with an accuracy below 15%), new soundscape recordings containing time-coded bird species annotations were integrated in 2017 in the test set (so as to better understand what makes state-of-the-art methods fail on such contents). This new data was specifically created for BirdCLEF thanks to the work of Paula Caycedo Rosales (ornithologist from the Biodiversa Foundation of Colombia and Instituto Alexander von Humboldt, Xeno-Canto member), Hervé Glotin (bio-accoustician, co-author of this paper) and Lucio Pando (field guide and ornithologist in Peru). In total, about 6.5 h of audio recordings were collected and annotated in the form of time-coded segments with associated species name. A baseline and validation package developed by Chemnitz University of Technology was shared with the participants[11]. The validation package contains 20 min of annotated soundscapes split into 5 recordings took of the last year test dataset. The baseline package offers a tools and a workflow to assist the participants in the development of their system: spectrograms extraction, deep neural network training, audio classification task, local validation (more details can be found in [26]).

Task Description: Participants were asked to run their system so as to identify all the actively vocalising birds species in each test recording (or in each test segment of 5 s for the soundscapes). The submission *run files* had to contain as many lines as the total number of identifications, with a maximum of 100 identifications per test segment). Each prediction had to be composed of a species name belonging to the training set and a normalized score in the range $[0, 1]$ reflecting the likelihood that this species is singing in the segment. The used evaluation metric was the classification mean Average Precision (*cmAP*), considering each class c of the ground truth as a query. This means that for each class c, all predictions with $ClassId = c$ are extracted from the run file and

---

[11] https://github.com/kahst/BirdCLEF-Baseline.

ranked by decreasing probability in order to compute the average precision for that class. Then, the mean across all classes is computed as the main evaluation metric. More formally:

$$cmAP = \frac{\sum_{c=1}^{C} AveP(c)}{C}$$

where C is the number of classes (species) in the ground truth and $AveP(c)$ is the average precision for a given species c computed as:

$$AveP(c) = \frac{\sum_{k=1}^{n_c} P(k) \times rel(k)}{n_{rel}(c)}.$$

where k is the rank of an item in the list of the predicted segments containing c, n_c is the total number of predicted segments containing c, $P(k)$ is the precision at cut-off k in the list, $rel(k)$ is an indicator function equaling 1 if the segment at rank k is a relevant one (*i.e.* is labeled as containing c in the ground truth) and $n_{rel}(c)$ is the total number of relevant segments for class c.

3.2 Participants and Results

29 research groups registered for the BirdCLEF 2018 challenge and downloaded the data. Six of them finally submitted run files and technical reports. Details of the systems and the methods used in the runs are synthesized in the overview working note of the task [16] and further developed in the individual working notes of the participants [20, 25, 28, 34, 37]. Below we give more details about the 2 systems that performed the best:

MFN System [28]: this participant trained an ensemble of fine-tuned Inception-V3 models [44] feeded by mel spectrograms and using various data augmentation techniques in the temporal and frequency domains. According to some preliminary experiments they conducted [28], Inception-V3 is likely to outperform more recent and/or larger architectures (such as ResNet152, DualPathNet92, InceptionV4, DensNet, InceptionResNetV2, Xception, NasNet), presumably because of its auxiliary branch that acts as an effective regularizer. Among all the data augmentation techniques they experimented [28], the most contributing one is the addition of background noise or sounds from other files belonging to the same bird species with random intensity, in order to simulate artificially numerous contexts where a given species can be recorded. The other data augmentation types, all together, also improve the prediction but none of them is prevalent. Among them, we can mention a low-quality degradation based on a MP3 encoding-decoding, jitter on duration (± 0.5 s), random factor to signal amplitude, random cyclic shift, random time interval dropouts, global and local pitch shift and frequency stretch, color jitter (brightness, contrast, saturation, hue). MfN Run 1 selected for each subtask the best single model learned during preliminary evaluations. The two models mainly differ in the pre-processing of audio files and choice of FFT parameters. MfN Run 2 combines both models, MfN Run 3 added a third declination of the model with other FFT parameters, but combined the predictions of the two best snapshots per model (regarding performance on the validation set) for averaging 3 × 2 predictions per species. MfN Run 4 added 4 more models and snapshots, reaching a total combination of 18 predictions per species.

OFAI System [37]: this participant used a quite different approach than MFN, without massive data augmentation and without relying on very deep image-oriented CNN architectures. OFAI rather used an ensemble of more shallow and compact CNN architectures (4 networks in total in OFAI Run 1). The first one, called *Sparrow*, was initially built for detecting the presence of bird calls in audio recordings [18]. *Sparrow* has a total of 10 layers (7 convolution, 2 pooling, 1 dense+softmax), taking as input rectangular gray mel spectrograms pictures. The second model is a variant of *Sparrow* where two pairs of convolution layers were replaced by two residual network blocks. During the training, the first model focused on the foreground species as targets, while the second one used also the background species. Additional models were based on the same architectures but were learned as Born-Again Networks (BANs), a distillation technique where student models are not designed for compacting teacher models but where they are parameterized identically to them, surpassing finally the performance of the teachers [9]. For the species prediction a temporal pooling with log-mean-exp is applied for combining the outputs given by the *Sparrow* model for all chunks of 5 s from a single audio recording, while a temporal attention is used for the second model *Sparrow-resnet*. The predictions are combined after temporal pooling, but before the softmax. In addition to the four convolutional neural networks, eight Multi-Layer Perceptrons (MLPs) with two hidden leaky ReLU layers were learned on the meta-data vector associated to each audio recording (yearly circular date, longitude, latitude and elevation). A Gaussian blurring was applied to that data as a data augmentation technique to avoid overfitting. The 4 CNN and the 8 MLPs were finally combined into a single ensemble that was evaluated through the submission of OFAI Run 2. OFAI Run 3 is the same as Run 2 but exploited the information of the year of introduction of the test samples in the challenge as a mean to post-filter the predictions. OFAI Run 4 corresponds to the performance of a single *Sparrow* model.

The main conclusions we can draw from the results of Figs. 3 and 4 are the following:

The Overall Performance Improved Significantly over Last Year for the Mono-Species Recordings But Not for the Soundscapes: The best evaluated system achieves an impressive MRR score of 0.83 this year whereas the best system evaluated on the same dataset last year [38] achieved a MRR of 0.71. On the other side, we do not measured any strong progress on the soundscapes. The best system of MfN this year actually reaches a c-mAP of 0.193 whereas the best system of last year on the same test dataset [38] achieved a c-mAP of 0.182.

Using Dates and Locations of the Observations Provides Some Improvements: Contrary to all previous editions of LifeCLEF, one participant succeeded this year in improving significantly the predictions of its system by using the date and location of the observations. More precisely, OFAI Run 2 combining CNNs and metadata-based MLPs achieves a mono-species MRR of 0.75 whereas OFAI Run 1, relying solely on the CNNs, achieves a MRR of 0.72.

Shallow and Compact Architectures Can Compete with State-of-the-Art Architectures: on one hand one, can say that network architecture plays a crucial role and taking an heavy and deep state-of-the-art architecture such as Inception-v3 (MfN) with massive data augmentation is the best performing approach. On the other hand systems with shallow and compact architectures such as the OFAI system can reach very competitive results, even with a minimal number of data augmentation techniques.

The Use of Ensembles of Networks Still Improves the Performance Consistently: this can be seen for instance through OFAI Run 4 (single model) that is consistently outperformed by OFAI Run 1 (11 models), or through the MfN Run 1 vs MfN Run 4 (18 models).

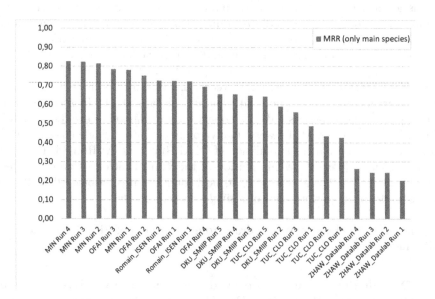

Fig. 3. BirdCLEF 2018 monophone identification results - Mean Reciprocal Rank. The blue dot line represents the last year's best system obtained by DYNI UTLN (Run 1) with a MRR of 0.714 [38]). (Color figure online)

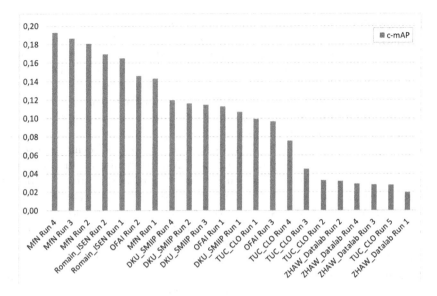

Fig. 4. BirdCLEF 2018 soundscape identification results - classification Mean Average Precision.

4   Task3: GeoLifeCLEF

The goal of the GeoLifeCLEF task is to automatically predict the list of plant species that are the most likely to be observed at a given location. This is useful for many scenarios in biodiversity informatics. First of all, it could improve species identification processes and tools by reducing the list of candidate species that are observable at a given location (be they automated, semi-automated or based on classical field guides or flora). More generally, it could facilitate biodiversity inventories through the development of location-based recommendation services (typically on mobile phones) as well as the involvement of non-expert nature observers. Last but not least, it might serve educational purposes thanks to biodiversity discovery applications providing innovative features such as contextualized educational pathways.

4.1   Data and Evaluation Procedure

A detailed description of the protocol used to build the GeoLifeCLEF 2018 dataset is provided in [5]. In a nutshell, the dataset was built from occurrences data of the Global Biodiversity Information Facility (GBIF[12]), the world's largest open data infrastructure in this domain, funded by governments. It is composed of 291,392 occurrences of $N = 3,336$ plant species observed on the French territory between 1835 and 2017. Each occurrence is characterized by 33 local environmental images of 64×64 pixels. These environmental images are windows

---

[12] https://www.gbif.org/.

cropped from wider environmental rasters and centered on the occurrence spatial location. They were constructed from various open datasets including Chelsea Climate, ESDB V2 soil pedology data, Corine Land Cover 2012 soil occupation data, CGIAR-CSI evapotranspiration data, USGS Elevation data (Data available from the U.S. Geological Survey.) and BD Carthage hydrologic data.

This dataset was split in 3/4 for training and 1/4 for testing with the constraints that: (i) for each species in the test set, there is at least one observation of it in the train set. and (ii), an observation of a species in the test set is distant of more than 100 meters from all observations of this species in the train set.

In the following, we usually denote as $x \in X$ a particular occurrence, each x being associated to a spatial position $p(x)$ in the spatial domain D, a species label $y(x)$ and an environmental tensor $\mathbf{g}(x)$ of size $64 \times 64 \times 33$. We denote as P the set of all spatial positions p covered by X. It is important to note that a given spatial position $p_0 \in P$ usually corresponds to several occurrences $x_j \in X, p(x_j) = p_0$ observed at that location (18,000 spatial locations over a total of 60,000, because of quantized GPS coordinates or Names-to-GPS transforms). In the training set, up to several hundreds of occurrences can be located at the same place (be they of the same species or not). The occurrences in the test set might also occur at identical locations but, by construction, the occurrence of a given species does never occur at a location closer than 100 m from the occurrences of the same species in the training set.

The used evaluation metric is the Mean Reciprocal Rank (MRR). The MRR is a statistic measure for evaluating any process that produces a list of possible responses to a sample of queries ordered by probability of correctness. The reciprocal rank of a query response is the multiplicative inverse of the rank of the correct answer. The MRR is the average of the reciprocal ranks for the whole test set:

$$MRR = \frac{1}{Q} \sum_{q=1}^{Q} \frac{1}{rank_q}$$

where Q is the total number of query occurrences x_q in the test set and $rank_q$ is the rank of the correct species $y(x_q)$ in the ranked list of species predicted by the evaluated method for x_q.

4.2   Participants and Results

29 research groups registered to the GeoLifeCLEF 2018 challenge and downloaded the dataset. Three research groups finally succeeded in submitting *runs*, i.e., files containing the predictions of the system(s) they ran. Details of the methods and systems used in the runs are synthesized in the overview working note of the task [5] and further developed in the individual working notes of the participants (FLO [3], ST [41] and SSN [35]). In a nutshell, the FLO team [3] developed four prediction models, (i) one convolutional neural network trained on environmental data (FLO_3), (ii) one neural network trained

on co-occurrences data (FLO_2) and two other models only based on the spatial occurrences of species: (iii) a closest-location classifier (FLO_1) and (iv) a random forest fitted on the spatial coordinates (FLO_4). Other runs correspond to late fusions of that base models. The ST team [41] experimented two main types of models, convolutional neural networks on environmental data (ST_1, ST_3, ST_11, ST_14, ST_15, ST_18, ST_19) and Boosted Trees (XGBoost) on vectors of environmental variables concatenated with spatial positions (ST_6, ST_9, ST_10, ST_12, ST_13, ST_16, ST_17). For analysis purposes, ST_2 corresponds to a random predictor and ST_7 to a constant predictor returning always the 100 most frequent species (ranked by decreasing value of their frequency in the training set). The last team SSN [35], attempted to learn a CNN-LSTM hybrid model, based on a ResNext architecture [48] extended with an LSTM layer [11] aimed at predicting the plant categories at 5 different levels of the taxonomy (class, then order, then family, then genus and finally species).

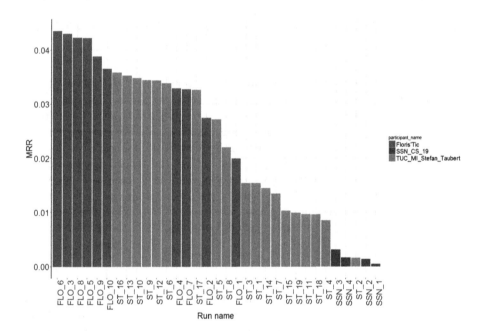

Fig. 5. GeoLifeCLEF 2018 results - Mean Reciprocal Rank of the evaluated systems

We report in Fig. 5 the performance achieved by the 33 submitted runs. The main conclusions we can draw from the results are the following:

Convolutional Neural Networks Outperformed Boosted Trees: Boosted trees are known to provide state-of-the-art performance for environmental modelling. They are actually used in a wide variety of ecological and studies [8,19,31,32]. Our evaluation, however, demonstrate that they can be consistently outperformed by convolutional neural networks trained on environmental data tensors. The best submitted run that does not result from a fusion of different models (**FLO_3**), is actually a convolutional neural network trained on the environmental patches. It achieved a MRR of 0.043 whereas the best boosted tree (**ST_16**) achieved a MRR of 0.035. As another evidence of the better performance of the CNN model, the six best runs of the challenge result from the combination of it with the other models of the Floris'Tic team. Now, it is important to notice that the CNN models trained by the ST team (ST_1, ST_3, ST_11, ST_14, ST_15, ST_18, ST_19) and SSN teams did not obtain good performance at all (often worse than the constant predictor based on the class prior distribution). This illustrates the difficulty of designing and fitting deep neural networks on new problems without former references in the literature. In particular, the approaches trying to adapt existing complex CNN architectures that are popular in the image domain (such as VGG [40], DenseNet [22], ResNEXT [48] and LSTM [11]) were not successful. High difference of performances in CNN learned with homemade architectures ($FLO_6, FLO_3, FLO_8, FLO_5, FLO_9, FLO_10$ compared to ST_3, ST_1) underlines the importance of architecture choices.

Purely Spatial Models are Not So Bad: the random forest model of the FLO team, fitted on spatial coordinates solely (FLO_4), achieved a fair MRR of 0.0329, close to the performance of the boosted trees of the ST team (that were trained on environmental & spatial data). Purely spatial models are usually not used for species distribution modelling because of the heterogeneity of the observations density across different regions. Indeed, the spatial distribution of the observed specimens is often more correlated with the geographic preferences of the observers than with the abundance of the observed species. However the goal of GeoLifeClef is to predict the most likely species to observe given the real presence of a plant. Thus, the heterogeneity sampling effort should induce less bias than in ecological studies.

It is Likely That the Convolutional Neural Network Already Captured the Spatial Information: The best run of the whole challenge (**FLO_6**) results from the combination of the best environmental model (CNN **FLO_3**) and the best spatial model (Random forest **FLO_4**). However, it is noticeable that the improvement of the fused run compared to the CNN alone is extremely tight (+0.0005), and actually not statistically significant. In other words, it seems that the information learned by the spatial model was already captured by the CNN. The CNN might actually have learned to recognize some particular locations thanks to specific shapes of the landscape in the environmental tensors.

A Significant Margin of Progress But Still Very Promising Results: even if the best MRR scores appear to be very low at a first glance, it is important to relativize them with regard to the nature of the task. Many species (tens to hundred) are actually living at the same location so that achieving very high MRR scores is not possible. The MRR score is useful to compare the methods between each others but it should not be interpreted as for a classical information retrieval task. In the test set itself, several species are often observed at exactly the same location. So that there is a max bound on the achievable MRR equal to 0.56. The best run (**FLO_3**) is still far from this max bound (MRR = 0.043) but it is much better than the random or the prior distribution based MRR. Concretely, it retrieves the right species in the top-10 results in 25% of the cases, or in the top-100 in 49% of the cases (over 3,336 species in the training set), which means that it is not so bad at predicting the set of species that might be observed at that location.

5   Conclusions and Perspectives

The main outcome of this collaborative evaluation is a snapshot of the performance of state-of-the-art computer vision, bio-acoustic and machine learning techniques towards building real-world biodiversity monitoring systems. The results did show that very high identification rates can be reached by the evaluated systems, even on large number of species (up to 10,000 species). The most noticeable progress came from the deployment of new convolutional neural network architectures, confirming the fast growing progress of that techniques. Concerning the identification of plant images, our study did show that the performance of the best models is now very close from the expertise of highly skilled botanists. Concerning bird sounds identification, our study reports impressive performance when using monospecies recordings of good quality such as the one recorded by the Xeno-Canto community. Identifying birds in raw, multi-directional soundscapes, however, remains a very challenging task. We actually did not measure any progress compared to the previous year despite several participants are working hard on this problem. Last but not least, a new challenge was introduced this year for the evaluation of location-based species recommendation methods based on environmental and spatial data. Here again, CNNs trained on environmental tensors appeared to be the most promising models. They outperformed boosted trees which are usually known as the state-of-the-art in ecology. We believe this is the beginning of a new integrative approach to environmental modelling, involving multi-task deep learning models trained on very big multi-modal datasets.

Acknowledgements. The organization of LifeCLEF 2018 was supported by the French project Floris'Tic (Tela Botanica, INRIA, CIRAD, INRA, IRD) funded in the context of the national investment program PIA. The organization of the BirdCLEF task was supported by the Xeno-Canto foundation for nature sounds as well as the French CNRS project SABIOD.ORG and EADM GDR CNRS MADICS, BRILAAM STIC-AmSud. The annotations of some soundscape were prepared with regreted wonderful Lucio Pando at Explorama Lodges, with the support of Pam Bucur, Marie Trone and H. Glotin.

References

1. Atito, S., et al.: Plant identification with deep learning ensembles. In: Working Notes of CLEF 2018 (Cross Language Evaluation Forum) (2018)
2. Baillie, J., Hilton-Taylor, C., Stuart, S.N.: 2004 IUCN red list of threatened species: a global species assessment. IUCN (2004)
3. Deneu, B., Maximilien Servajean, C.B., Joly, A.: Location-based species recommendation using co-occurrences and environment - GeoLifeCLEF 2018 challenge. In: CLEF Working Notes 2018 (2018)
4. Bonnet, P., et al.: Plant identification: experts vs. machines in the era of deep learning. In: Joly, A., Vrochidis, S., Karatzas, K., Karppinen, A., Bonnet, P. (eds.) Multimedia Technologies for Environmental & Biodiversity Informatics. MMSA, pp. 131–149. Springer, Cham (2018). https://doi.org/10.1007/978-3-319-76445-0_8
5. Botella, C., Bonnet, P., Joly, A.: Overview of GeoLifeCLEF 2018: location-based species recommendation. In: CLEF Working Notes 2018 (2018)
6. Briggs, F., et al.: Acoustic classification of multiple simultaneous bird species: a multi-instance multi-label approach. J. Acoust. Soc. Am. **131**, 4640 (2012)
7. Cai, J., Ee, D., Pham, B., Roe, P., Zhang, J.: Sensor network for the monitoring of ecosystem: bird species recognition. In: 3rd International Conference on Intelligent Sensors, Sensor Networks and Information, ISSNIP 2007 (2007)
8. De'Ath, G.: Boosted trees for ecological modeling and prediction. Ecology **88**(1), 243–251 (2007)
9. Furlanello, T., Lipton, Z.C., Itti, L., Anandkumar, A.: Born again neural networks. In: Metalearn 2017 NIPS Workshop, pp. 1–5, December 2017
10. Gaston, K.J., O'Neill, M.A.: Automated species identification: why not? Philos. Trans. Roy. Soc. Lond. B: Biol. Sci. **359**(1444), 655–667 (2004)
11. Gers, F.A., Schmidhuber, J., Cummins, F.: Learning to forget: continual prediction with LSTM (1999)
12. Goëau, H., Bonnet, P., Joly, A.: Overview of ExpertLifeCLEF 2018: how far automated identification systems are from the best experts? LifeCLEF experts vs. machine plant identification task 2018. In: CLEF 2018 (2018)
13. Goëau, H., et al.: The ImageCLEF 2013 plant identification task. In: CLEF 2013, Valencia (2013)
14. Goëau, H., et al.: The ImageCLEF 2011 plant images classification task. In: CLEF 2011 (2011)
15. Goëau, H., et al.: ImageCLEF 2012 plant images identification task. In: CLEF 2012, Rome (2012)
16. Goëau, H., Glotin, H., Planqué, R., Vellinga, W.P., Kahl, S.: Overview of Bird-CLEF 2018: monophone vs. soundscape bird identification. In: CLEF Working Notes 2018 (2018)
17. Goëau, H., Glotin, H., Vellinga, W., Planqué, B., Joly, A.: LifeCLEF bird identification task 2017. In: Working Notes of CLEF 2017 - Conference and Labs of the Evaluation Forum, Dublin, Ireland, 11–14 September 2017 (2017)
18. Grill, T., Schlüter, J.: Two convolutional neural networks for bird detection in audio signals. In: 2017 25th European Signal Processing Conference (EUSIPCO), pp. 1764–1768, August 2017
19. Guisan, A., Thuiller, W., Zimmermann, N.E.: Habitat Suitability and Distribution Models: With Applications in R. Cambridge University Press, Cambridge (2017)
20. Haiwei, W., Ming, L.: Construction and improvements of bird songs' classification system. In: Working Notes of CLEF 2018 (Cross Language Evaluation Forum) (2018)

21. Haupt, J., Kahl, S., Kowerko, D., Eibl, M.: Large-scale plant classification using deep convolutional neural networks. In: Working Notes of CLEF 2018 (Cross Language Evaluation Forum) (2018)
22. Huang, G., Liu, Z., Weinberger, K.Q., van der Maaten, L.: Densely connected convolutional networks. In: Proceedings of the IEEE Conference on Computer Vision and Pattern Recognition, vol. 1, p. 3 (2017)
23. Joly, A., et al.: Interactive plant identification based on social image data. Ecol. Inform. **23**, 22–34 (2014)
24. Joly, A., et al.: The ImageCLEF plant identification task 2013. In: International Workshop on Multimedia Analysis for Ecological Data (2013)
25. Kahl, S., Wilhelm-Stein, T., Klinck, H., Kowerko, D., Eibl, M.: A baseline for large-scale bird species identification in field recordings. In: Working Notes of CLEF 2018 (Cross Language Evaluation Forum) (2018)
26. Kahl, S., Wilhelm-Stein, T., Klinck, H., Kowerko, D., Eibl, M.: Recognizing birds from sound - the 2018 BirdCLEF baseline system. arXiv preprint arXiv:1804.07177 (2018)
27. Lasseck, M.: Image-based plant species identification with deep convolutional neural networks. In: Working Notes of CLEF 2017 (Cross Language Evaluation Forum) (2017)
28. Lasseck, M.: Audio-based bird species identification with deep convolutional neural networks. In: Working Notes of CLEF 2018 (Cross Language Evaluation Forum) (2018)
29. Lasseck, M.: Machines vs. experts: working note on the ExpertLifeCLEF 2018 plant identification task. In: Working Notes of CLEF 2018 (Cross Language Evaluation Forum) (2018)
30. Lee, D.J., Schoenberger, R.B., Shiozawa, D., Xu, X., Zhan, P.: Contour matching for a fish recognition and migration-monitoring system. In: Optics East, pp. 37–48. International Society for Optics and Photonics (2004)
31. Messina, J.P., et al.: Mapping global environmental suitability for Zika virus. eLife **5**, e15272 (2016)
32. Moyes, C.L., et al.: Predicting the geographical distributions of the macaque hosts and mosquito vectors of plasmodium knowlesi malaria in forested and non-forested areas. Parasit. Vectors **9**(1), 242 (2016)
33. Müller, H., Clough, P., Deselaers, T., Caputo, B. (eds.): ImageCLEF - Experimental Evaluation in Visual Information Retrieval. The Springer International Series On Information Retrieval, vol. 32. Springer, Heidelberg (2010). https://doi.org/10.1007/978-3-642-15181-1
34. Müller, L., Marti, M.: Two bachelor students' adventures in machine learning. In: Working Notes of CLEF 2018 (Cross Language Evaluation Forum) (2018)
35. Moudhgalya, N.B., Sharan Sundar, S.D.M.P., Bose, C.A.: Hierarchically embedded taxonomy with CLNN to predict species based on spatial features. In: CLEF Working Notes 2018 (2018)
36. Polyak, B.T., Juditsky, A.B.: Acceleration of stochastic approximation by averaging. SIAM J. Control Optim. **30**(4), 838–855 (1992)
37. Schlüter, J.: Bird identification from timestamped, geotagged audio recordings. In: Working Notes of CLEF 2018 (Cross Language Evaluation Forum) (2018)
38. Sevilla, A., Glotin, H.: Audio bird classification with inception v4 joint to an attention mechanism. In: Working Notes of CLEF 2017 (Cross Language Evaluation Forum) (2017)
39. Silvertown, J., et al.: Crowdsourcing the identification of organisms: a case-study of iSpot. ZooKeys **480**, 125 (2015)

40. Simonyan, K., Zisserman, A.: Very deep convolutional networks for large-scale image recognition. CoRR abs/1409.1556 (2014)
41. Taubert, S., Max Mauermann, S.K.D.K., Eibl, M.: Species prediction based on environmental variables using machine learning techniques. In: CLEF Working Notes 2018 (2018)
42. Sulc, M., Picek, L., Matas, J.: Plant recognition by inception networks with test-time class prior estimation. In: Working Notes of CLEF 2018 (Cross Language Evaluation Forum) (2018)
43. Sullivan, B.L., et al.: The eBird enterprise: an integrated approach to development and application of citizen science. Biol. Conserv. **169**, 31–40 (2014)
44. Szegedy, C., Vanhoucke, V., Ioffe, S., Shlens, J., Wojna, Z.: Rethinking the inception architecture for computer vision. In: Proceedings of the IEEE Conference on Computer Vision and Pattern Recognition, pp. 2818–2826 (2016)
45. Towsey, M., Planitz, B., Nantes, A., Wimmer, J., Roe, P.: A toolbox for animal call recognition. Bioacoustics **21**(2), 107–125 (2012)
46. Trifa, V.M., Kirschel, A.N., Taylor, C.E., Vallejo, E.E.: Automated species recognition of antbirds in a Mexican rainforest using hidden Markov models. J. Acoust. Soc. Am. **123**, 2424 (2008)
47. Wäldchen, J., Rzanny, M., Seeland, M., Mäder, P.: Automated plant species identification-trends and future directions. PLOS Comput. Biol. **14**(4), 1–19 (2018). https://doi.org/10.1371/journal.pcbi.1005993
48. Xie, S., Girshick, R., Dollár, P., Tu, Z., He, K.: Aggregated residual transformations for deep neural networks. In: 2017 IEEE Conference on Computer Vision and Pattern Recognition (CVPR), pp. 5987–5995. IEEE (2017)

Overview of PAN 2018
Author Identification, Author Profiling, and Author Obfuscation

Efstathios Stamatatos[1]([✉]), Francisco Rangel[2,3], Michael Tschuggnall[4],
Benno Stein[5], Mike Kestemont[6], Paolo Rosso[3], and Martin Potthast[7]

[1] Department of Information and Communication Systems Engineering,
University of the Aegean, Samos, Greece
pan@webis.de
[2] Autoritas Consulting S.A., Valencia, Spain
[3] PRHLT Research Center, Universitat Politècnica de València, Valencia, Spain
[4] Department of Computer Science, University of Innsbruck, Innsbruck, Austria
[5] Web Technology and Information Systems, Bauhaus-Universität Weimar,
Weimar, Germany
[6] University of Antwerp, Antwerp, Belgium
http://pan.webis.de
[7] Leipzig University, Leipzig, Germany

Abstract. PAN 2018 explores several authorship analysis tasks enabling a systematic comparison of competitive approaches and advancing research in digital text forensics. More specifically, this edition of PAN introduces a shared task in cross-domain authorship attribution, where texts of known and unknown authorship belong to distinct domains, and another task in style change detection that distinguishes between single-author and multi-author texts. In addition, a shared task in multimodal author profiling examines, for the first time, a combination of information from both texts and images posted by social media users to estimate their gender. Finally, the author obfuscation task studies how a text by a certain author can be paraphrased so that existing author identification tools are confused and cannot recognize the similarity with other texts of the same author. New corpora have been built to support these shared tasks. A relatively large number of software submissions (41 in total) was received and evaluated. Best paradigms are highlighted while baselines indicate the pros and cons of submitted approaches.

1 Introduction

Nowadays, a huge amount of digital texts is produced daily in Internet media. In many cases, the originality and credibility of this information is questionable. In addition, information about the authors of texts may be missing or hidden behind aliases. It is, therefore, essential to attempt to estimate credibility of texts and unmask author information in order to avoid social media misuse, enhance cyber-security, and enable digital text forensics. PAN is an evaluation

© Springer Nature Switzerland AG 2018
P. Bellot et al. (Eds.): CLEF 2018, LNCS 11018, pp. 267–285, 2018.
https://doi.org/10.1007/978-3-319-98932-7_25

lab dedicated to study originality (is this information new or re-used?), trust (can we trust this information?), and authorship (who wrote this?) of digital texts. Several shared tasks have been organized during the last 10 years covering many aspects of this field.

PAN 2018 follows the trend of recent years and focuses on authorship analysis exclusively. This research area attempts to reveal information about the authors of texts based mainly on their stylistic preferences. Every author has her unique characteristics (stylistic fingerprint) but she also shares some properties with other people of similar background (age, gender, education, etc.) It is quite challenging to define or measure both personal style (for each individual author) and collective style (males, females, young people, old people, etc.). In addition, it remains unclear what one should modify in her texts in order to attempt to hide her identity or to mimic the style of another author. This edition of PAN deals with these challenging issues.

Author identification puts emphasis on the personal style of individual authors. The most common task is authorship attribution where there is a set of candidate authors (suspects), with samples of their texts, and one of them is selected as the most likely author of a text of disputed authorship [32]. This can be a closed-set (one of the suspects is surely the true author) or an open-set (the true author may not be among the suspects) attribution case. This edition of PAN focuses on closed-set *cross-domain authorship attribution*, that is, when the texts unquestionably written by the suspects and the texts of disputed authorship belong to different domains. This is a realistic scenario suitable for several applications. For example, imagine the case of a crime novel published anonymously when all candidate authors have only published fantasy novels [14] or a disputed tweet when the available texts written by the suspects are newspaper articles. To be able to control the domain of texts, we turned to so-called *fanfiction* [12]. This term refers to the large body of contemporary fiction that is nowadays created by non-professional authors ('fans'), who write in the tradition of a well-known source work, such as the *Harry Potter* series by J.K. Rowling, that is sometimes called the 'canon'. These writings or 'fics' within such a 'fandom' heavily borrow characters, motives, settings, etc. from the source fandom. Fanfiction provides excellent material to study cross-domain authorship attribution since most fans are active in multiple fandoms.

Another important dimension in author identification is to intrinsically analyse a document, possibly written by multiple authors and identify the contribution of each co-author. The previous edition of PAN aimed to find the exact border positions within a document where the authorship changes. Taking the respective results into account which have shown that the problem is quite hard [40], we substantially relaxed the task this year and broke it down to the simple question: Given a document, are there any style changes or not? An alternative formulation would thus be to solely predict whether a document is written by a single author or by multiple collaborators, whereby it is irrelevant to the task to identify the exact border positions between authors. While the evaluation of the two preceding tasks relied on the Webis-TRC-12 data set [22], we created a novel data set by utilizing the StackExchange network[1]. Containing millions of publicly available questions and answers regarding several topics and subtopics, it represents a rich source which we exploited to build a comprehensive, but still realistic data set for the style change detection task.

When the collective style of groups of authors is considered, *author profiling* attempts to predict demographic and social characteristics, like age, gender, education, and personality traits. It is a research area associated with important applications in social media analytics and marketing as well as cyber forensics. In this edition of PAN, for the first time, multimodal information is considered. Both texts and images posted by social media users are used to predict their gender.

Finally, *author obfuscation* views authorship analysis from a different perspective. Given that author identification tools are available and are able to recognize the similarity within a set of texts of a certain author, the task examines what should be changed in one of these texts, maintaining its meaning, so that the author identification tools are confused. This task is strongly associated with maintaining privacy in online texts to ensure that anyone can freely express her opinion, even in countries and conditions where freedom of speech is restricted.

2   Previous Work

Two previous editions of PAN included shared tasks in authorship attribution [1,13]. However, they only examined the case where both training and test documents belong to the same domain. A relatively limited number of cross-domain authorship attribution studies has been published in the last decade. Most frequently, emphasis is put on cross-topic conditions using novels, journalistic texts, or scientific books belonging to clearly distinguished thematic areas [17,31,33,34]. Another trend is to examine cross-genre conditions using mainly literature works or social media texts (aiming to link accounts by the same user in different social networks) [15,18]. Novels in English and Spanish have also been used in the extreme case of cross-language authorship attribution [3]. To the best of our knowledge, so far there is no authorship attribution study focusing on fanfiction in cross-domain conditions.

With respect to intrinsic analyses of texts, PAN included several shared tasks in the last years. Starting from intrinsic plagiarism detection [20], the focus went from clustering authors within documents [36] to the detection of positions where the style, i.e., the authorship, changes [40]. Nevertheless, especially for the latter tasks the performances of submitted approaches were inferior to what was expected or even to simple baselines (e.g., [7]). Thereby approaches utilized typical stylometric features such as bags of character n-grams, frequencies of function words and other lexical metrics, processed by algorithms operating on top to detect outliers (e.g., [29]). In general, only few approaches target a segmentation by other criteria than topic, i.e., especially by authors (e.g., [8,9,39]).

---

[1] https://stackexchange.com, visited June 2018.

With respect to the proposed style change detection task at PAN'18, i.e., to solely separate single-authored documents from multi-authored ones, no prior studies exist to the best of our knowledge.

In all previous editions of PAN, author profiling tasks focused on textual information exclusively aiming at recognizing specific demographic and social characteristics, like age, gender, native language, and personality traits of authors [23,24,26–28]. Most of the author profiling corpora are based on online texts, like blogs, tweets, reviews, etc.

Regarding author masking, this is the third time this task has been offered in a row [10,21]. Given the significant challenge this task offers because of the need to paraphrase a given text under the constraint to change its writing style sufficiently, we have not changed it much compared to previous years, but have kept it as is so that new submissions are immediately comparable to those of previous years: With two additional submissions this year, the total number of automatic obfuscation approaches aiming at masking authors are now up to a total of 9 submission. Instead of changing the task, we continue to investigate new ways of evaluating and measuring the performance of obfuscation approaches, which, too, provides for an excellent challenge.

3   Author Identification

3.1   Cross-Domain Authorship Attribution

Fanfiction presents an interesting benchmark case for computational authorship identification. Most of the fanfiction is nowadays produced on online platforms (such as fanfiction.net or archiveofourown.org) that are not strongly moderated, so that they accurately reflect an author's individual style. Interestingly, many fans are moreover active across different fandoms a fact that facilitate the study of authorship attribution in cross-domain conditions. Because of the explicit intertextuality (i.e. borrowings from the original canon), it can be anticipated that the style and content of the original canons have a strong influence on the fanfics, because these often aim to imitate the style of the canon's original authors. Fanfiction thus allows for exciting authorship research: do fanfiction authors generally succeed in imitating the author's stylome or does their individual fingerprint still show in the style of their fics?

Closed-set authorship attribution attempts to identify the most likely author of a text. Given a sample of reference documents from a restricted and finite set of candidate authors, the task is to determine the most likely author of a previously unseen document of unknown authorship. This task becomes quite challenging when documents of known and unknown authorship come from different domains (e.g., thematic area, genre), i.e., cross-domain authorship attribution. In this edition of PAN all documents of unknown authorship are fics of the same fandom (target fandom) while the documents of known authorship by the candidate authors are fics of several fandoms (other than the target-fandom). This can be more accurately described as *cross-fandom attribution in fanfiction*. The participants are asked to prepare a method that can handle multiple cross-fandom attribution problems. t In more detail, a cross-domain authorship attribution problem is a tuple (A, K, U), where A is the set of candidate authors, K is the set of reference (known authorship) texts, and U is the set of unknown authorship texts. For each candidate author $a \in A$, we are given $K_a \subset K$, a set of texts unquestionably written by a. Each text in U should be assigned to exactly one $a \in A$. From a text categorization point of view, K is the training corpus and U is the test corpus. Let D_K be the set of fandoms of texts in K. Then, all texts in U belong to a single (target) fandom $d_U \notin D_K$.

Corpora. For this edition of PAN, we have collected a large number of fanfics and their associated metadata from the authoritative community platform *Archive of Our Own*, a project of the Organization for Transformative Works[2]. We limited our initial selection to fanfics in English (en), French (fr), Italian (it), Polish (pl), and Spanish (sp) that counted at least 500 tokens, according to the platform's own internal word count. Across all datasets, 'Harry Potter - J. K. Rowling' was typically the most frequent fandom. We therefore selected fanfics from this fandom as the target domain of all attribution problems. Only authors were admitted who contributed at least 7 texts to the non-target fandoms and at least 1 text to the target fandom.

For each language we constructed two separate datasets: a development set that participants could use to calibrate their system and an evaluation set on which the competing systems were eventually evaluated. Crucially, there was no overlap in authors between the development set and the test set (to discourage systems from overfitting on the characteristics of specific authors in the development set). To maximize the comparability of the data sets across languages, we randomly sampled 20 authors for each language and exactly 7 training texts from the non-target fandoms from their entire oeuvre. No sampling was carried out in the test material so that the number of test texts varies per author or problem. No texts shorter than 500 tokens were included and to normalize the length of longer fics, we only included the middle 1,000 tokens of texts that were longer than 1,000 tokens. Tokenization was done using NLTK's 'WordPunctTokenizer' [2]; our scripts heavily used the scikit-learn library [19]. The word count statistics are presented in the overview table below (Table 1). All texts were encoded as plain text (UTF8). To investigate the effect of the number of authors in an attribution problem, we provide several (downsampled) versions, containing random subsets of 5, 10, 15 and 20 authors respectively. For the early-bird evaluation, we only considered the problems of maximal number of authors (20) for each language.

Evaluation Framework. Given that we deal with a closed-set classification task and the fact that the evaluation dataset is not equally distributed over the candidate authors, we decided to use the macro-averaged F1 score as an evaluation measure. Given an authorship attribution problem, for each candidate

---

2 https://github.com/radiolarian/AO3Scraper.

Table 1. The cross-domain authorship attribution corpus.

	Language	Problems	Authors	Training texts per author	Test texts per author		Text length (avg. words)
					Min	Max	
Development	English	2	5, 20	7	1	22	795
	French	2	5, 20	7	1	10	796
	Italian	2	5, 20	7	1	17	795
	Polish	2	5, 20	7	1	21	800
	Spanish	2	5, 20	7	1	21	832
Evaluation	English	4	5, 10, 15, 20	7	1	17	820
	French	4	5, 10, 15, 20	7	1	20	782
	Italian	4	5, 10, 15, 20	7	1	29	802
	Polish	4	5, 10, 15, 20	7	1	42	802
	Spanish	4	5, 10, 15, 20	7	1	24	829

author recall and precision of the provided answers are calculated and a F1 score is provided. Then, the average F1 score over all candidate authors is used to estimate the performance of submissions for that attribution problem. Finally, submissions are ranked according to their mean macro-averaged F1 score over all available attribution problems.

To estimate the difficulty of a cross-domain authorship attribution problem and provide a challenging baseline for participants, we developed a simple but quite effective approach [30,31,34]. This method is based on character n-gram features and a support vector machine (SVM) classifier. First, all character 3-grams that occur at least 5 times in the training texts of an attribution problem are extracted and used as features to represent both training and test texts. Then, a SVM with linear kernel is trained based on the training texts and can be used to predict the most likely author of the test texts. As shown in previous work, this simple model can be very effective in cross-domain conditions given that the number of features is appropriately defined for each specific attribution problem [33]. However, in this shared task, we use a simple version where the cutoff frequency threshold (i.e., practically, this defines the number of features) is the same (5) for any attribution problem. This approach is called PAN18-BASELINE in the rest of this paper. A Python implementation of this approach has been released to enable participants experiment with its possible variations.

Evaluation Results. We received 11 submissions from research teams from several countries (Austria, Brazil, Germany, Iran (2), Israel (2), Mexico, the Netherlands, Spain, and Switzerland). All software submissions were deployed and evaluated in TIRA experimentation framework. Each submission had to analyse all attribution problems included in the evaluation corpus and it was given information about the language of the texts of each problem. Table 2 presents the mean macro-averaged F1 scores for all participants in the whole

Table 2. The evaluation results of the cross-domain authorship attribution task.

Submission	Overall	English	French	Italian	Polish	Spanish	Runtime
Custódio and Paraboni	**0.685**	0.744	**0.668**	0.676	0.482	**0.856**	00:04:27
Murauer et al.	0.643	**0.762**	0.607	0.663	0.450	0.734	00:19:15
Halvani and Graner	0.629	0.679	0.536	**0.752**	0.426	0.751	00:42:50
Mosavat	0.613	0.685	0.615	0.601	0.435	0.731	00:03:34
Yigal et al.	0.598	0.672	0.609	0.642	0.431	0.636	00:24:09
Martín dCR et al.	0.588	0.601	0.510	0.571	**0.556**	0.705	00:11:01
PAN18-BASELINE	0.584	0.697	0.585	0.605	0.419	0.615	00:01:18
Miller et al.	0.582	0.573	0.611	0.670	0.421	0.637	00:30:58
Schaetti	0.387	0.538	0.332	0.337	0.388	0.343	01:17:57
Gagala	0.267	0.376	0.215	0.248	0.216	0.280	01:37:56
López-Anguita et al.	0.139	0.190	0.065	0.161	0.128	0.153	00:38:46
Tabealhoje	0.028	0.037	0.048	0.014	0.024	0.018	02:19:14

evaluation dataset and for the subset of problems in each of the five available languages.

As can be seen, 6 submissions were able to surpass the baseline, another one was very close to it and 4 submissions were clearly below it. The overall top-performing submission by Custódio and Paraboni was also the most effective one for French and especially Spanish (with a remarkable difference from the second-best approach). Moreover, the method of Halvani and Graner achieved quite remarkable results for Italian in comparison to the rest of submissions. The most difficult cases appear to be the Polish ones while the highest average results are obtained for English and Spanish. With respect to the total runtime cost of the submitted approaches, in general, the top-performing methods are also relatively fast. On the contrary, most of the methods that perform significantly lower than the baseline are also the least efficient ones.

Table 3 shows the performance (macro-averaged F1 score) of the submitted methods for a varying candidate set size (from 20 authors to 5 authors). Apparently, the overall top-performing method of Custódio and Paraboni remains the most effective one for each of the examined candidate set sizes. In most cases, the ranking of participants is very similar to their overall ranking. It's also remarkable that the PAN18-BASELINE is especially effective when there are only a few (5) authors. In general, the performance of submissions improves when the candidate set becomes shorter. However, it seems that the best-performing approaches are less accurate in problems with 5 candidate authors in comparison to problems with 10 authors.

The winning method of Custódio and Paraboni [5] is an ensemble of three simple authorship attribution approaches based on character and word n-gram features and a distorted version of texts [34]. In each attribution, the most likely model is selected. The success of this approach provides evidence that the combination of several independent attribution methods is a very promising direc-

Table 3. Performance of the cross-domain authorship attribution submissions per candidate set size.

Submission	20 authors	15 authors	10 authors	5 authors
Custódio and Paraboni	**0.648**	**0.676**	**0.739**	**0.677**
Murauer et al.	0.609	0.642	0.680	0.642
Halvani and Graner	0.609	0.605	0.665	0.636
Mosavat	0.569	0.575	0.653	0.656
Yigal et al.	0.570	0.566	0.649	0.607
Martín dCR et al.	0.556	0.556	0.660	0.582
PAN18-BASELINE	0.546	0.532	0.595	0.663
Miller et al.	0.556	0.550	0.671	0.552
Schaetti	0.282	0.352	0.378	0.538
Gagala	0.204	0.240	0.285	0.339
López-Anguita et al.	0.064	0.065	0.195	0.233
Tabealhoje	0.012	0.015	0.030	0.056

tion. Similar conclusions were drawn in previous shared tasks on author verification [35]. The second-best method according to the overall ranking is a variation of the PAN18-BASELINE that uses dynamic adaptation of parameter values for each attribution problem separately. The third-best submission is based on text compression. Apparently, methods using simple and language-independent features are more effective in this task in comparison to more sophisticated approaches based on linguistic analysis and deep learning. A more comprehensive review of submitted methods is included in the task overview paper [16].

3.2   Style Change Detection

The style change detection task at PAN 2018 attaches to a series of subtasks of previous PAN events that focused on intrinsic characteristics of text documents [20, 36, 40]. Considering the relatively low accuracies achieved by participants of those tasks we therefore proposed a substantially simplified task at PAN 2018 while still beeing a continuation of the previous year's style breach detection task: Given a text document, participants should apply intrinsic analyses to decide whether it is written by one or more authors, i.e., if there exist any style changes or not. With respect to the intended, task simplification it was thereby irrelevant to identify the number of style changes, the specific positions, or to build clusters of authors.

Evaluation Data. To evaluate the approaches, three distinct data sets for training, validation and testing have been created using an approximate 50/25/25 split, whereby the solutions for the first two were provided. All data set are

Table 4. Overview of the style change detection data set.

Topic/site	Training				Validation				Test			
	Problems	Authors			Problems	Authors			Problems	Authors		
		1	2	3		1	2	3		1	2	3
Bicycles	160	80	47	33	82	41	28	13	70	35	27	8
Christianity	358	179	107	72	176	88	48	40	172	86	45	41
Gaming	178	89	47	42	86	43	23	20	78	39	21	18
History	354	177	104	73	178	89	54	35	170	85	46	39
Islam	166	83	49	34	86	43	31	12	72	36	20	16
Linguistics	144	72	46	26	72	36	22	14	64	32	12	20
Meta	196	98	56	42	94	47	30	17	90	45	30	15
Parenting	178	89	54	35	92	46	32	14	78	39	27	12
Philosophy	468	234	146	88	232	116	63	53	224	112	65	47
Poker	100	50	35	15	48	24	14	10	42	21	13	8
Politics	204	102	57	45	102	51	34	17	90	45	22	23
Project man	104	52	24	28	50	25	12	13	44	22	14	8
Sports	102	51	34	17	54	27	20	7	40	20	12	8
Stackoverflow	112	56	23	33	60	30	16	14	48	24	12	12
Writers	156	78	43	35	80	40	25	15	70	35	18	17
	2980	**1490**	**872**	**618**	**1492**	**746**	**452**	**294**	**1352**	**676**	**384**	**292**

based on user posts from 15 heterogeneous sites of the Q&A network StackExchange[3], covering different topics (e.g., *programming, politics, sports* or *religion*) and subtopics (e.g., *law, economy* or *european union* for the *politics* topic). Using the questions and answers of users belonging to the same topic and subtopic, the final documents have been assembled by varying the following parameters:

- number of style changes (including 0 for single-authored documents)
- number of collaborating authors (1–3)
- document length (300–1000 tokens)
- allow changes only at the end or within paragraphs
- uniform or random distribution of changes with respect to segment lengths

An overview of the dataset showing the number of problems per topic, i.e., StackExchange site, is depicted in Table 4. In total 2980 training, 1492 validation and 1352 test documents have been created, whereby each text consists of the same topic/subtopic and thus making the task single-genre and single-topic. Finally, for each data set and topic the number of single-authored documents is equal to the number of multi-authored documents, resulting in a 50% accuracy baseline for random guessing. A detailed description of the data set and the creation thereof is presented in the respective task overview paper [16].

Results. This year, six teams participated in the style change detection task, whereby five of them submitted their software to TIRA. The performance was thereby measured by computing the accuracy of correct predictions.

---

[3] https://stackexchange.com, visited June 2018.

At a glance, most approaches applied a binary classification based on different more or less complex models computed from stylometric features, and only one approach used an algorithmic method based on similarity measures. The best performing approach by Zlatkova et al. utilizes a stacking technique to combine an ensemble of multiple learners. Using several feature groups (e.g., including word n-grams and typical beginnings and endings), they at first build four different classifiers (i.e., an SVM, Random Forest, AdaBoost Trees and a multilayer perceptron) for each group to compute weighted models. Finally, a logistic regression combines these models together with a tf-idf-based gradient boosting approach to predict the final output. Safin and Ogaltsov also rely on an ensemble of three classifiers trained from common text statistics like number of sentences or punctuation frequencies, character n-grams and word n-grams. The final prediction is then calculated by a weighted sum of the classifier predictions, whereby the weightings have been tuned during preliminary experiments.

The approaches by Hosseinia et al. and Schaetti make use of different neural networks. Hosseinia et al. use two parallel recurrent neural networks (RNN) solely based on features extracted from the grammatical structure, i.e., the parse tree of sentences. To predict the appearance of style changes, they reverse the sentence order of a document, compute the respective parse tree features and integrate several similarity measures in their fusion layer to compare the reverse-order features with the original ones. On the other hand, Schaetti utilizes a character-based convolutional neural network (CNN) with three convolutional layers and 25 filters each, which does the final classification using a binary, linear layer. To train the network with more examples, the original training corpus was artificially extended by approximately a factor of 10 by sampling new documents from the available training corpus.

Finally, Khan used an algorithmic approach that at first splits a document into single sentences, builds groups thereof and computes simple word-based features. Using a sliding window technique, two consecutive sentence groups are then compared by calculating a matching score, whereby a tuned threshold determines the existence of a style change.

To be able to compare the results, three baselines have been used: (i) rnd1-BASELINE is simply guessing, (ii) rnd2-BASELINE uses a slightly enhanced guessing technique by incorporating the statistics of the training/validation datasets, which reveal that longer documents are a bit more likely to be multi-authored, and (iii) C99-BASELINE utilizes the C99 text segmentation algorithm [4] by predicting style changes if C99 found more than one segment and no changes in case it yielded only a single segment.

The final results of the five submitting teams are presented in Table 5. Zlatkova et al. could achieve the significantly best accuracy by predicting correctly 89% of all documents across all topics and subtopics. Moreover, all approaches could outperform all baselines. With respect to the runtime the two best performing approaches also needed significantly more time (due to the ensemble techniques and parse tree generation, respectively), compared to the other participants who could produce predictions within minutes for the roughly 1,300 documents in the test data set. Finally, fine-grained performances depend-

Table 5. Evaluation results of the style change detection task.

Submission	Accuracy	Runtime
Zlatkova et al.	**0.893**	01:35:25
Hosseinia and Mukherjee	0.825	10:12:28
Safin and Ogaltsov	0.803	00:05:15
Khan	0.643	00:01:10
Schaetti	0.621	00:03:36
C99-BASELINE	0.589	00:00:16
rnd2-BASELINE	0.560	-
rnd1-BASELINE	0.500	-

ing on the different topics, subtopics and data set configurations are presented in the respective overview paper of this task [16].

4   Author Profiling

The objective of author profiling is to classify authors depending on their sociolect aspect, that is, how language is shared by people. This may allow to identify personal traits such as age, gender, native language, language variety or personality type. The interest in author profiling can be seen in the number of participants in this shared task over the last years[4], as well as the number of investigations in the field[5]. Its importance relies on the possibility of improving marketing segmentation, security or forensics. For example, using the language as evidence to detect possible cases of abuse or harassing messages, and then to profile the authors.

The Author Profiling shared task at PAN 2018 focuses on the following aspects:

- *Gender identification.* As in previous editions, the task addresses gender identification, but from a new multimodal perspective.
- *Multimodality.* Besides textual data, images can be used to profile the authors. This multimodal perspective allows to investigate whether images can help to improve gender identification beyond considering only textual features.
- *Multilinguality.* Data is provided in Arabic, English and Spanish.
- *Twitter.* Data was collected from Twitter, where its idiosyncratic characteristics may show the daily real use of the language.

---

[4] In the six editions of the author profiling shared task we have had respectively 21 (2013: age and gender identification [26]), 10 (2014: age and gender identification in different genre social media [24]), 22 (2015: age and gender identification and personality recognition in Twitter [23]), 22 (2016: cross-genre age and gender identification [28]), 22 (2017: gender and language variety identification [27], and 23 (2018: multimodal gender identification [25]) participating teams.

[5] The search of "author profiling" raises 1,560 results in Google Scholar: https://scholar.google.es/scholar?q=%22author+profiling%22.

4.1   Evaluation Framework

To build the PAN-AP-2018 corpus we have used a subset from the PAN-AP-2017 corpus in Arabic, English and Spanish. For each author, we tried to collect all the images shared in her timeline. Since some authors did not share images (other users closed their accounts), the PAN-AP-2018 corpus contains the subset of authors from the PAN-AP-2017 corpus that still exist and have shared at least 10 images. In Table 6 the corpus figures are shown. The corpus is completely balanced per gender and each author is composed of exactly 100 tweets.

Table 6. Number of authors per language and subset, half of them per gender. Each author is composed of 100 tweets and 10 images.

	(AR) Arabic	(EN) English	(ES) Spanish
Training	1,500	3,000	3,000
Test	1,000	1,900	2,200

The participants were asked to send three predictions per author (namely *modalities*), by using: *(a)* a textual-based approach; *(b)* an image-based approach; *(c)* a combination of both approaches. The participants were allowed to approach the task in any language and to use any of these three approaches, although we encouraged them to participate in all languages and *modalities*[6].

The accuracy has been used for evaluation. For each language, we obtain the accuracy for each *modality*. The accuracy obtained with the combined approach has been selected as the accuracy for the given language. If the author only used the textual approach, this accuracy has been used. The final ranking has been calculated as the average accuracy per language, as shown in the following equation:

$$ranking = \frac{gender_{ar} + variety_{en} + gender_{es}}{3} \tag{1}$$

4.2   Results

This year 23 have been the teams who participated in the shared task. In Table 7 the overall performance per language and user's ranking are shown. The best results have been obtained in English (85.84%), followed by Spanish (82%) and Arabic (81.80%). As can be observed, all of them are over 80% of accuracy and most of the systems over 70% of accuracy.

---

[6] From the 23 participants, 22 participated in Arabic and Spanish, and all of them in English. All of them approached the task with textual features, and 12 also used images.

The overall best result (81.98%) has been obtained by the authors in [37]. They have approached the task with deep neural networks. For textual processing, they used word embeddings from a stream of tweets with FastText skip-grams and trained a Recurrent Neural Network. For images, they used a pre-trained Convolutional Neural Network. They combined both approaches with fusion component. The authors in [6] have obtained the second best result on average (81.70%) by approaching the task only from the textual perspective. They used SVM with different types of word and character n-grams. The third best overall result (80.68%) has been obtained by the authors in [38]. They used SVM with combinations of word and character n-grams for texts and a variant of the Bag of Visual Words for images, combining both predictions with a convex linear combination. Nevertheless, there is no statistical significance among the three of them. With respect to the different languages, the best results have been obtained by the same authors. For instance, the best result in Arabic (81.80%) has been obtained by the authors in [38], the best ones in English (85.84%) by the authors in [37], and the best ones in Spanish (82%) by the authors in [6]. It is worth to mention that the only result that is significantly higher is the one obtained in English (85.84%).

Table 7. Accuracy per language and global ranking as average per language.

Ranking	Team	Arabic	English	Spanish	Average
1	Takahashi *et al.*	0.7850	**0.8584**	0.8159	**0.8198**
2	Daneshvar	0.8090	0.8221	**0.8200**	0.8170
3	Tellez *et al.*	**0.8180**	0.8068	0.7955	0.8068
4	Ciccone *et al.*	0.7940	0.8132	0.8000	0.8024
5	Kosse *et al.*	0.7920	0.8074	0.7918	0.7971
6	Nieuwenhuis and Wilkens	0.7870	0.8095	0.7923	0.7963
7	Sierra-Loaiza *et al.*	0.8100	0.8063	0.7477	0.7880
8	Martinc *et al.*	0.7780	0.7926	0.7786	0.7831
9	Veenhoven *et al.*	0.7490	0.7926	0.8036	0.7817
10	ópez-Santillán *et al.*	0.7760	0.7847	0.7677	0.7761
11	Hacohen-Kerner *et al.* (A)	0.7570	0.7947	0.7623	0.7713
12	Gopal-Patra *et al.*	0.7680	0.7737	0.7709	0.7709
13	Hacohen-Kerner *et al.* (B)	0.7570	0.7889	0.7591	0.7683
14	Stout *et al.*	0.7640	0.7884	0.7432	0.7652
15	Von Däniken *et al.*	0.7320	0.7742	0.7464	0.7509
16	Schaetti	0.7390	0.7711	0.7359	0.7487
17	Aragon and Lopez	0.6670	0.8016	0.7723	0.7470
18	Bayot and Gonçalves	0.6760	0.7716	0.6873	0.7116
19	Garibo	0.6750	0.7363	0.7164	0.7092
20	Sezerer *et al.*	0.6920	0.7495	0.6655	0.7023
21	Raiyani *et al.*	0.7220	0.7279	0.6436	0.6978
22	Sandroni-Dias and Paraboni	0.6870	0.6658	0.6782	0.6770
23	Karlgren *et al.*	-	0.5521	-	-

In Table 8 the best results per language and *modality* are shown. Results obtained with the textual approach are higher than the ones obtained with images, although very similar in case of English. It should be highlighted that the best results where obtained by combining texts and images, especially in the case of English where the improvement is higher. A more in-depth analysis of the results and the different approaches can be found in [25].

Table 8. Best results per language and modality.

Language	Textual	Images	Combined
Arabic	0.8170	0.7720	0.8180
English	0.8221	0.8163	0.8584
Spanish	0.8200	0.7732	0.8200

5   Author Obfuscation

The author obfuscation task at PAN 2018 focuses on *author masking*, which can be viewed as an attack to existing authorship verification technology. More specifically, given a pair of texts written by the same author, the task is to change the style of one of these texts so that verification algorithms are led astray and cannot detect the unique authorship anymore. Pan 2018 features the third edition of this task, whose specification follows the evaluation framework of the two previous editions [10,21]. In order to be self-contained, the following paragraphs will repeat basic information of both the data and the setup.

5.1   Evaluation Datasets

The evaluation data consist of the English portion of the combined datasets of the PAN 2013–2015 authorship verification tasks, separated by training datasets and test datasets. The datasets cover a broad range of genres: excerpts from computer science textbooks, essays from language learners, excerpts from horror fiction novels, and dialog lines from plays. As usual, the (combined) training dataset was handed out to participants, while the (combined) test dataset was held back, being accessible only via the TIRA experimentation platform. The test dataset contains a total of 464 problem instances, each consisting of a to-be-obfuscated text and one or more other texts from the same author. The approaches submitted by participants were supposed to process each problem instance and to return for each of the to-be-obfuscated texts a paraphrased version. The paraphrasing procedure was allowed to exploit the other texts from the same author in order to learn about potential style modifications that may render the writing styles of the two texts dissimilar.

5.2   Performance Measures

To measure an algorithmically achieved obfuscation performance we propose to distinguish the following three orthogonal dimensions. We call an obfuscation (similarly: an obfuscation software)

- **safe**, if the obfuscated text cannot be attributed to the original authors,
- **sound**, if the obfuscated text is textually entailed by the original text, and
- **sensible**, if the obfuscated text is well-formed and inconspicuous.

From these dimensions the safety can be automatically calculated using the TIRA versions of 44 authorship verification approaches that are at our disposal: in this regard, we count the number of cases for which a true positive prediction of an authorship verifier is flipped to a false negative prediction after having applied the to-be-evaluated obfuscator. This is repeated for all 44 state-of-the-art verifiers.

With the current state of the art the soundness and the sensibleness of an author obfuscation approach can hardly assessed automatically; the values for these dimensions are hence based on human judgment (our as well as peer-review judgements). For this purpose, we grade a selection on a Likert scale of 1–5 with regard to sensibleness, and on 3-point scale with regard to soundness.

5.3   Results

We received 2 submissions for the author obfuscation task in addition to the 7 from the previous two years. A detailed evaluation of the results of these methods together with baselines (submissions from previous two years) is still underway at the time of writing this paper, since it requires the re-execution of the 44 authorship verifiers that have been submitted to the PAN authorship verification tasks. Evaluation results and analysis will be included in the task overview paper [11].

6   Summary

PAN 2018 shared tasks attracted a relatively large number of participants (41 submissions in total for all the tasks), comparable to previous editions of this evaluation lab. This demonstrates that there is a large and active research community in digital text forensics and PAN has become the main forum of this community. New datasets were built to support the PAN 2018 shared tasks covering several languages. One more year we required software submissions and all participant methods were evaluated in TIRA, ensuring replicability of results and facilitating the re-evaluation of these approaches using other datasets in the future.

Fanfiction texts provide an excellent material for evaluating authorship analysis methods. Focusing on cross-domain authorship attribution we were able to study how differences in fandom affect the effectiveness of attribution techniques. In general, submissions that do not require a deep linguistic analysis of texts were found to be both the most effective and the most efficient ones for this task. Heterogeneous ensembles of simple base methods and compression models outperformed more sophisticated approaches based on deep learning. Furthermore, the candidate set size is inversely correlated with the attribution accuracy especially when more than 10 authors are considered.

With the relaxation of the style change detection task at PAN 2018 we achieved to not only attract more participants, but also to significantly improve the performances of the submitted approaches. On a novel data set created from a popular Q&A network containing more than 4,000 problems, all participants achieved to surpass all provided baselines significantly by applying various techniques from machine learning ensembles to deep learning. Achieved accuracies of up to nearly 90% over the whole data set represent a good starting point to further develop and tighten the style change detection task in future PAN editions.

Author profiling was for another edition of PAN the most popular task with 23 submissions. The combination of information coming from texts and images posted by social media users seems to slightly improve the results of gender recognition. It is also notable that textual information and images when considered separately achieve comparable results. It remains to be seen whether they can be combined more effectively.

A key conclusion for author masking so far is that the task continues to be of interest to the community, albeit, it cannot compete in terms of number of participants with the other tasks. This is by no means to the detriment of the task, since we believe that the detection and prediction tasks of PAN can only truly be appreciated if the risks posed by an adversary are taken into account. In this regard, each of the aforementioned tasks have the potential of being attacked in the future, either by well-equipped individuals, or even at large by initiatives to subvert online surveillance. In this regard, we plan on recasting the obfuscation task next year, making it a bit easier to participate, yet extending its reach to other tasks.

Acknowledgments. Our special thanks go to all of PAN's participants, to Symanto Group (https://www.symanto.net/) for sponsoring PAN and to MeaningCloud (https://www.meaningcloud.com/) for sponsoring the author profiling shared task award. The work at the Universitat Politècnica de València was funded by the MINECO research project SomEMBED (TIN2015-71147-C2-1-P).

References

1. Argamon, S., Juola, P.: Overview of the international authorship identification competition at PAN-2011. In: Petras, V., Forner, P., Clough, P. (eds.) Notebook Papers of CLEF 2011 Labs and Workshops, 19–22 September 2011, Amsterdam, Netherlands, September 2011. http://www.clef-initiative.eu/publication/working-notes
2. Bird, S., Klein, E., Loper, E.: Natural Language Processing with Python. O'Reilly Media, Sebastopol (2009)
3. Bogdanova, D., Lazaridou, A.: Cross-language authorship attribution. In: Proceedings of the 9th International Conference on Language Resources and Evaluation, LREC 2014, pp. 2015–2020 (2014)
4. Choi, F.Y.: Advances in domain independent linear text segmentation. In: Proceedings of the 1st North American Chapter of the Association for Computational Linguistics Conference (NAACL), pp. 26–33. Association for Computational Linguistics, Seattle, April 2000
5. Custódio, J.E., Paraboni, I.: EACH-USP ensemble cross-domain authorship attribution. In: Working Notes Papers of the CLEF 2018 Evaluation Labs, September 2018, to be announced
6. Daneshvar, S.: Gender identification in Twitter using n-grams and LSA. In: Working Notes Papers of the CLEF 2018 Evaluation Labs, September 2018, to be announced
7. Daniel Karaś, M.S., Sobecki, P.: OPI-JSA at CLEF 2017: author clustering and style breach detection. In: Working Notes Papers of the CLEF 2017 Evaluation Labs. CEUR Workshop Proceedings. CLEF and CEUR-WS.org, September 2017
8. Giannella, C.: An improved algorithm for unsupervised decomposition of a multi-author document. The MITRE Corporation. Technical Papers, February 2014
9. Glover, A., Hirst, G.: Detecting stylistic inconsistencies in collaborative writing. In: Sharples, M., van der Geest, T. (eds.) The New Writing Environment, pp. 147–168. Springer, London (1996). https://doi.org/10.1007/978-1-4471-1482-6_12
10. Hagen, M., Potthast, M., Stein, B.: Overview of the author obfuscation task at PAN 2017: safety evaluation revisited. In: Cappellato, L., Ferro, N., Goeuriot, L., Mandl, T. (eds.) Working Notes Papers of the CLEF 2017 Evaluation Labs. CEUR Workshop Proceedings, CLEF and CEUR-WS.org, September 2017
11. Hagen, M., Potthast, M., Stein, B.: Overview of the author obfuscation task at PAN 2018. In: Working Notes Papers of the CLEF 2018 Evaluation Labs. CEUR Workshop Proceedings, CLEF and CEUR-WS.org (2018)
12. Hellekson, K., Busse, K. (eds.): The Fan Fiction Studies Reader. University of Iowa Press, Iowa City (2014)
13. Juola, P.: An overview of the traditional authorship attribution subtask. In: Forner, P., Karlgren, J., Womser-Hacker, C. (eds.) CLEF 2012 Evaluation Labs and Workshop - Working Notes Papers, 17–20 September 2012, Rome, Italy, September 2012. http://www.clef-initiative.eu/publication/working-notes
14. Juola, P.: The rowling case: a proposed standard analytic protocol for authorship questions. Digital Sch. Humanit. **30**(suppl–1), i100–i113 (2015)
15. Kestemont, M., Luyckx, K., Daelemans, W., Crombez, T.: Cross-genre authorship verification using unmasking. Engl. Stud. **93**(3), 340–356 (2012)
16. Kestemont, M., et al.: Overview of the author identification task at PAN-2018: cross-domain authorship attribution and style change detection. In: Working Notes Papers of the CLEF 2018 Evaluation Labs. CEUR Workshop Proceedings, CLEF and CEUR-WS.org (2018)

17. Koppel, M., Schler, J., Bonchek-Dokow, E.: Measuring differentiability: unmasking pseudonymous authors. J. Mach. Learn. Res. **8**, 1261–1276 (2007)
18. Overdorf, R., Greenstadt, R.: Blogs, Twitter feeds, and reddit comments: cross-domain authorship attribution. Proc. Priv. Enhanc. Technol. **2016**(3), 155–171 (2016)
19. Pedregosa, F., et al.: Scikit-learn: machine learning in Python. J. Mach. Learn. Res. **12**, 2825–2830 (2011)
20. Potthast, M., Eiselt, A., Barrón-Cedeño, A., Stein, B., Rosso, P.: Overview of the 3rd international competition on plagiarism detection. In: Notebook Papers of the 5th Evaluation Lab on Uncovering Plagiarism, Authorship and Social Software Misuse (PAN), Amsterdam, The Netherlands, September 2011
21. Potthast, M., Hagen, M., Stein, B.: Author obfuscation: attacking the state of the art in authorship verification. In: Working Notes Papers of the CLEF 2016 Evaluation Labs. CEUR Workshop Proceedings, CLEF and CEUR-WS.org, September 2016. http://ceur-ws.org/Vol-1609/
22. Potthast, M., Hagen, M., Völske, M., Stein, B.: Crowdsourcing interaction logs to understand text reuse from the web. In: Fung, P., Poesio, M. (eds.) Proceedings of the 51st Annual Meeting of the Association for Computational Linguistics (ACL 2013), pp. 1212–1221. Association for Computational Linguistics, August 2013. http://www.aclweb.org/anthology/P13-1119
23. Rangel, F., Celli, F., Rosso, P., Potthast, M., Stein, B., Daelemans, W.: Overview of the 3rd author profiling task at PAN 2015. In: Cappellato, L., Ferro, N., Jones, G., San Juan, E. (eds.) CLEF 2015 Evaluation Labs and Workshop - Working Notes Papers, Toulouse, France, pp. 8–11. CEUR-WS.org, September 2015
24. Rangel, F., et al.: Overview of the 2nd author profiling task at PAN 2014. In: Cappellato, L., Ferro, N., Halvey, M., Kraaij, W. (eds.) CLEF 2014 Evaluation Labs and Workshop - Working Notes Papers, Sheffield, UK, pp. 15–18. CEUR-WS.org, September 2014
25. Rangel, F., Rosso, P., G'omez, M.M., Potthast, M., Stein, B.: Overview of the 6th author profiling task at pan 2018: multimodal gender identification in Twitter. In: CLEF 2018 Labs and Workshops, Notebook Papers. CEUR Workshop Proceedings. CEUR-WS.org (2017)
26. Rangel, F., Rosso, P., Koppel, M., Stamatatos, E., Inches, G.: Overview of the author profiling task at PAN 2013. In: Forner, P., Navigli, R., Tufis, D. (eds.) CLEF 2013 Evaluation Labs and Workshop - Working Notes Papers, 23–26 September 2013, Valencia, Spain, September 2013
27. Rangel, F., Rosso, P., Potthast, M., Stein, B.: Overview of the 5th author profiling task at PAN 2017: gender and language variety identification in Twitter. In: Cappellato, L., Ferro, N., Goeuriot, L., Mandl, T. (eds.) Working Notes Papers of the CLEF 2017 Evaluation Labs. CEUR Workshop Proceedings, CLEF and CEUR-WS.org, September 2017
28. Rangel, F., Rosso, P., Verhoeven, B., Daelemans, W., Potthast, M., Stein, B.: Overview of the 4th author profiling task at PAN 2016: cross-genre evaluations. In: Balog, K., Cappellato, L., Ferro, N., Macdonald, C. (eds.) CLEF 2016 Labs and Workshops, Notebook Papers. CEUR Workshop Proceedings. CEUR-WS.org, September 2016
29. Safin, K., Kuznetsova, R.: Style breach detection with neural sentence embeddings. In: Working Notes Papers of the CLEF 2017 Evaluation Labs. CEUR Workshop Proceedings, CLEF and CEUR-WS.org, September 2017

30. Sapkota, U., Bethard, S., Montes, M., Solorio, T.: Not all character n-grams are created equal: a study in authorship attribution. In: Proceedings of the 2015 Conference of the North American Chapter of the Association for Computational Linguistics: Human Language Technologies, pp. 93–102 (2015)

31. Sapkota, U., Solorio, T., Montes, M., Bethard, S., Rosso, P.: Cross-topic authorship attribution: will out-of-topic data help? In: Proceedings of the 25th International Conference on Computational Linguistics. Technical Papers, pp. 1228–1237 (2014)

32. Stamatatos, E.: Intrinsic plagiarism detection using character n-gram Profiles. In: Stein, B., Rosso, P., Stamatatos, E., Koppel, M., Agirre, E. (eds.) SEPLN 2009 Workshop on Uncovering Plagiarism, Authorship, and Social Software Misuse (PAN 2009), pp. 38–46. Universidad Politécnica de Valencia and CEUR-WS.org, September 2009. http://ceur-ws.org/Vol-502

33. Stamatatos, E.: On the robustness of authorship attribution based on character n-gram features. J. Law Policy 21, 421–439 (2013)

34. Stamatatos, E.: Authorship attribution using text distortion. In: Proceedings of the 15th Conference of the European Chapter of the Association for Computational Linguistics, Long Papers, vol. 1, pp. 1138–1149. Association for Computational Linguistics (2017)

35. Stamatatos, E., et al.: Overview of the author identification task at PAN 2015. In: Cappellato, L., Ferro, N., Jones, G., San Juan, E. (eds.) CLEF 2015 Evaluation Labs and Workshop - Working Notes Papers, 8–11 September 2015, Toulouse, France. CEUR-WS.org, September 2015

36. Stamatatos, E., et al.: Clustering by authorship within and across documents. In: Working Notes Papers of the CLEF 2016 Evaluation Labs. CEUR Workshop Proceedings, CLEF and CEUR-WS.org, September 2016. http://ceur-ws.org/Vol-1609/

37. Takahashi, T., Tahara, T., Nagatani, K., Miura, Y., Taniguchi, T., Ohkuma, T.: Text and image synergy with feature cross technique for gender identification. In: Working Notes Papers of the CLEF 2018 Evaluation Labs, September 2018, to be announced

38. Tellez, E.S., Miranda-Jiménez, S., Moctezuma, D., Graff, M., Salgado, V., Ortiz-Bejar, J.: Gender identification through multi-modal tweet analysis using microtc and bag of visual words. In: Working Notes Papers of the CLEF 2018 Evaluation Labs, September 2018, to be announced

39. Tschuggnall, M., Specht, G.: Automatic decomposition of multi-author documents using grammar analysis. In: Proceedings of the 26th GI-Workshop on Grundlagen von Datenbanken. CEUR-WS, Bozen, October 2014

40. Tschuggnall, M., et al.: Overview of the author identification task at PAN-2017: style breach detection and author clustering. In: Cappellato, L., Ferro, N., Goeuriot, L., Mandl, T. (eds.) Working Notes Papers of the CLEF 2017 Evaluation Labs. CEUR Workshop Proceedings, vol. 1866. CLEF and CEUR-WS.org, September 2017. http://ceur-ws.org/Vol-1866/

Overview of the CLEF eHealth Evaluation Lab 2018

Hanna Suominen[1,2]([✉]), Liadh Kelly[3], Lorraine Goeuriot[4], Aurélie Névéol[5],
Lionel Ramadier[5], Aude Robert[6], Evangelos Kanoulas[7], Rene Spijker[8],
Leif Azzopardi[9], Dan Li[7], Jimmy[10], João Palotti[11,12], and Guido Zuccon[10]

[1] University of Turku, Turku, Finland
[2] The Australian National University (ANU),
Data61/Commonwealth Scientific and Industrial Research Organisation (CSIRO),
University of Canberra, Canberra, ACT, Australia
hanna.suominen@anu.edu.au
[3] Maynooth University, Maynooth, Ireland
liadh.kelly@mu.ie
[4] Univ. Grenoble Alpes, CNRS, Grenoble INP, LIG, 38000 Grenoble, France
Lorraine.Goeuriot@imag.fr
[5] LIMSI CNRS UPR 3251 Université Paris-Saclay, 91405 Orsay, France
Aurelie.Neveol@limsi.fr
[6] INSERM - CépiDc 80 rue du Général Leclerc,
94276 Le Kremlin-Bicêtre Cedex, France
aude.robert@inserm.fr
[7] Informatics Institute, University of Amsterdam, Amsterdam, Netherlands
E.Kanoulas@uva.nl
[8] Cochrane Netherlands and UMC Utrecht, Julius Center for Health Sciences
and Primary Care, Utrecht, Netherlands
R.Spijker-2@umcutrecht.nl
[9] Computer and Information Sciences, University of Strathclyde, Glasgow, UK
leif.azzopardi@strath.ac.uk
[10] Queensland University of Technology, Brisbane, QLD, Australia
jimmy@hdr.qut.edu.au, g.zuccon@qut.edu.au
[11] Vienna University of Technology, Vienna, Austria
palotti@ifs.tuwien.ac.at
[12] Qatar Computing Research Institute, Doha, Qatar
jpalotti@hbku.edu.qa

Abstract. In this paper, we provide an overview of the sixth annual edition of the CLEF eHealth evaluation lab. CLEF eHealth 2018 continues our evaluation resource building efforts around the easing and support of patients, their next-of-kins, clinical staff, and health scientists in understanding, accessing, and authoring eHealth information in a multilingual setting. This year's lab offered three tasks: Task 1 on multilingual information extraction to extend from last year's task on French and English corpora to French, Hungarian, and Italian; Task 2 on technologically assisted reviews in empirical medicine building on last year's pilot task

---

G. Zuccon—In alphabetical order by forename, HS, LK & LG co chaired the lab. AN & LR & AR, EK & RS & LA & DL, and J & JP & GZ led Tasks 1–3, respectively.

P. Bellot et al. (Eds.): CLEF 2018, LNCS 11018, pp. 286–301, 2018.
https://doi.org/10.1007/978-3-319-98932-7_26

in English; and Task 3 on Consumer Health Search (CHS) in mono- and multilingual settings that builds on the 2013–17 Information Retrieval tasks. In total 28 teams took part in these tasks (14 in Task 1, 7 in Task 2 and 7 in Task 3). Herein, we describe the resources created for these tasks, outline our evaluation methodology adopted and provide a brief summary of participants of this year's challenges and results obtained. As in previous years, the organizers have made data and tools associated with the lab tasks available for future research and development.

Keywords: Evaluation · Entity linking · Information retrieval
Health records · Information extraction · Medical informatics
Systematic reviews · Total recall · Test-set generation
Text classification · Text segmentation · Self-diagnosis

1 Introduction

In today's information overloaded society it is increasingly difficult to retrieve and digest valid and relevant information to make health-centered decisions. Medical content is becoming available electronically in a variety of forms ranging from patient records and medical dossiers, scientific publications and health-related websites to medical-related topics shared across social networks. Laypeople, clinicians and policy-makers need to easily retrieve, and make sense of medical content to support their decision making. *Information retrieval* (IR) systems have been commonly used as a means to access health information available online. However, the reliability, quality, and suitability of the information for the target audience varies greatly while high recall or coverage, that is finding all relevant information about a topic, is often as important as high precision, if not more. Furthermore, the information seekers in the health domain also experience difficulties in expressing their information needs as search queries.

CLEF eHealth aims to bring together researchers working on related information access topics and provide them with datasets to work with and validate the outcomes. The vision for the Lab is two-fold: (1) to develop tasks that potentially impact patient understanding of medical information and (2) to provide the community with an increasingly sophisticated dataset of clinical narrative, enriched with links to standard knowledge bases, evidence-based care guidelines, systematic reviews, and other further information, to advance the state-of-the-art in multilingual information extraction and IR in health care. Furthermore, we aim to support reproducible research by encouraging participants to reflect on methods and practical steps to take to facilitate the replication of their experiments. In particular, each year we call participants to submit their systems and configuration files, and independent researchers to reproduce the results of the participating teams.

This, the sixth year of the lab, aiming to build upon the resource development and evaluation approaches offered in the previous five years of the lab [7, 8, 13, 14, 26], offered the following three tasks:

- *Task 1.* Multilingual Information Extraction: *International Classification of Diseases, Version 10* (ICD10) coding of death certificates [21],
- *Task 2.* Technologically Assisted Reviews in Empirical Medicine [12], and
- *Task 3.* Consumer Health Search [10].

The *Multilingual Information Extraction* task challenged participants to information extraction in written text with its focus on unexplored languages corpora, specifically French, Hungarian, and Italian this year. This built upon the 2016 and 2017 tasks [19,20] which already addressed the analysis of French and English biomedical text with the extraction of causes of death from a corpus of death reports in French (2016 and 2017) and English (2017). This task can be treated as a named entity recognition and normalization task, but also as a text classification task. Each language can be addressed independently, but we encouraged participants to explore multilingual approaches. Only fully automated means were allowed, that is, human-in-the-loop approaches were not permitted. The goal of the task was to automatically assign ICD10 codes to the text content of death certificates. The results of high performing systems could be used within the workflow of institutes mandated by the *World Health Organisation* (WHO) to provide national death statistics.

The *Technologically Assisted Reviews in Empirical Medicine* task was a high-recall IR task in English that aimed at evaluating search algorithms that seek to identify all studies relevant for conducting a systematic review in empirical medicine. This year's task, similar to last year [11], had a focus on *Diagnostic Test Accuracy* (DTA) reviews. Search in this area is generally considered the hardest, and a breakthrough in this field would likely be applicable to other areas as well [15]. The typical process of searching for scientific publications to conduct a systematic review consists of three stages: (a) specifying a number of inclusion criteria that characterize the articles relevant to the review and constructing a complex Boolean Query to express them, (b) screening the abstracts and titles that result from the Boolean query, and (c) screening the full documents that passed the Abstract and Title Screening. Building on the 2017 task, which focused on the second stage of the process, that is, Abstract and Title Screening, the 2018 task focused on the first stage (*subtask 1*) and second stage (*subtask 2*) of the process, that is, Boolean Search and Abstract and Title Screening. More precisely, these tasks were defined as follows:

- *Subtask 1.* Prior to constructing a Boolean Query researchers have to design and write a search protocol that in written and in detail defines what constitutes a relevant study for their review. For the challenge associated with the first stage of the process, participants were provided with the relevant pieces of a protocol, in an attempt to complete search effectively and efficiently bypassing the construction of the Boolean query.
- *Subtask 2.* Given the results of the Boolean Search from stage 1 as the starting point, participants were required to rank the set of *abstracts* (A). The task had the following two goals: (i) to produce an efficient ordering of the documents, such that all of the relevant abstracts are retrieved as early as possible, and

(ii) to identify a subset of A which contains all or as many of the relevant abstracts for the least effort (i.e., total number of abstracts to be assessed).

The *Consumer Health Search* (CHS) task was a continuation of the previous CLEF eHealth IR tasks that ran in 2013, 2014, 2015, 2016, and 2017 [4–6,22,23,27], and embraced the *Text REtrieval Conference* (TREC) -style evaluation process, with a shared collection of documents and queries, the contribution of runs from participants and the subsequent formation of relevance assessments and evaluation of the participants submissions. The 2018 task used a new web corpus and a new set of queries compared to previous years. The subtasks within the IR challenge were similar to 2017's: ad hoc search, query variation, methods to personalize health search, and multilingual search. A new subtask was also introduced this year which required participants to classify queries with respect to the underlying query intent as detailed in [3]. Query variations were generated based on the fact that there are multiple ways to express a single information need. Translations of the English queries into several languages were also provided. Participants were required to translate the queries back to English and use the English translation to search the collection.

The remainder of this paper is structured as follows: in Sect. 2 we detail the tasks, evaluation and datasets created; in Sect. 3 we describe the submission and results for each task; and in Sect. 4 we provide conclusions.

2 Materials and Methods

In this section, we describe the materials and methods used in the three tasks of the CLEF eHealth evaluation lab 2018. After specifying our text documents to process in Sect. 2.1, we address their human annotations, queries, and relevance assessments in Sect. 2.2. Finally, in Sect. 2.3 we introduce our evaluation methods.

2.1 Text Documents

Task 1. The multilingual information extraction: ICD10 coding of death certificates task challenged its participants to information extraction in written text with focus on unexplored languages corpora, specifically French, Hungarian, and Italian this year to supplement last year's task on French and English. Its data set, called the *CepiDC Causes of Death Corpus*, comprised free-text descriptions of causes of death as reported by physicians in the standardized causes of death forms. Each document was manually coded by experts with ICD10 per international WHO standards.

Task 2. The technologically assisted reviews in empirical medicine task used the PubMed document collection for its Boolean Search challenge and a subset of PubMed documents for its challenge to make Abstract and Title Screening more effective. More specifically, for the Abstract and Title Screening subtask the PubMed Document Identifiers (PMIDs) of potentially relevant PubMed Document abstracts were provided for each training and test topic. The PMIDs were collected by the task coordinators by re-running the MEDLINE Boolean query used in the original systematic reviews conducted by Cochrane to search PubMed.

Task 3. The document corpus used in the Consumer Health Search task consists of web pages acquired from the CommonCrawl[1]. An initial list of websites was identified for acquisition. The list was built by submitting the task queries to the Microsoft Bing APIs (through Azure Cognitive Services) repeatedly over a period of a few weeks to incorporate possibly evolving results and variations in the Bing APIs services [9]; results were acquired as URLs and pooled. The domains of the URLs were then included in the list, except some domains that were excluded for decency reasons. The list was further augmented by including a number of known reliable health websites and other known unreliable health websites, from lists previously compiled by health institutions and agencies. We decided to include also known unreliable websites so that the collection can serve also for the study of methods that account for the reliability and trustworthiness of the search results.

2.2 Human Annotations, Queries, and Relevance Assessments

Task 1. The task consisted of extracting ICD10 codes from the raw lines of death certificate text (the process of identifying a single ICD code per certificate as the primary cause of death was not evaluated). This task relied on the text supplied to extract ICD10 codes from the certificates, line by line. The extraction system was to generate the ICD10 codes relevant to assign to each line. Systems were encouraged to report evidence text supporting the ICD10 code recommendations in the form of an excerpt of the original text that supports the ICD code prediction. For French, two data formats were supported. The so-called raw format supplied the text of each certificate line separately from the gold standard codes that were supplied at the certificate level. The so-called aligned format reconciled the gold standard codes to the specific certificate line that yielded them. For the French subtask, a training set of $125,384$ death certificates and an independent test set of $11,932$ death certificates was annotated with respect to ICD10 codes and supporting text evidence by professional coders. For the Hungarian subtask, a training set of $84,703$ death certificates and an independent test set of $21,176$ death certificates was assigned ICD10 codes by professional coders. For the Italian subtask, a training set of $14,502$ death certificates and an independent test set of $3,618$ death certificates was assigned ICD10 codes by professional coders.

Task 2. In Task 2 Subtask 1, for the No-Boolean-Search challenge as input for each topic participants were provided with:

---

[1] http://commoncrawl.org/.

1. Topic-ID.
2. The title of the review, written by Cochrane experts.
3. A part of the protocol: The Objective, the Type of Study, the Participants, the Index Tests, the Target Conditions, and the Reference Standards.
4. The entire PubMED database (which was available for downloaded directly from PubMED).

Participants were provided with 30 topics of Diagnostic Test Accuracy (DTA) reviews.

In Task 2 Subtask 2, focusing on title and abstract screening, topics consisted of the Boolean Search from the first step of the systematic review process. Specifically, for each topic the following information was provided:

1. Topic-ID.
2. The title of the review, written by Cochrane experts.
3. The Boolean query manually constructed by Cochrane experts.
4. The set of PubMed Document Identifiers (PMID's) returned by running the query in MEDLINE.

The CLEF 2017 TAR 42 topics (which excludes topics that were reviewed and found unreliable) were used as training set. A new test set consisting of 30 topics of Diagnostic Test Accuracy (DTA) reviews was generated for this year's challenge. The total number of unique PMID's released for the training set was 241, 669 (an average of 5, 754 per topic) and for the test set 218, 496 (an average of 7, 283 per topic).

The original systematic reviews written by Cochrane experts included a reference section that listed Included, Excluded, and Additional references to medical studies. The union of Included and Excluded references are the studies that were screened at a Title and Abstract level and were considered for further examination at a full content level. These constituted the relevant documents at the abstract level, while the Included references constituted the relevant documents at the full content level. The average percentage of relevant documents at Abstract level in the training set is 3.8% of the total number of PMID's released, and in the test set 4.7%, while at the content level the average percentage is 1.5% in the training set, and 1% in the test set.

References in the original systematic reviews were collected from a variety of resources, not only MEDLINE. Therefore, studies that were cited but did not appear in the results of the Boolean query were excluded from the label set for Subtask 2, but included for Subtask 1. Hence, the total number of relevant abstracts in the test set for Subtask 1 increased to 4, 656 from 3, 964 in Subtask 2, and the total number of relevant studies increased to 759 from 678. An important note here is that the additional studies are also included in the MEDLINE database, they were simply not retrieved by the Boolean query.

Task 3. The CHS task, Task 3, uses a new set of 50 queries issued by the general public to the HON search services, manually labeled with search intent and translated into French, German and Czech [3]. Subtask 1 uses these 50 queries. For subtask 2 and 3, each topic is augmented with 6 query variations issued by 6 research students at QUT with no medical knowledge. Each student was asked to formulate a query for each of the 50 queries' narrative. No post-processing was done to the formulated query variations and duplicates might exist within the 6 variations of a query. Subtask 4 uses parallel queries in the following languages: French, German, and Czech. These queries are manual translations of Subtask 1's 50 queries. Subtask 5 contains the same 50 topics labeled with search intents: (1) Disease/illness/syndrome/pathological condition, (2) Drugs and medicinal substances, (3) Healthcare, (4) Test & procedures, (5) First aid, (6) Healthy lifestyle, (7) Human anatomy, (8) Organ systems.

Relevance assessments are currently in progress. Similar to the 2016 and 2017 pools, we created the pool using the RBP-based Method A (Summing contributions) by Moffat et al. [17], in which documents are weighted according to their overall contribution to the effectiveness evaluation as provided by the RBP formula (with $p = 0.8$, following Park and Zhang [24]). This strategy, named RBPA, was chosen because it was shown that it should be preferred over traditional fixed-depth or stratified pooling when deciding upon the pooling strategy to be used to evaluate systems under fixed assessment budget constraints [16], as it is the case for this task.

Along with relevance assessments, readability/understandability and reliability/trustworthiness judgments will also be collected for the assessment pool; these will be used to evaluate systems across different dimensions of relevance. We plan to use crowdsourcing for the acquisition of the relevance assessments.

2.3 Evaluation Methods

Task 1. After completing our data use agreement, authorized participants were able to obtain training sets from March 2018. The test data for CLEF eHealth 2018 Task 1 was released on 27 April 2018. Teams could submit up to 2 runs per dataset by 12 May 2018. Hence, the maximum was 8 runs for all four datasets. System performance was assessed by the precision, recall and F-measure for ICD code extraction at the document level for Hungarian and Italian and both at the line and document level for French. Evaluation measures were computed overall for all ICD codes. A baseline was also implemented by the organizers [21].

Task 2. Teams could submit up to 3 runs per task. Hence a maximum of 6 runs for both subtasks. In addition, for Subtask 2, participants were also encouraged to submit ANY number of runs that result from their 2017 frozen systems. System performance was assessed using the same evaluation approach as that used for the 2017 TAR challenge [11]. The assumption behind this evaluation approach is the following: The user of your system is the researcher that performs the abstract and title screening of the retrieved articles. Every time an abstract is returned (i.e., ranked) there is an incurred cost/effort, while the abstract is either irrelevant (in which case no further action will be taken) or relevant (and hence passed to the next stage of document screening) to the topic under review. Evaluation measures were: Area under the recall-precision curve, that is, Average Precision; Minimum number of documents returned to retrieve all R relevant documents; Work Saved over Sampling at different Recall levels; Area under the cumulative recall curve normalized by the optimal area; Recall @ 0% to 100% of documents shown; a number of newly constructed cost-based measures; and reliability [1]. More details on the evaluation are provided in the Task 2 overview paper [12].

Task 3. For Subtasks 1, 2, and 3, participants could submit up to 4 runs in TREC format. For Subtask 4, participants could submit up to 4 runs per language. For Subtask 5, teams could submit runs containing up to 3 candidate intent per query, with up to 4 variation run. Evaluation measures for Subtasks 1 and 4 were NDCG@10, BPref and RBP. Subtask 2 used uRBP (with alpha value capturing the user expertise). Subtask 3 used NDCG@10, BPref and RBP - in the MVE framework. For Subtask 5, the evaluation measures are Mean Reciprocal Rank, nDCG@1, 2, 3.

3 Results

The number of groups who registered their interest in CLEF eHealth tasks was 26, 42, and 46 respectively (and a total of 70 unique teams). In total, 28 teams submitted to the three shared tasks.

Task 1 received considerable interest with 14 teams submitting runs, including one team from Algeria (techno), one team from Canada (TorontoCL), two teams from China (ECNU and WebIntelligentLab), three teams from France (APHP, IAM, ISPED), one team from Germany (WBI), one team from Italy (UNIPD), three teams from Spain (IxaMed, SINAI and UNED), one team from Switzerland (SIB) and one team from the United Kingdom (KCL). The training datasets were released at the beginning of March 2018 and the test datasets by 27 April 2018. The ICD-10 coding task submission on French, Hungarian and Italian death certificates were due by 12 May 2018.

For the Hungarian raw dataset, we received 9 official runs from 5 teams (Table 3). For the Italian raw dataset, we received 12 official runs from 7 teams (Table 4). For the French raw dataset, we received 18 official runs from 12 teams (Table 2). For the French aligned dataset, we received 16 official runs from 8 teams (Table 1). In addition to these official runs, unofficial runs were submitted by some participants after the test submission deadline[2].

Participants relied on a diverse range approaches including classification methods (often leveraging neural networks), information retrieval techniques and

---

[2] See Task 1 paper for details on unofficial runs [20].

Table 1. System performance for ICD10 coding on the **French aligned** test corpus in terms of Precision (P), recall (R) and F-measure (F). A horizontal dash line places the frequency baseline performance. The top part of the table displays official runs, while the bottom part displays the baseline

Team	P	R	F
IxaMed-run2	0.841	**0.835**	**0.838**
IxaMed-run1	**0.846**	0.822	0.834
IAM-run2	0.794	0.779	0.786
IAM-run1	0.782	0.772	0.777
SIB-TM	0.763	0.764	0.764
TorontoCL-run2	0.810	0.720	0.762
TorontoCL-run1	0.815	0.712	0.760
KCL-Health-NLP-run1	0.787	0.553	0.649
KCL-Health-NLP-run2	0.769	0.537	0.632
SINAI-run2	0.733	0.534	0.618
SINAI-run1	0.725	0.528	0.611
WebIntelligentLab	0.673	0.491	0.567
ECNUica-run1	0.771	0.437	0.558
ECNUica-run2	0.771	0.437	0.558
techno	0.489	0.356	0.412
KR-ISPED	0.029	0.020	0.023
Average	0.712	0.581	0.634
Median	0.771	0.545	0.641
Frequency baseline	0.452	0.450	0.451

dictionary matching accommodating for different levels of lexical variation. Most participants (12 teams out of 14) used the dictionaries that were supplied as part of the training data as well as other medical terminologies and ontologies (at least one team).

Task 2 attracted the interest of 7 teams submitting runs, including one team from Canada (UWA), one team from the USA (UIC/OHSU), one team from the UK (Sheffield), one team from China (ECNU), one team from Greece (AUTH), one team from Italy (UNIPD), one team from France (Limsi-CNRS). For the subtask 1, we received 12 runs from 4 teams. The results on a selected subset of metrics are shown in Table 5. For the subtask 2, we received 19 runs from 7 teams. The results on a selected subset of metrics are shown in Table 6. The 7 teams used a variety of learning methods including batch supervised learning, continuous active learning, a variety of learning algorithms including logistic regression, support vector machines, and neural networks, as well as unsupervised retrieval methods, such as TT-IDF, BM25, with or without traditional relevance feedback

Table 2. System performance for ICD10 coding on the **French raw** test corpus in terms of Precision (P), recall (R) and F-measure (F). A horizontal dash line places the frequency baseline performance. The top part of the table displays official runs, while the bottom part displays the baseline.

Team	P	R	F
IxaMed-run1	0.872	**0.597**	**0.709**
IxaMed-run2	0.877	0.588	0.704
LSI-UNED-run1	0.842	0.556	0.670
LSI-UNED-run2	0.879	0.540	0.669
IAM-run2	0.820	0.560	0.666
IAM-run1	0.807	0.555	0.657
TorontoCL-run2	0.842	0.522	0.644
TorontoCL-run1	0.847	0.515	0.641
WebIntelligentLab	0.702	0.495	0.580
ECNUica-run1	0.790	0.456	0.578
KCL-Health-NLP-run1	0.738	0.405	0.523
KCL-Health-NLP-run2	0.724	0.394	0.510
ims-unipd	0.653	0.396	0.493
techno	0.569	0.286	0.380
WBI-run2	0.512	0.253	0.339
WBI-run1	0.494	0.246	0.329
KR-ISPED	0.043	0.021	0.028
ECNUica-run2	**1.000**	0.000	0.000
Average	0.723	0.410	0.507
Median	0.798	0.475	0.579
Frequency baseline	0.341	0.201	0.253

methods, such as the Rocchio's Algorithm, and a variety of text representation methods including simple count-based methods to neural embeddings.

The training datasets were released on February 2018 and the test datasets on March 2018. The relevance labels on the testing data (required by active learning techniques) were provided to participants on 1 May 2018, four days before the submission deadline so that participants could not tune their systems towards the actual labels.

Task 3 had seven teams submitting runs: one team from Australia (QUT), one team from Botswana (UB-Botswana), one team from Czech Republic (CUNI), one team from Italy (IMS Unipd), one team from Portugal (UEvora), one team from Spain (SINAI), and one team from Tunisia (MIRACL). Participants submissions were due by June 8th 2018 and the relevance assessments are being collected at the time of writing of this paper. See the Task 3 overview paper for further details and the results of the evaluation [10].

Table 3. System performance for ICD10 coding on the **Hungarian raw** test corpus in terms of Precision (P), recall (R) and F-measure (F).

Hungarian (raw)			
Team	P	R	F
IxaMed run2	**0.970**	**0.955**	**0.963**
IxaMed run1	0.968	0.954	0.961
LSI UNED-run2	0.946	0.911	0.928
LSI UNED-run1	0.932	0.922	0.927
TorontoCL-run2	0.922	0.897	0.910
TorontoCL-run1	0.901	0.887	0.894
ims unipd	0.761	0.748	0.755
WBI-run2	0.522	0.388	0.445
WBI-run1	0.518	0.384	0.441
Average	0.243	0.174	0.202
Median	0.646	0.606	0.611
Frequency baseline	0.115	0.085	0.097

Table 4. System performance for ICD10 coding on the **Italian raw** test corpus in terms of Precision (P), recall (R) and F-measure (F).

Italian (raw)			
Team	P	R	F
IxaMed run1	**0.960**	**0.945**	**0.952**
IxaMed run2	0.945	0.922	0.934
LSI UNED-run1	0.917	0.875	0.895
LSI UNED-run2	0.931	0.861	0.895
TorontoCL-run1	0.908	0.824	0.864
TorontoCL-run2	0.900	0.829	0.863
WBI-run2	0.862	0.689	0.766
WBI-run1	0.857	0.685	0.761
KCL-Health-NLP-run1	0.746	0.636	0.687
KCL-Health-NLP-run2	0.725	0.616	0.666
ims unipd	0.535	0.484	0.509
Average	0.844	0.761	0.799
Median	0.900	0.824	0.863
Frequency baseline	0.165	0.172	0.169

Table 5. Average scores for the submitted runs in task 2 - subtask 1.

Run	MAP	R@50	R@100	R@200	R@300	R@400	R@500	R@1000	R@2000	R@k
auth_run1	0.113	0.188	0.341	0.51	0.61	0.66	0.693	0.787	0.802	0.816
auth_run2	0.113	0.188	0.341	0.51	0.61	0.66	0.693	0.787	0.802	0.809
auth_run3	0.113	0.188	0.341	0.51	0.61	0.66	0.693	0.787	0.802	0.787
ECNU_RUN1	0.072	0.17	0.242	0.339	0.393	0.431	0.472	0.561	0.561	0.472
ECNU_RUN2	0.041	0.076	0.145	0.216	0.281	0.34	0.378	0.378	0.378	0.378
ECNU_RUN3	0.072	0.173	0.246	0.341	0.411	0.452	0.485	0.561	0.561	0.485
shef-bm25	0.026	0.045	0.063	0.108	0.149	0.169	0.187	0.261	0.315	0.426
shef-tfidf	0.002	0.005	0.005	0.017	0.029	0.042	0.057	0.086	0.126	0.266
shef-bool	0.008	0.022	0.049	0.069	0.097	0.111	0.124	0.17	0.221	0.299
UWA	0.124	**0.256**	**0.428**	**0.592**	**0.693**	**0.771**	**0.806**	**0.912**	**0.947**	0.951
UWX	**0.154**	0.254	0.386	0.564	0.673	0.743	0.784	0.884	0.95	0.951
UWG	0.080	0.121	0.273	0.462	0.59	0.675	0.729	0.883	0.959	**0.962**

Table 6. Average scores for the submitted runs in task 2 - subtask 2.

Run	MAP	R@10%	R@20%	R@30%	R@K	K	Last_Rel	WSS95	WSS100
auth_run1	0.400	0.655	**0.883**	0.943	1.000	7283	3405	0.749	0.611
auth_run2	0.400	0.655	**0.883**	0.943	0.944	880	3405	0.749	0.611
auth_run3	0.393	0.653	0.874	0.931	0.943	880	4295	0.734	0.563
cnrs_RF_bi	0.314	0.560	0.776	0.862	1.000	7283	5173	0.617	0.460
cnrs_comb	0.337	0.557	0.774	0.862	1.000	7283	4378	0.657	0.510
cnrs_RF_uni	0.313	0.554	0.766	0.833	1.000	7283	5708	0.513	0.349
ECNU_RUN1	0.142	0.259	0.462	0.580	0.520	465	7173	0.027	0.026
ECNU_RUN2	0.081	0.232	0.414	0.539	0.371	466	4725	0.019	0.000
ECNU_RUN3	0.146	0.303	0.511	0.614	0.534	465	7172	0.029	0.025
unipd_t1500	0.316	0.544	0.761	0.843	0.945	2188	4259	0.543	0.396
unipd_t1000	0.317	0.542	0.765	0.857	0.920	1600	4101	0.572	0.410
unipd_t500	0.321	0.556	0.786	0.865	0.856	873	3935	0.616	0.475
shef-fb	**0.607**	0.554	0.774	0.856	1.000	7283	5171	0.635	0.444
shef-general	0.258	0.373	0.635	0.773	1.000	7283	5519	0.552	0.431
shef-query	0.224	0.338	0.591	0.734	1.000	7283	5736	0.506	0.377
uci_model8	0.174	0.289	0.462	0.562	0.513	1752	6385	0.255	0.154
uic_model7	0.180	0.296	0.473	0.579	0.576	2120	6185	0.264	0.164
UWB	0.378	**0.656**	**0.883**	0.944	0.927	1764	2655	0.756	0.610
UWA	0.362	0.651	0.877	**0.945**	0.990	2926	**2545**	0.751	0.608

4   Conclusions

In this paper, we provided an overview of the CLEF eHealth 2018 evaluation lab. The CLEF eHealth workshop series was established in 2012 as a scientific workshop with an aim of establishing an evaluation lab [25]. Since 2013, this annual workshop has been supplemented with two or more preceding shared tasks each year, in other words, the CLEF eHealth 2013–2018 evaluation labs [7,8,13,14,26]. During these past seven years, the CLEF eHealth series has offered a recurring contribution to the creation and dissemination of text analytics resources, methods, test collections, and evaluation benchmarks in order to ease and support patients, their next-of-kins, clinical staff, and health scientists in understanding, accessing, and authoring eHealth information in a multilingual setting.

Test collections generated by each of the three CLEF eHealth 2018 tasks offered a specific task definition, implemented in a dataset distributed together with an implementation of relevant evaluation metrics to allow for direct comparability of the results reported by systems evaluated on the collections. The established CLEF eHealth IE and IR tasks (Task 1 and Task 3) used a traditional shared task model for evaluation in which a community-wide evaluation is executed in a controlled setting: independent training and test datasets are used and all participants gain access to the test data at the same time, following which no further updates to systems are allowed. Shortly after releasing the test data (without labels or other solutions), the participating teams are to submit their outputs from the frozen systems to the task organizers, who are to evaluate these results and report the resulting benchmarks to the community.

Instead of continuing our replication track from 2016 and 2017 [18,19], we recommended interested teams participate to *ClEf/Ntcir/Trec REproducibility* (CENTRE)[3]. This CENTRE at CLEF 2018 evaluation lab ran a joint CLEF, *NII Testbeds and Community for Information access Research* (NTCIR), and TREC task on challenging participants to study the replicability of selected methods on the same experimental collections as its Task 1; study the reproducibility of selected methods on the different experimental collections as its Task 2; and study the re-reproducibility by using the components developed in aforementioned two tasks and made available by the other participants to replicate/reproduce their results [2]. The CLEF eHealth replication tracks 2016 and 2017 [18,19] gave our participating teams the opportunity to submit their processing methods to organizers, who then attempted to replicate the runs submitted by participants. Three and five participating teams of the CLEF eHealth 2016 Task 2 and the CLEF eHealth 2017 Task 1, respectively, took this opportunity. The teams submitted a total of seven and 22 methods to replication tracks 2016 and 2017, respectively. Both in 2016 and 2017, the organizers were able to achieve a perfect replication, but in some cases, this was only after contacting the submitting team for some further technical clarification on system requirements, installation procedure, and practical use. We were delighted to observe

---

[3] http://www.centre-eval.org/ (last accessed on 7 June 2018).

an overall improvement in method documentation as an outcome of running the track twice.

The annual CLEF eHealth workhops and evaluation labs have matured and established their presence in 2012–2018. In total, 70 unique teams registered their interest and 28 teams took part in the 2018 tasks (14 in Task 1, 7 in Task 2 and 7 in Task 3). In comparison, in 2017, 2016, 2015, 2014, and 2013, the number of team registrations was 67, 116, 100, 220, and 175, respectively and the number of participating teams was 32, 20, 20, 24, and 53 [7,8,13,14,26]. Given the significance of the tasks, all problem specifications, test collections, and text analytics resources associated with the lab have been made available to the wider research community through our CLEF eHealth website[4].

Acknowledgements. The CLEF eHealth 2018 evaluation lab has been supported in part by (in alphabetical order) the ANU, the CLEF Initiative, the Data61/CSIRO, and the French National Research Agency (ANR), under grant CABeRneT ANR-13-JS02-0009-01. We are also thankful to the people involved in the annotation, query creation, and relevance assessment exercise. Last but not least, we gratefully acknowledge the participating teams' hard work. We thank them for their submissions and interest in the lab.

References

1. Cormack, G.V., Grossman, M.R.: Engineering quality and reliability in technology-assisted review. In: Proceedings of the 39th International ACM SIGIR Conference on Research and Development in Information Retrieval, SIGIR 2016, pp. 75–84. ACM, New York (2016). https://doi.org/10.1145/2911451.2911510

2. Ferro, N., Maistro, M., Sakai, T., Soboroff, I.: Overview of CENTRE @ CLEF 2018. In: Ferro, N., et al. (eds.) CLEF 2018. LNCS, vol. 11018, pp. 239–246 (2018)

3. Goeuriot, L., et al.: D7.3 meta-analysis of the second phase of empirical and user-centered evaluations. Technical report, Khresmoi Project, August 2014

4. Goeuriot, L., et al.: ShARe/CLEF eHealth evaluation lab 2013, Task 3: information retrieval to address patients' questions when reading clinical reports. CLEF 2013 Online Working Notes 8138 (2013)

5. Goeuriot, L., et al.: An analysis of evaluation campaigns in ad-hoc medical information retrieval: CLEF eHealth 2013 and 2014. Inf. Retr. J. **21**, 1–34 (2018)

6. Goeuriot, L., et al.: ShARe/CLEF eHealth evaluation lab 2014, Task 3: user-centred health information retrieval. In: CLEF 2014 Evaluation Labs and Workshop: Online Working Notes. Sheffield, UK (2014)

7. Goeuriot, L., et al.: Overview of the CLEF eHealth evaluation lab 2015. In: Mothe, J., et al. (eds.) CLEF 2015. LNCS, vol. 9283, pp. 429–443. Springer, Cham (2015). https://doi.org/10.1007/978-3-319-24027-5_44

8. Goeuriot, L., et al.: CLEF 2017 eHealth evaluation lab overview. In: Jones, G.L.F., et al. (eds.) CLEF 2017. LNCS, vol. 10456, pp. 291–303. Springer, Cham (2017). https://doi.org/10.1007/978-3-319-65813-1_26

9. Jimmy, Zuccon, G., Demartini, G.: On the volatility of commercial search engines and its impact on information retrieval research. In: SIGIR 2018 (2018)

---

[4] https://sites.google.com/view/clef-ehealth-2018/home (last accessed on 7 June 2018).

10. Jimmy, Zuccon, G., Palotti, J., Goeuriot, L., Kelly, L.: Overview of the CLEF 2018 consumer health search task. In: Working Notes of Conference and Labs of the Evaluation (CLEF) Forum. CEUR Workshop Proceedings (2018)

11. Kanoulas, E., Li, D., Azzopardi, L., Spijker, R.: CLEF 2017 technologically assisted reviews in empirical medicine overview. In: Working Notes of Conference and Labs of the Evaluation (CLEF) Forum. CEUR Workshop Proceedings (2017)

12. Kanoulas, E., Li, D., Azzopardi, L., Spijker, R.: CLEF 2018 technologically assisted reviews in empirical medicine overview. In: Working Notes of Conference and Labs of the Evaluation (CLEF) Forum. CEUR Workshop Proceedings (2018)

13. Kelly, L., Goeuriot, L., Suominen, H., Névéol, A., Palotti, J., Zuccon, G.: Overview of the CLEF eHealth evaluation lab 2016. In: Fuhr, N., et al. (eds.) CLEF 2016. LNCS, vol. 9822, pp. 255–266. Springer, Cham (2016). https://doi.org/10.1007/978-3-319-44564-9_24

14. Kelly, L., et al.: Overview of the ShARe/CLEF eHealth evaluation lab 2014. In: Kanoulas, E., et al. (eds.) CLEF 2014. LNCS, vol. 8685, pp. 172–191. Springer, Cham (2014). https://doi.org/10.1007/978-3-319-11382-1_17

15. Leeflang, M.M., Deeks, J.J., Takwoingi, Y., Macaskill, P.: Cochrane diagnostic test accuracy reviews. Syst. Rev. **2**(1), 82 (2013)

16. Lipani, A., Palotti, J., Lupu, M., Piroi, F., Zuccon, G., Hanbury, A.: Fixed-cost pooling strategies based on IR evaluation measures. In: Jose, J.M., et al. (eds.) ECIR 2017. LNCS, vol. 10193, pp. 357–368. Springer, Cham (2017). https://doi.org/10.1007/978-3-319-56608-5_28

17. Moffat, A., Zobel, J.: Rank-biased precision for measurement of retrieval effectiveness. ACM Trans. Inf. Syst. **27**(1), 2:1–2:27 (2008). https://doi.org/10.1145/1416950.1416952

18. Névéol, A., et al.: CLEF eHealth 2017 multilingual information extraction task overview: ICD10 coding of death certificates in English and French. In: Cappellato, L., Ferro, N., Goeuriot, L., Mandl, T. (eds.) CLEF 2017 Working Notes. CEUR Workshop Proceedings (CEUR-WS.org) (2017). ISSN 1613–0073. http://ceur-ws.org/Vol-1866/

19. Névéol, A., et al.: Clinical information extraction at the CLEF eHealth evaluation lab 2016. In: Balog, K., Cappellato, L., Ferro, N., Macdonald, C. (eds.) CLEF 2016 Working Notes. CEUR Workshop Proceedings (CEUR-WS.org) (2016). ISSN 1613–0073. http://ceur-ws.org/Vol-1609/

20. Névéol, A., et al.: CLEF eHealth 2017 multilingual information extraction task overview: ICD10 coding of death certificates in English and French. In: CLEF 2017 Online Working Notes. CEUR-WS (2017)

21. Névéol, A., et al.: CLEF eHealth 2018 multilingual information extraction task overview: ICD10 coding of death certificates in French, Hungarian and Italian. In: CLEF 2018 Online Working Notes. CEUR-WS (2018)

22. Palotti, J., et al.: CLEF eHealth evaluation lab 2015, task 2: retrieving information about medical symptoms. In: CLEF 2015 Online Working Notes. CEUR-WS (2015)

23. Palotti, J., et al.: CLEF 2017 task overview: the IR Task at the eHealth evaluation lab. In: Working Notes of Conference and Labs of the Evaluation (CLEF) Forum. CEUR Workshop Proceedings (2017)

24. Park, L.A., Zhang, Y.: On the distribution of user persistence for rank-biased precision. In: Proceedings of the 12th Australasian Document Computing Symposium, pp. 17–24 (2007)

25. Suominen, H.: In: Forner, P., Karlgren, J., Womser-Hacker, C., Ferro, N. (eds.) CLEF 2012 Working Notes. CEUR Workshop Proceedings (CEUR-WS.org) (2012). ISSN 1613–0073. http://ceur-ws.org/Vol-1178/

26. Suominen, H., et al.: Overview of the ShARe/CLEF eHealth evaluation lab 2013. In: Forner, P., Müller, H., Paredes, R., Rosso, P., Stein, B. (eds.) CLEF 2013. LNCS, vol. 8138, pp. 212–231. Springer, Heidelberg (2013). https://doi.org/10. 1007/978-3-642-40802-1_24

27. Zuccon, G., et al.: The IR task at the CLEF eHealth evaluation lab 2016: user-centred health information retrieval. In: CLEF 2016 Evaluation Labs and Workshop: Online Working Notes, CEUR-WS, September 2016

CLEF MC2 2018 Lab Overview

Malek Hajjem[1,2], Jean Valére Cossu[3], Chiraz Latiri[2], and Eric SanJuan[1(✉)]

[1] LIA, Avignon University, Avignon, France
{malek.hajjem,eric.sanjuan}@univ-avignon.fr
[2] LIPAH, Tunis Manar University, Tunis, Tunisia
chiraz.latiri@gnet.tn
[3] MyLI, My Local Influence, Marseille, France
jvcossu@gmail.com

Abstract. MC2 lab mainly focuses on developing processing methods and resources to mine the social media (SM) sphere surrounding cultural events such as festivals, music, books, movies and museums. Following previous editions (CMC 2016 and MC2 2017), the 2018 edition focused on argumentative mining and multilingual cross SM search. Public microblogs about cultural events like festivals are promotional announcements by organizers or artists, very few are personal and argumentative, the challenge is to find them before they eventually become viral. We report the main lessons learned from this 2018 CLEF task.

Keywords: Argumentation mining · Microblogs
Information Retrieval · Ranking

1 Introduction

Following previous editions, MC2 Lab 2018 was centered on multilingual culture mining and retrieval process over the large corpus of cultural microblogs [7] considered in the two previous editions [6,8]. Two main tasks were considered: cross language cultural microblog search and argumentation mining.

The initial challenge for 2018 was, given a short movie review on the French VodKaster[1] Social Media, find related microblogs in the MC2 corpus in four different target languages (French, English, Spanish and Portuguese). Indeed, browsing the VodKaster website, French readers get personal short comments about movies. Since similar posts can be found on twitter we decided to display to the reader a concise summary of microblogs related to the comment he/she is reading, considering bilingual and trilingual users that would read microblogs in other languages than French. In this user's context, personal and argumentative microblogs are expected to be more relevant than news or official announcements. Microblogs sharing similar arguments can be considered as highly relevant even though they are about different movies. From this initial task, came the idea of

---

[1] http://www.vodkaster.com/.

© Springer Nature Switzerland AG 2018
P. Bellot et al. (Eds.): CLEF 2018, LNCS 11018, pp. 302–308, 2018.
https://doi.org/10.1007/978-3-319-98932-7_27

a second one focusing on argument mining in a multilingual collection. It consisted in finding personal and argumentative microblogs in the corpus. Public posts about cultural events like festivals are mostly promotional announcements by organizers or artists. Personal argumentative microblogs about specific festivals provide real insights into public reception but both their variety and rarity make them difficult to seek. Therefore, argumentative mining captured most of participant efforts during this lab edition. The cold start scenario of finding them without any specific learning resource motivated the use of IR approaches based on language model or specialized linguistic resources.

The rest of this paper focus on this specific task. Related work is presented in Sect. 2. Section 3 is devoted to task thorough description an motivations. Data including a baseline run is fully described in Sect. 4. Result and participant approaches are reported in Sect. 5.

2 Related Work

Argumentation (or argument) mining is the automatic extraction of structured arguments from unstructured textual corpora [10]. This task represents a new problem in corpus-based text analysis that addresses the challenging task [13] of automatically identifying the justifications provided by opinion holders for their judgments. The initial research of argumentation mining has been proposed for legal documents, on-line debates, product reviews, political debates and newspaper articles, court cases, as well as in the dialogical domain [3,12,13].

As a result of the advent of social media platforms, argumentation mining for social media text and user generated content has been proposed [5,14]. The goal of argumentation mining with short and unstructured data is to improve our ability to process and infer meaning from social media text. In fact, this kind of data is characterized to be ambiguous by nature which makes it hard for a user to effectively understand what the opinion tweet is about. Generally, such tweets are indispensable to form a view about a new topic or make a decision based on users feedback. In such a case, expressed argument is all what we are looking for.

Regarding short texts, developed approaches for microblogs differ from techniques dedicated to other genres. These are usually longer, such as forums, product reviews, blogs and news. In fact high quality social media data sets annotated with argumentation structure are rare which affects the use of machine learning techniques. In this context we cite DART [4], a dataset to support the development of frameworks addressing the argument mining pipeline on Twitter.

This lack of resources and challenges to extract arguments from social media text could be explained by the fact that social media platforms such as comment boards on news portals, product review sites, or microblogs are less controlled communication environments where the communicative intention is not to engage in an argumentative discussion but rather to simply express an opinion on the subject matter [14]. To solve this issue, argumentation mining within social media text has to deal with several sets of features to capture the above mentioned characteristics for persuasive comment identification from user generated data. This was the case of [17] where authors propose and evaluate other features to rank comments for their persuasive scores, including textual information in the comments and social interaction related features.

3 Task

The proposed task is inspired from the field of focused retrieval. This later aims to provide users with direct access to relevant information in retrieved documents. For this task, a relevant information is expressed in the form of argument that supports or criticizes an event. So, we presume that the proposed method must perform:

1. a search process that focus on claims about a given topic out in a massive collection.
2. a ranking process that has a potential argumentative coming first.

Following such steps, a synthesis of many argument facets about a specific event is automatically constructed. Such an output could be treated more easily, on priority, by a festival organizer.

Argumentation mining is considered as an extension of the opinion mining issue from social network content. The main objective of this field is to automatically identify reason-conclusion structures that can lead to model social web user's positions about a service, product or event expressed through social media platforms. As explored in [10] most argumentation mining approaches have tackled the challenging task of extracting arguments based on machine learning methods. However, in case of argumentation mining from social media like Facebook and Twitter, the lack of labeled corpora with argumentation information and the informal nature of user-generated content make this task more complicated.

Argumentation mining in this task tend to act in the same way of an Information Retrieval (IR) system where potential argumentative microblogs had to come first. A similar approach that addresses such purpose was presented in RepLab task [2], where the output of the priority task will be a ranking of microblogs according to their probability of being a potential threat to the reputation of some entity.

Following the task proposition described above, the argumentation mining task of MC2 lab is then defined as **argumentation detection** combined with **priority ranking** of argumentative microblogs. The detection of argumentation content will depend on a search process that arranged microblogs based on the amount of claims about a given culture event or festival name.

The evidence related to such claims would be an invaluable information for festival organizers, journalists and communication departments. It would be useful even to normal festival spectator, since it would summarize all argumentation facets that one needs to access in order to obtain a satisfactory overview about a festival name.

Participants were welcome to present systems that attempt the whole task objective (argumentation detection + argumentation ranking). These two phases are explicitly considered in Argumentation mining task as following:

- Argumentation detection: Given a festival name as query (Topic), participants have to induce, from the microblog collection, the set of the most argumentative microblogs about this culture event.
- Argumentation ranking: Participants are asked to judge the relevance of each microblog of the set in term of argumentation.

4   Data

4.1   Corpus

The MC2 corpus is a microblog stream, covering 18 months from May 2015 to November 2016, about festivals in different languages [7]. This corpus was provided to registered participants by ANR GAFES project[2]. It consists of a pool with more than 50M unique microblogs from different sources with their meta-information.

4.2   Topics

Given a cultural query about festivals in English or French. The task proposes to search for the 100 most argumentative microblogs.

We chose to gather microblogs based on the most visible festival names on FlickR (the famous photos sharing site)[3] in order to avoid getting microblogs from official pages of festival organizers and getting a maximum of personal microblogs

Only the subset of festivals with at least 300 photos has been considered. The selection was done through a manual exploration on the microblog corpus to ensure providing queries with enough argumentation content for our target audience.

4.3   Baseline

The baseline approach consisted in using Indri language model to search for argumentative microblogs. For each festival, a query including lexical features expressing opinion and argumentation was defined following [1]. In argumentative microblogs, users usually use comparison language to compare and contrast ideas (*More, less*). Authors also tend to use pronouns like (*my, mine, myself,I*). Verbs like *believe, think, agree* and adverbs play an important role to identify argument components. They indicate the presence of a major claim and adverbs like *also,often or really* emphasize the importance of some premise [15]. Verbs like *should, could* are frequently used in argumentative context to express what users were expecting. In addition to this argumentative keywords list, we use a list expression opinion used in [9].

---

[2] http://www.agence-nationale-recherche.fr/?Projet=ANR-14-CE24-0022.
[3] https://www.flickr.com/.

5 Results

Argumentative mining received considerable interest with 31 registered participants, but only 5 teams submitted a total of 18 runs per language. Organizers baselines were added to this pool. The NDGC has been adopted as the main official measure, but precision at 100 could have been used since it provided the exact same rankings.

Two reference sets of argumentative structures represented as regular expresions have been assigned to each query (festival name). One has been exracted apriori from the manual interactive run provided as baseline. A second one has been extracted from participant runs. To avoid duplicated content, only microblog textual content has been considered. All meta-data like URLs, #hashtags and @replies were removed. Most argumentative phrases have been extracted from this material and been modeled as generic Regular Expressions. These steps were both applied to the English and French runs.

Table 1 describes average NDGC results for English queries. Results on French are similar but due to a smaller number of queries, differences are not statistically significant. All participant systems relied on an initial step of pretreatment to filter the original dataset by language and topic.

ERTIM Team found the highest number of argumentative microblogs using lexical data enrichment [16]. This resource associates a score to each lemma according to the affective. Besides these lexicon based measures, opinion was detected based on the proportion of adjectives among all part of speech tags. In addition to this opinion scoring process, ERTIM tackled the argumentation detection in the same way by scoring opinion tweets based on the number of conjunctions. Conjunctions are discourse connector commonly used to structure a text. This was a systematic approach applied to all microblogs in the corpus. Although they found a number of argumentative microblogs higher than other participants for almost all queries, there was no overlap with argumentative microblogs found in the baseline runs.

Teams relying on language model using queries mixing multiword terms with argumentative connectors found less argumentative microblogs but a larger overlap with the reference extracted from the baseline run.

Table 1. Best average NDGC scores for top participants (English)

Team	Organizer-Ref	Pooling-Ref
ERTIM	0.0092	**0.6011*****
ECNUica	0.03333	0.082
LIA-run2	**0.0609***	0.0632

6   Conclusion

Previous editions of the MC2 lab focused on contextualization [6] and timeline illustration [8,11] of cultural events over a 18 months period based on the ANR GaFes corpus [7]. In 2018 the main challenge has been to find authentic personal microblogs in this massive collection. This is required to portrait festival reputation among participants. Among them, public argumentative microblogs are the most important since they could have a direct impact on reputation. However, promotional microblogs by festival organizers tend to use similar syntax and form. The main finding of this year is that lexical filtering combined with part of speech analysis is the most efficient to detect these microblogs and rank them by priority. However, this extraction is not exhaustive. An interactive search using complex queries based on Indri language model[4] lead to discover undetected relevant personal argumentative microblogs.

References

1. Aker, A., et al.: What works and what does not: classifier and feature analysis for argument mining. In: Proceedings of the 4th Workshop on Argument Mining, ArgMining@EMNLP 2017, pp. 91–96. Association for Computational Linguistics (2017)
2. Amigó, E., et al.: Overview of RepLab 2013: evaluating online reputation monitoring systems. In: Forner, P., Müller, H., Paredes, R., Rosso, P., Stein, B. (eds.) CLEF 2013. LNCS, vol. 8138, pp. 333–352. Springer, Heidelberg (2013). https://doi.org/10.1007/978-3-642-40802-1_31
3. Bal, B.K., Dizier, P.S.: Towards building annotated resources for analyzing opinions and argumentation in news editorials. In: Proceedings of the Seventh International Conference on Language Resources and Evaluation (LREC 2010). European Language Resources Association (ELRA), Valletta, Malta, May 2010
4. Bosc, T., Cabrio, E., Villata, S.: DART: a dataset of arguments and their relations on Twitter. In: European Language Resources Association (ELRA) (2016)
5. Dusmanu, M., Cabrio, E., Villata, S.: Argument mining on Twitter: arguments, facts and sources. In: Proceedings of the 2017 Conference on Empirical Methods in Natural Language Processing, EMNLP 2017, pp. 2317–2322. Association for Computational Linguistics (2017)
6. Goeuriot, L., Mothe, J., Mulhem, P., Murtagh, F., SanJuan, E.: Overview of the CLEF 2016 cultural micro-blog contextualization workshop. In: Fuhr, N., et al. (eds.) CLEF 2016. LNCS, vol. 9822, pp. 371–378. Springer, Cham (2016). https://doi.org/10.1007/978-3-319-44564-9_30
7. Goeuriot, L., Mothe, J., Mulhem, P., SanJuan, E.: Building evaluation datasets for cultural microblog retrieval. In: Proceedings of the Eleventh International Conference on Language Resources and Evaluation, LREC 2018. European Language Resources Association (ELRA) (2018)
8. Goeuriot, L., Mulhem, P., SanJuan, E.: CLEF 2017 MC2 search and time line tasks overview. In: Working Notes of CLEF 2017 - Conference and Labs of the Evaluation Forum, 11–14 September 2017, Dublin, Ireland (2017)

---

[4] http://www.cs.cmu.edu/lemur/3.1/IndriQueryLanguage.html.

9. Hu, M., Liu, B.: Mining and summarizing customer reviews. In: Proceedings of the Tenth ACM SIGKDD International Conference on Knowledge Discovery and Data Mining, KDD 2004, pp. 168–177. ACM, New York (2004)

10. Lippi, M., Torroni, P.: Argumentation mining: state of the art and emerging trends. ACM Trans. Internet Technol. **16**(2), 10:1–10:25 (2016)

11. Mulhem, P., Goeuriot, L., Dogra, N., Ould Amer, N.: TimeLine illustration based on microblogs: when diversification meets metadata re-ranking. In: Jones, G.J.F., et al. (eds.) CLEF 2017. LNCS, vol. 10456, pp. 224–235. Springer, Cham (2017). https://doi.org/10.1007/978-3-319-65813-1_22

12. Newman, S.E., Marshall, C.C.: Pushing Toulmin too far: learning from an argument representation scheme (1992)

13. Palau, R.M., Moens, M.: Argumentation mining. Artif. Intell. Law **19**(1), 1–22 (2011)

14. Snajder, J.: Social media argumentation mining: the quest for deliberateness in raucousness. CoRR abs/1701.00168 (2017). http://arxiv.org/abs/1701.00168

15. Stab, C., Gurevych, I.: Identifying argumentative discourse structures in persuasive essays. In: EMNLP, pp. 46–56 (2014)

16. Warriner, A.B., Kuperman, V., Brysbaert, M.: Norms of valence, arousal, and dominance for 13,915 English lemmas. Behav. Res. Methods **45**(4), 1191–1207 (2013)

17. Wei, Z., Liu, Y., Li, Y.: Is this post persuasive? Ranking argumentative comments in online forum. In: ACL (2016)

Overview of ImageCLEF 2018: Challenges, Datasets and Evaluation

Bogdan Ionescu[1]([✉]), Henning Müller[2], Mauricio Villegas[3],
Alba García Seco de Herrera[4], Carsten Eickhoff[5], Vincent Andrearczyk[2],
Yashin Dicente Cid[2], Vitali Liauchuk[6], Vassili Kovalev[6], Sadid A. Hasan[7],
Yuan Ling[7], Oladimeji Farri[7], Joey Liu[7], Matthew Lungren[8],
Duc-Tien Dang-Nguyen[9], Luca Piras[10], Michael Riegler[11,12], Liting Zhou[9],
Mathias Lux[13], and Cathal Gurrin[9]

[1] University Politehnica of Bucharest, Bucharest, Romania
bionescu@alpha.imag.pub.ro
[2] University of Applied Sciences Western Switzerland (HES-SO), Sierre, Switzerland
[3] omni:us, Berlin, Germany
[4] University of Essex, Colchester, UK
[5] Brown University, Providence, RI, USA
[6] United Institute of Informatics Problems, Minsk, Belarus
[7] Artificial Intelligence Lab, Philips Research North America, Cambridge, MA, USA
[8] Department of Radiology, Stanford University, Stanford, CA, USA
[9] Dublin City University, Dublin, Ireland
[10] University of Cagliari and Pluribus One, Cagliari, Italy
[11] University of Oslo, Oslo, Norway
[12] Simula Metropolitan Center for Digital Engineering, Oslo, Norway
[13] Klagenfurt University, Klagenfurt, Austria

Abstract. This paper presents an overview of the ImageCLEF 2018 evaluation campaign, an event that was organized as part of the CLEF (Conference and Labs of the Evaluation Forum) Labs 2018. ImageCLEF is an ongoing initiative (it started in 2003) that promotes the evaluation of technologies for annotation, indexing and retrieval with the aim of providing information access to collections of images in various usage scenarios and domains. In 2018, the 16th edition of ImageCLEF ran three main tasks and a pilot task: (1) a *caption prediction* task that aims at predicting the caption of a figure from the biomedical literature based only on the figure image; (2) a *tuberculosis* task that aims at detecting the tuberculosis type, severity and drug resistance from CT (Computed Tomography) volumes of the lung; (3) a *LifeLog* task (videos, images and other sources) about daily activities understanding and moment retrieval, and (4) a pilot task on *visual question answering* where systems are tasked with answering medical questions. The strong participation, with over 100 research groups registering and 31 submitting results for the tasks, shows an increasing interest in this benchmarking campaign.

© Springer Nature Switzerland AG 2018
P. Bellot et al. (Eds.): CLEF 2018, LNCS 11018, pp. 309–334, 2018.
https://doi.org/10.1007/978-3-319-98932-7_28

1   Introduction

One or two decades ago getting access to large visual data sets for research was a problem and open data collections that could be used to compare algorithms of researchers were rare. Now, it is getting easier to access data collections but it is still hard to obtain annotated data with a clear evaluation scenario and strong baselines to compare against. Motivated by this, ImageCLEF has for 16 years been an initiative that aims at evaluating multilingual or language independent annotation and retrieval of images [5,21,23,25,39]. The main goal of ImageCLEF is to support the advancement of the field of visual media analysis, classification, annotation, indexing and retrieval. It proposes novel challenges and develops the necessary infrastructure for the evaluation of visual systems operating in different contexts and providing reusable resources for benchmarking. It is also linked to initiatives such as Evaluation-as-a-Service (EaaS) [17,18].

Many research groups have participated over the years in these evaluation campaigns and even more have acquired its datasets for experimentation. The impact of ImageCLEF can also be seen by its significant scholarly impact indicated by the substantial numbers of its publications and their received citations [36].

There are other evaluation initiatives that have had a close relation with ImageCLEF. LifeCLEF [22] was formerly an ImageCLEF task. However, due to the need to assess technologies for automated identification and understanding of living organisms using data not only restricted to images, but also videos and sound, it was decided to be organised independently from ImageCLEF. Other CLEF labs linked to ImageCLEF, in particular the medical task, are: CLEFeHealth [14] that deals with processing methods and resources to enrich difficult-to-understand eHealth text and the BioASQ [4] tasks from the Question Answering lab that targets biomedical semantic indexing and question answering but is now not a lab anymore. Due to their medical orientation, the organisation is coordinated in close collaboration with the medical tasks in ImageCLEF. In 2017, ImageCLEF explored synergies with the MediaEval Benchmarking Initiative for Multimedia Evaluation [15], which focuses on exploring the "multi" in multimedia: speech, audio, visual content, tags, users, context. MediaEval was founded in 2008 as VideoCLEF, a track in the CLEF Campaign.

This paper presents a general overview of the ImageCLEF 2018 evaluation campaign[1], which as usual was an event organised as part of the CLEF labs[2].

The remainder of the paper is organized as follows. Section 2 presents a general description of the 2018 edition of ImageCLEF, commenting about the overall organisation and participation in the lab. Followed by this are sections dedicated to the four tasks that were organised this year: Sect. 3 for the Caption Task, Sect. 4 for the Tuberculosis Task, Sect. 5 for the Visual Question Answering Task, and Sect. 6 for the Lifelog Task. For the full details and complete results on the participating teams, the reader should refer to the corresponding task

---

[1] http://imageclef.org/2018/.

[2] http://clef2018.clef-initiative.eu/.

overview papers [7,11,19,20]. The final section concludes the paper by giving an overall discussion, and pointing towards the challenges ahead and possible new directions for future research.

2   Overview of Tasks and Participation

ImageCLEF 2018 consisted of three main tasks and a pilot task that covered challenges in diverse fields and usage scenarios. In 2017 [21] the proposed challenges were almost all new in comparison to 2016 [40], the only exception being Caption Prediction that was a subtask already attempted in 2016, but for which no participant submitted results. After such a big change, for 2018 the objective was to continue most of the tasks from 2017. The only change was that the 2017 Remote Sensing pilot task was replaced by a novel one on Visual Question Answering. The 2018 tasks are the following:

- **ImageCLEFcaption:** Interpreting and summarizing the insights gained from medical images such as radiology output is a time-consuming task that involves highly trained experts and often represents a bottleneck in clinical diagnosis pipelines. Consequently, there is a considerable need for automatic methods that can approximate this mapping from visual information to condensed textual descriptions. The task addresses the problem of bio-medical image concept detection and caption prediction from large amounts of training data.
- **ImageCLEFtuberculosis:** The main objective of the task is to provide a tuberculosis severity score based on the automatic analysis of lung CT images of patients. Being able to extract this information from the image data alone allows to limit lung washing and laboratory analyses to determine the tuberculosis type and drug resistances. This can lead to quicker decisions on the best treatment strategy, reduced use of antibiotics and lower impact on the patient.
- **ImageCLEFlifelog:** An increasingly wide range of personal devices, such as smart phones, video cameras as well as wearable devices that allow capturing pictures, videos, and audio clips of every moment of life are becoming available. Considering the huge volume of data created, there is a need for systems that can automatically analyse the data in order to categorize, summarize and also to retrieve query-information that the user may desire. Hence, this task addresses the problems of lifelog data understanding, summarization and retrieval.
- **ImageCLEF-VQA-Med (pilot task):** Visual Question Answering is a new and exciting problem that combines natural language processing and computer vision techniques. With the ongoing drive for improved patient engagement and access to the electronic medical records via patient portals, patients can now review structured and unstructured data from labs and images to text reports associated with their healthcare utilization. Such access can help them better understand their conditions in line with the details received from their healthcare provider. Given a medical image accompanied with a set of

clinically relevant questions, participating systems are tasked with answering the questions based on the visual image content.

In order to participate in the evaluation campaign, the research groups first had to register by following the instructions on the ImageCLEF 2018 web page. To ease the overall management of the campaign, this year the challenge was organized through the crowdAI platform[3]. To get access to the datasets, the participants were required to submit a signed End User Agreement (EUA) form. Table 1 summarizes the participation in ImageCLEF 2018, including the number of registrations (counting only the ones that downloaded the EUA) and the number of signed EUAs, indicated both per task and for the overall Lab. The table also shows the number of groups that submitted results (runs) and the ones that submitted a working notes paper describing the techniques used.

The number of registrations could be interpreted as the initial interest that the community has for the evaluation. However, it is a bit misleading because several persons from the same institution might register, even though in the end they count as a single group participation. The EUA explicitly requires all groups that get access to the data to participate, even though this is not enforced. Unfortunately, the percentage of groups that submit results is often limited. Nevertheless, as observed in studies of scholarly impact [36,37], in subsequent years the datasets and challenges provided by ImageCLEF often get used, in part due to the researchers that for some reason (e.g. alack of time, or other priorities) were unable to participate in the original event or did not complete the tasks by the deadlines.

After a decrease in participation in 2016, the participation again increased in 2017 and for 2018 it increased further. The number of signed EUAs is considerably higher, mostly due to the fact that this time each task had an independent EUA. Also, due to the change to crowdAI, the online registration became easier and attracted other research groups than usual, which made the registration-to-participation ratio lower than in previous years. Nevertheless, in the end, 31 groups participated and 28 working notes papers were submitted, which is a slight increase with respect to 2017. The following four sections are dedicated to each of the tasks. Only a short overview is reported, including general objectives, description of the tasks and datasets and a short summary of the results.

3   The Caption Task

This task studies algorithmic approaches to medical image understanding. As a testbed for doing so, teams were tasked with automatically "guessing" fitting keywords or free-text captions that best describe an image from a collection of images published in the biomedical literature.

---

[3] https://www.crowdai.org/.

Table 1. Key figures of participation in ImageCLEF 2018.

Task	Registered & downloaded EUA	Signed EUA	Groups that subm. results	Submitted working notes
Caption	84	46	8	6
Tuberculosis	85	33	11	11
VQA-Med	58	28	5	5
Lifelog	38	25	7	7
Overall	265*	132*	31	29

*Total for all tasks, not unique groups/emails.

3.1 Task Setup

Following the structure of the 2017 edition, two sub tasks were proposed. The first task, concept detection, aims to extract the main biomedical concepts represented in an image based only on its visual content. These concepts are UMLS (Unified Medical Language System®) Concept Unique Identifiers (CUIs). The second task, caption prediction, aims to compose coherent free-text captions describing the image based only on the visual information. Participants were, of course, allowed to use the UMLS CUIs extracted in the first task to compose captions from individual concepts. Figure 1 shows an example of the information available in the training set. An image is accompanied by a set of UMLS CUIs and a free-text caption. Compared to 2017 the data sets was modified strongly to respond to some of the difficulties with the task in the past [13].

3.2 Dataset

The dataset used in this task is derived from figures and their corresponding captions extracted from biomedical articles on PubMed Central® (PMC)[4]. This data set was changed strongly compared to the same task run in 2017 to reduce the diversity on the data and limit the number of compound figures. A subset of clinical figures was automatically obtained from the overall set of 5.8 million PMC figures using a deep multimodal fusion of Convolutional Neural Networks (CNN), described in [2]. In total, the dataset is comprised of 232,305 image–caption pairs split into disjoint training (222,305 pairs) and test (10,000 pairs) sets. For the Concept Detection subtask, concepts present in the caption text were extracted using the QuickUMLS library [30]. After having observed a strong breadth of concepts and image types in the 2017 edition of the task, this year's continuation focused on radiology artifacts, introducing a greater topical focus to the collection.

---

[4] https://www.ncbi.nlm.nih.gov/pmc/.

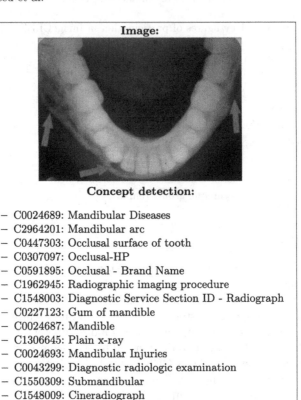

Image:

Concept detection:

- C0024689: Mandibular Diseases
- C2964201: Mandibular arc
- C0447303: Occlusal surface of tooth
- C0307097: Occlusal-HP
- C0591895: Occlusal - Brand Name
- C1962945: Radiographic imaging procedure
- C1548003: Diagnostic Service Section ID - Radiograph
- C0227123: Gum of mandible
- C0024687: Mandible
- C1306645: Plain x-ray
- C0024693: Mandibular Injuries
- C0043299: Diagnostic radiologic examination
- C1550309: Submandibular
- C1548009: Cineradiograph

Caption prediction: *Mandibular* true *occlusal radiograph.*

Fig. 1. Example of an image and the information provided in the training set in the form of the original caption and the extracted UMLS concepts.

3.3   Participating Groups and Submitted Runs

In 2018, 46 groups registered for the caption task compared with the 37 groups registered in 2017. 8 groups submitted runs, one less than in 2017. 28 runs were submitted to the concept detection subtask and 16 to the caption prediction task. Although the caption prediction task appears like an extension of the concept detection task, only two groups participated in both, and 4 groups participated only in the caption prediction task.

3.4   Results

The submitted runs are summarized in Tables 2 and 3, respectively. Similar to 2017, there were two main approaches used on the concept detection subtask: multi-modal classification and retrieval.

Table 2. Concept detection performance in terms of F_1 scores.

Team	Run	$MeanF_1$
UA.PT_Bioinformatics	aae-500-o0-2018-04-30_1217	0.1108
UA.PT_Bioinformatics	aae-2500-merge-2018-04-30_1812	0.1082
UA.PT_Bioinformatics	lin-orb-500-o0-2018-04-30_1142	0.0978
ImageSem	run10extended_results_concept_1000_steps_25000_learningrate_0.03_batch_20	0.0928
ImageSem	run02extended_results-testdata	0.0909
ImageSem	run4more1000	0.0907
ImageSem	run01candidate_image_test_0.005	0.0894
ImageSem	run05extended_results_concept_1000_top20	0.0828
UA.PT_Bioinformatics	faae-500-o0-2018-04-27_1744	0.0825
ImageSem	run06top2000_extended_results	0.0661
UA.PT_Bioinformatics	knn-ip-aae-train-2018-04-27_1259	0.0569
UA.PT_Bioinformatics	knn-aae-all-2018-04-26_1233	0.0559
IPL	DET_IPL_CLEF2018_w_300_annot_70_gboc_200	0.0509
UMass	result_concept_new	0.0418
AILAB	results_v3	0.0415
IPL	DET_IPL_CLEF2018_w_300_annot_40_gboc_200	0.0406
AILAB	results	0.0405
IPL	DET_IPL_CLEF2018_w_300_annot_30_gboc_200	0.0351
UA.PT_Bioinformatics	knn-orb-all-2018-04-24_1620	0.0314
IPL	DET_IPL_CLEF2018_w_200_annot_30_gboc_200	0.0307
UA.PT_Bioinformatics	knn-ip-faae-all-2018-04-27_1512	0.0280
UA.PT_Bioinformatics	knn-ip-faae-all-2018-04-27_1512	0.0272
IPL	DET_IPL_CLEF2018_w_200_annot_20_gboc_200	0.0244
IPL	DET_IPL_CLEF2018_w_200_annot_15_gboc_200	0.0202
IPL	DET_IPL_CLEF2018_w_100_annot_20_gboc_100	0.0161
AILAB	results_v3	0.0151
IPL	DET_IPL_CLEF2018_w_200_annot_5_gboc_200	0.0080
ImageSem	run03candidate_image_test_0.005douhao	0.0001

ImageSem [41] was the only group applying a retrieval approach this year achieving 0.0928 in terms of mean F1 scores. They retrieved similar images from the training set and clustered concepts of those images. The multi–modal classification approach was more popular [27, 28, 38]. Best results were achieved by UA.PT Bioinformatics [27] using a traditional bag-of-visual-words algorithm. They experimented with logistic regression and k-Nearest Neighbors (k-NN) for the classification step. Morgan State University [28] used a deep learning based approach by using both image and text (caption) features of the training set for modeling. However, instead of using the full 220K-image collection, they relied on a subset of 4K images, applying the Keras[5] framework to generate deep learning based features. IPL [38] used and encoder of the ARAE [44] model creating a textual representation for all captions. In addition, the images were mapped to continuous representation space with a CNN.

---

[5] https://keras.io/.

Table 3. Caption prediction performance in terms of BLEU scores.

Team	Run	Mean BLEU
ImageSem	run04Captionstraining	0.2501
ImageSem	run09Captionstraining	0.2343
ImageSem	run13Captionstraining	0.2278
ImageSem	run19Captionstraining	0.2271
ImageSem	run03Captionstraining	0.2244
ImageSem	run07Captionstraining	0.2228
ImageSem	run08Captionstraining	0.2221
ImageSem	run06Captionstraining	0.1963
UMMS	test_captions_output4_13_epoch	0.1799
UMMS	test_captions_output2_12_epoch	0.1763
Morgan	result_caption	0.1725
UMMS	test_captions_output1	0.1696
UMMS	test_captions_output5_13_epoch	0.1597
UMMS	test_captions_output3_13_epoch	0.1428
KU Leuven	23_test_valres_0.134779058389_out_file_greedy	0.1376
WHU	CaptionPredictionTesting-Results-zgb	0.0446

In the Caption Prediction subtask, ImageSem [41] achieved the best results using an image retrieval strategy and tuning the parameters such as the most similar images and the number of candidate concepts. The other 4 groups used different deep learning approaches in very interesting ways from generating captions word by word or in sequences of words. Morgan State University [28] and WHU used a long short-term memory (LSTM) network while UMass [33] and KU Leuven [32] applied different CCNs.

After discussions in the 2017 submissions where groups used external data and possibly included part of the test data, no group augmented the training set in 2018. It is further noticeable that, despite the dataset being less noisy than in 2018, the achieved results were slightly lower than observed in the previous year, in both tasks.

3.5 Lessons Learned and Next Steps

Interestingly and despite this year's focus on radiology modalities, a large number of target concepts was extracted in the training set. Such settings with hundreds of thousands of classes are extremely challenging and fall into the realm of extreme classification methods. In future editions of the task, we plan to focus on detecting only the most commonly used UMLS concepts and truncate the concept distribution in order to shift the intellectual challenge away from extreme or one-shot classification settings that were not originally meant to be the key challenge in this task.

The new filtering for finding images with lower variability and fewer combined figures helped to make the task more realistic and considering the difficulty of the task the results are actually fairly good.

Most techniques used relied on deep learning but best results were often obtained also with other techniques, such as using retrieval and handcrafted features. This may be due to the large number of concepts and in this case limited amount of training data. As PMC is increasing in size very quickly it should be easy to find more data for future contests.

4   The Tuberculosis Task

Tuberculosis (TB) remains a persistent threat and a leading cause of death worldwide also in recent years with multiple new strains appearing worldwide. Recent studies report a rapid increase of drug-resistant cases [29] meaning that the TB organisms become resistant to two or more of the standard drugs. One of the most dangerous forms of drug-resistant TB is so-called multi-drug resistant (MDR) tuberculosis that is simultaneously resistant to several of the most powerful antibiotics. Recent published reports show statistically significant links between drug resistance and multiple thick-walled caverns [42]. However, the discovered links are not sufficient for a reliable early recognition of MDR TB. Therefore, assessing the feasibility of MDR detection based on Computed Tomography (CT) imaging remains an important but very challenging task. Other tasks proposed in the ImageCLEF 2018 tuberculosis challenge are automatic classification of TB types and TB severity scoring using CT volumes.

4.1   Task Setup

Three subtasks were proposed in the ImageCLEF 2018 tuberculosis task [11]:

- Multi-drug resistance detection (MDR subtask);
- Tuberculosis type classification (TBT subtask);
- Tuberculosis severity scoring (SVR subtask).

The goal of the MDR subtask is to assess the probability of a TB patient having a resistant form of tuberculosis based on the analysis of a chest CT. Compared to 2017, datasets for the MDR detection subtask were extended by means of adding several cases with extensively drug-resistant tuberculosis (XDR TB), which is a rare and the most severe subtype of MDR TB.

Table 4. Dataset for the MDR subtask.

# Patients	Train	Test
DS	134	99
MDR	125	137
Total patients	259	236

Table 5. Dataset for the TBT subtask.

# Patients (# CTs)	Train	Test
Type 1 – Infiltrative	228 (376)	89 (176)
Type 2 – Focal	210 (273)	80 (115)
Type 3 – Tuberculoma	100 (154)	60 (86)
Type 4 – Miliary	79 (106)	50 (71)
Type 5 – Fibro-cavernous	60 (99)	38 (57)
Total patients (CTs)	677 (1008)	317 (505)

Table 6. Dataset for the SVR subtask.

# Patients	Train	Test
Low severity	90	62
High severity	80	47
Total patients	170	109

The goal of the TBT subtask is to automatically categorize each TB case into one of the following five types: Infiltrative, Focal, Tuberculoma, Miliary, and Fibro-cavernous. The SVR subtask is dedicated to assess the TB severity based on a single CT image of a patient. The severity score is the results of a cumulative score of TB severity assigned by a medical doctor.

4.2   Dataset

For all three subtasks 3D CT volumes were provided with a size of 512×512 pixels and number of slices varying from 50 to 400. All CT images were stored in the NIFTI file format with .nii.gz file extension (g-zipped .nii files). This file format stores raw voxel intensities in Hounsfield Units (HU) as well as the corresponding image metadata such as image dimensions, voxel size in physical units, slice thickness, etc. For all patients automatically extracted masks of the lungs were provided. The details of the lung segmentation used can be found in [9].

Tables 4, 5 and 6 present for each of the subtasks the division of the datasets between training and test sets (columns), and the corresponding ground truth labels (rows). The dataset for the MDR subtask was composed of 262 MDR and 233 Drug-Sensitive (DS) patients, as shown in Table 4. In addition to CT image data, age and gender for each patient were provided for this subtask. The TBT task contained in total 1,513 CT scans of 994 unique patients divided as shown in Table 5. Patient metadata includes only age. The dataset for the SVR subtask was represented by a total number of 279 patients with a TB severity score assigned for each case by medical doctors. The scores were presented as numbers from 1 to 5, so for a regression task. In addition, for the 2-class prediction task the severity labels were binarized so that scores from 1 to 3 corresponded to "high severity" and 4–5 corresponded to "low severity" (see Table 6).

4.3 Participating Groups and Submitted Runs

In the second year of the task, 11 groups from 9 countries submitted at least one run to one of the subtasks. There were 7 groups participating in the MDR subtask, 8 in the TBT subtask, and 7 groups participating in the SVR subtask. Each group could submit up to 10 runs. Finally, 39 runs were submitted by the groups in the MDR subtask, 39 in the TBT and 36 in the SVR subtasks. Several Deep Learning approaches were employed by 8 out of the 11 participating groups. The approaches were based on using 2D and 3D Convolutional Neural Networks (CNNs) for both classification and feature extraction, transfer learning and a few other techniques. In addition, one group used texture-based graph models of the lungs, one group used texture-based features combined with classifiers and one group used features based on image binarization and morphology.

4.4 Results

The MDR subtask is designed as a 2-class problem. The participants submitted for each patient in the test set the probability of belonging to the MDR group. The Area Under the ROC Curve (AUC) was chosen as the measure to rank the results. The accuracy was provided as well. For the TBT subtask, the participants had to submit the tuberculosis type. Since the 5-class problem was not balanced, Cohen's Kappa[6] coefficient was used to compare the methods. Again, the accuracy was provided for this subtask. Finally, the SVR subtask was considered in two ways: as a regression problem with scores from 1 to 5, and as a 2-class classification problem (low/high severity). The regression problem was evaluated using Root Mean Square Error (RMSE), and AUC was used to evaluate the classification approaches. Tables 7, 8 and 9 show the final results for each run and its rank.

---

[6] https://en.wikipedia.org/wiki/Cohen's_kappa.

Table 7. Results for the MDR subtask.

Group Name	Run	AUC	Rank AUC	Acc	Rank Acc
VISTA@UEvora	MDR-Run-06-Mohan-SL-F3-Personal.txt	0.6178	1	0.5593	8
San Diego VA HCS/UCSD	MDSTest1a.csv	0.6114	2	0.6144	1
VISTA@UEvora	MDR-Run-08-Mohan-voteLdaSmoF7-Personal.txt	0.6065	3	0.5424	17
VISTA@UEvora	MDR-Run-09-Sk-SL-F10-Personal.txt	0.5921	4	0.5763	3
VISTA@UEvora	MDR-Run-10-Mix-voteLdaSl-F7-Personal.txt	0.5824	5	0.5593	9
HHU-DBS	MDR_FlattenCNN_DTree.txt	0.5810	6	0.5720	4
HHU-DBS	MDR_FlattenCNN2_DTree.txt	0.5810	7	0.5720	5
HHU-DBS	MDR_Conv68adam_fl.txt	0.5768	8	0.5593	10
VISTA@UEvora	MDR-Run-07-Sk-LDA-F7-Personal.txt	0.5730	9	0.5424	18
UniversityAlicante	MDRBaseline0.csv	0.5669	10	0.4873	32
HHU-DBS	MDR_Conv48sgd.txt	0.5640	11	0.5466	16
HHU-DBS	MDR_Flatten.txt	0.5637	12	0.5678	7
HHU-DBS	MDR_Flatten3.txt	0.5575	13	0.5593	11
UIIP_BioMed	MDR_run_TBdescs2_zparts3_thrprob50_rf150.csv	0.5558	14	0.4576	36
UniversityAlicante	testSVM_SMOTE.csv	0.5509	15	0.5339	20
UniversityAlicante	testOpticalFlowwFrequencyNormalized.csv	0.5473	16	0.5127	24
HHU-DBS	MDR_Conv48sgd_fl.txt	0.5424	17	0.5508	15
HHU-DBS	MDR_CustomCNN_DTree.txt	0.5346	18	0.5085	26
HHU-DBS	MDR_FlattenX.txt	0.5322	19	0.5127	25
HHU-DBS	MDR_MultiInputCNN.txt	0.5274	20	0.5551	13
VISTA@UEvora	MDR-Run-01-sk-LDA.txt	0.5260	21	0.5042	28
MedGIFT	MDR_Riesz_std_correlation_TST.csv	0.5237	22	0.5593	12
MedGIFT	MDR_HOG_std_euclidean_TST.csv	0.5205	23	0.5932	2
VISTA@UEvora	MDR-Run-05-Mohan-RF-F3I650.txt	0.5116	24	0.4958	30
MedGIFT	MDR_AllFeats_std_correlation_TST.csv	0.5095	25	0.4873	33
UniversityAlicante	DecisionTree25v2.csv	0.5049	26	0.5000	29
MedGIFT	MDR_AllFeats_std_euclidean_TST.csv	0.5039	27	0.5424	19
LIST	MDRLIST.txt	0.5029	28	0.4576	37
UniversityAlicante	testOFFullVersion2.csv	0.4971	29	0.4958	31
MedGIFT	MDR_HOG_mean_correlation_TST.csv	0.4941	30	0.5551	14
MedGIFT	MDR_Riesz_AllCols_correlation_TST.csv	0.4855	31	0.5212	22
UniversityAlicante	testOpticalFlowFull.csv	0.4845	32	0.5169	23
MedGIFT	MDR_Riesz_mean_euclidean_TST.csv	0.4824	33	0.5297	21
UniversityAlicante	testFrequency.csv	0.4781	34	0.4788	34
UniversityAlicante	testflow1.csv	0.4740	35	0.4492	39
MedGIFT	MDR_HOG_AllCols_euclidean_TST.csv	0.4693	36	0.5720	6
VISTA@UEvora	MDR-Run-06-Sk-SL.txt	0.4661	37	0.4619	35
MedGIFT	MDR_AllFeats_AllCols_correlation_TST.csv	0.4568	38	0.5085	27
VISTA@UEvora	MDR-Run-04-Mix-Vote-L-RT-RF.txt	0.4494	39	0.4576	38

4.5   Lessons Learned and Next Steps

Similarly to 2017 [10], in the MDR task all participants achieved a relatively low performance, which is only slightly higher than the performance of a random classifier. The best accuracy achieved by participants was 0.6144, and the best reached AUC was 0.6178. These results are better than in the previous years but still remain unsatisfactory for clinical use. The overall increase of performance compared to 2017 may be partly explained by the introduction of patient age and gender, and also by adding more severe cases with XDR TB. For the TBT subtask, the results are slightly worse compared to 2017 in terms of Cohen's Kappa with the best run scoring a 0.2312 Kappa value (0.2438 in 2017) and slightly better with respect to the best accuracy of 0.4227 (0.4067 in 2017). It is worth to notice that none of the groups achieving best performance in the

Table 8. Results for the TBT subtask.

Group Name	Run	Kappa	Rank Kappa	Acc	Rank Acc
UIIP_BioMed	TBT_run_TBdescs2_zparts3_thrprob50_rf150.csv	0.2312	1	0.4227	1
fau_ml4cv	TBT_m4_weighted.txt	0.1736	2	0.3533	10
MedGIFT	TBT_AllFeats_std_euclidean_TST.csv	0.1706	3	0.3849	2
MedGIFT	TBT_Riesz_AllCols_euclidean_TST.csv	0.1674	4	0.3849	3
VISTA@UEvora	TBT-Run-02-Mohan-RF-F20I1500S20-317.txt	0.1664	5	0.3785	4
fau_ml4cv	TBT_m3_weighted.txt	0.1655	6	0.3438	12
VISTA@UEvora	TBT-Run-05-Mohan-RF-F20I2000S20.txt	0.1621	7	0.3754	5
MedGIFT	TBT_AllFeats_AllCols_correlation_TST.csv	0.1531	8	0.3691	7
MedGIFT	TBT_AllFeats_mean_euclidean_TST.csv	0.1517	9	0.3628	8
MedGIFT	TBT_Riesz_std_euclidean_TST.csv	0.1494	10	0.3722	6
San Diego VA HCS/UCSD	Task2Submission64a.csv	0.1474	11	0.3375	13
San Diego VA HCS/UCSD	TBTTask_2_128.csv	0.1454	12	0.3312	15
MedGIFT	TBT_AllFeats_AllCols_correlation_TST.csv	0.1356	13	0.3628	9
VISTA@UEvora	TBT-Run-03-Mohan-RF-7FF20I1500S20-Age.txt	0.1335	14	0.3502	11
San Diego VA HCS/UCSD	TBTLast.csv	0.1251	15	0.3155	20
fau_ml4cv	TBT_w_combined.txt	0.1112	16	0.3028	22
VISTA@UEvora	TBT-Run-06-Mix-RF-5FF20I2000S20.txt	0.1005	17	0.3312	16
VISTA@UEvora	TBT-Run-04-Mohan-VoteRFLMT-7F.txt	0.0998	18	0.3186	19
MedGIFT	TBT_HOG_AllCols_euclidean_TST.csv	0.0949	19	0.3344	14
fau_ml4cv	TBT_combined.txt	0.0898	20	0.2997	23
MedGIFT	TBT_HOG_std_correlation_TST.csv	0.0855	21	0.3218	18
fau_ml4cv	TBT_m2p01_small.txt	0.0839	22	0.2965	25
MedGIFT	TBT_AllFeats_std_correlation_TST.csv	0.0787	23	0.3281	17
fau_ml4cv	TBT_m2.txt	0.0749	24	0.2997	24
MostaganemFSEI	TBT_mostaganemFSEI_run4.txt	0.0629	25	0.2744	27
MedGIFT	TBT_HOG_std_correlation_TST.csv	0.0589	26	0.3060	21
fau_ml4cv	TBT_modelsimple_lmbdap1_norm.txt	0.0504	27	0.2839	26
MostaganemFSEI	TBT_mostaganemFSEI_run1.txt	0.0412	28	0.2650	29
MostaganemFSEI	TBT_MostaganemFSEI_run2.txt	0.0275	29	0.2555	32
MostaganemFSEI	TBT_MostaganemFSEI_run6.txt	0.0210	30	0.2429	33
UniversityAlicante	3nnconProbabilidad2.txt	0.0204	31	0.2587	30
UniversityAlicante	T23nnFinal.txt	0.0204	32	0.2587	31
fau_ml4cv	TBT_m1.txt	0.0202	33	0.2713	28
LIST	TBTLIST.txt	-0.0024	34	0.2366	34
MostaganemFSEI	TBT_mostaganemFSEI_run3.txt	-0.0260	35	0.1514	37
VISTA@UEvora	TBT-Run-01-sk-LDA-Update-317-New.txt	-0.0398	36	0.2240	35
VISTA@UEvora	TBT-Run-01-sk-LDA-Update-317.txt	-0.0634	37	0.1956	36
UniversityAlicante	T2SVMFinal.txt	-0.0920	38	0.1167	38
UniversityAlicante	SVMirene.txt	-0.0923	39	0.1136	39

2017 edition participated in 2018. The group obtaining best results in this task this year (the UIIP group) obtained a 0.1956 Kappa value and 0.3900 accuracy in the 2017 edition. This shows a strong improvement, possibly linked to the increased size of the dataset. The newly-introduced SVR subtask demonstrated good performance in both regression and classification problems. The best result in terms of regression achieved a 0.7840 RMSE, which is less than 1 grade of error in a 5-grade scoring system. The best classification run demonstrated a 0.7708 AUC. These results are promising taking into consideration the fact that TB severity was scored by doctors using not only CT images but also additional clinical data. The good participation also highlights the importance of the task.

Table 9. Results for the SVR subtask.

Group Name	Run	RMSE	Rank RMSE	AUC	Rank AUC
UIIP_BioMed	SVR_run_TBdescs2_zparts3_thrprob50_rf100.csv	0.7840	1	0.7025	6
MedGIFT	SVR_HOG_std_euclidean_TST.csv	0.8513	2	0.7162	5
VISTA@UEvora	SVR-Run-07-Mohan-MLP-6FTT100.txt	0.8883	3	0.6239	21
MedGIFT	SVR_AllFeats_AllCols_euclidean_TST.csv	0.8883	4	0.6733	10
MedGIFT	SVR_AllFeats_AllCols_correlation_TST.csv	0.8934	5	0.7708	1
MedGIFT	SVR_HOG_mean_euclidean_TST.csv	0.8985	6	0.7443	3
MedGIFT	SVR_HOG_mean_correlation_TST.csv	0.9237	7	0.6450	18
MedGIFT	SVR_HOG_AllCols_euclidean_TST.csv	0.9433	8	0.7268	4
MedGIFT	SVR_HOG_AllCols_correlation_TST.csv	0.9433	9	0.7608	2
HHU-DBS	SVR_RanFrst.txt	0.9626	10	0.6484	16
MedGIFT	SVR_Riesz_AllCols_correlation_TST.csv	0.9626	11	0.5535	34
MostaganemFSEI	SVR_mostaganemFSEI_run3.txt	0.9721	12	0.5987	25
HHU-DBS	SVR_RanFRST_depth_2_new_new.txt	0.9768	13	0.6620	13
HHU-DBS	SVR_LinReg_part.txt	0.9768	14	0.6507	15
MedGIFT	SVR_AllFeats_mean_euclidean_TST.csv	0.9954	15	0.6644	12
MostaganemFSEI	SVR_mostaganemFSEI_run6.txt	1.0046	16	0.6119	23
VISTA@UEvora	SVR-Run-03-Mohan-MLP.txt	1.0091	17	0.6371	19
MostaganemFSEI	SVR_mostaganemFSEI_run4.txt	1.0137	18	0.6107	24
MostaganemFSEI	SVR_mostaganemFSEI_run1.txt	1.0227	19	0.5971	26
MedGIFT	SVR_Riesz_std_correlation_TST.csv	1.0492	20	0.5841	29
VISTA@UEvora	SVR-Run-06-Mohan-VoteMLPSL-5F.txt	1.0536	21	0.6356	20
VISTA@UEvora	SVR-Run-02-Mohan-RF.txt	1.0580	22	0.5813	31
MostaganemFSEI	SVR_mostaganemFSEI_run2.txt	1.0837	23	0.6127	22
Middlesex University	SVR-Gao-May4.txt	1.0921	24	0.6534	14
HHU-DBS	SVR_RanFRST_depth_2_Ludmila_new_new.txt	1.1046	25	0.6862	8
VISTA@UEvora	SVR-Run-05-Mohan-RF-3FI300S20.txt	1.1046	26	0.5812	32
VISTA@UEvora	SVR-Run-04-Mohan-RF-F5-I300-S200.txt	1.1088	27	0.5793	33
VISTA@UEvora	SVR-Run-01-sk-LDA.txt	1.1770	28	0.5918	27
HHU-DBS	SVR_RanFRST_depth_2_new.txt	1.2040	29	0.6484	17
San Diego VA HCS/UCSD	SVR9.csv	1.2153	30	0.6658	11
San Diego VA HCS/UCSD	SVRSubmission.txt	1.2153	31	0.6984	7
HHU-DBS	SVR_DTree_Features_Best_Bin.txt	1.3203	32	0.5402	36
HHU-DBS	SVR_DTree_Features_Best.txt	1.3203	33	0.5848	28
HHU-DBS	SVR_DTree_Features_Best_All.txt	1.3714	34	0.6750	9
MostaganemFSEI	SVR_mostaganemFSEI.txt	1.4207	35	0.5836	30
Middlesex University	SVR-Gao-April27.txt	1.5145	36	0.5412	35

5   The VQA-Med Task

5.1   Task Description

Visual Question Answering is a new and exciting problem that combines natural language processing and computer vision techniques. Inspired by the recent success of visual question answering in the general domain[7] [3], we propose a pilot task to focus on visual question answering in the medical domain (VQA-Med). Given medical images accompanied with clinically relevant questions, participating systems were tasked with answering questions based on the visual image content. Figure 2 shows a few example images with associated questions and ground truth answers.

---

[7] http://www.visualqa.org/.

Table 10. Participating groups in the VQA-Med task.

Team	Institution	# Runs
FSTT	Abdelmalek Essaadi University, Faculty of Sciences and Techniques, Tangier, Morocco	2
JUST	Jordan University of Science and Technology, Jordan	3
NLM	Lister Hill National Center for Biomedical Communications, National Library of Medicine, Bethesda, MD, USA	5
TU	Tokushima University, Japan	3
UMMS	University of Massachusetts Medical School, Worcester, MA, USA	4

5.2   Dataset

We considered medical images along with their captions extracted from PubMed Central articles[8] (essentially a subset of the ImageCLEF 2017 caption prediction task [13]) to create the datasets for the proposed VQA-Med task.

We used a semi-automatic approach to generate question-answer pairs from captions of the medical images. First, we automatically generated all possible question-answer pairs from captions using a rule-based question generation (QG) system[9]. The candidate questions generated via the automatic approach contained noise due to rule mismatch with the clinical domain sentences. Therefore, two expert human annotators manually checked all generated question-answer pairs associated with the medical images in two passes. In the first pass, syntactic and semantic correctness were ensured while in the second pass, well-curated validation and test sets were generated by verifying the clinical relevance of the questions with respect to associated medical images.

The final curated corpus was comprised of 6,413 question-answer pairs associated with 2,866 medical images. The overall set was split into 5,413 question-answer pairs (associated with 2,278 medical images) for training, 500 question-answer pairs (associated with 324 medical images) for validation, and 500 questions (associated with 264 medical images) for testing.

5.3   Participating Groups and Runs Submitted

Out of 58 online registrations, 28 participants submitted signed end user agreement forms. Finally, 5 groups submitted a total of 17 runs, indicating a considerable interest in the VQA-Med task. Table 10 gives an overview of all participants and the number of submitted runs[10].

---

[8] https://www.ncbi.nlm.nih.gov/pmc/.
[9] http://www.cs.cmu.edu/~ark/mheilman/questions/.
[10] There was a limit of maximum 5 run submissions per team.

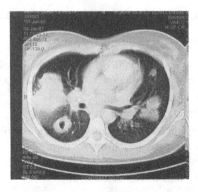

Question: What does the CT scan of thorax show?
Answer: bilateral multiple pulmonary nodules

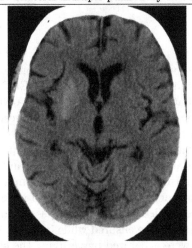

Question: Is the lesion associated with a mass effect?
Answer: no

Fig. 2. Example images with question-answer pairs in the VQA-Med task.

5.4   Results

The evaluation of the participant systems of the VQA-Med task was conducted based on three metrics: BLEU, WBSS (Word-based Semantic Similarity), and CBSS (Concept-based Semantic Similarity) [19]. BLEU [26] is used to capture the similarity between a system-generated answer and the ground truth answer. The overall methodology and resources for the BLEU metric are essentially similar to the ImageCLEF 2017 caption prediction task[11]. The WBSS metric is created based on Wu-Palmer Similarity (WUPS[12]) [43] with WordNet ontology

---

[11] http://www.imageclef.org/2017/caption.
[12] https://datasets.d2.mpi-inf.mpg.de/mateusz14visualturing/calculate_wups.py.

Table 11. Scores of all submitted runs in the VQA-Med task.

(a) BLEU			(b) WBSS			(c) CBSS		
Team	Run ID	BLEU	Team	Run ID	WBSS	Team	Run ID	CBSS
UMMS	6113	0.162	UMMS	6069	0.186	NLM	6120	0.338
UMMS	5980	0.160	UMMS	6113	0.185	TU	5521	0.334
UMMS	6069	0.158	UMMS	5980	0.184	TU	5994	0.330
UMMS	6091	0.155	UMMS	6091	0.181	NLM	6087	0.327
TU	5994	0.135	NLM	6084	0.174	TU	6033	0.324
NLM	6084	0.121	TU	5994	0.174	FSTT	6183	0.269
NLM	6135	0.108	NLM	6135	0.168	FSTT	6220	0.262
TU	5521	0.106	TU	5521	0.160	NLM	6136	0.035
NLM	6136	0.106	NLM	6136	0.157	NLM	6084	0.033
TU	6033	0.103	TU	6033	0.148	NLM	6135	0.032
NLM	6120	0.085	NLM	6120	0.144	JUST	6086	0.029
NLM	6087	0.083	NLM	6087	0.130	UMMS	6069	0.023
JUST	6086	0.061	JUST	6086	0.122	UMMS	5980	0.021
FSTT	6183	0.054	JUST	6038	0.104	UMMS	6091	0.017
JUST	6038	0.048	FSTT	6183	0.101	UMMS	6113	0.016
JUST	6134	0.036	JUST	6134	0.094	JUST	6038	0.015
FSTT	6220	0.028	FSTT	6220	0.080	JUST	6134	0.011

in the backend by following a recent algorithm to calculate semantic similarity in the biomedical domain [31]. WBSS computes a similarity score between a system-generated answer and the ground truth answer based on word-level similarity. CBSS is similar to WBSS, except that instead of tokenizing the system-generated and ground truth answers into words, we use MetaMap[13] via the pymetamap wrapper[14] to extract biomedical concepts from the answers, and build a dictionary using these concepts. Then, we build one-hot vector representations of the answers to calculate their semantic similarity using the cosine similarity measure.

The overall results of the participating systems are presented in Table 11a to c for the three metrics in a descending order of the scores (the higher the better).

5.5   Lessons Learned and Next Steps

In general, participants used deep learning techniques to build their VQA-Med systems [19]. In particular, participant systems leveraged sequence to sequence learning and encoder-decoder-based frameworks utilizing deep convolutional neural networks (CNN) to encode medical images and recurrent neural networks

---

[13] https://metamap.nlm.nih.gov/.
[14] https://github.com/AnthonyMRios/pymetamap.

(RNN) to generate question encoding. Some participants used attention-based mechanisms to identify relevant image features to answer the given questions. The submitted runs also varied with the use of various VQA networks such as stacked attention networks (SAN), the use of advanced techniques such as multimodal compact bilinear (MCB) pooling or multimodal factorized bilinear (MFB) pooling to combine multimodal features, the use of different hyperparameters etc. Participants did not use any additional datasets except the official training and validation sets to train their models.

The relatively low BLEU scores and WBSS scores of the runs in the results table denote the difficulty of the VQA-Med task in generating similar answers as the ground truth, while higher CBSS scores suggest that some participants were able to generate relevant clinical concepts in their answers similar to the clinical concepts present in the ground truth answers. To leverage the power of advanced deep learning algorithms towards improving the state-of-the-art in visual question answering in the medical domain, we plan to increase the dataset size in the future editions of this task.

6   The Lifelog Task

6.1   Motivation and Task Setup

An increasingly wide range of personal devices, such as smart phones, video cameras as well as wearable devices that allow capturing pictures, videos, and audio clips pf every moment of life have now become inseparable companions and, considering the huge volume of data created, there is an urgent need for systems that can automatically analyze the data in order to categorize, summarize and also retrieve information that the user may require. This kind of data, commonly referred to as *lifelogs*, gathered increasing attention in recent years within the research community above all because of the precious information that can be extracted from this kind of data and for the remarkable effects in the technological and social field.

Despite the increasing number of successful related workshops and panels (e.g., JCDL 2015[15], iConf 2016[16], ACM MM 2016[17], ACM MM 2017[18]) lifelogging has seldom been the subject of a rigorous comparative benchmarking exercise as, for example, the lifelog evaluation task at NTCIR-14[19] or last year's edition of the ImageCLEFlifelog task [6]. Also in this second edition of the task we aim to bring the attention of lifelogging to a wider audience and to promote research into some of its key challenges such as on multi-modal analysis of large data collections. The ImageCLEF 2018 LifeLog task [7] aims to be a comparative evaluation of information access and retrieval systems operating over personal

---

[15] http://www.jcdl.org/archived-conf-sites/jcdl2015/www.jcdl2015.org/panels.html.
[16] http://irlld2016.computing.dcu.ie/index.html.
[17] http://lta2016.computing.dcu.ie.
[18] http://lta2017.computing.dcu.ie.
[19] http://ntcir-lifelog.computing.dcu.ie.

lifelog data. The task consists of two sub-tasks and both allow participation independently. These sub-tasks are:

- Lifelog moment retrieval (LMRT);
- Activities of Daily Living understanding (ADLT).

Lifelog Moment Retrieval Task (LMRT)
The participants have to retrieve a number of specific moments in a lifelogger's life. "Moments" were defined as semantic events or activities that happened throughout the day. For example, participants should return the relevant moments for the query *"Find the moment(s) when I was shopping for wine in the supermarket."* Particular attention should be paid to the diversification of the selected moments with respect to the target scenario. The ground truth for this subtask was created using manual annotation.

Activities of Daily Living Understanding Task (ADLT)
The participants should analyze the lifelog data from a given period of time (e.g., *"From August 13 to August 16"* or *"Every Saturday"*) and provide a summarization based on the selected concepts provided by the task organizers of Activities of Daily Living (ADL) and the environmental settings/contexts in which these activities take place.

In the following it is possible to see some examples of ADL concepts:

- *"Commuting (to work or another common venue)"*
- *"Traveling (to a destination other than work, home or another common social event)"*
- *"Preparing meals (include making tea or coffee)"*
- *"Eating/drinking"*

Some examples of contexts are:

- *"In an office environment"*
- *"In a home"*
- *"In an open space"*

The summarization is described as the total duration and the number of times the queried concepts happens.

- ADL: "Eating/drinking: 6 times, 90 min", "Traveling: 1 time, 60 min".
- Context: "In an office environment: 500 min", "In a church: 30 min".

6.2   Dataset Employed

This year a completely new multimodal dataset was provided to participants. This consists of 50 days of data from a lifelogger. The data contain a large collection of wearable camera images (1,500–2,500 per day), visual concepts (automatically extracted visual concepts with varying rates of accuracy), semantic content (semantic locations, semantic activities) based on sensor readings (via

Table 12. Statistics of ImageCLEFlifelog2018 Dataset.

Size of the collection	**18.854** GB
Number of images	**80,440** images
Number of known locations	**135** locations
Concepts	Fully annotated (by Microsoft Computer Vision API)
Biometrics	Fully provided (24 × 7)
Human activities	Provided
Number of ADLT topics	**20** (10 for devset, 10 for testset)
Number of LMRT topics	**20** (10 for devset, 10 for testset)

the Moves App) on mobile devices, biometric information (heart rate, galvanic skin response, calorie burn, steps, etc.), music listening history. The dataset is built based on the data available for the NTCIR-13 - Lifelog 2 task [16]. A summary of the data collection is shown in Table 12.

Evaluation Methodology

For assessing performance in the *Lifelog moment retrieval task* classic metrics were employed. These metrics are:

- Cluster Recall at $X(CR@X)$—a metric that assesses how many different clusters from the ground truth are represented among the top X results;
- Precision at $X(P@X)$—measures the number of relevant photos among the top X results;
- F1-measure at $X(F1@X)$—the harmonic mean of the previous two measures.

Various cut off points were considered, e.g., $X = 5, 10, 20, 30, 40, 50$. Official ranking metric this year was the **F1-measure@10**, which gives equal importance to diversity (via $CR@10$) and relevance (via $P@10$).

Participants were allowed to undertake the sub-tasks in an interactive or automatic manner. For interactive submissions, a maximum of five minutes of search time is allowed per topic. In particular, the organizers would like to emphasize methods that allow interaction with real users (via Relevance Feedback, RF, for example), i.e., beside the best performance, the method of interaction (e.g. the number of iterations using relevance feedback), or innovation level of the method (for example, new way to interact with real users) are encouraged.

In the *Activities of daily living understanding*, the evaluation metric is the percentage of dissimilarity between the ground-truth and the submitted values, measured as average of the time and minute differences, as follows:

$$ADL_{score} = \frac{1}{2} \left(max(0, 1 - \frac{|n - n_{gt}|}{n_{gt}}) + max(0, 1 - \frac{|m - m_{gt}|}{m_{gt}}) \right)$$

where n, n_{gt} are the submitted and ground-truth values for how many times the events occurred, respectively, and m, m_{gt} are the submitted and ground-truth values for how long (in minutes) the events happened, respectively.

Table 13. Submitted runs for ImageCLEFlifelog2018 LMRT task.

Team	Run name	F1@10
Organizers [45]	Run 1*	0.077
	Run 2*	0.131
	Run 3*,†	0.407
	Run 4*,†	0.378
	Run 5*,†	0.365
AILab-GTI [24]	Subm#1	0.504
	Subm#2	**0.545**
	Subm#3	0.477
	Subm#4	0.536
	Subm#5	0.477
	Subm#6	0.480
	exps5	0.512
	Subm#0†	0.542
Regim Lab [1]	Run 1	0.065
	Run 2	0.364
	Run 3	0.411
	Run 4	0.411
	Run 5	0.424
NLP-Lab [34]	Run 1	0.177
	Run 3	0.223
	Run 4	0.395
	Run 5	0.354
HCMUS [35]	Run 1	0.355
	Run 2	0.479
CAMPUS-UPB [12]	Run 1	0.216
	Run 2†	0.169
	Run 3†	0.168
	Run 4†	0.166
	Run 5†	0.443

Notes: *Submissions from the organizer teams are just for reference.
†Submissions submitted after the official competition.

6.3 Participating Groups and Runs Submitted

This year the number of participants was considerably higher with respect to 2017: we received in total 41 runs: 29 (21 official, 8 additional) for LMRT and 12 (8 official, 4 additional) for ADLT, from 7 teams from Brunei, Taiwan, Vietnam,

Table 14. Submitted runs for ImageCLEFlifelog2018 ADLT task.

Team	Run name	Score (% dissimilarity)
Organizers [45]	Run 1[*]	0.816
	Run 2[*,†]	0.456
	Run 3[*,†]	0.344
	Run 4[*,†]	0.481
	Run 5[*,†]	0.485
CIE@UTB [8]	Run 1	**0.556**
NLP-Lab [34]	Run 1	0.243
	Run 2	0.285
	Run 3	0.385
	Run 4	0.459
	Run 5	0.479
HCMUS [35]	Run 1	0.059

Notes: [*]Submissions from the organizer teams are just for reference.
[†]Submissions submitted after the official competition.

Greece-Spain, Tunisia, Romania, and a multi-nation team from Ireland, Italy, Austria, and Norway. The received approaches range from fully automatic to fully manual, from using a single information source provided by the task to using all information as well as integrating additional resources, from traditional learning methods (e.g. SVMs) to deep learning and ad-hoc rules. Submitted runs and their results are summarized in Tables 13 and 14.

6.4   Lessons Learned and Next Steps

We learned that the majority of the approaches this year exploit and combine visual, text, location and other information to solve the task, which is different from last year when often only one type of data was analysed. Furthermore, we learned that lifelogging is following the trend in data analytics, meaning that participants are using deep learning in many cases. However, there still is room for improvement, since the best results are coming from the fine-tuned queries, which means we need more advanced techniques on bridging the gap between the abstract of human needs and the multi-modal data. Regarding the number of the signed-up teams and the submitted runs, we received a significant improvement compared to last year. This shows how interesting and challenging lifelog data is and that it holds much research potential. As next steps we do not plan to enrich the dataset but rather provide richer data and narrow down the application of the challenges (e.g., extend to health-care application).

7   Conclusions

This paper presents a general overview of the activities and outcomes of the ImageCLEF 2018 evaluation campaign. Four tasks were organised covering challenges in: caption prediction, tuberculosis type and drug resistance detection, medical visual question answering and lifelog retrieval.

The participation increased slightly compared to 2017, with over 130 signed user agreements, and in the end 31 groups submitting results. This is remarkable as three of the tasks are only in the second edition and one was in the first edition. Whereas several of the participants had participated in the past there was also a large number of groups totally new to ImageCLEF and also collaborations of research groups in several tasks.

As is now becoming commonplace, many of the participants employ deep neural networks to address all proposed tasks. In the tuberculosis task, the results in multi-drug resistance are still limited for practical use, though good performance was obtained in the new severity scoring subtask. In the visual question answering task the scores were relatively low, even though some approaches do seem to predict concepts present. In the lifelog task, in contrast to the previous year, several approaches used a combination of visual, text, location and other information.

The use of crowdAI was a change for many of the traditional participants and created many questions and also much work for the task organizers. On the other hand it is a much more modern platform that offers new possibilities, for example continuously running the challenge even beyond the workshop dates. The benefits of this will likely only be seen in the coming years.

ImageCLEF 2018 again brought together an interesting mix of tasks and approaches and we are looking forward to the fruitful discussions at the workshop.

Acknowledgements. Bogdan Ionescu—part of this work was supported by the Ministry of Innovation and Research, UEFISCDI, project SPIA-VA, agreement 2SOL/2017, grant PN-III-P2-2.1-SOL-2016-02-0002.

Duc-Tien Dang-Nguyen, Liting Zhou and Cathal Gurrin—part of this work has emanated from research supported in part by research grants from the Irish Research Council (IRC) under Grant Number GOIPG/2016/741 and Science Foundation Ireland (SFI) under grant number SFI/12/RC/2289.

References

1. Abdallah, F.B., Feki, G., Ezzarka, M., Ammar, A.B., Amar, C.B.: Regim Lab Team at ImageCLEFlifelog LMRT Task 2018, 10–14 September 2018
2. Andrearczyk, V., Henning, M.: Deep multimodal classification of image types in biomedical journal figures. In: Ferro, N., et al. (eds.) CLEF 2018. LNCS, vol. 11018, pp. 3–14. Springer, Cham (2018)
3. Antol, S., et al.: VQA: visual question answering. In: International Conference on Computer Vision (ICCV) (2015)

4. Balikas, G., Krithara, A., Partalas, I., Paliouras, G.: BioASQ: a challenge on large-scale biomedical semantic indexing and question answering. In: Müller, H., Jimenez del Toro, O.A., Hanbury, A., Langs, G., Foncubierta Rodríguez, A. (eds.) MRDM 2015. LNCS, vol. 9059, pp. 26–39. Springer, Cham (2015). https://doi.org/10.1007/978-3-319-24471-6_3

5. Clough, P., Müller, H., Sanderson, M.: The CLEF 2004 cross-language image retrieval track. In: Peters, C., Clough, P., Gonzalo, J., Jones, G.J.F., Kluck, M., Magnini, B. (eds.) CLEF 2004. LNCS, vol. 3491, pp. 597–613. Springer, Heidelberg (2005). https://doi.org/10.1007/11519645_59

6. Dang-Nguyen, D.T., Piras, L., Riegler, M., Boato, G., Zhou, L., Gurrin, C.: Overview of ImageCLEFlifelog 2017: lifelog retrieval and summarization. In: CLEF 2017 Labs Working Notes. CEUR Workshop Proceedings, Dublin, Ireland, 11–14 September 2017. CEUR-WS.org (2017). http://ceur-ws.org

7. Dang-Nguyen, D.T., Piras, L., Riegler, M., Zhou, L., Lux, M., Gurrin, C.: Overview of ImageCLEFlifelog 2018: daily living understanding and lifelog moment retrieval. In: CLEF 2018 Working Notes. CEUR Workshop Proceedings, Avignon, France, 10–14 September 2018. CEUR-WS.org (2018). http://ceur-ws.org

8. Dao, M.S., Kasem, A., Nazmudeen, M.S.H.: Leveraging Content and Context to Foster Understanding of Activities of Daily Living, 10–14 September 2018

9. Dicente Cid, Y., Jimenez-del-Toro, O., Depeursinge, A., Müller, H.: Efficient and fully automatic segmentation of the lungs in CT volumes. In: Goksel, O., Jimenez-del-Toro, O., Foncubierta-Rodriguez, A., Müller, H. (eds.) Proceedings of the VISCERAL Challenge at ISBI. No. 1390 in CEUR Workshop Proceedings, April 2015

10. Dicente Cid, Y., Kalinovsky, A., Liauchuk, V., Kovalev, V., Müller, H.: Overview of ImageCLEFtuberculosis 2017 - predicting tuberculosis type and drug resistances. In: CLEF 2017 Labs Working Notes. CEUR Workshop Proceedings, Dublin, Ireland, 11–14 September 2017. CEUR-WS.org (2017). http://ceur-ws.org

11. Dicente Cid, Y., Liauchuk, V., Kovalev, V., Müller, H.: Overview of ImageCLEFtuberculosis 2018 - detecting multi-drug resistance, classifying tuberculosis type, and assessing severity score. In: CLEF 2018 Working Notes. CEUR Workshop Proceedings, Avignon, France, 10–14 September 2018. CEUR-WS.org (2018). http://ceur-ws.org

12. Dogariu, M., Ionescu, B.: Multimedia Lab @ CAMPUS at ImageCLEFlifelog 2018 Lifelog Moment Retrieval, 10–14 September 2018

13. Eickhoff, C., Schwall, I., García Seco de Herrera, A., Müller, H.: Overview of ImageCLEFcaption 2017 - image caption prediction and concept detection for biomedical images. In: CLEF 2017 Labs Working Notes. CEUR Workshop Proceedings, Dublin, Ireland, 11–14 September 2017. CEUR-WS.org (2017). http://ceur-ws.org

14. Goeuriot, L., et al.: CLEF 2017 eHealth evaluation lab overview. In: Jones, G.J.F., et al. (eds.) CLEF 2017. LNCS, vol. 10456, pp. 291–303. Springer, Cham (2017). https://doi.org/10.1007/978-3-319-65813-1_26

15. Gravier, G., et al.: Working notes proceedings of the mediaeval 2017 workshop. In: MediaEval 2017 Working Notes. CEUR Workshop Proceedings, Dublin, Ireland, 13–15 September 2017. CEUR-WS.org (2017). http://ceur-ws.org

16. Gurrin, C., et al.: Overview of NTCIR-13 Lifelog-2 task. In: Proceedings of the 13th NTCIR Conference on Evaluation of Information Access Technologies (2017)

17. Hanbury, A., et al.: Evaluation-as-a-service: overview and outlook. ArXiv arXiv:1512.07454 (2015)

18. Hanbury, A., Müller, H., Langs, G., Weber, M.A., Menze, B.H., Fernandez, T.S.: Bringing the algorithms to the data: cloud–based benchmarking for medical image analysis. In: Catarci, T., Forner, P., Hiemstra, D., Peñas, A., Santucci, G. (eds.) CLEF 2012. LNCS, vol. 7488, pp. 24–29. Springer, Heidelberg (2012). https://doi.org/10.1007/978-3-642-33247-0_3

19. Hasan, S.A., Ling, Y., Farri, O., Liu, J., Lungren, M., Müller, H.: Overview of the ImageCLEF 2018 medical domain visual question answering task. In: CLEF2018 Working Notes. CEUR Workshop Proceedings, Avignon, France, 10–14 September 2018. CEUR-WS.org (2018). http://ceur-ws.org

20. García Seco de Herrera, A., Eickhoff, C., Andrearczyk, V., Müller, H.: Overview of the ImageCLEF 2018 caption prediction tasks. In: CLEF 2018 Working Notes. CEUR Workshop Proceedings, Avignon, France, 10–14 September 2018. CEUR-WS.org (2018). http://ceur-ws.org

21. Ionescu, B., et al.: Overview of ImageCLEF 2017: information extraction from images. In: Jones, G.J.F., et al. (eds.) CLEF 2017. LNCS, vol. 10456, pp. 315–337. Springer, Cham (2017). https://doi.org/10.1007/978-3-319-65813-1_28

22. Joly, A., et al.: LifeCLEF 2017 lab overview: multimedia species identification challenges. In: Proceedings of CLEF 2017 (2017)

23. Kalpathy-Cramer, J., García Seco de Herrera, A., Demner-Fushman, D., Antani, S., Bedrick, S., Müller, H.: Evaluating performance of biomedical image retrieval systems: overview of the medical image retrieval task at ImageCLEF 2004–2014. Comput. Med. Imaging Graph. **39**, 55–61 (2015)

24. Kavallieratou, E., del Blanco, C.R., Cuevas, C., García, N.: Retrieving Events in Life Logging, 10–14 September 2018

25. Müller, H., Clough, P., Deselaers, T., Caputo, B. (eds.): ImageCLEF - Experimental Evaluation in Visual Information Retrieval. Information Retrieval Series, vol. 32. Springer, Heidelberg (2010). https://doi.org/10.1007/978-3-642-15181-1

26. Papineni, K., Roukos, S., Ward, T., Zhu, W.J.: BLEU: a method for automatic evaluation of machine translation. In: Proceedings of the 40th Annual Meeting on Association for Computational Linguistics, pp. 311–318. Association for Computational Linguistics (2002)

27. Pinho, E., Costa, C.: Feature learning with adversarial networks for concept detection in medical images: UA.PT Bioinformatics at ImageCLEF 2018. In: CLEF2018 Working Notes. CEUR Workshop Proceedings, Avignon, France, 10–14 September 2018. CEUR-WS.org (2018). http://ceur-ws.org

28. Rahman, M.M.: A cross modal deep learning based approach for caption prediction and concept detection by CS Morgan State. In: CLEF2018 Working Notes. CEUR Workshop Proceedings, Avignon, France, 10–14 September 2018. CEUR-WS.org (2018). http://ceur-ws.org

29. Sharma, A., et al.: Estimating the future burden of multidrug-resistant and extensively drug-resistant tuberculosis in India, the Philippines, Russia, and South Africa: a mathematical modelling study. Lancet Infect. Dis. **17**(7), 707–715 (2017). http://www.sciencedirect.com/science/article/pii/S1473309917302475

30. Soldaini, L., Goharian, N.: QuickUMLS: a fast, unsupervised approach for medical concept extraction. In: MedIR Workshop, SIGIR (2016)

31. Soğancıoğlu, G., Öztürk, H., Özgür, A.: BIOSSES: a semantic sentence similarity estimation system for the biomedical domain. Bioinformatics **33**(14), i49–i58 (2017)

32. Spinks, G., Moens, M.F.: Generating text from images in a smooth representation space. In: CLEF2018 Working Notes. CEUR Workshop Proceedings, Avignon, France, 10–14 September 2018. CEUR-WS.org (2018). http://ceur-ws.org

33. Su, Y., Liu, F.: UMass at ImageCLEF caption prediction 2018 task. In: CLEF2018 Working Notes. CEUR Workshop Proceedings, Avignon, France, 10–14 September 2018. CEUR-WS.org (2018). http://ceur-ws.org

34. Tang, T.H., Fu, M.H., Huang, H.H., Chen, K.T., Chen, H.H.: NTU NLP-Lab at ImageCLEFlifelog 2018: Visual Concept Selection with Textual Knowledge for Understanding Activities of Daily Living and Life Moment Retrieval, 10–14 September 2018

35. Tran, M.T., Truong, T.D., Dinh-Duy, T., Vo-Ho, V.K., Luong, Q.A., Nguyen, V.T.: Lifelog Moment Retrieval with Visual Concept Fusion and Text-based Query Expansion, 10–14 September 2018

36. Tsikrika, T., de Herrera, A.G.S., Müller, H.: Assessing the scholarly impact of ImageCLEF. In: Forner, P., Gonzalo, J., Kekäläinen, J., Lalmas, M., de Rijke, M. (eds.) CLEF 2011. LNCS, vol. 6941, pp. 95–106. Springer, Heidelberg (2011). https://doi.org/10.1007/978-3-642-23708-9_12

37. Tsikrika, T., Larsen, B., Müller, H., Endrullis, S., Rahm, E.: The scholarly impact of CLEF (2000–2009). In: Forner, P., Müller, H., Paredes, R., Rosso, P., Stein, B. (eds.) CLEF 2013. LNCS, vol. 8138, pp. 1–12. Springer, Heidelberg (2013). https://doi.org/10.1007/978-3-642-40802-1_1

38. Valavanis, L., Kalamboukis, T.: IPL at ImageCLEF 2018: a kNN-based concept detection approach. In: CLEF2018 Working Notes. CEUR Workshop Proceedings, Avignon, France, 10–14 September 2018. CEUR-WS.org (2018). http://ceur-ws.org

39. Villegas, M., et al.: General overview of ImageCLEF at the CLEF 2015 labs. In: Mothe, J., et al. (eds.) CLEF 2015. LNCS, vol. 9283, pp. 444–461. Springer, Cham (2015). https://doi.org/10.1007/978-3-319-24027-5_45

40. Villegas, M., et al.: General overview of ImageCLEF at the CLEF 2016 labs. In: Fuhr, N., et al. (eds.) CLEF 2016. LNCS, vol. 9822, pp. 267–285. Springer, Cham (2016). https://doi.org/10.1007/978-3-319-44564-9_25

41. Wang, X., Zhang, Y., Guo, Z., Li, J.: ImageSem at ImageCLEF 2018 caption task: image retrieval and transfer learning. In: CLEF2018 Working Notes. CEUR Workshop Proceedings, Avignon, France, 10–14 September 2018. CEUR-WS.org (2018). http://ceur-ws.org

42. Wang, Y.X.J., Chung, M.J., Skrahin, A., Rosenthal, A., Gabrielian, A., Tartakovsky, M.: Radiological signs associated with pulmonary multi-drug resistant tuberculosis: an analysis of published evidences. Quant. Imaging Med. Surg. 8(2), 161–173 (2018)

43. Wu, Z., Palmer, M.: Verbs semantics and lexical selection. In: Proceedings of the 32nd Annual Meeting on Association for Computational Linguistics, pp. 133–138. Association for Computational Linguistics (1994)

44. Zhao, J.J., Kim, Y., Zhang, K., Rush, A.M., LeCun, Y.: Adversarially regularized autoencoders for generating discrete structures. CoRR, abs/1706.04223 (2017)

45. Zhou, L., Piras, L., Riegler, M., Lux, M., Dang-Nguyen1, D.T., Gurrin, C.: An interactive lifelog retrieval system for activities of daily living understanding, 10–14 September 2018

Evaluation of Personalised Information Retrieval at CLEF 2018 (PIR-CLEF)

Gabriella Pasi[1], Gareth J. F. Jones[2], Keith Curtis[2], Stefania Marrara[3(✉)],
Camilla Sanvitto[1], Debasis Ganguly[4], and Procheta Sen[2]

[1] University of Milano Bicocca, Milan, Italy
`pasi@disco.unimib.it`
[2] Dublin City University, Dublin, Ireland
[3] Consorzio C2T, Milan, Italy
`stefania.marrara@consorzioc2t.it`
[4] IBM Research Labs, Dublin, Ireland

Abstract. The series of Personalised Information Retrieval (PIR-CLEF) Labs at CLEF is intended as a forum for the exploration of methodologies for the repeatable evaluation of personalised information retrieval (PIR). The PIR-CLEF 2018 Lab is the first full edition of this series after the successful pilot edition at CLEF 2017, and provides a Lab task dedicated to personalised search, while the workshop at the conference will form the basis of further discussion of strategies for the evaluation of PIR and suggestions for improving the activities of the PIR-CLEF Lab. The PIR-CLEF 2018 Task is the first PIR evaluation benchmark based on the Cranfield paradigm, with the potential benefits of producing evaluation results that are easily reproducible. The task is based on search sessions over a subset of the ClueWeb12 collection, undertaken by volunteer searchers using a methodology developed in the CLEF 2017 pilot edition of PIR-CLEF. The PIR-CLEF test collection provides a detailed set of data gathered during the activities undertaken by each subject during the search sessions, including their search queries and details of relevant documents as marked by the searchers. The PIR-CLEF 2018 workshop is intended to review the design and construction of the collection, and to consider the topic of reproducible evaluation of PIR more generally with the aim of improving future editions of the evaluation benchmark.

1 Introduction

The PIR CLEF Lab organized within CLEF 2018 has the aim of providing a framework for the evaluation of Personalised Information Retrieval (PIR). PIR systems are aimed at enhancing traditional IR systems to better satisfy the information needs of individual users by providing search results that are not only relevant to the query in general, but specifically to the user who submitted the query. In order to provide a personalised service, a PIR system leverages various kinds of information about the users and their preferences and interests,

© Springer Nature Switzerland AG 2018
P. Bellot et al. (Eds.): CLEF 2018, LNCS 11018, pp. 335–342, 2018.
https://doi.org/10.1007/978-3-319-98932-7_29

which are also inferred through a variety of interactions of the user with the system. The information gathered is then represented in a user model, which is typically employed to either improve the user's query or to re-rank retrieved results list obtained using the standard query, so that documents that are more relevant to the user, are presented in the top positions of the list.

In the literature, the issue of evaluating the effectiveness of personalised approaches to search has been the source of previous investigations, generally within the scope of research related to interactive information retrieval. The notion of relevance is user centered, and can vary during a search session, depending both on the task at hand and on the user's interactions with the search system. Existing work on the evaluation of PIR has investigated this issue under different perspectives. A category of approaches (the prominent ones) has relied on user-centered evaluations, mostly based on user studies; this approach involves real users undertaking search tasks in a supervised environment, and by posing the user at the centre of the evaluation activity can produce relevant and informed feedbacks. However, while this methodology has the advantage of enabling the detailed study of the activities of real users, it has the significant drawback of not being easily reproducible, thus greatly limiting the scope for algorithmic exploration. Among some previous attempts to define PIR benchmark tasks based on the Cranfield paradigm, the closest experiment to the PIR Lab is the TREC Session track[1] conducted annually between 2010 and 2014. This track focused on stand-alone search sessions, where a "session" is a continuous sequence of query reformulations on the same topic, along with any user interaction with the retrieved results in service of satisfying a specific information need; however no details of the searcher undertaking the task have been made available. Thus, the TREC Session track did not exploit any user model to personalise the search experience, nor did it allow user actions over multiple search session to be taken into consideration in the ranking of the search output.

The PIR-CLEF 2018 Lab provided search data from a single search session gathered by the activities of volunteer users within the context of a search carried out in a user selected broad search category. The data collected were the same as those for the earlier Pilot Lab in 2017 [9]. We plan in the future to gather data across multiple sessions to enable the construction and exploitation of persistent user behaviour across the multiple search sessions focusing on the same topical area, in the same manner as user searching consistently within a topical area of ongoing interest.

PIR-CLEF 2018 thus provides an evaluation framework and test collection to enable research groups working on PIR to both experiment with and provide feedback on our proposed PIR evaluation methodology.

The remainder of this paper is organised as follows: Sect. 2 outlines existing related work, Sect. 3 provides an overview of the PIR-CLEF 2018 task, Sect. 3.2 discusses the metrics available for the evaluation of the task, and Sect. 5 concludes the paper.

---

[1] http://trec.nist.gov/data/session.html.

2   Related Work

Recent years have seen increasing interest in the study of contextual search: in particular, several research contributions have addressed the task of personalizing search by incorporating knowledge of user preferences into the search process [2]. This user-centered approach to search has raised the related issue of how to properly evaluate the effectiveness of personalized search in a scenario where relevance is strongly dependent on the interpretation of the individual user. The essential question here is, what is the impact on search effectiveness which arises from the inclusion of personal information relating to the preferences of the individual user. To this purpose several user-based evaluation frameworks have been developed, as discussed in [3].

A first category of approaches aimed at evaluating PIR systems is focused on performing a user-centered evaluation by providing a kind of extension to the laboratory based evaluation paradigm. The TREC Interactive track [4] and the TREC HARD track [5] are examples of this kind of evaluation framework. These tracks aimed at involving users in interactive tasks to get additional information about the user and the query context. The evaluation was done by comparing a baseline run ignoring the user/topic metadata with another run considering it.

The more recent TREC Contextual Suggestion track [6] was proposed with the purpose of investigating search techniques for complex information needs that are highly dependent on both context and the user's interests. Participants in the track were given, as input, a set of geographical contexts and a set of user profiles that contain a list of attractions the user has previously rated. The task was to produce a list of ranked suggestions for each profile-context pair by exploiting the given contextual information. However, despite these extensions, the overall evaluation Was still system controlled and only a few contextual features were available in the process.

TREC also introduced a Session track [7] the focus of which was to exploit user interactions during a query session to incrementally improve the results within this session. The novelty of this task was the evaluation of system performance over entire sessions instead of a single query.

However, the above attempts had various limitations in satisfactorily injecting the user's behaviour into the evaluation; for this reason the problem of defining a standard approach to the evaluation of personalized search is a hot research topic, which needs effective solutions.

A first attempt to create a collection satisfactorily accounting for individual user behaviour in search was done in the FIRE Conference held in 2011. The Personalised and Collaborative Information Retrieval track [8] was organised with the aim of extending a standard IR ad-hoc test collection by gathering additional meta-information during the topic development process to facilitate research on personalised and collaborative IR. However, since no runs were submitted to this track, only preliminary studies have been carried out and reported using it.

As introduced above, within CLEF 2017 we organised the PIR-CLEF pilot study for the purpose of providing a forum to enable the exploration of the evaluation of PIR [9]. The Pilot Lab provided a preliminary edition of the 2018

PIR-CLEF Lab. One of the achievements of the PIR-CLEF 2017 Pilot Task was the establishment of an evaluation benchmark combining elements of a user-centered and the Cranfield evaluation paradigm, with the potential benefits of producing evaluation results that are easily reproducible. The task was based on search sessions over a subset of the ClueWeb12 collection, undertaken by 10 users by using a clearly defined and novel methodology. The collection was defined by relying on data gathered by the activities undertaken during the search sessions by each participant, including details of relevant documents as marked by the searchers. An important point is that the collection was developed but not used by any group participating at the pilot task. For this reason we were able to use this data collection as the develop dataset for the CLEF 2018 PIR-CLEF task This dataset was distributed to the 16 groups registered to the Lab. We have also prepared a second collection for PIR CLEF 2018, as well as a system able to perform a comparative evaluation of the algorithms developed by the participating groups.

3   Overview of the PIR-CLEF 2018 Task

As described in the previous sections, the goal of the PIR-CLEF 2018 Task was to investigate the potentiality of using a laboratory-based methodology to enable a comparative evaluation of PIR methodologies. The collection of data used during both PIR-CLEF 2017 and PIR-CLEF 2018 was carried out with the cooperation of volunteer users. In each case, the data collection was organized into two sequential phases:

- *Data gathering.* This phase involved the volunteer users carrying out a task-based search session during which the activities of the user were recorded (e.g., formulated queries, bookmarked documents, etc.). Each search session was composed of a phase of query development, refinement and modification, and associated search with each query on a specific topical domain selected by the user, followed by a relevance assessment phase where the user indicated the relevance of documents returned in response to each query and a short report writing activity based on the search activity undertaken. Further details of this procedure are provided in [1].
- *Data cleaning and preparation.* This phase took place once the data gathering had been completed, and did not involve any user participation. It consisted of filtering and elaborating the information collected in the previous phase in order to prepare a dataset with various kinds of information related to the specific user's preferences. In addition, a bag-of-words representation of the participant's user profile was created to allow comparative evaluation of PIR algorithms using the same simple user model.

For the PIR-CLEF 2018 Task we made available the user profile data and raw search data produced by guided search sessions undertaken by 10 volunteer users created for the IT-CLEF 2017 pilot, as detailed in Sect. 3.1. The data provided included the submitted queries, baseline ranked lists of documents retrieved using a standard search system in response to each query, the items clicked by the user in response to this list, and document relevance information provided by the user on a 4-grade scale. Each session was performed by the users on a topic of their choosing, and search was carried out over a subset of the ClueWeb12 web collection.

The aim of the task was to use the provided information to improve the ranking of the search results list over a baseline ranking of documents judged relevant to the query by the user who entered the query.

The data was provided in csv format to the registered participants in the task. Access to the search service for the indexed subset of the ClueWeb12 collection was provided by Dublin City University via an API.

3.1   Dataset

To create datasets for distribution to the task participants, the data collected from the volunteer users was extracted and stored in csv files, and provided to the Lab participants in a zip folder.

Table 1. The PIR-CLEF dataset

cvs file	Content
cvs1	Info about the query session
cvs2	User's search log
cvs3	Relevance assessment of documents
cvs4	User's personal info
cvs5	TREC-style topic description
cvs6a	Simple user profile
cvs6b	User profile with stop words removal

As shown in Table 1, the file *user's session* (csv1) contains the information about each phase of the query sessions performed by each user. It also contains information about the user carrying the search including username, query_session ID and category, task and several timestamps of the session.

The file *user's log* (csv2) contains the search logs of each user, i.e. every search event that has been triggered by a user's action.

The file *user's assessment* (csv3) contains the relevance assessments of a pool of documents with respect to every single query developed by each user to fulfill the given task.

The file *user's info* (csv4) contains some personal information about the users such as age range, gender, occupation or native language.

The file *user's topic* (csv5) contains TREC-style final topic descriptions about the user's information needs that were developed in the final step of each search session, including also a short description provided by the searcher giving details of the topic about which they were searching and a description of which documents are relevant to the topic and which are not.

The file *simple user profile* (csv6a) for each user contains simple profiles computed as *bag of words* (simple version - the applied indexing included tokenization, shingling, and index terms weighting).

The file *complex user profile* (csv6b) contains, for each user, the same information provided in csv6a, with the difference that the applied indexing was enriched by also including stop word removal.

The source used to extract the information employed to construct the two user profiles is the set of documents that the participant has assessed as relevant at the end of the tasks. The user's log file (cvs2) contains for each user all the queries.

Participants had the possibility to contribute to the task in two ways:

– The two user profile files (csv6a and csv6b) provide bag-of words profiles for the volunteer users, extracted by applying different indexing procedures to the considered documents. Participants could compare the results obtained by applying their personalisation algorithm on these queries with the results obtained and evaluated by the users on the same queries (and included in the user assessment file csv3). Their search had to be carried out on the ClueWeb12 collection, by using the API provided by DCU. Then, by using the 4-graded scale evaluations of the documents (relevant, somewhat relevant, non relevant, off topic) provided by the users and contained in the user assessment file csv3, it was possible to compute evaluation metrics for the created ranked lists. Note that documents that do not appear in csv3 were considered non-relevant.
– The challenge here was to use the raw data provided in the files csv1, csv2, csv3, csv4, and csv5 to create user profiles. In the approaches proposed in the literature, user profiles are formally represented as bags of words, as vectors, or as conceptual taxonomies, generally defined based on external knowledge resources (such as the WordNet and the ODP - Open Directory Project). The task here was more research oriented: to examine whether the information provided in test collection is sufficient to create a useful user profile. Also to consider whether there is information not present in the current test collection that could be included to improve the profile.

In the Lab we encouraged participants to be involved in this task by using existing or new algorithms and/or to explore new ideas. We also welcomed contributions that make an analysis of the task and/or of the dataset.

3.2 Performance Measures

At this first edition of the Lab, well known information retrieval metrics, such as Average Precision (AP) and Normalized Discounted Cumulative Gain (NDCG) were used to evaluate partcipants' results. However, a key objective of PIR-CLEF is to examine new methods of evaluating PIR, particularly within our Cranfield based framework. In the pursuit of this we have developed a tool to enable comparative analysis of retrieval results for multiple runs across a session which is being used for explorative analysis of runs carried out using the PIR-CLEF collections. Further details on this tool are available in [10].

4 Towards More Realistic Evaluation of PIR

The PIR-CLEF 2018 Task gathered data from the volunteer searchers over only a single search session, in practice a user exploiting a certain information need is generally expected to gather information across multiple sessions. Over the course of these sessions the searcher will have multiple topics associated with their informations. Some topics will typically recur over a number of sessions, and while some search topics may be entirely semantically separate, others will overlap, and in all cases the users knowledge of the topic will progress over time and recall of earlier sessions may in some cases assist the searcher in later sessions looking at the same topic. Obviously, a personalisation model should imitate this behaviour. How to extend the data gathering methodology to this more realistic and complex situation requires further investigation.

There are multiple issues which must be considered, not least how to engage volunteer participants in these more complex tasks over the longer collections periods that will required. Given the multiple interacting factors highlighting above, work will also be required to consider how to account for these in the design of such an extended PIR test collection and the process of the information collection, to enable meaningful experiments to be conducted to investigate personalisation models and their use in search algorithms.

The design of the PIR-CLEF 2018 task makes the additional simplifying assumption of a simple relevance relationship between individual queries posed to the search engine by the retrieved documents. However, it is observed that users often approach an IR system with a more complex information seeking intention which can require multiple search interactions to satisfy. Further we can consider the relationship between the information seeking intention as it develops incrementally during the multiple search interactions and item retrieved at each stage in terms of usefulness to the searcher rather than simple relevance to the information need [11]. However, to operationalise these more complex factors in the development of a framework for evaluation of PIR is clearly challenging.

5 Conclusions and Future Work

This paper introduced the PIR-CLEF 2018 Personalised Information Retrieval (PIR) Workshop and the associated Task. The paper first introduced relevant existing work in the evaluation of PIR. The task is the first edition of a Lab dedicated to the theme of personalised search, after a successful pilot held at CLEF 2017. This is the first evaluation benchmark in this field based on the Cranfield paradigm, with the significant benefit of producing results easily reproducible.

An evaluation using this collection has been run to allow research groups working on personalised IR to both experience with and provide feedback about our proposed PIR evaluation methodology. While the Task moves beyond the state-of-the-art in evaluation of PIR, it nevertheless makes simplifying assumptions in terms of the user's interactions during a search session; we briefly considered these here, and how to incorporate these into more evaluation of PIR that is closer to real-world user experience will be the subject of further work.

References

1. Sanvitto, C., Ganguly, D., Jones, G.J.F., Pasi, G.: A laboratory-based method for the evaluation of personalised search. In: Proceedings of the Seventh International Workshop on Evaluating Information Access (EVIA 2016), a Satellite Workshop of the NTCIR-12 Conference, Tokyo Japan (2016)
2. Pasi, G.: Issues in personalising information retrieval. IEEE Intell. Inform. Bull. **11**(1), 3–7 (2010)
3. Tamine-Lechani, L., Boughanem, M., Daoud, M.: Evaluation of contextual information retrieval effectiveness: overview of issues and research. Knowl. Inf. Syst. **24**(1), 1–34 (2009)
4. Harman, D.: Overview of the fourth text retrieval conference (TREC-4). In: Proceedings of the Fourth Text REtrieval Conference (TREC-4), Gaithersburg, Maryland (1995)
5. Allan, J.: HARD track overview in TREC 2003: high accuracy retrieval from documents. In: Proceedings of The Twelfth Text REtrieval Conference (TREC 2003), Gaithersburg, Maryland, USA, pp. 24–37 (2003)
6. Dean-Hall, A., Clarke, C.L.A., Kamps, J., Thomas, P., Voorhees, E.M.: Overview of the TREC 2012 contextual suggestion track. In: Proceedings of the Twenty-First Text REtrieval Conference (TREC 2012), Gaithersburg, Maryland (2012)
7. Carterette, B., Kanoulas, E., Hall, M.M., Clough, P.D.: Overview of the TREC 2014 session track. In: Proceedings of The Twenty-Third Text REtrieval Conference (TREC 2014), Gaithersburg, Maryland, USA (2014)
8. Ganguly, D., Leveling, J., Jones, G.J.F.: Overview of the personalized and collaborative information retrieval (PIR) track at FIRE-2011. In: Majumder, P., Mitra, M., Bhattacharyya, P., Subramaniam, L.V., Contractor, D., Rosso, P. (eds.) FIRE 2010-2011. LNCS, vol. 7536, pp. 227–240. Springer, Heidelberg (2013). https://doi.org/10.1007/978-3-642-40087-2_22
9. Pasi, G., Jones, G.J.F., Marrara, S., Sanvitto, C., Ganguly, D., Sen, P.: Overview of the CLEF 2017 personalised information retrieval pilot lab (PIR-CLEF 2017). In: Jones, G.J.F., et al. (eds.) CLEF 2017. LNCS, vol. 10456, pp. 338–345. Springer, Cham (2017). https://doi.org/10.1007/978-3-319-65813-1_29
10. Pasi, G., et al.: Overview of the CLEF 2018 personalised information retrieval pilot lab (PIR-CLEF 2018): methods for comparative evaluation of PIR. In: Working Notes of CLEF 2018 - Conference and Labs of the Evaluation Forum, Avignon, France (2018)
11. Belkin, N.J., Hienert, D., Mayr-Schlegel, P., Shah, C.: Data requirements for evaluation of personalization of information retrieval - a position paper. In: Proceedings of Working Notes of the CLEF 2017 Labs, Dublin, Ireland (2017)

Overview of eRisk: Early Risk Prediction on the Internet

David E. Losada[1]([✉]), Fabio Crestani[2], and Javier Parapar[3]

[1] Centro Singular de Investigación en Tecnoloxías da Información (CiTIUS),
Universidade de Santiago de Compostela, Santiago de Compostela, Spain
david.losada@usc.es
[2] Faculty of Informatics, Universitá della Svizzera italiana (USI),
Lugano, Switzerland
fabio.crestani@usi.ch
[3] Information Retrieval Lab, University of A Coruña, A Coruña, Spain
javierparapar@udc.es

Abstract. This paper provides an overview of eRisk 2018. This was the second year that this lab was organized at CLEF. The main purpose of eRisk was to explore issues of evaluation methodology, effectiveness metrics and other processes related to early risk detection. Early detection technologies can be employed in different areas, particularly those related to health and safety. The second edition of eRisk had two tasks: a task on early risk detection of depression and a task on early risk detection of anorexia.

1 Introduction

The main purpose of this lab is to explore issues of evaluation methodologies, performance metrics and other aspects related to building test collections and defining challenges for early risk detection. Early detection technologies are potentially useful in different areas, particularly those related to safety and health. For example, early alerts could be sent when a person starts showing signs of a mental disorder, when a sexual predator starts interacting with a child, or when a potential offender starts publishing antisocial threats on the Internet. In 2017, our main goal was to pioneer a new interdisciplinary research area that would be potentially applicable to a wide variety of profiles, such as potential paedophiles, stalkers, individuals with a latent tendency to fall into the hands of criminal organisations, people with suicidal inclinations, or people susceptible to depression.

The 2017 lab had two possible ways to participate. One of them followed a classical workshop pattern. This workshop was open to the submission of papers describing test collections or data sets suitable for early risk prediction or early risk prediction challenges, tasks and evaluation metrics. This open submission format was discontinued in 2018. eRisk 2017 also included an exploratory task on early detection of depression. This pilot task was based on the evaluation methodology and test collection presented in a CLEF 2016 paper [1]. The interaction between depression and language use is interesting for early risk detection

© Springer Nature Switzerland AG 2018
P. Bellot et al. (Eds.): CLEF 2018, LNCS 11018, pp. 343–361, 2018.
https://doi.org/10.1007/978-3-319-98932-7_30

algorithms. We shared this collection with all participating teams and the 2017 participants approached the problem with multiple technologies and models (e.g. Natural Language Processing, Machine Learning, Information Retrieval, etc.). However, the effectiveness of all participating systems was relatively low [2]. For example, the highest F1 was 64%. This suggests that the 2017 task was challenging and there was still much room from improvement.

In 2018, the lab followed a standard campaign-style format. It was composed of two different tasks: early risk detection of depression and early risk detection of anorexia. The first task is a continuation of the eRisk 2017 pilot task. The teams had access to the eRisk 2017 data as training data, and new depression and non-depression test cases were extracted and provided to the participants during the test stage. The second task followed the same format as the depression task. The organizers of the task collected data on anorexia and language use, the data were divided into a training subset and a test subset, and the task followed the same iterative evaluation schedule implemented in 2017 (see below).

2   Task 1: Early Detection of Signs of Depression

This is an exploratory task on early detection of signs of depression. The challenge consists of sequentially processing pieces of evidence –in the form of writings posted by depressed or non-depressed users– and learn to detect early signs of depression as soon as possible. The lab focuses on Text Mining solutions and, thus, it concentrates on Social Media submissions (posts or comments in a Social Media website). Texts should be processed by the participating systems in the order they were created. In this way, systems that effectively perform this task could be applied to sequentially track user interactions in blogs, social networks, or other types of online media.

The test collection for this task has the same format as the collection described in [1]. It is a collection of submissions or writings (posts or comments) done by Social Media users. There are two classes of users, depressed and non-depressed. The positive group was obtained by searching for explicit expressions related to a diagnosis (e.g. "diagnosed with depression") and doing a manual check of the retrieved posts. The control group was obtained by random sampling from the large set of social media users available. To make the collection realistic, we also included in the control group users who often post about depression (e.g. individuals who actively participate in the depression threads because they have a close relative suffering from depression). For every user, we collected all his submissions (up to 1000 posts + 1000 comments, which is the limit imposed by the platform), organized them in chronological order, and split this sequence in 10 chunks. The first chunk has the oldest 10% of the submissions, the second chunk has the second oldest 10%, and so forth.

The task was organized into two different stages:

- **Training stage.** Initially, the teams that participated in this task had access to some training data. In this stage, the organizers of the task released the

Table 1. Task1 (depression). Main statistics of the train and test collections

	Train		Test	
	Depressed	*Control*	*Depressed*	*Control*
Num. subjects	135	752	79	741
Num. submissions (posts & comments)	49,557	481,837	40,665	504,523
Avg num. of submissions per subject	367.1	640.7	514.7	680.9
Avg num. of days from first to last submission	586.43	625.0	786.9	702.5
Avg num. words per submission	27.4	21.8	27.6	23.7

entire history of submissions done by a set of training users. All chunks of all training users were sent to the participants. Additionally, the actual class (depressed or non-depressed) of each training user was also provided (i.e. whether or not the user explicitly mentioned that they were diagnosed with depression). In 2018, the training data consisted of all 2017 users (2017 training split + 2017 test split). The participants could therefore tune their systems with the training data and build up from 2017's results. The training dataset was released on Nov 30th, 2017.

– **Test stage.** The test stage had 10 releases of data (one release per week). The first week we gave the 1st chunk of data to the teams (oldest submissions of all test users), the second week we gave the 2nd chunk of data (second oldest submissions of all test users), and so forth. After each release, the teams had to process the data and, before the next week, each team had to choose between: (a) emitting a decision on the user (i.e. depressed or non-depressed), or (b) making no decision (i.e. waiting to see more chunks). This choice had to be made for each user in the test split. If the team emitted a decision then the decision was considered as final. The systems were evaluated based on the accuracy of the decisions and the number of chunks required to take the decisions (see below). The first release of test data was done on Feb 6th, 2018 and the last (10th) release of test data was done on April 10th, 2018.

Table 1 reports the main statistics of the train and test collections. The two splits are unbalanced (there are more non-depression cases than depression cases). In the training collection the percentage of depressed cases was about 15% and in the test collection this percentage was about 9%. The number of users is not large, but each user has a long history of submissions (on average, the collections have several hundred submissions per user). Additionally, the mean range of dates from the first submission to the last submission is wide (more than 500 days). Such wide history permits to analyze the evolution of the language from the oldest post or comment to the most recent one.

2.1   Evaluation Measures

The evaluation of the tasks considered standard classification measures, such as F1, Precision and Recall (computed with respect to the positive class –depression or anorexia, respectively–) and an early risk detection measure proposed in [1]. The standard classification measures can be employed to assess the teams' estimations with respect to golden truth judgments that inform us about users that are really positive cases. We include them in our evaluation report because these metrics are well-known and easily interpretable.

However, standard classification measures are time-unaware and do not penalize late decisions. Therefore, the evaluation of the tasks also considered a newer measure of performance that rewards early alerts. More specifically, we employed ERDE, an error measure for early risk detection [1] for which the fewer writings required to make the alert, the better. For each user the evaluation proceeds as follows. Given a chunk of data, if a team's system does not emit a decision then it has access to the next chunk of data (i.e. more submissions from the same user). However, the team's system gets a penalty for *late emission*.

ERDE, which stands for *early risk detection error*, takes into account the correctness of the (binary) decision and the delay taken by the system to make the decision. The delay is measured by counting the number (k) of distinct submissions (posts or comments) seen before taking the decision. For instance, imagine a user u who posted a total number of 250 posts or comments (i.e. exactly 25 submissions per chunk to simplify the example). If a team's system emitted a decision for user u after the second chunk of data then the delay k would be 50 (because the system needed to see 50 pieces of evidence in order to make its decision).

Another important factor is that data are unbalanced (many more negative cases than positive cases) and, thus, the evaluation measure needs to weight different errors in a different way. Consider a binary decision d taken by a team's system with delay k. Given golden truth judgments, the prediction d can be a true positive (TP), true negative (TN), false positive (FP) or false negative (FN). Given these four cases, the ERDE measure is defined as:

$$ERDE_o(d, k) = \begin{cases} c_{fp} & \text{if } d\text{=positive AND ground truth=negative (FP)} \\ c_{fn} & \text{if } d\text{=negative AND ground truth=positive (FN)} \\ lc_o(k) \cdot c_{tp} & \text{if } d\text{=positive AND ground truth=positive (TP)} \\ 0 & \text{if } d\text{=negative AND ground truth=negative (TN)} \end{cases}$$

How to set c_{fp} and c_{fn} depends on the application domain and the implications of FP and FN decisions. We will often deal with detection tasks where the number of negative cases is several orders of magnitude larger than the number of positive cases. Hence, if we want to avoid building trivial systems that always say no, we need to have $c_{fn} >> c_{fp}$. In evaluating the systems, we fixed c_{fn} to 1 and c_{fp} was set according to the proportion of positive cases in 2017's test data (e.g. we set c_{fp} to 0.1296).

The factor $lc_o(k)(\in [0,1])$ represents a cost associated to the delay in detecting true positives. We set c_{tp} to c_{fn} (i.e. c_{tp} was set to 1) because late detection can have severe consequences (as a late detection is considered as equivalent to not detecting the case at all).

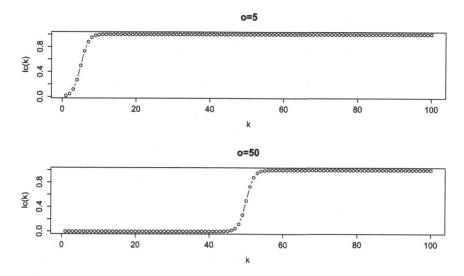

Fig. 1. Latency cost functions: $lc_5(k)$ and $lc_{50}(k)$

The function $lc_o(k)$ is a monotonically increasing function of k:

$$lc_o(k) = 1 - \frac{1}{1 + e^{k-o}} \qquad (1)$$

The function is parameterised by o, which controls the place in the X axis where the cost grows more quickly (Fig. 1 plots $lc_5(k)$ and $lc_{50}(k)$).

The latency cost factor was only used for the true positives because we understand that late detection is not an issue for true negatives. True negatives are non-risk cases that, of course, would not demand early intervention (i.e. these cases just need to be effectively filtered out from the positive cases). The systems must therefore focus on early detecting risk cases and detecting non-risk cases (regardless of when these non-risk cases are detected).

To further understand the effect of this penalty let us consider a positive case. Imagine that this positive user is detected by system A after analyzing two texts ($k = 2$), while system B also detects the case but it makes the alert after analyzing 8 texts ($k = 8$). $ERDE_5$ would assign system A an error of 0.047 and system B an error of 0.9526.

All cost weights are in $[0, 1]$ and, thus, ERDE is in the range $[0, 1]$. Systems had to take one decision for each subject and the overall error is the mean of the p ERDE values.

2.2   Results

Each team could submit up to 5 runs or variants. We received 45 contributions from 11 different institutions. This is a substantial increase with respect to erisk

2017, which had 8 institutions and 30 contributed runs. Table 3 reports the institutions that contributed to eRisk 2018 and the labels associated to their runs.

First, let us analyze the behaviour of the systems in terms of how fast they emitted decisions. Figure 2 shows a boxplot graph of the number of chunks required to make the decisions. The test collection has 820 users and, thus, each boxplot represents the statistics of 820 cases.

Some systems (RKMVERIB, RKMVERIC, RKMVERID, RKMVERIE, TBSA, UPFC, UPFD) took all decisions after the last chunk (i.e. did not emit any earlier decision). These variants were extremely conservative: they waited to see the whole history of submissions for all users and, next, they emitted their decisions. Remember that all teams were forced to emit a decision for each user at the last chunk.

Many other runs also took most of the decisions after the last chunk. For example, FHDO-BCSGA assigned a decision at the last chunk in 725 out of 820 users. Only a few runs were really quick at emitting decisions. Notably, most UDC's runs and LIIRA had a median of 1 chunk needed to emit decisions.

Figure 3 shows a boxplot of the number of submissions required by each run in order to emit decisions. Most of the time the teams waited to see hundreds of writings for each user. Only a few submissions (UDCA, UDCB, UDCD, UDCE, UNSLD, some LIIRx runs) had a median number of writings analyzed below 100. It appears that the teams have concentrated on accuracy (rather than delay) and, thus, they did not care much about penalties for late decisions. A similar behaviour was found in the runs submitted in 2017.

The number of user submissions has a high variance. Some users have only 10 submissions, while other users have more than a thousand submissions. It would be interesting to study the interaction between the number of user submissions and the effectiveness of the estimations done by the participating systems. This study could help to shed light on issues such as the usefulness of a large (vs short) history of submissions and the effect of off-topic submissions (e.g. submissions totally unrelated to depression).

Another intriguing issue relates to potential false positives. For instance, a doctor who is active on the depression community because he gives support to people suffering from depression, or a wife whose husband has been diagnosed with depression. These people would often write about depression and possibly use a style that might imply they are depressed, but obviously they are not. The collection contains this type of non-depressed users and these cases are challenging for automatic classification. Arguably, these non-depressed users are much different from other non-depressed users who do not engage in any depression-related conversation. In any case, this issue requires further investigation. For example, it will be interesting to do error analysis with the systems' decisions and check the characteristics of the false positives.

Figure 4 helps to analyze another aspect of the decisions emitted by the teams. For each user class, it plots the percentage of correct decisions against the number of users. For example, the last two bars of the upper plot show that about 5 users were correctly identified by more than 90% of the runs. Similarly, the rightmost bar of the lower plot means that a few non-depressed users were correctly classified by all runs (100% correct decisions). The graphs show that the teams tend to be more effective with non-depressed users. This is as expected because most non-depressed cases do not engage in depression-related conversations and, therefore, they are easier to distinguish from depressed users. The distribution of correct decisions for non-depressed users has many cases where more than 80% of the systems are correct. The distribution of correct decisions for depressed users is flatter, and many depressed users are only identified by a low percentage of the runs. This suggests that the teams implemented a wide range of strategies that detect different portions of the depression class. Furthermore, there are not depressed users that are correctly identified by all systems. However, an interesting point is that no depressed user has 0% of correct decisions. This means that every depressed user was classified as such by at least one run. In the future, it will be interesting to perform error analysis and try to understand why some positive cases are really hard to detect (e.g. is it that we have little evidence on such cases?).

Let us now analyze the effectiveness results (see Table 4). The first conclusion we can draw is that the task is as difficult as in 2017. In terms of F1, performance is again low. The highest F1 is 0.64 and the highest precision is 0.67. This might be related to the effect of false positives discussed above. The lowest $ERDE_{50}$ was achieved by the FHDO-BCSG team, which also submitted the runs that performed the best in terms of $F1$. The run with the lowest $ERDE_5$ was submitted by the UNSLA team and the run with the highest precision was submitted by RKMVERI. The UDC team submitted a high recall run (0.95) but its precision was extremely low.

In terms of $ERDE_5$, the best performing run is UNSLA, which has poor F1, Precision and Recall. This run was not good at identifying many depressed users but, still, it has low $ERDE_5$. This suggests that the true positives were emitted by this run at earlier chunks (quick emissions). $ERDE_5$ is extremely stringent with delays (after 5 writings, penalties grow quickly, see Fig. 1). This promotes runs that emit few but quick depression decisions. $ERDE_{50}$, instead, gives smoother penalties to delays. This makes that the run with the lowest $ERDE_{50}$, FHDO-BCSGB, has much higher F1 and Precision. Such difference between $ERDE_5$ and $ERDE_{50}$ is highly relevant in practice. For example, a mental health agency seeking an automatic tool for screening depression could set the penalty weights depending on the consequences of late detection of signs of depression.

3   Task 2: Early Detection of Signs of Anorexia

Task 2 was an exploratory task on early detection of signs of anorexia. The format of the task, data extraction methods and evaluation methodology (training stage followed by a test stage with on sequential releases of user data) was the same used for Task 1. This task was introduced in 2018 and, therefore, all users (training + test) were collected just for this new task.

Table 2. Task2 (anorexia). Main statistics of the train and test collections

	Train		Test	
	Anorexia	*Control*	*Anorexia*	*Control*
Num. subjects	20	132	41	279
Num. submissions (posts & comments)	7,452	77,514	17,422	151,364
Avg num. of submissions per subject	372.6	587.2	424.9	542.5
Avg num. of days from first to last submission	803.3	641.5	798.9	670.6
Avg num. words per submission	41.2	20.9	35.7	20.9

Table 2 reports the main statistics of the train and test collections of Task 2. The collection shares the main characteristics of Task 1's collections: the two splits are unbalanced (of course, there are more non-anorexia cases than anorexia cases). Contrary to the depression case, the number of users is not large (and, again, each user has a long history of submissions). The mean range of dates from the first submission to the last submission is also wide (more than 500 days).

3.1   Results

Each team could submit up to 5 runs or variants. We received 35 contributions from 9 different institutions. All institutions participating in Task 2 had also sent results for Task 1. Table 5 reports the institutions that contributed to this second task of eRisk 2018 and the labels associated to their runs.

The behaviour of the systems in terms of how fast they emitted decisions is shown in Fig. 5, which includes boxplot graphs of the number of chunks required to make the decisions. The test collection of Task 2 has 320 users and, thus, each boxplot represents the statistics of 320 cases. The trends are similar to those found in Task 1. Mosf of the systems emitted decisions at a late stage with only a few exceptions (notably, LIIRA and LIIRB). LIIRA and LIIRB had a median number of chunks analyzed of 3 and 6, respectively. The rest of the systems had a median number of chunks analized equal to or near 10.

Figure 6 shows a boxplot of the number of submissions required by each run in order to emit decisions. Again, most of the variants analyzed hundred of submissions before emitting decisions. Only the two LIIR runs discussed above and LIRMMD opted for emitting decisions after a fewer number of user submissions. In Task 2, again, most of the teams have ignored the penalties for late decisions and they have mostly focused on classification accuracy.

Figure 7 plots the percentage of correct decisions against the number of users. The plot shows again a clear distinction between the positive class (anorexia) and the negative class (non-anorexia). Most of the non-anorexia users are correctly identified by most of the systems (nearly all non-anorexia users fall in the range

Table 3. Task 1 (depression). Participating institutions and submitted results

Institution	Submitted files
FH Dortmund, Germany	FHDO-BCSGA
	FHDO-BCSGB
	FHDO-BCSGC
	FHDO-BCSGD
	FHDO-BCSGE
IRIT, France	LIIRA
	LIIRB
	LIIRC
	LIIRD
	LIIRE
LIRMM, University of Montpellier, France	LIRMMA
	LIRMMB
	LIRMMC
	LIRMMD
	LIRMME
Instituto Tecnológico Superior del Oriente del Estado de Hidalgo, Mexico	PEIMEXA
Instituto Nacional de Astrofísica, Óptica y Electrónica, Mexico	PEIMEXB
Universidad de Houston, USA	PEIMEXC
& Universidad Autónoma del Estado de Hidalgo, Mexico	PEIMEXD
	PEIMEXE
Ramakrishna Mission Vivekananda Educational and Research Institute, Belur Math, West Bengal, India	RKMVERIA
	RKMVERIB
	RKMVERIC
	RKMVERID
	RKMVERIE
University of A Coruña, Spain	UDCA
	UDCB
	UDCC
	UDCD
	UDCE
Universidad Nacional de San Luis, Argentina	UNSLA
	UNSLB
	UNSLC
	UNSLD
	UNSLE
Universitat Pompeu Fabra, Spain	UPFA
	UPFB
	UPFC
	UPFD
Université du Québec à Montréal, Canada	UQAMA
The Black Swan, Taiwan	TBSA
Tokushima University, Japan	TUA1A
	TUA1B
	TUA1C
	TUA1D

80%–100%, meaning that at least 80% of the systems labeled them as non-anorexic). In contrast, the distribution of anorexia users is flatter and, in many cases, they are only identified by less than half of the systems. An interesting result is that all anorexia users were identified by at least 10% of the systems.

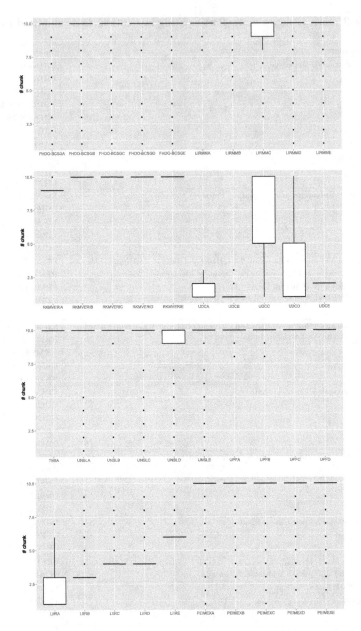

Fig. 2. Number of chunks required by each contributing run in order to emit a decision.

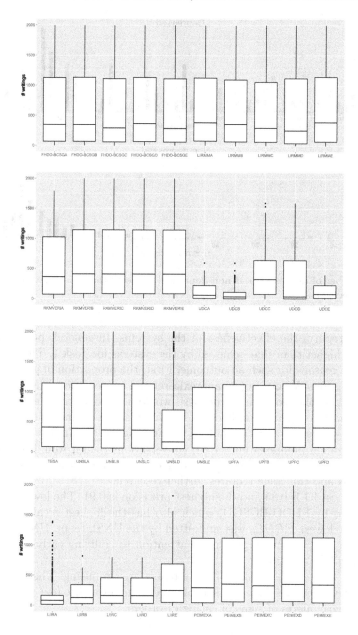

Fig. 3. Number of writings required by each contributing run in order to emit a decision.

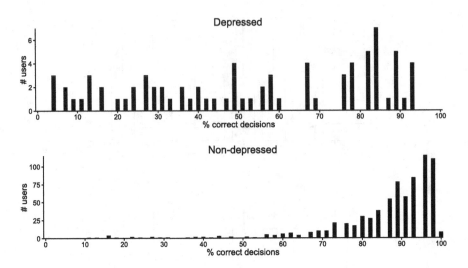

Fig. 4. Number of depressed and non-depressed subjects that had a given percentage of correct decisions.

Table 6 reports the effectiveness of the systems. In general, performance is remarkably higher than that achieved by the systems for Task 1. There could be a number of reasons for such an outcome. First, the proportion of potential false positives (e.g. people engaging in anorexia-related conversations) might be lower in Task 2's test collection. This hypothesis would need to be investigated through a careful analysis of the data. Second, the submissions of anorexia users might be extremely focused on eating habits, losing weights, etc. If they do not often engage in general (anorexia unrelated) conversations then it would be easier for the systems to distinguish them from other users. In any case, these are only speculations and this issue requires further research.

The highest F1 is 0.85 and the highest precision is 0.91. The lowest $ERDE_{50}$ was achieved by FHDO-BCSGD, which also has the highest recall (0.88). The run with the lowest $ERDE_5$ was submitted by the UNSL team (UNSLB), which shows again that this team paid more attention to emitting early decisions (at least for the true positives).

Overall, the results obtained by the teams are promising. The high performance achieved suggest that it is feasible to design automatic text analysis tools that make early alerts of signs of eating disorders.

Table 4. Task 1 (depression). Results

	$ERDE_5$	$ERDE_{50}$	F1	P	R
FHDO-BCSGA	9.21%	6.68%	0.61	0.56	0.67
FHDO-BCSGB	9.50%	**6.44%**	**0.64**	0.64	0.65
FHDO-BCSGC	9.58%	6.96%	0.51	0.42	0.66
FHDO-BCSGD	9.46%	7.08%	0.54	0.64	0.47
FHDO-BCSGE	9.52%	6.49%	0.53	0.42	0.72
LIIRA	9.46%	7.56%	0.50	0.61	0.42
LIIRB	10.03%	7.09%	0.48	0.38	0.67
LIIRC	10.51%	7.71%	0.42	0.31	0.66
LIIRD	10.52%	7.84%	0.42	0.31	0.66
LIIRE	9.78%	7.91%	0.55	0.66	0.47
LIRMMA	10.66%	9.16%	0.49	0.38	0.68
LIRMMB	11.81%	9.20%	0.36	0.24	0.73
LIRMMC	11.78%	9.02%	0.35	0.23	0.71
LIRMMD	11.32%	8.08%	0.32	0.22	0.57
LIRMME	10.71%	8.38%	0.37	0.29	0.52
PEIMEXA	10.30%	7.22%	0.38	0.28	0.62
PEIMEXB	10.30%	7.61%	0.45	0.37	0.57
PEIMEXC	10.07%	7.35%	0.37	0.29	0.51
PEIMEXD	10.11%	7.70%	0.39	0.35	0.44
PEIMEXE	10.77%	7.32%	0.35	0.25	0.57
RKMVERIA	10.14%	8.68%	0.52	0.49	0.54
RKMVERIB	10.66%	9.07%	0.47	0.37	0.65
RKMVERIC	9.81%	9.08%	0.48	**0.67**	0.38
RKMVERID	9.97%	8.63%	0.58	0.60	0.56
RKMVERIE	9.89%	9.28%	0.21	0.35	0.15
UDCA	10.93%	8.27%	0.26	0.17	0.53
UDCB	15.79%	11.95%	0.18	0.10	**0.95**
UDCC	9.47%	8.65%	0.18	0.13	0.29
UDCD	12.38%	8.54%	0.18	0.11	0.61
UDCE	9.51%	8.70%	0.18	0.13	0.29
UNSLA	**8.78%**	7.39%	0.38	0.48	0.32
UNSLB	8.94%	7.24%	0.40	0.35	0.46
UNSLC	8.82%	6.95%	0.43	0.38	0.49
UNSLD	10.68%	7.84%	0.45	0.31	0.85
UNSLE	9.86%	7.60%	0.60	0.53	0.70
UPFA	10.01%	8.28%	0.55	0.56	0.54
UPFB	10.71%	8.60%	0.48	0.37	0.70
UPFC	10.26%	9.16%	0.53	0.48	0.61
UPFD	10.16%	9.79%	0.42	0.42	0.42
UQAMA	10.04%	7.85%	0.42	0.32	0.62
TBSA	10.81%	9.22%	0.37	0.29	0.52
TUA1A	10.19%	9.70%	0.29	0.31	0.27
TUA1B	10.40%	9.54%	0.27	0.25	0.28
TUA1C	10.86%	9.51%	0.47	0.35	0.71
TUA1D	-	-	0.00	0.00	0.00

Table 5. Task 2 (anorexia). Participating institutions and submitted results

Institution	Submitted files
FH Dortmund, Germany	FHDO-BCSGA
	FHDO-BCSGB
	FHDO-BCSGC
	FHDO-BCSGD
	FHDO-BCSGE
IRIT, France	LIIRA
	LIIRB
LIRMM, University of Montpellier, France	LIRMMA
	LIRMMB
	LIRMMC
	LIRMMD
	LIRMME
Instituto Tecnológico Superior del Oriente del Estado de Hidalgo, Mexico	PEIMEXA
Instituto Nacional de Astrofísica, Óptica y Electrónica, Mexico	PEIMEXB
Universidad de Houston, USA & Universidad Autónoma del Estado de	PEIMEXC
Hidalgo, Mexico	PEIMEXD
	PEIMEXE
Ramakrishna Mission Vivekananda Educational and Research Institute,	RKMVERIA
Belur Math, West Bengal, India	RKMVERIB
	RKMVERIC
	RKMVERID
	RKMVERIE
Universidad Nacional de San Luis, Argentina	UNSLA
	UNSLB
	UNSLC
	UNSLD
	UNSLE
Universitat Pompeu Fabra, Spain	UPFA
	UPFB
	UPFC
	UPFD
The Black Swan, Taiwan	TBSA
Tokushima University, Japan	TUA1A
	TUA1B
	TUA1C

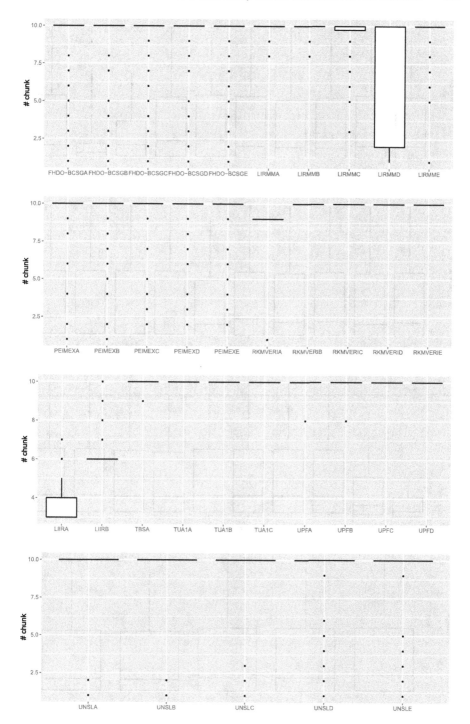

Fig. 5. Number of chunks required by each contributing run in order to emit a decision.

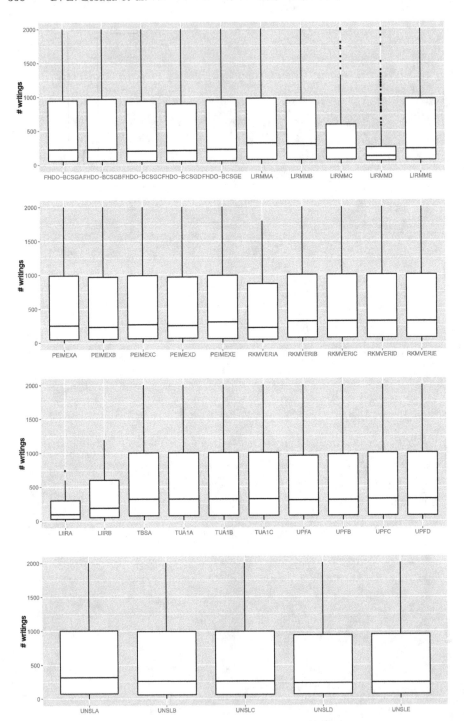

Fig. 6. Number of writings required by each contributing run in order to emit a decision.

Table 6. Task 2 (anorexia). Results

	$ERDE_5$	$ERDE_{50}$	F1	P	R
FHDO-BCSGA	12.17%	7.98%	0.71	0.67	0.76
FHDO-BCSGB	11.75%	6.84%	0.81	0.84	0.78
FHDO-BCSGC	13.63%	9.64%	0.55	0.47	0.66
FHDO-BCSGD	12.15%	**5.96%**	0.81	0.75	**0.88**
FHDO-BCSGE	11.98%	6.61%	**0.85**	0.87	0.83
LIIRA	12.78%	10.47%	0.71	0.81	0.63
LIIRB	13.05%	10.33%	0.76	0.79	0.73
LIRMMA	13.65%	13.04%	0.54	0.52	0.56
LIRMMB	14.45%	12.62%	0.52	0.41	0.71
LIRMMC	16.06%	15.02%	0.42	0.28	0.78
LIRMMD	17.14%	14.31%	0.34	0.22	0.76
LIRMME	14.89%	12.69%	0.41	0.32	0.59
PEIMEXA	12.70%	9.25%	0.46	0.39	0.56
PEIMEXB	12.41%	7.79%	0.64	0.57	0.73
PEIMEXC	13.42%	10.50%	0.43	0.37	0.51
PEIMEXD	12.94%	9.86%	0.67	0.61	0.73
PEIMEXE	12.84%	10.82%	0.31	0.28	0.34
RKMVERIA	12.17%	8.63%	0.67	0.82	0.56
RKMVERIB	12.93%	12.31%	0.46	0.81	0.32
RKMVERIC	12.85%	12.85%	0.25	0.86	0.15
RKMVERID	12.89%	12.89%	0.31	0.80	0.20
RKMVERIE	12.93%	12.31%	0.46	0.81	0.32
UNSLA	12.48%	12.00%	0.17	0.57	0.10
UNSLB	**11.40%**	7.82%	0.61	0.75	0.51
UNSLC	11.61%	7.82%	0.61	0.75	0.51
UNSLD	12.93%	9.85%	0.79	**0.91**	0.71
UNSLE	12.93%	10.13%	0.74	0.90	0.63
UPFA	13.18%	11.34%	0.72	0.74	0.71
UPFB	13.01%	11.76%	0.65	0.81	0.54
UPFC	13.17%	11.60%	0.73	0.76	0.71
UPFD	12.93%	12.30%	0.60	0.86	0.46
TBSA	13.65%	11.14%	0.67	0.60	0.76
TUA1A	-	-	0.00	0.00	0.00
TUA1B	19.90%	19.27%	0.25	0.15	0.76
TUA1C	13.53%	12.57%	0.36	0.42	0.32

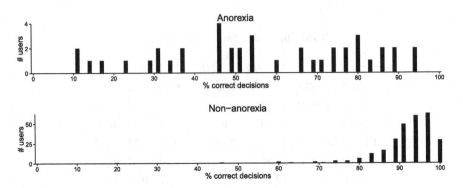

Fig. 7. Number of anorexia and non-anorexia users that had a given percentage of correct decisions.

4 Conclusions

This paper provided an overview of eRisk 2018. This was the second year that this lab was organized at CLEF and the lab's activities concentrated on two tasks (early detection of signs of depression and early detection of signs of anorexia). Overall, the tasks received 80 variants or runs and the teams focused on tuning different classification solutions. The tradeoff between early detection and accuracy was ignored by most participants.

The effectiveness of the solutions implemented to early detect signs of depression is similar to that achieved for eRisk 2017. This performance is still modest, suggesting that it is challenging to tell depressed and non-depressed users apart. In contrast, the effectiveness of the systems that detect signs of anorexia was much higher. This promising result encourages us to further explore the creation of benchmarks for text-based screening of eating disorders. In the future, we also want to instigate more research on the tradeoff between accuracy and delay.

Acknowledgements. We thank the support obtained from the Swiss National Science Foundation (SNSF) under the project "Early risk prediction on the Internet: an evaluation corpus", 2015.

We also thank the financial support obtained from the (i) "Ministerio de Economía y Competitividad" of the Government of Spain and FEDER Funds under the research project TIN2015-64282-R, (ii) Xunta de Galicia (project GPC 2016/035), and (iii) Xunta de Galicia – "Consellería de Cultura, Educación e Ordenación Universitaria" and the European Regional Development Fund (ERDF) through the following 2016–2019 accreditations: ED431G/01 ("Centro singular de investigacion de Galicia") and ED431G/08.

References

1. Losada, D.E., Crestani, F.: A test collection for research on depression and language use. In: Fuhr, N., et al. (eds.) CLEF 2016. LNCS, vol. 9822, pp. 28–39. Springer, Cham (2016). https://doi.org/10.1007/978-3-319-44564-9_3
2. Losada, D.E., Crestani, F., Parapar, J.: eRISK 2017: CLEF lab on early risk prediction on the internet: experimental foundations. In: Jones, G.J.F., et al. (eds.) CLEF 2017. LNCS, vol. 10456, pp. 346–360. Springer, Cham (2017). https://doi.org/10.1007/978-3-319-65813-1_30

Overview of the CLEF Dynamic Search Evaluation Lab 2018

Evangelos Kanoulas[1]($\boxtimes$), Leif Azzopardi[2], and Grace Hui Yang[3]

[1] Informatics Institute, University of Amsterdam, Amsterdam, Netherlands
e.kanoulas@uva.nl
[2] Computer and Information Sciences, University of Strathclyde, Glasgow, UK
leif.azzopardi@strath.ac.uk
[3] Department of Computer Science, Georgetown University, Washington, D.C., USA
huiyang@cs.georgetown.edu

Abstract. In this paper we provide an overview of the CLEF 2018 Dynamic Search Lab. The lab ran for the first time in 2017 as a workshop. The outcomes of the workshop were used to define the tasks of this year's evaluation lab. The lab strives to answer one key question: how can we evaluate, and consequently build, dynamic search algorithms? Unlike static search algorithms, which consider user request's independently, and consequently do not adapt their ranking with respect to the user's sequence of interactions and the user's end goal, dynamic search algorithms try to infer the user's intentions based on their interactions and adapt their ranking accordingly. Session personalization, contextual search, conversational search, dialog systems are some examples of dynamic search. Herein, we describe the overall objectives of the CLEF 2018 Dynamic Search Lab, the resources created, and the evaluation methodology designed.

Keywords: Evaluation · Information retrieval · Dynamic search
Interactive search · Conversational search · User simulations
Query suggestion · Query generation · Meta-search · Result re-ranking

1 Introduction

Information Retrieval (IR) research has traditionally focused on serving the best results for a single query – so-called ad-hoc retrieval. However, users typically search iteratively, refining and reformulating their queries during a session. IR systems can still respond to each query in a session independently of the history of user interactions, or alternatively adopt their model of relevance in the context of these interactions. A key challenge in the study of algorithms and models that dynamically adapt their response to a user's query on the basis of prior interactions is the creation of suitable evaluation resources and the definition of suitable evaluation metrics to assess their effectiveness. Over the years various initiatives have been proposed which have tried to make progress on this long standing challenge.

© Springer Nature Switzerland AG 2018
P. Bellot et al. (Eds.): CLEF 2018, LNCS 11018, pp. 362–371, 2018.
https://doi.org/10.1007/978-3-319-98932-7_31

The TREC Interactive Track [12], which ran between 1994 and 2002, investigated the evaluation of interactive IR systems and resulted in an early standardization of the experimental design. However, it did not lead to a reusable test collection methodology. The TREC High Accuracy Retrieval of Documents (HARD) Track [1] followed the Interactive track, with the primary focus on single-cycle user-system interactions. These interactions were embodied in clarification forms which could be used by retrieval algorithms to elicit feedback from assessors. The track attempted to further standardize the retrieval of interactive algorithms, however it also did not lead to a reusable collection that supports adaptive and dynamic search algorithms. The TREC Session Track [2], which ran from 2010 through 2014, made some headway in this direction. The track produced test collections, where included with the topic description was the history of user interactions with a system, that could be used to improve the performance of a given query. While, this mean adaptive and dynamic algorithms could be evaluated for one iteration of the search process, the collection's are not suitable for assessing the quality of retrieval over an entire session. Further, algorithms that learn to optimize ranking over entire sessions are not feasible to be built. In 2015, the TREC Tasks Track [16,21] took a different direction, where the test collection provided queries for which all possible sub-tasks needed to be inferred, and the documents relevant to those sub-tasks identified. Even though the produced test collections could be used in testing whether a system could help the user to perform a task end-to-end, the focus was not on adapting and learning from the user's interactions as in the case of dynamic search algorithms. The Dynamic Domain Track [18], which ran in parallel to the Tasks Track, between 2015 and 2017, focused on domains of special interests, which usually produces complex and exploratory searches with multiple runs of user and search engine interactions. It was search in multiple runs of interactions where the participting systems were expected to adjust their systems dynamically based on the relevance judgments provided along the way. Figure 1 provides an overview of the task in this track. The user simulator, was practically feedback on the relevance of the returned documents and the passages in these document, to be used by retrieval systems in any way they could for the next iteration. Despite this over-simplification of what constitutes a user simulation the Dynamic Domain Track was the first benchmark collection that was designed to allow the development of dynamic retrieval systems in a controlled laboratory setting. The CLEF Dynamic Search Lab takes this effort one step forward, and instead of focusing on developing dynamic search algorithm, it focuses on developing effective user simulations.

In the related domain of dialogue systems, the advancement of deep and reinforcement learning methods has led to a new generation of data-driven dialog systems. Broadly-speaking, dialog systems can be categorized along two dimensions, (a) goal-driven vs. non-goal-driven, and (b) open-domain vs. closed domain dialog systems. Goal-driven open-domain dialog systems are in par with dynamic search engines: as they seek to provide assistance, advice and answers to a user over unrestricted and diverse topics, helping them complete their task, by not only taking into account the conversation history but optimizing the overall

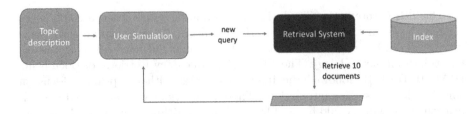

Fig. 1. TREC Dynamic Domain framework depicting the overall process and the task of ranking.

dialogue towards a specific user goal. While, a variety of corpora is available for training such dialog systems [15], when it comes to the evaluation, the existing corpora are inappropriate. This is because they only contain a static set of dialogues and any dialog that does not develop in a way similar to the static set cannot be evaluated. Often, the evaluation of goal-driven dialogue systems focuses on goal-related performance criteria, such as goal completion rate, dialogue length, and user satisfaction. Automatically determining whether a task has been solved however is an open problem, while task-completion is not the only quality criterion of interest in the development of dialog systems. Thus, simulated data is often generated by a simulated user [3,6,14]. Given a sufficiently accurate model of how user's converse, the interaction between the dialog system and the user can be simulated over a large space of possible topics. Using such data, it is then possible to deduce the desired metrics. This suggests that a similar approach could be taken in the context of interactive IR. However, while significant effort has been made to render the simulated data as realistic as possible [11,13], generating realistic user simulation models remains an open problem.

2   Lab Overview and Tasks

The focus of CLEF Dynamic Search is the evaluation and development of dynamic information retrieval algorithms that solve a user's complex task by continuously interacting with the user. When it comes to dynamic systems, the response of the system affects the user's next action. For instance, in dialog systems the response of the system highly affects how the user will continue the dialog, in search-based retrieval, the ranked results by the search engine highly affect the next query of the user. In these setups the evaluation of the systems becomes a really hard task, and it remains an open problem. Given the absence of a reliable evaluation framework in such a conversational/dynamic setup, the development of dynamic/conversational search engines also remains an open problem.

The CLEF 2018 Dynamic Search Lab focuses on the development of a dynamic search system evaluation framework, on the basis of the conclusions of the CLEF 2018 Dynamic Search Lab workshop [7,8]. The framework constitutes two agents – a question-agent and an answer-agent – which interact to solve a user's task. The answer agent corresponds to the dynamic search system, or dynamic question answering system, while the question agent corresponds to the simulated user. In this 2018 edition, we focus on the development of a question agent, the goal of which is the production of effective queries given a verbose description of a user's information need (*query suggestion*). The question-agent will produce queries in a multi-round fashion; at every round a query is produced, submitted to the answer-agent, an Indri query language model over the New York Time corpus (more in Sect. 3), and the top-10 results of the query are fed back to the question-agent for the production of the next query. Potential participants are provided with a RESTful API to query the Indri index. The question-agent is running for 10 rounds, submitting in total 10 queries and obtaining 100 results retrieved by the answer agent. These 100 results, 10 per query, are then ranked in final ranking (*result composition*). Therefore, the lab offers two tasks to potential participants:

- Task 1: Query generation/suggestion
- Task 2: Results composition.

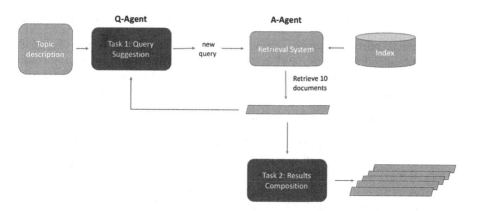

Fig. 2. CLEF 2018 Dynamic Search Lab framework depicting the overall process and the two tasks of query generation and result composition.

The two tasks are also depicted in red boxes in Fig. 2. In Task 1, participants were provided with a set of topics, split in a development and a test set. During the first search iteration, the participating runs in Task 1, were asked to generate a query to be submitted to a predefined, and provided by the participants retrieval system. In all follow up iterations, beyond the topic descriptions, the participating runs could use any information from the top-10 per-query returned documents resulted from all previous iterations. Participants were asked generate queries for 10 rounds of interactions. At the end of the 10 rounds, participants had to submit a run, with the following format:

```
TOPIC QUESTION DOCNO RANK SCORE RUN
```

TOPIC is the topic id and could be found in the released topics. QUESTION is the suggested by the participant query of this round. The question should be included within quotes, e.g. "london hotels". Each suggested query should be repeated over a maximum of 10 rows. DOCNO is the document id in the corpus. RANK is the rank of the document returned for this given round (in increasing order) SCORE is the score of the ranking/classification algorithm. RUN is an identifier/name for the system producing the run. Below is an example of a run:

```
dd17-51 "Katrina most costly hurricane" 1783276 10  ILPS-run1
dd17-51 "Katrina most costly hurricane" 1775816 9   ILPS-run1
dd17-51 "Katrina most costly hurricane" 1718269 8   ILPS-run1
dd17-51 "Katrina most costly hurricane" 1724162 7   ILPS-run1
dd17-51 "Katrina most costly hurricane" 1701311 6   ILPS-run1
dd17-51 "Katrina most costly hurricane" 1834929 5   ILPS-run1
dd17-51 "Katrina most costly hurricane" 1818307 4   ILPS-run1
dd17-51 "Katrina most costly hurricane" 1780634 3   ILPS-run1
dd17-51 "Katrina most costly hurricane" 1704548 2   ILPS-run1
dd17-51 "Katrina most costly hurricane" 1704526 1   ILPS-run1
dd17-51 "Hurricane Katrina's path of destruction"  1704322 10  ILPS-run1
... ... ... ...
dd17-60 "Tupac Amaru and Shining Path relationship" 0896459 1   ILPS-run1
```

In Task 2, participants were provided with all the top-10 results of the 10 queries submitted to the retrieval system, and they were asked to re-rank these 100 documents into a single ranking. The run to be submitted should have the following format:

```
TOPIC DUMMY DOCNO RANK SCORE RUN
```

TOPIC is the topic id and can be found in the released topics. DUMMY is a dummy column to be filled in with 0. DOCNO is the document number in the corpus. RANK is the rank of the document returned for this given round (in increasing order). SCORE is the score of the ranking/classification algorithm. RUN is an identifier/name for the system producing the run

Below is an example run:

```
dd17-51 0   1783276 100 ILPS-run1
dd17-51 0   1704322 99  ILPS-run1
dd17-51 0   1718269 98  ILPS-run1
dd17-51 0   1724162 97  ILPS-run1
dd17-51 0   1704548 96  ILPS-run1
dd17-51 0   1834929 95  ILPS-run1
dd17-51 0   1818307 94  ILPS-run1
dd17-51 0   1780634 93  ILPS-run1
dd17-51 0   1701311 92  ILPS-run1
dd17-51 0   1704526 91  ILPS-run1
dd17-51 0   1775816 90  ILPS-run1
... ... ... ...
dd17-60 0   0896459 1   ILPS-run1
```

3   Data Sets and Answer Agent

The collection that is used in the 2018 Dynamic Search Lab is the New York Times corpus[1]. The New York Times dataset consists of 1,855,658 articles published in New York Times from January 1, 1987 to June 19, 2007 with metadata provided by the New York Times Newsroom, the New York Times Indexing Service and the online production staff at nytimes.com. Most articles are manually summarized and tagged by professional staffs. The original form of this dataset is in News Industry Text Format (NITF).

The corpus was indexed by Indri and a Query Language Model with Dirichlet Smoothing has been implemented on the top of the Indri index, using Pyndri [4][2]. Potential participants are provided with a RESTful API to query the index[3].

The topics used are the topics developed by NIST assessors for the TREC 2017 Dynamic Domain Track [19]. A topic contains a title, which is like a query of few words, a more extended description of the user's information need, and a narrative that elaborates on what makes a document relevant and what not. It is the main search target for one complete run of dynamic search. An example of a topic provided to participants can be found below:

```
<topic name="Return of Klimt paintings to Maria Altmann"
      id="dd17-1">
    <description>Find information about the artwork by Austrian
    painter Gustav Klimt that was stolen by Nazis from its Austrian
    owners and subsequently returned to the rightful heir, Maria
    Altmann. </description>
    <narrative>This topic follows developments in the case of six
    specific paintings stolen by the Nazis during WWII.  The stolen
    paintings were given to a relative of the artist (Gustav Klimt),
    who in turn gave them to the Austrian government. ... Only the
    six paintings that comprised the Altmann case are relevant;
    work by other artists and other work by Klimt that had been
    confiscated by the Nazis is not relevant. </narrative>
</topic>
```

Each topic contains multiple subtopics, each of which addresses one aspect of the topic. The NIST assessors have tried produce a complete set of subtopics for each topic, and so they are treated as the complete set used in the evaluation. An example of a topic with subtopics is shown below:

---

[1] https://catalog.ldc.upenn.edu/ldc2008t19.
[2] https://github.com/cvangysel/pyndri.
[3] https://bitbucket.org/cvangysel/pyndri-flask.

```
<topic name="Hurricane Katrina's Effects" id="dd17-51"
        num_of_subtopics="4">
    <description>Hurricane Katrina, the most costly hurricane ever,
    effected millions of people ... </description>
    <narrative>Relevant documents report on how ... </narrative>
    <subtopic name="Katrina most costly hurricane" id="505"
            num_of_passages="10">
        <passage id="3628">
            <docno>1783276</docno>
            <rating>2</rating>
            <text><![CDATA[A federal judge in Mississippi ...]]>
            </text>
            <type>MANUAL</type>
        </passage>
        ...
```

Ten topics were released as a development set on April 15, 2018, and fifty topics as the test set on May 5, 2018. Subtopics for the test topics were not be released. The relevance judgments for these topics also followed the same sub-topic structure.

4   Evaluation

4.1   Task 1: Query Suggestion

The objective of task 1 is to generate a sequence of queries, in a sequential fashion, given a verbose description of a task (topic) and results of the answer agent for all previous queries. Each developed question agent is allowed to go over 10 rounds of query generations. At each round one query is submitted to the answer agent, and the top 10 results are collected. At the end of round 10, 100 search results will have been collected.

Therefore, in task 1 we focus on session based evaluation, with the quality of the A-Agent quantified by the Cube Test [10], sDCG [5], Expected Utility [20], and expected session nDCG [9]; other diagnostic measures such as precision and recall are to be reported. Cube Test is a search effectiveness measurement evaluating the speed of gaining relevant information (could be documents or passages) in a dynamic search process. It measures the amount of relevant information a system could gather and the time needed in the entire search process. The higher the Cube Test score, the better the IR system. sDCG extends the classic DCG to a search session which consists of multiple iterations. The relevance scores of results that are ranked lower or returned in later iterations get more discounts. The discounted cumulative relevance score is the final results of this metric. Expected Utility scores different runs by measuring the relevant information a system found and the length of documents. The relevance scores of documents are discounted based on ranking order and novelty. The document length is discounted only based on ranking position. The difference between the cumulative relevance score and the aggregated document length is the final score of each run. Expected session DCG is an extension of the probabilistic model of the Expected Utility measure, that allows for modeling users that do not always see all the reformulations of a static set of them, i.e. allows for early abandonment.

4.2   Task 2: Results Composition

The objective of Task 2 is given the rankings obtained in Task 1 to merge them in a single composite ranking. At the end of round 10, 100 search results will have been collected. These 100 results coming from 10 queries should be re-ranked in a single optimal ranking. The evaluation of the quality of the composed ranking is done with traditional measures, such as nDCG, and diversity-based measures such as α-nDCG.

5   Lab Participation

Setting up the lab required more time than was originally anticipated. As a result, both the benchmark collection and the answer agent service were provided to participants only by mid-April, which did not allow the construction of a community around the lab. Hence, while 13 groups registered for the lab and 3 groups expressed very strong interest in participating, the lab received no submissions.

6   Conclusions

The CLEF Dynamic Search for Complex Tasks lab strives to answer one key question: how can we evaluate, and consequently build, dynamic search algorithms? The 2018 lab focused on how to devise an evaluation framework for dynamic search. Inspired by the Dynamic Domain framework, the lab sought for participants who would build user simulators, in terms of generated queries along multiple search iterations. The lab organizers decided to evaluate the effectiveness of the generated queries, rather than how close they are to actual user queries, and hence the main task of the lab (task 1) turned into a query suggestion task. This task was also followed by a result composition task (task 2) which focused on re-ranking the documents produced by a controlled retrieval system on the basis of the suggested queries.

Acknowledgements. This work was partially supported by the Google Faculty Research Award program. All content represents the opinion of the authors, which is not necessarily shared or endorsed by their respective employers and/or sponsors.

References

1. Allan, J.: HARD track overview in TREC 2003 high accuracy retrieval from documents. Technical report, DTIC Document (2005)
2. Carterette, B., Clough, P.D., Hall, M.M., Kanoulas, E., Sanderson, M.: Evaluating retrieval over sessions: the TREC session track 2011–2014. In: Perego, R., Sebastiani, F., Aslam, J.A., Ruthven, I., Zobel, J. (eds.) Proceedings of the 39th International ACM SIGIR Conference on Research and Development in Information Retrieval, SIGIR 2016, Pisa, Italy, 17–21 July 2016, pp. 685–688. ACM (2016). https://doi.org/10.1145/2911451.2914675
3. Georgila, K., Henderson, J., Lemon, O.: User simulation for spoken dialogue systems: learning and evaluation. In: Interspeech, pp. 1065–1068 (2006)
4. Van Gysel, C., Kanoulas, E., de Rijke, M.: Pyndri: a Python interface to the indri search engine. In: Jose, J.M., et al. (eds.) ECIR 2017. LNCS, vol. 10193, pp. 744–748. Springer, Cham (2017). https://doi.org/10.1007/978-3-319-56608-5_74
5. Järvelin, K., Price, S.L., Delcambre, L.M.L., Nielsen, M.L.: Discounted cumulated gain based evaluation of multiple-query IR sessions. In: Macdonald, C., Ounis, I., Plachouras, V., Ruthven, I., White, R.W. (eds.) ECIR 2008. LNCS, vol. 4956, pp. 4–15. Springer, Heidelberg (2008). https://doi.org/10.1007/978-3-540-78646-7_4
6. Jung, S., Lee, C., Kim, K., Jeong, M., Lee, G.G.: Data-driven user simulation for automated evaluation of spoken dialog systems. Comput. Speech Lang. $23(4)$, 479–509 (2009). https://doi.org/10.1016/j.csl.2009.03.002
7. Kanoulas, E., Azzopardi, L.: CLEF 2017 dynamic search evaluation lab overview. In: Jones, G.J.F., et al. (eds.) CLEF 2017. LNCS, vol. 10456, pp. 361–366. Springer, Cham (2017). https://doi.org/10.1007/978-3-319-65813-1_31
8. Kanoulas, E., Azzopardi, L.: CLEF 2017 dynamic search lab overview and evaluation. In: Cappellato, L., Ferro, N., Goeuriot, L., Mandl, T. (eds.) Working Notes of CLEF 2017 - Conference and Labs of the Evaluation Forum, Dublin, Ireland, 11–14 September 2017. CEUR Workshop Proceedings, vol. 1866. CEUR-WS.org (2017). http://ceur-ws.org/Vol-1866/invited_paper_13.pdf
9. Kanoulas, E., Carterette, B., Clough, P.D., Sanderson, M.: Evaluating multi-query sessions. In: Proceedings of the 34th International ACM SIGIR Conference on Research and Development in Information Retrieval, SIGIR 2011, pp. 1053–1062. ACM, New York (2011). https://doi.org/10.1145/2009916.2010056
10. Luo, J., Wing, C., Yang, H., Hearst, M.A.: The water filling model and the cube test: multi-dimensional evaluation for professional search. In: 22nd ACM International Conference on Information and Knowledge Management, CIKM 2013, San Francisco, CA, USA, 27 October–1 November 2013, pp. 709–714 (2013). https://doi.org/10.1145/2505515.2523648
11. Maxwell, D., Azzopardi, L.: Agents, simulated users and humans: an analysis of performance and behaviour. In: Proceedings of the 25th ACM International on Conference on Information and Knowledge Management, pp. 731–740. CIKM 2016 (2016)
12. Over, P.: The TREC interactive track: an annotated bibliography. Inf. Process. Manag. $37(3)$, 369–381 (2001)
13. Pääkkönen, T., Kekäläinen, J., Keskustalo, H., Azzopardi, L., Maxwell, D., Järvelin, K.: Validating simulated interaction for retrieval evaluation. Inf. Retr. J. 20, 1–25 (2017)
14. Pietquin, O., Hastie, H.: A survey on metrics for the evaluation of user simulations. Knowl. Eng. Rev. $28(01)$, 59–73 (2013)

15. Serban, I.V., Lowe, R., Henderson, P., Charlin, L., Pineau, J.: A survey of available corpora for building data-driven dialogue systems. CoRR abs/1512.05742 (2015). http://arxiv.org/abs/1512.05742

16. Verma, M., et al.: Overview of the TREC tasks track 2016. In: Voorhees and Ellis [17] (2016). http://trec.nist.gov/pubs/trec25/papers/Overview-T.pdf

17. Voorhees, E.M., Ellis, A. (eds.): Proceedings of The Twenty-Fifth Text REtrieval Conference, TREC 2016, Gaithersburg, Maryland, USA, 15–18 November 2016, vol. Special Publication 500-321. National Institute of Standards and Technology (NIST) (2016). http://trec.nist.gov/pubs/trec25/trec2016.html

18. Yang, G.H., Soboroff, I.: TREC 2016 dynamic domain track overview. In: Voorhees and Ellis [17] (2016). http://trec.nist.gov/pubs/trec25/papers/Overview-DD.pdf

19. Yang, G.H., Soboroff, I.: TREC 2017 dynamic domain track overview. In: Voorhees, E.M., Ellis, A. (eds.) Proceedings of The Twenty-Sixth Text REtrieval Conference, TREC 2017, Gaithersburg, Maryland, USA, 15–18 November 2017. National Institute of Standards and Technology (NIST) (2017)

20. Yang, Y., Lad, A.: Modeling expected utility of multi-session information distillation. In: Azzopardi, L., et al. (eds.) ICTIR 2009. LNCS, vol. 5766, pp. 164–175. Springer, Heidelberg (2009). https://doi.org/10.1007/978-3-642-04417-5_15

21. Yilmaz, E., Verma, M., Mehrotra, R., Kanoulas, E., Carterette, B., Craswell, N.: Overview of the TREC 2015 tasks track. In: Voorhees, E.M., Ellis, A. (eds.) Proceedings of The Twenty-Fourth Text REtrieval Conference, TREC 2015, Gaithersburg, Maryland, USA, 17–20 November 2015, vol. Special Publication 500–319. National Institute of Standards and Technology (NIST) (2015). http://trec.nist.gov/pubs/trec24/papers/Overview-T.pdf

Overview of the CLEF-2018 CheckThat! Lab on Automatic Identification and Verification of Political Claims

Preslav Nakov[1]([⊠]), Alberto Barrón-Cedeño[1], Tamer Elsayed[2],
Reem Suwaileh[2], Lluís Màrquez[3], Wajdi Zaghouani[4], Pepa Atanasova[5],
Spas Kyuchukov[6], and Giovanni Da San Martino[1]

[1] Qatar Computing Research Institute, HBKU, Doha, Qatar
{pnakov,albarron,gmartino}@qf.org.qa
[2] Computer Science and Engineering Department, Qatar University, Doha, Qatar
{telsayed,reem.suwaileh}@qu.edu.qa
[3] Amazon, Barcelona, Spain
lluismv@amazon.com
[4] College of Humanities and Social Sciences, HBKU, Doha, Qatar
wzaghouani@hbku.edu.qa
[5] SiteGround, Sofia, Bulgaria
pepa.gencheva@siteground.com
[6] Sofia University "St Kliment Ohridski", Sofia, Bulgaria
spas.kyuchukov@gmail.com

Abstract. We present an overview of the CLEF-2018 CheckThat! Lab on Automatic Identification and Verification of Political Claims. In its starting year, the lab featured two tasks. Task 1 asked to predict which (potential) claims in a political debate should be prioritized for fact-checking; in particular, given a debate or a political speech, the goal was to produce a ranked list of its sentences based on their worthiness for fact-checking. Task 2 asked to assess whether a given check-worthy claim made by a politician in the context of a debate/speech is factually true, half-true, or false. We offered both tasks in English and in Arabic. In terms of data, for both tasks, we focused on debates from the 2016 US Presidential Campaign, as well as on some speeches during and after the campaign (we also provided translations in Arabic), and we relied on comments and factuality judgments from factcheck.org and snopes.com, which we further refined manually. A total of 30 teams registered to participate in the lab, and 9 of them actually submitted runs. The evaluation results show that the most successful approaches used various neural networks (esp. for Task 1) and evidence retrieval from the Web (esp. for Task 2). We release all datasets, the evaluation scripts, and the submissions by the participants, which should enable further research in both check-worthiness estimation and automatic claim verification.

Keywords: Computational journalism
Check-worthiness estimation · Fact-checking · Veracity

1   Introduction

The current coverage of the political landscape in both the press and in social media has led to an unprecedented situation. Like never before, a statement in an interview, a press release, a blog note, or a tweet can spread almost instantaneously across the globe. This speed of proliferation has left little time for double-checking claims against the facts, which has proven critical in politics. For instance, the 2016 US Presidential Campaign was arguably influenced by fake news in social media and by false claims. Indeed, some politicians were fast to notice that when it comes to shaping public opinion, facts were secondary, and that appealing to emotions and beliefs worked better. It has been even proposed that this was marking the dawn of a post-truth age.

As the problem became evident, a number of fact-checking initiatives have started, led by organizations such as FactCheck[1] and Snopes[2] among many others. Yet, this has proved to be a very demanding manual effort, which means that only a relatively small number of claims could be fact-checked.[3] This makes it important to prioritize the claims that fact-checkers should consider first, and then to help them discover the veracity of those claims.

The **CheckThat! Lab** at CLEF-2018 aims at helping in that respect, by promoting the development of tools for computational journalism. Figure 1 illustrates the fact-checking pipeline, which includes three steps: (*i*) *check-worthiness estimation*, (*ii*) *claim normalization*, and (*iii*) *fact-checking*. The CheckThat! Lab focuses on the first and the last steps, while taking for granted (and thus excluding) the intermediate claim normalization step.

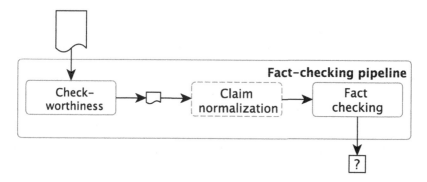

Fig. 1. The general fact-checking pipeline. First, the input document is analyzed to identify sentences containing check-worthy claims, then these claims are extracted and normalized (to be self-contained), and finally they are fact-checked.

---

[1] http://www.factcheck.org.

[2] http://www.snopes.com.

[3] Fully automating the process of fact-checking is not yet a viable alternative, partly because of limitations of the existing technology, and partly due to low trust in such methods by human users.

Hillary Clinton:	I think my husband did a pretty good job in the 1990s.	
Hillary Clinton:	I think a lot about what worked and how we can make it work again...	
Donald Trump:	Well, he approved NAFTA...	⊘

(a) Fragment from the First 2016 US Presidential Debate.

| Hillary Clinton: | He provided a good middle-class life for us, but the people he worked for, he expected the bargain to be kept on both sides. | |
| Hillary Clinton: | And when we talk about your business, you've taken business bankruptcy six times. | ⊘ |

(b) Another fragment from the First 2016 US Presidential Debate.

Fig. 2. English debate fragments: check-worthy sentences are marked with ⊘ .

Task 1 (Check-Worthiness) aims to help fact-checkers prioritize their efforts. In particular, it asks participants to build systems that can mimic the selection strategies of a particular fact-checking organization: factcheck.org. The task is defined as follows:

> Given a transcription of a political debate/speech, predict which claims should be prioritized for fact-checking.

Figure 2 shows examples of English debate fragments with annotations for Task 1. In example 2a, Hillary Clinton discusses the performance of her husband Bill Clinton while he was US president. Donald Trump fires back with a claim that is worth fact-checking: that Bill Clinton approved NAFTA. In example 2b, Donald Trump is accused of having filed for bankruptcy six times, which is also worth checking.

Task 1 is a *ranking* task. The goal is to produce a *ranked list* of sentences ordered by their worthiness for fact-checking. Each of the identified claims then becomes an input for the next step (after being manually normalized, i.e., edited to be self-contained with no ambiguous or unresolved references).

Task 2 (Fact-Checking) focuses on tools intended to verify the factuality of a check-worthy claim. The task is defined as follows:

> Given a check-worthy claim in the form of a (transcribed) sentence, determine whether the claim is likely to be true, half-true, or false.

For example, the sentence *"Well, he approved NAFTA..."* from example 2a is normalized to *"President Bill Clinton approved NAFTA."* and the target label is set to HALF-TRUE. Similarly, the sentence *"And when we talk about your business, you've taken business bankruptcy six times."* from example 2b is normalized to *"Donald Trump has filed for bankruptcy of his business six times."* and the target label is set to TRUE.

Task 2 is a *classification* task. The goal is to *label* each check-worthy claim with an estimated/predicted veracity. Note that we provide the participants not only with the normalized claim, but also with the original sentence it originated from, which is in turn given in the context of the entire debate/speech. Thus, this is a novel task for fact-checking claims *in context*, an aspect that has been largely ignored in previous research on fact-checking.

Note that the intermediate task of *claim normalization* is challenging and requires dealing with anaphora resolution, paraphrasing, and dialogue analysis, and thus we decided not to offer it as a separate task.

We produced data based on professional fact-checking annotations of debates and speeches from factcheck.org, which we modified in three ways: (*i*) we did some minor adjustments of which sentences were selected for fact-checking, (*ii*) we generated normalized versions of the claims in the selected sentences, and (*iii*) we generated veracity labels for each normalized claim based on the fact-checker's free-text analysis. As a result, we created CT-C-18, the Check-That! 2018 corpus, which combines two sub-corpora: CT-CWC-18 to predict check-worthiness, and CT-FCC-18 to assess the veracity of claims. We offered each of the two tasks in two languages: English and Arabic. For Arabic, we hired professional translators to translate the English data, and we also had a separate Arabic-only part for Task 2, based on claims from snopes.com.

Nine teams participated in the lab this year. The most successful systems relied on supervised models using a manifold of representations. We believe that there is still large room for improvement, and thus we release the corpora, the evaluation scripts, and the participants' predictions, which should enable further research on check-worthiness estimation and automatic claim verification.[4]

The remainder of the paper is organized as follows. Section 2 presents an overview of related work. Section 3 describes the datasets. Section 4 discusses Task 1 (check-worthiness) in detail, including the evaluation framework and the setup, the approaches used by the participating teams, and the official results. Section 5 provides similar details for Task 2 (fact-checking). Finally, Sect. 6 draws some conclusions.

2   Related Work

Journalists, online users, and researchers are well aware of the proliferation of false information, and topics such as credibility and fact-checking are becoming increasingly important. For example, there was a 2016 special issue of the ACM Transactions on Information Systems journal on Trust and Veracity of Information in Social Media [24], and there is a Workshop on Fact Extraction and Verification at EMNLP'2018. Moreover, there is a SemEval-2017 shared task on Rumor Detection [7], an ongoing FEVER challenge on Fact Extraction and VERification at EMNLP'2018, the present CLEF'2018 Lab on Automatic Identification and Verification of Claims in Political Debates, and an upcoming task at SemEval'2019 on Fact-Checking in Community Question Answering Forums.

---

[4] https://github.com/clef2018-factchecking.

Automatic fact-checking was envisioned in [31] as a multi-step process that includes (*i*) identifying check-worthy statements [9,14,16], (*ii*) generating questions to be asked about these statements [18], (*iii*) retrieving relevant information to create a knowledge base [29], and (*iv*) inferring the veracity of the statements, e.g., using text analysis [6,28] or external sources [18,27].

The first work to target check-worthiness was the ClaimBuster system [14]. It was trained on data that was manually annotated by students, professors, and journalists, where each sentence was annotated as *non-factual, unimportant factual*, or *check-worthy factual*. The data consisted of transcripts of historical US election debates covering the period from 1960 until 2012 for a total of 30 debates and 28,029 transcribed sentences. In each sentence, the speaker was marked: candidate vs. moderator. The ClaimBuster used an SVM classifier and a manifold of features such as sentiment, TF.IDF word representations, part-of-speech (POS) tags, and named entities. It produced a check-worthiness ranking on the basis of the SVM prediction scores. The ClaimBuster system did not try to mimic the check-worthiness decisions for any specific fact-checking organization; yet, it was later evaluated against CNN and PolitiFact [15]. In contrast, our dataset is based on actual annotations by a fact-checking organization, and we release freely all data and associated scripts (while theirs is not available).

More relevant to the setup of Task 1 of this Lab is the work of [9], who focused on debates from the US 2016 Presidential Campaign and used pre-existing annotations from nine respected fact-checking organizations (PolitiFact, FactCheck, ABC, CNN, NPR, NYT, Chicago Tribune, The Guardian, and Washington Post): a total of four debates and 5,415 sentences. Beside many of the features borrowed from ClaimBuster—together with sentiment, tense, and some other features, their model pays special attention to the context of each sentence. This includes whether it is part of a long intervention by one of the actors and even its position within such an intervention. The authors predicted both (*i*) whether any of the fact-checking organizations would select the target sentence, and also (*ii*) whether a specific one would select it.

In follow-up work, [16] developed ClaimRank, which can mimic the claim selection strategies for each and any of the nine fact-checking organizations, as well as for the union of them all. Even though trained on English, it further supports Arabic, which is achieved via cross-language English-Arabic embeddings.

The work of [25] also focused on the 2016 US Election campaign, and they also used data from nine fact-checking organizations (but slightly different set from above). They used presidential (three presidential one vice-presidential) and primary debates (seven Republican and eight Democratic) for a total of 21,700 sentences. Their setup asked to predict whether any of the fact-checking sources would select the target sentence. They used a boosting-like model that takes SVMs focusing on different clusters of the dataset and the final outcome was considered as that coming from the most confident classifier. The features considered ranged from LDA topic-modeling to POS tuples and bag-of-words representations.

For Task 1, we follow a setup that is similar to that of [9,16,25], but we manually verify the selected sentences, e.g., to adjust the boundaries of the check-worthy claim, and also to include all instances of a selected check-worthy claim (as fact-checkers would only comment on one instance of a claim). We further have an Arabic version of the dataset. Finally, we chose to focus on a single fact-checking organization.

Regarding Task 2, which targets fact-checking a claim, there have been several datasets that focus on rumor detection. The gold labels are typically extracted from fact-checking websites such as Politifact with datasets ranging in size from 300 for the Emergent dataset [8] to 12.8 K claims for the Liar dataset [33]. Another fact-checking source that has been used is snopes.com, with datasets ranging in size from 1k claims [20] to 5k claims [26].

Less popular as a source has been Wikipedia with datasets ranging in size from 100 claims [26] to 185k for the FEVER dataset [30]. These datasets rely on crowdsourced annotations, which allows them to get large-scale, but risks having lower quality standards compared to the rigorous annotations by fact-checking organizations. Other crowdsourced efforts include the SemEval-2017's shared task on Rumor Detection [7] with 5.5k annotated rumorous tweets, and CREDBANK with 60M annotated tweets [22]. Finally, there have been manual annotation efforts, e.g., for fact-checking the answers in a community question answering forums with size of 250 [21]. Note that while most datasets have been targeting English, there have been also efforts focusing on other languages, e.g., Chinese [20], Arabic [3], and Bulgarian [13].

Unlike the above work, our focus in Task 2 is on claims in both their normalized and unnormalized form and in the context of a political debate or speech.

3   Corpora

We produced the CT-C-18 corpus, which stands for CheckThat! 2018 corpus. It is composed of CT-CWC-18 (check-worthiness corpus) and CT-FCC-18 (fact-checking corpus). CT-C-18 includes transcripts from debates, together with political speeches, and isolated claims. Table 1 gives an overview.

The training sets for both tasks come from the first and the second Presidential debates and the Vice-Presidential debate in the 2016 US campaign. The labels for both tasks were derived from manual fact-checking analysis published on factcheck.org. For Task 1, a claim was considered check-worthy if a journalist had fact-checked it. For Task 2 a judgment was generated based on the free-text discussion by the fact-checking journalists: true, half-true, or false. We followed the same procedure for texts in the test set: two other debates and five speeches by Donald Trump, which occurred after he took office as a US President. Note that there are cases in which the number of claims intended for predicting factuallity is lower than the reported number of check-worthy claims. The reason is that claims exist which were formulated more than once in both debates and speeches and, whereas we do consider them all as positive instances for Task 1, we consider them only once for Task 2.

Table 1. Overview of the debates, speeches, and isolated claims in the CT-C-18 corpus. It includes the number of utterances, those identified as check-worthy (task 1), and those claims identified as factually- true, half-true, and false. The debates/speeches that are available in Arabic are marked with 🏴. Note that the claims from snopes.com were released in Arabic only, and are marked with ●.

| | Set | Claims | Check-worthy | Factuallity | | |
				true	half-true	false
Debates						
🏴 1st Presidential	training	1,403	37	8	9	13
🏴 2nd Presidential	training	1,303	25	4	7	14
🏴 Vice-Presidential	training	1,358	28	7	6	14
🏴 3rd Presidential	test	1,351	77	19	8	21
🏴 9th Democratic	test	1,464	17	3	3	4
D. Trump Speeches						
🏴 Acceptance	test	375	21	8	5	7
World Economic Forum	test	245	11	6	2	3
Tax Reform Event	test	412	16	4	4	4
Address to Congress	test	390	15	6	3	4
Miami Speech	test	645	35	4	9	12
● **Snopes.com claims**	test	–	150	30	10	110

The Arabic version of the corpus was produced manually by professional translators who translated some of the English debates/speeches to Arabic as shown in Table 1. We used this strategy for all three training debates, for the two testing debates, and for one of the five speeches that we used for testing. In order to balance the number of examples for Task 2, we included fresh Arabic-only instances by selecting 150 claims from snopes.com that were related to the Arab world or to Islam. As the language of snopes.com is English, we translated these claims to Arabic but this time using Google Translate, and then some of the task organizers (native Arabic speakers) post-edited the result in order to come up with proper Arabic versions. Further details about the construction of the CT-CWC-18 and the CT-FCC-18 corpora can be found in [2,4].

4   Task 1: Check-Worthiness

4.1   Evaluation Measures

As we shaped this task as an information retrieval problem, in which check-worthy instances should be ranked at the top of the list, we opted for using mean average precision as the official evaluation measure. It is defined as follows:

$$MAP = \frac{\sum_{d=1}^{D} AveP(d)}{D} \tag{1}$$

Table 2. Task 1 (check-worthiness): overview of the learning models and of the representations used by the participants.

Learning Models	[1]	[11]	[12]	[35]	[36]		Representations	[1]	[11]	[12]	[35]	[36]
Recurrent neural nets		✓					Bag of words					✓
Multilayer perceptron					✓		Character n-grams		✓			
Support vector machines	✓				✓		Part of speech tags			✓	✓	✓
Random forest	✓						Verbal forms					✓
k-nearest neighbors	✓						Negations					✓
Gradient boosting					✓		Named entities				✓	✓

Representations	[1]	[11]	[12]	[35]	[36]
Sentiment				✓	✓
Topics					✓
IR nutritional labels ✓					
Clauses					✓
Syntactic dependency	✓				✓
Word embeddings			✓	✓	✓

Teams

[1] RNCC — [–] fragarach
[11] UPV-INAOE-Autoritas — [–] blue
[12] Copenhagen
[35] bigIR
[36] Prise de Fer

where $d \in D$ is one of the debates/speeches, and $AveP$ is the average precision:

$$AveP = \frac{\sum_{k=1}^{K}(P(k) \times \delta(k))}{\#\text{check-worthy claims}} \qquad (2)$$

where $P(k)$ refers to the value of precision at rank k and $\delta(k) = 1$ iff the claim at that position is check-worthy.

Following [9], we further report the results for some other measures: (*i*) mean reciprocal rank (MRR), (*ii*) mean R-Precision (MR-P), and (*iii*) mean precision@k (P@k). Here *mean* refers to macro-averaging over the testing debates/speeches.

4.2   Evaluation Results

The participants were allowed to submit one primary and up to two contrastive runs in order to test variations or alternative models. For ranking purposes, only the primary submissions were considered. A total of seven teams submitted runs for English, and two of them also did so for Arabic.

English. Table 4 shows the results for English. The best primary submission was that of the *Prise de Fer* team [35], which used a multilayer perceptron and a feature-rich representation. We can see that they had the best overall performance not only on the official MAP measure, but also on six out of nine evaluation measures (and they were 2nd or 3rd on the rest).

Interestingly, the top-performing run for English was an unofficial one, namely the contrastive 1 run by the *Copenhagen* team [12]. This model consisted of a recurrent neural network on three representations. They submitted a system that combined their neural network with the model of [9] as their primary submission, but their neural network alone (submitted as contrastive 1), performed better on the test set. This can be due to the model of [9] relying on structural information, which was not available for the speeches included in the test set.

To put these results in perspective, the bottom of Table 4 shows the results for two baselines: (*i*) a random permutation of the input sentences, and (*ii*) an n-gram based classifier. We can see that all systems managed to outperform the *random* baseline on all measures by a margin. However, only two runs managed to beat the *n-gram* baseline: the primary run of the *Prise de Fer* team, and the contrastive 1 run of the *Copenhagen* team.

Arabic. Only two teams participated in the Arabic task [11,34], using basically the same models that they had for English. The *bigIR* [34] team translated automatically the test input to English and then ran their English system, while *UPV–INAOE–Autoritas* translated to Arabic the English lexicons their representation was based on, and then trained an Arabic system on the Arabic training data, which they finally ran on the Arabic test input. It is worth noting that for English *UPV–INAOE–Autoritas* outperformed *bigIR*, but for Arabic it was the other way around. We suspect that a possible reason might be the direction of machine translation and also the presence/lack of context. On one hand, translation into English tends to be better than into Arabic. Moreover, the translation of sentences is easier as there is context, whereas such a context is missing when translating lexicon entries in isolation.

Finally, similarly to English, all runs managed to outperform the *random* baseline by a margin, while the *n-gram* baseline was strong yet possible to beat.

5   Task 2: Factuality

5.1   Evaluation Measures

Task 2 (factuality) the claims have to be labeled as *true*, *half-true*, or *false*. Note that, unlike standard multi-way classification problems, here we have a natural ordering between the classes and confusing one extreme with the other one is more harmful than confusing it with a neighboring class. This is known as an *ordinal classification* problem (aka *ordinal regression*), and it requires an evaluation measure that would take this ordering into account. Therefore, we opted for using mean absolute error (MAE), which is standard for such kinds of problems, as the official measure. MAE is defined as follows:

$$MAE = \frac{\sum_{c=1}^{C} |y_c - x_c|}{C} \tag{3}$$

where y_c and x_c are gold and predicted labels of claim c and $|\cdot|$ is the difference between them: either zero, one, or two.

Following [23], we also compute macro-average mean absolute error, accuracy, macro-averaged F_1, and macro-averaged recall.[5]

5.2 Evaluation Results

When dealing with the factuality task, participants opted for retrieving evidence from the Web in order to assess the factuality of the claims. After retrieving a number of search engine snippets or full documents, they performed different operations, including calculating similarities or levels of contradiction and stance between the supporting document and the claim. For example, the Copenhagen team [32] concatenating the representations of claim and of the document in a neural network. Table 3 gives a brief overview. Refer to [4] and the corresponding participants' reports for further details.

Table 3. Task 2 (factuality): overview of the learning models and of the representations used by the participants.

	[10]	[20]	[33]	[35]	f(claim, doc)	[10]	[20]	[33]	[35]
Learning Models					Similarity	✓		✓	
Logistic regression				✓	Alexa rank	✓			
Long short-term memory	✓				Stance				✓
Conv. neural network			✓		Contradiction				✓
Support vector machine			✓		NN concatenation			✓	
Random forests	✓			✓					
Search Engines					**Teams**				
Google	✓		✓	✓	[10] UPV-INAOE-Autoritas				
Bing	✓				[33] Copenhagen				
Representations					[20] Check it out				
Bag of words	✓		✓	✓	[35] bigIR				
Word embeddings	✓	✓	✓	✓	[—] FACTR				

Note that the *bigIR* team [34] tried to identify the relevant fragments in the supporting documents by considering only those with high similarity against the claim. Various approaches [32,34] are based at some extent on [17]. Only one team, Check it out [19], did not use external supporting documents (Table 5).

English. Table 6 shows the results on the English dataset. Overall, the top-performing system is the one by the Copenhagen team [32]. One aspect that

---

[5] The implementation of the evaluation measures is available at https://github.com/clef2018-factchecking/clef2018-factchecking/.

Table 4. Task 1 (check-worthiness): English results, ranked based on MAP, the official evaluation measure. The best score per evaluation measure is in shown in bold.

	MAP	MRR	MR-P	MP@1	MP@3	MP@5	MP@10	MP@20	MP@50
Prise de Fer [35]									
primary	**.1332**$_{(1)}$	**.4965**$_{(1)}$	**.1352**$_{(1)}$	**.4286**$_{(1)}$	**.2857**$_{(1)}$	.2000$_{(2)}$	.1429$_{(3)}$	**.1571**$_{(1)}$	.1200$_{(2)}$
cont. 1	.1366	.5246	.1475	.4286	.2857	.2286	.1571	.1714	.1229
cont. 2	.1317	.4139	.1523	.2857	.1905	.1714	.1571	.1571	.1429
Copenhagen [12]									
primary	.1152$_{(2)}$	.3159$_{(5)}$	.1100$_{(5)}$	.1429$_{(3)}$	.1429$_{(4)}$	.1143$_{(3)}$	.1286$_{(4)}$	.1286$_{(2)}$	**.1257**$_{(1)}$
cont. 1	.1810	.6224	.1875	.5714	.4286	.3143	.2571	.2357	.1514
UPV–INAOE–Autoritas [11]									
primary	.1130$_{(3)}$	.4615$_{(2)}$	.1315$_{(2)}$	.2857$_{(2)}$	.2381$_{(2)}$	**.3143**$_{(1)}$	**.2286**$_{(1)}$	.1214$_{(3)}$	.0886$_{(4)}$
cont. 1	.1232	.3451	.1022	.1429	.2857	.2286	.1429	.1143	.0771
cont. 2	.1253	.5535	.0849	.4286	.4286	.2571	.1429	.1286	.0771
bigIR [34]									
primary	.1120$_{(4)}$	.2621$_{(6)}$	.1165$_{(4)}$	.0000$_{(4)}$	.1429$_{(4)}$	.1143$_{(3)}$	.1143$_{(5)}$	.1000$_{(5)}$	.1114$_{(3)}$
cont. 1	.1319	.2675	.1505	.1429	.0952	.0857	.1714	.1786	.1343
cont. 2	.1116	.2195	.1294	.0000	.1429	.1429	.1857	.1429	.0886
fragarach									
primary	.0812$_{(5)}$	.4477$_{(3)}$	.1217$_{(3)}$	.2857$_{(2)}$	.1905$_{(3)}$	.2000$_{(2)}$	.1571$_{(2)}$	.1071$_{(4)}$	.0743$_{(5)}$
blue									
primary	.0801$_{(6)}$	.2459$_{(7)}$	.0576$_{(7)}$	.1429$_{(3)}$	.0952$_{(5)}$	.0571$_{(4)}$	.0571$_{(6)}$	.0857$_{(6)}$	.0600$_{(6)}$
RNCC [1]									
primary	.0632$_{(7)}$	.3775$_{(4)}$	.0639$_{(6)}$	.2857$_{(2)}$	.1429$_{(4)}$	.1143$_{(3)}$	.0571$_{(6)}$	.0571$_{(7)}$	.0486$_{(7)}$
cont. 1	.0886	.4844	.0945	.4286	.1429	.1714	.1286	.1000	.0714
cont. 2	.0747	.2198	.0984	.0000	.0952	.1143	.1000	.1000	.0829
Baselines									
n-gram	.1201	.4087	.1280	.1429	.2857	.1714	.1571	.1357	.1143
random	.0485	.0633	.0359	.0000	.0000	.0000	.0286	.0214	.0429

Table 5. Task 1 (check-worthiness): Arabic results, ranked based on MAP, the official evaluation measure. The best score per evaluation measure is in bold.

	MAP	MRR	MR-P	MP@1	MP@3	MP@5	MP@10	MP@20	MP@50
bigIR [34]									
primary	**.0899**$_{(1)}$	.1180$_{(2)}$	**.1105**$_{(1)}$	.0000$_{(2)}$	.0000$_{(2)}$	.0000$_{(2)}$	**.1333**$_{(1)}$	**.1000**$_{(1)}$	**.1133**$_{(1)}$
cont. 1	.1497	.2805	.1760	.0000	.3333	.3333	.2667	.2333	.1533
cont. 2	.0962	.1660	.0895	.0000	.1111	.2000	.1667	.1000	.0867
UPV–INAOE–Autoritas [11]									
primary	.0585$_{(2)}$	**.3488**$_{(1)}$	.0087$_{(2)}$	**.3333**$_{(1)}$	**.1111**$_{(1)}$	**.0667**$_{(1)}$	.0333$_{(2)}$	.0167$_{(2)}$	.0400$_{(2)}$
cont. 1	.1168	.6714	.0649	.6667	.6667	.4000	.2000	.1000	.0733
Baselines									
n-gram	.0861	.2817	.0981	.0000	.3333	.2667	.1667	.1667	.0867
random	.0460	.0658	.0375	.0000	.0000	.0000	.0333	.0167	.0333

might explain the relatively large difference in performance compared to the other teams is the use of additional training material. The Copenhagen team incorporated hundreds of labeled claims from Politifact to their training set. Their model combines the claim and supporting texts to build representations. Their primary submission is an SVM, whereas their contrastive one uses a CNN.

Table 6. Task 2 (factuality): English results, ranked based on MAE, the official evaluation measure. The best score per evaluation measure is in bold.

	MAE	Macro MAE	Acc	Macro F1	Macro AvgR
Copenhagen [32]					
primary	**.7050**$_{(1)}$	**.6746**$_{(1)}$	**.4317**$_{(1)}$	**.4008**$_{(1)}$	**.4502**$_{(1)}$
cont. 1	.7698	.7339	.4676	.4681	.4721
FACTR					
primary	.9137$_{(2)}$	.9280$_{(2)}$	.4101$_{(2)}$	.3236$_{(2)}$	.3684$_{(2)}$
cont. 1	.9209	.9358	.4029	.3063	.3611
cont. 2	.9281	.9314	.4101	.3420	.3759
UPV–INAOE–Autoritas [10]					
primary	.9496$_{(3)}$	.9706$_{(3)}$	.3885$_{(4)}$	.2613$_{(3)}$	.3403$_{(3)}$
bigIR [34]					
primary	.9640$_{(4)}$	1.0000$_{(4)}$	.3957$_{(3)}$	.1890$_{(4)}$	.3333$_{(4)}$
cont. 1	.9640	1.0000	.3957	.1890	.3333
cont. 2	.9424	.9256	.3525	.3297	.3405
Check It Out [19]					
primary	.9640$_{(4)}$	1.0000$_{(4)}$	.3957$_{(3)}$	.1890$_{(4)}$	.3333$_{(4)}$
Baselines					
n-gram	.9137	.9236	.3957	.3095	.3588
random	.8345	.8139	.3597	.3569	.3589

Unfortunately, not much information is available regarding team FACTR, as no paper was submitted to describe their model. They used a similar approach as most other teams: converting the claim into a query for a search engine, computing stance, sentiment and other features over the supporting documents, and using them in a supervised model.

Arabic. Table 7 shows the results of the two teams that participated in the Arabic task. In order to deal with it, FACTR translated all the claims into English and performed the rest of the process in that language. In contrast, UPV–INAOE–Autoritas [10] translated the claims into English, but only in order to query the search engines,[6] and then translated the retrieved evidence into Arabic in order to keep working in that language. Perhaps, the noise generated by using two imperfect translations caused their performance to decrease (the performance of the two teams in the English task was much closer).

---

[6] The reason is that the Arabic dataset was produced by translating the datasets from an English version. Hence it was difficult to find evidence in Arabic.

Table 7. Task 2 (factuality): Arabic results, ranked based on MAE, the official evaluation measure. The best score per evaluation measure is in bold.

	MAE	Macro MAE	Acc	Macro F1	Macro AvgR
FACTR					
primary	**.6579**$_{(1)}$	**.8914**$_{(1)}$	**.5921**$_{(1)}$	**.3730**$_{(1)}$	**.3804**$_{(1)}$
cont. 1	.7018	.9461	.5833	.3691	.3766
cont. 2	.6623	.9153	.5965	.3657	.3804
UPV–INAOE–Autoritas [10]					
primary	.8202$_{(2)}$	1.0417$_{(2)}$	.5175$_{(2)}$	.2796$_{(2)}$	.3027$_{(2)}$
Baselines					
n-gram	.6798	.9850	.5789	.2827	.3267
random	.9868	.9141	.3070	.2733	.2945

Overall, the performance of the models in Arabic is better than in English. The reason is that the isolated claims from snopes.com—which were released only in Arabic (cf. Table 1)—were easier to verify.

6   Conclusions and Future Work

We have presented an overview of the CLEF-2018 CheckThat! Lab on Automatic Identification and Verification of Political Claims. Task 1 asked to predict which claims in a political debate or speech should be prioritized for fact-checking. Task 2 asked to assess whether a claim made by a politician is factually true, half-true, or false. We proposed both tasks in English and Arabic, relying on comments and factuality judgments from both factcheck.org and snopes.com to obtain a further-refined gold standard and on translation for the Arabic versions of the corpus. A total of 30 teams registered to participate in the lab, and 9 of them actually submitted runs. The evaluation results showed that the most successful approaches used various neural networks (esp. for Task 1) and evidence retrieved from the Web (esp. for Task 2). The corpora and the evaluation measures we have released as a result of this lab should enable further research in check-worthiness estimation and in automatic claim verification.

In future iterations of the lab, we plan to add more debates and speeches, both annotated and unannotated, which would enable semi-supervised learning. We further want to add annotations for the same debates/speeches from different fact-checking organizations, which would allow using multi-task learning [9].

Acknowledgments. This work was made possible in part by NPRP grant# NPRP 7-1313-1-245 from the Qatar National Research Fund (a member of Qatar Foundation). Statements made herein are solely the responsibility of the authors.

References

1. Agez, R., Bosc, C., Lespagnol, C., Mothe, J., Petitcol, N.: IRIT at CheckThat! 2018. In: Cappellato et al. [5]
2. Atanasova, P., et al.: Overview of the CLEF-2018 CheckThat! Lab on automatic identification and verification of political claims. Task 1: Check-worthiness. In: Cappellato et al. [5]
3. Baly, R., Mohtarami, M., Glass, J., Màrquez, L., Moschitti, A., Nakov, P.: Integrating stance detection and fact checking in a unified corpus. In: Proceedings of the 2018 Conference of the North American Chapter of the Association for Computational Linguistics: Human Language Technologies. NAACL-HLT 2018, New Orleans, Louisiana, USA, pp. 21–27 (2018)
4. Barrón-Cedeño, A., et al.: Overview of the CLEF-2018 CheckThat! Lab on automatic identification and verification of political claims. Task 2: Factuality. In: Cappellato et al. [5]
5. Cappellato, L., Ferro, N., Nie, J.Y., Soulier, L. (eds.): Working Notes of CLEF 2018-Conference and Labs of the Evaluation Forum. CEUR Workshop Proceedings, CEUR-WS.org, Avignon, France (2018)
6. Castillo, C., Mendoza, M., Poblete, B.: Information credibility on Twitter. In: Proceedings of the 20th International Conference on World Wide Web, WWW 2011, Hyderabad, India, pp. 675–684 (2011)
7. Derczynski, L., Bontcheva, K., Liakata, M., Procter, R., Wong Sak Hoi, G., Zubiaga, A.: SemEval-2017 task 8: RumourEval: determining rumour veracity and support for rumours. In: Proceedings of the 11th International Workshop on Semantic Evaluation, SemEval 2017, Vancouver, Canada, pp. 60–67 (2017)
8. Ferreira, W., Vlachos, A.: Emergent: a novel data-set for stance classification. In: Proceedings of the 2016 Conference of the North American Chapter of the Association for Computational Linguistics: Human Language Technologies. NAACL-HLT 2016, San Diego, California, USA, pp. 1163–1168 (2016)
9. Gencheva, P., Nakov, P., Màrquez, L., Barrón-Cedeño, A., Koychev, I.: A context-aware approach for detecting worth-checking claims in political debates. In: Proceedings of the International Conference Recent Advances in Natural Language Processing. RANLP 2017, Varna, Bulgaria, pp. 267–276 (2017)
10. Ghanem, B., Montes-y Gómez, M., Rangel, F., Rosso, P.: UPV-INAOE-Autoritas - check that: an approach based on external sources to detect claims credibility. In: Cappellato et al. [5]
11. Ghanem, B., Montes-y Gómez, M., Rangel, F., Rosso, P.: UPV-INAOE-Autoritas - check that: preliminary approach for checking worthiness of claims. In: Cappellato et al. [5]
12. Hansen, C., Hansen, C., Simonsen, J., Lioma, C.: The Copenhagen team participation in the check-worthiness task of the competition of automatic identification and verification of claims in political debates of the CLEF-2018 fact checking lab. In: Cappellato et al. [5]
13. Hardalov, M., Koychev, I., Nakov, P.: In search of credible news. In: Proceedings of the 17th International Conference on Artificial Intelligence: Methodology, Systems, and Applications. AIMSA 2016, Varna, Bulgaria, pp. 172–180 (2016)
14. Hassan, N., Li, C., Tremayne, M.: Detecting check-worthy factual claims in presidential debates. In: Proceedings of the 24th ACM International Conference on Information and Knowledge Management, CIKM 2015, Melbourne, Australia, pp. 1835–1838 (2015)

15. Hassan, N., Tremayne, M., Arslan, F., Li, C.: Comparing automated factual claim detection against judgments of journalism organizations. In: Computation + Journalism Symposium, Stanford, California, USA, September 2016
16. Jaradat, I., Gencheva, P., Barrón-Cedeño, A., Màrquez, L., Nakov, P.: ClaimRank: detecting check-worthy claims in Arabic and English. In: Proceedings of the 16th Annual Conference of the North American Chapter of the Association for Computational Linguistics, NAACL-HLT 2018, New Orleans, Louisiana, USA, pp. 26–30 (2018)
17. Karadzhov, G., Nakov, P., Màrquez, L., Barrón-Cedeño, A., Koychev, I.: Fully automated fact checking using external sources. In: Proceedings of the International Conference Recent Advances in Natural Language Processing, RANLP 2017, pp. 344–353. INCOMA Ltd., Varna (2017)
18. Karadzhov, G., Nakov, P., Màrquez, L., Barrón-Cedeño, A., Koychev, I.: Fully automated fact checking using external sources. In: Proceedings of the Conference on Recent Advances in Natural Language Processing, RANLP 2017, Varna, Bulgaria, pp. 344–353 (2017)
19. Lal, Y.K., Khattar, D., Kumar, V., Mishra, A., Varma, V.: Check it out : politics and neural networks. In: Cappellato et al. [5]
20. Ma, J., et al.: Detecting rumors from microblogs with recurrent neural networks. In: Proceedings of the 25th International Joint Conference on Artificial Intelligence, IJCAI 2016, New York, New York, USA, pp. 3818–3824 (2016)
21. Mihaylova, T., et al.: Fact checking in community forums. In: Proceedings of the Thirty-Second AAAI Conference on Artificial Intelligence, AAAI 2018, New Orleans, Louisiana, USA, pp. 879–886 (2018)
22. Mitra, T., Gilbert, E.: CREDBANK: a large-scale social media corpus with associated credibility annotations. In: Cha, M., Mascolo, C., Sandvig, C. (eds.) Proceedings of the Ninth International Conference on Web and Social Media, ICWSM 2015, Oxford, UK, pp. 258–267 (2015)
23. Nakov, P., Ritter, A., Rosenthal, S., Sebastiani, F., Stoyanov, V.: SemEval-2016 task 4: Sentiment analysis in Twitter. In: Proceedings of the 10th International Workshop on Semantic Evaluation, SemEval 2016, San Diego, California, USA, pp. 1–18 (2016)
24. Papadopoulos, S., Bontcheva, K., Jaho, E., Lupu, M., Castillo, C.: Overview of the special issue on trust and veracity of information in social media. ACM Trans. Inf. Syst. 34(3), 14:1–14:5 (2016)
25. Patwari, A., Goldwasser, D., Bagchi, S.: TATHYA: a multi-classifier system for detecting check-worthy statements in political debates. In: Proceedings of the 2017 ACM on Conference on Information and Knowledge Management, CIKM 2017, Singapore, pp. 2259–2262 (2017)
26. Popat, K., Mukherjee, S., Strötgen, J., Weikum, G.: Credibility assessment of textual claims on the web. In: Proceedings of the 25th ACM International on Conference on Information and Knowledge Management, CIKM 2016, pp. 2173–2178. ACM, Indianapolis (2016)
27. Popat, K., Mukherjee, S., Strötgen, J., Weikum, G.: Where the truth lies: explaining the credibility of emerging claims on the web and social media. In: Proceedings of the 26th International Conference on World Wide Web Companion, WWW 2017, Perth, Australia, pp. 1003–1012 (2017)
28. Rashkin, H., Choi, E., Jang, J.Y., Volkova, S., Choi, Y.: Truth of varying shades: analyzing language in fake news and political fact-checking. In: Proceedings of the Conference on Empirical Methods in Natural Language Processing, EMNLP 2017, pp. 2931–2937 (2017)

29. Shiralkar, P., Flammini, A., Menczer, F., Ciampaglia, G.L.: Finding streams in knowledge graphs to support fact checking. In: Proceedings of the IEEE International Conference on Data Mining, ICDM 2017, New Orleans, Louisiana, USA, pp. 859–864 (2017)
30. Thorne, J., Vlachos, A., Christodoulopoulos, C., Mittal, A.: FEVER: a large-scale dataset for fact extraction and verification. In: Proceedings of the 2018 Conference of the North American Chapter of the Association for Computational Linguistics: Human Language Technologies. NAACL-HLT 2018, New Orleans, Louisiana, USA, pp. 809–819 (2018)
31. Vlachos, A., Riedel, S.: Fact checking: task definition and dataset construction. In: Proceedings of the ACL 2014 Workshop on Language Technologies and Computational Social Science, Baltimore, Maryland, USA, pp. 18–22 (2014)
32. Wang, D., Simonsen, J., Larseny, B., Lioma, C.: The Copenhagen team participation in the factuality task of the competition of automatic identification and verification of claims in political debates of the CLEF-2018 fact checking lab. In: Cappellato et al. [5]
33. Wang, W.Y.: "Liar, liar pants on fire": a new benchmark dataset for fake news detection. In: Proceedings of the 55th Annual Meeting of the Association for Computational Linguistics, ACL 2017, Vancouver, Canada, pp. 422–426 (2017)
34. Yasser, K., Kutlu, M., Elsayed, T.: bigIR at CLEF 2018: detection and verification of check-worthy political claims. In: Cappellato et al. [5]
35. Zuo, C., Karakas, A., Banerjee, R.: A hybrid recognition system for check-worthy claims using heuristics and supervised learning. In: Cappellato et al. [5]

Author Index

Printed in the United States
By Bookmasters